THE GUINNESS ENCYCLOPAEDIA OF SPORTS RECORDS & RESULTS

PETER MATTHEWS
AND IAN MORRISON

GUINNESS BOOKS

The authors Peter Matthews (general editor) and
Ian Morrison are well-known sports experts.

Peter Matthews, a sports consultant
to *The Guinness Book of Records*, is
athletics commentator for ITV and
Channel 4, and he is also editor of the
International Athletics Annual.

Previous works include: *Track & Field
Athletics: The Records* (1986), the
sports section of the *Guinness Book of
Winners & Champions* (1981), *Piccolo
Encyclopaedia of Sport* (1974).

Ian Morrison, an established Guinness
author and professional sports
statistician, has written books on
Motor Racing, Horse Racing, Rugby
League, Rugby Union, Cycling and
Boxing. His two most recent books
published by Guinness in their
'Records' series are *Boxing* (1986) and
Motor Racing (1987). He has also
provided biographical information on
sports personalities, from sports as far
apart as Archery and Weightlifting, for
many publications, including several for
the 1984 Los Angeles Olympics.

Editor: Beatrice Frei
Design and Layout: Michael Morey

© Peter Matthews, Ian Morrison and Guinness Superlatives Ltd, 1987

Published in Great Britain by Guinness Superlatives Ltd, 33 London Road, Enfield,
Middlesex

Typeset in Frutiger and Sabon by Peter MacDonald, Twickenham
Printed and bound in Great Britain by Butler and Tanner Ltd, Frome, Somerset

'Guinness' is a registered trade mark of Guinness Superlatives Ltd

British Library Cataloguing in Publication Data

Matthews, Peter, 1945-
Guinness encyclopaedia of sports records and results
1. Sports—Records 2. Games—Records
I. Title II. Morrison, Ian, 1947-
796'.09 GV741

ISBN 0–85112–492–5

CONTENTS

INTRODUCTION

Our aim in this book has been to gather together a comprehensive collection of the statistics of international sport. We have given brief introductions to the sports and to the major events within these sports, together with lists of records and champions.

It has been many years since any work approaching the extent of this compendium has been published. Nonetheless such is the magnitude of this task, that in order to contain the extent of this book to a reasonable size we have had to face difficult decisions on what to include and what to leave out. There are an enormous number of sports that are practised in different parts of the world, but we have tried to include as many as possible, and in particular all those that are widespread. The world records and world champions of the sports have first priority for inclusion. Of course the major international sports, such as soccer or athletics have the most space. We have tried to pack in as much data as possible. In lists of team champions we have brought together the wins by each team. In these and other lists we have shown consecutive wins as e.g. 1973-7, for wins in each year from 1973 to 1977.

Country abbreviations have been used throughout as shown in the list that follows.

Space has not always permitted the inclusion of complete lists for long-established events, but we have given summaries to include the champions who have won the most titles, thus ensuring that the 'greats' of the past are recognised. Complete lists of Olympic champions are included, but under each sport rather than in the separate Olympic section.

Peter Matthews and Ian Morrison

ABBREVIATIONS

av.	average
cc	cubic capacity
d	days
hr	hours
kg	kilograms
km	kilometres
km/h	kilometres per hour
m	metres
min	minutes
mph	miles per hour
m/s	metres per second
sec	seconds
y	yards
yr	years

In dates, months are usually abbreviated to their first three digits.

COUNTRIES

Alb	Albania
Alg	Algeria
Arg	Argentina
Aus	Australia
Aut	Austria
Bah	Bahamas
Bar	Barbados
Bel	Belgium
Ber	Bermuda
Bhn	Bahrain * (BHR)
Bra	Brazil
Bul	Bulgaria
Bur	Burma * (BIR)
Cam	Cameroon * (CMR)
Can	Canada
Chl	Chile * (CHI)
Chn	China (People's Republic) * (PRC)
Col	Colombia
Con	Congo * (CGO)
Cs	Czechoslovakia * (TCH)
Cub	Cuba
Cyp	Cyprus
Den	Denmark
Dji	Djibouti
Dom	Dominican Republic
Ecu	Ecuador
Egy	Egypt
Eng	England
Est	Estonia
Eth	Ethiopia
Fij	Fiji
Fin	Finland
Fra	France
FRG	Federal Republic of Germany
Gab	Gabon
Gam	The Gambia
GDR	German Democratic Republic
Ger	Germany (pre 1945)
Gha	Ghana
Gre	Greece
Gua	Guatemala
Guy	Guyana
Haw	Hawaii
HK	Hong Kong * (HKG)
Hol	Holland/Netherlands
Hun	Hungary
Ice	Iceland * (ISL)
Ina	Indonesia
Ind	India
IOM	Isle of Man
Ire	Ireland * (IRE)
Irn	Iran
Irq	Iraq
Isr	Israel
Ita	Italy
IvC	Ivory Coast * (CIV)
Jam	Jamaica
Jap	Japan
Ken	Kenya
Kuw	Kuwait
Lat	Latvia
Lie	Liechtenstein
Lux	Luxembourg
Mal	Malaysia
Maw	Malawi
Mex	Mexico
Mgl	Mongolia
Mlt	Malta
Mon	Monaco
Mor	Morocco * (MAR)
NI	Northern Ireland
Nic	Nicaragua * (NCA)
Nig	Nigeria * (NGR)
NKo	North Korea (Korean PDR) * (PRK)
Nor	Norway
NZ	New Zealand * (NZL)
Pak	Pakistan
Pan	Panama
Par	Paraguay
Per	Peru
Phi	Philippines
PNG	Papua New Guinea
Pol	Poland
Por	Portugal
PR	Puerto Rico * (PUR)
Qat	Qatar
Rho	Rhodesia
Rom	Romania
Rus	Russia (USSR from 1917)
SAf	South Africa
Sco	Scotland
Sen	Senegal
Sin	Singapore
SKo	Korea (South) * (KOR)
Som	Somalia
Spa	Spain * (ESP)
SRho	Southern Rhodesia (now Zimbabwe)
Sri	Sri Lanka
Sud	Sudan
SVI	St Vincent
Swe	Sweden
Swi	Switzerland * (SUI)
Tai	Taiwan * (TPE)
Tan	Tanzania
Tha	Thailand
Tri	Trinidad & Tobago
Tun	Tunisia
Tur	Turkey
Uga	Uganda
UK	United Kingdom of Great Britain & N.Ireland * (GBR)
Uru	Uruguay
USA	United States
USSR	Soviet Union * (URS)
Ven	Venezuela
Wal	Wales
WI	West Indies
Yug	Yugoslavia
Zam	Zambia
Zim	Zimbabwe (formerly Rhodesia)

* These abbreviations differ in some cases from those used by the IOC (which are shown in brackets). The latter are always three digits and often French language based; we have prefered English or those of the countries concerned.

GOVERNING BODIES OF SPORT
Specified here in English; see relevant sports for translations and dates of founding.

AAA	Amateur Athletic Association (UK)
AAU	Amateur Athletic Union (USA)
AIBA	International Amateur Boxing Federation
FEI	International Equestrian Federation
FIA	International Automobile Association
FIAC	International Amateur Cycling Federation
FIBA	International Amateur Basketball Federation
FIC	International Canoeing Federation
FIDE	International Chess Federation
FIE	International Fencing Federation
FIFA	International Football Association Federation
FIG	International Gymnastic Federation
FIH	International Hockey Federation
FIL	International Luge Federation
FILA	International Amateur Wrestling Federation
FIM	International Motorcycling Federation
FINA	International Amateur Swimming Federation
FIQ	International Bowling Federation
FIRA	International Amateur Rugby Federation
FIS	International Ski Federation
FISA	International Rowing Federation
FITA	International Archery Federation
FIVB	International Volleyball Federation
GAA	Gaelic Athletic Federation
IAAF	International Amateur Athletic Federation
IBF	International Badminton Federation
	International Boxing Federation
IBSF	International Billiards & Snooker Federation
ICF	International Curling Federation
IHF	International Handball Federation
IIHF	International Ice Hockey Federation
IJF	International Judo Federation
IOF	International Orienteering Federation
IRFB	International Rugby Football Board
ISF	International Softball Federation
ISU	International Skating Union
ITF	International Tennis Federation
ITTF	International Table Tennis Federation
IWF	International Weightlifting Federation
IYRU	International Yacht Racing Union
LPGA	Ladies Professional Golfers Association
MCC	Marylebone Cricket Club
NBA	National Basketball Federation (USA)
NBL	National Basketball League (USA)
NCAA	National Collegiate Athletic Association (USA)
NFL	National Football League (USA)
NHL	National Hockey League (USA)
PGA	Professional Golfers Association
PRCA	Professional Rodeo Cowboys Association
TCCB	Test and County Cricket Board
UCI	International Cycling Union
UIPMB	International Union of Modern Pentathlon and Archery
UIT	International Shooting Union
WBA	World Boxing Association
WBC	World Boxing Council
WTF	World Taekwan-Do Federation
WWSU	World Water Skiing Union

Other abbreviations for sports bodies are given under their respective sports.

AMERICAN FOOTBALL

American football evolved from the British games of soccer and rugby in the latter part of the 19th century. There were conflicting versions of football, but an important development was the first match under Harvard Rules by Harvard University against McGill University, Montreal in May 1874. In 1876 the Intercollegiate Football Association was formed, and in that year Harvard agreed to reduce the number of players per side from 15 to 11, which it is today. The first professional game was between Latrobe and Jeanette in Pennsylvania on 31 Aug 1895, and by the end of the century it had become the national game, although exceptionally rough at the time. After many fatalities in the early part of the 20th century considerable modifications were made to the rules, including the introduction of the forward pass in 1906. The first Rose Bowl game between the leading college teams was held in 1902.

The American Professional Football Association was formed in 1920 and twelve teams contested the first league season. The association became the National Football League in 1922.

NATIONAL FOOTBALL LEAGUE CHAMPIONS

From 1921-32 there was just one league.
Winners
1921 Chicago Staleys
1922 Canton Bulldogs (Ohio)
1923 Canton Bulldogs (Ohio)
1924 Cleveland Bulldogs
1925 Chicago Cardinals
1926 Frankford Yellowjackets
1927 New York Giants
1928 Providence Steamroller
1929 Green Bay Packers
1930 Green Bay Packers
1931 Green Bay Packers
1932 Chicago Bears

Walter Payton of the Chicago Bears holds the career record for yards gained rushing. (All-Sport/Tony Duffy)

From 1933 the NFL was divided into two divisions with the winners playing off for the NFL Championship.

	EASTERN DIVISION	WESTERN DIVISION	CHAMPIONSHIP
1933	New York Giants	Chicago Bears	Bears 23 Giants 21
1934	New York Giants	Chicago Bears	Giants 30 Bears 13
1935	New York Giants	Detroit Lions	Lions 26 Giants 7
1936	Boston Redskins	Green Bay Packers	Packers 21 Redskins 6
1937	Washington Redskins	Chicago Bears	Redskins 28 Bears 21
1938	New York Giants	Green Bay Packers	Giants 23 Packers 17
1939	New York Giants	Green Bay Packers	Packers 27 Giants 0
1940	Washington Redskins	Chicago Bears	Bears 73 Redskins 0
1941	New York Giants	Chicago Bears	Bears 37 Giants 9
1942	Washington Redskins	Chicago Bears	Redskins 14 Bears 6
1943	Washington Redskins	Chicago Bears	Bears 41 Redskins 21
1944	New York Giants	Green Bay Packers	Packers 14 Giants 7
1945	Washington Redskins	Cleveland Rams	Rams 15 Redskins 14
1946	New York Giants	Chicago Bears	Bears 24 Giants 14
1947	Philadelphia Eagles	Chicago Cardinals	Cardinals 28 Eagles 21
1948	Philadelphia Eagles	Chicago Cardinals	Eagles 7 Cardinals 0
1949	Philadelphia Eagles	Los Angeles Rams	Eagles 14 Rams 0

AMERICAN CONFERENCE	**NATIONAL CONFERENCE**	**CHAMPIONSHIP**
1950 Cleveland Browns	Los Angeles Rams	Browns 30 Rams 28
1951 Cleveland Browns	Los Angeles Rams	Rams 24 Browns 17
1952 Cleveland Browns	Detroit Lions	Lions 17 Browns 7
EASTERN CONFERENCE	**WESTERN CONFERENCE**	**CHAMPIONSHIP**
1953 Cleveland Browns	Detroit Lions	Lions 17 Browns 16
1954 Cleveland Browns	Detroit Lions	Browns 56 Lions 10
1955 Cleveland Browns	Los Angeles Rams	Browns 38 Rams 14
1956 New York Giants	Chicago Bears	Giants 47 Bears 7
EASTERN CONFERENCE	**WESTERN CONFERENCE**	**CHAMPIONSHIP**
1957 Cleveland Browns	Detroit Lions	Lions 59 Browns 14
1958 New York Giants	Baltimore Colts	Colts 23 Giants 17
1959 New York Giants	Baltimore Colts	Colts 31 Giants 16

The AFL was formed in 1960 with an Eastern and Western Division while the NFL still had its Eastern and Western Conferences. Both the AFL and NFL had end of season Championships.

AFL CHAMPIONSHIP
1960 Houston Oilers 24 Los Angeles Chargers 16
1961 Houston Oilers 10 San Diego Chargers 3
1962 Dallas Texans 20 Houston Oilers 17
1963 San Diego Chargers 51 Boston Patriots 10
1964 Buffalo Bills 20 San Diego Chargers 7
1965 Buffalo Bills 23 San Diego Chargers 0
1966 Kansas City Chiefs 31 Buffalo Bills 7
1967 Oakland Raiders 40 Houston Oilers 7
1968 New York Jets 27 Oakland Raiders 23
1969 Kansas City Chiefs 17 Oakland Raiders 17

NFL CHAMPIONSHIP
1960 Philadelphia Eagles 17 Green Bay Packers 13
1961 Green Bay Packers 37 New York Giants 0
1962 Green Bay Packers 16 New York Giants 7
1963 Chicago Bears 14 New York Giants 10
1964 Cleveland Browns 27 Baltimore Colts 0
1965 Green Bay Packers 23 Cleveland Browns 12
1966 Green Bay Packers 34 Dallas Cowboys 27
1967 Green Bay Packers 21 Dallas Cowboys 17
1968 Baltimore Colts 34 Cleveland Browns 0
1969 Minnesota Vikings 27 Cleveland Browns 7

From 1970 the NFL has consisted of the AFC and the NFC, each with Eastern, Central and Western divisions. End of season play-offs result in each Conference providing their own champions who meet in the Super Bowl.

AFC CHAMPIONSHIP
1970 Baltimore Colts 27 Oakland Raiders17
1971 Miami Dolphins 21 Baltimore Colts 0
1972 Miami Dolphins 21 Pittsburgh Steelers 17
1973 Miami Dolphins 27 Oakland Raiders 10
1974 Pittsburgh Steelers 24 Oakland Raiders 13
1975 Pittsburgh Steelers 16 Oakland Raiders 10
1976 Oakland Raiders 24 Pittsburgh Steelers 7
1977 Denver Broncos 20 Oakland Raiders 17
1978 Pittsburgh Steelers 34 Houston Oilers 5
1979 Pittsburgh Steelers 27 Houston Oilers 13
1980 Oakland Raiders 34 San Diego Chargers 27
1981 Cincinnati Bengals 27 San Diego Chargers 7
1982 Miami Dolphins 14 New York Jets 0
1983 Los Angeles Raiders 24 Dallas Cowboys 17
1984 Miami Dolphins 45 Pittsburgh Steelers 28
1985 New England Patriots 31 Miami Dolphins 14
1986 Denver Broncos 23 Cleveland Browns 20

NFC CHAMPIONSHIP
1970 Dallas Cowboys 17 San Francisco 49ers 10
1971 Dallas Cowboys 14 San Francisco 49ers 3
1972 Washington Redskins 26 Dallas Cowboys 3
1973 Minnesota Vikings 27 Dallas Cowboys 10
1974 Minnesota Vikings 14 Los Angeles Rams 10
1975 Dallas Cowboys 37 Los Angeles Rams 7
1976 Minnesota Vikings 24 Los Angeles Rams 13
1977 Dallas Cowboys 23 Minnesota Vikings 6
1978 Dallas Cowboys 28 Los Angeles Rams 0
1979 Los Angeles Rams 9 Tampa Bay Buccaneers 0
1980 Philadelphia Eagles 20 Dallas Cowboys 7
1981 San Francisco 49ers 28 Dallas Cowboys 27
1982 Washington Redskins 31 Dallas Cowboys 17
1983 Washington Redskins 24 San Francisco 49ers 21
1984 San Francisco 49ers 23 Chicago Bears 0
1985 Chicago Bears 24 Los Angeles Rams 0
1986 New York Giants 17 Washington Redskins 0

MAJOR NFL RECORDS
Most games: 340 George Blanda (Chicago Bears, Baltimore, Houston, Oakland) 1949-75
Most season as head coach: 40 George Halas (Chicago Bears) 1920-9, 1933-42, 1946-55, 1958-67
Most points (career): 2,002 George Blanda (Chicago Bears, Baltimore, Houston, Oakland) 1949-75
Most points (season): 176 Paul Hornung (Green Bay) 1960
Most points (game): 40 Ernie Nevers (Chicago Cardinals v Chicago Bears) 28 Nov 1929
Most touchdowns (career): 126 Jim Brown (Cleveland) 1957-65
Most touchdowns (season): 24 John Riggins (Washington) 1983
Most touchdowns (game):
6 Ernie Nevers (Chicago Cardinals v Chicago Bears) 28 Nov 1929
6 William Jones (Cleveland v Chicago Bears) 25 Nov 1951
6 Gale Sayers (Chicago v San Francisco) 12 Dec 1965
Most field goals (career): 373 Jan Stenerud (Kansas City, Green Bay, Minnesota) 1967-85
Most field goals (season): 35 Ali Haji-Sheikh (New York Giants) 1983
Most field goals (game): 7 Jim Bakken (St.Louis v Pittsburgh) 24 Sep 1967

Rushing
Most yards gained (career): 16,193 Walter Payton (Chicago) 1975-86
Most yards gained (season): 2,105 Eric Dickerson (Los Angeles Rams) 1984

Most yards gained (game): 275 Walter Payton (Chicago v Minnesota) 20 Nov 1977

Passing

Most passes completed (career): 3,686 Fran Tarkenton (Minnesota, New York Giants) 1961-78
Most passes completed (season): 378 Dan Marino (Miami) 1986
Most passes completed (game): 42 Richard Todd (New York Jets v San Francisco) 21 Sep 1980
Most yards gained (career): 47,003 Fran Tarkenton (Minnesota, New York Giants) 1961-78
Most yards gained (season): 5,084 Dan Marino (Miami) 1984
Most yards gained (game): 554 Norm Van Brocklin (Los Angeles v New York Yanks) 28 Sep 1951

SUPER BOWL

Inaugurated in 1966 it is a match between the AFC and NFC champions. It is held in January each year, at the end of the regular season.

1967	Green Bay Packers	35	Kansas City Chiefs	10
1968	Green Bay Packers	33	Oakland Raiders	14
1969	New York Jets	16	Baltimore Colts	7
1970	Kansas City Chiefs	23	Minnesota Vikings	7
1971	Baltimore Colts	16	Dallas Cowboys	13
1972	Dallas Cowboys	24	Miami Dolphins	3
1973	Miami Dolphins	14	Washington Redskins	7
1974	Miami Dolphins	24	Minnesota Vikings	7
1975	Pittsburgh Steelers	16	Minnesota Vikings	6
1976	Pittsburgh Steelers	21	Dallas Cowboys	17
1977	Oakland Raiders	32	Minnesota Vikings	14
1978	Dallas Cowboys	27	Denver Broncos	10
1979	Pittsburgh Steelers	35	Dallas Cowboys	31
1980	Pittsburgh Steelers	31	Los Angeles Rams	19
1981	Oakland Raiders	27	Philadelphia Eagles	10
1982	San Francisco 49ers	26	Cincinnati Bengals	21
1983	Washington Redskins	27	Miami Dolphins	17
1984	Los Angeles Raiders	38	Washington Redskins	9
1985	San Francisco 49ers	38	Miami Dolphins	16
1986	Chicago Bears	46	New England Patriots	10
1987	New York Giants	39	Denver Broncos	20

SUPERBOWL RECORDS

Most wins: 4 Pittsburgh Steelers; 3 Oakland/Los Angeles Raiders; 2 Green Bay Packers, San Francisco 49ers, Dallas Cowboys, Miami Dolphins
Most appearances: 5 Dallas Cowboys, Miami Dolphins 4 Pittsburgh Steelers, Oakland/Los Angeles Raiders, Minnesota Vikings
Most games (player): 5 Marv Fleming (Green Bay 1967-8, Miami 1972-4)
5 Larry Cole (Dallas 1971-2, 1976, 1978-9)
5 Cliff Harris (Dallas 1971-2, 1976, 1978-9)
5 D.D.Lewis (Dallas 1971-2, 1976, 1978-9)
5 Preston Pearson (Baltimore 1969, Pittsburgh 1975, Dallas 1976, 1978-9)
5 Charlie Waters (Dallas 1971-2, 1976, 1978-9)
5 Rayfield Wright (Dallas 1971-2, 1976, 1978-9)
Most games (coach): 6 Don Schula (Baltimore 1969, Miami 1972-4, 1983, 1985)
Most points (career): 24 Franco Harris (Pittsburgh)
Most points (game): 18 Roger Craig (San Francisco, 1985)

Most touchdowns (career): 4 Franco Harris (Pittsburgh)
Most touchdowns (game): 3 Roger Craig (San Francisco, 1985)
Most field goals (career): 5 Ray Wersching (San Francisco)
Most field goals (game): 4 Don Chandler (Green Bay v Oakland, 1968)
4 Ray Wersching (San Francisco v Cincinnati, 1982)

COLLEGE FOOTBALL

More than 650 colleges, affiliated to the National Collegiate Athletic Association compete throughout the United States each year. The ultimate aim of them all is to reach one of the many Bowl finals held at the end of the season. The 'Big Four' bowls are the Rose Bowl, Sugar Bowl, Cotton Bowl and Orange Bowl, all traditionally played on 1 January each year.

Most Bowl appearances: 39 Alabama, 33 Texas, 30 USC, 28 Tennessee

Gale Sayers of the Chicago Bears set the NFL record of 22 touchdowns in a rookie season, including six in one game.

Most wins: 22 Alabama, 21 USC, 18 Oklahoma, 15 Texas, Georgia Tech.
Most 'Big Four' appearances: 29 Alabama, 24 USC, 23 Texas
Most 'Big Four' wins: 18 USC, 17 Alabama, 14 Oklahoma

Major College career records:
Most points scored: 368 Luis Zendejas (Arizona State) 1981-4
Most touchdowns: 59 Glenn Davis (Army) 1943-6
59 Tony Dorsett (Pittsburgh) 1973-6

Most field goals: 79 John Lee (UCLA) 1982-5
Most yards gained rushing: 6082 Tony Dorsett (Pittsburgh) 1973-6
Most yards gained passing: 10,579 Doug Flutie (Boston College) 1981-4
Most passes completed: 900 Brian McClure (Bowling Green) 1982-5

HEISMAN TROPHY

Awarded annually since 1935 by the Downtown Athletic Club of New York to the top college footballer as determined by a poll of journalists. It was originally called the D.A.C. Trophy but changed its name in 1936. Its full title is the John W. Heisman Memorial Trophy, named after the first athletic director of the Downtown club.

Recent winners:
1970 Jim Plunkett (Stanford)
1971 Pat Sullivan (Auburn)
1972 Johnny Rodgers (Nebraska)
1973 John Cappelletti (Penn State)
1974 Archie Griffin (Ohio State)
1975 Archie Griffin (Ohio State)
1976 Tony Dorsett (Pittsburgh)
1977 Earl Campbell (Texas)
1978 Billy Sims (Oklahoma)
1979 Charles White (USC)
1980 George Rogers (South Carolina)

1981 Marcus Allen (USC)
1982 Herschel Walker (Georgia)
1983 Mike Rozier (Nebraska)
1984 Doug Flutie (Boston College)
1985 Bo Jackson (Auburn)
1986 Vinny Testaverde (Miami)
Most wins: 2 Archie Griffin 1974-5

NATIONAL CHAMPIONS

At the end of December each year journalists throughout the United States engage in a national poll to vote for the outstanding college team of the year. The poll has been conducted since 1936.

Recent winners:
1977 Notre Dame
1978 Alabama
1979 Alabama
1980 Georgia
1981 Clemson
1982 Penn State
1983 Miami, Florida
1984 Brigham Young
1985 Oklahoma
1986 Penn State
Most wins: 7 Notre Dame 1943, 1946-7, 1949, 1966, 1973, 1977

ANGLING

Angling is the art of catching fish with rod, line and hook. Such an activity naturally dates back to civilised man's earliest days. The oldest club still in existence is the Ellem fishing club in Scotland, formed in 1829. English national championships were first held in 1906 and the International Confederation of Anglers (CIPS – see below) was formed in Rome in 1952.

WORLD FLY FISHING CHAMPIONSHIPS

The first world fly fishing championship was held in 1981, organised by the Confédération Internationale de la Pêche Sportive (CIPS).

Year	Venue	Individual winner	Team winner
1981	Lake Echternach (Lux)	C.Wittkamp (Hol)	Netherlands
1982	Narcea River (Spa)	Viktor Diez y Diez (Spa)	Italy
1983	Sesia River (Ita)	Segismondo Fernandez (Spa)	Italy
1984	Tormes River (Spa)	Tony Pawson (Eng)	Italy
1985	San River (Pol)	Leslaw Frasik (Pol)	Poland
1986	Ourthe River (Bel)	Slivoj Svoboda (Cs)	Italy
1987	Various locations (Eng)	Brian Leadbetter (Eng)	England

WORLD CHAMPIONSHIPS

The first World Fresh Water Championships were held in 1957, three years after the staging of the first European championships.

Winners:

	INDIVIDUAL	TEAM
1957	Mandeli (Ita)	Italy
1958	Garroit (Bel)	Belgium
1959	Robert Tesse (Fra)	France
1960	Robert Tesse (Fra)	Belgium
1961	Ramon Legogue (Fra)	GDR
1962	Raimondo Tedasco (Ita)	Italy
1963	William Lane (Eng)	France
1964	Joseph Fontanet (Fra)	France
1965	Robert Tesse (Fra)	Romania
1966	Henri Guiheneuf (Fra)	France
1967	Jacques Isenbaert (Bel)	Belgium
1968	Günter Grebenstein (FRG)	France
1969	Robin Harris (Eng)	Holland
1970	Marcel Van den Eynde (Bel)	Belgium
1971	Dino Bassi (Ita)	Italy
1972	Hubert Levels (Hol)	France
1973	Pierre Michiels (Bel)	Belgium
1974	Aribert Richter (FRG)	France
1975	Ian Heaps (Eng)	France
1976	Dino Bassi (Ita)	Italy
1977	Jean Mainil (Bel)	Luxembourg
1978	Jean-Pierre Fouquet (Fra)	France

1979 Gerard Heulard (Fra)	France
1980 Wolf-Rüdiger Kremkus (FRG)	FR Germany
1981 Dave Thomas (Eng)	France
1982 Kevin Ashurst (Eng)	Holland
1983 Wolf-Rüdiger Kremkus (FRG)	Belgium
1984 Bobby Smithers (Ire)	Luxembourg
1985 Dave Roper (Eng)	England
1986 Lud Wever (Hol)	Italy

Most Wins (Ind): 3 Robert Tesse
(Team): 11 France

ARCHERY

From the use of bow and arrow in hunting and in warfare, archery developed as one of man's earliest known organized sports.

The world governing body is the Fédération Internationale de Tir à l'Arc (FITA), which was founded in 1931.

WORLD CHAMPIONSHIPS

World target archery championships were first staged in 1931 and are now held bienially. From 1957 the contests have been over Double FITA rounds of 36 arrows at 90m, 70m, 50m and 30m for men; 70m, 60m, 50m and 30m for women; scores are given for these. As from 1987 the championships are conducted on a knockout basis with scores not being accumulated over the rounds.

Winners:

MEN'S INDIVIDUAL
1931 Michal Sawicki (Pol)
1932 Laurent Reith (Bel)
1933 Donald Mackenzie (USA)
1934 Henry Kjellson (Swe)
1935 Adriaan van Kohlen (Bel)
1936 Emil Heilborn (Swe)
1937 George De Rons (Bel)
1938 Frantisek Hadas (Cs)
1939 Roger Beday (Fra)
1946 Einar Tang Holbek (Den)
1947-50 Hans Deutgen (Swe)
1952 Stellan Andersson (Swe)
1953 Bror Lundgren (Swe)
1955 Nils Andersson (Swe)
1957 Ozziek Smathers (USA) 2231
1958 Stig Thysell (Swe) 2101
1959 James Caspers (USA) 2247
1961 Joseph Thornton (USA) 2310
1963 Charles Sandlin (USA) 2332
1965 Matti Haikonen (Fin) 2313
1967 Ray Rogers (USA) 2298
1969 Hardy Ward (USA) 2423
1971 John Williams (USA) 2445
1973 Viktor Sidoruk (USSR) 2185
1975 Darrell Pace (USA) 2548
1977 Richard McKinney (USA) 2501
1979 Darrell Pace (USA) 2474
1981 Kysti Laasonen (Fin) 2541
1983 Richard McKinney (USA) 2617
1985 Richard McKinney (USA) 2601
1987 Vladimir Yesheyev (USSR)

Most wins: 4 Hans Deutgen, 3 Richard McKinney

MEN'S TEAM WINS:
14 USA	1957, each championship 1959-83
6 Sweden	1934, 1948, 1950, 1952-3, 1955
4 Czechoslovakia	1936, 1938, 1947, 1949
2 France	1931, 1939
2 Poland	1932, 1937
2 Belgium	1933, 1935
2 South Korea	1985, 1987
1 Denmark	1946
Finland	1958
F.R. Germany	1987

Record score: 7817 USA 1983

WOMEN'S INDIVIDUAL:
1931-4 Janina Kurkowska (Pol)
1935 Ina Catani (Swe)
1936 Janina Kurkowska (Pol)
1937 Ingo Simon (UK)
1938 Nora Weston Martyr (UK)
1939 Janina Kurkowska (Pol)
1946 Nilla de Wharton Burr (UK)
1947 Janina Kurkowska (Pol)
1948 Nilla de Wharton Burr (UK)
1949 Barbara Waterhouse (UK)
1950 Jean Lee (USA)
1952 Jean Lee (USA)
1953 Jean Richards (USA)
1955 Katarzyna Wisniowska (Pol)
1957 Carole Meinhart (USA) 2120
1958 Sigrid Johansson (Swe) 2053
1959 Ann Corby (née Weber) (USA) 2023
1961 Nancy Vanderheide (USA) 2173
1963 Victoria Cook (USA) 2253
1965 Maire Lindholm (Fin) 2214
1967 Maria Maczynska (Pol) 2240
1969 Dorothy Lidstone (Can) 2361
1971 Emma Gapchenko (USSR) 2380
1973 Linda Myers (USA) 2204
1975 Zebiniso Rustamova (USSR) 2465
1977 Luann Ryon (USA) 2515
1979 Kim Jin-Ho (SKo) 2507
1981 Natalya Butuzova (USSR) 2514
1983 Kim Jin-Ho (SKo) 2616
1985 Irina Soldatova (USSR) 2595
1987 Ma Xiagjun (Chn)

Most wins: 7 Janina Kurkowska (née Spychajowa) (Pol)

WOMEN'S TEAM WINS:
8 USA	1952, 1957-9, 1961, 1963, 1965, 1977
7 Poland	1933-4, 1936, 1938-9, 1967, 1971
6 USSR	1969, 1973, 1975, 1981, 1985, 1987
5 United Kingdom	1935, 1937, 1946, 1949, 1955
2 Finland	1950, 1953
2 South Korea	1979, 1983
1 Denmark	1947
1 Czechoslovakia	1948

Record score: 7721 USSR 1985

Rick McKinney has won three world titles, and the 1984 Olympic silver medal. (All-Sport/Tony Duffy)

OLYMPIC GAMES

The sport was included in the Olympic Games from 1900 to 1908, then again in 1920 (at the Belgian style of shooting), and was re-introduced in 1972.

Hubert van Innis (Bel) won a record six gold and three silver medals: two gold and a silver in 1900 and the rest in 1920.

Olympic archery is now contested at double FITA rounds.

Winners:

MEN
1972 John Williams (USA) 2528
1976 Darrell Pace (USA) 2571
1980 Tomi Poikolainen (Fin) 2455
1984 Darrell Pace (USA) 2616

WOMEN
1972 Doreen Wilber (USA) 2424
1976 Luann Ryan (USA) 2499
1980 Keto Lossaberidze (USSR) 2491
1984 Seo Hyang-Soon (SKo) 2568

Team events for men and women are to be contested from 1988.

WORLD RECORDS

for single FITA rounds (maximum 360 points for each set)

MEN
FITA	1341	Darrell Pace (USA) 1979
90m	322	Vladimir Yesheyev (USSR) 1980
70m	342	Richard McKinney (USA) 1985
50m	345	Richard McKinney (USA) 1982
30m	357	Takayoshi Matsushita (Jap) 1986
Team	3912	USA (Richard McKinney, Darrell Pace, Jerry Pylpchuk) 1985

WOMEN
FITA	1331	Lyudmila Arzhanikova (USSR) 1986
70m	328	Natalya Butuzova (USSR) 1979
60m	338	Lyudmila Arzhanikova (USSR) 1984
	338	Kim Jin-Ho (SKo) 1986
50m	335	Yanzhina Tsyrenzhapova (USSR) 1985
30m	354	Kim Mi-Ja (SKo) 1986
Team	3935	South Korea (Kim Mi-Ja, Kim Jin-Ho, Park Jung-Ah) 1986

WORLD INDOOR RECORDS
Indoor FITA Round at 18 metres, maximum score 600
Men: 590   Thierry Venant (Fra) 1987
Women: 583   Natalya Butuzova (USSR) 1983

Indoor Double FITA Rounds at 25 metres:
Men: 589   Darrell Pace (USA) 1984
Women: 588   Yelena Margel (USSR) 1985

Archery is a sport at which practitioners can remain at the top for a long time. A most notable example is that of Alice Blanche Legh who won a record 23 British ladies' titles between 1881 and 1922, when she was 67.

WORLD FIELD ARCHERY CHAMPIONSHIPS

Held in 1969, 1971 and biennially from 1972 at bare bow and freestyle categories for men and women.

Most wins: 3 Anders Rosenberg (Swe) men's bare bow 1978, 1980, 1982.

ASSOCIATION FOOTBALL

The Chinese played a form of football, *Tsu chu* (meaning 'to kick a ball of stuffed leather'), over 2500 years ago, other versions may have been played in various parts of the world, but much of the game's development came in England. An early reference to the sport came in 1314 when Edward II issued a prohibition on the game due to the excessive noise people were making in the streets of London hustling over footballs. Three subsequent British monarchs also banned the sport, for one reason or another, until it became an organised sport in the 19th century. The first rules were drawn up at Cambridge University in 1848 and there were various modifications over the next decades. The Sheffield club, the oldest club still in existence, was formed in 1855, and the Football Association was founded in 1863. The sport grew rapidly in popularity world-wide, and the Fédération Internationale de Football Association (FIFA), the world governing body, was formed in Paris in 1904. It now has 150 members.

WORLD CUP

The first World Cup for the Jules Rimet Trophy was held in Uruguay in 1930. The competition has been staged every four years since then, with the exception of the war years. Brazil won the trophy outright in 1970 following their third win and teams now compete for the FIFA World Cup.

Finals:
(Goalscorers are shown beneath each team)

Year	Winners		Runners-up		Venue	Attendance
1930	URUGUAY Dorado, Cea, Iriarte, Castro	4	ARGENTINA Peucelle, Stabile	2	Montevideo, Uruguay	90,000
1934	ITALY Orsi, Schiavio	2	CZECHOSLOVAKIA Puc	1*	Rome, Italy	55,000
1938	ITALY Colaussi (2), Piola (2)	4	HUNGARY Titkos, Sarosi	2	Paris France	50,000
1950	URUGUAY Schiaffino, Ghiggia	2	BRAZIL Friaca	1§	Rio de Janeiro, Brazil	199,854
1954	F.R.GERMANY Rahn (2), Morlock	3	HUNGARY Puskas, Czibor	2	Berne, Switzerland	55,000
1958	BRAZIL Vava (2), Pele (2) Zagalo	5	SWEDEN Liedholm, Simonsson	2	Stockholm, Sweden	49,737
1962	BRAZIL Amarildo, Zito, Vava	3	CZECHOSLOVAKIA Masopust	1	Santiago, Chile	69,068
1966	ENGLAND Hurst (3), Peters	4	F.R.GERMANY Haller, Weber	2*	Wembley, London England	93,000
1970	BRAZIL Gerson, Jairzinho, Pele, Carlos Alberto	4	ITALY Boninsegna	1	Mexico City, Mexico	110,000
1974	F.R.GERMANY Breitner (pen), Muller	2	HOLLAND Neeskens (pen)	1	Munich, F.R.Germany	77,833
1978	ARGENTINA Kempes (2), Bertoni	3	HOLLAND Nanninga	1*	Buenos Aires, Argentina	77,000
1982	ITALY Rossi, Tardelli, Altobelli	3	F.R.GERMANY Breitner	1	Madrid, Spain	92,000
1986	ARGENTINA Brown, Valdano, Burruchaga	3	F.R.GERMANY Rummenigge, Voller	2	Mexico City, Mexico	114,580

(*) after extra time
(§) deciding match of final pool

THE LEADING NATIONS

A summary of the leading nations' records in the final stages of the World Cup.

	Winner	Runner-up	3rd	Played	Games Won	Drawn	Lost	Goals For	Against
Brazil	3	1	2	62	41	11	10	144	63
Italy	3	1	-	47	25	11	11	79	52
F.R.Germany	2	3	2	61	34	13	14	130	85
Argentina	2	1	-	41	22	6	13	77	55
Uruguay	2	-	-	33	14	7	12	59	47
England	1	-	-	34	15	9	10	47	32

Note: F.R.Germany includes Germany.

Most appearances in final stages:
13 Brazil (all competitions)
11 F.R.Germany
11 Italy
 9 Argentina
 8 England
 8 Uruguay
Highest score (Final rounds): 10-1 Hungary v El Salvador, 15 Jun 1982
Highest score (Qualifying rounds): 13-0 New Zealand v Fiji, 15 Aug 1981

FINAL TOURNAMENT RECORDS:

Most appearances:
21 Uwe Seeler (FRG) 1958-70
21 Wladyslaw Zmuda (Pol) 1974-86
Most final tournaments: 5 Antonio Carbajal (Mex) 1950-66
Most goals in career: 14 Gerd Müller (FRG) 1970-74
Most goals in one tournament: 13 Just Fontaine (Fra) 1958
Most goals in one game:
4 Leonidas (Bra) v Poland 1938
4 Ernest Willimowski (Pol) v Brazil 1938
4 Gustav Wetterstrom (Swe) v Cuba 1938
4 Juan Schiaffino (Uru) v Bolivia 1950
4 Ademir (Bra) v Sweden 1950
4 Sandor Kocsis (Hun) v F.R.Germany 1954
4 Just Fontaine (Fra) v F.R.Germany 1958
4 Eusebio (Por) v North Korea 1966
4 Emilio Butragueno (Spa) v Denmark 1986

Edison Arantes do Nascimento, better known as Pele, played in three winning World Cup teams.

Bobby Moore, England's victorious World Cup skipper in 1966.

EUROPEAN CHAMPIONSHIP

Held every four years, the championship is played over a two-year period. Originally called the European Nations Cup it changed to its present name in 1968. Competing nations compete for the Henri Delaunay Cup, named after the former General Secretary of the Union of European Football Associations (UEFA).

Finals:

Year	Winners		Runners-up		Venue	Attendance
1960	USSR Metreveli, Ponedelnik	2	YUGOSLAVIA Netto (og)	1*	Paris	17,966
1964	SPAIN Pereda, Marcellino	2	USSR Khusainov	1	Madrid	120,000
1968	ITALY Domenghini	1	YUGOSLAVIA Dzajic	1*	Rome	75,000
Replay	ITALY Riva, Anastasi	2	YUGOSLAVIA	0	Rome	60,000
1972	F.R.GERMANY Muller (2), Wimmer	3	USSR	0	Brussels	43,437
1976	CZECHOSLOVAKIA (Czechoslovakia won 5-3 on penalties) Svehlik, Dobias	2	F.R.GERMANY Muller, Holzenbein	2*	Belgrade	45,000
1980	F.R.GERMANY Hrubesch (2)	2	BELGIUM Van der Eychen	1	Rome	47,864
1984	FRANCE Platini, Bellone	2	SPAIN	0	Paris	80,000

(*) after extra time
Most wins: 2 F.R.Germany 1972, 1980
Most finals: 3 USSR 1960, 1964, 1972; F.R.Germany 1972, 1976, 1980

EUROPEAN CHAMPION CLUBS' CUP

Popularly known as the European Cup it is an annual knockout competition for the league champions of all UEFA affiliated countries. It was first held in 1955-56, shortly after the formation of UEFA, and was the idea of Gabriel Hanot, the soccer editor of the French daily newspaper *L'Equipe*.

Finals:

Year	Winners		Runners-up		Venue	Attendance
1956	REAL MADRID Rial (2), Di Stefano, Marquitos	4	STADE DE REIMS Leblond, Templin, Hidalgo	3	Paris	38,000
1957	REAL MADRID Di Stefano (pen), Gento	2	FIORENTINA	0	Madrid	124,000
1958	REAL MADRID Di Stefano, Rial, Gento	3	AC MILAN Schiaffino, Grillo	2	Brussels	67,000
1959	REAL MADRID Mateos, Di Stefano	2	STADE DE REIMS	0	Stuttgart	80,000
1960	REAL MADRID Puskas (4), Di Stefano (3)	7	EINTRACHT FRANKFURT Stein (2), Kress	3	Glasgow	127,621
1961	BENFICA Aguas, Coluna, Ramallets (og)	3	BARCELONA Kocsis, Czibor	2	Berne	28,000
1962	BENFICA Eusebio (2, 1 pen) Aguas, Cavem, Coluna	5	REAL MADRID Puskas (3)	3	Amsterdam	65,000
1963	AC MILAN Altafini (2)	2	BENFICA Eusebio	1	London	45,000

Year	Winners		Runners-up		Venue	Attendance
1964	INTER MILAN Mazzola (2), Milani	3	REAL MADRID Felo	1	Vienna	74,000
1965	INTER MILAN Jair	1	BENFICA	0	Milan	80,000
1966	REAL MADRID Amancio, Serena	2	PARTIZAN BELGRADE Vasovic	1	Brussels	55,000
1967	GLASGOW CELTIC Gemmell, Chalmers	2	INTER MILAN Mazzola (pen)	1	Lisbon	56,000
1968	MANCHESTER UNITED Charlton (2), Best Kidd	4	BENFICA Graca	1*	London	100,000
1969	AC MILAN Prati (3), Sormani	4	AJAX Vasovic (pen)	1	Madrid	50,000
1970	FEYENOORD Israel, Kindvall	2	GLASGOW CELTIC Gemmell	1*	Milan	50,000
1971	AJAX van Dijk, Haan	2	PANATHINAIKOS	0	London	90,000
1972	AJAX Cruyff (2)	2	INTER MILAN	0	Rotterdam	67,000
1973	AJAX Rep	1	JUVENTUS	0	Belgrade	93,500
1974	BAYERN MUNICH Schwarzenbeck	1	ATLETICO MADRID Luis	1	Brussels	65,000
Replay	BAYERN MUNICH Hoeness (2), Muller (2)	4	ATLETICO MADRID	0	Brussels	65,000

The marvellous Real Madrid team of the early 1960s.

Year	Winners		Runners-up		Venue	Attendance
1975	BAYERN MUNICH Roth, Muller	2	LEEDS UNITED	0	Paris	48,000
1976	BAYERN MUNICH Roth	1	ST.ETIENNE	0	Glasgow	54,864
1977	LIVERPOOL McDermott, Smith Neal (pen)	3	BORUSSIA MOENCHENGLADBACH Simonsen	1	Rome	57,000
1978	LIVERPOOL Dalglish	1	FC BRUGES	0	London	92,000
1979	NOTTINGHAM FOREST Francis	1	MALMO	0	Munich	57,500
1980	NOTTINGHAM FOREST Robertson	1	SV HAMBURG	0	Madrid	50,000
1981	LIVERPOOL A.Kennedy	1	REAL MADRID	0	Paris	48,360
1982	ASTON VILLA Withe	1	BAYERN MUNICH	0	Rotterdam	46,000
1983	SV HAMBURG Magath	1	JUVENTUS	0	Athens	80,000
1984	LIVERPOOL (Liverpool won 4-2 on penalties) Neal	1	AS ROMA Pruzzo	1*	Rome	69,693
1985	JUVENTUS Platini (pen)	1	LIVERPOOL	0	Brussels	58,000
1986	STEAUA BUCHAREST (Steaua won 2-0 on penalties)	0	BARCELONA	0*	Seville	70,000
1987	FC PORTO Madjer, Juary	2	BAYERN MUNICH Kögl	1	Vienna	59,000

(*) after extra time

Biggest win: 12-2 Feyenoord v Reykjavik (1st round) 17 Sep 1969
(final): 7-3 Real Madrid v Eintracht 18 May 1960
Biggest win (aggregate): 18-0 (8-0 & 10-0) Benfica v Stade Dudelange
(preliminary round) Sep & Oct 1965

Franz Beckenbauer, twice European Footballer of the Year, points the way. He captained Bayern Munich and played 103 times for West Germany, 1965-77

EUROPEAN CUP-WINNERS' CUP

The second most important European club competition after the Champions' Cup, the Cup-Winners' Cup is open to winners of domestic senior cup competitions in UEFA-affiliated countries. The first final in 1961 was over two legs, but all subsequent finals have been at a single game.

Finals:

Year	Winners		Runners-up		Venue	Attendance
1961	FIORENTINA Milan (2)	2	GLASGOW RANGERS	0	Glasgow	80,000
	FIORENTINA Milan, Hamrin (Fiorentina won 4-1 on aggregate)	2	GLASGOW RANGERS Scott	1	Florence	50,000
1962	ATLETICO MADRID Peiro	1	FIORENTINA Hamrin	1	Glasgow	27,289
Replay	ATLETICO MADRID Jones, Mendonca, Peiro	3	FIORENTINA	0	Stuttgart	38,120
1963	TOTTENHAM HOTSPUR Greaves (2), Dyson (2) White	5	ATLETICO MADRID Collar (pen)	1	Rotterdam	49,143
1964	SPORTING LISBON Figueiredo (2), Dansky (og)	3	MTK BUDAPEST Sandor (2), Kuti	3*	Brussels	3,208
Replay	SPORTING LISBON Morais	1	MTK BUDAPEST	0	Antwerp	19,924
1965	WEST HAM UNITED Sealey (2)	2	MUNICH 1860	0	London	97,974
1966	BORUSSIA DORTMUND Held, Yeats (og)	2	LIVERPOOL Hunt	1*	Glasgow	41,657
1967	BAYERN MUNICH Roth	1	GLASGOW RANGERS	1*	Nuremberg	69,480
1968	AC MILAN Hamrin (2)	2	SV HAMBURG	0	Rotterdam	53,276
1969	SLOVAN BRATISLAVA Cvetler, Hrivnak, Jan Capkovich	3	BARCELONA Zaluda, Rexach	2	Basle	19,478
1970	MANCHESTER CITY Young, Lee (pen)	2	GORNIK ZABRZE Ozlizlo	1	Vienna	7,968
1971	CHELSEA Osgood	1	REAL MADRID Zoco	1*	Athens	42,000
Replay	CHELSEA Dempsey, Osgood	2	REAL MADRID Fleitas	1	Athens	24,000
1972	GLASGOW RANGERS Johnston (2), Stein	3	DYNAMO MOSCOW Estrekov, Makovikov	2	Barcelona	24,701
1973	AC MILAN Chiarugi	1	LEEDS UNITED	0	Salonika	45,000
1974	FC MAGDEBURG Lanzi (og), Seguin	2	AC MILAN	0	Rotterdam	4,641
1975	DYNAMO KIEV Onischenko (2), Blokhin	3	FERENCVAROS	0	Basle	10,897
1976	ANDERLECHT Rensenbrink (2, 1 pen) Van der Elst (2)	4	WEST HAM UNITED Holland, Robson	2	Brussels	58,000

Year	Winners		Runners-up		Venue	Attendance
1977	SV HAMBURG Volkert (pen), Magath	2	ANDERLECHT	0	Amsterdam	65,000
1978	ANDERLECHT Rensenbrink (2), Van Binst (2)	4	AUSTRIA WAC	0	Paris	48,679
1979	BARCELONA Sanchez, Asensi, Rexach, Krankl	4	FORTUNA DUSSELDORF Seel (2), K.Allofs	3*	Basle	58,000
1980	VALENCIA (Valencia won 5-4 on penalties)	0	ARSENAL	0*	Brussels	40,000
1981	DYNAMO TBILISI Gutsayev, Daraselia	2	CARL ZEISS JENA Hoppe	1	Dusseldorf	9,000
1982	BARCELONA Simonsen, Quini	2	STANDARD LIEGE Vandermissen	1	Barcelona	100,000
1983	ABERDEEN Black, Hewitt	2	REAL MADRID Juanito (pen)	1*	Gothenburg	17,804
1984	JUVENTUS Vignola, Boniek	2	FC PORTO Sousa	1	Basle	60,000
1985	EVERTON Gray, Steven, Sheedy	3	RAPID VIENNA Krankl	1	Rotterdam	35,000
1986	DYNAMO KIEV Zavarov, Blokhin, Yevtushenko	3	ATLETICO MADRID	0	Lyon	39,300
1987	AJAX AMSTERDAM Van Basten	1	LOKOMOTIV LEIPZIG	0	Athens	35,000

(*) after extra time

Biggest win: 16-1 Sporting Lisbon v Apoel Nicosia (1st round) 13 Nov 1963
Biggest win (final): 5-1 Tottenham Hotspur v Atletico Madrid 15 May 1963
Biggest win (aggregate): 21-0 (8-0 & 13-0) Chelsea v Jeunesse Hautcharage (1st round) 15 & 29 Sep 1971

UEFA CUP

Established in 1955 it was initially intended as a tournament for European cities that sponsored international industrial fairs, hence the competition's original name, the International Industries Fairs Inter-Cities Cup, commonly known as the Fairs Cup. The first tournament took three years to complete. The second Fairs Cup predominently involved club sides and from 1960-1 it became an annual event. The competition became known as the European Fairs Cup in 1966 and in 1971 it became the UEFA Cup. The competition is open to leading sides not eligible for the other two main European competitions. The final, unlike the other European tournaments, is played over two legs on a home and away basis.

Finals:

Year		Home team		Away team		Attendance
1958	1st leg	LONDON Greaves, Langley (pen)	2	BARCELONA Tejada, Martinez	2	45,466
	2nd leg	BARCELONA Suarez(2), Evaristo(2), Martinez, Verges	6	LONDON	0	62,000
		(Barcelona won 8-2 on aggregate)				
1960	1st leg	BIRMINGHAM CITY	0	BARCELONA	0	40,500
	2nd leg	BARCELONA Czibor(2), Martinez, Coll	4	BIRMINGHAM CITY Hooper	1	70,000
		(Barcelona won 4-1 on aggregate)				
1961	1st leg	BIRMINGHAM CITY Hellawell, Orritt	2	AS ROMA Manfredini(2)	2	21,005

Year	Home team		Away team		Attendance
	2nd leg AS ROMA Farmer(og), Pestrin (AS Roma won 4-2 on aggregate)	2	BIRMINGHAM CITY	0	60,000
1962	1st leg VALENCIA Guillot(3), Yosu(2) H.Nunez	6	BARCELONA Kocsis(2)	2	65,000
	2nd leg BARCELONA Kocsis (Valencia won 7-3 on aggregate)	1	VALENCIA Guillot	1	60,000
1963	1st leg DYNAMO ZAGREB Zambata	1	VALENCIA Waldo, Urtiaga	2	40,000
	2nd leg VALENCIA Mano, Nunez (Valencia won 4-1 on aggregate)	2	DYNAMO ZAGREB	0	55,000
1964	REAL ZARAGOZA (Played over one leg, at Barcelona) Villa, Marcelino	2	VALENCIA Urtiaga	1	50,000
1965	FERENCVAROS (Played over one leg, at Turin) Fenyvesi	1	JUVENTUS	0	25,000
1966	1st leg BARCELONA Canario	0	REAL ZARAGOZA	1	70,000
	2nd leg REAL ZARAGOZA Marcelino(2) (Barcelona won 4-3 on aggregate)	2	BARCELONA Pujol(3), Zaballa	4*	70,000
1967	1st leg DYNAMO ZAGREB Cercer(2)	2	LEEDS UNITED	0	40,000
	2nd leg LEEDS UNITED (Dynamo Zagreb won 2-0 on aggregate)	0	DYNAMO ZAGREB	0	35,604
1968	1st leg LEEDS UNITED Jones	1	FERENCVAROS	0	25,368
	2nd leg FERENCVAROS (Leeds United won 1-0 on aggregate)	0	LEEDS UNITED	0	70,000
1969	1st leg NEWCASTLE UNITED Moncur(2), Scott	3	UJPEST DOZSA	0	60,000
	2nd leg UJPEST DOZSA Bene, Gorocs (Newcastle United won 6-2 on aggregate)	2	NEWCASTLE UNITED Moncur, Arentoft, Foggon	3	37,000
1970	1st leg ANDERLECHT Mulder(2), Devrindt	3	ARSENAL Kennedy	1	37,000
	2nd leg ARSENAL Kelly, Radford, Sammels (Arsenal won 4-3 on aggregate)	3	ANDERLECHT	0	51,612
1971	1st leg JUVENTUS (abandoned after 51 minutes, waterlogged pitch)	0	LEEDS UNITED	0	40,000
	Replay JUVENTUS Bettega, Capello	2	LEEDS UNITED Madeley, Bates	2	42,000
	2nd leg LEEDS UNITED Clarke (Leeds United won on the away goals rule)	1	JUVENTUS Anastasi	1	42,483
1972	1st leg WOLVERHAMPTON W.	1	TOTTENHAM HOTSPUR Chivers(2)	2	38,362
	2nd leg TOTTENHAM HOTSPUR Mullery (Tottenham Hotspur won 3-2 on aggregate)	1	WOLVERHAMPTON W. Wagstaffe	1	54,303
1973	1st leg LIVERPOOL (abandoned after 27 minutes, waterlogged pitch)	0	BORUSSIA MOENCHENGLADBACH	0	44,967

Year	Home team		Away team		Attendance
	Replay LIVERPOOL Keegan(2), Lloyd	3	BORUSSIA MOENCHENGLADBACH	0	41,169
	2nd leg BORUSSIA MOENCHENGLADBACH Heynckes(2)	2	LIVERPOOL	0	35,000
	(Liverpool won 3-2 on aggregate)				
1974	1st leg TOTTENHAM HOTSPUR England, van Daele(og)	2	FEYENOORD van Hanegem, De Jong	2	46.281
	2nd leg FEYENOORD Rijsbergen, Ressel	2	TOTTENHAM HOTSPUR	0	59,317
	(Feyenoord won 4-2 on aggregate)				
1975	1st leg BORUSSIA MOENCHENGLADBACH	0	TWENTE ENSCHEDE	0	42,368
	2nd leg TWENTE ENSCHEDE Drost	1	BORUSSIA MOENCHENGLADBACH Heynckes(3), Simonsen(2-1 pen)	5	21,767
	(Borussia Moenchengladbach won 5-1 on aggregate)				
1976	1st leg LIVERPOOL Kennedy, Case, Keegan(pen)	3	FC BRUGES Lambert, Cools	2	49,981
	2nd leg FC BRUGES Lambert(pen)	1	LIVERPOOL Keegan	1	32,000
	(Liverpool won 4-3 on aggregate)				
1977	1st leg JUVENTUS Tardelli	1	ATLETICO BILBAO	0	75,000
	2nd leg ATLETICO BILBAO Irureta, Carlos	2	JUVENTUS Bettega	1	43,000
	(Juventus won on the away-goals rule)				
1978	1st leg BASTIA	0	PSV EINDHOVEN	0	15,000
	2nd leg PSV EINDHOVEN W.van der Kerkhof, Deykers, van der Kuylen	3	BASTIA	0	27,000
	(Eindhoven won 3-0 on aggregate)				
1979	1st leg RED STAR BELGRADE Sestic	1	BORUSSIA MOENCHENGLADBACH Juristic(og)	1	87.500
	2nd leg BORUSSIA MOENCHENGLADBACH Simonsen(pen)	1	RED STAR BELGRADE	0	45,000
	(Borussia Moenchengladbach won 2-1 on aggregate)				
1980	1st leg BORUSSIA MOENCHENGLADBACH Kulik(2), Matthaus	3	EINTRACHT FRANKFURT Karger, Holzenbein	2	25,000
	2nd leg EINTRACHT FRANKFURT Schaub	1	BORUSSIA MOENCHENGLADBACH	0	60,000
	(Eintracht won on the away-goals rule)				
1981	1st leg IPSWICH TOWN Wark(pen), Thijssen, Mariner	3	AZ 67 ALKMAAR	0	27,532
	2nd leg AZ 67 ALKMAAR Welzl, Metgod, Tol, Jonker	4	IPSWICH TOWN Thijssen, Wark	2	28,500
	(Ipswich Town won 5-4 on aggregate)				
1982	1st leg IFK GOTHENBURG Tord Holmgren	1	SV HAMBURG	0	42,548
	2nd leg SV HAMBURG	0	IFK GOTHENBURG Corneliusson, Nilsson, Fredriksson(pen)	3	60,000
	(Gothenburg won 4-0 on aggregate)				

Year		Home team		Away team		Attendance
1983	1st leg	ANDERLECHT Brylle	1	BENFICA	0	60,000
	2nd leg	BENFICA Sheu	1	ANDERLECHT Lozano	1	80,000
	(Anderlecht won 2-1 on aggregate)					
1984	1st leg	ANDERLECHT Olsen	1	TOTTENHAM HOTSPUR Miller	1	40,000
	2nd leg	TOTTENHAM HOTSPUR Roberts	1	ANDERLECHT Czerniatynski	1*	46,205
	(Tottenham Hotspur won 4-3 on penalties)					
1985	1st leg	VIDEOTON	0	REAL MADRID Michel, Santillana, Juanito	3	30,000
	2nd leg	REAL MADRID	0	VIDEOTON Majer	1	90,000
	(Real Madrid won 3-1 on aggregate)					
1986	1st leg	REAL MADRID Valdano(2), Sanchez, Gordillo, Santillana	5	COLOGNE K.Allofs	1	80,000
	2nd leg	COLOGNE Bein, Geilenkirchen	2	REAL MADRID	0	15,000
	(Real Madrid won 5-3 on aggregate)					
1987	1st leg	IFK GOTHENBURG Petterson	1	DUNDEE UNITED	0	50,023
	2nd leg	DUNDEE UNITED Clark	1	IFK GOTHENBURG Nilsson	1	20,911
	(Gothenburg won 2-1 on aggregate)					

(*) after extra time
Biggest win: 13-0 Cologne v Union Luxembourg (1st round) 5 Oct 1965
Biggest win (final, aggregate): 8-2 (2-2 & 6-0) Barcelona v London 5 Mar & 1 May 1958
Biggest win (aggregate): 21-0 (9-0 & 12-0) Feyenoord v US Rumelange (1st round) 13 & 27 Sep 1972

EUROPE'S LEADING TEAMS

The following is a table of all teams that have won two or more major European tournaments

	Champions Cup	Cup-winners Cup	UEFA/Fairs Cup	Total
Real Madrid	6	-	2	8
Liverpool	4	-	2	6
Barcelona	-	2	3	5
Bayern Munich	3	1	-	4
AC Milan	2	2	-	4
Ajax	3	1	-	4
Juventus	1	1	1	3
Anderlecht	-	2	1	3
Tottenham Hotspur	-	1	2	3
Valencia	-	1	2	3
Borussia Moenchengladbach	-	-	3	3
Benfica	2	-	-	2
Inter Milan	2	-	-	2
Nottingham Forest	2	-	-	2
SV Hamburg	1	1	-	2
Feyenoord	1	-	1	2
Dynamo Kiev	-	2	-	2
Leeds United	-	-	2	2
IFK Gothenburg	-	-	2	2

DISTRIBUTION OF NATIONS

The following countries have provided winners of the three main European competitions

	European Cup	Cup-winners Cup	UEFA/Fairs Cup	Total
England	8	5	9	22
Spain	6	4	8	18
Italy	5	4	2	11
F.R.Germany	4	3	3	10
Holland	4	1	2	7
Portugal	3	1	-	4
Scotland	1	2	-	3
Belgium	-	2	1	3
USSR	-	3	-	3
Sweden	-	-	2	2
Romania	1	-	-	1
Czechoslovakia	-	1	-	1
GDR	-	1	-	1
Hungary	-	-	1	1
Yugoslavia	-	-	1	1

EUROPEAN SUPER CUP

After Ajax won the European Cup for the second successive year in 1972 the Dutch newspaper *De Telegraaf* suggested they play the winners of the Cup-Winners' Cup for a Super Cup. They played, and beat, Glasgow Rangers over two legs and became the first winners. UEFA did not officially recognise the event until 1974. There was no competition in 1981 and 1985. In 1984 and 1986 the cup was decided on one match.

Year	Winners	Runners-up	Scores
1972 a	Ajax *	Glasgow Rangers	3-1, 3-2
1973 b	Ajax *	AC Milan	0-1, 6-0
1974 c	Bayern Munich *	FC Magdeburg	3-2, 2-1
1975	Dynamo Kiev	Bayern Munich *	1-0, 2-0
1976	Anderlecht	Bayern Munich *	1-2, 4-1
1977	Liverpool *	SV Hamburg	1-1, 6-0
1978	Anderlecht	Liverpool *	3-1, 1-2
1979	Nottingham F *	Barcelona	1-0, 1-1
1980	Valencia	Nottingham F *	1-2, 1-0

(Valencia won on the away goals rule)

1982	Aston Villa *	Barcelona	0-1, 3-0
1983	Aberdeen	SV Hamburg *	0-0, 2-0
1984	Juventus	Liverpool *	2-0
1986 d	Steaua Bucharest *	Dynamo Kiev	1-0

* indicates European Cup holders
a played in 1973
b played in 1974
c The two scheduled clubs, Bayern Munich and Magdeburg, were drawn together in the second round of the 1974-75 European Champions Cup. They decided the results of that match would decide that season's Super Cup winners.
d Played in 1987
Most wins: 2 Ajax, Anderlecht

SOUTH AMERICAN CHAMPIONSHIP

In 1910 an Argentine national side, composed mainly of British exiles, suggested a tournament against Uruguay and Chile. This was the forerunner of the South American Championship which was inaugurated in 1916, the year of the formation of the South American Football Confederation. The championship is now held every four years but organisation has left a lot to be desired over the years and the popularity of the event dropped considerably in the 1960s, particularly after the introduction of the Libertadores Cup, when club soccer was regarded as more important than the international game in some countries. The championship was revived in 1975, after a gap of eight years, and is now played on a home and away league basis with the ten competing nations split into three groups. It becomes a knockout competition from the semi-final stage.

Winners:

13	Uruguay	1916-7, 1920, 1923-4, 1926, 1935*, 1942, 1956*, 1959*, 1967, 1983, 1987
12	Argentina	1921, 1925, 1927, 1929, 1937, 1941*, 1945*, 1946*, 1947, 1955, 1957, 1959
3	Brazil	1919, 1922, 1949
2	Peru	1939, 1975
2	Paraguay	1953, 1979
1	Bolivia	1963

* extraordinary tournament

SOUTH AMERICAN CUP

The South American Cup was first contested in 1960 when its full title was the South American Champion's Club Cup. Like the European Cup it was open to national league champions of countries affiliated to the South American Confederation. In 1965 league runners-up were also allowed to enter the competition and, that year, it changed its name to the Copa Libertadores.

Winners:

1960	Penarol (Uru)	1974	Independiente (Arg)
1961	Penarol (Uru)	1975	Independiente (Arg)
1962	Santos (Bra)	1976	Cruzeiro (Bra)
1963	Santos (Bra)	1977	Boca Juniors (Arg)
1964	Independiente (Arg)	1978	Boca Juniors (Arg)
1965	Independiente (Arg)	1979	Olimpia (Par)
1966	Penarol (Uru)	1980	Nacional (Uru)
1967	Racing Club (Arg)	1981	Flamengo (Bra)
1968	Estudiantes (Arg)	1982	Penarol (Uru)
1969	Estudiantes (Arg)	1983	Gremio (Bra)
1970	Estudiantes (Arg)	1984	Independiente (Arg)
1971	Nacional (Uru)	1985	Argentinos Juniors (Arg)
1972	Independiente (Arg)		
1973	Independiente (Arg)	1986	River Plate (Arg)

Most wins: 7 Independiente 4 Penarol 3 Estudiantes

NORTH AMERICAN SOCCER LEAGUE

The North American Soccer League (NASL) was formed in 1968 through the merger of the United States Soccer Association and the National Professional Soccer League. The recruiting of such big international names as Pele and Franz Beckenbauer in the 1970s saw crowds top the 70,000 mark. After that, however, the league declined and from a peak of 24 teams in 1979, the numbers dwindled until the NASL folded in 1985.

Champions:

1968	Atlanta Chiefs	1977	New York Cosmos
1969	Kansas City Spurs	1978	New York Cosmos
1970	Rochester Lancers	1979	Vancouver Whitecaps
1971	Dallas Tornado		
1972	New York Cosmos	1980	New York Cosmos
1973	Philadelphia Atoms	1981	Chicago Sting
1974	Los Angeles Aztecs	1982	New York Cosmos
1975	Tampa Bay Rowdies	1983	Tulsa Roughnecks
1976	Toronto Metro-Croatia	1984	Chicago Sting

Most wins: 5 New York Cosmos

WORLD CLUB CHAMPIONSHIP

The World Club Championship was first held in 1960 and was a meeting between the winners of the European Champions Cup and the South American Champions Cup. The two competing teams played each other on a home and away basis (with the exception of 1973) but since 1980 the winners have been decided by one match (for the Toyota Cup) played in Tokyo. There were no championship matches in 1975 and 1978. During the 1970s many of the matches became very physical affairs and on five occasions the European Cup holders refused to take part; their places were taken by runners-up. Prior to 1969, if both sides won a match, a third match was played.

Below left: *Diego Maradona, for whom the record transfer fee of £6.9 million was paid by Napoli to Barcelona.*

Below right: *Brazil's captain, Socrates.*

Bottom right: *Michel Platini of France, European Footballer of the Year three times with Juventus.*

Results:

Year	Winners	Runners-up	Scores	Play-off
1960	Real Madrid (Spa)	Penarol (Uru)	0-0, 5-1	
1961	Penarol (Uru)	Benfica (Por)	0-1, 5-0	2-1
1962	Santos (Bra)	Benfica (Por)	3-2, 5-2	
1963	Santos (Bra)	AC Milan (Ita)	2-4, 4-2	1-0
1964	Inter Milan (Ita)	Independiente (Arg)	0-1, 2-0	1-0
1965	Inter Milan (Ita)	Independiente (Arg)	3-0, 0-0	
1966	Penarol (Uru)	Real Madrid (Spa)	2-0, 2-0	
1967	Racing Club (Arg)	Glasgow Celtic (Sco)	0-1, 2-1	1-0
1968	Estudiantes (Arg)	Manchester U (Eng)	1-0, 1-1	
1969	AC Milan (Ita)	Estudiantes (Arg)	3-0, 1-2	
1970	Feyenoord (Hol)	Estudiantes (Arg)	2-2, 1-0	
1971	Nacional (Uru)	Panathinaikos (Gre)	1-1, 2-1	
1972	Ajax (Hol)	Independiente (Arg)	1-1, 3-0	

Results:

Year	Winners	Runners-up	Result(s)
1973	Independiente (Arg)	Juventus (Ita)	1-0
1974	Atletico Madrid (Spa)	Independiente (Arg)	0-1, 2-0
1976	Bayern Munich (FRG)	Cruzeiro (Bra)	2-0, 0-0
1977	Boca Juniors (Arg)	Borussia Moenchenglabach (FRG)	2-2, 3-0
1979	Olimpia (Par)	Malmo (Swe)	1-0, 2-1
1980	Nacional (Uru)	Nottingham F (Eng)	1-0
1981	Flamengo (Bra)	Liverpool (Eng)	3-0
1982	Penarol (Uru)	Aston Villa (Eng)	2-0
1983	Gremio (Bra)	SV Hamburg (FRG)	2-1
1984	Independiente (Arg)	Liverpool (Eng)	1-0
1985	Juventus (Ita)	Argentinos Juniors (Arg)	2-2
	(Juventus won 4-2 on penalties)		
1986	River Plate (Arg)	Steaua Bucharest (Rom)	1-0

Wins: 3 Penarol 2 Santos, Inter Milan, Nacional, Independiente
European wins: 9. South American wins: 16
Not one European team won a match in South America. Real Madrid (1960), Feyenoord (1970), Ajax (1972) and Bayern Munich (1976) all managed to draw.
Biggest attendance: 150,000 Santos v AC Milan (2nd leg 1963) Rio de Janeiro

BRITISH INTERNATIONAL CHAMPIONSHIP

The oldest international championship in the world, the four home countries of England, Scotland, Wales and Northern Ireland (formerly Ireland) contested the series annually from 1883-84 until 1983-84. The four countries played each other once with two points for a win and one for a draw. If two or more nations obtained the same number of points they shared the title. From 1979-80 however, goal difference decided the champions in case of a tie. With a decline in interest in the 1960s and 70s, the championship, often referred to as the Home International Championship, ended after the 1983-84 season. Only the England v Scotland fixture remains on a regular basis. The championship was not completed in 1980-81 and no champions were declared.

Outright Wins:

34	England	1888, 1891-3, 1895, 1898-9, 1901, 1904-5, 1909, 1911, 1913, 1930, 1932, 1938, 1947-8, 1950, 1954-5, 1957, 1961, 1965-6, 1968-9, 1971, 1973, 1975, 1978-9, 1982-3
24	Scotland	1884-5, 1887, 1889, 1894, 1896-7, 1900, 1902, 1910, 1921-3, 1925-6, 1929, 1936, 1949, 1951, 1962-3, 1967, 1976-77
7	Wales	1907, 1920, 1924, 1928, 1933-4, 1937
3	N.Ireland/Ireland	1914, 1980, 1984

Four-way tie: In 1955-6 all four nations shared the title with three points each.

INTERNATIONAL CAPS

England's Billy Wright was the first player to reach the milestone of making 100 senior international appearances. His 100th match was against Scotland at Wembley on 11 April 1959. Since then many players have passed the 100 mark.

The most capped players have been:
150 * Hector Chumpitaz (Per) 1963-82
120 * Rivelino (Bra) 1968-79
119 Pat Jennings (NI) 1964-86
115 Bjorn Nordqvist (Swe) 1963-78
112 Dino Zoff (Ita) 1968-83
111 * Pele (Bra) 1957-71

* Includes matches against club sides and other representative selections.

In addition to Jennings, *the following British players have won 100 caps:*
108 Bobby Moore (Eng) 1962-73
106 Bobby Charlton (Eng) 1958-70
105 Billy Wright (Eng) 1946-59
102 Kenny Dalglish (Sco) 1971-86

OLYMPIC GAMES

Soccer was unofficially played in the first Modern Olympics in 1896. It was included in the Paris Games four years later but some sources still regard it as an unofficial competition, as was the 1904 competition. All sources agree, however, that all subsequent Olympic soccer tournaments have been regarded as official. Because of the strength of the so called 'non-professional' Eastern-bloc nations, FIFA ruled that all players who had competed in the 1982 World Cup could not compete in the Los Angeles Olympics two years later. As it turned out, the ban had no effect on the eastern European nations because of their boycott of the Games. The only time soccer has not been included in the Olympic programme since 1908 was at Los Angeles in 1932.

Finals:

1900	Upton Park FC (UK)	4	UFSA (Fra)	0
1904	Galt FC, Ontario (Can)	7	Christian Brothers College (USA)	1
1906	Denmark	5	Smyrna (Gre)	1
1908	Great Britain	2	Denmark	0
1912	Great Britain	4	Denmark	2
1920	Belgium	2	Czechoslovakia	0

(Czechoslovakia disqualified after walking off the pitch as a protest against refereeing decisions. Spain were awarded the silver medal)

1924	Uruguay	3	Switzerland	0
1928	Uruguay (after 1-1 draw)	2	Argentina	1
1936	Italy	2	Austria	1*
1948	Sweden	3	Yugoslavia	1
1952	Hungary	2	Yugoslavia	0
1956	USSR	1	Yugoslavia	0
1960	Yugoslavia	3	Denmark	1
1964	Hungary	2	Czechoslovakia	1
1968	Hungary	4	Bulgaria	1
1972	Poland	2	Hungary	1
1976	GDR	3	Poland	1
1980	Czechoslovakia	1	GDR	0

1984 France   2   Brazil   0
* after extra time

Leading medalists:

	Gold	Silver	Bronze	Total
Hungary	3	1	1	5
Yugoslavia	1	3	1	5
Denmark	1	3	1	5
USSR	1	-	3	4
Great Britain	3	-	-	3
GDR	1	1	1	3
Sweden	1	-	2	3
Holland	-	-	3	3

Most wins: 3 Great Britain 1900,1908,1912, Hungary 1952, 1964, 1968
Biggest win: 17-1 Denmark v France 'A' 1908
Olympic champions/World Cup holders simultaneously:
Uruguay 1928 Olympics, 1930 World Cup
Italy 1934 World Cup, 1936 Olympics, 1938 World Cup
Most goals in an Olympic tournament: 12 Ferenc Bene (Hun) 1964

FOOTBALL LEAGUE

The Football League was the brainchild of William McGregor of Aston Villa who called the first meeting of interested clubs to the Anderton's Hotel, Fleet Street, London on 22 March 1888. The first formal meeting took place less than a month later, on 17 April, at the Royal Hotel, Manchester when 12 members agreed to form the Football League. The first matches were played the following September, and Preston North End emerged as the inaugural champions. A Second Division was formed in 1892 when most members of the old Football Alliance joined the League. A Third Division was added in 1920 and when 20 northern clubs joined the League in 1921 the Third Division was constituted into Northern and Southern sections. The current compliment of 92 clubs was reached in 1950 and in 1958 the geographically divided Third Divisions were split into Third and Fourth Divisions.

THE FOUNDER MEMBERS of the Football League were: Accrington, Aston Villa, Blackburn Rovers, Bolton Wanderers, Burnley, Derby County, Everton, Notts County, Preston North End, Stoke City, West Bromwich Albion, Wolverhampton Wanderers.
THE FIRST EVER Football League fixtures on 8 September 1888 were as follows:

Bolton Wanderers	3	Derby County	6
Everton	2	Accrington	1
Preston North End	5	Burnley	2
Stoke City	0	West Bromwich A.	2
Wolverhampton W.	1	Aston Villa	1

(Blackburn Rovers and Notts County did not play)

FIRST DIVISION CHAMPIONS

Season	Champions	Pts.	Max.Pts.
1888-89	Preston North End	40	44
1889-90	Preston North End	33	44
1890-91	Everton	29	44
1891-92	Sunderland	42	52
1892-93	Sunderland	48	60
1893-94	Aston Villa	44	60
1894-95	Sunderland	47	60
1895-96	Aston Villa	45	60
1896-97	Aston Villa	47	60
1897-98	Sheffield United	42	60
1898-99	Aston Villa	45	68
1899-00	Aston Villa	50	68
1900-01	Liverpool	45	68
1901-02	Sunderland	44	68
1902-03	Sheffield Wednesday	42	68
1903-04	Sheffield Wednesday	47	68
1904-05	Newcastle United	48	68
1905-06	Liverpool	51	76
1906-07	Newcastle United	51	76
1907-08	Manchester United	52	76
1908-09	Newcastle United	53	76
1909-10	Aston Villa	53	76
1910-11	Manchester United	52	76
1911-12	Blackburn Rovers	49	76
1912-13	Sunderland	54	76
1913-14	Blackburn Rovers	51	76
1914-15	Everton	46	76
1919-20	West Bromwich Albion	60	84
1920-21	Burnley	59	84
1921-22	Liverpool	57	84
1922-23	Liverpool	60	84
1923-24	Huddersfield Town	57	84
1924-25	Huddersfield Town	58	84
1925-26	Huddersfield Town	57	84
1926-27	Newcastle United	56	84
1927-28	Everton	53	84
1928-29	Sheffield Wedensday	52	84
1929-30	Sheffield Wednesday	60	84
1930-31	Arsenal	66	84
1931-32	Everton	56	84
1932-33	Arsenal	58	84
1933-34	Arsenal	59	84
1934-35	Arsenal	58	84
1935-36	Sunderland	56	84
1936-37	Manchester City	57	84
1937-38	Arsenal	52	84
1938-39	Everton	59	84
1946-47	Liverpool	57	84
1947-48	Arsenal	59	84
1948-49	Portsmouth	58	84
1949-50	Portsmouth	56	84
1950-51	Tottenham Hotspur	60	84
1951-52	Manchester United	57	84
1952-53	Arsenal	54	84
1953-54	Wolverhampton W.	57	84
1954-55	Chelsea	52	84
1955-56	Manchester United	60	84
1956-57	Manchester United	64	84
1957-58	Wolverhampton W.	64	84
1958-59	Wolverhampton W.	61	84
1959-60	Burnley	55	84
1960-61	Tottenham Hotspur	66	84
1961-62	Ipswich Town	56	84
1962-63	Everton	61	84
1963-64	Liverpool	57	84
1964-65	Manchester United	61	84
1965-66	Liverpool	61	84
1966-67	Manchester United	60	84
1967-68	Manchester City	58	84
1968-69	Leeds United	67	84

Season	Champions	Pts.	Max.Pts.
1969-70	Everton	66	84
1970-71	Arsenal	65	84
1971-72	Derby County	58	84
1972-73	Liverpool	60	84
1973-74	Leeds United	62	84
1974-75	Derby County	53	84
1975-76	Liverpool	60	84
1976-77	Liverpool	57	84
1977-78	Nottingham Forest	64	84
1978-79	Liverpool	68	84
1979-80	Liverpool	60	84
1980-81	Aston Villa	60	84
1981-82	Liverpool	87	126
1982-83	Liverpool	82	126
1983-84	Liverpool	80	126
1984-85	Everton	90	126
1985-86	Liverpool	88	126
1986-87	Everton	86	126

FOOTBALL LEAGUE STATISTICS

Most titles
Division 1: 16 Liverpool
Division 2: 6 Leicester City, Manchester City
Division 3: 2 Portsmouth, Oxford United
Division 4: 2 Chesterfield, Doncaster Rovers,
Peterborough United

Most points in a season
Division 1 a: 68 Liverpool 1978-9
b: 90 Everton 1984-5
Division 2 a: 70 Tottenham Hotspur 1919-20
b: 88 Luton Town 1981-2
88 Chelsea 1983-4
88 Sheffield Wednesday 1983-4
Division 3 a: 70 Aston Villa 1971-2
b: 97 Bournemouth 1986-7
Division 4 a: 74 Lincoln City 1975-6
b: 102 Swindon Town 1985-6
a indicates under old system of two points for a win,
1888-1981
b indicates current scoring system of three points for a
win, from 1981

Most goals for in a season
Division 1: 128 Aston Villa 1930-1
Division 2: 122 Middlesbrough 1926-7
Division 3: 111 Queen's Park Rangers 1961-2
Division 4: 134 Peterborough United 1960-1

Highest scores
13-0 Stockport County v Halifax Town (Division 3N - 6 Jan 1934)
13-0 Newcastle United v Newport County (Division 2 - 5 Oct 1946)
13-4 Tranmere Rovers v Oldham Athletic (Division 3N - 26 Dec 1935)
12-0 West Bromwich Albion v Darwen (Division 1 - 4 Apr 1892)
12-0 Small Heath (later Birmingham City) v Walsall Town Swifts (Division 2 - 17 Dec 1892)
12-0 Arsenal v Loughborough Town (Division 2 - 12 Mar 1900)
12-0 Small Heath (later Birmingham City) v Doncaster Rovers (Division 2 - 11 Apr 1903)
12-0 Nottingham Forest v Leicester Fosse (Division 1 - 21 Apr 1909)

The successful management team of Peter Taylor (left) and Brian Clough (right) who took Nottingham Forest to victory in four major competitions.

12-0 Chester v York City (Division 3N - 1 Feb 1936)
12-0 Luton Town v Bristol Rovers (Division 3S - 13 Apr 1936)

Other divisional records:
11-0 Oldham Athletic v Southport (Division 4 - 26 Dec 1962)
9-0 Tranmere Rovers v Accrington Stanley (Division 3 - 18 Apr 1959)
Brentford v Wrexham (Division 3 - 15 Oct 1963)

Most individual goals in a game
10 Joe Payne (Luton Town v Bristol Rovers) Division 3S - 13 Apr 1936
9 Robert Bell (Tranmere Rovers v Oldham Athletic) Division 3N - 26 Dec 1935
7 Arthur Whitehurst (Bradford City v Tranmere Rovers) Division 3N - 6 Mar 1929)
7 Ted Drake (Arsenal v Aston Villa) Division 1 - 14 Dec 1935
7 Ted Harston (Mansfield Town v Hartlepool United) Division 3N - 23 Jan 1937
7 Eric Gemmell (Oldham Athletic v Chester) Division 3N - 19 Jan 1952
7 Tommy Briggs (Blackburn Rovers v Bristol Rovers) Division 2 - 5 Feb 1955
7 Neville Coleman (Stoke City v Lincoln City) Division 2 - 23 Feb 1957

Most individual goals in a season:
60 Dixie Dean (Everton) Division 1 - 1927-8
59 George Camsell (Middlesbrough) Division 2 - 1926-7
55 Joe Payne (Luton Town) Division 3S - 1936-7
55 Ted Harston (Mansfield Town) Division 3N - 1936-7
52 Terry Bly (Peterborough United) Division 4 - 1960-1

FA CUP

The idea of the Football Association Challenge Cup came from Charles Alcock, secretary of the Football Association. He put forward his plans at a meeting attended by 12 clubs on 18 October 1871. The following 15 teams eventually entered the first competition: Wanderers, Harrow Chequers, Clapham Rovers, Upton Park, Crystal Palace, Hitchin, Maidenhead, Great Marlow, Barnes, Civil Service, Royal Engineers, Reigate Priory, Donington School, Hampstead Heathens, Queen's Park (Glasgow)

Year	Winners		Runners-up		Venue	Attendance
1872	WANDERERS Betts	1	ROYAL ENGINEERS	0	Kennington Oval	2,000
1873	WANDERERS Kinnaird, Wollaston	2	OXFORD UNIVERSITY	0	Lillie Bridge	3,000
1874	OXFORD UNIVERSITY Mackarness, Patton	2	ROYAL ENGINEERS	0	Kennington Oval	2,000
1875	ROYAL ENGINEERS Renny-Tailyour	1	OLD ETONIANS Bonsor	1*	Kennington Oval	3,000
Replay	ROYAL ENGINEERS Renny-Tailyour, Stafford	2	OLD ETONIANS	0	Kennington Oval	3,000
1876	WANDERERS Edwards	1	OLD ETONIANS Bonsor	1	Kennington Oval	3,000
Replay	WANDERERS Hughes (2), Wollaston	3	OLD ETONIANS	0	Kennington Oval	3,500
1877	WANDERERS Lindsay, Kenrick	2	OXFORD UNIVERSITY Kinnaird (og)	1*	Kennington Oval	3,000
1878	WANDERERS Kenrick(2), Kinnaird	3	ROYAL ENGINEERS unknown	1	Kennington Oval	4,500
1879	OLD ETONIANS Clerke	1	CLAPHAM ROVERS	0	Kennington Oval	5,000
1880	CLAPHAM ROVERS Lloyd-Jones	1	OXFORD UNIVERSITY	0	Kennington Oval	6,000
1881	OLD CARTHUSIANS Wyngard, Parry, Todd	3	OLD ETONIANS	0	Kennington Oval	4,500
1882	OLD ETONIANS Macauley	1	BLACKBURN ROVERS	0	Kennington Oval	6,500
1883	BLACKBURN OLYMPIC Matthews, Crossley	2	OLD ETONIANS Goodhart	1*	Kennington Oval	8,000
1884	BLACKBURN ROVERS Sowerbutts, Forrest	2	QUEEN'S PARK Christie	1	Kennington Oval	4,000
1885	BLACKBURN ROVERS Forrest, Brown	2	QUEEN'S PARK	0	Kennington Oval	12,500
1886	BLACKBURN ROVERS	0	WEST BROMWICH ALBION	0	Kennington Oval	15,000
Replay	BLACKBURN ROVERS Brown, Sowerbutts	2	WEST BROMWICH ALBION	0	Racecourse Ground, Derby	12,000
1887	ASTON VILLA Hunter, Hodgetts	2	WEST BROMWICH ALBION	0	Kennington Oval	15,500
1888	WEST BROMWICH ALBION Woodhall, Bayliss	2	PRESTON NORTH END Dewhurst	1	Kennington Oval	19,000
1889	PRESTON NORTH END Dewhurst, Ross, Thomson	3	WOLVERHAMPTON W.	0	Kennington Oval	22,000
1890	BLACKBURN ROVERS Townley (3),Walton John Southworth, Lofthouse	6	SHEFFIELD WEDNESDAY Bennett	1	Kennington Oval	20,000
1891	BLACKBURN ROVERS Southworth, Dewar Townley	3	NOTTS COUNTY Oswald	1	Kennington Oval	23,000
1892	WEST BROMWICH ALBION Nicholls, Geddes, Reynolds	3	ASTON VILLA	0	Kennington Oval	32,810
1893	WOLVERHAMPTON W. Allen	1	EVERTON	0	Fallowfield	45,000
1894	NOTTS COUNTY Logan (3), Watson	4	BOLTON WANDERERS Cassidy	1	Goodison Park	37,000

Year	Winners		Runners-up		Venue	Attendance
1895	ASTON VILLA Devey	1	WEST BROMWICH ALBION	0	Crystal Palace	42,560
1896	SHEFFIELD WEDNESDAY Spiksley (2)	2	WOLVERHAMPTON W. Black	1	Crystal Palace	48,836
1897	ASTON VILLA Devey, Campbell Crabtree	3	EVERTON Bell, Hartley	2	Crystal Palace	65,891
1898	NOTTINGHAM FOREST Capes (2), McPherson	3	DERBY COUNTY Bloomer	1	Crystal Palace	62,017
1899	SHEFFIELD UNITED Bennett, Priest, Beers, Almond	4	DERBY COUNTY Boag	1	Crystal Palace	73,833
1900	BURY McLuckie (2), Wood, Plant	4	SOUTHAMPTON	0	Crystal Palace	68,945
1901	TOTTENHAM HOTSPUR Brown(2)	2	SHEFFIELD UNITED Bennett, Priest	2	Crystal Palace	110,820
Replay	TOTTENHAM HOTSPUR Cameron, Smith Brown	3	SHEFFIELD UNITED Priest	1	Burnden Park	20,470
1902	SHEFFIELD UNITED Common	1	SOUTHAMPTON Wood	1	Crystal Palace	76,914
Replay	SHEFFIELD UNITED Hedley, Barnes	2	SOUTHAMPTON Brown	1	Crystal Palace	33,068
1903	BURY Leeming (2), Ross, Sagar, Plant, Wood	6	DERBY COUNTY	0	Crystal Palace	63,102
1904	MANCHESTER CITY Meredith	1	BOLTON WANDERERS	0	Crystal Palace	61,374
1905	ASTON VILLA Hampton (2)	2	NEWCASTLE UNITED	0	Crystal Palace	101,117
1906	EVERTON Young	1	NEWCASTLE UNITED	0	Crystal Palace	75,609
1907	SHEFFIELD WEDNESDAY Stewart, Simpson	2	EVERTON Sharp	1	Crystal Palace	84,584
1908	WOLVERHAMPTON W. Hunt, Hedley, Harrison	3	NEWCASTLE UNITED Howie	1	Crystal Palace	74,967
1909	MANCHESTER UNITED A.Turnbull	1	BRISTOL CITY	0	Crystal Palace	71,401
1910	NEWCASTLE UNITED Rutherford	1	BARNSLEY Tuffnell	1	Crystal Palace	77,747
Replay	NEWCASTLE UNITED Shepherd (2-1 pen)	2	BARNSLEY	0	Goodison Park	69,000
1911	BRADFORD CITY	0	NEWCASTLE UNITED	0	Crystal Palace	69,098
Replay	BRADFORD CITY Spiers	1	NEWCASTLE UNITED	0	Old Trafford	58,000
1912	BARNSLEY	0	WEST BROMWICH ALBION	0	Crystal Palace	54,556
Replay	BARNSLEY Tuffnell	1	WEST BROMWICH ALBION	0*	Bramhall Lane	38,555
1913	ASTON VILLA Barber	1	SUNDERLAND	0	Crystal Palace	120,081
1914	BURNLEY Freeman	1	LIVERPOOL	0	Crystal Palace	72,778
1915	SHEFFIELD UNITED Simmons, Kitchen, Fazackerley	3	CHELSEA	0	Old Trafford	49,557

Year	Winners		Runners-up		Venue	Attendance
1920	ASTON VILLA Kirton	1	HUDDERSFIELD TOWN	0*	Stamford Bridge	50,018
1921	TOTTENHAM HOTSPUR Dimmock	1	WOLVERHAMPTON W.	0	Stamford Bridge	72,805
1922	HUDDERSFIELD TOWN Smith	1	PRESTON NORTH END	0	Stamford Bridge	53,000
1923	BOLTON WANDERERS Jack, J.R.Smith	2	WEST HAM UNITED	0	Wembley	126,047
1924	NEWCASTLE UNITED Harris, Seymour	2	ASTON VILLA	0	Wembley	91,695
1925	SHEFFIELD UNITED Tunstall	1	CARDIFF CITY	0	Wembley	91,763
1926	BOLTON WANDERERS Jack	1	MANCHESTER CITY	0	Wembley	91,447
1927	CARDIFF CITY Ferguson	1	ARSENAL	0	Wembley	91,206
1928	BLACKBURN ROVERS Roscamp (2), McLean	3	HUDDERSFIELD TOWN Jackson	1	Wembley	92,041
1929	BOLTON WANDERERS Butler, Blackmore	2	PORTSMOUTH	0	Wembley	92,576
1930	ARSENAL James, Lambert	2	HUDDERSFIELD TOWN	0	Wembley	92,488
1931	WEST BROMWICH ALBION W.G.Richardson (2)	2	BIRMINGHAM Bradford	1	Wembley	92,406
1932	NEWCASTLE UNITED Allen (2)	2	ARSENAL John	1	Wembley	92,298
1933	EVERTON Stein, Dean, Dunn	3	MANCHESTER CITY	0	Wembley	92,950
1934	MANCHESTER CITY Tilson (2)	2	PORTSMOUTH Rutherford	1	Wembley	93,258
1935	SHEFFIELD WEDNESDAY Rimmer (2), Hooper Palethorpe	4	WEST BROMWICH ALBION Boyes, Sandford	2	Wembley	93,204
1936	ARSENAL Drake	1	SHEFFIELD UNITED	0	Wembley	93,384
1937	SUNDERLAND Gurney, Carter, Burbanks	3	PRESTON NORTH END F.O'Donnell	1	Wembley	93,495
1938	PRESTON NORTH END Mutch (pen)	1	HUDDERSFIELD TOWN	0*	Wembley	93,497
1939	PORTSMOUTH Parker (2), Barlow, Anderson	4	WOLVERHAMPTON W. Dorsett	1	Wembley	99,370
1946	DERBY COUNTY Stamps (2), Doherty H.Turner(og)	4	CHARLTON ATHLETIC H.Turner	1*	Wembley	98,215
1947	CHARLTON ATHLETIC Duffy	1	BURNLEY	0*	Wembley	99,000
1948	MANCHESTER UNITED Rowley (2), Pearson, Anderson	4	BLACKPOOL Shimwell (pen), Mortensen	2	Wembley	99,000
1949	WOLVERHAMPTON W. Pye (2), Smyth	3	LEICESTER CITY Griffiths	1	Wembley	99,500
1950	ARSENAL Lewis (2)	2	LIVERPOOL	0	Wembley	100,000

Year	Winners		Runners-up		Venue	Attendance
1951	NEWCASTLE UNITED Milburn (2)	2	BLACKPOOL	0	Wembley	100,000
1952	NEWCASTLE UNITED G.Robledo	1	ARSENAL	0	Wembley	100,000
1953	BLACKPOOL Mortensen (3), Perry	4	BOLTON WANDERERS Lofthouse, Moir, Bell	3	Wembley	100,000
1954	WEST BROMWICH ALBION Allen (2,1 pen), Griffin	3	PRESTON NORTH END Morrison, Wayman	2	Wembley	100,000
1955	NEWCASTLE UNITED Milburn, Mitchell, Hannah	3	MANCHESTER CITY Johnstone	1	Wembley	100,000
1956	MANCHESTER CITY Hayes, Dyson, Johnstone	3	BIRMINGHAM CITY Kinsey	1	Wembley	100,000
1957	ASTON VILLA McParland (2)	2	MANCHESTER UNITED Taylor	1	Wembley	100,000
1958	BOLTON WANDERERS Lofthouse (2)	2	MANCHESTER UNITED	0	Wembley	100,000
1959	NOTTINGHAM FOREST Dwight, Wilson	2	LUTON TOWN Pacey	1	Wembley	100,000
1960	WOLVERHAMPTON W. McGrath (og), Deeley (2)	3	BLACKBURN ROVERS	0	Wembley	100,000
1961	TOTTENHAM HOTSPUR Smith, Dyson	2	LEICESTER CITY	0	Wembley	100,000
1962	TOTTENHAM HOTSPUR Greaves, Smith, Blanchflower (pen)	3	BURNLEY Robson	1	Wembley	100,000
1963	MANCHESTER UNITED Herd (2), Law	3	LEICESTER CITY Keyworth	1	Wembley	100,000
1964	WEST HAM UNITED Sissons, Hurst, Boyce	3	PRESTON NORTH END Holden, Dawson	2	Wembley	100,000
1965	LIVERPOOL Hunt, St.John	2	LEEDS UNITED Bremner	1*	Wembley	100,000
1966	EVERTON Trebilcock (2), Temple	3	SHEFFIELD WEDNESDAY McCalliog, Ford	2	Wembley	100,000
1967	TOTTENHAM HOTSPUR Robertson, Saul	2	CHELSEA Tambling	1	Wembley	100,000
1968	WEST BROMWICH ALBION Astle	1	EVERTON	0*	Wembley	100,000
1969	MANCHESTER CITY Young	1	LEICESTER CITY	0	Wembley	100,000
1970	CHELSEA Houseman, Hutchinson	2	LEEDS UNITED Charlton, Jones	2*	Wembley	100,000
Replay	CHELSEA Osgood, Webb	2	LEEDS UNITED Jones	1*	Old Trafford	62,078
1971	ARSENAL Kelly, George	2	LIVERPOOL Heighway	1*	Wembley	100,000
1972	LEEDS UNITED Clarke	1	ARSENAL	0	Wembley	100,000
1973	SUNDERLAND Porterfield	1	LEEDS UNITED	0	Wembley	100,000
1974	LIVERPOOL Keegan (2), Heighway	3	NEWCASTLE UNITED	0	Wembley	100,000
1975	WEST HAM UNITED A.Taylor (2)	2	FULHAM	0	Wembley	100,000
1976	SOUTHAMPTON Stokes	1	MANCHESTER UNITED	0	Wembley	100,000

Year	Winners		Runners-up		Venue	Attendance
1977	MANCHESTER UNITED Pearson, J.Greenhoff	2	LIVERPOOL Case	1	Wembley	100,000
1978	IPSWICH TOWN Osborne	1	ARSENAL	0	Wembley	100,000
1979	ARSENAL Talbot, Stapleton, Sunderland	3	MANCHESTER UNITED McQueen, McIlroy	2	Wembley	100,000
1980	WEST HAM UNITED Brooking	1	ARSENAL	0	Wembley	100,000
1981	TOTTENHAM HOTSPUR Hutchison (og)	1	MANCHESTER CITY Hutchison	1*	Wembley	100,000
Replay	TOTTENHAM HOTSPUR Villa (2), Crooks	3	MANCHESTER CITY Mackenzie, Reeves (pen)	2	Wembley	92,000
1982	TOTTENHAM HOTSPUR Hoddle	1	QUEEN'S PARK RANGERS Fenwick	1*	Wembley	100,000
Replay	TOTTENHAM HOTSPUR Hoddle (pen)	1	QUEEN'S PARK RANGERS	0	Wembley	90,000
1983	MANCHESTER UNITED Stapleton, Wilkins	2	BRIGHTON & HOVE A. Smith, Stevens	2*	Wembley	100,000
Replay	MANCHESTER UNITED Robson (2), Whiteside, Muhren (pen)	4	BRIGHTON & HOVE A.	0	Wembley	92,000
1984	EVERTON Sharp, Gray	2	WATFORD	0	Wembley	100,000
1985	MANCHESTER UNITED Whiteside	1	EVERTON	0*	Wembley	100,000
1986	LIVERPOOL Rush (2), Johnston	3	EVERTON Lineker	1	Wembley	98,000
1987	COVENTRY CITY Bennett, Houchen Mabbutt (og)	3	TOTTENHAM HOTSPUR C. Allen, Mabbutt	2*	Wembley	98,000

* after extra time

FA CUP STATISTICS

Biggest win:
26-0 Preston North End v Hyde United (1st round) 15
   Oct 1887
Biggest win (final):
6-0 Bury v Derby County 18 Apr 1903
Most wins:
7 Aston Villa, Tottenham Hotspur
6 Blackburn Rovers, Manchester United, Newcastle
   United
Most finals:
11 Arsenal, Newcastle United
10 Everton, Manchester United, West Bromwich Albion
Most semi-finals:
21 Everton
19 West Bromwich Albion
Most winners' medals
5 James Forrest (Blackburn Rovers) 1884-6, 1890-1
5 Hon. A. F. Kinnaird (Wanderers) 1873, 1877-8 (Old
   Etonians) 1879, 1882
5 Charles Wollaston (Wanderers) 1873, 1876-8

Second division finalists
Since the formation of the second division of the
Football League in 1892-3, the following clubs from that
division have reached the FA Cup final:

1894 Notts County *
1904 Bolton Wanderers
1908 Wolverhampton Wanderers *
1910 Barnsley
1912 Barnsley *
1920 Huddersfield Town
1921 Wolverhampton Wanderers
1923 West Ham United
1931 West Bromwich Albion *
1936 Sheffield United
1947 Burnley
1949 Leicester City
1964 Preston North End
1973 Sunderland *
1975 Fulham
1976 Southampton *
1980 West Ham United *
1982 Queen's Park Rangers

No clubs from the 3rd or 4th divisions have reached the
FA Cup final but the following non-league clubs have,
since the formation of the League, reached the final.

1900 Southampton
1901 Tottenham Hotspur *
1902 Southampton

* indicates winners

FOOTBALL LEAGUE CUP

Instituted in 1960-1 it was not until the 1969-70 season that all 92 Football League teams took part. All finals up to 1966 were played on a two-legged basis but since then they have been played at Wembley Stadium. Following sponsorship from the Milk Marketing Board in 1982 the Cup changed its name to the Milk Cup, and in 1986 it became known as the Littlewoods Cup.

Year		Home team		Away team		Attendance
1961	1st leg	ROTHERHAM UNITED Webster, Kirkman	2	ASTON VILLA	0	12,226
	2nd leg	ASTON VILLA O'Neill, Burrows, McParland	3	ROTHERHAM UNITED	0*	31,202
		(Aston Villa won 3-2 on aggregate)				
1962	1st leg	ROCHDALE	0	NORWICH CITY Lythgoe (2), Punton	3	11,123
	2nd leg	NORWICH CITY Hill	1	ROCHDALE	0	19,708
		(Norwich City won 4-0 on aggregate)				
1963	1st leg	BIRMINGHAM CITY Leek (2), Bloomfield	3	ASTON VILLA Thomson	1	31,850
	2nd leg	ASTON VILLA	0	BIRMINGHAM CITY	0	37,920
		(Birmingham City won 3-1 on aggregate)				
1964	1st leg	STOKE CITY Bebbington	1	LEICESTER CITY Gibson	1	22,309
	2nd leg	LEICESTER CITY Stringfellow, Gibson, Riley	3	STOKE CITY Viollet, Kinnell	2	25,372
		(Leicester City won 4-3 on aggregate)				
1965	1st leg	CHELSEA Tambling, McCreadie, Venables (pen)	3	LEICESTER CITY Appleton, Goodfellow	2	20,690
	2nd leg	LEICESTER CITY	0	CHELSEA	0	26,958
		(Chelsea won 3-2 on aggregate)				
1966	1st leg	WEST HAM UNITED Moore, Byrne	2	WEST BROMWICH ALBION Astle	1	28,341
	2nd leg	WEST BROMWICH ALBION Kaye, Brown, Clark, Williams	4	WEST HAM UNITED Peters	1	31,925
		(West Bromwich Albion won 5-3 on aggregate)				

Year	Winners		Runners-up		Venue	Attendance
1967	QUEEN'S PARK RANGERS R.Morgan, Marsh, Lazarus	3	WEST BROMWICH ALBION Clark (2)	2	Wembley	97,952
1968	LEEDS UNITED Cooper	1	ARSENAL	0	Wembley	97,887
1969	SWINDON TOWN Rogers (2), Smart	3	ARSENAL Gould	1	Wembley	98,189
1970	MANCHESTER CITY Doyle, Pardoe	2	WEST BROMWICH ALBION Astle	1	Wembley	97,963
1971	TOTTENHAM HOTSPUR Chivers (2)	2	ASTON VILLA	0	Wembley	100,000
1972	STOKE CITY Conroy, Eastham	2	CHELSEA Osgood	1	Wembley	100,000
1973	TOTTENHAM HOTSPUR Coates	1	NORWICH CITY	0	Wembley	100,000
1974	WOLVERHAMPTON W. Hibbitt, Richards	2	MANCHESTER CITY Bell	1	Wembley	100,000
1975	ASTON VILLA Graydon	1	NORWICH CITY	0	Wembley	100,000

Year	Winners		Runners-up		Venue	Attendance
1976	MANCHESTER CITY Barnes, Tueart	2	NEWCASTLE UNITED Gowling	1	Wembley	100,000
1977	ASTON VILLA	0	EVERTON	0	Wembley	100,000
Replay	ASTON VILLA Kenyon (og)	1	EVERTON Latchford	1*	Hillsborough	55,000
Replay	ASTON VILLA Little (2), Nicholl	3	EVERTON Latchford, Lyons	2*	Old Trafford	54,749
1978	NOTTINGHAM FOREST	0	LIVERPOOL	0*	Wembley	100,000
Replay	NOTTINGHAM FOREST Robertson (pen)	1	LIVERPOOL	0	Old Trafford	54,375
1979	NOTTINGHAM FOREST Birtles (2), Woodcock	3	SOUTHAMPTON Peach, Holmes	2	Wembley	100,000
1980	WOLVERHAMPTON W. Gray	1	NOTTINGHAM FOREST	0	Wembley	100,000
1981	LIVERPOOL A.Kennedy	1	WEST HAM UNITED Stewart (pen)	1*	Wembley	100,000
Replay	LIVERPOOL Dalglish, Hansen	2	WEST HAM UNITED Goddard	1	Villa Park	36.693
1982	LIVERPOOL Whelan (2), Rush	3	TOTTENHAM HOTSPUR Archibald	1*	Wembley	100,000
1983	LIVERPOOL Kennedy, Whelan	2	MANCHESTER UNITED Whiteside	1*	Wembley	100,000
1984	LIVERPOOL	0	EVERTON	0*	Wembley	100,000
Replay	LIVERPOOL Souness	1	EVERTON	0	Maine Road	52,089
1985	NORWICH CITY Chisholm (og)	1	SUNDERLAND	0	Wembley	100,000
1986	OXFORD UNITED Hebberd, Houghton, Charles	3	QUEEN'S PARK RANGERS	0	Wembley	90,396
1987	ARSENAL Nicholas (2)	2	LIVERPOOL Rush	1	Wembley	96,000

* after extra time

LEAGUE CUP STATISTICS
Biggest win:
10-0 West Ham United v Bury (2nd round, 2nd leg) 25 Oct 1983
10-0 Liverpool v Fulham (2nd round, 1st Leg) 23 Sep 1986
Biggest win (final):
4-1 West Bromwich A v West Ham United (2nd leg) 23 Mar 1966
Most wins:
4 Liverpool
3 Aston Villa

Most finals:
6 Liverpool
5 Aston Villa
4 Norwich City
Most semi-finals:
8 Aston Villa, Liverpool
Most winners' medals:
4 Phil Neal, Alan Kennedy, Kenny Dalglish, Sammy Lee, Ian Rush, Graeme Souness (all Liverpool)

Ian Rush of Liverpool was, in the 1983-4 season, the first British player to win the Golden Boot award as Europe's leading scorer. (ASP)

Non-first division finalists
The following non-first division sides have reached the final:
1961 Rotherham United (Division 2)
1962 Norwich City * (Division 2)
1962 Rochdale (Division 4)
1967 Queen's Park Rangers * (Division 3)
1969 Swindon Town * (Division 3)
1971 Aston Villa (Division 3)
1975 Aston Villa * (Division 2)
1975 Norwich City (Division 2)
1981 West Ham United
* indicates winners

THE LEADING FOOTBALL LEAGUE CLUBS

Based on number of divisional titles, FA Cup Final wins and Football League/Milk/Littlewoods Cup Final wins.

	Football League Divisions						FA Cup	FL Cup	TOTAL
	1	2	3	4	3N	3S			
Liverpool	16	4	-	-	-	-	3	4	27
Aston Villa	7	2	1	-	-	-	7	3	20
Manchester U	7	2	-	-	-	-	6	-	15
Manchester C	2	6	-	-	-	-	4	2	14
Everton	9	1	-	-	-	-	4	-	14
Arsenal	8	-	-	-	-	-	5	1	14
Tottenham H	2	2	-	-	-	-	7	2	13
Sheffield W	4	5	-	-	-	-	3	-	12
Wolverhampton W	3	2	-	-	1	-	4	2	12
Newcastle U	4	1	-	-	-	-	6	-	11
Blackburn R	2	1	1	-	-	-	6	-	10

Champions of Divisions 1, 2 and 3 (incl. 3N & 3S):
Aston Villa, Wolverhampton W., Preston North End, Burnley, Derby County, Ipswich Town, Nottingham Forest
Champions of Divisions 1 and 4:
Huddersfield Town, Sheffield United

Champions of most divisions:
4 Grimsby Town have been champions of the 2nd, 3rd, 4th and 3rd division (north)
Most titles by clubs that have not won the 1st division:

		Div. 2	3	3S	3N	4
6	Leicester City	6	-	-	-	-
6	Notts County	3	-	2	-	1
6	Grimsby Town	2	1	-	2	1
5	Doncaster Rovers	-	-	-	3	2

Dual FA Cup/League Cup winners:
Liverpool, Aston Villa, Wolverhampton W., Manchester City, Tottenham Hotspur, Leeds United, Chelsea, West Bromwich A., Nottingham Forest, Arsenal

ALL-TIME LEAGUE TABLE

Our own league table based on the following points system:
12 points for winning the 1st Division title, 10 for winning the FA Cup and 8 for winning the League/Milk/Littlewoods Cup, with half those points for finishing runners-up.

Club	points
1 Liverpool	326
2 Aston Villa	244
3 Everton	228
4 Manchester United	216
5 Arsenal	210
6 Tottenham Hotspur	143
7 Wolverhampton W	142
8 Newcastle United	137
9 Sunderland	131
10 Manchester City	122
11 West Bromwich A	115
12 Preston North End	105

Liverpool heroes: Kenny Dalglish (l) and Ian Rush (r) – both won footballer of the year awards. They play for Scotland and Wales respectively. (All-Sport)

SCOTTISH FOOTBALL LEAGUE

The Scottish League was formed in 1890, two years after the Football League. A second division was added in 1893 and the biggest re-organisation in the League since its formation came in 1975-6 when it was completely re-structured. The leading 10 teams formed a new Premier division while the remaining teams were divided into Divisions 1 and 2. The number of teams in the Premier Division was extended to 12 in 1986-7.

First Division/Premier Division champions

Season	Champions	Pts.	Max.Pts.
1890-91	Dumbarton	29	36
	Rangers	29	36
1891-92	Dumbarton	37	44
1892-93	Celtic	29	36
1893-94	Celtic	29	36
1894-95	Hearts	31	36
1895-96	Celtic	30	36
1896-97	Hearts	28	36
1897-98	Celtic	33	36
1898-99	Rangers	36	36
1899-00	Rangers	32	36
1900-01	Rangers	35	40
1901-02	Rangers	28	36
1902-03	Hibernian	37	44
1903-04	Third Lanark	43	52
1904-05	Celtic	41	52
1905-06	Celtic	49	60
1906-07	Celtic	55	68
1907-08	Celtic	55	68
1908-09	Celtic	51	68
1909-10	Celtic	54	68
1910-11	Rangers	52	68
1911-12	Rangers	51	68
1912-13	Rangers	53	68
1913-14	Celtic	65	76
1914-15	Celtic	65	76
1915-16	Celtic	67	76
1916-17	Celtic	64	76
1917-18	Rangers	56	68
1918-19	Celtic	58	68
1919-20	Rangers	71	84
1920-21	Rangers	76	84
1921-22	Celtic	67	84
1922-23	Rangers	55	76
1923-24	Rangers	59	76
1924-25	Rangers	60	76
1925-26	Celtic	58	76
1926-27	Rangers	56	76
1927-28	Rangers	60	76
1928-29	Rangers	67	76
1929-30	Rangers	60	76
1930-31	Rangers	60	76
1931-32	Motherwell	66	76
1932-33	Rangers	62	76
1933-34	Rangers	66	76
1934-35	Rangers	55	76
1935-36	Celtic	66	76
1936-37	Rangers	61	76
1937-38	Celtic	61	76
1938-39	Rangers	59	76
1946-47	Rangers	46	68
1947-48	Hibernian	48	68

Season	Champions	Pts.	Max.Pts.
1948-49	Rangers	46	68
1949-50	Rangers	50	68
1950-51	Hibernian	48	68
1951-52	Hibernian	45	68
1952-53	Rangers	43	68
1953-54	Celtic	43	68
1954-55	Aberdeen	49	68
1955-56	Rangers	52	68
1956-57	Rangers	55	68
1957-58	Hearts	62	68
1958-59	Rangers	50	68
1959-60	Hearts	54	68
1960-61	Rangers	51	68
1961-62	Dundee	54	68
1962-63	Rangers	57	68
1963-64	Rangers	55	68
1964-65	Kilmarnock	50	68
1965-66	Celtic	57	68
1966-67	Celtic	58	68
1967-68	Celtic	63	68
1968-69	Celtic	54	68
1969-70	Celtic	57	68
1970-71	Celtic	56	68
1971-72	Celtic	60	68
1972-73	Celtic	57	68
1973-74	Celtic	53	68
1974-75	Rangers	56	68

Premier Division

Season	Champions	Pts.	Max.Pts.
1975-76	Rangers	54	72
1976-77	Celtic	55	72
1977-78	Rangers	55	72
1978-79	Celtic	48	72
1979-80	Aberdeen	48	72
1980-81	Celtic	56	72
1981-82	Celtic	55	72
1982-83	Dundee United	56	72
1983-84	Aberdeen	57	72
1984-85	Aberdeen	59	72
1985-86	Celtic	50	72
1986-87	Rangers	69	88

SCOTTISH LEAGUE STATISTICS

Most wins: 38 Rangers; 34 Celtic

Biggest win: 13-2 East Fife v Edinburgh City (Division 2 - 11 Dec 1937)

Biggest win (Division 1/Premier Division)
11-0 Celtic v Dundee 26 Oct 1895

Most individual goals in a match:
8 Owen McNally (Arthurlie v Armadale) Division 2 - 1 Oct 1927
8 Jimmy McGrory (Celtic v Dunfermline Athletic) Division 1 - 14 Jan 1928
8 Jim Dyet (King's Park v Forfar Athletic) Division 2 - 2 Jan 1930
8 John Calder (Morton v Raith Rovers) Division 2- 18 Mar 1936

Most individual goals in a season:
66 Jim Smith (Ayr United) Division 2 - 1927-8
53 Robert Skinner (Dunfermline Athletic) Division 2 - 1925-6
52 Bill McFadyen (Motherwell) Division 1 - 1931-2
50 Jimmy McGrory (Celtic) Division 1 - 1935-6

SCOTTISH FA CUP

When Queen's Park called a meeting of clubs on 13 March 1873 it was with the intention of organising a cup competition, similar to the FA Cup. Seven clubs attended that first meeting and Queen's Park's wishes were granted but, at the same meeting, it was decided to form the Scottish Football Association and so the new cup competition was called the Scottish Football Association Cup.

Year	Winners		Runners-up		Venue	Attendance
1874	Queen's Park	2	Clydesdale	0	Hampden Park	3,500
1875	Queen's Park	3	Renton	0	Hampden Park	7,000
1876	Queen's Park	1	Third Lanark	1	Hamilton Cres	10,000
Replay	Queen's Park	2	Third Lanark	0	Hamilton Cres	6,000
1877	Vale of Leven	1	Rangers	1	Hamilton Cres	10,000
Replay	Vale of Leven	1	Rangers	1	Hamilton Cres	15,000
Replay	Vale of Leven	3	Rangers	2	Hampden Park	12,000
1878	Vale of Leven	1	Third Lanark	0	Hampden Park	5,000
1879	Vale of Leven	1	Rangers	1	Hampden Park	9,000
	(awarded trophy, Rangers refused to appear for the replay)					
1880	Queen's Park	3	Thornlibank	0	Cathkin Park	4,000
1881	Queen's Park	2	Dumbarton	1	Kinning Park	15,000
	(replayed due to spectator invasion of pitch)					
Replay	Queen's Park	3	Dumbarton	1	Kinning Park	7,000
1882	Queen's Park	2	Dumbarton	2	Cathkin Park	12,500
Replay	Queen's Park	4	Dumbarton	1	Cathkin Park	14,000
1883	Dumbarton	2	Vale of Leven	2	Hampden Park	9,000
Replay	Dumbarton	2	Vale of Leven	1	Hampden Park	12,000
1884	Queen's Park awarded cup due to Vale of Leven failing to appear					
1885	Renton	0	Vale of Leven	0	Hampden Park	2,500
Replay	Renton	3	Vale of Leven	1	Hampden Park	3,500
1886	Queen's Park	3	Renton	1	Cathkin Park	7,000
1887	Hibernian	2	Dumbarton	1	Hampden Park	12,000
1888	Renton	6	Cambuslang	1	Hampden Park	11,000
1889	Third Lanark	3	Celtic	1	Hampden Park	18,000
	(game declared void due to snowstorm)					
Replay	Third Lanark	2	Celtic	1	Hampden Park	13,000
1890	Queen's Park	1	Vale of Leven	1	Ibrox	11,000
Replay	Queen's Park	2	Vale of Leven	1	Ibrox	14,000
1891	Hearts	1	Dumbarton	0	Hampden Park	10,836
1892	Celtic	1	Queen's Park	0	Ibrox	40,000
	(replayed due to spectator disruption)					
Replay	Celtic	5	Queen's Park	1	Ibrox	26,000
1893	Queen's Park	0	Celtic	1	Ibrox	18,771
	(replayed due to frosty pitch)					
Replay	Queen's Park	2	Celtic	1	Ibrox	13,239
1894	Rangers	3	Celtic	1	Hampden Park	17,000
1895	St.Bernard's	2	Renton	1	Ibrox	15,000
1896	Hearts	3	Hibernian	1	Logie Green	17,034
1897	Rangers	5	Dumbarton	1	Hampden Park	14,000
1898	Rangers	2	Kilmarnock	0	Hampden Park	13,000
1899	Celtic	2	Rangers	0	Hampden Park	25,000
1900	Celtic	4	Queen's Park	3	Ibrox	15,000
1901	Hearts	4	Celtic	3	Ibrox	12,000
1902	Hibernian	1	Celtic	0	Celtic Park	16,000
1903	Rangers	1	Hearts	1	Celtic Park	40,000
Replay	Rangers	0	Hearts	0	Celtic Park	35,000
Replay	Rangers	2	Hearts	0	Celtic Park	32,000
1904	Celtic	3	Rangers	2	Hampden Park	65,000
1905	Third Lanark	0	Rangers	0	Hampden Park	54,000
Replay	Third Lanark	3	Rangers	1	Hampden Park	55,000
1906	Hearts	1	Third Lanark	0	Ibrox	25,000
1907	Celtic	3	Hearts	0	Hampden Park	50,000
1908	Celtic	5	St.Mirren	1	Hampden Park	55,000
1909	Celtic	2	Rangers	2	Hampden Park	70,000

Year	Winners		Runners-up		Venue	Attendance
Replay	Celtic	1	Rangers	1	Hampden Park	61,000
(Owing to a riot, cup withheld after two drawn games)						
1910	Dundee	2	Clyde	2	Ibrox	62,300
Replay	Dundee	0	Clyde	0	Ibrox	24,500
Replay	Dundee	2	Clyde	1	Ibrox	25,400
1911	Celtic	0	Hamilton A.	0	Ibrox	45,000
Replay	Celtic	2	Hamilton A.	0	Ibrox	24,700
1912	Celtic	2	Clyde	0	Ibrox	46,000
1913	Falkirk	2	Raith Rovers	0	Celtic Park	45,000
1914	Celtic	0	Hibernian	0	Ibrox	56,000
Replay	Celtic	4	Hibernian	1	Ibrox	40,000
1920	Kilmarnock	3	Albion Rovers	2	Hampden Park	95,000
1921	Partick Thistle	1	Rangers	0	Celtic Park	28,300
1922	Morton	1	Rangers	0	Hampden Park	75,000
1923	Celtic	1	Hibernian	0	Hampden Park	80,100
1924	Airdrieonians	2	Hibernian	0	Ibrox	59,218
1925	Celtic	2	Dundee	1	Hampden Park	75,137
1926	St.Mirren	2	Celtic	0	Hampden Park	98,620
1927	Celtic	3	East Fife	1	Hampden Park	80,070
1928	Rangers	4	Celtic	0	Hampden Park	118,115
1929	Kilmarnock	2	Rangers	0	Hampden Park	114,708
1930	Rangers	0	Partick Thistle	0	Hampden Park	107,475
Replay	Rangers	2	Partick Thistle	1	Hampden Park	103,686
1931	Celtic	2	Motherwell	2	Hampden Park	105,000
Replay	Celtic	4	Motherwell	2	Hampden Park	98,579
1932	Rangers	1	Kilmarnock	1	Hampden Park	111,982
Replay	Rangers	3	Kilmarnock	0	Hampden Park	104,965
1933	Celtic	1	Motherwell	0	Hampden Park	102,339
1934	Rangers	5	St.Mirren	0	Hampden Park	113,403
1935	Rangers	2	Hamilton A.	1	Hampden Park	87,286
1936	Rangers	1	Third Lanark	0	Hampden Park	88,859
1937	Celtic	2	Aberdeen	1	Hampden Park	147,365
1938	East Fife	1	Kilmarnock	1	Hampden Park	80,091
Replay	East Fife	4	Kilmarnock	2	Hampden Park	92,716
1939	Clyde	4	Motherwell	0	Hampden Park	94,799
1947	Aberdeen	2	Hibernian	1	Hampden Park	82,140
1948	Rangers	1	Morton	1	Hampden Park	129,176
Replay	Rangers	1	Morton	0	Hampden Park	133,570
1949	Rangers	4	Clyde	1	Hampden Park	108,435
1950	Rangers	3	East Fife	0	Hampden Park	118,262
1951	Celtic	1	Motherwell	0	Hampden Park	131,943
1952	Motherwell	4	Dundee	0	Hampden Park	136,274
1953	Rangers	1	Aberdeen	1	Hampden Park	129,681
Replay	Rangers	1	Aberdeen	0	Hampden Park	112,619
1954	Celtic	2	Aberdeen	1	Hampden Park	129,926
1955	Clyde	1	Celtic	1	Hampden Park	106,111
Replay	Clyde	1	Celtic	0	Hampden Park	68,735
1956	Hearts	3	Celtic	1	Hampden Park	133,339
1957	Falkirk	1	Kilmarnock	1	Hampden Park	83,000
Replay	Falkirk	2	Kilmarnock	1	Hampden Park	79,785
1958	Clyde	1	Hibernian	0	Hampden Park	95,124
1959	St.Mirren	3	Aberdeen	1	Hampden Park	108,591
1960	Rangers	2	Kilmarnock	0	Hampden Park	108,017
1961	Dunfermline A.	0	Celtic	0	Hampden Park	113,618
Replay	Dunfermline A.	2	Celtic	0	Hampden Park	87,866
1962	Rangers	2	St.Mirren	0	Hampden Park	126,930
1963	Rangers	1	Celtic	1	Hampden Park	129,527
Replay	Rangers	3	Celtic	0	Hampden Park	120,263
1964	Rangers	3	Dundee	1	Hampden Park	120,982
1965	Celtic	3	Dunfermline A.	2	Hampden Park	108,800
1966	Rangers	0	Celtic	0	Hampden Park	126,552
Replay	Rangers	1	Celtic	0	Hampden Park	98,202

Year	Winners		Runners-up		Venue	Attendance
1967	Celtic	2	Aberdeen	0	Hampden Park	127,117
1968	Dunfermline A.	3	Hearts	1	Hampden Park	56,366
1969	Celtic	4	Rangers	0	Hampden Park	132,874
1970	Aberdeen	3	Celtic	1	Hampden Park	108,434
1971	Celtic	1	Rangers	1	Hampden Park	120,092
Replay	Celtic	2	Rangers	1	Hampden Park	103,332
1972	Celtic	6	Hibernian	1	Hampden Park	106,102
1973	Rangers	3	Celtic	2	Hampden Park	122,714
1974	Celtic	3	Dundee United	0	Hampden Park	75,959
1975	Celtic	3	Airdrieonians	1	Hampden Park	75,457
1976	Rangers	3	Hearts	1	Hampden Park	85,354
1977	Celtic	1	Rangers	0	Hampden Park	54,252
1978	Rangers	2	Aberdeen	1	Hampden Park	61,563
1979	Rangers	0	Hibernian	0	Hampden Park	50,610
Replay	Rangers	0	Hibernian	0	Hampden Park	33,506
Replay	Rangers	3	Hibernian	2	Hampden Park	30,602
1980	Celtic	1	Rangers	0	Hampden Park	70,303
1981	Rangers	0	Dundee United	0	Hampden Park	55,000
Replay	Rangers	4	Dundee United	1	Hampden Park	43,009
1982	Aberdeen	4	Rangers	1*	Hampden Park	53,788
1983	Aberdeen	1	Rangers	0*	Hampden Park	62,979
1984	Aberdeen	2	Celtic	1*	Hampden Park	58,900
1985	Celtic	2	Dundee United	1	Hampden Park	60,346
1986	Aberdeen	3	Hearts	0	Hampden Park	62,841
1987	St Mirren	1	Dundee United	0	Hampden Park	51,792

* after extra time

SCOTTISH FA CUP STATISTICS
Most wins: 27 Celtic; 24 Rangers
Biggest win: 36-0 Arbroath v Bon Accord (1st round) 12 Sep 1885
Biggest win (final):
6-1 Renton v Cambuslang 4 Feb 1888
6-1 Celtic v Hibernian 6 May 1972
Most individual goals in one match:
13 John Petrie (Arbroath v Bon Accord) 1st round 12 Sep 1885
Most winner's medals:
8 Charles Campbell (Queen's Park) 1874-6, 1880-2, 1884, 1886

SCOTTISH LEAGUE CUP

The Scottish League Cup was founded in 1946-7 and replaced the Southern League Cup that had been played during the war. Prior to 1977-8 the teams were split into eight or nine groups, with the winners going through to a knockout competition. Since 1977, however, it has been run on a strict knockout basis. The Cup became known as the Skol Cup in 1984-5. All finals have been at Hampden Park, unless otherwise stated.

Year	Winners		Runners-up	
1947	Rangers	4	Aberdeen	0
1948	East Fife	1	Falkirk	1*
Replay	East Fife	4	Falkirk	1
1949	Rangers	2	Raith Rovers	0
1950	East Fife	3	Dunfermline A	0
1951	Motherwell	3	Hibernian	0
1952	Dundee	3	Rangers	2
1953	Dundee	2	Kilmarnock	0
1954	East Fife	3	Partick Thistle	2
1955	Hearts	4	Motherwell	2
1956	Aberdeen	2	St.Mirren	1
1957	Celtic	0	Partick Thistle	0*
Replay	Celtic	3	Partick Thistle	0
1958	Celtic	7	Rangers	1
1959	Hearts	5	Partick Thistle	1
1960	Hearts	2	Third Lanark	1
1961	Rangers	2	Kilmarnock	0
1962	Rangers	1	Hearts	1*
Replay	Rangers	3	Hearts	1
1963	Hearts	1	Kilmarnock	0
1964	Rangers	5	Morton	0
1965	Rangers	2	Celtic	1
1966	Celtic	2	Rangers	1
1967	Celtic	1	Rangers	0
1968	Celtic	5	Dundee	3
1969	Celtic	6	Hibernian	2
1970	Celtic	1	St.Johnstone	0
1971	Rangers	1	Celtic	0
1972	Partick Thistle	4	Celtic	1
1973	Hibernian	2	Celtic	1
1974	Dundee	1	Celtic	0
1975	Celtic	6	Hibernian	3
1976	Rangers	1	Celtic	0
1977	Aberdeen	2	Celtic	1
1978	Rangers	2	Celtic	1
1979	Rangers	2	Aberdeen	1
1980	Dundee United	0	Aberdeen	0
Replay	Dundee United	3	Aberdeen	0§
1981	Dundee United	3	Dundee	0§
1982	Rangers	2	Dundee United	1
1983	Celtic	2	Rangers	1

Year	Winners		Runners-up	
1984	Rangers	3	Celtic	2*
1985	Rangers	1	Dundee United	0
1986	Aberdeen	3	Hibernian	0
1987	Rangers	2	Celtic	1

* after extra time, § Played at Dens Park, Dundee

SCOTTISH LEAGUE CUP STATISTICS

Most wins: 14 Rangers; 9 Celtic
Biggest win (final): 7-1 Celtic v Rangers 19 Oct 1957

Kenny Dalglish (All-Sport)

THE RANGERS AND CELTIC MONOPOLY

The following table of the most successful Scottish clubs shows the domination of the two Glasgow giants.

	League Titles	FA Cup Wins	League Cup Wins	Total
RANGERS	38	24	14	76
CELTIC	34	27	9	70
Hearts	5	5	4	14
Aberdeen	4	6	3	13
Queen's Park	-	10	-	10

FA AMATEUR CUP

Inaugurated in 1893-4 the Amateur Cup's correct name was the Football Association Amateur Challenge Cup. When the Football Association dropped the word 'amateur' from its rules in 1974 the Amateur Cup was discontinued, with Bishop's Stortford beating Ilford 4-1 in the last final.

Most wins:
10 Bishop Auckland 1896, 1900, 1914, 1921-2, 1935, 1939, 1955-7
 5 Clapton 1907, 1909, 1915, 1924-5
 5 Crook Town 1901, 1954, 1959, 1962, 1964
Biggest win:
Northern Nomads 7 Stockton 1, 17 Apr 1926
Dulwich Hamlet 7 Marine 1, 16 Apr 1932

FA CHALLENGE TROPHY

Non-league football's premier competition, the FA Challenge Trophy was first contested in 1970 and is open to senior professional, or semi-professional clubs not in the Football League. The final is played at Wembley.

Finals:

Year	Winners		Runners-up	
1970	Macclesfield Town	2	Telford United	0
1971	Telford United	3	Hillingdon Borough	2
1972	Stafford Rangers	3	Barnet	0
1973	Scarborough	2	Wigan Athletic	1*
1974	Morecambe	2	Dartford	1
1975	Matlock	4	Scarborough	0
1976	Scarborough	3	Stafford Rangers	2*
1977	Scarborough	2	Dagenham	1
1978	Altrincham	3	Leatherhead	1
1979	Stafford Rangers	2	Kettering Town	0
1980	Dagenham	2	Mossley	1
1981	Bishop's Stortford	1	Sutton United	0
1982	Enfield	1	Altrincham	0*
1983	Telford United	2	Northwich Victoria	1
1984	Northwich Victoria	2	Bangor City	1
1985	Wealdstone (after 1-1 draw)	2	Boston United	1
1986	Altrincham	1	Runcorn	0
1987	Kidderminster (after 0-0 draw)	2	Burton Albion	1

* after extra time

Most wins: 3 Scarborough 1973, 1976-7
Biggest attendance: 32,000 Stafford Rangers v Kettering Town 1979

GM VAUXHALL CONFERENCE

Leading clubs from the Northern Premier and Southern Leagues combined to form the new Alliance Premier League in 1979-80 with the ultimate objective of becoming a feeder to the Football League. That aim was achieved in 1986-7 season when the champions automatically gained Football League status, subject to ground suitability and the possession of an acceptable financial structure. The league became known as the Gola League in 1984-5, and changed to its current style in 1986-7.

Champions:
1979-80 Altrincham
1980-1 Altrincham
1981-2 Runcorn
1982-3 Enfield
1983-4 Maidstone United
1984-5 Wealdstone
1985-6 Enfield
1986-7 Scarborough

FA VASE

First held in 1974-75, the FA Vase replaced the Amateur Cup. Clubs that retained their 'amateur' status, and minor semi-professional sides take part in the Vase. The final is played at Wembley.

Finals:

1975	Hoddesdon Town	2	Epsom & Ewell	1
1976	Billericay Town	1	Stamford	0*
1977	Billericay Town (after 1-1 draw)	2	Sheffield	1
1978	Blue Star	2	Barton Rovers	1
1979	Billericay Town	4	Almondsbury G	1
1980	Stamford	2	Guisborough Town	0
1981	Whickham	3	Willenhall Town	2*
1982	Forest Green R	3	Rainworth MW	0
1983	VS Rugby	1	Halesowen Town	0
1984	Stansted	3	Stamford	2
1985	Halesowen Town	3	Fleetwood Town	1
1986	Halesowen Town	3	Southall	0
1987	St Helens Town	3	Warrington Town	2

* after extra time
Most wins: 3 Billericay Town 1976-7, 1979
Biggest attendance: 18,340 Halesowen Town v Southall 1986

FREIGHT ROVER TROPHY

A regionalised knockout tournament for third and fourth division clubs, it was first held in 1984-5 and replaced the Associate Members' Cup. The final is played at Wembley.

Year	Winners		Runners-up		Attendance
1985	Wigan Athletic	3	Brentford	1	39,897
1986	Bristol City	3	Bolton W.	0	54,502
1987	Mansfield T.	1	Bristol City	1	58,586

(Mansfield won 5-4 on penalties)

Stanley Matthews became, in 1965, the first footballer to be knighted. That year he played in the First Division at the age of 50.

AWARDS

FOOTBALL WRITERS' PLAYER OF THE YEAR

The Football Writers Association was founded in 1947 and since 1947-48 its members have voted for their Player of the Year.

Winners:
1948 Stanley Matthews (Blackpool)
1949 Johnny Carey (Manchester United)
1950 Joe Mercer (Arsenal)
1951 Harry Johnston (Blackpool)
1952 Billy Wright (Wolverhampton Wanderers)
1953 Nat Lofthouse (Bolton Wanderers)
1954 Tom Finney (Preston North End)
1955 Don Revie (Manchester City)
1956 Bert Trautmann (Manchester City)
1957 Tom Finney (Preston North End)
1958 Danny Blanchflower (Tottenham Hotspur)
1959 Syd Owen (Luton Town)
1960 Bill Slater (Wolverhampton Wanderers)
1961 Danny Blanchflower (Tottenham Hotspur)
1962 Jimmy Adamson (Burnley)
1963 Stanley Matthews (Stoke City)
1964 Bobby Moore (West Ham United)
1965 Bobby Collins (Leeds United)
1966 Bobby Charlton (Manchester United)
1967 Jackie Charlton (Leeds United)
1968 George Best (Manchester United)
1969 Tony Book (Manchester City) &
        Dave Mackay (Derby County)

1970 Billy Bremner (Leeds United)
1971 Frank McLintock (Arsenal)
1972 Gordon Banks (Stoke City)
1973 Pat Jennings (Tottenham Hotspur)
1974 Ian Callaghan (Liverpool)
1975 Alan Mullery (Fulham)
1976 Kevin Keegan (Liverpool)
1977 Emlyn Hughes (Liverpool)
1978 Kenny Burns (Nottingham Forest)
1979 Kenny Dalglish (Liverpool)
1980 Terry McDermott (Liverpool)
1981 Frans Thijssen (Ipswich Town)
1982 Steve Perryman (Tottenham Hotspur)
1983 Kenny Dalglish (Liverpool)
1984 Ian Rush (Liverpool)
1985 Neville Southall (Everton)
1986 Gary Lineker (Everton)
1987 Clive Allen (Tottenham Hotspur)

Most wins: 2 Tom Finney, Danny Blanchflower, Stanley Matthews, Kenny Dalglish
Most wins (clubs): 7 Liverpool; 4 Tottenham Hotspur; 3 Leeds United, Manchester City, Manchester United
Uncapped winners: The following winners of the award never won a full international cap: Jimmy Adamson (1962), Tony Book (1969)
Second Division winners: The only players to win the award while with a second division club were: Stanley Matthews (Stoke City, 1963), Dave Mackay (Derby County, 1969), Alan Mullery (Fulham, 1975)

PROFESSIONAL FOOTBALLERS' ASSOCIATION PLAYER OF THE YEAR

At the end of each season the professional players vote for their Player of the Year, a trophy much cherished by its winners. The first such award was made in 1974. A Young Player award is also presented annually, as well as a Merit Award.

Winners:

Player of the Year
1974 Norman Hunter (Leeds United)
1975 Colin Todd (Derby County)
1976 Pat Jennings (Tottenham Hotspur)
1977 Andy Gray (Aston Villa)
1978 Peter Shilton (Nottingham Forest)
1979 Liam Brady (Arsenal)
1980 Terry McDermott (Liverpool)
1981 John Wark (Ipswich Town)
1982 Kevin Keegan (Southampton)
1983 Kenny Dalglish (Liverpool)
1984 Ian Rush (Liverpool)
1985 Peter Reid (Everton)
1986 Gary Lineker (Everton)
1987 Clive Allen (Tottenham Hotspur)

Young Player of the Year
1974 Kevin Beattie (Ipswich Town)
1975 Mervyn Day (West Ham United)
1976 Peter Barnes (Manchester City)
1977 Andy Gray (Aston Villa)
1978 Tony Woodcock (Nottingham Forest)
1979 Cyrille Regis (West Bromwich Albion)
1980 Glenn Hoddle (Tottenham Hotspur)
1981 Gary Shaw (Aston Villa)
1982 Steve Moran (Southampton)

1983 Ian Rush (Liverpool)
1984 Paul Walsh (Luton Town)
1985 Mark Hughes (Manchester United)
1986 Tony Cottee (West Ham United)
1987 Tony Adams (Arsenal)

Merit Award
1974 Bobby Charlton & Cliff Lloyd
1975 Denis Law
1976 George Eastham
1977 Jack Taylor
1978 Bill Shankly
1979 Tom Finney
1980 Sir Matt Busby
1981 John Trollope
1982 Joe Mercer
1983 Bob Paisley
1984 Bill Nicholson
1985 Ron Greenwood
1986 Alf Ramsey, Harold Shepherdson & the 1966 England World Cup winning squad
1987 Stanley Matthews

Dual winners:
The following players have won the Player of the Year, and Young Player of the Year awards:
Andy Gray (both in 1977), Ian Rush (Young Player 1983, Player 1984)
The following clubs have provided the winners of both major PFA awards in the same season:
Aston Villa (1977 Andy Gray, both)
Nottingham Forest (1978 Peter Shilton & Tony Woodcock)
Southampton (1982 Kevin Keegan & Steve Moran)
Liverpool (1983 Kenny Dalglish & Ian Rush)

Winners of the Football Writers' and PFA Player of the Year Awards:
Pat Jennings (FWA 1973, PFA 1976)
Kevin Keegan (FWA 1976, PFA 1982)
Kenny Dalglish (FWA 1979, 1983, PFA 1983)
Terry McDermott (FWA 1980, PFA 1980)
Ian Rush (FWA 1984, FWA 1984)
Gary Lineker (FWA 1986, PFA 1986)
Clive Allen (FWA 1987, PFA 1987)

EUROPEAN FOOTBALLER OF THE YEAR

Le Ballon D'Or (Golden Ball) is awarded each year by the French newspaper *France Football* who ask various journalists in UEFA affiliated countries to draw up a list of their five nominees.

Winners:
1956 Stanley Matthews (Blackpool)
1957 Alfredo di Stefano (Real Madrid)
1958 Raymond Kopa (Real Madrid)
1959 Alfredo di Stefano (Real Madrid)
1960 Luis Suarez (Barcelona)
1961 Omar Sivori (Juventus)
1962 Josef Masopust (Dukla Prague)
1963 Lev Yashin (Dynamo Moscow)
1964 Denis Law (Manchester United)
1965 Eusebio (Benfica)
1966 Bobby Charlton (Manchester United)
1967 Florian Albert (Ferencvaros)
1968 George Best (Manchester United)
1969 Gianni Rivera (AC Milan)
1970 Gerd Müller (Bayern Munich)

1971 Johan Cruyff (Ajax)
1972 Franz Beckenbauer (Bayern Munich)
1973 Johan Cruyff (Barcelona)
1974 Johan Cruyff (Barcelona)
1975 Oleg Blokhin (Dynamo Kiev)
1976 Franz Beckenbauer (Bayern Munich)
1977 Allan Simonsen (B.Moenchengladbach)
1978 Kevin Keegan (SV Hamburg)
1979 Kevin Keegan (SV Hamburg)
1980 Karl-Heinz Rummenigge (Bayern Munich)
1981 Karl-Heinz Rummenigge (Bayern Munich)
1982 Paolo Rossi (Juventus)
1983 Michel Platini (Juventus)
1984 Michel Platini (Juventus)
1985 Michel Platini (Juventus)
1986 Igor Belanov (Dynamo Kiev)

Most wins: 3 Johan Cruyff, Michel Platini; 2 Alfredo di Stefano, Franz Beckenbauer, Kevin Keegan, Karl-Heinz Rummenigge
Most wins (clubs): 5 Bayern Munich; 4 Juventus; 3 Real Madrid, Barcelona, Manchester United

THE MOST HONOURED BRITISH PLAYERS

The following players have been honoured on three or more occasions with awards from the three main associations.

	FWA	PFA	European	Total
Kevin Keegan	1	1	2	4
Stanley Matthews	2	-	1	3
Tom Finney	2	1	-	3
Kenny Dalglish	2	1	-	3
Bobby Charlton	1	1	1	3
Ian Rush	1	2	-	3

BELL'S SCOTCH WHISKY MANAGER OF THE YEAR

Instituted in 1965-6 the trophy and accompanying cheque is presented to the Manager of the Season. In addition to the annual prize, monthly awards are made to the Manager of the Month, and divisional awards are also made monthly.

Winners:
1966 Jock Stein (Glasgow Celtic)
1967 Jock Stein (Glasgow Celtic)
1968 Matt Busby (Manchester United)
1969 Don Revie (Leeds United)
1970 Don Revie (Leeds United)
1971 Bertie Mee (Arsenal)
1972 Don Revie (Leeds United)
1973 Bill Shankly (Liverpool)
1974 Jack Charlton (Middlesbrough)
1975 Ron Saunders (Aston Villa)
1976 Bob Paisley (Liverpool)
1977 Bob Paisley (Liverpool)
1978 Brian Clough (Nottingham Forest)
1979 Bob Paisley (Liverpool)
1980 Bob Paisley (Liverpool)
1981 Ron Saunders (Aston Villa)
1982 Bob Paisley (Liverpool)
1983 Bob Paisley (Liverpool)
1984 Joe Fagan (Liverpool)
1985 Howard Kendall (Everton)
1986 Kenny Dalglish (Liverpool)
1987 Howard Kendall (Everton)
Most wins: 6 Bob Paisley; 3 Don Revie; 2 Ron Saunders, Jock Stein, Howard Kendall

Michel Platini of France (All-Sport)

THE MOST SUCCESSFUL MANAGER

Bob Paisley's nine-year reign as Liverpool's manager was the most successful ever in the history of English football. His complete record was:

	League Champs.	League/ Milk Cup	FA Cup	European Cup	UEFA Cup	European Super Cup
Wins	6	3	-	3	1	1
Runners-up	2	1	1	-	-	-

ADIDAS GOLDEN BOOT AWARD

An annual award made by the sportswear manufacturers who present a Golden Boot to the European player who scores the most goals in the domestic League season. They also make an award to their Team of the Year.

Golden Boot winners

Year	Player	Club	Goals
1968	Eusebio	Benfica	43
1969	Petar Jekov	CSKA Sofia	36
1970	Gerd Müller	Bayern Munich	38
1971	Josip Skoblar	Marseille	44
1972	Gerd Müller	Bayern Munich	40
1973	Eusebio	Benfica	40
1974	Hector Yazalde	Sporting Lisbon	46
1975	Dudu Georgescu	Dinamo Bucharest	33
1976	Sotiris Kaiafas	Omonia Nicosia	39
1977	Dudu Georgescu	Dinamo Bucharest	47
1978	Hans Krankl	Rapid Vienna	41
1978	Kees Kist	AZ 67 Alkmaar	34
1980	Erwin van den Bergh	Lierse	39
1981	Georgi Slavkov	Trakia	31
1982	Wim Kieft	Ajax	32

1983 Francisco Gomes   FC Porto   36
1984 Ian Rush   Liverpool   32
1985 Francisco Gomes   FC Porto   39
1986 Marco van Basten   Ajax   37

Team of the Year
1968 Benfica & AC Milan (shared)
1969 Ajax
1970 Glasgow Celtic
1971 Ajax & Arsenal (shared)
1972 Ajax
1973 Ajax
1974 Bayern Munich & Feyenoord (shared)
1975 Borussia Moenchengladbach
1976 Liverpool
1977 Juventus
1978 Liverpool
1979 Nottingham Forest
1980 Real Madrid
1981 Ipswich Town
1982 Liverpool
1983 Liverpool
1984 Liverpool
1985 Everton
1986 Real Madrid

INDIVIDUAL GOALSCORING RECORDS

For first class matches

MOST GOALS IN ONE GAME
World record: 16 Stephan Stanis (Racing Club Lens v Aubry-Asturies) 13 Dec 1942
International: 10 Sofus Nielsen (Denmark v France) 1908 Olympics
10 Gotfried Fuchs (Germany v Russia) 1912 Olympics
British international record: 6 Joe Bambrick (N.Ireland v Wales) 1 Feb 1930
World Cup: several players have scored four goals in one game (q.v.)
Major European competition: 6 Lothar Emmerich (Borussia Dortmund v Floriana) Cup-Winners' Cup 1st round 13 Oct 1965
FA Cup (proper): 9 Ted MacDougall (Bournemouth v Margate) 1st round 20 Nov 1971
(preliminary round): 10 Chris Marron (South Shields v Radcliffe) 20 Sep 1947
Football League/Milk/Littlewoods Cup:
5 Derek Reeves (Southampton v Leeds U) 4th round 5 Dec 1960
5 Alan Wilks (QPR v Oxford U) 3rd round 10 Oct 1967
Football League: 10 Joe Payne (Luton T v Bristol R) Div.3S 13 Apr 1936
Scottish Cup: 13 John Petrie (Arbroath v Bon Accord) 12 Sep 1885
Scottish League: 8 Jimmy McGrory (Celtic v Dunfermline A) Div 1 14 Jan 1928

MOST GOALS IN A CAREER
World record: 1329 Artur Friedenreich (Germania, CA Ipiranga, Americano, CA Paulistano, Sao Paulo, Flamengo) 1909-35
Full Internationals: 97 Pele (Bra) 1957-70

Bobby Charlton.

(British record): 49 Bobby Charlton (Eng) 1958-70
World Cup: 14 Gerd Müller (FRG) 1970-74
European Cup: 49 Alfredo di Stefano (Real Madrid) 1955-64
Football League: 434 Arthur Rowley (West Bromwich A, Fulham, Leicester C, Shrewsbury T) 1946-65
Scottish League: 410 Jimmy McGrory (Celtic, Clydebank) 1922-38

HAT TRICKS
Most in a career: 92 Pele 1956-77
(British record): 37 Dixie Dean 1924-39

HAT TRICKS IN MAJOR FINALS
World Cup:
Geoff Hurst (England v West Germany) 30 Jul 1966
European Championship: None
European Cup:
Ferenc Puskas (4 goals) (Real Madrid v Eintracht) 18 May 1960
Alfredo di Stefano (Real Madrid v Eintracht) 18 May 1960
Ferenc Puskas (Real Madrid v Benfica) 2 May 1962
Pierino Prati (AC Milan v Ajax) 28 May 1969
European Cup-Winners' Cup: None
UEFA/Fairs Cup:
Vicente Guillot (Valencia v Barcelona) 8 Sep 1962
Luis Pujol (Barcelona v Real Zaragoza) 21 Sep 1966
Jupp Heynckes (B.Moenchengladbach v Twente Enschede) 21 May 1975
FA Cup:
William Townley (Blackburn R v Sheffield W) 29 Mar 1890
Jimmy Logan (Notts County v Bolton Wanderers) 31 Mar 1894

Don Quarrie (left) and Alan Wells (right), both won Olympic sprint gold medals, with six and four Commonwealth golds respectively.

Stan Mortensen (Blackpool v Bolton Wanderers) 2 May 1953
Football League/Milk/Littlewoods Cup: None
Scottish FA Cup:
Jimmy Quinn (Celtic v Rangers) 16 Apr 1904
Dixie Deans (Celtic v Hibernian) 6 May 1972
Scottish League Cup:
Davie Duncan (East Fife v Falkirk) 1 Nov 1948
Willie Bauld (Hearts v Motherwell) 23 Oct 1954
John McPhail (Celtic v Rangers) 19 Oct 1957
Jim Forrest (4 goals) (Rangers v Morton) 26 Oct 1963
Bobby Lennox (Celtic v Hibernian) 5 Apr 1969
Dixie Deans (Celtic v Hibernian) 26 Oct 1974
Joe Harper (Hibernian v Celtic) 26 Oct 1974
Ally McCoist (Rangers v Celtic) 25 Mar 1984

ATHLETICS

Competition in running, jumping or throwing naturally dates back into pre-history. The earliest evidence we have of organised running is from about 3800BC in Egypt, and athletic achievements were particularly prized at the ancient Olympic Games in Greece. Those Games were more than just sporting contests for they were also great artistic and cultural festivals maintaining the Greek ideal of perfection of mind and body. They provided the inspiration for the modern Olympic Games, which have provided the focus for athletics, since their re-introduction in 1896. At least that is until recently, for separate world championships for all events were instituted in 1983, and nowadays there is a plethora of top-class competition.

The first national championships were those of England in 1866, organised by the Amateur Athletic Club. These preceded the formation of the Amateur Athletic Association in 1880.

International governing body: The International Amateur Athletic Federation (IAAF), formed in 1912 initially with 17 members. It ratified the first list of world records in 1914. The IAAF now has 179 nations affiliated to it, more than any other international organisation, sporting or otherwise.

OLYMPIC GAMES

The first Olympic Games of the modern era were staged in Athens, Greece from 6 to 15 April 1896, when just 59 athletes from ten nations contested the athletics events. The 1900 and 1904 Games were also small-scale affairs, with just over 100 athletes at each, but from 1908 the Games grew rapidly in importance to true world championships. Women's events were first included in 1928, and the number of contestants in athletics passed 1000 for the first time at the 1960 Games.

OLYMPIC ATHLETICS CHAMPIONS

Note that automatic timing was first used at the Olympic Games in 1932. In this list of champions, automatic times are given, where known, for proper comparisons. Olympic records are shown by OR.

MEN

100 METRES
1896 Thomas Burke (USA) 12.0
1900 Francis Jarvis (USA) 11.0
1904 Archie Hahn (USA) 11.0
1906 Archie Hahn (USA) 11.2
1908 Reginald Walker (SAf) 10.8
1912 Ralph Craig (USA) 10.8
1920 Charles Paddock (USA) 10.8
1924 Harold Abrahams (UK) 10.6
1928 Percy Williams (Can) 10.8
1932 Eddie Tolan (USA) 10.38
1936 Jesse Owens (USA) 10.3
1948 Harrison Dillard (USA) 10.3
1952 Lindy Remigino (USA) 10.79
1956 Bobby Morrow (USA) 10.62
1960 Armin Hary (FRG) 10.32
1964 Robert Hayes (USA) 10.06
1968 James Hines (USA 9.95 OR
1972 Valeriy Borzov (USSR) 10.14
1976 Hasely Crawford (Tri) 10.06
1980 Allan Wells (UK) 10.25
1984 Carl Lewis (USA) 9.99

200 METRES
1900 Walter Tewksbury (USA) 22.2
1904 Archie Hahn (USA) 21.6
1908 Robert Kerr (Can) 22.6
1912 Ralph Craig (USA) 21.7
1920 Allen Woodring (USA) 22.0
1924 Jackson Scholz (USA) 21.6
1928 Percy Williams (Can) 21.8
1932 Eddie Tolan (USA) 21.12
1936 Jesse Owens (USA) 20.7
1948 Melvin Patton (USA) 21.1
1952 Andrew Stanfield (USA) 20.81
1956 Bobby Morrow (USA) 20.75
1960 Livio Berrutti (Ita) 20.62
1964 Henry Carr (USA) 20.36
1968 Tommie Smith (USA) 19.83
1972 Valeriy Borzov (USSR) 20.00
1976 Donald Quarrie (Jam) 20.22
1980 Pietro Mennea (Ita) 20.19
1984 Carl Lewis (USA) 19.80 OR

400 METRES
1896 Thomas Burke (USA) 54.2
1900 Maxie Long (USA) 49.4
1904 Harry Hillman (USA) 49.2
1906 Paul Pilgrim (USA) 53.2
1908 Wyndham Halswelle (UK) 50.0
1912 Charles Reidpath (USA) 48.2
1920 Bevil Rudd (SAf) 49.6
1924 Eric Liddell (UK) 47.6
1928 Ray Barbuti (USA) 47.8
1932 Bill Carr (USA) 46.28
1936 Archie Williams (USA) 46.66
1948 Arthur Wint (Jam) 46.2
1952 George Rhoden (Jam) 46.09
1956 Charles Jenkins (USA) 46.86
1960 Otis Davis (USA) 45.07
1964 Michael Larrabee (USA) 45.15
1968 Lee Evans (USA) 43.86 OR
1972 Vincent Matthews (USA) 44.66

1976 Alberto Juantorena (Cub) 44.26
1980 Viktor Markin (USSR) 44.60
1984 Alonzo Babers (USA) 44.27

800 METRES
1896 Edwin Flack (Aus) 2:11.0
1900 Alfred Tysoe (UK) 2:01.2
1904 James Lightbody (USA) 1:56.0
1906 Paul Pilgrim (USA) 2:01.5
1908 Mel Sheppard (USA) 1:52.8
1912 James Meredith (USA) 1:51.9
1920 Albert Hill (UK) 1:53.4
1924 Douglas Lowe (UK) 1:52.4
1928 Douglas Lowe (UK) 1:51.8
1932 Tom Hampson (UK) 1:49.70
1936 John Woodruff (USA) 1:52.9
1948 Malvin Whitfield (USA) 1:49.2
1952 Malvin Whitfield (USA) 1:49.34
1956 Thomas Courtney (USA) 1:47.75
1960 Peter Snell (NZ) 1:46.48
1964 Peter Snell (NZ) 1:45.1
1968 Ralph Doubell (Aus) 1:44.40
1972 David Wottle (USA) 1:45.86
1976 Alberto Juantorena (Cub) 1:43.50
1980 Steven Ovett (UK) 1:45.40
1984 Joaquim Cruz (Bra) 1:43.00 OR

1500 METRES
1896 Edwin Flack (Aus) 4:33.2
1900 Charles Bennett (UK) 4:06.2
1904 James Lightbody (USA) 4:05.4
1906 James Lightbody (USA) 4:12.0
1908 Mel Sheppard (USA) 4:03.4
1912 Arnold Jackson (UK) 3:56.8
1920 Albert Hill (UK) 4:01.8
1924 Paavo Nurmi (Fin) 3:53.6
1928 Harri Larva (Fin) 3:53.2
1932 Luigi Beccali (Ita) 3:51.20
1936 Jack Lovelock (NZ) 3:47.8
1948 Henry Eriksson (Swe) 3:49.8
1952 Josef Barthel (Lux) 3:45.28
1956 Ron Delany (Ire) 3:41.49
1960 Herbert Elliott (Aus) 3:35.6
1964 Peter Snell (NZ) 3:38.1
1968 Kipchoge Keino (Ken) 3:34.91
1972 Pekka Vasala (Fin) 3:36.33
1976 John Walker (NZ) 3:39.17
1980 Sebastian Coe (UK) 3:38.40
1984 Sebastian Coe (UK) 3:32.53 OR

5000 METRES
1912 Hannes Kolehmainen (Fin) 14:36.6
1920 Joseph Guillemot (Fra) 14:55.6
1924 Paavo Nurmi (Fin) 14:31.2
1928 Ville Ritola (Fin) 14:38.0
1932 Lauri Lehtinen (Fin) 14:29.91
1936 Gunnar Hockert (Fin) 14:22.2
1948 Gaston Reiff (Bel) 14:17.6
1952 Emil Zatopek (Cs) 14:06.72
1956 Vladimir Kuts (USSR) 13:39.86
1960 Murray Halberg (NZ) 13:43.4
1964 Robert Schul (USA) 13:48.8
1968 Mohamed Gammoudi (Tun) 14:05.0
1972 Lasse Viren (Fin) 13:26.42
1976 Lasse Viren (Fin) 13:24.76

Above: *Alberto Juantarena wins the Olympic 800 in 1976 from Ivo van Damme (103) and Rick Wohlhuter. The bearded Steve Ovett is fifth.*
Below: *Herb Elliott.*

1980 Miruts Yifter (Eth) 13.20.91
1984 Said Aouita (Mor) 13:05.59 OR

10 000 METRES
1912 Hannes Kolehmainen (Fin) 31:20.8
1920 Paavo Nurmi (Fin) 31:45.8
1924 Ville Ritola (Fin) 30:23.2
1928 Paavo Nurmi (Fin) 30:18.8
1932 Janusz Kushocinski (Pol) 30:11.42
1936 Ilmari Salminen (Fin) 30:15.4
1948 Emil Zatopek (Cs) 29:59.6
1952 Emil Zatopek (Cs) 29:17.0
1956 Vladimir Kuts (USSR) 28:45.60
1960 Pyotr Bolotnikov (USSR) 28:32.18
1964 William Mills (USA) 28:24.4
1968 Naftali Temu (Ken) 29:27.4
1972 Lasse Viren (Fin) 27:38.35 OR
1976 Lasse Viren (Fin) 27:40.38
1980 Miruts Yifter (Eth) 27:42.69
1984 Alberto Cova (Ita) 27:47.54

MARATHON (42.295km)
1896 Spyridon Louis (Gre) 2:58:50.0 (40km)
1900 Michel Theato (Fra) 2:59:45.0 (40.26km)
1904 Thomas Hicks (USA) 3:28:35.0 (40km)
1906 William Sherring (Can) 2:51:23.6 (41.86km)
1908 John Hayes (USA) 2:55:18.4
1912 Kenneth McArthur (SAf) 2:36:54.8 (40.2km)
1920 Hannes Kolehmainen (Fin) 2:32:35.8 (42.75km)
1924 Albin Stenroos (Fin) 2:41:22.6
1928 Mohamed El Ouafi (Fra) 2:32:57.0
1932 Juan Zabala (Arg) 2:31:36.0
1936 Kitei Son (Jap)* 2:29:19.2
1948 Delfo Cabrera (Arg) 2:34:51.6
1952 Emil Zatopek (Cs) 2:23:03.2
1956 Alain Mimoun (Fra) 2:25:00.0
1960 Abebe Bikila (Eth) 2:15:16.2
1964 Abebe Bikila (Eth) 2:12:11.2
1968 Mamo Wolde (Eth) 2:20:26.4
1972 Frank Shorter (USA) 2:12:19.8
1976 Waldemar Cierpinski (GDR) 2:09:55
1980 Waldemar Cierpinski (GDR) 2:11:03
1984 Carlos Lopes (Por) 2:09:21 OR

* Actually the Korean Kee Chung Sohn

4×100 METRES RELAY
1912 UK 42.4
1920 USA 42.2
1924 USA 41.0
1928 USA 41.0
1932 USA 40.10
1936 USA 39.8
1948 USA 40.6
1952 USA 40.26
1956 USA 39.59
1960 FR Germany 39.66
1964 USA 39.06
1968 USA 38.23
1972 USA 38.19
1976 USA 38.83
1980 USSR 38.26
1984 USA 37.83 OR

MEDLEY RELAY (200M, 200M, 400M, 800M)
1908 USA 3:29.4

4×400 METRES RELAY
1912 USA 3:16.6
1920 UK 3:22.2
1924 USA 3:16.0
1928 USA 3:14.2
1932 USA 3:08.14
1936 UK 3:09.0
1948 USA 3:10.4
1952 Jamaica 3:04.04
1956 USA 3:04.80
1960 USA 3:02.37
1964 USA 3:00.71
1968 USA 2:56.16 OR
1972 Kenya 2:59.83
1976 USA 2:58.66
1980 USSR 3:01.08
1984 USA 2:57.91

110 METRES HURDLES
1896 Thomas Curtis (USA) 17.6
1900 Alvin Kraenzlein (USA) 15.4
1904 Fred Schule (USA) 16.0
1906 Robert Leavitt (USA) 16.2
1908 Forrest Smithson (USA) 15.0
1912 Fred Kelly (USA) 15.1
1920 Earl Thomson (Can) 14.8
1924 Daniel Kinsey (USA) 15.0
1928 Sydney Atkinson (SAf) 14.8
1932 George Saling (USA) 14.57
1936 Forrest Towns (USA) 14.2
1948 William Porter (USA) 13.9
1952 Harrison Dillard (USA) 13.91
1956 Lee Calhoun (USA) 13.70
1960 Lee Calhoun (USA) 13.98
1964 Hayes Jones (USA) 13.67
1968 Willie Davenport (USA) 13.33
1972 Rodney Milburn (USA) 13.24
1976 Guy Drut (Fra) 13.30
1980 Thomas Munkelt (GDR) 13.39
1984 Roger Kingdom (USA) 13.20 OR

400 METRES HURDLES
1900 Walter Tewksbury (USA) 57.6
1904 Harry Hillman (USA) 53.0
1908 Charles Bacon (USA) 55.0
1920 Frank Loomis (USA) 54.0
1924 Morgan Taylor (USA) 52.6
1928 Lord Burghley (UK) 53.4
1932 Robert Tisdall (Ire) 51.67
1936 Glenn Hardin (USA) 52.4
1948 Roy Cochran (USA) 51.1
1952 Charles Moore (USA) 51.06
1956 Glenn Davis (USA) 50.29
1960 Glenn Davis (USA) 49.51
1964 Rex Cawley (USA) 49.69
1968 David Hemery (UK) 48.12
1972 John Akii-Bua (Uga) 47.82
1976 Edwin Moses (USA) 47.63 OR
1980 Volker Beck (GDR) 48.70
1984 Edwin Moses (USA) 47.75

3000 METRES STEEPLECHASE
1920 Percy Hodge (UK) 10:00.4
1924 Ville Ritola (Fin) 9:33.6
1928 Toivo Loukola (Fin) 9:21.8

1932 Volmari Iso-Hollo (Fin) 10:33.4*
1936 Volmari Iso-Hollo (Fin) 9:03.8
1948 Tore Sjöstrand (Swe) 9:04.6
1952 Horace Ashenfelter (USA) 8:45.68
1956 Christopher Brasher (UK) 8:41.35
1960 Zdzislaw Kryszkowiak (Pol) 8:34.31
1964 Gaston Roelants (Bel) 8:30.8
1968 Amos Biwott (Ken) 8:51.0
1972 Kipchoge Keino (Ken) 8:23.64
1976 Anders Gärderud (Swe) 8:08.02 OR
1980 Bronislaw Malinowski (Pol) 8:09.70
1984 Julius Korir (Ken) 8:11.80

* due to lap counting error distance was 3460 metres

20 000 METRES WALK
1956 Leonid Spirin (USSR) 1:31:27.4
1960 Vladimir Golubnichiy (USSR) 1:34:07.2
1964 Kenneth Matthews (UK) 1:29:34.0
1968 Vladimir Golubnichiy (USSR) 1:33:58.4
1972 Peter Frenkel (GDR) 1:26:42.4
1976 Daniel Bautista (Mex) 1:24:40.6
1980 Maurizio Damilano (Ita) 1:23:35.5
1984 Ernesto Canto (Mex) 1:23.13 OR

50 000 METRES WALK
1932 Thomas Green (UK) 4:50:10.0
1936 Harold Whitlock (UK) 4:30:41.1
1948 John Ljunggren (Swe) 4:41:52.0
1952 Giuseppe Dordoni (Ita) 4:28:07.8
1956 Norman Read (NZ) 4:30:42.8
1960 Don Thompson (UK) 4:25:30.0
1964 Abdon Pamich (Ita) 4:11:12.4
1968 Christophe Höhne (GDR) 4:20:13.6
1972 Bernd Kannenberg (GDR) 3:56:11.6
1980 Hartwig Gauder (GDR) 3:49:24
1984 Raul Gonzales (Mex) 3:47:26 OR

HIGH JUMP
1896 Ellery Clark (USA) 1.81
1900 Irving Baxter (USA) 1.90
1904 Samuel Jones (USA) 1.80
1906 Con Leahy (UK/Ire) 1.77
1908 Harry Porter (USA) 1.90
1912 Alma Richards (USA) 1.93
1920 Richard Landon (USA) 1.94
1924 Harold Osborn (USA) 1.98
1928 Robert King (USA) 1.94
1932 Duncan McNaughton (Can) 1.97
1936 Cornelius Johnson (USA) 2.03
1948 John Winter (Aus) 1.98
1952 Walter Davis (USA) 2.04
1956 Charles Dumas (USA) 2.12
1960 Robert Shavlakadze (USSR) 2.16
1964 Valeriy Brumel (USSR) 2.18
1968 Dick Fosbury (USA) 2.24
1972 Yuriy Tarmak (USSR) 2.23
1976 Jacek Wszola (Pol) 2.25
1980 Gerd Wessig (GDR) 2.36 OR
1984 Dietmar Mögenburg (FRG) 2.35

POLE VAULT
1896 William Hoyt (USA) 3.30
1900 Irving Baxter (USA) 3.30
1904 Charles Dvorak (USA) 3.50
1906 Fernand Gonder (Fra) 3.40

1908 Edward Cooke & Alfred Gilbert (USA) 3.71
1912 Harry Babcock (USA) 3.95
1920 Frank Foss (USA) 4.09
1924 Lee Barnes (USA) 3.95
1928 Sabin Carr (USA) 4.20
1932 Bill Miller (USA) 4.31
1936 Earle Meadows (USA) 4.35
1948 Guinn Smith (USA) 4.30
1952 Robert Richards (USA) 4.55
1956 Robert Richards (USA) 4.56
1960 Donald Bragg (USA) 4.70
1964 Frederick Hansen (USA) 5.10
1968 Bob Seagren (USA) 5.40
1972 Wolfgang Nordwig (GDR) 5.50
1976 Tadeusz Slusarski (Pol) 5.50
1980 Wladyslaw Kozakiewicz (Pol) 5.78 OR
1984 Pierre Quinon (Fra) 5.75

LONG JUMP
1896 Ellery Clark (USA) 6.35
1900 Alvin Kraenzlein (USA) 7.18
1904 Myer Prinstein (USA) 7.34
1906 Myer Prinstein (USA) 7.20
1908 Francis Irons (USA) 7.48
1912 Albert Gutterson (USA) 7.60
1920 William Pettersson (Swe) 7.15
1924 William De Hart Hubbbard (USA) 7.44
1928 Edward Hamm (USA) 7.73
1932 Edward Gordon (USA) 7.64
1936 Jesse Owens (USA) 8.06
1948 William Steele (USA) 7.82
1952 Jerome Biffle (USA) 7.57
1956 Gregory Bell (USA) 7.83

Viktor Saneyev won three Olympic, two European outdoor and six European indoor triple jump titles. (All-Sport)

1960 Ralph Boston (USA) 8.12
1964 Lynn Davies (UK) 8.07
1968 Bob Beamon (USA) 8.90 OR
1972 Randy Williams (USA) 8.24
1976 Arnie Robinson (USA) 8.35
1980 Lutz Dombrowski (GDR) 8.54
1984 Carl Lewis (USA) 8.54

TRIPLE JUMP
1896 James Connolly (USA) 13.71
1900 Myer Prinstein (USA) 14.47
1904 Myer Prinstein (USA) 14.35
1906 Peter O'Connor (UK/Ire) 14.07
1·908 Tim Ahearne (UK/Ire) 14.91
1912 Gustaf Lindblom (Swe) 14.76
1920 Vilho Tuulos (Fin) 14.50
1924 Anthony Winter (Aus) 15.52
1928 Mikio Oda (Jap) 15.21
1932 Chuhei Nambu (Jap) 15.72
1936 Naoto Tajima (Jap) 16.00
1948 Arne Ahman (Swe) 15.40
1952 Adhemar Ferreira da Silva (Bra) 16.22
1956 Adhemar Ferreira da Silva (Bra) 16.35
1960 Jozef Schmidt (Pol) 16.81
1964 Jozef Schmidt (Pol) 16.85
1968 Viktor Saneyev (USSR) 17.39 OR
1972 Viktor Saneyev (USSR) 17.35
1976 Viktor Saneyev (USSR) 17.29
1980 Jaak Uudmae (USSR) 17.35
1984 Al Joyner (USA) 17.26

SHOT
1896 Robert Garrett (USA) 11.22
1900 Richard Sheldon (USA) 14.10
1904 Ralph Rose (USA) 14.80
1906 Martin Sheridan (USA) 12.32
1908 Ralph Rose (USA) 14.21
1912 Patrick McDonald (USA) 15.34
1920 Ville Pörhölä (Fin) 14.81
1924 Clarence Houser (USA) 14.99
1928 John Kuck (USA) 15.87
1932 Leo Sexton (USA) 16.00
1936 Hans Woellke (Ger) 16.20
1948 Wilbur Thompson (USA) 17.12
1952 Parry O'Brien (USA) 17.41
1956 Parry O'Brien (USA) 18.57
1960 William Nieder (USA) 19.68
1964 Dallas Long (USA) 20.33
1968 Randy Matson (USA) 20.54
1972 Wladyslaw Komar (Pol) 21.18
1976 Udo Beyer (GDR) 21.05
1980 Vladimir Kiselyov (USSR) 21.35 OR
1984 Alessandro Andrei (Ita) 21.26

DISCUS
1896 Robert Garrett (USA) 29.15
1900 Rudolf Bauer (Hun) 36.04
1904 Martin Sheridan (USA) 39.28
1906 Martin Sheridan (USA) 41.46
1908 Martin Sheridan (USA) 40.89
1912 Armas Taipale (Fin) 45.21
1920 Elmer Niklander (Fin) 44.68
1924 Clarence Houser (USA) 46.15
1928 Clarence Houser (USA) 47.32
1932 John Anderson (USA) 49.49

1936 Ken Carpenter (USA) 50.48
1948 Adolfo Consolini (Ita) 52.78
1952 Sim Iness (USA) 55.03
1956 Al Oerter (USA) 56.36
1960 Al Oerter (USA) 59.18
1964 Al Oerter (USA) 61.00
1968 Al Oerter (USA) 64.78
1972 Ludvik Danek (Cs) 64.40
1976 Mac Wilkins (USA) 67.50 (OR: 68.28 qualifying)
1980 Viktor Rashchupkin (USSR) 66.64
1984 Rolf Danneberg (FRG) 66.60

HAMMER
1900 John Flanagan (USA) 49.73
1904 John Flanagan (USA) 51.23
1908 John Flanagan (USA) 51.92
1912 Matt McGrath (USA) 54.74
1920 Patrick Ryan (USA) 52.87
1924 Fred Tootell (USA) 53.29
1928 Patrick O'Callaghan (Ire) 51.39
1932 Patrick O'Callaghan (Ire) 53.92
1936 Karl Hein (Ger) 56.49
1948 Imre Nemeth (Hun) 56.07
1952 Jozsef Csermak (Hun) 60.34
1956 Harold Connolly (USA) 63.19
1960 Vasiliy Rudenkov (USSR) 67.10
1964 Romuald Klim (USSR) 69.74
1968 Gyula Zsivotzky (Hun) 73.36
1972 Anatoliy Bondarchuk (USSR) 75.50
1976 Yuriy Sedykh (USSR) 77.52
1980 Yuriy Sedykh (USSR) 81.80 OR
1984 Juha Tiainen (Fin) 78.08

JAVELIN
1906 Erik Lemming (Swe) 53.90
1908 Erik Lemming (Swe) 54.82
1912 Erik Lemming (Swe) 60.64
1920 Jonni Myyrä (Fin) 65.78
1924 Jonni Myyrä (Fin) 62.96
1928 Erik Lundkvist (Swe) 66.60
1932 Matti Järvinen (Fin) 72.71
1936 Gerhard Stöck (Ger) 71.84
1948 Tapio Rautavaara (Fin) 69.77
1952 Cyrus Young (USA) 73.78
1956 Egil Danielsen (Nor) 85.71
1960 Viktor Tsibulenko (USSR) 84.64
1964 Pauli Nevala (Fin) 82.66
1968 Janis Lusis (USSR) 90.10
1972 Klaus Wolfermann (FRG) 90.48
1976 Miklos Nemeth (Hun) 94.58 OR
1980 Dainis Kula (USSR) 91.20
1984 Arto Harkönen (Fin) 86.76

DECATHLON
(scores on all re-scored on 1984 tables)
1912 Jim Thorpe (USA) 6564 §
1920 Helge Løvland (Nor) 5804
1924 Harold Osborn (USA) 6476
1928 Paavo Yrjölä (Fin) 6587*
1932 James Bausch (USA) 6735*
1936 Glenn Morris (USA) 7254
1948 Robert Mathias (USA) 6628
1952 Robert Mathias (USA) 7592
1956 Milton Campbell (USA) 7614
1960 Rafer Johnson (USA) 7926

1964 Willi Holdorf (FRG) 7794 est
1968 Bill Toomey (USA) 8144
1972 Nikolai Avilov (USSR) 8466
1976 Bruce Jenner (USA) 8634
1980 Daley Thompson (UK) 8522
1984 Daley Thompson (UK) 8847 OR
§ disqualified for professionalism, and gold given to
Hugo Weislander (Swe) 5965, but posthumously
re-instated in 1982
* On the 1984 tables, the second placed Akilles Järvinen
scored 6645 in 1928 and 6879 in 1932!

WOMEN

100 METRES
1928 Elizabeth Robinson (USA) 12.2
1932 Stanislawa Walasiewicz (Pol) 11.9
1936 Helen Stephens (USA) 11.5
1948 Fanny Blankers-Koen (Hol) 11.9
1952 Marjorie Jackson (Aus) 11.65
1956 Betty Cuthbert (Aus) 11.82
1960 Wilma Rudolph (USA) 11.08
1964 Wyomia Tyus (USA) 11.49
1968 Wyomia Tyus (USA) 11.08
1972 Renate Stecher (GDR) 11.07
1976 Annegret Richter (FRG) 11.08
1980 Lyudmila Kondratyeva (USSR) 11.06
1984 Evelyn Ashford (USA) 10.97 OR

200 METRES
1948 Fanny Blankers-Koen (Hol) 24.4
1952 Marjorie Jackson (Aus) 23.89
1956 Betty Cuthbert (Aus) 23.55
1960 Wilma Rudolph (USA) 24.03
1964 Edith Maguire (USA) 23.05
1968 Irena Szewinska (Pol) 22.58
1972 Renate Stecher (GDR) 22.40
1976 Barbel Eckert (GDR) 22.37
1980 Barbel Wöckel (née Eckert) (GDR) 22.03
1984 Valerie Brisco-Hooks (USA) 21.81 OR

400 METRES
1964 Betty Cuthbert (Aus) 52.01
1968 Colette Besson (Fra) 52.03
1972 Monika Zehrt (GDR) 51.08
1976 Irena Szewinska (Pol) 49.29
1980 Marita Koch (GDR) 48.88
1984 Valerie Brisco-Hooks (USA) 48.83 OR

800 METRES
1928 Lina Radke (Ger) 2:16.8
1960 Lyudmila Shevtsova (USSR) 2:04.50
1964 Ann Packer (UK) 2:01.1
1968 Madeline Manning (USA) 2:00.92
1972 Hildegard Falck (FRG) 1:58.55
1976 Tatyana Kazankina (USSR) 1:54.94
1980 Nadezhda Olizarenko (USSR) 1:53.43 OR
1984 Doina Melinte (Rom) 1:57.60

1500 METRES
1972 Lyudmila Bragina (USSR) 4:01.38
1976 Tatyana Kazankina (USSR) 4:05.48
1980 Tatyana Kazankina (USSR) 3.56.56 OR
1984 Gabriella Doria (Ita) 4:03.25

3000 METRES
1984 Maricica Puica (Rom) 8:35.96 OR

MARATHON
1984 Joan Benoit (USA) 2:24:52 OR

80 METRES HURDLES
1932 Mildred Didrikson (USA) 11.7
1936 Trebisonda Valla (Ita) 11.75
1948 Fanny Blankers-Koen (Hol) 11.2
1952 Shirley Strickland (Aus) 11.03
1956 Shirley Strickland (Aus) 10.96
1960 Irina Press (USSR) 10.94
1964 Karin Balzer (GDR) 10.54
1968 Maureen Caird (Aus) 10.39

100 METRES HURDLES
1972 Annelie Ehrhardt (GDR) 12.59
1976 Johanna Schaller (GDR) 12.77
1980 Vera Komisova (USSR) 12.56 OR
1984 Benita Fitzgerald-Brown (USA) 12.84

400 METRES HURDLES
1984 Nawal el Moutawakil (Mor) 54.61 OR

HIGH JUMP
1928 Ethel Catherwood (Can) 1.59
1932 Jean Shiley (USA) 1.65
1936 Ibolya Csak (Hun) 1.60
1948 Alice Coachman (USA) 1.68
1952 Esther Brand (SAf) 1.67
1956 Mildred McDaniel (USA) 1.76
1960 Iolanda Balas (Rom) 1.85
1964 Iolanda Balas (Rom) 1.90
1968 Miloslava Rezkova (Cs) 1.82
1972 Ulrike Meyfarth (FRG) 1.92
1976 Rosi Ackermann (GDR) 1.93
1980 Sara Simeoni (Ita) 1.97
1984 Ulrike Meyfarth (FRG) 2.02 OR

LONG JUMP
1948 Olga Gyarmati (Hun) 5.69
1952 Yvette Williams (NZ) 6.24
1956 Elzbieta Krzesinska (Pol) 6.35
1960 Vyera Krepkina (USSR) 6.37
1964 Mary Rand (UK) 6.76
1968 Viorica Viscopoleanu (Rom) 6.82
1972 Heide Rosendahl (FRG) 6.78
1976 Angela Voigt (GDR) 6.72
1980 Tatyana Kolpakova (USSR) 7.06 OR
1984 Anisora Stanciu (Rom) 6.96

SHOT
1948 Micheline Ostermeyer (Fra) 13.75
1952 Galina Zybina (USSR) 15.28
1956 Tamara Tishkyevich (USSR) 16.59
1960 Tamara Press (USSR) 17.32
1964 Tamara Press (USSR) 18.14
1968 Margitta Gummel (GDR) 19.61
1972 Nadezhda Chizhova (USSR) 21.03
1976 Ivanka Khristova (Bul) 21.16
1980 Ilona Slupianek (GDR) 22.41 OR
1984 Claudia Losch (FRG) 20.48

DISCUS
1928 Helena Konopacka (Pol) 39.62
1932 Lillian Copeland (USA) 40.58
1936 Gisela Mauermayer (Ger) 47.63
1948 Micheline Ostermeyer (Fra) 41.92
1952 Nina Ponomaryeva (USSR) 51.42

1956 Olga Fikotova (Cs) 53.69
1960 Nina Ponomaryeva (USSR) 55.10
1964 Tamara Press (USSR) 57.27
1968 Lia Manoliu (Rom) 58.28
1972 Faina Melnik (USSR) 66.62
1976 Evelin Schlaak (GDR) 69.00
1980 Evelin Jahl (née Schlaak) (GDR) 69.96 OR
1984 Ria Stalmach (Hol) 65.36

JAVELIN
1932 Mildred Didrikson (USA) 43.68
1936 Tilly Fleischer (Ger) 45.18
1948 Herma Bauma (Aut) 45.57
1952 Dana Zatopkova (Cs) 50.47
1956 Inese Jaunzeme (USSR) 53.86
1960 Elvira Ozolina (USSR) 55.98
1964 Mihaela Penes (Rom) 60.54
1968 Angela Nemeth (Hun) 60.36
1972 Ruth Fuchs (GDR) 63.88
1976 Ruth Fuchs (GDR) 65.94
1980 Maria Colon (Cub) 68.40
1984 Tessa Sanderson (UK) 69.56 OR

4×100 METRES RELAY
1928 Canada 48.4
1932 USA 46.86
1936 USA 46.9
1948 Netherlands 47.5
1952 USA 46.14
1956 Australia 44.65
1960 USA 44.72
1964 Poland 43.69
1968 USA 42.87
1972 FR Germany 42.81
1976 GDR 42.55
1980 GDR 41.60 OR
1984 USA 41.65

4×400 METRES RELAY
1972 GDR 3:22.95
1976 GDR 3:19.23
1980 USSR 3:20.12
1984 USA 3:18.29 OR

PENTATHLON
(80m hurdles, high jump, shot, long jump, 200m
1964-8. 100m hurdles replaced 80m hurdles from 1972,
and 800m replaced 200m from 1976. All scored on
1971 tables.)
1964 Irina Press (USSR) 4702
1968 Ingrid Becker (FRG) 4559
1972 Mary Peters (UK) 4801
1976 Sigrun Siegl (GDR) 4745
1980 Nadezhda Tkachenko (USSR) 5083

HEPTATHLON
1984 Glynis Nunn (Aus) 6387 OR

DISCONTINUED EVENTS

60 METRES
1900 Alvin Kraenzlein (USA) 7.0
1904 Archie Hahn (USA) 7.0

5 MILES
1906 Henry Hawtrey (UK) 26:11.8
1908 Emil Voigt (UK) 25:11.2

Faina Melnik (All-Sport)

TEAM RACE
1900 Great Britain (5000m)
1908 Great Britain (3 Miles)
1912 USA (3000m)
1920 USA (3000m)
1924 Finland (3000m)

STEEPLECHASE
1900 George Orton (Can) 7:34.4 (2500m)
1900 John Rimmer (UK) 12:58.4 (4000m)
1904 James Lightbody (USA) 7:39.6 (2590m)
1908 Arthur Russell (UK) 10:47.8 (3200m)

CROSS-COUNTRY INDIVIDUAL
1912 Hannes Kolehmainen (Fin) 45:11.6 (12 000m)
1920 Paavo Nurmi (Fin) 27:15.0 (8000m)
1924 Paavo Nurmi (Fin) 32:54.8 (10 000m)

CROSS-COUNTRY TEAM
1904 USA
1912 Sweden
1920 Finland
1924 Finland

200 METRES HURDLES
1900 Alvin Kraenzlein (USA) 25.4
1904 Harry Hillman (USA) 24.6

PENTATHLON
In 1906 consisted of standing long jump, Greek style
discus, javelin, 192m race and Greco-Roman wrestling:
in 1912-24 of long jump, javelin, 200m, discus and
1500m.
1906 Hjalmar Mellander (Swe)
1912 Jim Thorpe (USA)*
     Ferdinand Bie (Nor)
1920 Eero Lehtonen (Fin)
1924 Eero Lehtonen (Fin)

* posthumously reinstated as winner

STANDING HIGH JUMP
1900 Ray Ewry (USA) 1.655
1904 Ray Ewry (USA) 1.50
1906 Ray Ewry (USA) 1.565
1908 Ray Ewry (USA) 1.575
1912 Platt Adams (USA) 1.63

STANDING LONG JUMP
1900 Ray Ewry (USA) 3.21
1904 Ray Ewry (USA) 3.476
1906 Ray Ewry (USA) 3.30
1908 Ray Ewry (USA) 3.335
1912 Konstantin Tsiklitiras (Gre) 3.37

STANDING TRIPLE JUMP
1900 Ray Ewry (USA) 10.58
1904 Ray Ewry (USA) 10.55

56LB WEIGHT
1904 Etienne Desmarteau (Can) 10.465
1920 Patrick McDonald (USA) 11.265

STONE (6.4KG) PUT
1906 Nicolaos Georgantas (Gre) 19.925

SHOT – BOTH HANDS
(aggregate of throws with right and left hands)
1912 Ralph Rose (USA) 27.70

DISCUS – GREEK STYLE
1906 Werner Järvinen (Fin) 35.17
1908 Martin Sheridan (USA) 38.00

DISCUS – BOTH HANDS
1912 Armas Taipale (Fin) 82.86

JAVELIN – FREE STYLE
1908 Erik Lemming (Swe) 54.445

JAVELIN – BOTH HANDS
1912 Julius Saaristo (Fin) 109.42

1500 METRES WALK
1906 George Bonhag (USA) 7:12.6

3000 METRES WALK
1906 György Sztantics (Hun) 15:13.2
1920 Ugo Frigerio (Ita) 13:14.2

3500 METRES WALK
1908 George Larner (UK) 14:55.0

10 000 METRES WALK
1912 George Goulding (Can) 46:28.4
1920 Ugo Frigerio (Ita) 48:06.2
1924 Ugo Frigerio (Ita) 47:49.0
1948 John Mikaelsson (Swe) 45:13.2
1952 John Mikaelsson (Swe) 45:02.8

10 MILES WALK
1908 George Larner (UK) 1:15:57.4

MOST MEDALS

MEN

	Gold	Silver	Bronze	Years
12 Paavo Nurmi (Fin)	9	3	-	1920-8
10 Raymond Ewry (USA)	10	-	-	1900-8
9 Martin Sheridan (USA)	5	3	1	1906-8
8 Ville Ritola (Fin)	5	3	-	1924-8
7 Erik Lemming (Swe)	4	-	3	1906-12

Others to win four gold medals:
James Lightbody (USA) 1904-6
Alvin Kraenzlein (USA) 1900
Archie Hahn (USA) 1904-06
James Lightbody (USA) 1904-06
Myer Prinstein (USA) 1900-06
Erik Lemming (Swe) 1906-12
Mel Sheppard (USA) 1908-12
Hannes Kolehmainen (Fin) 1912-20
Jesse Owens (USA) 1936
Emil Zatopek (Cs) 1948-52
Harrison Dillard (USA) 1948-52
Al Oerter (USA) 1956-68
Lasse Viren (Fin) 1972-76
Carl Lewis (USA) 1984

WOMEN

	Gold	Silver	Bronze	Years
7 Shirley de la Hunty (Aus)	3	1	3	1948-56
7 Irena Szewinska (Pol)	3	2	2	1964-76

Others to win four gold medals:
Fanny Blankers-Koen (Hol) 1948
Betty Cuthbert (Aus) 1956-64
Bärbel Wöckel (GDR) 1976-80

Al Oerter – the only Olympian to win four consecutive titles. (All-Sport)

Most gold medals at one Games:
MEN 5 Paavo Nurmi (Fin) 1924; 4 Alvin Kraenzlein (USA) 1900, Ville Ritola (Fin) 1924, Jesse Owens (USA) 1936, Carl Lewis (USA) 1984.
WOMEN 4 Fanny Blankers-Koen (Hol) 1948

Most medals at one Games: 6 Ville Ritola (Fin) 4 gold, 2 silver 1924

Most Games contested: 6 Lia Manoliu (Rom) 1952-72, women's discus, successively 6th, 9th, 3rd, 3rd, 1st, 9th.

Oldest gold medallists:
MEN 42 years 23 days Pat McDonald (USA) 56lb weight 1920
WOMEN 36 years 176 days Lia Manoliu (Rom) discus 1968

Oldest medallists:
MEN 48y 115d Tebbs Lloyd Johnson (UK) 3rd 50km walk 1948
WOMEN 37 years 348 days Dana Zatopkova (Cs) 2nd javelin 1960

Youngest gold medallists:
MEN 17y 263d Bob Mathias (USA) decathlon 1948
WOMEN 15y 123d Barbara Pearl Jones (USA) 4x100m relay 1952.

Sergey Bubka, the first six-metre pole vaulter (All-Sport)

LEADING NATIONS BY MEDALS AT THE OLYMPIC GAMES IN ATHLETICS
(including 1906 Games)

| | MEN | | | WOMEN | | | TOTAL |
Nation	Gold	Silver	Bronze	Gold	Silver	Bronze	Medals
USA	234	177	147	26	19	10	613
USSR	29	31	36	25	18	28	167
United Kingdom	40	52	38	4	18	11	163
Finland	46	32	28	-	2	-	108
F.R.Germany *	10	23	32	11	13	11	100
GDR	11	16	11	22	20	17	97
Sweden	17	24	40	-	-	3	84
Australia	6	9	11	10	7	11	54
France	7	19	16	3	1	2	48
Italy	12	6	18	3	4	2	45
Canada	9	9	14	2	5	6	45
Poland	9	7	4	6	8	7	41
Hungary	6	13	16	3	1	2	41

* Germany 1896-1952, since then the Federal Republic of Germany. Medals won by the combined German teams of 1956, 1960 and 1964 have been allocated to FRG or GDR according to the athlete's origin.

WORLD CHAMPIONSHIPS

Athletics events at the Olympic Games have had world championship status, but the first championships for athletics alone were staged in the Olympic Stadium, Helsinki, Finland in 1983. The second world championships are set for Rome in September 1987.

1983 CHAMPIONS

MEN

100m:	Carl Lewis (USA) 10.07
200m:	Calvin Smith (USA) 20.14
400m:	Bert Cameron (Jam) 45.05
800m:	Willi Wülbeck (FRG) 1:43.65
1500m:	Steve Cram (UK) 3:41.59
5000m:	Eamonn Coghlan (Ire) 13:28.53
10000m:	Alberto Cova (Ita) 28:01.04
Marathon:	Rob de Castella (Aus) 2:10:03
3000m steeple:	Patriz Ilg (FRG) 8:15.06
110m hurdles:	Greg Foster (USA) 13.42
400m hurdles:	Edwin Moses (USA) 47.50
High jump:	Gennadiy Avdeyenko (USSR) 2.32
Pole vault:	Sergey Bubka (USSR) 5.70
Long jump:	Carl Lewis (USA) 8.55
Triple jump:	Zdzislaw Hoffmann (Pol) 17.42
Shot:	Edward Sarul (Pol) 21.39
Discus:	Imrich Bugar (Cs) 67.72
Hammer:	Sergey Litvinov (USSR) 82.68
Javelin:	Detlef Michel (GDR) 89.48
Decathlon:	Daley Thompson (UK) 8714
4×100m relay:	USA 37.86
4×400m relay:	USSR 3:00.79
20km walk:	Ernesto Canto (Mex) 1:20:49
50km walk:	Ronald Weigel (GDR) 3:43:08

WOMEN

100m:	Marlies Göhr (GDR) 10.97
200m:	Marita Koch (GDR) 22.13
400m:	Jarmila Kratochvilova (Cs) 47.99
800m:	Jarmila Kratochvilova (Cs) 1:54.68
1500m:	Mary Decker (USA) 4:00.90
3000m:	Mary Decker (USA) 8:34.62
Marathon:	Grete Waitz (Nor) 2:28:09
100m hurdles:	Bettina Jahn (GDR) 12.35
400m hurdles:	Yekaterina Fesenko (USSR) 54.14
High jump:	Tamara Bykova (USSR) 2.01
Long jump:	Heike Daute (GDR) 7.27w
Shot:	Helena Fibingerova (Cs) 21.05
Discus:	Martina Opitz (GDR) 68.94
Javelin:	Tiina Lillak (Fin) 70.82
Heptathlon:	Ramona Neubert (GDR) 6770
4×100m relay:	GDR 41.76
4×400m relay:	GDR 3:19.73

Winner of the most medals: Marita Koch (GDR) with golds at the women's 200m, 4×100m and 4×400m relays and silver at 100m. Carl Lewis (USA) also won three gold medals, at 100m, LJ and 4×100m relay.
Oldest world champion: Helena Fibingerova SP at 34yr 30d.
Youngest world champion: Heike Daute LJ 18yr 241d.

Winners of events not included on the Olympic programme for which there were separate world championships prior to 1983:
1976 MEN 50km walk: Venyamin Soldatenko (USSR) 3:54:40
1980 WOMEN 3000m: Birgit Friedmann (FRG) 8:48.1
          400mh: Barbara Broschat (GDR) 54.55

WORLD INDOOR CHAMPIONSHIPS

An unofficial World Indoor Games was staged at Bercy, Paris in January 1985. These were succeeded by the first World Indoor Championships at Indianapolis, USA in March 1987, when the champions were:

MEN

60m:	Ben Johnson (Can) 6.41
200m:	Kirk Baptiste (USA) 20.73
400m:	Antonio McKay (USA) 45.98
800m:	José Luis Barbosa (Bra) 1:47.49
1500m:	Marcus O'Sullivan (Ire) 3:39.04
3000m:	Frank O'Mara (Ire) 8:03.32
60m hurdles:	Tonie Campbell (USA) 7.51
High jump:	Igor Paklin (USSR) 2.38
Pole vault:	Sergey Bubka (USSR) 5.85
Long jump:	Larry Myricks (USA) 8.23
Triple jump:	Mike Conley (USA) 17.54
Shot:	Ulf Timmermann (GDR) 22.24
5km walk:	Mikhail Shchennikov (USSR) 18:27.79

WOMEN

60m:	Nellie Fiere-Cooman (Hol) 7.08
200m:	Heike Drechsler (GDR) 22.27
400m:	Sabine Busch (GDR) 51.66
800m:	Christine Wachtel (GDR) 2:01.32
1500m:	Doina Melinte (Rom) 4:05.68
3000m:	Tatyana Samolenko (USSR) 8:46.52
60m hurdles:	Cornelia Oschkenat (GDR) 7.82
High jump:	Stefka Kostadinova (Bul) 2.05
Long jump:	Heike Drechsler (GDR) 7.10
Shot:	Natalya Lisovskaya (USSR) 20.52
3km walk:	Olga Krishtop (USSR) 12:05.49

IAAF WORLD CUP

First held in 1977. The competing teams represent each of the five continents, with national teams from the USA and the top two men's and women's teams from the European Cup. Host nation Italy competed as a ninth team in 1981. Each team enters one competitor per event.

Winners:

Year	Men	Women
1977	GDR	Europe
1979	USA	GDR
1981	Europe	GDR
1985	USA	GDR

INDIVIDUAL EVENT WINNERS
MEN

100 METRES
1977 Steve Williams (USA) 10.13
1979 James Sanford (USA) 10.17
1981 Allan Wells (Eur/UK) 10.20
1985 Ben Johnson (Ame/Can) 10.00

200 METRES
1977 Clancy Edwards (USA) 20.17
1979 Silvio Leonard (Ame/Cub) 20.34
1981 Mel Lattany (USA) 20.21
1985 Robson Caetano Da Silva (Ame/Bra) 20.44

400 METRES
1977 Alberto Juantorena (Ame/Cub) 45.36
1979 Hassan El Kashief (Afr/Sud) 45.39
1981 Cliff Wiley (USA) 44.88
1985 Mike Franks (USA) 44.47

800 METRES
1977 Alberto Juantorena (Ame/Cub) 1:44.04
1979 James Maina (Afr/Ken) 1:47.69
1981 Sebastian Coe (Eur/UK) 1:46.16
1985 Sammy Koskei (Afr/Ken) 1:45.14

1500 METRES
1977 Steve Ovett (Eur/UK) 3:34.45
1979 Thomas Wessinghage (Eur/FRG) 3:46.00
1981 Steve Ovett (Eur/UK) 3:34.95
1985 Omer Khalifa (Afr/Sud) 3:41.16

5000 METRES
1977 Miruts Yifter (Afr/Eth) 13:13.82
1979 Miruts Yifter (Afr/Eth) 13:35.9
1981 Eamonn Coghlan (Eur/Ire) 14:08.39
1985 Doug Padilla (USA) 14:04.11

10 000 METRES
1977 Miruts Yifter (Afr/Eth) 28:32.3
1979 Miruts Yifter (Afr/Eth) 27:53.07
1981 Werner Schildhauer (GDR) 27:38.43
1985 Wodajo Bulti (Afr/Eth) 29:22.96

3000 METRES STEEPLECHASE
1977 Michael Karst (FRG) 8:21.6
1979 Kiprotich Rono (Afr/Ken) 8:25.97
1981 Boguslaw Maminski (Eur/Pol) 8:19.89
1985 Julius Kariuki (Afr/Ken) 8:39.51

110 METRES HURDLES
1977 Thomas Munkelt (GDR) 13.41
1979 Renaldo Nehemiah (USA) 13.39
1981 Greg Foster (USA) 13.32
1985 Tonie Campbell (USA) 13.35w

400 METRES HURDLES
1977 Ed Moses (USA) 47.58
1979 Ed Moses (USA) 47.53
1981 Ed Moses (USA) 47.37
1985 Andre Phillips (USA) 48.42

HIGH JUMP
1977 Rolf Beilschmidt (GDR) 2.30
1979 Franklin Jacobs (USA) 2.27
1981 Tyke Peacock (USA) 2.28
1985 Patrik Sjöberg (Eur/Swe) 2.31

POLE VAULT
1977 Mike Tully (USA) 5.60
1979 Mike Tully (USA) 5.45
1981 Konstantin Volkov (USSR) 5.70
1985 Sergey Bubka (USSR) 5.85

LONG JUMP
1977 Arnie Robinson (USA) 8.19
1979 Larry Myricks (USA) 8.52
1981 Carl Lewis (USA) 8.15
1985 Mike Conley (USA) 8.20

TRIPLE JUMP
1977 João de Oliveira (Ame/Bra) 16.68
1979 João de Oliveira (Ame/Bra) 17.02
1981 João de Oliveira (Ame/Bra) 17.37
1985 Willie Banks (USA) 17.58

SHOT
1977 Udo Beyer (GDR) 21.74
1979 Udo Beyer (GDR) 20.45
1981 Udo Beyer (GDR) 21.40
1985 Ulf Timmermann (GDR) 22.00

DISCUS
1977 Wolfgang Schmidt (GDR) 67.14
1979 Wolfgang Schmidt (GDR) 66.02
1981 Armin Lemme (GDR) 66.38
1985 Gennadiy Kolnootchenko (USSR) 69.08

HAMMER
1977 Karl-Hans Riehm (FRG) 75.64
1979 Sergey Litvinov (USSR) 78.70
1981 Yuriy Sedykh (USSR) 77.42
1985 Juri Tamm (USSR) 82.12

JAVELIN
1977 Michael Wessing (FRG) 87.46
1979 Wolfgang Hanisch (GDR) 86.48
1981 Dainis Kula (USSR) 89.74
1985 Uwe Hohn (GDR) 96.96

4 × 100 METRES RELAY
1977 USA 38.03
1979 Americas 38.70
1981 Europe 38.73
1985 USA 38.10

4 × 400 METRES RELAY
1977 F.R.Germany 3:01.34
1979 USA 3:00.70
1981 USA 2:59.12
1985 USA 3:00.71

WOMEN

100 METRES
1977 Marlies Oelsner (GDR) 11.16
1979 Evelyn Ashford (USA) 11.06
1981 Evelyn Ashford (USA) 11.02
1985 Marlies Göhr (née Oelsner) (GDR) 11.10

200 METRES
1977 Irena Szewinska (Eur/Pol) 22.72
1979 Evelyn Ashford (USA) 21.83
1981 Evelyn Ashford (USA) 22.18
1985 Marita Koch (GDR) 21.90

400 METRES
1977 Irena Szewinska (Eur/Pol) 49.52
1979 Marita Koch (GDR) 48.97
1981 Jarmila Kratochvilova (Eur/Cs) 48.61
1985 Marita Koch (GDR) 47.60

800 METRES
1977 Totka Petrova (Eur/Bul) 1:59.20
1979 Nikolina Shtereva (Eur/Bul) 2:00.52
1981 Lyudmila Veselkova (USSR) 1:57.48
1985 Christine Wachtel (GDR) 2:01.57

1500 METRES
1977 Tatyana Kazankina (USSR) 4:12.7
1979 Totka Petrova (Eur/Bul) 4:06.46*
1981 Tamara Sorokina (USSR) 4:03.33
1985 Hildegard Körner (GDR) 4:10.86

3000 METRES
1977 Grete Waitz (Eur/Nor) 8:43.5
1979 Svyetlana Ulmasova (USSR) 8:36.32
1981 Angelika Zauber (GDR) 8:54.89
1985 Ulrike Bruns (GDR) 9:14.65

10 000 METRES
1985 Aurora Cunha (Eur/Por) 32:07.50

100 METRES HURDLES
1977 Grazyna Rabsztyn (Eur/Pol) 12.70
1979 Grazyna Rabsztyn (Eur/Pol) 12.67
1981 Tatyana Anisimova (USSR) 12.85
1985 Cornelia Oschkenat (GDR) 12.71

400 METRES HURDLES
1979 Barbara Klepp (GDR) 55.83
1981 Ellen Neumann (GDR) 54.82
1985 Sabine Busch (GDR) 54.45

HIGH JUMP
1977 Rosemarie Ackermann (GDR) 1.98
1979 Debbie Brill (Ame/Can) 1.96
1981 Ulrike Meyfarth (Eur/FRG) 1.96
1985 Stefka Kostadinova (Eur/Bul) 2.00

LONG JUMP
1977 Lynette Jacenko (Oce/Aus) 6.54
1979 Anita Stukane (USSR) 6.64
1981 Sigrid Ulbricht (GDR) 6.80
1985 Heike Drechsler (GDR) 7.27

SHOT
1977 Ilona Slupianek (GDR) 20.93 *
1979 Ilona Slupianek (GDR) 20.98

1981 Ilona Slupianek (GDR) 20.60
1985 Natalya Lisovskaya (USSR) 20.69

DISCUS
1977 Faina Melnik (USSR) 68.10
1979 Evelin Jahl (GDR) 65.18
1981 Evelin Jahl (GDR) 66.70
1985 Martina Opitz (GDR) 69.78

JAVELIN
1977 Ruth Fuchs (GDR) 62.36
1979 Ruth Fuchs (GDR) 66.10
1981 Antoaneta Todorova (Eur/Bul) 70.08
1985 Olga Gavrilova (USSR) 66.80

4 × 100 METRES RELAY
1977 Europe 42.51
1979 Europe 42.19
1981 GDR 42.22
1985 GDR 41.37

4 × 400 METRES RELAY
1977 GDR 3:24.04
1979 GDR 3:20.38
1981 GDR 3:20.62
1985 GDR 3:19.49

Most individual event wins
MEN
4 Miruts Yifter (Afr/Eth) 5000m & 10 000m 1977-79
3 Ed Moses (USA) 400mh 1977-79-81
3 João de Oliveira (Ame/Bra) TJ 1977-79-81
3 Udo Beyer (GDR) SP 1977-79-81

WOMEN
4 Evelyn Ashford (USA) 100m & 200m 1981-83
3* Ilona Slupianek (GDR) SP 1977*-79-81
3 Marita Koch (GDR) 400m 1979-85, 200m 1985

* Slupianek subsequently disqualified for infringing the doping regulations at the preceding European Cup.

IAAF WORLD RACE WALKING CUP

This competition is held biennially for the Lugano Trophy (men) and the Eschborn Cup (women). It has been officially recognised by the IAAF with the above name since 1977. The finalists are nations from each continent, with additional European nations qualifying for the final from three qualifying matches.

THE LUGANO TROPHY
Contested by men's national teams walking over 20km and 50km.

Wins:
5 GDR   1965, 1967, 1970, 1973, 1985
3 USSR   1975, 1983, 1987
2 United Kingdom 1961, 1963
2 Mexico   1977, 1979
1 Italy   1981

THE ESCHBORN CUP
Contested by women's national teams walking over 10km (5km 1979-81).

Wins:
2 USSR   1981, 1987
2 China   1983, 1985
1 United Kingdom 1979, USSR 1981

IAAF WORLD CUP MARATHON

Staged at Hiroshima, Japan in 1985 and at Seoul, Korea in 1987.

Winners:	1985	1987
Men's team:	Djibouti	Italy
Individual:	Ahmed Saleh (Dji) 2:08:09	Ahmed Saleh (Dji) 2:10:55
Women's team:	Italy	USSR
Individual:	Katrin Dörre (GDR) 2:33:30	Zoya Ivanova (USSR) 2:30:39

IAAF WOMEN'S WORLD ROAD RACE CHAMPIONSHIP

Held annually, at 15km (10km 1983-4).

Winners:

	TEAM	INDIVIDUAL
1983	USA	Wendy Sly (UK) 32:23
1984	UK	Aurora Cunha (Por) 33:04
1985	UK	Aurora Cunha (Por) 49:17
1986	USSR	Aurora Cunha (Por) 48:31

COMMONWEALTH GAMES

See Commonwealth Games section for all winners.

Most gold medals:
MEN
6 Don Quarrie (Jam) 1970-78

WOMEN
7 Marjorie Nelson (née Jackson) (Aus) 1950-54
7 Raelene Boyle (Aus) 1970-82
6 Pam Kilborn/Ryan (Aus) 1962-70

Most medals:

MEN	Gold	Silver	Bronze	
6 Don Quarrie (Jam)	6	-	-	1970-78
6 Harry Hart (SAf)	4	1	1	1930-34
6 Allan Wells (Sco)	4	1	1	1978-82
WOMEN				
9 Raelene Boyle (Aus)	7	2	-	1970-82
8 Denise Robertson/Boyd (Aus)	2	3	3	1974-82
7 Marjorie Jackson (Aus)	7	-	-	1950-54
7 Valerie Sloper/Young (NZ)	5	1	1	1958-74
7 Kathy Smallwood/Cook (Eng)	3	3	1	1978-86
7 Angella Taylor/Issajenko (Can)	3	2	2	1982-86
6 Pam Kilborn/Ryan (Aus)	6	-	-	1962-70

Most medals at one Games:

	Gold	Silver	Bronze	
5 Decima Norman (Aus)	5	-	-	1938
5 Shirley Strickland (Aus)	3	2	-	1950

EUROPEAN CUP

The European Cup is contested biennially by European nations, with each team entering one athlete per event and one team in each relay. The Cup is dedicated to the memory of Dr Bruno Zauli, the former President of the European Committee of the IAAF, who died suddenly in 1963, soon after the decision had been made to start this competition.

From 1965 until 1981 the competition was staged with a qualifying round, semi-finals and final, but from 1983 the nations have been arranged into groups according to strength, with eight men's and eight women's teams in 'A' and 'B' groups, with additional nations in C1 and C2 groups. There is one up and one down promotion and relegation between A and B, and two up and two down between B and C.

Men's final wins:
6 GDR 1970, 1975, 1977, 1979, 1981, 1983
5 USSR 1965, 1967, 1973, 1985, 1987

Women's final wins:
8 GDR 1970, 1973, 1975, 1977, 1979, 1981,
        1983, 1987
3 USSR 1965, 1967, 1985

Most event wins in finals (individual/relay)

MEN
8 Harald Schmid (FRG) 5/3

WOMEN
12 Marlies Göhr (GDR) 6/6
 9 Marita Koch (GDR) 4/5
 7 Renate Stecher (GDR) 5/2
 5 Irena Szewinska (Pol) 4/1

EUROPEAN COMBINED EVENTS CUP

Held biennially at decathlon for men and heptathlon (pentathlon 1973-9) for women since 1973. As with the European Cup, nations are now divided into A, B, C1 and C2 groups.

Wins:

MEN
3 USSR 1975, 1977, 1985
2 FR Germany 1981, 1983
2 GDR 1979, 1987
1 Poland 1973

WOMEN
6 GDR 1973, 1975, 1979, 1981, 1983, 1985
2 USSR 1977, 1987

EUROPEAN MARATHON CUP

Held biennially since 1981.

Team winners:
MEN: Italy 1981; GDR 1983, 1985
WOMEN: GDR 1985

IAAF/MOBIL GRAND PRIX

Introduced in 1986, half the standard men's and women's events are contested each year for individual events Grand Prix and an overall Grand Prix over a series of 15-16 international meetings throughout the world. Overall champions have been:

Year	**MEN**	**WOMEN**
1985	Doug Padilla (USA)	Mary Slaney (USA)
1986	Said Aouita (Mor)	Yordanka Donkova (Bul)

EUROPEAN CHAMPIONSHIPS

The first European Championships were staged at the Stadio Communale, Turin in 1934 for men only. Women's championships were held separately in 1938, but men's and women's events were combined at one venue from

Brendan Foster leads Nick Rose in the European Cup. Foster won at 5000m in 1973 and 1977 and at 10000m in 1979, and Rose at 5000m in 1977.

1946. The championships are held at four-yearly intervals, although there was a break in that pattern when they were held in 1969 and 1971.

Winners at the last two championships (1982 and 1986), championships bests (CBP), and athletes to have won a particular event twice:

MEN

100 METRES
1982 Frank Emmelmann (GDR) 10.21
1986 Linford Christie (UK) 10.15 *CBP*
Most: 3 Valeriy Borzov (USSR) 1969, 1971, 1974

200 METRES
1982 Olaf Prenzler (GDR) 20.46
1986 Vladimir Krylov (USSR) 20.52
Most: 2 Pietro Mennea (Ita) 1974, 1978 (20.16 *CBP*)

400 METRES
1982 Hartmut Weber (FRG) 44.72
1986 Roger Black (UK) 44.59 CBP

800 METRES
1982 Hans-Peter Ferner (FRG) 1:46.33
1986 Sebastian Coe (UK) 1:44.50
CBP: 1:43.84 Olaf Beyer (GDR) 1978
Most: 2 Manfred Matuschewski (GDR) 1962, 1966

1500 METRES
1982 Steve Cram (UK) 3:36.49
1986 Steve Cram (UK) 3:41.09

Steve Cram (left) beats Joaquin Cruz (right) at 800 metres in Zürich in 1985.

CBP: 3:35.59 Steve Ovett (UK) 1978
Most: 2 Steve Cram

5000 METRES
1982 Thomas Wessinghage (FRG) 13:28.90
1986 Jack Buckner (UK) 13:10.15 *CBP*

10 000 METRES
1982 Alberto Cova (Ita) 27:41.03
1986 Stefano Mei (Ita) 27:56.79
CBP: 27:30.99 Martti Vainio (Fin) 1978
Most: 2 Ilmari Salminen (Fin) 1934, 1938; Emil Zatopek (Cs) 1950, 1954; Jürgen Haase (GDR) 1966, 1969

MARATHON
1982 Gerard Nijboer (Hol) 2:15:16
1986 Gelindo Bordin (Ita) 2:10:54 *CBP*

3000 METRES STEEPLECHASE
1982 Patriz Ilg (FRG) 8:18.52
1986 Hagen Melzer (GDR) 8:16.65
Most: 2 Bronislaw Malinowski (Pol) 1974 (8:15.04 *CBP*), 1978

110 METRES HURDLES
1982 Thomas Munkelt (GDR) 13.41
1986 Stéphane Caristan (Fra) 13.20 *CBP*
Most: 2 Eddy Ottoz (Ita) 1966, 1969; Thomas Munkelt 1978, 1982

400 METRES HURDLES
1982 Harald Schmid (FRG) 47.48 *CBP*
1986 Harald Schmid (FRG) 48.65
Most: 3 Harald Schmid 1978, 1982, 1986

4 × 100 METRES RELAY
1982 USSR 38.60
1986 USSR 38.29 *CBP*

4 × 400 METRES RELAY
1982 FR Germany 3:00.51
1986 United Kingdom 2:59.84 *CBP*

20 KM WALK
1982 José Marin (Spa) 1:23:43
1986 Jozef Pribilinec (Cs) 1:21:15 *CBP*

50 KM WALK
1982 Reima Salonen (Fin) 3:55:29
1986 Hartwig Gauder (GDR) 3:40:55 *CBP*
Most: 2 Abdon Pamich (Ita) 1962, 1966; Christoph Höhne (GDR) 1969, 1974

HIGH JUMP
1982 Dietmar Mögenburg (FRG) 2.30
1986 Igor Paklin (USSR) 2.34 *CBP*

POLE VAULT
1982 Aleksandr Krupskiy (USSR) 5.60
1986 Sergey Bubka (USSR) 5.85 *CBP*
Most: 3 Wolfgang Nordwig (GDR) 1966, 1969, 1971; 2 Eeles Landström (Fin) 1954, 1958

LONG JUMP
1982 Lutz Dombrowski (GDR) 8.41w
1986 Robert Emmiyan (USSR) 8.41 *CBP*
Most: 3 Igor Ter-Ovanesyan (USSR) 1958, 1962, 1969; 2 Wilhelm Leichum (Ger) 1934, 1938

TRIPLE JUMP
1982 Keith Connor (UK) 17.29

1986 Khristo Markov (Bul) 17.66 *CBP*
Most: 2 Leonid Shcherbakov (USSR) 1950, 1954; Jozef Schmidt (Pol) 1958, 1962; Viktor Saneyev (USSR) 1969, 1974

SHOT
1982 Udo Beyer (GDR) 21.50
1986 Werner Günthör (Swi) 22.22 *CBP*
Most: 2 Gunnar Huseby (Ice) 1946, 1950; Vilmos Varju (Hun) 1962, 1966; Hartmut Briesenick (GDR) 1971, 1974; Udo Beyer (GDR) 1978, 1982

DISCUS
1982 Imrich Bugar (Cs) 66.64
1986 Romas Ubartas (USSR) 67.08
CBP: 67.20 Wolfgang Schmidt (GDR) 1978 (qualifying round)
Most: 3 Adolfo Consolini (Ita) 1946, 1950, 1954

HAMMER
1982 Yuriy Sedykh (USSR) 81.66
1986 Yuriy Sedykh (USSR) 86.74 *CBP*
Most: 3 Yuriy Sedykh 1978, 1982, 1986

JAVELIN
1982 Uwe Hohn (GDR) 91.34
1986 Klaus Tafelmeier (FRG) 84.76 *CBP* (new javelin)
Most: 4 Janis Lusis (USSR) 1962, 1966, 1969 (CBP old javelin 91.52), 1971; 2 Matti Järvinen (Fin) 1934, 1938; Janusz Sidlo (Pol) 1954, 1958

DECATHLON
1982 Daley Thompson (UK) 8774
1986 Daley Thompson (UK) 8811 *CBP*
Most: 3 Vasiliy Kuznetsov (USSR) 1954, 1958, 1962; 2 Joachim Kirst (GDR) 1969, 1971; Daley Thompson

WOMEN
100 METRES
1982 Marlies Göhr (GDR) 11.01
1986 Marlies Göhr (GDR) 10.91 *CBP*
Most: 3 Marlies Göhr 1978, 1982, 1986

200 METRES
1982 Bärbel Wöckel (GDR) 22.04
1986 Heike Drechsler (GDR) 21.71 *CBP*
Most: 2 Irena Szewinska (Pol) 1966, 1974

400 METRES
1982 Marita Koch (GDR) 48.15 *CBP*
1986 Marita Koch (GDR) 48.22
Most: 3 Marita Koch 1978, 1982, 1986; 2 Mariya Itkina (USSR) 1958, 1962

800 METRES
1982 Olga Mineyeva (USSR) 1:55.41 *CBP*
1986 Nadezhda Olizarenko (USSR) 1:57.15
Most: 2 Vera Nikolic (Yug) 1966, 1971

1500 METRES
1982 Olga Dvirna (USSR) 3:57.80 *CBP*
1986 Ravilya Agletdinova (USSR) 4:01.19

3000 METRES
1982 Svetlana Ulmasova (USSR) 8:30.28 *CBP*
1986 Olga Bondarenko (USSR) 8:33.99
Most: 2 Svetlana Ulmasova 1978, 1982

Irena Szewinska beats Bärbel Eckert at 200 metres in the first World Cup in 1977. Between them they won seven Olympic gold medals. (All-Sport)

10 000 METRES
1986 Ingrid Kristiansen (Nor) 30:23.25 *CBP*

MARATHON
1982 Rosa Mota (Por) 2:36:04
1986 Rosa Mota (Por) 2:28:38 *CBP*
Most: 2 Rosa Mota

100 METRES HURDLES
1982 Lucyna Kalek (Pol) 12.45
1986 Yordanka Donkova (Bul) 12.38 *CBP*
Most: 3 Karin Balzer (GDR) 1966 (80mh), 1969, 1971; 2
Fanny Blankers-Koen (Hol) 1946, 1950 (both at 80mh)

400 METRES HURDLES
1982 Ann-Louise Skoglund (Swe) 54.58
1986 Marina Styepanova (USSR) 53.32 *CBP*

4 × 100 METRES RELAY
1982 GDR 42.19
1986 GDR 41.84 *CBP*

4 × 400 METRES RELAY
1982 GDR 3:19.05
1986 GDR 3:16.87 *CBP*

10 KM WALK
1986 Maria Cruz Diaz (Spa) 46:09 *CBP*

HIGH JUMP
1982 Ulrike Meyfarth (FRG) 2.02 *CBP*
1986 Stefka Kostadinova (Bul) 2.00
Most: 2 Iolanda Balas (Rom) 1958, 1962

LONG JUMP
1982 Vali Ionescu (Rom) 6.79
1986 Heike Drechsler (GDR) 7.27 *CBP*

SHOT
1982 Ilona Slupianek (GDR) 21.59 *CBP*
1986 Heidi Krieger (GDR) 21.10
Most: 4 Nadezhda Chizhova (USSR) 1966, 1969, 1971,
1974; 2 Ilona Slupianek 1978, 1982

DISCUS
1982 Tsvetanka Khristova (Bul) 68.34
1986 Diane Sachse (GDR) 71.36 *CBP*
Most: 2 Nina Dumbadze (USSR) 1946, 1950; Tamara Press
(USSR) 1958, 1962; Faina Melnik (USSR) 1971, 1974

JAVELIN
1982 Anna Verouli (Gre) 70.02
1986 Fatima Whitbread (UK) 76.32 (77.44 *CBP* in
qualifying)
Most: 2 Dana Zatopkova (Cs) 1954, 1958; Ruth Fuchs
(GDR) 1974, 1978

HEPTATHLON
1982 Ramona Neubert (GDR) 6664
1986 Anke Behmer (GDR) 6717 *CBP*
Most (at pentathlon): 2 Galina Bystrova (USSR) 1958,
1962

Most gold medals at all events:

MEN
5 Harald Schmid (FRG) 1978-86
4 Janis Lusis (USSR) 1962-71
4 Valeriy Borzov (USSR) 1969-74

WOMEN
6 Marita Koch (GDR) 1978-86
5 Fanny Blankers-Koen (Hol) 1946-50
5 Irena Szewinska (Pol) 1966-74
5 Marlies Göhr (GDR) 1978-86
4 Maria Itkina (USSR) 1954-62
4 Nadezhda Chizhova (USSR) 1966-74
4 Renate Stecher (GDR) 1969-74

Most medals:

MEN
		Gold	Silver	Bronze	
6	Harald Schmid (FRG)	5	1	-	1978-86
6	Pietro Mennea (Ita)	3	2	1	1971-74

WOMEN
		Gold	Silver	Bronze	
10	Irena Szewinska (Pol)	5	1	4	1966-78
8	Fanny Blankers-Koen (Hol)	5	1	2	1938-50
8	Renate Stecher (GDR)	4	4	-	1969-74
7	Marlies Göhr (GDR)	5	1	1	1978-86
6	Yevgeniya Sechenova (USSR)	2	2	2	1946-50
6	Marita Koch (GDR)	6	-	-	1978-86

Most medals at one event: (long jump)
5	Igor Ter-Ovanesyan (USSR)	3	2	-	1966-71

Most medals at one Championships:
4	Fanny Blankers-Koen (Hol)	3	1	-	1950
4	Irena Kirszenstein* (Pol)	3	1	-	1966
4	Stanislawa Walasiewicz (Pol)	2	2	-	1938

* later Szewinska

EUROPEAN INDOOR CHAMPIONSHIPS

European Indoor Games were held for the first time on 27 Mar 1966 at the Westfallenhalle in Dortmund. From 1970 they received IAAF sanction as the official European Indoor Championships.

Most wins:

MEN
7 Valeriy Borzov (USSR) 60m 1970-1, 1974-7; 50m 1972
6 Viktor Saneyev (USSR) triple jump 1970-2, 1975-7
5 Marian Woronin (Pol) 60m 1979-82, 1987

WOMEN
8 Helena Fibingerova (Cs) shot 1973-4, 1977-8, 1980, 1983-5
5 Karin Balzer (GDR) 50m hurdles 1967-9, 60m hurdles 1970-1
5 Nadezhda Chizhova (USSR) shot 1967-8, 1970-2
5 Marlies Göhr (GDR) 60m 1977-9, 1982-3

WORLD RECORDS

World records for athletics were first officially recognised by the IAAF in 1913. Initially records were recognised for 96 men's events, and this list has been reduced at various times, including the elimination of Imperial distances, except the 1 mile, in 1977. Women's records were first accepted by the Fédération Sportive Féminine Internationale (FSFI), from its formation in 1921. The FSFI merged with the IAAF in 1936. Women's records at distances from 1500m upwards have only been added to the official lists over the past two decades.

From 1977 all records at sprint distances up to 400 metres have been accepted only if timed fully automatically.

Records are shown for each of the currently recognised events, with the records at 15-year intervals. Many of the performances at 1912 and those indicated by (u) were not, for various reasons, ratified by the IAAF, but they are considered as the best acceptable. Also listed are those athletes to have set most records at each event.

MEN
100 METRES
1912 10.5 Richard Rau (Ger) 13 Aug 1911
1927 10.2 Charles Paddock (USA) 18 Jun 1921 (u)
1942 10.2 by four men
1957 10.1 Lloyd La Beach (Pan) 7 Oct 1950 (u) and by three men in 1956
1972 9.9 by five men
    9.95 Jim Hines (USA) 14 Oct 1968
1987 9.93 Calvin Smith (USA) 3 Jul 1983
The records set by Hines and Smith were at high altitude. The best time at low altitude is 9.95 by Ben Johnson (Can) in Moscow on 9 Jul 1986.
Most officially ratified: 4 Steve Williams (USA) all at 9.9 1974-6

200 METRES (y- 220 yards)
1912 21.4y James Maybury (USA) 5 Jun 1897
    21.4y Robert Kerr (USA) 26 Sep 1908
1927 21.2y William Applegarth (UK) 4 Jul 1914
    21.2 Charles Paddock (USA) 6 May 1923 (u)
    21.2y H.T.Evans (USA) 17 May 1924 (u)
1942 20.6y James Carlton (Aus) 18 Jun 1932 (u)
1957 20.6y Andy Stanfield (USA) 26 May 1951 and two other men
1972 19.83 Tommie Smith (USA) 16 Oct 1968
1987 19.72 Pietro Mennea (Italy) 12 Sep 1979
The records of Smith and Mennea were at the high altitude of Mexico City. The best time at low altitude is 19.75 Carl Lewis (USA) 19 Jun 1983.
Most: 5 Ray Norton (USA) 20.6 - 20.5 1959-60

400 METRES (y- 440 yards)
1912 47.8y Maxie Long (USA) 29 Sep 1900
1927 47.4y Ted Meredith (USA) 27 May 1916
    47.4y Binga Desmond (USA) Jun 1916 (u)
1942 46.0 Rudolf Harbig (Ger) 12 Aug 1939
    46.0 Grover Klemmer (USA) 29 Jun 1941
1957 45.2 Lou Jones (USA) 30 Jun 1956
1987 43.86 Lee Evans (USA) 18 Oct 1968
Most: 4 Herb McKenley (Jam) 46.2y - 45.9 1946-8
Evans ran his record at Mexico City. The best at low altitude is 44.10 Butch Reynolds (USA) 1987.

Seb Coe sets his fourth world record, 2:13.40 for 1000 metres at Oslo in 1980. (Keystone Press)

800 METRES (y- 880 yards)

1912	1:51.9	Ted Meredith (USA) 8 Jul 1912
1927	1:51.6y	Otto Peltzer (Ger) 3 Jul 1926
1942	1:46.6	Rudolf Harbig (Ger) 15 Jul 1939
1957	1:45.7	Roger Moens (Bel) 3 Aug 1955
1972	1:44.3	Peter Snell (NZ 3 Feb 1962
	1:44.3	Ralph Doubell (Aus) 15 Oct 1968
	1:44.3	Dave Wottle (USA) 1 Jul 1972
1987	1:41.73	Sebastian Coe (UK) 10 Jun 1981

Most: 7 Lawrence 'Lon' Myers (USA) 1:56.2y - 1:55.4y 1880-5

1000 METRES

1912	2:31.0	Emilio Lunghi (Ita) 31 May 1908
1927	2:25.8	Otto Peltzer (Ger) 18 Sep 1927
1942	2:21.5	Rudolf Harbig (Ger) 24 May 1941
1957	2:19.0	Auden Boysen (Nor) 30 Aug 1955
	2:19.0	Istvan Rozsavolgyi (Hun) 21 Sep 1955
1972	2:16.2	Jürgen May (GDR) 20 Jul 1965
	2:16.2	Franz-Josef Kemper (FRG) 21 Sep 1966
1987	2:12.18	Sebastian Coe (UK) 11 Jul 1981

Most: 3 Auden Boysen (Nor) 2:20.4 - 2:19.0 1953-5

1500 METRES

1912	3:55.8	Abel Kiviat (USA) 8 Jun 1912
1927	3:51.0	Otto Peltzer (Ger) 11 Sep 1926
1942	3:45.8	Gunder Hägg (Swe) 17 Jul 1942
1957	3:38.1	Stanislav Jungwirth (Cs) 12 Jul 1957
1972	3:33.1	Jim Ryun (USA) 8 Jul 1967
1987	3:29.46	Saïd Aouita (Mor) 23 Aug 1985

Most: 3 Abel Kiviat (USA) 3:59.2 - 3:55.8 1912
3 Gunder Hägg (Swe) 3:47.6 - 3:43.0 1941-4
3 Steve Ovett (UK) 3:32.09 - 3:30.77 1980-3

1 MILE

1912	4:12¾	Walter George (UK) 23 Aug 1886 (professional)
1927	4:10.4	Paavo Nurmi (Fin) 23 Aug 1923
1942	4:04.6	Gunder Hägg (Swe) 4 Sep 1942
1957	3:57.2	Derek Ibbotson (UK) 19 Jul 1957
1972	3:51.1	Jim Ryun (USA) 23 Jun 1967
1985	3:46.32	Steve Cram (UK) Oslo 27 Jul 1985

Most: 3 Gunder Hägg (Swe) 4:06.1 - 4.01.3 1942-5
3 Arne Andersson (Swe) 4:06.2 - 4:01.6 1942-4
3 Sebastian Coe (UK) 3:48.95 - 3:47.33 1979-81

2000 METRES

1912	5:37.0	Alfred Shrubb (UK) 11 Jun 1904 (1.25 miles)
1927	5:23.4	Eino Borg (Purje) (Fin) 9 Aug 1927
1942	5:11.8	Gunder Hägg (Swe) 23 Aug 1942
1957	5:02.2	Istvan Rozsavolgyi (Hun) 2 Oct 1955
1972	4:56.2	Michel Jazy (Fra) 12 Oct 1966
1987	4:50.81	Saïd Aouita (Mor) 16 Jul 1987

3000 METRES

1912	8:36.9	Hannes Kolehmainen (Fin) 12 Jul 1912
1927	8:20.4	Paavo Nurmi (Fin) 13 Jul 1926
1942	8:01.2	Gunder Hägg (Swe) 28 Aug 1942
1957	7:52.8	Gordon Pirie (UK) 4 Sep 1956
1972	7:37.6	Emiel Puttemans (Bel) 14 Sep 1972
1987	7:32.1	Henry Rono (Ken) 27 Jun 1978

Most: 4 Paavo Nurmi (Fin) 8:28.6 - 8:20.4 1922-6

5000 METRES

1912	14:36.6	Hannes Kolehmainen (Fin) 10 Jul 1912
1927	14:28.2	Paavo Nurmi (Fin) 19 Jun 1924
1942	13:58.1	Gunder Hägg (Swe) 20 Sep 1942
1957	13:35.0	Vladimir Kuts (USSR) 13 Oct 1957
1972	13:13.0	Emiel Puttemans (Bel) 20 Sep 1972
1987	12:58.39	Saïd Aouita (Mor) 22 Jul 1987

Most: 4 Vladimir Kuts (USSR) 13:56.6 - 13:35.0 1954-7
Ron Clarke (Aus) 13:34.4 - 13:16.6 1965-6

10000 METRES

1912	30:58.8	Jean Bouin (Fra) 16 Nov 1911
1927	30:06.1	Paavo Nurmi (Fin) 31 Aug 1924
1942	29:52.6	Taisto Mäki (Fin) 17 Sep 1939
1957	28:30.4	Vladimir Kuts (USSR) 11 Sep 1956
1972	27:38.35	Lasse Viren (Fin) 3 Sep 1972
1987	27:13.81	Fernando Mamede (Por) 2 Jul 1984

Most: 5 Emil Zatopek (Cs) 29:28.2 - 28:54.2 1949-54

CURRENT RECORDS AT OTHER LONG DISTANCE EVENTS

20,000m	57:24.2	Jos Hermens (Hol) 1 May 1976
25,000m	1:13:55.8	Toshihiko Seko (Jap) 22 Mar 1981
30,000m	1:29:18.8	Toshihiko Seko (Jap) 22 Mar 1981
1 hour	20,944m	Jos Hermens (Hol) 1 May 1976

MARATHON

Note that records are not officially recognised for the marathon, for which times are affected by the nature of the road courses. Best times:

1912	2:40:34.2	Thure Johansson (Swe) 26 May 1909
1927	2:29:01.8	Al Michelsen (USA) 12 Oct 1925

The great Ed Moses, who won 122 successive races at 400m hurdles, 1977-87.

1942	2:26:42	Sohn Kee Chung (Kor) 3 Nov 1935
1957	2:17:39.4	Jim Peters (UK) 26 Jun 1954
1972	2:08:33.6	Derek Clayton (Aus) 30 May 1969
1987	2:07:11.6	Carlos Lopes (Por) 20 Apr 1985

Most: 4 Jim Peters (UK) 2:20:42.2 - 2:17:39.4 1952-4

3000 METRES STEEPLECHASE

1942	9:03.8	Volmari Iso-Hollo (Fin) 8 Aug 1936 (u)
1957	8:35.6	Sandor Rozsnyoi (Hun) 16 Sep 1957
1972	8:20.7	Anders Gärderud (Swe) 14 Sep 1972
1987	8:05.4	Henry Rono (Ken) 13 May 1978

Most: 4 Anders Gärderud (Swe) 8:20.7 - 8:08.02 1972-6

110 METRES HURDLES (y- 120 yards hurdles)

1912	15.0	Forrest Smithson (USA) 25 Jul 1908
1927	14.4y	Earl Thomson (USA) 29 May 1920
1942	13.7	Forrest Towns (USA) 27 Aug 1936
	13.7	Fred Wolcott (USA) 29 Jun 1941
1957	13.3y	Jack Davis (USA) 17 Nov 1956
1972	13.0y	Rod Milburn (USA) 20 Jun 1971
	13.24	Rod Milburn (USA) 7 Sep 1972
1987	12.93	Renaldo Nehemiah (USA) 19 Aug 1981

Most: 6 Forrest Towns (USA) 14.1 - 13.7 1936
6 Rod Milburn (USA) 13.2 - 13.0y/13.24 1971-5

400 METRES HURDLES

1912	55.0	Charles Bacon (USA) 22 Jul 1908
1927	52.1	Ivan Riley (USA) 31 May 1924 (u)
1942	50.6	Glenn Hardin (USA) 26 Jul 1934
1957	49.5	Glenn Davis (USA) 29 Jun 1956
1972	47.82	John Akii-Bua (Uga) 2 Sep 1972
1987	47.02	Edwin Moses (USA) 31 Aug 1983

Most: 4 Edwin Moses (USA) 47.63 - 47.02 1976-83

HIGH JUMP

1912	2.00m	George Horine (USA) 18 May 1912
1927	2.03m	Harold Osborn (USA) 27 May 1924
1942	2.11m	Lester Steers (USA) 17 Jun 1941
1957	2.15m	Charles Dumas (USA) 29 Jun 1956
	2.16m*	Yuriy Styepanov (USSR) 13 Jul 1957
1972	2.29m	Ni Chih-Chin (Chn) 8 Nov 1970 (u)
	2.29m	Pat Matzdorf (USA) 3 Jul 1971
1987	2.42m	Patrick Sjöberg (Swe) 30 Jun 1987

Most: 6 Valeriy Brumel (USSR) 2.23 - 2.28 1961-3
4 John Thomas (USA) 2.17 - 2.22 1960
* set with built-up shoe, subsequently disallowed

POLE VAULT

1912	4.02m	Marcus Wright (USA) 8 Jun 1912
1927	4.26m	Sabin Carr (USA) 27 May 1927
1942	4.77m	Cornelius Warmerdam (USA) 23 May 1942
1957	4.82m	Bob Gutowski (USA) 15 Jun 1957 (u)
1972	5.63m	Bob Seagren (USA) 2 Jul 1972
1987	6.03m	Sergey Bubka (USSR) 23 Jun 1987

Most: 9 John Pennel (USA) 4.95 - 5.44 1963-9
7 Cornelius Warmerdam (USA) 4.57 - 4.77 1940-2
7 Sergey Bubka (USSR) 5.85 - 6.03 1984-7
6 Bob Seagren (USA) 5.32 - 5.63
1966-72
5 Thierry Vigneron (Fra) 5.75 - 5.91 1980-4

LONG JUMP

1912	7.61m	Peter O'Connor (Ire) 5 Aug 1901
1927	7.89m	William DeHart Hubbard (USA) 13 Jun 1925
1942	8.13m	Jesse Owens (USA) 25 May 1935
1987	8.90m	Bob Beamon (USA) 18 Oct 1968

Bob Beamon's 8.90m was set at the 2240m altitude of Mexico City. The best low altitude jump is 8.79m by Carl Lewis (USA) at Indianapolis 19 Jun 1983
Most: 6 Ralph Boston (USA) 8.21 - 8.35 1960-5

TRIPLE JUMP

1912	15.52m	Daniel Ahearne (USA) 30 May 1911
1927	15.52m	Daniel Ahearne & Anthony Winter (Aus) 12 Jul 1924
1942	16.00m	Naoto Tajima (Jap) 6 Aug 1936
1957	16.56m	Adhemar Ferreira da Silva (Bra) 16 Mar 1955
1972	17.44m	Viktor Saneyev (USSR) 17 Oct 1972
1987	17.97m	Willie Banks (USA) 16 Jun 1985

Most: 5 Adhemar Ferreira da Silva (Bra) 16.00 - 16.56 1951-5

SHOT

1912/27 15.54m Ralph Rose (USA) 21 Aug 1909
1942 17.40m Jack Torrance (USA) 5 Aug 1934
1957 19.25m Parry O'Brien (USA) 1 Nov 1956
1972 21.78m Randy Matson (USA) 22 Apr 1967
1987 22.64m Udo Beyer (GDR) 20 Aug 1986
       22.86m Brian Oldfield (USA) 10 May 1975
              (professional)
Most: 14 Parry O'Brien (USA) 18.00 - 19.30 1953-9
9 Dallas Long (USA) 19.25 - 20.68 1959-64
7 George Gray (USA) 13.76 - 14.75 1889-98
7 Ralph Rose (USA) 14.81 - 15.54 1904-9
5 Jack Torrence (USA) 16.30 - 17.40 1934

DISCUS

1912 47.58m James Duncan (USA) 27 May 1912
1927 48.20m Clarence Houser (USA) 3 Apr 1926
1942 53.34m Adolfo Consolini (Ita) 26 Oct 1941
1957 59.28m Fortune Gordien (USA) 22 Aug 1953
1972 70.38m Jay Silvester (USA) 16 May 1971 (u)
1987 74.08m Jürgen Schult (GDR) 6 Jun 1986
Most: 6 Jay Silvester (USA) 60.56 - 70.38 1961-71
4 Fortune Gordien (USA) 56.46 - 59.28 1949-53
4 Al Oerter (USA) 61.10 - 62.94 1962-4
4 Mac Wilkins (USA) 69.18 - 70.86 1976

HAMMER

1912 57.10m Matt McGrath (USA) 29 Oct 1911
1927 57.77m Pat Ryan (USA) 17 Aug 1913
1942 59.55m Pat O'Callaghan (Ire) 22 Aug 1937 (u)
1957 68.54m Hal Connolly (USA) 2 Nov 1956
1972 76.40m Walter Schmidt (FGR) 4 Sep 1971
1987 86.74m Yuriy Sedykh (USSR) 30 Aug 1986
Most: 14 John Flanagan (USA) 44.46 - 56.19 1895-1909
7 Hal Connolly (USA) 66.71 - 71.26 1956-65
7 Mikhail Krivonosov (USSR) 63.34 - 67.32 1954-6
7 James Mitchell (USA) 36.40 - 44.21 1886-92
6 Yuriy Sedykh (USSR) 80.38 - 86.74 1980-6

JAVELIN – old specification

1912 62.32m Eric Lemming (Swe) 29 Sep 1912
1927 69.88m Eino Penttila (Fin) 8 Oct 1927
1942 78.70m Yrjö Nikkanen (Fin) 11 Oct 1938
1957 85.71m Egil Danielsen (Nor) 26 Nov 1956
1972 93.80m Janis Lusis (USSR) 6 Jul 1972
1986 104.80m Uwe Hohn (GDR) 20 Jul 1984
Most: 10 Matti Järvinen (Fin) 71.57 - 77.23 1930-6
9 Eric Lemming (Swe) 49.32 - 62.32 1899-1912
5 Jonni Myrrä (Fin) 63.29 - 68.56 1914-25
– new specification introduced 1987
1987 87.66m Jan Zelezny (Cs) 31 May 1987

Daley Thompson (All-Sport)

DECATHLON – all rescored on the 1984 Tables
1912	6564	Jim Thorpe (USA) 13/15 Jul 1912 (u)
1927	6566	Paavo Yrjölä (Fin) 16/17 Jul 1927
1942	7254	Glenn Morris (USA) 7/8 Aug 1936
1957	7608	Rafer Johnson (USA) 10/11 Jun 1955
1972	8466	Nikolay Avilov (USSR) 7/8 Sep 1972
1987	8847	Daley Thompson (UK) 8/9 Aug 1984

(100m: 10.44, LJ: 8.01m, SP: 15.72m, HJ: 2.03m, 400m: 46.97, 110m hurdles: 14.33, DT: 46.56m, PV: 5.00m, JT: 65.24m, 1500m: 4:35.00)
Most: 4 Paavo Yrjölä (Fin) 6460 - 6700 1926-30
4 Daley Thompson (UK) 8648 - 8847 1980-4

4 × 100 METRES RELAY
1912	42.3	Germany 8 Jul 1912
1927	41.0	USA 12 Jul 1924
1942	39.8	USA 9 Aug 1936
1957	39.59	USA 1 Dec 1956
1972	38.19	USA 10 Sep 1972
1985	37.83	USA 11 Aug 1984

(Sam Graddy, Ron Brown, Calvin Smith, Carl Lewis)

4 × 400 METRES RELAY
1912	3:16.6	USA 15 Jul 1912
1927	3:16.0	USA 13 Jul 1924
1942	3:08.2	USA 7 Aug 1932
1957	3:03.9	Jamaica 27 Jul 1952 (3:04.04 auto)
1987	2:56.16	USA 20 Oct 1968

(Vince Matthews, Ron Freeman II, Larry James, Lee Evans)

OTHER CURRENT RELAY WORLD RECORDS
4 × 200m 1:20.26 University of Southern California (USA) 27 May 1978
(Joel Andrews, James Sanford, Billy Mullins, Clancy Edwards)
4 × 800m 7:03.89 UK 30 Aug 1982
(Peter Elliott, Garry Cook, Steve Cram, Sebastian Coe)
4 × 1500m 14:38.8 FR Germany 17 Aug 1977
(Thomas Wessinghage, Harald Hudak, Michael Lederer, Karl Fleschen)

WOMEN
Events from 1500 metres upwards have been recognised comparatively recently. The years that the IAAF have first officially recognised records for such events are shown as IAAF 19...

100 METRES
1927	12.1	Gertrud Gladitsch (Ger) 3 Jul 1927
1942	11.5	Helen Stephens (USA) 15 May 1936 & 10 Aug 1936
1957	11.3	Shirley Strickland (Aus) 4 Aug 1955
1972	11.07	Renate Stecher 2 Sep 1972
	11.0	(hand timed) by five women
1987	10.76	Evelyn Ashford (USA) 22 Aug 1984

Most: 10 Stanisława Walasiewicz* (Pol) 11.9 - 11.6 1932-7
9 Renate Stecher (née Meissner) (GDR) 11.0 - 10.8 1970-3
* Note that Walasiewicz's femininity has subsequently been questioned.

200 METRES (y- 220 yards)
| 1927 | 25.3 | Eileen Edwards (UK) 12 Jun 1927 |
| 1942 | 23.6 | Stanisława Walasiewicz* (Pol) 15 Aug 1935 |

Marita Koch – perhaps the greatest woman athlete ever (All-Sport)

1957	23.2	Betty Cuthbert (Aus) 16 Sep 1956
1972	22.40	Renate Stecher (GDR) 7 Sep 1972
	22.4	Chi Cheng (Tai) 12 Jul 1970
1987	21.71	Marita Koch (GDR) 10 Jun 1979 & 21 Jul 1984
	21.71	Heike Drechsler (GDR) 29 Jun 1987 & 29 Aug 1987

Most: 4 Irena Szewinska (née Kirszenstein) (Pol) 22.7 - 22.21 1965-74
4 Marita Koch (GDR) 22.06 - 21.71 1978-84
4 Eileen Edwards (UK) 26.2y - 25.3 1924-7

400 METRES (y- 440 yards) IAAF 1957
1927	60.8y	Eileen Edwards (UK)	11 Jul 1924
1942	56.8y	Nellie Halstead (UK)	9 Jul 1932
1957	53.6	Mariya Itkina (USSR)	6 Jul 1967
1972	51.02	Marilyn Neufville (Jam)	25 Jul 1970
1987	47.60	Marita Koch (GDR)	6 Oct 1985

Most: 7 Marita Koch (GDR) 49.19 - 47.60 1978-85
5 Shin Keum Dan (NKo) 53.0 - 51.2 1962-4

800 METRES
1927	2:23.7	Lina Batschauer (Ger)	7 Aug 1927
1942	2:15.3	Yekdokiya Vasilyeva (USSR)	9 Sep 1938
	2:15.3	Kseniya Shilo (USSR)	26 Aug 1940
1957	2:05.0	Nina Otkalenko (USSR)	24 Sep 1955
1972	1:58.45	Hildegard Falck (FRG)	11 Jul 1971
1987	1:53.28	Jarmila Kratochvilova (Cs)	26 Jul 1983

Most: 7 Nina Otkalenko (née Pletnyova) 2:12.0 - 2:05.0 1951-5

1500 METRES IAAF 1967
1942	4:41.8	Anna Zaytseva (USSR)	10 Jun 1940
1957	4:25.0	Diane Leather (UK)	21 Sep 1955 u
1972	4:01.38	Lyudmila Bragina (USSR)	9 Sep 1972
1987	3:52.47	Tatyana Kazankina (USSR)	13 Aug 1980

Most: 4 Lyudmila Bragina (USSR) 4:06.9 - 4:01.38 1972

1 MILE IAAF 1967
1942	5:15.3	Evelyne Forster (UK)	22 Jul 1939
1957	4:45.0	Diane Leather (UK)	21 Sep 1955
1972	4:35.3	Ellen Tittel (FRG)	20 Aug 1971
1987	4:16.71	Mary Slaney (USA)	21 Aug 1985
	4:15.8	Natalya Artyemova (USSR)	5 Aug 1984 (u)

Most: 5 Diane Leather (UK) 5:07.6 - 4:45.0 1953-5

3000 METRES IAAF 1974
1972	8:53.0	Lyudmila Bragina (USSR)	12 Aug 1972
1987	8:22.62	Tatyana Kazankina (USSR)	26 Aug 1984

Most: 4 Paola Cacchi (née Pigni) (Ita) 9:42.8 - 9:09.4 1969-72
3 Lyudmila Bragina (USSR) 8:53.0 - 8:27.12 1972-6

5000 METRES IAAF 1981
1972	15:48.5	Adrienne Beames (Aus)	5 Jan 1972 u
1987	14:37.33	Ingrid Kristiansen (Nor)	5 Aug 1986

Most: 3 Ingrid Kristiansen (Nor) 15:28.43 - 14:37.33 1981-6

10000 METRES IAAF 1981
1972	34:08.0	Adrienne Beames (Aus)	28 Jan 1972 u
1987	30:13.74	Ingrid Kristiansen (Nor)	5 Aug 1987

CURRENT RECORDS AT OTHER DISTANCE EVENTS
1000m	2:30.6	Tatyana Providokhina (USSR)	20 Aug 1978
2000m	5:28.69	Maricica Puica (Rom)	11 Jul 1986

MARATHON
Note that records are not officially recognised for the marathon, for which times are affected by the nature of the road courses.

Best times:
1972 2:46:30 Adrienne Beames (Aus) 31 Aug 1971
1987 2:21:06 Ingrid Kristiansen (Nor) 21 Apr 1985

Most: 4 Grete Waitz (Nor) 2:32:30 - 2:25:29 1978-83

80 METRES HURDLES
The standard women's hurdles distance was 80 metres, over seven flights of 2ft 6in (76cm) hurdles from 1927 until replaced by the 100m over eight flights of 2ft 9in (84cm) hurdles in 1969.
1942	11.3	Claudia Testoni (Ita)	23 Jul 1939 & 13 Aug 1939
	11.3	Fanny Blankers-Koen (Hol)	20 Sep 1942
1957	10.6	Centa Gastl (FRG)	20 Jun 1959
1969	10.2	Vera Korsakova (USSR)	16 Jun 1968
	10.39	Maureen Caird (Aus)	18 Oct 1968 (auto)

Most: 6 Irina Press (USSR) 10.6 - 10.3 1960-5
5 Claudia Testoni (Ita) 11.6 - 11.3 1938-9

100 METRES HURDLES
Replaced the 80 metres hurdles in 1969
1972	12.59	Annelie Ehrhardt (GDR)	8 Sep 1972 (auto)
	12.5	Annelie Ehrhardt (GDR)	15 Jun 1972
	12.5	Pamela Ryan (Aus)	28 Jun 1972
1987	12.25	Ginka Zagorcheva (Bul)	8 Jul 1987

Most: 6 Karin Balzer (GDR) 13.3 - 12.6 1969-71
4 Yordanka Donkova (Bul) 12.36 - 12.26 1986

400 METRES HURDLES IAAF 1974
1987 52.94 Marina Styepanova (USSR) 17 Sep 1986

Most: 3 Marina Styepanova (née Makeyeva) (USSR) 54.78 - 52.94 1979-86

HIGH JUMP
1927	1.59m	Marjorie Clark (SAf)	15 Apr 1927
1942	1.66m	Dorothy Odam (UK)	29 May 1939
	1.66m	Esther Van Heerden (SAf)	29 Mar 1941
	1.66m	Ilsebill Pfenning (Swi)	27 Jul 1941
1957	1.77m*	Cheng Feng-Yung (Chn)	17 Nov 1957
1972	1.94m	Yordanka Blagoyeva (Bul)	24 Sep 1972
1985	2.08m	Stefka Kostadinova (Bul)	31 May 1986

Most: 14 Iolanda Balas (Rom) 1.75 - 1.91 1956-61
7 Rosemarie Ackermann (née Witschas) (GDR) 1.94 - 2.00 1974-7
* set with built-up shoe, subsequently disallowed

LONG JUMP
1927	5.75m	Kinue Hitomi (Jap)	5 Jun 1926
1942	6.12m	Christel Schulz (Ger)	30 Jul 1939
1957	6.35m	Elzbieta Krzesinska (Pol)	27 Nov 1956
1972	6.84m	Heide Rosendahl (GFR)	3 Sep 1970
1987	7.45m	Heike Drechsler (GDR)	21 Jun 1986 & 3 Jul 1986

Most: 4 Tatyana Shchelkanova (USSR) 6.48 - 6.70 1962-4
4 Anisoara Cusmir (Rom) 7.15 - 7.43 1982-3

SHOT
1927	11.37m	Ruth Lange (Ger)	4 Sep 1927
1942	14.38m	Gisela Mauermayer (Ger)	15 Jul 1934
1957	16.76m	Galina Zybina (USSR)	13 Oct 1956
1972	21.03m	Nadezhda Chizhova (USSR)	7 Sep 1972
1987	22.63m	Natalya Lisovskaya (USSR)	7 June 1987

Most: 15 Galina Zybina (USSR) 15.19 - 16.76 1952-6
10 Nadezhda Chizhova (USSR) 18.67 - 21.45 1968-73
 9 Grete Heublein (Ger) 10.86 - 13.70 1927-31
 6 Tamara Press (USSR) 17.25 - 18.59 1959-65
 5 Ruth Lange (Ger) 10.84 - 11.52 1927-8

DISCUS
1927 39.18m Halina Konopacka (Pol) 4 Sep 1927
1942 49.54m Nina Dumbadze (USSR) 29 Oct 1939
1957 57.04m Nina Dumbadze (USSR) 18 Oct 1952
1972 67.32m Argentina Menis (Rom) 23 Sep 1972
1987 74.56m Zdenka Silhava (Cs) 26 Aug 1984

Most: 11 Faina Melnik (USSR) 64.22 - 70.50 1971-6
9 Jadwiga Wajsowna (Pol) 40.34 - 44.19 1932-4
9 Gisela Mauermayer (Ger) 44.34 - 48.31 1935-6
7 Nina Dumbadze (USSR) 49.11 - 57.04 1939-52
6 Halina Konopacka (Pol) 31.24 - 39.62 1925-8
6 Tamara Press (USSR) 57.15 - 59.70 1960-5

JAVELIN
1927 38.80m Margaret Jenkins (USA) 3 Sep 1927
1942 47.24m Anneliese Steinheuer (Ger) 21 Jun 1942
1957 55.48m Nadezhda Konyayeva (USSR) 6 Aug 1954
1972 65.06m Ruth Fuchs (GDR) 11 Jun 1972
1985 78.90m Petra Falke (GDR) 29 Jul 1987

Most: 6 Ruth Fuchs (GDR) 65.06 - 69.96 1972-80
4 Elvira Ozolina (USSR) 57.92 - 61.38 1960-4

HEPTATHLON — all scored on the 1984 Tables
1987 7158   Jackie Joyner (USA) 1/2 Aug 1986
           (100m hurdles: 12.85, high jump: 1.88m, shot:
           14.76m, 200m: 23.00, long jump: 7.01m, javelin:
           49.86m, 800m: 2:10.02)

Most: 4 Ramona Neubert (GDR) 6670 - 6935 1981-3

The heptathlon has been the standard women's multi-event competition since 1981. Until 1980 the pentathlon was the standard competition. The events changed several times, and the scores given are all rescored on the 1984 tables.

Most: 8 Irina Press (USSR) 4121 - 4602 1959-64
    5 Aleksandra Chudina (USSR) 3564 - 4024
    1947-55

4 × 100 METRES RELAY
1927 49.8   Great Britain 29 Aug 1926
1942 46.4   Germany 8 Aug 1936
1957 44.65   Australia 1 Dec 1956
1972 42.81   FR Germany 10 Sep 1972
1987 41.37   GDR 31 Jul 1983

(Silke Gladisch, Sabine Rieger, Ingrid Auerswald, Marlies Göhr)

4 × 400 METRES RELAY IAAF 1969
1972 3:22.95 GDR 10 Sep 1972
1987 3:15.92 GDR 3 Jun 1984

(Gesine Walther, Sabine Busch, Dagmar Rübsam, Marita Koch)

OTHER CURRENT RELAY WORLD RECORDS
4 × 200m 1:28.15 GDR 9 Aug 1980
(Marlies Göhr, Romy Müller, Bärbel Wöckel, Marita Koch)
4 × 800m 7:50.17 USSR 5 Aug 1984
(Nadezhda Olizarenko, Lyubov Gurina, Lyudmila Borisova, Irina Podyalovskaya)

WORLD INDOOR RECORDS

From 1 January 1987 the IAAF recognize world indoor records. The best performances made before that date have been noted as World Bests, and world records must better these to be officially accepted. Track performances around a turn must be made on a track no larger than 200 metres.

Event	Mark	Athlete (Nation)	Venue	Date
MEN				
50 metres	5.55	Ben Johnson (Can)	Ottawa	31 Jan 1987
60 metres	6.41	Ben Johnson (Can)	Indianapolis	7 Mar 1987
200 metres	20.36	Bruno Marie-Rose (Fra)	Lievin	22 Feb 1987
400 metres	45.41	Thomas Schönlebe (GDR)	Vienna	9 Feb 1986
800 metres	1:44.91	Sebastian Coe (UK)	Cosford	12 Mar 1983
1000 metres	2:18.00	Igor Lotarev (USSR)	Moscow	14 Feb 1987
1500 metres	3:35.6 (u)	Eamonn Coghlan (Ire)	San Diego	20 Feb 1981
	3:36.04	José-Luis Gonzalez (Spa)	Oviedo	1 Mar 1986
1 mile	3:49.78	Eamonn Coghlan (Ire)	East Rutherford	27 Feb 1983
2000 metres	4:54.07	Eamonn Coghlan (Ire)	Inglewood	21 Feb 1987
3000 metres	7:39.2	Emiel Puttemans (Bel)	Berlin	18 Feb 1973
5000 metres	13:20.4	Suleiman Nyambui (Tan)	New York	6 Feb 1981
50m hurdles	6.25	Mark McKoy (Can)	Kobe	5 Mar 1986
60m hurdles	7.46	Greg Foster (USA)	Indianapolis	6 Mar 1987
High jump	2.41	Patrik Sjöberg (Swe)	Piraeus	1 Feb 1987
Pole vault	5.97	Sergey Bubka (USSR)	Turin	17 Mar 1987
Long jump	8.79	Carl Lewis (USA)	New York	27 Feb 1984
Triple jump	17.76	Mike Conley (USA)	New York	27 Feb 1987
Shot	22.26	Werner Günthör (Swi)	Magglingen	8 Feb 1987
4×200m relay	1:22.32	Italy	Turin	11 Feb 1984
4×400m relay	3:05.9	USSR	Vienna	14 Mar 1970
5000m walk	18:27.79	Mikhail Shchennikov (USSR)	Indianapolis	7 Mar 1987

Event	Mark	Athlete (Nation)	Venue	Date
WOMEN				
50 metres	6.06	Angella Issajenko (Can)	Ottawa	31 Jan 1987
60 metres	7.00	Nellie Cooman-Fiere (Hol)	Madrid	23 Feb 1986
200 metres	22.27	Heike Drechsler (GDR)	Indianapolis	7 Mar 1987
400 metres	49.59	Jarmila Kratochvilova (Cs)	Milan	7 Mar 1982
800 metres	1:58.42	Sigrun Wodars (GDR)	Vienna	10 Jan 1987
	1:58.4	Olga Vakhrusheva (USSR)	Moscow	16 Feb 1980
1000 metres	2:34.8	Brigitte Kraus (FRG)	Dortmund	19 Feb 1978
1500 metres	4:00.8	Mary Decker-Slaney (USA)	New York	8 Feb 1980
1 mile	4:20.5	Mary Decker-Slaney (USA)	San Diego	19 Feb 1982
3000 metres	8:39.79	Zola Budd (UK)	Cosford	8 Feb 1986
5000 metres	15:35.4	Margaret Groos (USA)	Blacksburg	20 Feb 1981
50m hurdles	6.71	Cornelia Oschekenat (GDR)	Berlin	9 Feb 1986
	6.71	Cornelia Oschekenat (GDR)	Berlin	24 Feb 1987
60m hurdles	7.74	Yordanka Donkova (Bul)	Sofia	14 Feb 1987
High jump	2.05	Stefka Kostadinova (Bul)	Indianapolis	8 Mar 1987
Long jump	7.32	Heike Drechsler (GDR)	New York	27 Feb 1987
Shot	22.50	Helena Fibingerova (Cs)	Jablonec	19 Feb 1977
3000m walk	12:05.49	Olga Krishtop (USSR)	Indianapolis	6 Mar 1987
4×200m relay	1:33.56	VfL Sindelfingen (FRG)	Sindelfingen	8 Feb 1986
4×400m relay	3:34.38	FR Germany	Dortmund	30 Jan 1981

WORLD BESTS – ULTRAMARATHON TRACK EVENTS

MEN	hr:min:sec			
30 miles	2:42:00	Jeff Norman (UK)	Timperley	7 Jun 1980
50 km	2:48:06	Jeff Norman (UK)	Timperley	7 Jun 1980
40 miles	3:48:35	Don Ritchie (UK)	Hendon, London	16 Oct 1982
50 miles	4:51:49	Don Ritchie (UK)	Hendon, London	12 Mar 1983
100 km	6:10:20	Don Ritchie (UK)	Crystal Palace	28 Oct 1978
100 miles	11:30:51	Don Ritchie (UK)	Crystal Palace	15 Oct 1977
200 km	15:11:10	Yiannis Kouros (Gre)	Montauban, Fra	15-16 Mar 1985
200 miles	27:48:35	Yiannis Kouros (Gre)	Montauban, Fra	15-16 Mar 1985
500 km	60:23:00	Yiannis Kouros (Gre)	Colac, Aus.	26-29 Nov 1984
500 miles	105:42:09	Yiannis Kouros (Gre)	Colac, Aus.	26-30 Nov 1984
1000 km	136:17:00	Yiannis Kouros (Gre)	Colac, Aus.	26-31 Nov 1984
1500 km	14d 20:10:13	Malcolm Campbell (UK)	Gateshead	11-26 Nov 1985
2000 km	15d 21:07:43	Malcolm Campbell (UK)	Gateshead	11-27 Nov 1985
	kilometres			
24 hrs	283.600	Yiannis Kouros (Gre)	Montauban, Fra	15-16 Mar 1985
48 hrs	452.270	Yiannis Kouros (Gre)	Montauban, Fra	15-17 Mar 1985
6 days	1023.2	Yiannis Kouros (Gre)	Colac, Aus.	26 Nov-1 Dec 1984

LOND DISTANCE ROAD BESTS

Where superior to track bests and run on properly measured road courses.

	hr:min:sec			
40 miles	3:46:31	Barney Klecker (USA)	Chicago	5 Oct 1980
50 miles	4:50:21	Bruce Fordyce (SAf)	London-Brighton	25 Sep 1983
1000 miles	11d 20:36	Stu Mittleman (USA)	Queens, New York	26 Apr-8 May 1986
	kilometres			
24 hours	286.463	Yiannis Kouros (Gre)	New York	28-29 Sep 1985

It should be noted that road times must be assessed with care as course conditions can vary considerably.

WORLD BESTS – ULTRAMARATHON TRACK EVENTS

WOMEN	hr:min:sec			
30 miles	3:28:12	Ann Franklin (UK)	Barry, Wales	9 Mar 1986
50 km	3:36:58	Ann Franklin (UK)	Barry, Wales	9 Mar 1986
40 miles	4:47:27	Ann Franklin (UK)	Barry, Wales	9 Mar 1986
50 miles	6:17:30 !	Monika Kuno (FRG)	Vogt	8-9 Jul 1983
100 km	8:01:01	Monika Kuno (FRG)	Vogt	8-9 Jul 1983

Event	Mark	Athlete (Nation)	Venue	Date
150 km	14:20:32 !	Eleanor Adams (UK)	Honefoss, Nor	12-13 Jul 1986
100 miles	15:25:46	Eleanor Adams (UK)	Honefoss, Nor	12-13 Jul 1986
200 km	20:09:28 !	Eleanor Adams (UK)	Honefoss, Nor	12-13 Jul 1986
200 miles	44:44:08	Eleanor Adams (UK)	Montauban, Fra	15-17 Mar 1985
500 km	86:31:21	Eleanor Adams (UK)	Colac, Aus.	24-28 Feb 1986
500 miles	143:38:55	Eleanor Adams (UK)	Colac, Aus.	24 Feb-2 Mar 1986
	kilometres			
24 hrs	222.8	Eleanor Adams (UK)	Nottingham	4-5 Aug 1985
48 hrs	347.420	Arlette Touchard (Fra)	Montauban, Fra	14-16 Mar 1986
6 days	808.0	Eleanor Adams (UK)	Colac, Aus.	24 Feb-2 Mar 1986

! Timed on one running watch only.

LONG DISTANCE ROAD BESTS

Where superior to track bests and run on properly measured road courses.

50 km	3:13:51	Janis Klecker (USA)	Tallahassee	17 Dec 1983
40 miles	4:43:22	Marcy Schwam (USA)	Chicago	3 Oct 1982
50 miles	5:59:26	Marcy Schwam (USA)	Chicago	3 Oct 1982
100 km	7:26:01	Chantal Langlacé (Fra)	Migennes	17 Jun 1984
100 miles	15:07:45	Christine Barrett (UK)	Forthampton	14 Apr 1984
500 km	82:10	Annie van der Meer (Hol)	Paris-Colmar	8-11 Jun 1983

INDOORS

24 hrs	227.261 km	Eleanor Adams (UK)	Milton Keynes	14-15 Feb 1987

WALKING WORLD RECORDS

The IAAF currently ratify records at just four track walking events - at 20, 30 and 50 kilometres and at 2 hours. At one time their list embraced a large number of distances, but the shorter distance records were dropped due in particular to difficulties in judging whether walkers were maintaining the strict disciplines of the event. The standard road walking events have become established at 20 and 50 kilometres.

WORLD RECORDS AND BESTS – TRACK WALKS

	hr:min:sec			
1500m	5:17.17 i	Tim Lewis (USA)	East Rutherford	14 Feb 1987
1 mile	5:38.2 i	Tim Lewis (USA)	Inglewood	21 Feb 1987
3000m	10:54.6 i	Carlo Mattioli (Ita)	Milan	6 Feb 1980
5000m	18:27.79 i	Mikhail Shchennikov (USSR)	Indianapolis	7 Mar 1987
10 km	38:02.60	Jozef Pribilinec (Cs)	Banska Bystrica	30 Aug 1985
15 km	58:22.4	Jozef Pribilinec (Cs)	Hildesheim	6 Sep 1987
10 miles	1:05:07.6	Domingo Colin (Mex)	Fana	26 May 1979
20 km	1:18:40.0	Ernesto Canto (Mex)	Fana	5 May 1984
15 miles	1:42:18.0	Reima Salonen (Fin)	Raisio	1 Sep 1979
25 km	1:44:54.0 *	Maurizio Damilano (Ita)	San Donato Milanese	5 May 1985
30 km	2:06:07.3 *	Maurizio Damilano (Ita)	San Donato Milanese	5 May 1985
20 miles	2:22:09.9	Raul Gonzales (Mex)	Frde	19 May 1978
30 miles	3:34:16.3	Raul Gonzales (Mex)	Fana	25 May 1979
50 km	3:41:38.4	Raul Gonzales (Mex)	Fana	25 May 1979
100 km	9:23:58.6	Roger Quemener (Fra)	Saint Maur	28 Mar 1976
	kilometres			
1 hour	15.547	Jozef Pribilinec (Cs)	Hildesheim	6 Sep 1986
2 hrs	28.565	Maurizio Damilano (Ita)	San Donato Milanese	5 May 1985

i indoors, * unratified

WORLD BESTS – ROAD WALKS

Where superior to track bests and walked on properly measured road courses.

25 km	1:45:52	Hartwig Gauder (GDR)	Grasleben	20 Jul 1980
30 km	2:03:06	Daniel Bautista (Mex)	Cherkassy	27 Apr 1980

Event	Mark	Athlete (Nation)	Venue	Date
50 km	3:38:17	Ronald Weigel (GDR)	Potsdam	25 May 1986
100 km	8:58:12	Gérard Lelièvre (Fra)	Laval	7 Oct 1984

It should be noted that road times must be assessed with care as course conditions can vary considerably.

WOMEN'S WALKING WORLD RECORDS

The IAAF have ratified records for women's track walking at 5km and 10km since 1981.

WORLD RECORDS AND BESTS – TRACK WALKS   i = indoors

	hr:min:sec			
1500m	6:01.16 i	Maryanne Torrellas (USA)	East Rutherford	14 Feb 1987
1 mile	6:28.46 i	Giuliana Salce (Ita)	Genoa	16 Feb 1985
3 km	12:05.49 i	Olga Krishtop (USSR)	Indianapolis	6 Mar 1987
5 km	21:20.2	Yan Hong (Chn)	Xinglong	29 Mar 1987
10 km	44:26.5	Xu Yongjiu (Chn)	Xinglong	31 Mar 1987
	kilometres			
1 hour	12.465	Giuliana Salce (Ita)	L'Aquila	9 Sep 1984

WORLD BESTS – ROAD WALKS
Where superior to track bests

10 km	43:22	Olga Krishtop (USSR)	New York	3 May 1987
15 km	1:11:24	Sue Cook (Aus)	Canberra	7 Jul 1984
20 km	1:33:30	Kerry Saxby (Aus)	Canberra	13 Jul 1985
25 km	2:12:38	Sue Cook (Aus)	Canberra	20 Jun 1981
30 km	2:45:52	Sue Cook (Aus)	Melbourne	5 Sep 1982
50 km	5:01:52	Lilian Millen (UK)	York	16 Apr 1983
100 km	11:40.07	Aaf de Rijk (Hol)	Hamm	17 Oct 1981
	kilometres			
24 hours	202.230	Annie van den Meer (Hol)	Rouen	30 Apr - 1 May 1984

It should be noted that road times must be assessed with care as course conditions (and accuracy of measurement) can vary considerably.

MAJOR MARATHON RACES

The marathon distance is 26 miles 385 yards (42.195km), the distance for the race at the 1908 Olympic Games, run from Windsor to the White City Stadium, London. That distance became standard from 1924.

BOSTON

The Boston marathon is the world's oldest annual race. It was first run by 15 men on 19 Apr 1897 over a distance of 24 miles 1232 yards (39.75km). Since then it has been run every year on or about the 19th April, Patriot's Day, which honours the famed ride of Paul Revere through Boston. The full marathon distance was first run in 1927.
Kathy Switzer (USA) contested the race in 1967, although the race director tried to prevent her, but her pioneering efforts helped force the acceptance of women runners, and they were admitted officially for the first time in 1972.

Winners from 1970:
1970 Ron Hill (UK) 2:10:30
1971 Alvaro Mejia (Col) 2:18:45
1972 Olavi Suomalainen (Fin) 2:15:39
1973 Jon Anderson (USA) 2:16:03
1974 Neil Cusack (Ire) 2:13:39

1975 Bill Rodgers (USA) 2:09:55
1976 Jack Fultz (USA) 2:20:19
1977 Jerome Drayton (Can) 2:14:46
1978 Bill Rodgers (USA) 2:10:13
1979 Bill Rodgers (USA) 2:09:27
1980 Bill Rodgers (USA) 2:12:11
1981 Toshihiko Seko (Jap) 2:09:26
1982 Alberto Salazar (USA) 2:08:51
1983 Greg Meyer (USA) 2:09:01
1984 Geoff Smith (UK) 2:10:34
1985 Geoff Smith (UK) 2:14:05
1986 Rob de Castella (Aus) 2:07:51
1987 Toshihiko Seko (Jap) 2:11:50

Most wins: 7 Clarence De Mar (USA) 1911, 1922–4, 1927–8, 1930; 4 Gérard Coté (Can) 1940, 1943–4, 1948; 4 Bill Rodgers (USA) 1975, 1978–80

WOMEN
1972 Nina Kuscsik (USA) 3:08:58
1973 Jackie Hansen (USA) 3:05:59
1974 Miki Gorman (USA) 2:47:11
1975 Liane Winter (FRG) 2:42:24
1976 Kim Merritt (USA) 2:47:10
1977 Miki Gorman (USA) 2:48:33
1978 Gayle Barron (USA) 2:44:52
1979 Joan Benoit (USA) 2:35:15

1980 Jacqueline Gareau (Can) 2:34:28
1981 Allison Roe (NZ) 2:26:46
1982 Charlotte Teske (FRG) 2:29:33
1983 Joan Benoit (USA) 2:22:43
1984 Lorraine Moller (NZ) 2:29:28
1985 Lisa Weidenbach (USA) 2:34:06
1986 Ingrid Kristiansen (Nor) 2:24:55
1987 Rosa Mota (Por) 2:25.21

Most wins: 2 Miki Gorman, Joan Benoit

CHICAGO

First held in 1977 as the Mayor Daley Marathon, world class fields have been attracted annually since 1983, and there have been large prize funds, especially rewarding for the world records for both men and women in 1985. *Winners from 1983:*

MEN
1983 Joseph Nzau (Ken) 2:09:45
1984 Steve Jones (UK) 2:08:05
1985 Steve Jones (UK) 2:07:13
1986 Toshihiko Seko (Jap) 2:08:27

WOMEN
1983 Rosa Mota (Por) 2:31:12
1984 Rosa Mota (Por) 2:26:01
1985 Joan Benoit (USA) 2:21:21
1986 Ingrid Kristiansen (Nor) 2:27:08

FUKUOKA

The Asahi marathon was first run in 1947 at Kumamoto. It was first held at Fukuoka in 1951, and the race was been held there every year since 1964 in early December. Over the past 20 years it has consistently attracted world class men's fields.

Winners from 1967, when Derek Clayton set a world best to win the race:

1967 Derek Clayton (Aus) 2:09:37
1968 Bill Adcocks (UK) 2:10:48
1969 Jerome Drayton (Can) 2:11:13
1970 Akio Usami (Jap) 2:10:38
1971 Frank Shorter (USA) 2:12:51
1972 Frank Shorter (USA) 2:10:30
1973 Frank Shorter (USA) 2:11:45
1974 Frank Shorter (USA) 2:11:32
1975 Jerome Drayton (Can) 2:10:09
1976 Jerome Drayton (Can) 2:12:25
1977 Bill Rodgers (USA) 2:10:56
1978 Toshihiko Seko (Jap) 2:10:21
1979 Toshihiko Seko (Jap) 2:10:35
1980 Toshihiko Seko (Jap) 2:09:45
1981 Rob de Castella (Aus) 2:08:18
1982 Paul Ballinger (NZ) 2:10:15
1983 Toshihiko Seko (Jap) 2:08:52
1984 Takeyuki Nakayama (Jap) 2:10:00
1985 Masanari Shintaku (Jap) 2:09:51
1986 Juma Ikangaa (Tan) 2:10:06

Most wins: 4 Frank Shorter, Toshihiko Seko

Grete Waitz, eight times New York marathon winner, here steps down in distance to win the L'Éggs 10km road race. (All-Sport)

LONDON

The first London marathon was run on 29 Mar 1981. Organised and inspired by the 1956 Olympic steeplechase gold medallist, Chris Brasher, it caught the public's imagination and was a great success, 7055 runners started and 6418 finished. Numbers increased each year to a record 19710 finishers in 1987.

Winners:

MEN
1981 Dick Beardsley (USA) & Inge Simonsen (Nor) 2:11:48
1982 Hugh Jones (UK) 2:09:24
1983 Mike Gratton (UK) 2:09:43
1984 Charlie Spedding (UK) 2:09:57
1985 Steve Jones (UK) 2:08:16
1986 Toshihiko Seko (Jap) 2:10:02
1987 Hiromi Taniguchi (Jap) 2:09.50

WOMEN
1981 Joyce Smith (UK) 2:29:57
1982 Joyce Smith (UK) 2:29:43
1983 Grete Waitz (Nor) 2:25:29
1984 Ingrid Kristiansen (Nor) 2:24:26
1985 Ingrid Kristiansen (Nor) 2:21:06
1986 Grete Waitz (Nor) 2:24:54
1987 Ingrid Kristiansen (Nor) 2:22.48

NEW YORK

Fred Lebow has organised the New York marathon annually from 1970. The race was run in Central Park until 1976, when, to celebrate the US Bicentennial the course was changed to a route through all five boroughs of the

city. From that year, when there were 2090 runners, the race has become one of the world's great sporting occasions, and in 1986 there were a record 20,502 runners, of whom 19,689 finished.

Winners since 1976:

MEN

1976 Bill Rodgers (USA) 2:10:10
1977 Bill Rodgers (USA) 2:11:29
1978 Bill Rodgers (USA) 2:12:12
1979 Bill Rodgers (USA) 2:11:42
1980 Alberto Salazar (USA) 2:09:41
1981 Alberto Salazar (USA) 2:08:13
1982 Alberto Salazar (USA) 2:09:29
1983 Rod Dixon (NZ) 2:08:59
1984 Orlando Pizzolato (Ita) 2:14:53
1985 Orlando Pizzolato (Ita) 2:11:34.
1986 Gianni Poli (Ita) 2:11:06

WOMEN

1976 Miki Gorman (USA) 2:39:11
1977 Miki Gorman (USA) 2:43:10
1978 Grete Waitz (Nor) 2:32:30
1979 Grete Waitz (Nor) 2:27:33
1980 Grete Waitz (Nor) 2:25:41
1981 Allison Roe (NZ) 2:25:29
1982 Grete Waitz (Nor) 2:27:14
1983 Grete Waitz (Nor) 2:27:00
1984 Grete Waitz (Nor) 2:29:30
1985 Grete Waitz (Nor) 2:28:34
1986 Grete Waitz (Nor) 2:28:06

Note that the course used from 1981 to 1983 was found to be 170 yards (155m) short of the full marathon distance, about 30 seconds at top men's pace. That sadly meant that the world best times set by Alberto Salazar and Allison Roe in 1981 were invalidated.

ROTTERDAM

Since its inception in 1981 Rotterdam has attracted elite fields.

Winners:

MEN

1981 John Graham (UK) 2:09:28
1982 Rodolfo Gomez (Mex) 2:11:57
1983 Rob de Castella (Aus) 2:08:37
1984 Gidamis Shahanga (Tan) 2:11:12
1985 Carlos Lopes (Por) 2:07:12
1986 Abebe Mekonnen (Eth) 2:09:08
1987 Belaine Densimo (Eth) 2:12.58

The women's best is 2:32.27 by Rosa Mota (Por) in 1983.

CROSS-COUNTRY RUNNING

WORLD CROSS-COUNTRY CHAMPIONSHIPS

The International Cross-Country Championships were first held at Hamilton Park Racecourse, Glasgow in 1903 over 8 miles (12.87km), contested by the four countries from the British Isles. The race was held annually, with France first entering in 1907, Belgium in 1923, and thereafter the event steadily gained in international prestige. A junior race was first added in 1961, although there had been an international race for juniors between England, France and Belgium in 1940, and the first women's race held in 1967. There were two women's races in 1970: included here is the one in the USA; the other, in France, was won by Paula Pigni (Ita), with the Netherlands team winners.

The event has had official world championship status from 1973, when the IAAF took control of the event from the International Cross-Country Union. The distances raced now are: Men – 12km, Women – 5km, Junior Men – 8km. Men's teams are of nine runners, with six to score; women and junior men of six runners, four to score.

Winning senior teams

MEN

44	England	1903-14, 1920-1, 1924-5, 1930-8, 1951, 1953-5, 1958-60, 1962, 1964-72, 1976, 1979-80
14	France	1922-3, 1926-9, 1939, 1946-7, 1949-50, 1952, 1956, 1978
7	Belgium	1948, 1957, 1961, 1963, 1973-4, 1977
5	Ethiopia	1981-5
2	Kenya	1986-7
1	New Zealand	1975

WOMEN

8	USA	1968-9, 1975, 1979, 1983-5, 1987
7	England	1967, 1970-74, 1986
5	USSR	1976-7, 1980-2
1	Romania	1978

There were record fields in 1986, when the number of finishers were: 328 men, 171 junior men and 161 women; with 39, 29 and 28 teams respectively placing.

**INDIVIDUAL WINNERS:
INTERNATIONAL CHAMPIONSHIPS 1903-72**

MEN

1903-4 Alfred Shrubb (Eng)
1905 Albert Aldridge (Eng)
1906 Charles Straw (Eng)
1907 Adam Underwood (Eng)
1908 Archie Robertson (Eng)
1909-10 Edward Wood (Eng)
1911-3 Jean Bouin (Fra)
1914 Arthur Nicholls (Eng)
1920 James Wilson (Sco)
1921 Walter Freeman (Eng)
1922 Joseph Guillemot (Fra)
1923 Charles Blewitt (Eng)
1924 William 'Joe' Cotterell (Eng)
1925 Jack Webster (Eng)
1926 Ernest Harper (Eng)
1927 Lewis Payne (Eng)
1928 Harry Eckersley (Eng)
1929 William 'Joe' Cotterell (Eng)
1930 Thomas Evenson (Eng)
1931 Tim Smythe (Ire)
1932 Thomas Evenson (Eng)
1933-5 Jack Holden (Eng)
1936 William Eaton (Eng)
1937 James Flockhart (Sco)
1938 John Emery (Eng)
1939 Jack Holden (Eng)

1946-7 Raphael Pujazon (Fra)
1948 John Doms (Bel)
1949 Alain Mimoun (Fra)
1950 Lucien Theys (Bel)
1951 Geoffrey Saunders (Eng)
1952 Alain Mimoun (Fra)
1953 Franjo Mihalic (Yug)
1954 Alain Mimoun (Fra)
1955 Frank Sando (Eng)
1956 Alain Mimoun (Fra)
1957 Frank Sando (Eng)
1958 Stan Eldon (Eng)
1959 Fred Norris (Eng)
1960 Rhadi ben Abdesselem (Mor)
1961 Basil Heatley (Eng)
1962 Gaston Roelants (Bel)
1963 Roy Fowler (Eng)
1964 Francesco Arizmendi (Spa)
1965 Jean Fayolle (Fra)
1966 Ben Assou El Ghazi (Mor)
1967 Gaston Roelants (Bel)
1968 Mohammed Gammoudi (Tun)
1969 Gaston Roelants (Bel)
1970 Michael Tagg (Eng)
1971 David Bedford (Eng)
1972 Gaston Roelants (Bel)

WOMEN
1967-71 Doris Brown (USA)
1972 Joyce Smith (Eng)

INDIVIDUAL CHAMPIONS – WORLD CHAMPIONSHIPS FROM 1973

Year	MEN	WOMEN
1973	Pekka Paivarinta (Fin)	Paola Cacchi (Ita)
1974	Eric De Beck (Bel)	Paola Cacchi (Ita)
1975	Ian Stewart (Sco)	Julie Brown (USA)
1976	Carlos Lopes (Por)	Carmen Valero (Spa)
1977	Leon Schots (Bel)	Carmen Valero (Spa)
1978	John Treacy (Ire)	Grete Waitz (Nor)
1979	John Treacy (Ire)	Grete Waitz (Nor)
1980	Craig Virgin (USA)	Grete Waitz (Nor)
1981	Craig Virgin (USA)	Grete Waitz (Nor)
1982	Mohamed Kedir (Eth)	Maricica Puica (Rom)
1983	Bekele Debele (Eth)	Grete Waitz (Nor)
1984	Carlos Lopes (Por)	Maricica Puica (Rom)
1985	Carlos Lopes (Por)	Zola Budd (Eng)
1986	John Ngugi (Ken)	Zola Budd (Eng
1987	John Ngugi (Ken)	Annette Sergent (Fra)

MEN
Most wins: 4 Jack Holden (Eng), Alain Mimoun (Fra), Gaston Roelants (Bel).
Most placings in first three: 7 Gaston Roelants four wins, three second.
Most placings in first ten: 10 Jack Holden 1930-46
Most appearances: 20 Marcel Van de Wattyne 1946-65

WOMEN
Most wins: 5 Doris Brown (USA), Grete Waitz (Nor).
Most placings in first three: 7 Grete Waitz five wins, two third.
Most placings in first ten: 7 Grete Waitz 1978-84
Most appearances: 16 Jean Lochhead (Wal) 1967-84
Greatest winning margins:
MEN: 56 sec Jack Holden (Eng) 1934
WOMEN: 40 sec Grete Waitz (Nor) 1980

ENGLISH NATIONAL CROSS-COUNTRY CHAMPIONSHIP

The 'National' is the oldest and largest of all national cross-country championships. It was first held in 1876, when all 32 runners went off course and the race was declared void. Held annually since then, apart from the war years; there was a peak field in the senior race of 2006 finishers and 223 teams in 1987.

Most wins (individual): 4 Percy Stenning 1877-80, Alfred Shrubb 1901-4; 3 Edward Parry 1888-9, 1891; Jack Holden 1938-9, 1946; Frank Aaron 1949-51; Gordon Pirie 1953-5; Basil Heatley 1960-1, 1963.

Recent winners:
1980 Nick Rose
1981 Julian Goater
1982 David Clarke
1984 Eamonn Martin
1983 Tim Hutchings
1985 David Lewis
1986 Tim Hutchings
1987 David Clarke

Most wins (team): 28 Birchfield Harriers; 6 Salford Harriers, Tipton Harriers, Gateshead Harriers.

The English women's cross-country championships were first held in 1927.
Most wins (individual): 6 Lillian Styles 1928-30, 1933-4, 1937; 5 Rita Ridley 1969-72, 1974; 4 Diane Leather 1953-6; Pam Davies 1965-8.

Recent winners:
1980 Ruth Smeeth
1981 Wendy Smith
1982 Paula Fudge
1983 Christine Benning
1984 Jane Furniss
1985 Angela Tooby
1986 Carole Bradford
1987 Jane Shields (née Furniss)

Most wins (team): 12 Birchfield Harriers, 7 London Olympiades, 6 Ilford, Sale Harriers

AUSTRALIAN RULES FOOTBALL

A predominantly kicking game, played by teams of 18-a-side. Its principal initiators were Henry Colden Harrison and Thomas Wills, who helped to form the Melbourne Football Club in 1858. In 1877 the Victorian Football Association was founded, from which eight clubs broke away to form the Victorian Football League (VFL). Four more teams had been admitted by 1925, and in 1987 teams from Queensland and Western Australia joined the league.

AUSTRALIAN NATIONAL FOOTBALL LEAGUE CHAMPIONSHIP

The first inter-state game was between Victoria and South Australia in 1879 and the first inter-state carnival in 1908.

Winners:
Victoria 1908, 1914, 1924, 1927, 1930, 1933, 1937, 1947, 1950, 1953, 1956, 1958, 1966, 1969, 1972, 1980
South Australia 1911, 1985
Western Australia 1921, 1961, 1979, 1983, 1984, 1986

NATIONAL FOOTBALL LEAGUE

Contested by the leading teams from all over Australia. First held in 1976, but Victoria withdrew in 1977-8, when it ran its own Premiership series (winners: 1977 Hawthorn, 1978 Fitzroy).

Winners:
1976 Hawthorn (Vic)
1977 Norwood (SA)
1978 South Adelaide (SA)
1979 Collingwood (Vic)
1980 North Melbourne (Vic)
1981 Essendon (Vic)
1982 Sydney Swans (NSW)
1983 Carlton (Vic)
1984 Essendon (Vic)
1985-6 Hawthorn (Vic)

VICTORIAN FOOTBALL LEAGUE

Australia's premier game is the VFL final for the Premiership Cup held annually at the Melbourne Cricket Ground, for which the attendance record is 121,696 in 1970.

Premiership wins:

14	Carlton	1906-8, 1914-5, 1938, 1945, 1947, 1968, 1970, 1972, 1979, 1981-2
14	Essendon	1897, 1901, 1911-2, 1923-4, 1942, 1946, 1949-50, 1962, 1965, 1984-5
13	Collingwood	1902-3, 1910, 1917, 1919, 1927-30, 1935-6, 1953, 1958
12	Melbourne	1900, 1926, 1939-41, 1948, 1955-7, 1959-60, 1964
10	Richmond	1920-1, 1932, 1934, 1943, 1967, 1969, 1973-4, 1980
8	Fitzroy	1898-9, 1904-5, 1913, 1916, 1922, 1944
6	Geelong	1925, 1931, 1937, 1951-2, 1963
6	Hawthorn	1961, 1971, 1976, 1978, 1983, 1986
3	South Melbourne	1909, 1918, 1933
2	North Melbourne	1975, 1977
1	Footscray	1954, St Kilda 1966

VFL Records:
Highest aggregate score: 345 St Kilda beat Melbourne 204-141, 6 May 1978
Record margin in Grand Final: 83 Hawthorn beat Essendon 140-57, 26 Sep 1983
Goals in career: 2191 Peter Hudson 1963-81
Goals in season: 150 Bob Pratt (South Melbourne) 1934, Peter Hudson (Hawthorn) 1971
Goals in Grand Final: 9 Gordon Coventry for Collingwood v Richmond 1928
Most games: 403 Kevin Bartlett (Richmond) 1965-83

Most premierships:
South Australia: 27 Port Adelaide 1884-1981
Western Australia: 26 East Fremantle 1900-85

BADMINTON

The name of the game comes from its playing at Badminton House in England by the family and guests of the Duke of Beaufort in the 19th century. Its origins, however, are most directly from the children's game of battledore and shuttlecock, and a similar game was played in China over two thousand years ago. Badminton was played considerably by Army officers in the 1870s in India, where the first modern rules were codified.

The Badminton Association was founded in England in 1893. The world governing body is the International Badminton Federation, formed in 1934.

THOMAS CUP

The international team competition for men's teams of six players who play five singles and four doubles in each contest, held every three years until 1982 when it became a biennial event. The cup was donated by Sir George Thomas, winner of 21 All-England titles, in 1940 but the competition could not start until after the war.

Winners:

1949	Malaya	1970	Indonesia
1952	Malaya	1973	Indonesia
1955	Malaya	1976	Indonesia
1958	Indonesia	1979	Indonesia
1961	Indonesia	1982	China
1964	Indonesia	1984	Indonesia
1967	Malaysia	1986	China

Most wins: 8 Indonesia

UBER CUP

The women's equivalent of the Thomas Cup, it was also contested triennially until 1984 when it became a biennial event. The cup was presented by Betty Uber who represented England a then record 37 times between 1926 and 1951. Each tie consists of three singles and four doubles.

Winners:

1957	United States	1975	Indonesia
1960	United States	1978	Japan
1963	United States	1981	Japan
1966	Japan	1984	China
1969	Japan	1986	China
1972	Japan		

Most wins: 5 Japan

WORLD CHAMPIONSHIPS

Instituted in 1977 and initially held every three years, but now held biennially.

Rudy Hartono (All-Sport)

Winners:

MEN'S SINGLES
1977 Flemming Delfs (Den)
1980 Rudy Hartono (Ina)
1983 Icuk Sugiarto (Ina)
1985 Han Jian (Chn)
1987 Yang Yang (Chn)

WOMEN'S SINGLES
1977 Lene Koppen (Den)
1980 Wiharjo Verawaty (Ina)
1983 Li Lingwei (Chn)
1985 Han Aiping (Chn)
1987 Han Aiping (Chn)

MEN'S DOUBLES
1977 Johan Wahjudi & Tjun Tjun (Ina)
1980 Ade Chandra & Hadinata Christian (Ina)
1983 Steen Fladberg & Jesper Helledie (Den)
1985 Park Joo Bong & Kim Moon Soo (SKo)
1987 Li Yongbo & Tian Bingyi (Chn)

WOMEN'S DOUBLES
1977 Etsuko Tuganoo & Emiko Vero (Jap)
1980 Nora Perry & Jane Webster (UK)
1983 Lin Ying & Wu Dixi (Chn)
1985 Han Aiping & Li Lingwei (Chn)
1987 Lin Ying & Guan Weizhen (Chn)

MIXED DOUBLES
1977 Steen Stovgaard & Lene Koppen (Den)
1980 Hadinata Christian & Imelda Wigoeno (Ina)
1983 Thomas Kihlstrom (Swe) & Nora Perry (UK)
1985 Park Joo Bong & Yoo Sang Hee (SKo)
1987 Wang Pengrin & Shi Fangjing (Chn)
Most titles: 3 Han Aiping

ALL ENGLAND CHAMPIONSHIPS
MEN'S SINGLES
1900 Sydney Smith (Eng)
1901 H. Davies (Eng)
1902-3 Ralph Watling (Eng)
1904-5 H. Marrett (Eng)
1906-7 Norman Wood (Eng)
1908 H. Marrett (Eng)
1909-10 Frank Chesterton (Eng)
1911-2 George Sautter (Eng)
1920-3 George Thomas (Eng)
1924 'Curly' Mack (Ire)
1925-9 Frank Devlin (Ire)
1930 Donald Hume (Eng)
1931 Frank Devlin (Ire)
1932 Ralph Nichols (Eng)
1933 Raymond White (Eng)
1934 Ralph Nichols (Eng)
1935 Raymond White (Eng)
1936-8 Ralph Nichols (Eng)
1939 Tage Madsen (Den)
1947 Conny Jepsen (Swe)
1948 Jörn Skaarup (Den)
1949 Dave Freeman (USA)
1950-2 Wong Peng Soon (Mal)
1953-4 Eddie Choong (Mal)
1955 Wong Peng Soon (Mal)
1956-7 Eddie Choong (Mal)
1958 Erland Kops (Den)
1959 Tan Joe Hok (Ina)
1960-3 Erland Kops (Den)
1964 Knud Nielsen (Den)
1965 Erland Kops (Den)
1966 Tan Aik Huang (Mal)
1967 Erland Kops (Den)
1968-74 Rudy Hartono (Ina)
1975 Svend Pri (Den)
1976 Rudy Hartono (Ina)
1977 Flemming Delfs (Den)
1978-9 Liem Swie King (Ina)
1980 Prakash Padukone (Ina)
1981 Liem Swie King (Ina)
1982 Morten Frost (Den)
1983 Luan Jin (Chn)
1984 Morten Frost (Den)
1985 Zhao Jianhua (Chn)
1986-7 Morten Frost (Den)
Most wins: 8 Rudy Hartono (Ina)

MEN'S DOUBLES
1899 D Oakes & Stewart Massey (Eng)
1900-2 H Mellersh & F Collier (Eng)
1903 Stewart Massey & E Huson (Eng)
1904 A Prebble & H Marrett (Eng)
1905 Stewart Massey & C Barnes (Eng)
1906 George Thomas & H Marrett (Eng)
1907 A Prebble & Norman Wood (Eng)
1908 George Thomas & H Marrett (Eng)

1909 A Prebble & Frank Chesterton (Eng)
1910 George Thomas & H Marrett (Eng)
1911 P Fitton & Edward Hawthorn (Eng)
1912 George Thomas & H Marrett (Eng)
1913-4 George Thomas & Frank Chesterton (Eng)
1920 Alfred Engelbach & Robert du Roveray (Eng)
1921 George Thomas & Francis Hodge (Eng)
1922 Frank Devlin (Ire) & George Sautter (Eng)
1923 Frank Devlin & 'Curly' Mack (Ire)
1924 George Thomas & Francis Hodge (Eng)
1925 Herbert Huber & A Jones (Eng)
1926-7 Frank Devlin & 'Curly' Mack (Ire)
1928 George Thomas & Francis Hodge (Eng)
1929-31 Frank Devlin & 'Curly' Mack (Ire)
1932-5 Donald Hume & Raymond White (Eng)
1936-8 Ralph Nichols & Leslie Nichols (Eng)
1939 Tom Boyle & James Rankin (Ire)
1947 Tage Madsen & Poul Holm (Den)
1948 Preben Dabelsteen & Borge Fredricksen (Den)
1949 Ooi Teik Hock & Teoh Seng Khoon (Mal)
1950 Preben Dabelsteen & Jörn Skaarup (Den)
1951-3 Eddie Choong & David Choong (Mal)
1954 Ooi Teik Hock & Ong Poh Lim (Mal)
1955-6 Finn Kobbero & Jurgen Hammergaard Hansen
    (Den)
1957 Joseph Alston (USA) & Hock Aun Heah (Mal)
1958 Erland Kops & Per Nielsen (Den)
1959 Lim Say Hup & Teh Kew San (Mal)
1960 Finn Kobbero & Per Neilsen (Den)
1961-4 Finn Kobbero & Jurgen Hammergaard Hansen
    (Den)
1965-6 Ng Boon Bee & Tan Yee Khan (Mal)
1967-9 Erland Kops & Henning Borch (Den)
1970 Tom Backer & Paul Petersen (Den)
1971 Ng Boon Bee & Punch Gunalan (Mal)
1972-3 Hadinata Christian & Ade Chandra (Ina)
1974-5 Tjun Tjun & Johan Wahjudi (Ina)
1976 Bengt Froman & Thomas Kihlstrom (Swe)
1977-80 Tjun Tjun & Johan Wahjudi (Ina)
1981 Hariamanto Kartono & Rudy Heryanto (Ina)
1982 Razif Sidek & Jalaini Sidek (Mal)
1983 Stefan Karlsson & Thomas Kihlstrom (Swe)
1984 Hariamanto Kartono & Rudy Heryanto (Ina)
1985-6 Kim Moon-Soo & Park Joo-Bong (SKo)
1987 Li Yongbo & Tian Bingyi (Chn)

WOMEN'S SINGLES

1900-1 Ethel Thomson (Eng)
1902 Meriel Lucas (Eng)
1903-4 Ethel Thomson (Eng)
1905 Meriel Lucas (Eng)
1906 Ethel Thomson (Eng)
1907-10 Meriel Lucas (Eng)
1911 Margaret Larminie (Eng)
1912 Margaret Tragett (née Larminie) (Eng)
1913-4 Lavinia Radeglia (Eng)
1920-2 Kitty McKane (Eng)
1923 Lavinia Radeglia (Eng)
1924 Kitty McKane (Eng)
1925 Margaret Stocks (Eng)
1926-7 Marjorie Barrett (Eng)
1928 Margaret Tragett (Eng)
1929-31 Marjorie Barrett (Eng)
1932 Leonie Kingsbury (Eng)

Lene Koppen, the first women's world champion.
(All-Sport)

1933 Alice Woodroffe (Eng)
1934 Leonie Kingsbury (Eng)
1935 Betty Uber (Eng)
1936-7 Thelma Kingsbury (Eng)
1938 Daphne Young (Eng)
1939 Dorothy Walton (Can)
1947 Marie Ussing (Den)
1948 Kirsten Thorndahl (Den)
1949 Aase Jacobsen (Den)
1950 Tonny Olsen-Ahm (Den)
1951 Aase Jacobsen (Den)
1952 Tonny Olsen-Ahm (Den)
1953 Marie Ussing (Den)
1954 Judy Devlin (USA)
1955-6 Margaret Varner (USA)
1957-8 Judy Devlin (USA)
1959 Heather Ward (Eng)
1960 Judy Devlin (USA)
1961-4 Judy Hashman (née Devlin)(USA)
1965 Ursula Smith (Eng)
1966-7 Judy Hashman (USA)
1968 Eva Twedberg (Swe)
1969 Hiroe Yuki (Jap)
1970 Etsuko Takenaka (Jap)
1971 Eva Twedberg (Swe)
1972 Noriko Nakayama (Jap)
1973 Margaret Beck (Eng)

1974-5 Hiroe Yuki (Jap)
1976 Gillian Gilks (Eng)
1977 Hiroe Yuki (Jap)
1978 Gillian Gilks (Eng)
1979-80 Lene Köppen (Den)
1981 Sun Ai Hwang (SKo)
1982-3 Zang Ailing (Chn)
1984 Li Lingwei (Chn)
1985 Han Aiping (Chn)
1986 Kim Yun-Ja (SKo)
1987 Kirsten Larsen (Den)

Most wins: 10 Judy Hashman (née Devlin)(USA)

WOMEN'S DOUBLES
1899-1900 Meriel Lucas & Miss Graeme (Eng)
1901 Miss St.John & E Moseley (Eng)
1902 Meriel Lucas & Ethel Thomson (Eng)
1903 M Hardy & Dorothea Douglass (Eng)
1904-6 Meriel Lucas & Ethel Thomson (Eng)
1907-9 Meriel Lucas & G Murray (Eng)
1910 Mary Bateman & Meriel Lucas (Eng)
1911-2 Alice Gowenlock & Dorothy Cundall (Eng)
1913 Hazel Hogarth & Mary Bateman (Eng)
1914 Margaret Tragett (née Larminie) & Eveline
       Peterson (Eng)
1920 Lavinia Radeglia & Violet Elton (Eng)
1921 Kitty McKane & Margaret McKane (Eng)
1922-3 Margaret Tragett & Hazel Hogarth (Eng)
1924 Margaret Stocks (née McKane) & Kitty McKane
       (Eng)
1925 Margaret Tragett & Hazel Hogarth (Eng)
1926 A Head & Violet Elton (Eng)
1927 Margaret Tragett & Hazel Hogarth (Eng)
1928-30 Marjorie Barrett & Violet Elton (Eng)
1931 Betty Uber & Marianne Horsley (Eng)
1932 Marjorie Barrett & Leonie Kingbury (Eng)
1933-6 Thelma Kingsbury & Marjorie Bell-Henderson
       (Eng)
1937-8 Betty Uber & Diana Doveton (Eng)
1939 Ruth Dalsgard & Tonny Olsen (Den)
1947-8 Tonny Olsen-Ahm & Kirsten Thorndahl (Den)
1949 Betty Uber & Queenie Allen (Eng)
1950-1 Tonny Olsen-Ahm & Kirsten Thorndahl (Den)
1952 Tonny Olsen-Ahn & Aase Jacobsen (Den)
1953 Iris Cooley & June White (Eng)
1954 Judy Devlin & Susan Devlin (USA)
1955 Iris Cooley & June White (Eng)
1956 Judy Devlin & Susan Devlin (USA)
1957 Kirsten Granlund (née Thorndahl) & Ami
       Hammergaard Hansen (Den)
1958 Margaret Varner & Heather Ward (Eng)
1959 Iris Cooley-Rogers & June White-Timperley (Eng)
1960 Judy Devlin & Susan Devlin (USA)
1961 Judy Hashman (née Devlin)(USA) & Susan Peard
       (née Devlin)(Ire)
1962 Judy Hashman (USA) & Tonny Holst-Christensen
       (Den)
1963 Judy Hashman (USA) & Susan Peard (Ire)
1964-5 Karen Jorgensen & Ulla Rasmussen (Den)
1966 Judy Hashman(USA) & Susan Peard (Ire)
1967 Irme Rietveld (Hol) & Ulla Strand (née
       Rasmussen)(Den)
1968 Retno Koestijah & Miss Minarni (Ina)
1969-70 Margaret Boxall & Sue Whetnall (Eng)

1971 Noriko Takagi & Hiroe Yuki (Jap)
1972-3 Machiko Aizawa & Etsuko Takenaka (Jap)
1974 Margaret Beck & Gillian Gilks (Eng)
1975 Machiko Aizawa & Etsuko Takenaka (Jap)
1976 Gillian Gilks & Sue Whetnall (Eng)
1977 Etsuko Tuganoo (née Takenaka) & Emiko Ueno
       (Jap)
1978 Atsuko Tokuda & Mikiko Takada (Jap)
1979 Wiharjo Verawaty & Imelda Wigoeno (Ina)
1980 Gillian Gilks & Nora Perry (Eng)
1981 Nora Perry & Jane Webster (Eng)
1982 Lin Ying & Wu Dixi (Chn)
1983 Xu Rong & Wu Jianqiu (Chn)
1984 Lin Ying & Wu Dixi (Chn)
1985 Li Lingwei & Han Aiping (Chn)
1986-7 Chung Myung-Hee & Hwang Hye-Young (SKo)

MIXED DOUBLES
1899-1900 D Oakes & Miss St.John (Eng)
1901 F Collier & Miss E Stawell-Brown (Eng)
1902 L Ransford & Miss E Moseley (Eng)
1903 George Thomas & Ethel Thomson (Eng)
1904 H Marrett & Dorothea Douglass (Eng)
1905 H Marrett & Hazel Hogarth (Eng)
1906 George Thomas & Ethel Thomson (Eng)
1907 Gearge Thomas & Miss G Murray (Eng)
1908 Norman Wood & Meriel Lucas (Eng)
1909 A Prebble & Dora Boothby (Eng)
1910 George Sautter & Dorothy Cundall (Eng)
1911 George Thomas & Margaret Larminie (Eng)
1912 Edward Hawthorn & Hazel Hogarth (Eng)
1913 George Sautter & Miss M Mayston (Eng)
1914 George Thomas & Hazel Hogarth (Eng)
1920-2 George Thomas & Hazel Hogarth (Eng)
1923 'Curly' Mack (Ire) & Margaret Tragett (née
       Larminie) (Eng)
1924-5 Frank Devlin (Ire) & Kitty McKane (Eng)
1926-7 Frank Devlin (Ire) & Eveline Peterson (Eng)
1928 A Harbot & Margaret Tragett (Eng)
1929 Frank Devlin (Ire) & Marianne Horseley (Eng)
1930-2 Herbert Uber & Betty Uber (Eng)
1933-6 Donald Hume & Betty Uber (Eng)
1937 Ian Maconachie (Ire) & Thelma Kingsbury (Eng)
1938 Raymond White & Betty Uber (Eng)
1939 Ralph Nichols & Bessie Staples (Eng)
1947 Poul Holm & Tonny Olsen-Ahm (Den)
1948 Jörn Skaarup & Kirsten Thorndahl (Den)
1949 Cliton Stephens & Patsey Stephens (USA)
1950-2 Poul Holm & Tonny Olsen-Ahm (Den)
1953 Eddie Choong (Mal) & June White (Eng)
1954 John Best & Iris Cooley (Eng)
1955 Finn Kobbero & Kirsten Thorndahl (Den)
1956 Tony Jordan & June Timperley (née White)(Eng)
1957 Finn Kobbero & Kirsten Granlund (née Thorndal)
       (Den)
1958 Tony Jordan & June Timperley (Eng)
1959 Per Nielsen & Mrs.I Hansen (Den)
1960-1 Finn Kobbero & Kirsten Granlund (Den)
1962-3 Finn Kobbero & Ulla Ramussen (Den)
1964 Tony Jordan & Jennifer Pritchard (Eng)
1965-6 Finn Kobbero & Ulla Strand (née Ramussen)
       (Den)
1967 Svend Andersen & Ulla Strand (Den)
1968 Tony Jordan & Sue Pound (Eng)

1969 Roger Mills & Gillian Perrin (Eng)
1970 Per Walsöe & Pernille Mölgaard Hansen (Den)
1971-2 Svend Pri (formerly Andersen) & Ulla Strand (Den)
1973 Derek Talbot & Gillian Gilks (Eng)
1974 David Eddy & Sue Whetnall (Eng)
1975 Elliott Stuart & Nora Gardner (Eng)
1976-7 Derek Talbot & Gillian Gillks (Eng)
1978 Mike Tredgett & Nora Perry (née Gardner) (Eng)
1979 Hadinata Christian & Imelda Wigoeno (Ina)
1980-1 Mike Tredgett & Nora Perry (Eng)
1982 Martin Dew & Gillian Gilks (Eng)
1983 Thomas Kihlstrom (Swe) & Nora Perry (Eng)
1984 Martin Dew & Gillian Gilks (Eng)
1985 Billy Gillibrand & Nora Perry (Eng)
1986 Park Joo-Bong & Chung Myung-Hee (SKo)
1987 Lee Deuk-Choon & Chung Myung-Hee (SKo)

Most titles:

MEN
21 George Thomas 1903-28
    4 singles, 9 men's doubles, 8 mixed doubles
18 Frank Devlin 1922-31
    6 singles, 7 men's doubles, 5 mixed doubles

WOMEN
17 Meriel Lucas 1899-1910
    6 singles, 10 women's doubles, 1 mixed doubles
17 Judy Hashman (née Devlin) 1954-67
    10 singles, 7 women's doubles

Champions who won Wimbledon titles at Lawn Tennis:
MEN: Sydney Smith 1900-6
WOMEN: Ethel Larcombe (née Thomson) 1900-14;
Dorothea Lambert Chambers (née Douglass) 1903-14;
Dora Boothby 1909-13; Kitty Godfree (née McKane)
1920-6

BANDY

An 11-a-side game similar to hockey but played on
ice-covered pitches. Unlike ice hockey, however, bandy is
played with a ball rather than a puck. It may have
originated in England c.1790, but is now played principally
in the Baltic regions.
  World Championships are held biennially, first in 1957.
The USSR have won 12 titles, every one from 1957, except
for 1981, 1983 and 1987 when the winners were
Sweden.
The record score in a World Championship match: USSR
beat USA 21-1 at Skövde on 1 Feb 1987.

BASEBALL

The English believe that Baseball is derived from the very
English game of Rounders. The Americans, however, are
adamant that Abner Doubleday, a West Point cadet, laid
out the first 'diamond' at Cooperstown in 1839. A special
commission was set up in the United States in 1905 to
establish the true 'birth' of Baseball, and their findings
credited it to Doubleday. The first rules were drawn up by
Alexander Cartwright Jr in 1845 and the first match under
the Cartwright rules was a year later between the New
York Base Ball Club and the sport's first organised club,
the New York Knickerbockers.

WORLD SERIES

There are two Baseball leagues in America, the National
League (NL) which was formed in 1876 and the American
League (AL) which was formed in 1901. A total of 26
teams make up the two leagues and after a regular season
of 162 matches against other teams in their own league, a
series of play-offs decides which team shall represent each
league in the best-of-seven game World Series played
each October.

Peter Rose holds the major league record for the most base hits in a career. (All-Sport)

Year	Winners	Runners-up	Score
1903	Boston Red Sox (AL)	Pittsburgh Pirates (NL)	5-3
1904	Not held		
1905	New York Giants (NL)	Philadelphia Athletics (AL)	4-1
1906	Chicago White Sox (AL)	Chicago Cubs (NL)	4-2
1907	Chicago Cubs (NL)	Detroit Tigers (AL)	4-0*
1908	Chicago Cubs (NL)	Detroit Tigers (AL)	4-1
1909	Pittsburgh Pirates (NL)	Detroit Tigers (AL)	4-3
1910	Philadelphia Athletics (AL)	Chicago Cubs (NL)	4-1
1911	Philadelphia Athletics (AL)	New York Giants (NL)	4-2
1912	Boston Red Sox (AL)	New York Giants (NL)	4-3*
1913	Philadelphia Athletics (AL)	New York Giants (NL)	4-1
1914	Boston Braves (NL)	Philadelphia Athletics (AL)	4-0
1915	Boston Red Sox (AL)	Philadelphia Phillies (NL)	4-1
1916	Boston Red Sox (AL)	Brooklyn Dodgers (NL)	4-1
1917	Chicago White Sox (AL)	New York Giants (NL)	4-2
1918	Boston Red Sox (AL)	Chicago Cubs (NL)	4-2
1919	Cincinnati Reds (NL)	Chicago White Sox (AL)	5-3
1920	Cleveland Indians (AL)	Brooklyn Dodgers (NL)	5-2
1921	New York Giants (NL)	New York Yankees (AL)	4-3
1922	New York Giants (NL)	New York Yankees (AL)	4-0*
1923	New York Yankees (AL)	New York Giants (NL)	4-2
1924	Washington Senators (AL)	New York Giants (NL)	4-3
1925	Pittsburgh Pirates (NL)	Washington Senators (AL)	4-3
1926	St.Louis Cardinals (NL)	New York Yankees (AL)	4-3
1927	New York Yankees (AL)	Pittsburgh Pirates (NL)	4-0
1928	New York Yankees (AL)	St.Louis Cardinals (NL)	4-0
1929	Philadelphia Athletics (AL)	Chicago Cubs (NL)	4-1
1930	Philadelphia Athletics (AL)	St.Louis Cardinals (NL)	4-2
1931	St.Louis Cardinals (NL)	Philadelphia Athletics (AL)	4-3
1932	New York Yankees (AL)	Chicago Cubs (NL)	4-0
1933	New York Giants (NL)	Washington Senators (AL)	4-1
1934	St.Louis Cardinals (NL)	Detroit Tigers (AL)	4-3
1935	Detroit Tigers (AL)	Chicago Cubs (NL)	4-2
1936	New York Yankees (AL)	New York Giants (NL)	4-2
1937	New York Yankees (AL)	New York Giants (NL)	4-1
1938	New York Yankees (AL)	Chicago Cubs (NL)	4-0
1939	New York Yankees (AL)	Cincinnati Reds (NL)	4-0
1940	Cincinnati Reds (NL)	Detroit Tigers (AL)	4-3
1941	New York Yankees (AL)	Brooklyn Dodgers (NL)	4-1
1942	St.Louis Cardinals (NL)	New York Yankees (AL)	4-1
1943	New York Yankees (AL)	St.Louis Cardinals (NL)	4-1
1944	St.Louis Cardinals (NL)	St.Louis Browns (AL)	4-2
1945	Detroit Tigers (AL)	Chicago Cubs (NL)	4-3
1946	St.Louis Cardinals (NL)	Boston Red Sox (AL)	4-3
1947	New York Yankees (AL)	Brooklyn Dodgers (NL)	4-3
1948	Cleveland Indians (AL)	Boston Braves (NL)	4-2
1949	New York Yankees (AL)	Brooklyn Dodgers (NL)	4-1
1950	New York Yankees (AL)	Philadelphia Phillies (NL)	4-0
1951	New York Yankees (AL)	New York Giants (NL)	4-2
1952	New York Yankees (AL)	Brooklyn Dodgers (NL)	4-3
1953	New York Yankees (AL)	Brooklyn Dodgers (NL)	4-2
1954	New York Giants (NL)	Cleveland Indians (AL)	4-0
1955	Brooklyn Dodgers (NL)	New York Yankees (AL)	4-3
1956	New York Yankees (AL)	Brooklyn Dodgers (NL)	4-3
1957	Milwaukee Braves (NL	New York Yankees (AL)	4-3
1958	New York Yankees (AL)	Milwaukee Braves (NL)	4-3
1959	Los Angeles Dodgers (NL)	Chicago White Sox (AL)	4-2
1960	Pittsburgh Pirates (NL)	New York Yankees (AL)	4-3
1961	New York Yankees (AL)	Cincinnati Reds (NL)	4-1
1962	New York Yankees (AL)	San Francisco Giants (NL)	4-3
1963	Los Angeles Dodgers (NL)	New York Yankees (AL)	4-0
1964	St.Louis Cardinals (NL)	New York Yankees (AL)	4-3
1965	Los Angeles Dodgers (NL)	Minnesota Twins (AL)	4-3

1966 Baltimore Orioles (AL)	Los Angeles Dodgers (NL)	4-0
1967 St.Louis Cardinals (NL)	Boston Red Sox (AL)	4-3
1968 Detroit Tigers (AL)	St.Louis Cardinals (NL)	4-3
1969 New York Mets (NL)	Baltimore Orioles (AL)	4-1
1970 Baltimore Orioles (AL)	Cincinnati Reds (NL)	4-1
1971 Pittsburgh Pirates (NL)	Baltimore Orioles (AL)	4-3
1972 Oakland 'A's (AL)	Cincinnati Reds (NL)	4-3
1973 Oakland 'A's (AL)	New York Mets (NL)	4-3
1974 Oakland 'A's (AL)	Los Angeles Dodgers (NL)	4-1
1975 Cincinnati Reds (NL)	Boston Red Sox (AL)	4-3
1976 Cincinnati Reds (NL)	New York Yankees (AL)	4-0
1977 New York Yankees (AL)	Los Angeles Dodgers (NL)	4-3
1978 New York Yankees (AL)	Los Angeles Dodgers (NL)	4-2
1979 Pittsburgh Pirates (NL)	Baltimore Orioles (AL)	4-3
1980 Philadelphia Phillies (NL)	Kansas City Royals (AL)	4-2
1981 Los Angeles Dodgers (NL)	New York Yankees (AL)	4-2
1982 St.Louis Cardinals (NL)	Milwaukee Brewers (AL)	4-3
1983 Baltimore Orioles (AL)	Philadelphia Phillies (NL)	4-1
1984 Detroit Tigers (AL)	San Diego Padres (NL)	4-1
1985 Kansas City Royals (AL)	St.Louis Cardinals (NL)	4-3
1986 New York Mets (NL)	Boston Red Sox (AL)	4-3

* Includes one drawn game
(AL) American League (NL) National League

Most wins: 22 New York Yankees; 9 St.Louis Cardinals; 5 Boston Red Sox, Pittsburgh Pirates, Philadelphia Athletics; 4 New York Giants, Cincinnati Reds, Cleveland Indians, Detroit Tigers, Los Angeles Dodgers; 3 Baltimore Orioles, Oakland A's

Most individual appearances: 14 Lawrence 'Yogi' Berra (New York Yankees) 1947, 1949-53, 1955-8, 1960-3 (he was on the winning team 10 times)

Most home runs in one game: 3 'Babe' Ruth (New York Yankees v St.Louis Cardinals, 4th game) 6 Oct 1926; Reggie Jackson (New York Yankees v Los Angeles Dodgers, 6th game) 18 Oct 1977 (Jackson hit three consecutive pitches out of the park for his homers)

Most runs in a series: 10 Reggie Jackson (New York Yankees, 1977)

Most home runs in a series: 5 Reggie Jackson (New York Yankees, 1977)

Perfect pitch (9 innings): Don Larsen (New York Yankees v Brooklyn Dodgers, 5th game) 8 Oct 1956

Record attendance (Series): 420,784 Los Angeles Dodgers v Chicago White Sox 1-8 Oct 1959

Record attendance (single game): 92,706 Los Angeles Dodgers v Chicago White Sox (5th game) at Memorial Coliseum, Los Angeles, 6 Oct 1959

MOST VALUABLE PLAYER AWARD

The only men to have won the coveted award twice are: Sandy Koufax (Los Angeles, NL 1963, 1965); Bob Gibson (St.Louis NL, 1964, 1967); Reggie Jackson (Oakland AL, New York AL, 1973, 1977)

MAJOR LEAGUE RECORDS

Most National League titles (from 1876):
17 New York Giants; 16 Chicago Cubs; 14 St.Louis Cardinals; 12 Brooklyn Dodgers; 9 Boston Braves, Pittsburgh Pirates; 8 Los Angeles Dodgers
Most American League titles (from 1901):
33 New York Yankees; 10 Boston Red Sox; 9 Detroit Tigers, Philadelphia Athletics

BATTING

Career

Best batting average: .367 Ty Cobb (Detroit AL, Philadelphia AL) 1905-28
Most runs: 2245 Ty Cobb (Detroit AL, Philadelphia AL) 1905-28
Most home runs: 755 Hank Aaron (Milwaukee NL, Atlanta NL, Milwaukee AL) 1954-76
Most runs batted in: 2297 Hank Aaron (Milwaukee NL, Atlanta NL, Milwaukee AL) 1954-76
Most base hits: 4256 Pete Rose (Cincinatti NL, Philadelphia NL) 1963-86
Total bases: 6856 Hank Aaron (Milwaukee NL, Atlanta NL, Milwaukee AL) 1954-76
Stolen bases: 938 Louis Brock (Chicago NL, St.Louis NL) 1961-79

Season

Best batting average: .438 Hugh Duffy (Boston NL) 1894
Most runs: 196 William Hamilton (Philadelphia NL) 1894
Most home runs: 61 Roger Maris (New York AL) 1961
Most runs batted in: 190 Hack Wilson (Chicago NL) 1930
Most base hits: 257 George Sisler (St.Louis AL) 1920
Total bases: 457 Babe Ruth (New York AL) 1921
Stolen bases: 130 Rickey Henderson (Oakland AL) 1982

General

Consecutive hits: 12 Pinky Higgins (Boston AL) 19-21 Jun 1938; Moose Dropo (Detroit AL) 14-15 Jul 1952
Consecutive games batted safely: 56 Joe DiMaggio (New York AL) 15 May-16 Jul 1941
Consecutive games played: 2130 Lou Gehrig (New York AL) 1 Jun 1925-30 Apr 1939

PITCHING

Career

Games won: 511 Cy Young (Cleveland NL, St.Louis AL, Boston NL, Boston AL, Cleveland AL) 1890-1911
Shutouts: 113 Walter Johnson (Washington AL) 1907-27
Strikeouts: 4373 Nolan Ryan (New York NL, California AL, Houston NL) 1968-87
No-hit games: 5 Nolan Ryan (California AL, Houston NL) 1968-86

Complete games: 751 Cy Young (Cleveland NL, St.Louis AL, Boston NL, Boston AL, Cleveland AL) 1890-1911

Season

Games won: 60 Charles Radbourne (Providence NL) 1884

Shutouts: 16 George Bradley (St.Louis NL) 1876; Grover Alexander (Philadelphia NL) 1916

Strikeouts: 383 Nolan Ryan (California AL) 1973

General

Consecutive games won: 24 Carl Owen Hubbell (New York NL) 1936-7

LEAGUE LEADERS

Post-war leaders – taking the best of the AL or NL each year:

BEST BATTING AVERAGE

1946	Stan Musial (St.Louis)	NL	.365
1947	Harry Walker (St.Louis/ Philadelphia)	NL	.363
1948	Stan Musial (St.Louis)	NL	.376
1949	George Kell (Detroit)	AL	.343
1950	Billy Goodman (Boston)	AL	.354
1951	Stan Musial (St.Louis)	NL	.355
1952	Stan Musial (St.Louis)	NL	.336
1953	Carl Furillo (Brooklyn)	NL	.344
1954	Willie Mays (New York Giants)	NL	.345
1955	Al Kaline (Detroit)	AL	.340
1956	Mickey Mantle (NY Yankees)	AL	.353
1957	Ted Williams (Boston)	AL	.388
1958	Richie Ashburn (Philadelphia)	NL	.350
1959	Hank Aaron (Milwaukee)	NL	.355
1960	Dick Groat (Pittsburgh)	NL	.325
1961	Norm Cash (Detroit)	AL	.361
1962	Tommy Davis (Los Angeles)	NL	.346
1963	Tommy Davis (Los Angeles)	NL	.326
1964	Roberto Clemente (Pittsburgh)	NL	.339
1965	Roberto Clemente (Pittsburgh)	NL	.329
1966	Maria Alou (Pittsburgh)	NL	.342
1967	Roberto Clemente (Pittsburgh)	NL	.357
1968	Pete Rose (Cincinatti)	NL	.335
1969	Pete Rose (Cincinatti)	NL	.348
1970	Rico Carty (Atlanta)	NL	.366
1971	Joe Torre (St.Louis)	NL	.363
1972	Billy Williams (Chicago)	NL	.333
1973	Rod Carew (Minnesota)	AL	.350
1974	Rod Carew (Minnesota)	AL	.364
1975	Rod Carew (Minnesota)	AL	.359
1976	Bill Madlock (Chicago)	NL	.339
1977	Rod Carew (Minnesota)	AL	.388
1978	Dave Parker (Pittsburgh)	NL	.334
1979	Keith Hernandez (St.Louis)	NL	.344
1980	George Brett (Kansas City)	AL	.390
1981	Bill Madlock (Pittsburgh)	NL	.341
1982	Willie Watson (Kansas City)	AL	.332
1983	Wade Boggs (Boston)	AL	.361
1984	Tony Gwynn (San Diego)	NL	.341
1985	Wade Boggs (Boston)	AL	.368
1986	Wade Boggs (Boston	AL	.357

Highest ever average: .438 Hugh Duffy (Boston NL) 1894

AL best: .421 Napolean Lajoie (Philadelphia) 1901

Most seasons with best average:
In NL: 8 John P. Wagner (Pittsburgh) 1900, 1903-4, 1906-9, 1911; 7 Rogers Hornsby (St.Louis) 1920-5, 1928; Stan Musial (St.Louis) 1943, 1946, 1948, 1950-2, 1957
In AL: 9 Ty Cobb (Detroit) 1907-15; 7 Rod Carew (Minnesota) 1969, 1972-5, 1977-8; 6 Ted Williams (Boston) 1941-2, 1947-8, 1957-8

MOST HOME RUNS IN SEASON

1946	Hank Greenberg (Detroit)	AL	44
1947	Ralph Kiner (Pittsburgh) & Johnny Mize (New York Giants)	NL	51
1948	Ralph Kiner (Pittsburgh) & Johnny Mize (New York Giants)	NL	40
1949	Ralph Kiner (Pittsburgh)	NL	54
1950	Ralph Kiner (Pittsburgh)	NL	47
1951	Ralph Kiner (Pittsburgh)	NL	42
1952	Ralph Kiner (Pittsburgh) & Hank Sauer (Chicago)	NL	37
1953	Eddie Mathews (Milwaukee)	NL	47
1954	Ted Kluszewski (Cincinnati)	NL	49
1955	Willie Mays (New York Giants)	NL	51
1956	Mickey Mantle (NY Yankees)	NL	52
1957	Hank Aaron (Milwaukee)	NL	44
1958	Ernie Banks (Chicago)	NL	47
1959	Eddie Mathews (Milwaukee)	NL	46
1960	Ernie Banks (Chicago)	NL	41
1961	Orlando Cepeda (San Francisco)	NL	46
1962	Willie Mays (San Francisco)	NL	49
1963	Harmon Killebrew (Minnesota)	AL	45
1964	Harmon Killebrew (Minnesota)	AL	49
1965	Willie Mays (San Francisco)	NL	52
1966	Frank Robinson (Baltimore)	AL	49
1967	Carl Yastrzemski (Boston) & Harmon Killebrew (Minnesota)	AL	44
1968	Frank Howard (Washington)	AL	44
1969	Harmon Killebrew (Minnesota)	AL	49
1970	Johnny Bench (Cincinnati)	NL	45
1971	Willie Stargel (Pittsburgh)	NL	48
1972	Johnny Bench (Cincinnati)	NL	40
1973	Willie Stargel (Pittsburgh)	NL	44
1974	Mike Schmidt (Philadelphia)	NL	36
1975	Mike Schmidt (Philadelphia)	NL	38
1976	Mike Schmidt (Philadelphia)	NL	38
1977	George Foster (Cincinnati)	NL	52
1978	Jim Rice (Boston)	AL	46
1979	Dave Kingman (Chicago)	NL	48
1980	Mike Schmidt (Philadelphia)	NL	48
1981	Mike Schmidt (Philadelphia)	NL	31
1982	Gorman Thomas (Milwaukee) & Reggie Jackson (California)	AL	39
1983	Mike Schmidt (Philadelphia)	NL	40
1984	Tony Armas (Boston)	AL	43
1985	Darrell Evans (Detroit)	AL	60
1986	Jesse Barfield (Toronto)	AL	40

Most seasons leading NL: 8 Mike Schmidt (Philadelphia) 1974-6, 1980-1, 1983-4, 1986; 7 Ralph Kiner (Pittsburgh) 1946-52; 6 Melvin Ott (New York) 1932, 1934, 1936-8, 1942)

Most seasons leading AL: 12 Babe Ruth (New York) 1918-21, 1923-4, 1926-31; 6 Harmon Killebrew (Minnesota) 1959, 1962-4, 1967, 1969

EARNED RUN AVERAGE

1946	Hal Newhouser (Detroit)	AL	1.94
1947	Warren Spahn (Boston)	NL	2.33
1948	Harry Brecheen (St.Louis)	NL	2.24
1949	Dave Koslo (New York)	NL	2.50
1950	Jim Hearn (St.Louis/New York)	NL	2.49
1951	Saul Rogovin (Detroit/Chicago)	AL	2.78
1952	Allie Reynolds (New York)	AL	2.07
1953	Warren Spahn (Milwaukee)	NL	2.10
1954	John Antonelli (New York)	NL	2.29
1955	Billy Pierce (Chicago)	AL	1.57
1956	Whitey Ford (New York)	AL	2.47
1957	Bobby Schantz (New York)	AL	2.45
1958	Whitey Ford (New York)	AL	2.01
1959	Hoyt Wilhelm (Baltimore)	AL	2.19
1960	Frank Baumann (Chicago)	AL	2.68
1961	Richard Donovan (Washington)	AL	2.40
1962	Hank Aguirre (Detroit)	AL	2.21
1963	Sandy Koufax (Los Angeles)	NL	1.88
1964	Dean Chance (Los Angeles)	AL	1.64
1965	Sandy Koufax (Los Angeles)	NL	2.04
1966	Sandy Koufax (Los Angeles)	NL	2.04
1967	Phil Niekro (Atlanta)	NL	1.87
1968	Bob Gibson (St.Louis)	NL	1.12
1969	Juan Marichal (San Francisco)	NL	2.10
1970	Diego Segui (Oakland)	AL	2.56
1971	Tom Seaver (New York)	NL	1.76
1972	Luis Tiant (Boston)	AL	1.91
1973	Tom Seaver (New York)	NL	2.07
1974	Buzz Capra (Atlanta)	NL	2.28
1975	Jim Palmer (Baltimore)	AL	2.09
1976	Mark Fidrych (Detroit)	AL	2.34
1977	John Candelaria (Pittsburgh)	NL	2.34
1978	Ron Guidry (New York)	AL	1.74
1979	J.R.Richard (Houston)	NL	2.71
1980	Don Sutton (Los Angeles)	NL	2.21
1981	Nolan Ryan (Houston)	NL	1.69
1982	Steve Rogers (Montreal)	NL	2.40
1983	Atlee Hammaker (San Francisco)	NL	2.25
1984	Alejandro Pena (Los Angeles)	NL	2.56
1985	Dwight Gooden (New York)	NL	1.53
1986	Mike Scott (Houston)	AL	2.22

Most times NL leader: 5 Pete Alekander (Philadelphia, Chicago) 1915-7, 1919-20; Sandy Koufax (Los Angeles) 1962-6; 3 Dazzy Vance (Brooklyn) 1924, 1928, 1930; Carl Hubbell (New York) 1933-4, 1936; Tom Seaver (New York) 1970-1, 1973
Most times AL leader: 8 Lefty Grove (Philadelphia, Boston) 1926, 1930-2, 1935-6, 1938-9; 4 Barney Johnson (Washington) 1913, 1918-9, 1924

MOST VALUABLE PLAYER OF THE YEAR

At the end of each season the Baseball Writer's Association vote for the Most Valuable Player of the Year in both the American and National leagues. The award was instituted in 1931.

Post-war winners:

AMERICAN LEAGUE

1946	Ted Williams (Boston)
1947	Joe DiMaggio (New York)
1948	Louis Boudreau (Cleveland)
1949	Ted Williams (Boston)
1950	Philip Rizzuto (New York)
1951	'Yogi' Berra (New York)
1952	Robert Shantz (Philadelphia)
1953	Albert Rosen (Cleveland)
1954	'Yogi' Berra (New York)
1955	'Yogi' Berra (New York)
1956	Mickey Mantle (New York)
1957	Mickey Mantle (New York)
1958	Jack Jensen (Boston)
1959	Nelson Fox (Chicago)
1960	Roger Maris (New York)
1961	Roger Maris (New York)
1962	Mickey Mantle (New York)
1963	Elston Howard (New York)
1964	Brooks Robinson (Baltimore)
1965	Zoilo Versalles (Minnesota)
1966	Frank Robinson (Baltimore)
1967	Carl Yastrzemski (Boston)
1968	Dennis McLain (Detroit)
1969	Harmon Killebrew (Minnesota)
1970	John Powell (Baltimore)
1971	Vida Blue (Oakland)
1972	Dick Allen (Chicago)
1973	Reggie Jackson (Oakland)
1974	Jeffrey Burroughs (Texas)
1975	Fredric Lynn (Boston)
1976	Thurman Munson (New York)
1977	Rod Carew (Minnesota)
1978	Jim Rice (Boston)
1979	Donald Baylor (California)
1980	George Brett (Kansas City)
1981	Rollie Fingers (Milwaukee)
1982	Robin Yount (Milwaukee)
1983	Cal Ripken Jr (Baltimore)
1984	Willie Hernandez (Detroit)
1985	Don Mattingly (New York)
1986	Roger Clemmens (Boston)

NATIONAL LEAGUE

1946	Stan Musial (St.Louis)
1947	Bob Elliott (Boston)
1948	Stan Musial (St.Louis)
1949	Jack Robinson (Brooklyn)
1950	Jim Konstanty (Philadelphia)
1951	Roy Campanella (Brooklyn)
1952	Hank Sauer (Chicago)
1953	Roy Campanella (Brooklyn)
1954	Willie Mays (New York)
1955	Roy Campanella (Brooklyn)
1956	Don Newcombe (Brooklyn)
1957	Hank Aaron (Milwaukee)
1958	Ernest Banks (Chicago)
1959	Ernest Banks (Chicago)
1960	Dick Groat (Pittsburgh)
1961	Frank Robinson (Cincinnati)
1962	Maurice Wills (Los Angeles)
1963	Sandy Koufax (Los Angeles)
1964	Kenton Boyer (St.Louis)
1965	Willie Mays (San Francisco)
1966	Roberto Clemente (Pittsburgh)
1967	Orlando Cepeda (St.Louis)
1968	Robert Gibson (St.Louis)
1969	Willie McCovey (San Francisco)
1970	Johnny Bench (Cincinnati)

1971 Joe Torre (St.Louis)
1972 Johnny Bench (Cincinnati)
1973 Pete Rose (Cincinnati)
1974 Steve Garvey (Los Angeles)
1975 Joe Morgan (Cincinnati)
1976 Joe Morgan (Cincinnati)
1977 George Foster (Cincinnati)
1978 Dave Parker (Pittsburgh)
1979 Keith Hernandez (St.Louis) &
     Willie Stargell (Pittsburgh)
1980 Mike Schmidt (Philadelphia)
1981 Mike Schmidt (Phildaelphia)
1982 Dale Murphy (Atlanta)
1983 Dale Murphy (Atlanta)
1984 Ryne Sandberg (Chicago)
1985 Willie McGee (St.Louis)
1986 Mike Schmidt (Philadelphia)

Most selections:
NL: 3 Stan Musial 1943, 1946, 1948; Roy Campanella, Mike Schmidt
AL: 3 James E.Foxx (Philadelphia) 1932-3, 1938; Joe Di Maggio 1939, 1941, 1947; Yogi Berra, Mickey Mantle

CY YOUNG AWARD
Awarded from 1956 to the outstanding pitcher on the major leagues. From 1967 awards have been made for both American and National leagues.

Most wins: 3 Sandy Koufax (Los Angeles AL) 1963, 1965-6; James Palmer (Baltimore AL) 1973, 1975-6; Thomas Seaver (New York NL) 1969, 1973, 1975; Steve Carlton (Philadelphia NL) 1977, 1980, 1982

WORLD AMATEUR WORLD CHAMPIONSHIP

Instituted 1938. Held biennially since 1974.

Winners:
18 Cuba   1939-40, 1942-3, 1950, 1952-3, 1961,
             1969-73*, 1976, 1978, 1980, 1984, 1986
3 Venezuela 1941, 1944-5,
2 Colombia   1947, 1965,
2 USA   1973*-4
1 United Kingdom 1938, Dominican Republic 1948, Puerto Rico 1951, South Korea 1982
*1973, Cuba and USA shared title

INTER-CONTINENTAL CUP

An amateur competition. Competing teams are selected by the host country, but must include the defending champions. First held 1973, and subsequently every two years.

Winners:
3 Cuba 1979, 1983, 1985; 2 USA 1975, 1981; 1 Japan 1973, South Korea 1977

OLYMPIC GAMES

American Baseball has appeared at five Olympic Games as a demonstration sport. In addition, Finnish Baseball was included in 1952.

Winners:
1912 USA

1936 'World Amateurs'
1956 American Services team
1964 USA
1984 Japan

BASKETBALL

The modern game of basketball was invented by Dr James Naismith at the Training School of the International YMCA College at Springfield, Massachusetts, USA in December 1891. Games bearing a resemblance to basketball have been played for thousands of years, the earliest being perhaps 'Pok-ta-Pok', played by the Olmecs in Mexico in the 10th century BC.

The early games of basketball had large numbers of players, but five-a-side as standard was agreed in 1895. The AAU organised the first national tournament in the USA in 1897. The first professional league was the National Basketball League (NBL), founded in 1898. This organization merged with the Basketball Association of America in 1949 to form the National Basketball Association (NBA).

The amateur governing body, the Fédération Internationale de Basketball (FIBA) was founded in 1932 and the sport added to the Olympic programme in 1936. FIBA membership reached 166 in 1986.

OLYMPIC GAMES

First played by men in 1936 and by women in 1976.

Winners:

MEN		WOMEN	
1936	USA	1976	USSR
1948	USA	1980	USSR
1952	USA	1984	USA
1956	USA		
1960	USA		
1964	USA		
1968	USA		
1972	USSR		
1976	USA		
1980	Yugoslavia		
1984	USA		

WORLD CHAMPIONSHIPS

First held for men in Buenos Aires in 1950, and for women in 1953. They are each now held quadrennially.

Winners:

MEN		WOMEN	
1950	Argentina	1953	USA
1954	USA	1957	USA
1959	Brazil	1959	USSR
1963	Brazil	1964	USSR
1967	USSR	1967	USSR
1970	Yugoslavia	1971	USSR
1974	USSR	1975	USSR
1978	Yugoslavia	1979	USA
1982	USSR	1983	USSR
1986	USA	1986	USA

EUROPEAN CHAMPIONSHIPS

Wins:

MEN

14 USSR 1947, 1951, 1953, 1957, 1959, 1961, 1963, 1965, 1967, 1969, 1971, 1979, 1981, 1985
3 Yugoslavia 1973, 1975, 1977
2 Lithuania 1937, 1939
1 Latvia 1935, Czechoslovakia 1946, Egypt 1949, Hungary 1955, Italy 1983, Greece 1987

WOMEN

18 USSR 1950, 1952, 1954, 1956, 1960, 1962, 1964, 1966, 1968, 1970, 1972, 1974, 1976, 1978, 1980, 1981, 1983, 1985
1 Italy 1938, Bulgaria 1958

EUROPEAN CHAMPIONS CUP

First held in 1958 for men and 1959 for women.

Wins:

MEN

7 Real Madrid (Spa) 1964-5, 1967-8, 1974, 1978, 1980
5 Varese (Ita): 1970, 1972-3, 1975-6
4 CSKA Moskva (USSR) 1961, 1963, 1969, 1971
3 ASK Riga (USSR) 1958-60
2 Cibona Zagreb (Yug) 1985-6
2 Maccabi Tel Aviv (Isr) 1977, 1981
2 Milan (Ita) 1966, 1987
1 Dynamo Tbilisi (USSR) 1962, Bosna Sarajevo (Yug) 1979, Cantu (Ita) 1982-3, Banco di Roma (Ita) 1984

WOMEN

18 Daugawa Riga (USSR) 1960-2, 1964-75, 1977, 1981-2
4 AS Vicenza (Ita) 1983, 1985-7
2 Slavia Sofia (Bul) 1959, 1963
1 CKD Praha (Cs) 1976, Sesto San Giovanni (Ita) 1978, Red Star Belgrade 1979, Turin (Ita) 1980, Levski Spartak Sofia 1984

NBA CHAMPIONS

The 23 American professional teams are divided into two conferences, the Eastern, subdivided into the Atlantic Division and the Central Division, and the Western, subdivided into the Midwest Division and the Pacific Division. The best teams contest play-offs annually to determine the champions. The American Basketball Association, which had begun in 1967, merged with the NBA in 1976.

National League Champions:
1938 Goodyears
1939-40 Firestones
1941-2 Oshkosh
1943-5 Fort Wayne Pistons
1946 Rochester Royals
1947 Chicago Stags
1948 Minneapolis Lakers
1949 Anderson Packers

NBA Champions:
1947 Philadelphia Warriors
1948 Baltimore Bullets
1949-50 Minneapolis Lakers
1951 Rochester Royals
1952-4 Minneapolis Lakers
1955 Syracuse Nationals
1956 Philadelphia Warriors
1957 Boston Celtics
1958 St Louis Hawks
1959-66 Boston Celtics
1967 Philadelphia 76ers
1968-9 Boston Celtics
1970 New York Knicks
1971 Milwaukee Bucks
1972 Los Angeles Lakers
1973 New York Knicks
1974 Boston Celtics
1975 Golden State Warriors
1976 Boston Celtics
1977 Portland Trail Blazers
1978 Washington Bullets
1979 Seattle Supersonics
1980 Los Angeles Lakers
1981 Boston Celtics
1982 Los Angeles Lakers
1983 Philadelphia 76ers
1984 Boston Celtics
1985 Los Angeles Lakers
1986 Boston Celtics
1987 Los Angeles Lakers

Most wins: 16 Boston Celtics

NBA RECORDS

Highest match aggregate: 370 Detroit Pistons beat Denver Nuggets 186-184, Denver, 13 Dec 1983. Extra time was played following a 145-145 tie in regulation time.

Most points in game: 100 Wilt Chamberlain, Philadelphia v New York, 2 Mar 1962.

Most points in play-offs game: 63 Michael Jordan, Chicago v Boston, Apr 1986

Season's record points: 4029 Wilt Chamberlain, Philadelphia, 1962

Most seasons as NBA scoring leader: 7 Wilt Chamberlain 1960-6

Career record points:
36,474 Kareem Abdul-Jabbar, Milwaukee Bucks & Los Angeles Lakers, 1969-87
31,419 Wilt Chamberlain, Philadelphia & San Francisco, 1960-73 (record average 30.1 points per game)

NBA MOST VALUABLE PLAYER

Voted annually by NBA players from 1956:
1956 Bob Pettit (St Louis)
1957 Bob Cousy (Boston)
1958 Bill Russell (Boston)
1959 Bob Pettit (St Louis)
1960 Wilt Chamberlain (Philadelphia)
1961-3 Bill Russell (Boston)
1964 Oscar Robertson (Cincinnati)
1965 Bill Russell (Boston)
1966-8 Wilt Chamberlain (Philadelphia)
1969 Wes Unseld (Baltimore)
1970 Willis Reed (New York)

Kareem Abdul-Jabbar (All-Sport)

1971-2 Kareem Abdul-Jabbar* (Milwaukee)
1973 Dave Cowens (Boston)
1974 Kareem Abdul-Jabbar (Milwaukee)
1975 Bob McAdoo (Buffalo)
1976-7 Kareem Abdul-Jabbar (Los Angeles)
1978 Bill Walton (Portland)
1979 Moses Malone (Houston)
1980 Kareem Abdul-Jabbar (Los Angeles)
1981 Julius Erving (Philadelphia)
1982 Moses Malone (Houston)
1983 Moses Malone (Philadelphia)
1984-6 Larry Bird (Boston)
1987 Earvin 'Magic' Johnson (Los Angeles Lakers)

Most wins: 6 Kareem Abdul-Jabbar; 5 Bill Russell; 4 Wilt
Chamberlain; 3 Moses Malone, Larry Bird
* still known as Lew Alcindor in 1971

NCAA CHAMPIONSHIPS

The most important inter-collegiate competition in the
USA, first contested in 1939.

Most wins in Division One:
10 UCLA 1964-5, 1967-73, 1975
 5 Kentucky 1948-9, 1951, 1958, 1978
 5 Indiana 1940, 1953, 1976, 1981, 1987

Men's winners from 1980:
1980 Louisville
1981 Indiana
1982 North Carolina
1983 North Carolina State
1984 Georgetown
1985 Villanova
1986 Louisville
1987 Indiana

One player has been voted the Most Valuable Player in the
NCAA final three times: Lew Alcindor of UCLA (University
College of Los Angeles) 1967-9. He subsequently changed
his name to Kareem Abdul-Jabbar.

Women's champions. First contested 1982.
1982 Louisiana Tech
1983-4 Un. Southern California
1985 Old Dominion
1986 Texas
1987 Tennessee

ENGLISH NATIONAL CHAMPIONS
MEN
First held in 1936

Winners:
1936-7 Hoylake YMCA
1938-9 Catford Saints
1940 Birmingham Athletic Institute
1947 Carpathians
1948-50 Latter Day Saints
1951 Birmingham Dolobran
1952-5 London Polytechnic
1957-8 Central YMCA
1959 Aspley Old Boys
1960 Central YMCA
1961 London University
1962-4 Central YMCA
1965 Aldershot Warriors
1966 Oxford University
1967 Central YMCA
1968 Oxford University
1969 Central YMCA
1970 Liverpool Police
1971 Manchester University
1972 Avenue
1973 London Latvian SK
1974 Crystal Palace
1975 Embassy All Stars
1976-80 Crystal Palace
1981 Sunderland
1982 Crystal Palace
1983 Sunderland
1984 Solent
1985 Manchester United
1986 Kingston
1987 Brunel & Crystal Palace

WOMEN
First held in 1965.

Winners:
1965-7 Malory
1968 Abbey Wood
1969 Malory
1970-1 Abbey Wood
1972-3 Turnford Tigers
1974 Eston Eagles
1975 Cleveland Eagles
1976 Turnford Tigers
1977-80 Tigers
1981-3 Southgate
1984-5 Northampton
1986 Crystal Palace
1987 Northampton

ENGLISH NATIONAL LEAGUE

MEN
First contested in the 1972/3 season.

Wins:
7 Crystal Palace 1974, 1976-8, 1980, 1982-3
1 Avenue (Leyton) 1973, Embassy (Islington) 1975,
Doncaster 1979, Birmingham 1981, Solent 1984,
Kingston 1985, Manchester United 1986, Portsmouth
1987

WOMEN
First contested in the 1975/6 season.

Wins:
3 Herts Tigers 1976-7, 1980
3 Southgate 1981-3
3 Northampton 1984-5, 1987
2 Cleveland 1978-9
1 Crystal Palace 1986

BIATHLON

Combined cross-country skiing and rifle shooting.
Competitors ski over prepared courses carrying a
small-bore rifle. Men compete individually over 10km or
20km distances. During the former they have two
shooting competitions and in the latter four, prone and
standing, at a target 50 metres away. The relay event is
four by 7.5km, each member shooting once prone and
once standing. Penalties are imposed for missing the
target. The women's equivalent distances are 5km, 10km
and 3 by 5km relay.
The sport's governing body is L'Union Internationale de
Pentathlon Moderne et Biathlon, the UIPMB, which took
on the administration of biathlon in 1957, and which
staged the first world championships the following year.

OLYMPIC GAMES

Winners:

10 KILOMETRES
1980 Frank Ullrich (GDR) 32:10.69
1984 Eirik Kvalfoss (Nor) 30:53.8

Frank Ullrich, six world and Olympic titles (All-Sport)

20 KILOMETRES
1960 Klas Lestander (Swe) 1:33:21.6
1964 Vladimir Melanin (USSR) 1:20:26.8
1968 Magnar Solberg (Nor) 1:13:45.9
1972 Magnar Solberg (Nor) 1:15:55.5
1976 Nikolay Kruglov (USSR) 1:14:12.26
1980 Anatoliy Alyabyev (USSR) 1:08:16.31
1984 Peter Angerer (FRG) 1:11:52.7

MEN'S 4 × 7.5km RELAY
1968 USSR 2:13:02.4
1972 USSR 1:51:44.92
1976 USSR 1:57:55.64
1980 USSR 1:34:03.27
1984 USSR 1:38:51.70

Most gold medals: 4 Aleksandr Tikhonov (USSR) relay
1968-72-76-80.

Most medals: 5 Aleksandr Tikhonov 4 relay gold, 20km
silver 1968.

WORLD CHAMPIONSHIPS

Held annually from 1958 with the exception of Olympic
years.

Winners:

10 KILOMETRES
1974 Juhani Suutarinen (Fin) 37:42.43
1975 Nikolay Kruglov (USSR) 35:27.7
1977 Aleksandr Tikhonov (USSR) 32:47.8
1978 Frank Ullrich (GDR) 32:17.44
1979 Frank Ullrich (GDR) 40:35.37
1981 Frank Ullrich (GDR) 33:08.57
1982 Eirik Kvalfoss (Nor) 33:03.26
1983 Eirik Kvalfoss (Nor) 31:12.03
1985 Frank-Peter Rötsch (GDR) 30:25.2
1986 Valeriy Medvetsev (USSR) 28:02.0
1987 Frank-Peter Rötsch (GDR) 29:49.60

20 KILOMETRES
1958 Alosh Wiklund (Swe) 1:33:44
1959 Vladimir Melanin (USSR) 1:41:05
1961 Kalevi Huuskonen (Fin) 1:32:11
1962 Vladimir Melanin (USSR) 1:23:30
1963 Vladimir Melanin (USSR) 1:32:06.8
1965 Olav Jordet (Nor) 1:23:34.9
1966 Jon Istad (Nor) 1:38:21.8
1967 Viktor Mamatov (USSR) 1:28:34.1
1969 Aleksandr Tikhonov (USSR) 1:22:46.2
1970 Aleksandr Tikhonov (USSR) 1:23:42.1
1971 Dieter Speer (GDR) 1:18:20.2
1973 Aleksandr Tikhonov (USSR) 1:26:30.20
1974 Juhani Suutarinen (Fin) 1:12:04.74
1975 Heikki Ikola (Fin) 1:13:52.3
1977 Heikki Ikola (Fin) 1:10:51.8
1978 Odd Lirhus (Nor) 1:05:26.39
1979 Klaus Siebert (GDR) 1:07:40.13
1981 Heikki Ikola (Fin) 1:13:07.29
1982 Frank Ullrich (GDR) 1:07:17.03
1983 Frank Ullrich (GDR) 1:05:00.09
1985 Yuriy Kashkarov (USSR) 57:50.3
1986 Valeriy Medvetzev (USSR) 57:05.0
1987 Frank-Peter Rötsch (GDR) 1:00:00.40

TEAM
Sweden   1958
USSR   1959, 1962-3
Finland   1961
Norway   1965
4 × 7.5 km RELAY
Norway   1965-7
USSR   1969-71, 1973-4, 1977, 1983, 1985-6
Finland   1975
GDR   1978-9, 1981-2, 1987

WOMEN'S 5km
1984 Venera Chernyshova (USSR) 23:00.1
1985 Sanna Grønlid (Nor) 21:58.90
1986 Kaya Parve (USSR) 20:07.0
1987 Yelena Golovina (USSR) 21:14.7

WOMEN'S 10km
1984 Venera Chernyshova (USSR) 44:21.7
1985 Kaya Parva (USSR) 43:31.40
1986 Eva Korpela (Swe) 41:56.0
1987 Sanna Grønlid (Nor) 42:42.0

WOMEN'S 3 × 5 km RELAY
USSR   1984-7

Most titles (including Olympics):
MEN
14 Aleksandr Tikhonov (USSR) 4 individual, 10 relay
    1968-80
10 Frank Ullrich (GDR) 6 individual, 4 relay 1978-83
 7 Vladimir Melanov (USSR) 4 individual, 3 team
    1959-63
WOMEN
5 Venera Chernyshova (USSR) and Kaya Parve (USSR)
   both 2 individual, 3 relay 1984-6.

WORLD CUP
Contested at 10km and 20km over a series of five
events during each winter.

Men's winners:
1979 Klaus Siebert (GDR)
1980-2 Frank Ullrich (GDR)
1983 Peter Angerer (FRG)
1984-5 Frank-Peter Rötsch (GDR)
1986 André Sehmisch (GDR)
1987 Frank-Peter Rötsch (GDR)

BILLIARDS

The earliest reference to Billiards, which is related to the
outdoor game of paille-malle, played on grass, dates to
the early 15th-century. Louis XI of France is believed to
have had a billiard table. The game became popular in
Britain at the turn of the 19th century and the governing
body, The Billiards Association (now the Billiards &
Snooker Control Council), was formed in 1885.

WORLD PROFESSIONAL CHAMPIONSHIP
First held in 1870, the championship was organised on a
challenge basis until 1909. From 1909 it was run on a
knockout basis under Billiard Control Club rules, until
becoming dormant in 1934. It was revived on a
challenge basis in 1951. In 1980 it was restored to a
tournament event and, since 1982, has been held
annually.

Winners:
1870 William Cook (Eng)
1870 John Roberts, Jnr (Eng)
1870 Joseph Bennett (Eng)
1871 John Roberts, Jnr (Eng)
1871 William Cook (Eng)
1875 John Roberts,Jnr (Eng)
1880 Joseph Bennett (Eng)
1885 John Roberts Jnr (Eng)
1889 Charles Dawson (Eng)
1901 H.W.Stevenson (Eng)
1901 Charles Dawson (Eng)
1901 H.W.Stevenson (Eng)
1903 Charles Dawson (Eng)
1908 Melbourne Inman (Eng)
1909-11 H.W.Stevenson (Eng)
1912-4 Melbourne Inman (Eng)
1919 Melbourne Inman (Eng)
1920 Willie Smith (Eng)
1921-2 Tom Newman (Eng)
1923 Willie Smith (Eng)
1924-7 Tom Newman (Eng)
1928-30 Joe Davis (Eng)
1931 no competition
1932 Joe Davis (Eng)
1933-4 Walter Lindrum (Aus)
1951 Clark McConachy (NZ)
1968 Rex Williams (Eng)
1971 Leslie Driffield (Eng)
1971 Rex Williams (Eng)
1980 Fred Davis (Eng)
1982 Rex Williams (Eng)

1983 Rex Williams (Eng)
1984 Mark Wildman (Eng)
1985 Ray Edmonds (Eng)
1986 Robbie Foldvari (Aus)
1987 Norman Dagley (Eng)

Most wins (pre-1909): John Roberts, Jnr made 8 successful defences of his title 1870-85
(post-1909): 7 Rex Williams 1968-76 (including 5 successful challenges)
Tom Newman won a record six titles under knockout conditions, 1921-7

WORLD AMATEUR CHAMPIONSHIP

Inaugurated in 1926 it is now held every two years and is organised by the International Billiards & Snooker Federation (IBSF). It is a round-robin event with the four leading players then competing in a knockout tournament.

1926 Joe Earlham (Eng)
1927 Allan Prior (SAf)
1929 Les Hayes (Aus)
1931 Laurie Steeples (Eng)
1933 Sydney Lee (Eng)
1935 Horace Coles (Wal)
1936 Robert Marshall (Aus)
1938 Robert Marshall (Aus)
1951 Robert Marshall (Aus)
1952 Leslie Driffield (Eng)
1954 Tom Cleary (Aus)
1958 Wilson Jones (Ind)
1960 Herbert Beetham (Eng)
1962 Robert Marshall (Aus)
1964 Wilson Jones (Ind)
1967 Leslie Driffield (Eng)
1969 Jack Karnehm (Eng)
1971 Norman Dagley (Eng)
1973 Mohammed Lafir (Sri)
1975 Norman Dagley (Eng)
1977 Michael Ferreira (Ind)
1979 Paul Mifsud (Malta)
1981 Michael Ferreira (Ind)
1983 Michael Ferreira (Ind)
1985 Geet Sethi (Ind)
1987 Geet Sethi (Ind)

Most wins: 4 Robert Marshall

UNITED KINGDOM PROFESSIONAL CHAMPIONSHIP

Instituted in 1934 it discontinued in 1951 but was revived in 1979 until 1983 when it was taken off the professional calender. It was revived once more in 1987.

Winners:
1934-9 Joe Davis
1946 John Barrie
1947 Joe Davis
1948 Sidney Smith
1950 John Barrie
1951 Fred Davis
1979 Rex Williams
1980 Jack Karnehm
1981 Rex Williams

Rex Williams, Amateur Snooker champion in 1951 and World Billiards 32 years later. (All-Sport)

1983 Mark Wildman
1987 Norman Dagley
Most wins: 7 Joe Davis

RECORD BREAKS

Highest break including the now outlawed cradle cannon:
499,135 Tom Reece 3 Jun-6 Jul 1907
Highest certified break using the anchor cannon:
42,746 William Cook 29 May-7 Jun 1907
Official world record break (since introduction of the 25-hazard rule in 1926)
4137 Walter Lindrum 20 June 1932
Highest break under the baulk-line rule:
1784 Joe Davis 29 May 1936
Highest official break in amateur competition:
1149 Michael Ferreira 15 Dec 1978
Highest break under current 'two pot' rule:
962 (unfinished) Michael Ferreira 29 Apr 1986

THREE CUSHION BILLIARDS

Played on a table without pockets, this variation of billiards dates to 1878. The governing body, the Union Mondiale de Billiard (UMB) was formed in 1928. Popular in the USA and Europe, the lack of pockets makes it a 'cannons-only' game, but there are several variations which demand a high level of skill. In Europe is it known as Carom.

Most UMB titles have been won by Raymond Ceulemans (Bel) with 19 (1963-6, 1968-73, 1975-81, 1983, 1985) Willie Hoppe (USA) won a total of 51 three-cushion championships throughout the United States.

BOBSLEIGH & TOBOGGANING

The first known bobsleigh races were run by British enthusiasts in Switzerland in the 1880s, when improvements were made to sleighs to make them go faster. Luge races had been held a few years earlier, and two special luge runs were constructed at Davos, Switzerland in 1879. The earliest known sledge is dated c.6500 BC and was found at Heinola, Finland.

The first purpose-built bobsleigh run was constructed at St Moritz in 1902. There are now Olympic bobsleigh events for two- and four-man teams, who sit in the bob. Skeleton one-man toboggans are used on the Cresta Run, and there was an Olympic event for them in 1924 and 1948. In the skeleton toboggans the riders lie face down, but this form of tobogganing has been superseded in the Olympics by Luge tobogganing, in which the rider sits up or lies back.

International governing bodies: Fédération Internationale de Bobsleigh et de Tobogganing (FIBT), founded in 1923. Luge tobogganing originally came under the auspices of the FIBT, but from 1957 has had its own governing body, the Fédération Internationale de Luge (FIL).

Bobsleigh runs are between 1100m and 1600m in length. The two-man bob has a maximum length of 2.7m and a maximum weight of bob and crew of 390kg; for a four-man bob the maxima are 3.8m and 630kg; luges are about 1.50m in length, and the maximum weight of the luge is 20kg for a single-seater or 22 kg for a two-seater. Luge runs are over a minimum of 1000m. Women are not permitted to contest international bobsleigh events, but contest single-seater luge races, an Olympic event from 1964.

OLYMPIC GAMES

Two-man bob winners:
1932 Hubert Stevens & Curtis Stevens (USA)
1936 Ivan Brown & Alan Washbond (USA)
1948 Felix Endrich & Friedrich Waller (Swi)
1952 Andreas Ostler & Lorenz Nieberl (FRG)
1956 Lamberto Dalla Costa & Giacomo Conti (Ita)
1964 Tony Nash & Robin Dixon (UK)
1968 Eugenio Monti & Luciano de Paolis (Ita)
1972 Wolfgang Zimmerer & Peter Utzschneider (FRG)
1976 Meinhard Nehmer & Bernhard Germeshausen (GDR)
1980 Erich Schärer & Josef Benz (Swi)
1984 Wolfgang Hoppe & Dietmar Schauerhammer (GDR)

Four-man bob winners:
1924 Switzerland
1928 USA
1932 USA
1936 Switzerland
1948 USA
1952 Germany (FRG)
1956 Switzerland
1964 Canada
1968 Italy
1972 Switzerland
1976 GDR
1980 GDR
1984 GDR

Skeleton bob winners:
1928 Jennison Heaton (USA)
1948 Nino Bibbia (Ita)

Most gold medals by an individual:
3 Meinhard Nehmer & Bernhard Germeshausen (GDR)
2-man 1976, 4-man 1976 and 1980

Most medals: 6 Eugenio Monti (Ita): two gold 1968, two silver 1956, two bronze 1964.

Luge tobogganing – men's single-seater winners:
1964 Thomas Köhler (GDR)
1968 Manfred Schmid (Aut)
1972 Wolfgang Scheidel (GDR)
1976 Detlef Günther (GDR)
1980 Bernhard Glass (GDR)
1984 Paul Hildgartner (Ita)

Luge – men's two-seater winners:
1964 Josef Feistmantl & Manfred Stengl (Aut)
1968 Thomas Köhler & Klaus Bonsack (GDR)
1972 Paul Hildgartner & Walter Plaikner (Ita) and
     Horst Hörnlein & Reinhard Bredow (GDR)
1976 Hans Rinn & Norbert Hahn (GDR)
1980 Hans Rinn & Norbert Hahn (GDR)
1984 Hans Stanggasinger & Franz Wembacher (FRG)

Luge – women's single-seater winners:
1964 Ortrun Enderlein (GDR)
1968 Erica Lechner (Ita)
1972 Anna-Maria Müller (GDR)
1976 Margit Schumann (GDR)
1980 Vera Sosulya (USSR)
1984 Steffi Martin (GDR)

BOBSLEIGH WORLD CHAMPIONSHIPS

Held annually from 1930 for the four-man bob and 1931 for the two-man bob. The Olympic events (qv) are the world championships in those years.

Two-man bob winners:
1931 Hanns Killian & Sebastian Huber (Ger)
1933 Alexandru Papana & Dumitru Hubert (Rom)
1934 Alexandru Frim & Vasile Dumitrescu (Rom)
1935 Reto Capadrutt & Emil Diener (Swi)
1937 Frederic McEnvoy & B.H.Black (UK)
1938 Bibo Fischer & Rolf Thielacke (Ger)
1939 René Lundnen & J.Kuffer (Bel)
1947 Fritz Feierabend & Stephan Waser (Swi)
1949 Felix Endrich & Friedrich Waller (Swi)
1950 Fritz Feierabend & Stephan Waser (Swi)

1951 Andreas Osterl & Lorenz Nieberl (FRG)
1953 Felix Endrich & Fritz Stoeckli (Swi)
1954 Guglielmo Scheibmeier & Andrea Zambelli (Ita)
1955 Fritz Feierabend & Harry Warburton (Swi)
1957-9 Eugenio Monti & Renzo Alvera (Ita)
1961 Eugenio Monti & Sergio Siorpaes (Ita)
1962 Rinaldo Ruatti & Enrico De Lorenzo (Ita)
1963 Eugenio Monti & Sergio Siorpaes (Ita)
1965 Tony Nash & Robin Dixon (UK)
1966 Eugenio Monti & Sergio Siorpaes (Ita)
1967 Erwin Thaler & Reinhold Durnthaler (Aut)
1969 Nevio de Zordo & Adriano Frassinelli (Ita)
1970 Horst Floth & Pepi Bader (FRG)
1971 Gianfranco Gaspari & Mario Armano (Ita)
1973-4 Wolfgang Zimmerer & Peter Utzschneider (FRG)
1975 Giorgio Alvera & Franco Perruquet (Ita)
1977 Hans Hiltebrand & Heinz Meier (Swi)
1978-9 Erich Schärer & Josef Benz (Swi)
1981 Bernhard Germeshausen & Hans-Jürgen Gerhardt (GDR)
1982 Erich Schärer & Josef Benz (Swi)
1983 Ralf Pichler & Urs Leuthold (Swi)
1985-6 Wolfgang Hoppe & Dietmar Schauerhammer (GDR)
1987 Ralf Pichler & Celest Poltera (Swi)

Four-man winners:

12	Switzerland	1939, 1947, 1954-5, 1957, 1971, 1973, 1975, 1982-3, 1986-7
6	FR Germany	1951, 1958, 1962, 1969, 1974, 1979
4	Italy	1930, 1961, 1963, 1970
4	USA	1949-50, 1953, 1959
4	GDR	1977-8, 1981, 1985
3	Germany	1931, 1934-5
2	United Kingdom	1937-8
1	Canada	1965

Not decided in 1966 due to a fatal accident and in 1967 because of a thaw.

Most bobsleigh world titles (including Olympics):
2-man/4-man
11 Eugenio Monti (Ita) 8/3
 8 Erich Schärer (Swi) 4/4
 6 Fritz Feierabend (Swi) 3/3
 6 Bernhard Germeshausen (GDR) 2/4

BOBSLEIGH WORLD CUP

First held over a series of events in 1984-5.
Winners:
1985 Anton Fischer (FRG), 1986 Ekkehard Fasser (Swi), 1987 Matt Roy (USA)

LUGE WORLD CHAMPIONSHIPS

Held annually from 1955, with the exception of years in which luge events were included in the Olympics, with which they are now merged, to 1981 and now biennially

The 1987 World bobsleigh champions. (All-Sport)

on artificial runs. Separate world championships on natural runs were held in 1979 and biennially from 1980.

Men's single seater winners:
1955 Anton Salvesen (Nor)
1957 Hans Schaller (FRG)
1958 Jerzy Wojnar (Pol)
1959 Herbert Thaler (Aut)
1960 Helmuth Berndt (FRG)
1961 Jerzy Wojnar (Pol)
1962 Thomas Köhler (GDR)
1963 Fritz Nachmann (FRG)
1965 Hans Plenk (FRG)
1966 event cancelled
1967 Thomas Köhler (GDR)
1969 Josef Feistmantl (Aut)
1970 Josef Fendt (FRG)
1971 Karl Brunner (Ita)
1973 Hans Rinn (GDR)
1974 Josef Fendt (FRG)
1975 Wolfram Fiedler (GDR)
1977 Hans Rinn (GDR)
1978 Paul Hildgartner (Ita)
1979 Detlef Günther (GDR)
1981 Sergey Danilin (USSR)
1983 Miroslav Zajonc (Can)
1985 Michael Walter (GDR)
1987 Markus Prock (Aut)

Men's two-seater:
1955 Hans Krausner & Herbert Thaler (Aut)
1957-8 Josef Strillinger & Fritz Nachmann (FRG)
1960 Reinhold Frosch & Ewald Walch (Aut)
1961 Roman Pichler & Raimondo Prinoth (Ita)
1962 Giovanni Graber & Gianpoulo Ambrosi (Ita)
1963 Ryszard Pedrak & Lucjan Kudzia (Pol)
1965 Wolfgang Scheidel & Thomas Köhler (GDR)
1967 Klaus Bonsack & Thomas Köhler (GDR)
1969-70 Manfred Schmid & Ewald Walch (Aut)
1971 Paul Hildgartner & Walter Plaikner (Ita)
1973 Horst Hörnlein & Reinhard Bredow (GDR)
1974-5 Bernd Hann & Ulrich Hann (GDR)
1977 Hans Rinn & Norbert Hahn (GDR)
1978 Dainis Bremse & Aigars Krikis (USSR)
1979 Hans Brandner & Balthasar Schwarm (FRG)
1980 Hans Rinn & Norbert Hahn (GDR)
1981 Bernd Hann & Ulrich Hann (GDR)
1983 Jörg Hoffmann & Jochen Pietzsch (GDR)
1985 Jörg Hoffmann & Jochen Pietzsch (GDR)
1987 Jörg Hoffmann & Jochen Pietzsch (GDR)
Cancelled in 1959 and 1966

Most luge world titles (including Olympics):
6 Thomas Köhler (GDR), Hans Rinn (GDR).

Women's single-seater:
1955 Karla Kienzl (Aut)
1956 Maria Isser (Aut)
1957 Maria Semczyszak (Pol)
1959 Elly Lieber (Aut)
1960 Maria Isser (Aut)
1961 Elisabeth Nagele (Swi)
1962-3 Ilse Geisler (GDR)
1965 Ortrun Enderlein (GDR)
1966 event cancelled
1967 Ortrun Enderlein (GDR)
1969 Petra Tierlich (GDR)
1970 Barbara Piecha (Pol)
1971 Elisabeth Demleitner (FRG)
1973-5 Margrit Schumann (GDR)
1977 Margrit Schumann (GDR)
1978 Vera Sosulya (USSR)
1979 Melitta Sollmann (GDR)
1980 Vera Sosulya (USSR)
1981 Melitta Sollmann (GDR)
1983 Steffi Martin (GDR)
1985 Steffi Martin (GDR)
1987 Cerstin Schmidt (GDR)

Most wins (including Olympics):
5 Margrit Schumann (GDR).

LUGE WORLD CUP

Held over a series of events annually from the 1977/8 season.

Men's single-seater winners:
1978 Anton Winkler (GDR)
1979 Paul Hildgartner (Ita)
1980 Ernst Haspinger (Ita)
1981 Ernst Haspinger (Ita) & Paul Hildgartner (Ita)
1982 Ernst Haspinger (Ita)
1983 Paul Hildgartner (Ita)
1984 Michael Walter (GDR)
1985-7 Norbert Huber (Ita)

Men's two-seater winners:
1978-9 Peter Gschnitzer & Karl Brunner (Ita)
1980-2 Günther Lemmerer & Reinhold Sulzbacher (Aut)
1983 Hansjörg Raffl & Norbert Huber (Ita)
1984 Jörg Hoffmann & Jochen Pietzsch (GDR)
1985-6 Hansjörg Raffl & Norbert Huber (Ita)
1987 Thomas Schwab & Wolfgang Staudinger (FRG)

Women's single-seater winners:
1978 Regina König (FRG)
1979-81 Angelika Schafferer (Aut)
1982 Vera Sosulya (USSR)
1983 Ute Weiss (GDR)
1984 Steffi Martin (GDR) & Bettina Schmidt (GDR)
1985 Cerstin Schmidt (GDR)
1986 Maria Rainer (Ita)
1987 Cerstin Schmidt (GDR)

BOWLING (TENPIN)

Bowling at 'pins' has existed as a pastime since 5200 BC but it only started to take shape in its present form in the early 19th century. Dutch or German migrants took the game of ninepins to the United States and the game became immensely popular – so popular that it attracted much gambling and consequently the game was banned. To get round the law, a tenth pin was added, and they were laid out in a diamond shape. The new game, once again, became very popular. The American Bowling Congress was formed in 1895, and they standardised the rules. The Women's International Bowling Congress (WIBC) was formed in 1915.

The world governing body of the amateur game is the

Fédération Internationale des Quilleurs (FIQ). Prior to the last war the International Bowling Association (IBA) governed the sport.

WORLD CHAMPIONSHIPS

The IBA organised four world championships between 1923-36. Since 1954 the championships have been organised by the FIQ, and since 1963 have been held every four years. Women took part for the first time in 1963

Winners:

MEN

INDIVIDUAL

Year	Winner	Score	No.of Games	Average
1923	Thure Sandström (Swe)	414	2	207.00
1926	Hugo Lillier (Swe)	829	4	207.25
1929	Schirgio (USA)	836	4	209.00
1936	Goldtammer (Ger)	921	4	230.25
1954	Gösta Algeskog (Swe)	4932	25	197.28
1955	Nils Bäckström (Swe)	4838	25	193.52
1958	Kaarlo Asukas (Fin)	5034	25	201.36
1960	Tito Reynolds (Mex)	4963	25	198.52
1963	Les Zikes (USA)	5519	28	197.11
1967	David Pond (UK)	5708	28	203.86
1971	Ed Luther (USA)	5963	28	212.96
1975	Bud Staudt (USA)	5816	28	207.71
1979	Ollie Ongtawco (Phi)	1278	6	213.00
1983	Armando Marino (Col)	1357	6	226.17
1987	Rolland Patrick (Fra)	1332	6	222.00

MASTERS

Winners:
1979 Gerry Bugden (UK)
1983 Tony Cariello (USA)
1987 Roger Pieters (Bel)

ALL-EVENTS

(score from all four events, singles, doubles, trios & team, to count.)
1983 Mats Karlsson 5242 pts (av. 218.42)
1987 Rick Steelsmith (USA) 5261 pts (av. 219.21)

DOUBLES

Wins:
4 Sweden 1923, 1955, 1958, 1987
3 Great Britain 1967, 1975, 1983*
2 Finland 1926, 1954
2 USA 1936, 1963
2 Australia 1979, 1983*
1 Mexico 1960
1 Puerto Rico 1971
* Shared title

Best average score: 219.83 Sweden (1987) 2638 pts from 6 games

TEAMS OF 5 PLAYERS

Wins:
4 Finland 1958, 1967, 1975, 1983
4 Sweden 1923, 1926, 1954, 1987
3 USA 1936, 1963, 1971
1 FR Germany 1955
1 Venezuela 1960
1 Australia 1979

Best average score: 211.83 Finland (1983) 6355 pts from 6 games

TEAMS OF 8 PLAYERS

(discontinued 1975)
Wins:
3 USA 1963, 1967, 1971
2 Sweden 1954, 1958
1 Finland 1955
1 Mexico 1960
1 FR Germany 1975

Best average score: 198.30 United States (1971) 12,691 pts from 8 games

TRIOS

Wins:
1 Malaysia 1979, Sweden 1983, USA 1987

Best average score: 216.61 Sweden (1983) 3899 pts from 6 games

WOMEN

INDIVIDUAL

Year	Winner	Score	No.of Games	Average
1963	Helen Shablis (USA)	4535	24	188.96
1967	Helen Weston (USA)	4585	24	191.04
1971	Ashie Gonzales (PR)	4535	24	188.96
1975	Annedore Haefker (FRG)	4615	24	192.29
1979	Lita de la Rosa (Phi)	1220	6	203.33
1983	Lena Sulkanen (Swe)	1293	6	215.50
1987	Edda Piccini (Ita)	1259	6	209.83

MASTERS

Winners:
1979 Lita de la Rosa (Phi)
1983 Lena Sulkanen (Swe)
1987 Annette Hagre (Swe)

ALL-EVENTS

1983 Bong Coo (Phi) 4806 pts (av.200.25)
1987 Sandra Jo Shiery (USA) 4894 pts (av. 203.92)

DOUBLES

Wins:
2 USA 1963, 1987
1 Mexico 1960
1 Japan 1971
1 Sweden 1975
1 Philippines 1979
1 Denmark 1983

Best average score: 213.83 USA (1987) 2566 pts

TEAMS OF 4 PLAYERS

(discontinued 1975)
Wins:
2 USA 1963*, 1971
1 Mexico 1963*
1 Finland 1967
1 Japan 1975
* There were two titles in 1963

Best average score: 194.00 United States (1971) 4656 pts from 6 games

TEAMS OF 5 PLAYERS

Wins:
3 USA 1971, 1979, 1987
1 Finland 1967
1 Japan 1975
1 Sweden 1983

Best average score: 200.37 USA (1987) 6011 pts from 6 games

TRIOS
Wins:
2 USA 1979, 1987
1 FR Germany 1983

Best average score: 200.17 USA (1987) 3603 pts from 6 games
The only perfect game (300) in the World Championships was rolled by Rick Steelsmith (USA) during the Trios event at the 1987 championships.

THE AMERICAN BOWLING CONGRESS

The men's governing body in the USA was founded in 1895. Its most important event is the annual Masters Bowling Tournament.

Winners have been:

1951	Lee Jouglard	1970	Don Glover
1952	Willard Taylor	1971	Jim Godman
1953	Rudy Habetler	1972	Bill Beach
1954	Eugene Elkins	1973	Dave Soutar
1955	Buzz Fazio	1974	Paul Colwell
1956-7	Dick Hoover	1975	Ed Ressler Jr.
1958	Tom Hennessey	1976	Nelson Burton Jr.
1959	Ray Bluth	1977	Earl Anthony
1960	Bill Golembiewski	1978	Frank Ellenburg
1961	Don Carter	1979	Doug Meyers
1962	Bill Golembiewski	1980	Neil Burton
1963	Harry Smith	1981	Randy Lightfoot
1964-5	Billy Welu	1982	Joe Berardi
1966	Bob Strampe	1983	Mike Lastowski
1967	Lou Scalia	1984	Earl Anthony
1968	Pete Tountas	1985	Steve Wunderlich
1969	Jim Chestney	1986	Mark Fahy

Most wins: 2 Hoover, Golembiewski, Welu, Anthony

Earl Anthony, the first bowler to achieve career winnings of $1 million. (American Bowling Congress)

ABC Champions

Held annually from 1901 at the following categories: all-events, singles, doubles and five-man team.

All-events champions from 1970:
1970 Mike Berlin 2004
1971 Al Cohn 2063
1972 Mac Lowry 2026
1973 Ron Woolet 2104
1974 Bob Hart 2087
1975 Bobby Meadows 2033
1976 Jim Lindquist 2071
1977 Bub Debenham 2117
1978 Chris Cobus 1994
1979 Bob Basacchi 2097
1980 Steve Fehr 2076
1981 Rod Toft 2107
1982 Rich Wonders 2076
1983 Tony Cariello 2059
1984 Bob Goike 2142
1985 Barry Asher 2033
1986 Ed Marzka 2116

Most wins: 2 Barney Spinella 1922, 1927; Joe Wilman 1939, 1946; Frank Santore 1950, 1953

ABC RECORDS FOR LEAGUE AND TOURNAMENT PLAY

Team series	3858	Budweiser Beer, St Louis 1958
Team game	1365	Edwards Concrete, Moscow, Pa. 1982
Doubles series	1639	Bob Perry & Mike Foti, Lodi, NJ 1986
Doubles game	600	John Cotta & Steve Larsen, Manteca, Cal. 1981
Individual series	886	Albert Brandt, Lockport, NY 1939

A perfect score, strikes in all ten frames of a game, is 300. Thus the singles total maximum for three sanctioned games is 900.

The most 300 games in ABC tournaments: 27 Elvin Mesger, 24 John Wilcox Jr., 21 Ron Woolet, Teata Semiz, 20 Mark Stibora.

Most scores of over 800 in ABC tournaments: 21 Elvin Mesger.

THE PROFESSIONAL BOWLERS ASSOCIATION

The PBA was formed in the USA in 1958. Its annual Tournament of Champions is held its home in Akron, Ohio, and is sponsored by Firestone.

Year	Tournament of Champions winners	PBA leading money winners	$
1962	Joe Joseph	Don Carter	49,972
1963	Not held	Dick Weber	46,333
1964	Not held	Bob Strampe	33,592
1965	Billy Hardwick	Dick Weber	47,674
1966	Wayne Zahn	Wayne Zahn	54,720
1967	Jim Stefanich	Dave Davis	54,165
1968	Dave Davis	Jim Stefanich	67,377
1969	Jim Godman	Billy Hardwick	64,160
1970	Don Johnson	Mike McGrath	52,049

1971	Johnny Petraglia	Johnny Petraglia	85,065
1972	Mike Durbin	Don Johnson	56,648
1973	Jim Godman	Don McCune	69,000
1974	Earl Anthony	Earl Anthony	99,585
1975	Dave Davis	Earl Anthony	107,585
1976	Marshall Holman	Earl Anthony	110,833
1977	Mike Berlin	Mark Roth	105,583
1978	Earl Anthony	Mark Roth	134,500
1979	George Pappas	Mark Roth	124,517
1980	Wayne Webb	Wayne Webb	116,700
1981	Steve Cook	Earl Anthony	164,735
1982	Mike Durbin	Earl Anthony	134,760
1983	Joe Berardi	Earl Anthony	135,605
1984	Mike Durbin	Mark Roth	158,712
1985	Mark Williams	Mike Aulby	201,200
1986	Marshall Holman	Walter Williams	145,550
1987	Peter Weber	–	–

PRO CAREER EARNINGS AND MOST PBA TITLES WON

(to end of 1986 season)	Earnings	Titles
Earl Anthony	$1,265,171	41
Mark Roth	1,185,262	32
Marshall Holman	1,061,718	20
Mike Durbin	728,745	14
Wayne Webb	727,681	16
Dick Weber	726,234	28
George Pappas	720,531	10
Nelson Burton Jr.	684,925	17
Mike Aulby	659,588	13
Dave Davis	620,812	18

Others with more than 18 titles
Don Johnson 26, Dick Ritger 20, Camen Salvino 18

THE WOMEN'S INTERNATIONAL BOWLING CONGRESS

The WIBC was founded in the USA in 1916, and WIBC Championships have been held annually from then, except for 1943-5. Their tournament attracted a record 75,480 entrants in 1983 for the event held over a three-month period.

All-events winners from 1970:
1970 Dorothy Fothergill 1984
1971 Lorrie Nicholls 1840
1972 Mildred Martorella 1877
1973 Toni Starin 1910
1974 Judy Soutar 1944
1975 Virginia Norton 1821
1976 Betty Morris 1866
1977 Akiko Yamaga 1895
1978 Annese Kelly 1896
1979 Betty Morris 1945
1980 Cheryl Robinson 1945
1981 Virginia Norton 1905
1982 Aleta Sill 1905
1983 Virginia Norton 1922
1984 Shinobu Saitoh (Jap) 1921
1985 Aleta Sill 1900
1986 Robin Romeo & Maria Lewis 1877

Most wins: 4 Emma Jaeger 1918, 1921, 1928-9; 3 Virginia Norton

THE QUEEN'S TOURNAMENT

The WIBC's most prestigious event, winners from its inception in 1961:

1961 Janet Harman
1962 Dorothy Wilkinson
1963 Irene Monterosso
1964 D.D.Jacobson
1965 Betty Kuczynski
1966 Judy Lee
1967 Mildred Martorella
1968 Phyllis Massey
1969 Ann Feigel
1970-1 Mildred Martorella
1972-3 Dorothy Fothergill
1974 Judy Soutar
1975 Cindy Powell
1976 Pamela Buckner
1977 Dana Stewart
1978 Loa Boxberger
1979-80 Donna Adamek
1981-2 Katsuko Sugimoto
1983 Aleta Sill
1984 Kazue Inahashi
1985 Aleta Sill
1986 Cora Fiebig

Queen's leading money winners: $62,140 Aleta Sill, $37,420 Katsuko Sugimoto, $31,845 Donna Adamek

WIBC records:

Team series	3379	Freeway Washer & Stamping Co., Cleveland 1959-60
Team game	1210	Sheraton Inn, Scranton, Pa. 1981-2
Doubles series	1496	Patty Ann & Pat Costello 1981-2
Doubles game	553	Jean Reeder & Janice James, Cleveland 1982-3
Individual series	864	Jeanne Maiden, Solon, Ohio 1986-7

Most sanctioned 300 games: 11 Jeanne Maiden, 7 Donna Adamek, Betty Morris

US OPENS

Now the biggest money tournament on the US tour. First held in 1941.

Most wins:

MEN
4 Don Carter 1952, 1954, 1956, 1958
4 Dick Weber 1962-3, 1965-6

WOMEN
8 Marion Ladewig 1949-52, 1954, 1956, 1959, 1963
3 Pat Costello 1974, 1976, 1980

BOWLS

The ancient Egyptians are believed to have played a game similar to bowls around 5200 BC but the earliest recorded green is at Southampton in 1299 although a green was claimed in Chesterfield in 1294. The modern rules for bowls were drawn up in Scotland in 1848-9 by Glasgow solicitor William Mitchell. The English Bowling Association was founded in 1903 with Test cricketer W.G.Grace as its first president, although this was preceded by the founding of the International (later Imperial) Bowling Association in 1899, but this lasted only until 1905, when the present world governing body, the International Bowling Board, was formed. The Women's International Bowling Board was formed in 1969.

WORLD OUTDOOR CHAMPIONSHIPS

Instituted in 1966 the championships are now held every four years. The first women's championships were held in 1969.

MEN

SINGLES
1966 David Bryant (Eng)
1972 Malwyn Evans (Wal)
1976 Doug Watson (SAf)
1980 David Bryant (Eng)
1984 Peter Belliss (NZ)

PAIRS
1966 Geoff Kelly & Bert Palm (Aus)
1972 Clementi Delgado & Eric Liddell (HK)
1976 Doug Watson & William Moseley (SAf)
1980 Alf Sandercock & Peter Rheuben (Aus)
1984 George Adrain & Skippy Arculli * (USA)
* substituted for Jim Candelet

TRIPLES
1966 Australia
1972 United States
1976 South Africa
1980 England
1984 Ireland

FOURS
1966 New Zealand
1972 England
1976 South Africa
1980 Hong Kong
1984 England

LEONARD TROPHY
(Presented to the winning team based on performances in all categories at the world championship)
1966 Australia
1972 Scotland
1976 South Africa
1980 England
1984 Scotland

Most wins overall: 4 David Bryant (singles 1966, 1980; triples and team 1980)

WOMEN

SINGLES
1969 Gladys Doyle (PNG)
1973 Elsie Wilke (NZ)
1977 Elsie Wilke (NZ)
1981 Norma Shaw (Eng)
1985 Merle Richardson (Aus)

David Bryant (All-Sport)

PAIRS
1969 E.McDonald & M.Cridlan (SAf)
1973 Lorna Lucas & Dot Jenkinson (Aus)
1977 Helen Wong & Elvie Chok (HK)
1981 Eileen Bell & Nan Allely (Ire)
1985 Merle Richardson & Fay Craig (Aus)

TRIPLES
1969 South Africa
1973 New Zealand
1977 Wales

1981 Hong Kong
1985 Australia

FOURS
1969 South Africa
1973 New Zealand
1977 Australia
1981 England
1985 Scotland

TEAM
1969 South Africa
1973 New Zealand
1977 Australia
1981 England
1985 Australia

Most wins overall: 3 Merle Richardson (fours 1977, singles and pairs 1985)

WORLD INDOOR CHAMPIONSHIP
Instituted 1979 and sponsored by Embassy.
1979 David Bryant (Eng)
1980 David Bryant (Eng)
1981 David Bryant (Eng)
1982 John Watson (Sco)
1983 Bob Sutherland (Sco)
1984 Jim Baker (Ire)
1985 Terry Sullivan (Wal)
1986-7 Tony Allcock (Eng)

Most wins: 3 David Bryant

World Indoor Pairs were instituted in 1986. Winners 1986 and 1987 were Tony Allcock and David Bryant.

INTERNATIONAL CHAMPIONSHIP
First held in 1903 it is a Home International Championship involving the four Home Countries. There was no championship in 1976.

Wins:

34 Scotland	1904, 1907-10, 1912-4, 1919, 1921-3, 1928, 1932, 1935-6, 1950, 1952-3, 1963, 1965-75, 1977, 1979-80
24 England	1903, 1906, 1911, 1924, 1926-7, 1929, 1939, 1947, 1949, 1954-6, 1958-62, 1964, 1983-7
13 Wales	1920, 1925, 1930-1, 1933-4, 1937-8, 1946, 1948, 1957, 1978, 1982
3 Ireland	1905, 1951, 1981

ENGLISH BOWLING ASSOCIATION CHAMPIONSHIP
First held in 1903, the year of the formation of the EBA. The most titles is 16 won by David Bryant between 1957-75. He won six singles, three pairs, three triples, and four fours titles.

Recent winners:

SINGLES
1981 Andy Thomson
1982 Chris Ward

1983 John Bell
1984 Wynne Richards
1985 Roy Keating
1986 Wynne Richards

Most wins: 6 David Bryant 1960, 1966, 1971-3, 1975
4 Percy Baker 1932, 1946, 1952, 1955

PAIRS
1981 Burton House, Lincs. (Alan Bates & Richard White)
1982 Bedford Borough, Bucks (David Hurst & John McConnell)
1983 Eldon Grove, Durham (George Turley & Mal Hughes)
1984 Lenham, Kent (Ollie Jones & Len Hayes)
1985 Haxby Road, Yorks (Peter Richardson & Frank Maxwell)
1986 Owton Lodge, Durham (Dave Kilner & Cliff Simpson)

TRIPLES
1981 St.Peter's, Hants.
1982 Lenham, Kent
1983 Marlborough, Suffolk
1984 Clevedon, Avon
1985 Clevedon, Avon
1986 Poole Park, Dorset

FOURS
1981 Owton Lodge, Durham
1982 Castle, Notts
1983 Bolton, Gtr.Manchester
1984 Boscombe Cliff, Hants
1985 Aldersbrook, Essex
1986 Stony Stratford, Bucks

GATEWAY INTERNATIONAL MASTERS
A popular spring tournament played at Worthing annually since 1978. Originally sponsored by Kodak, Gateway became the new sponsors in 1984.
1978-9 David Bryant (Eng)
1980-1 William Moseley (SAf)
1982 David Bryant (Eng)
1983 George Souza (HK)
1984-7 David Bryant (Eng)

WATERLOO CUP
Crown Green bowling's premier tournament, the Waterloo Handicap, has been held since 1907 and has its home at Blackpool's Waterloo Hotel.

Recent winners:
1977 Len Barrett
1978 Arthur Murray
1979 Brian Duncan
1980 Vernon Lee
1981 Roy Nicholson
1982 Dennis Mercer
1983 Stan Frith
1984 Steve Ellis
1985 Tommy Johnstone
1986 Brian Duncan

Most wins: 2 Brian Duncan, Bernard Kelly (1953-4), Arthur Murray (1973, 1978)

BOXING

From the beginning of time man has fought his fellow man but the first record of a boxing match was in Britain in 1681. In 1719 James Figg of Oxfordshire set up his school of arms in London and he is regarded as the first boxing champion. The first boxing rules were drawn up by John Broughton in 1743 and the famous Queensberry Rules, to which the sport adheres, were drawn up in 1865.

WORLD CHAMPIONS

The first World Championship fight with gloves and under the Queensberry Rules was on 30 July 1884 when Irish-born Jack Dempsey beat George Fulljames of the United States for the middleweight title. The following is a list of all generally recognised world champions. Most weight divisions currently have three different champions as recognised by the WBA (World Boxing Association), WBC (World Boxing Council) and IBF (International Boxing Federation). Because the IBF is relatively new, and because its records are sketchy, only their heavyweight champions are included in this list, but all IBF world champions as at 1 August 1987 can be found at the end of these lists. The dates indicate when the title changed hands.

Champions:

HEAVYWEIGHT
Undisputed Champions
1892 James J. Corbett (USA)
1897 Bob Fitzsimmons (UK)
1899 James J. Jeffries (USA)
1905 Marvin Hart (USA)
1906 Tommy Burns (Can)
1908 Jack Johnson (USA)
1915 Jess Willard (USA)
1919 Jack Dempsey (USA)
1926 Gene Tunney (USA)
1930 Max Schmeling (FRG)
1932 Jack Sharkey (USA)
1933 Primo Carnera (Ita)
1934 Max Baer (USA)
1935 James J. Braddock (USA)
1937 Joe Louis (USA)
1949 Ezzard Charles (USA)
1951 Jersey Joe Walcott (USA)
1952 Rocky Marciano (USA)
1956 Floyd Patterson (USA)
1959 Ingemar Johansson (Swe)
1960 Floyd Patterson (USA)
1962 Sonny Liston (USA)
1964 Cassius Clay (USA)
1970 Joe Frazier (USA)
1973 George Foreman (USA)
1974 Muhammad Ali (USA)
(formerly Cassius Clay)
1978 Leon Spinks (USA)
1987 Mike Tyson (USA)

WBC Champions
1978 Ken Norton (USA)
1978 Larry Holmes (USA)
1984 Tim Witherspoon (USA)
1984 Pinklon Thomas (USA)
1986 Trevor Berbick (Can)
1986 Mike Tyson (USA)

WBA Champions
1965 Ernie Terrell (USA)
1968 Jimmy Ellis (USA)
1978 Muhammad Ali (USA)
1979 John Tate (USA)
1980 Mike Weaver (USA)
1982 Mike Dokes (USA)
1983 Gerrie Coetzee (SAf)
1984 Greg Page (USA)
1985 Tony Tubbs (USA)
1986 Tim Witherspoon (USA)
1986 James 'Bonecrusher' Smith (USA)
1987 Mike Tyson (USA)

IBF Champions
1984 Larry Holmes (USA)
1985 Michael Spinks (USA)
1987 Tony Tucker (USA)

CRUISERWEIGHT (195lb)
WBC Champions
1979 Marvin Camel (USA)
1980 Carlos de Leon (PR)
1982 S.T. Gordon (USA)
1983 Carlos de Leon (PR)
1985 Alfonso Ratliff (USA)
1985 Bernard Benton (USA)
1986 Carlos de Leon (PR)

WBA Junior Heavyweight Champions
1982 Osvaldo Ocasio (PR)
1984 Piet Crous (SAf)
1985 Dwight Muhammad Qawi (USA) (formerly Dwight Braxton)
1986 Evander Holyfield (USA)
1987 Francesco Damiani (Ita)

Muhammad Ali (Syndication International)

LIGHT HEAVYWEIGHT (175lb)
Undisputed Champions
1903 Jack Root (Aut)
1903 George Gardner (Ire)
1903 Bob Fitzsimmons (UK)
1905 Jack O'Brien (USA)
1912 Jack Dillon (USA)
1916 Battling Levinsky (USA)
1920 Georges Carpentier (Fra)
1922 Battling Siki (Fra/Sen)
1923 Mike McTigue (USA)
1925 Paul Berlenbach (USA)
1926 Jack Delaney (Can)
1927 Tommy Loughran (USA)
1930 Maxie Rosenbloom (USA)
1934 Bob Olin (USA)
1935 John Henry Lewis (USA)
1939 Billy Conn (USA)
1941 Gus Lesnevich (USA)
1948 Freddie Mills (UK)
1950 Joey Maxim (USA)
1952 Archie Moore (USA)
1962 Harold Johnson (USA)
1963 Willie Pastrano (USA)
1965 Jose Torres (PR)
1966 Dick Tiger (Nig)
1968 Bob Foster (USA)
1983 Michael Spinks (USA)

WBC Champions
1970 Bob Foster (USA)
1974 John Conteh (UK)
1977 Miguel Cuello (Arg)
1978 Mate Parlov (Yug)
1978 Marvin Johnson (USA)
1979 Matthew Saad Muhammad
 (USA)
 (formerly Matthew Franklin)
1981 Dwight Muhammad Braxton
 (USA)
 (formerly Dwight Braxton)
1985 J.B. Williamson (USA)
1986 Dennis Andries (UK)
1987 Thomas Hearns (USA)

WBA Champions
1971 Vicente Rondon (Ven)
1974 Victor Galindez (Arg)
1978 Mike Rossman (USA)
1979 Victor Galindez (Arg)
1980 Eddie Mustaffa Muhammad (USA)
 (formerly Eddie Gregory)
1981 Michael Spinks (USA)
1986 Marvin Johnson (USA)
1987 Leslie Stewart (Tri)

MIDDLEWEIGHT (160lb)
Undisputed Champions
1891 Nonpareil Jack Dempsey (Ire)
1891 Bob Fitzsimmons (UK)
1897 Kid McCoy (USA)
1898 Tommy Ryan (USA)
1908 Stanley Ketchel (USA)
1908 Billy Papke (USA)
1908 Stanley Ketchel (USA)

Above: *Marvin Hagler lost on points to Sugar Ray Leonard at Caesar's Palace, Las Vegas on 6 Apr 1987. This middleweight contest was the most expensive ever.* (All-Sport)   Below: *Sugar Ray Robinson stopped Randolph Turpin in 1951.* (The Photo Source)

1910 Billy Papke (USA)
1911 Cyclone Thompson (USA)
1913 George Chip (USA)
1914 Al McCoy (USA)
1917 Mike O'Dowd (USA)
1920 Johnny Wilson (USA)
1923 Harry Greb (USA)
1926 Tiger Flowers (USA)
1926 Mickey Walker (USA)
1936 Freddie Steele (USA)
1941 Tony Zale (USA)
1947 Rocky Graziano (USA)
1948 Tony Zale (USA)
1948 Marcel Cerdan (Fra)
1949 Jake La Motta (USA)
1951 Sugar Ray Robinson (USA)
1951 Randolph Turpin (UK)
1951 Sugar Ray Robinson (USA)
1953 Carl Bobo Olson (USA)
1955 Sugar Ray Robinson (USA)
1957 Gene Fullmer (USA)
1957 Carmen Basilio (USA)
1958 Sugar Ray Robinson (USA)
1960 Paul Pender (USA)
1961 Terry Downes (UK)
1962 Paul Pender (USA)
1962 Dick Tiger (Nig)
1963 Joey Giardello (USA)
1965 Dick Tiger (Nig)
1966 Emile Griffith (USA)
1967 Nino Benvenuti (Ita)
1967 Emile Griffith (USA)
1968 Nino Benvenuti (Ita)
1970 Carlos Monzon (Arg)
1976 Carlos Monzon (Arg)
1977 Rodrigo Valdez (Col)
1978 Hugo Corro (Arg)
1979 Vito Antuofermo (Ita)
1980 Alan Minter (UK)
1980 Marvin Hagler (USA)

WBC Champions
1974 Rodrigo Valdez (Col)
1987 Sugar Ray Leonard

WBA Champions
1974 Carlos Monzon (Arg)

LIGHT MIDDLEWEIGHT (154lb)
Undisputed Champions
1962 Denny Moyer (USA)
1963 Ralph Dupas (USA)
1963 Sandro Mazzinghi (Ita)
1965 Nino Benvenuti (Ita)
1966 Ki-Soo Kim (SKo)
1968 Sandro Mazzinghi (Ita)
1969 Freddie Little (USA)
1970 Carmelo Bossi (Ita)
1971 Koichi Wajima (Jap)
1974 Oscar Albarado (USA)
1975 Koichi Wajima (Jap)

WBC Super Welterweight Champions
1975 Miguel de Oliviera (Bra)
1975 Elisha Obed (Bah)
1976 Eckhard Dagge (FRG)

Henry Armstrong, the only man to hold three world titles simultaneously. (The Photo-Source)

1977 Rocky Mattioli (Ita)
1979 Maurice Hope (UK)
1981 Wilfred Benitez (USA)
1982 Thomas Hearns (USA)
1986 Duane Thomas (USA)
1987 Lupe Aquino (Mex)

WBA Junior Middleweight Champions
1975 Jae-Do Yuh (SKo)
1976 Koichi Wajima (Jap)
1976 Jose Duran (Spa)
1976 Miguel Angel Castellini (Arg)
1977 Eddie Gazo (Nic)
1978 Masashi Kudo (Jap)
1979 Ayub Kalule (Uga)
1981 Sugar Ray Leonard (USA)
1981 Tadashi Mihara (Jap)
1982 Davey Moore (USA)
1983 Roberto Duran (Pan)
1984 Mike McCallum (Jam)

WELTERWEIGHT (147lb)
Undisputed Champions
1888 Paddy Duffy (USA)
1892 Billy Smith (USA)
1894 Tommy Ryan (USA)
1896 Charles McCoy (USA)
1898 Billy Smith (USA)
1900 Rube Ferns (USA)
1900 Matty Matthews (USA)
1901 Rube Ferns (USA)
1901 Joe Walcott (USA)
1904 Dixie Kid (USA)
1906 Honey Mellody (USA)
1907 Mike Sullivan (USA)
1915 Ted Kid Lewis (UK)
1916 Jack Britton (USA)

1917 Ted Kid Lewis (UK)
1919 Jack Britton (USA)
1922 Mickey Walker (USA)
1926 Pete Latzo (USA)
1927 Joe Dundee (Ita)
1929 Jackie Fields (USA)
1930 Jack Thompson (USA)
1930 Tommy Freeman (USA)
1931 Jack Thompson (USA)
1931 Lou Brouillard (Can)
1932 Jackie Fields (USA)
1933 Young Corbett III (Ita)
1933 Jimmy McLarnin (Ire)
1934 Barney Ross (USA)
1934 Jimmy McLarnin (Ire)
1935 Barney Ross (USA)
1938 Henry Armstrong (USA)
1940 Fritzie Zivic (USA)
1941 Red Cochrane (USA)
1946 Marty Servo (USA)
1946 Sugar Ray Robinson (USA)
1951 Kid Gavilan (Cub)
1954 Johnny Saxton (USA)
1955 Tony de Marco (USA)
1955 Carmen Basilio (USA)
1956 Johnny Saxton (USA)
1956 Carmen Basilio (USA)
1958 Virgil Atkins (USA)
1958 Don Jordon (USA)
1960 Benny Paret (Cub)
1961 Emile Griffith (USA)
1961 Benny Paret (Cub)
1962 Emile Griffith (USA)
1963 Luis Rodriguez (Cub)
1963 Emile Griffith (USA)
1966 Curtis Cokes (USA)
1969 Jose Napoles (Cub)

1970 Billy Backus (USA)
1971 Jose Napoles (Cub)
1981 Sugar Ray Leonard (USA)
1985 Don Curry (USA)
1986 Lloyd Honeyghan (UK)

WBC Champions
1975 John H. Stracey (UK)
1976 Carlos Palomino (Mex)
1979 Wilfred Benitez (USA)
1979 Sugar Ray Leonard (USA)
1980 Roberto Duran (Pan)
1980 Sugar Ray Leonard (USA)
1983 Milton McCrory (USA)

WBA Champions
1966 Curtis Cokes (USA)
1975 Angel Espada (PR)
1976 Pipino Cuevas (Mex)
1980 Thomas Hearns (USA)
1983 Don Curry (USA)
1987 Mark Breland (USA)

LIGHT WELTERWEIGHT (140lb)
Undisputed Champions
1926 Mushy Callahan (USA)
1930 Jackie Berg (UK)
1931 Tony Canzoneri (USA)
1932 Johnny Jaddick (USA)
1933 Battling Shaw (Mex)
1933 Tony Canzoneri (USA)
1933 Barney Ross (USA)
1946 Tippy Larkin (USA)
1959 Carlos Ortiz (PR)
1960 Duilio Loi (Ita)
1962 Eddie Perkins (USA)
1962 Duilio Loi (Ita)
1963 Roberto Cruz (Phi)
1963 Eddie Perkins (USA)
1965 Carlos Hernandez (Ven)
1966 Sandro Lopopolo (Ita)
1967 Paul Fujii (Haw)

WBC Super Lightweight Champions
1968 Pedro Adigue (Phi)
1970 Bruno Arcari (Ita)
1974 Perico Fernandez (Spa)
1975 Saensak Muangsurin (Tha)
1976 Miguel Velasquez (Spa)
1976 Saensak Muangsurin (Tha)
1978 Sang-Hyun Kim (SKo)
1980 Saoul Mamby (USA)
1982 Leroy Haley (USA)
1983 Bruce Curry (USA)
1984 Billy Costello (USA)
1985 Lonnie Smith (USA)
1986 Rene Arredondo (Mex)
1986 Tsuyoshi Hamada (Jap)
1987 Rene Arredondo (Mex)

WBA Champions
1968 Nicolino Loche (Arg)
1972 Alfonso Frazer (Pan)
1972 Antonio Cervantes (Col)
1976 Wilfred Benitez (USA)
1977 Antonio Cervantes (Col)
1980 Aaron Pryor (USA)

Sugar Ray Leonard (r) regained his world welterweight title from Roberto Duran (l) in 1980. (All-Sport)

1984 Johnny Bumphus (USA)
1984 Gene Hatcher (USA)
1985 Ubaldo Sacco (Arg)
1986 Patrizio Oliva (Ita)
1987 Juan Martin Coggi (Arg)

LIGHTWEIGHT (135lb)
Undisputed Champions
1888 Jack McAuliffe (Ire)
1896 George Lavigne (USA)
1899 Frank Erne (Swi)
1902 Joe Gans (USA)
1908 Battling Nelson (Den)
1910 Ad Wolgast (USA)
1912 Willie Ritchie (USA)
1914 Freddie Welsh (UK)
1917 Benny Leonard (USA)
1925 Jimmy Goodrich (USA)
1926 Sammy Mandell (USA)
1930 Al Singer (USA)
1930 Tony Canzeroni (USA)
1933 Barney Ross (USA)
1935 Tony Canzeroni (USA)
1936 Lou Ambers (USA)
1938 Henry Armstrong (USA)
1939 Lou Ambers (USA)
1941 Sammy Angott (USA)
1947 Ike Williams (USA)
1951 Jimmy Carter (USA)
1952 Lauro Salas (Mex)
1952 Jimmy Carter (USA)
1954 Paddy de Marco (USA)
1954 Jimmy Carter (USA)
1955 Wallace Smith (USA)
1956 Joe Brown (USA)
1962 Carlos Ortiz (PR)
1965 Ismael Laguna (Pan)

1965 Carlos Ortiz (PR)
1967 Carlos Ortiz (PR)
1968 Carlos Teo Cruz (Dom)
1969 Mando Ramos (USA)
1970 Ismael Laguna (Pan)
1970 Ken Buchanan (UK)
1978 Roberto Duran (Pan)

WBC Champions
1971 Pedro Carrasco (Spa)
1972 Mando Ramos (USA)
1972 Chango Carmona (Mex)
1972 Rodolfo Gonzalez (Mex)
1974 Guts Ishimatsu (Jap)
1976 Esteban de Jesus (PR)
1979 Jim Watt (UK)
1981 Alexis Arguello (Nic)
1983 Edwin Rosario (PR)
1984 Jose Luis Ramirez (Mex)
1985 Hector Camacho (PR)
1987 Jose Luis Ramirez (Mex)

WBA Champions
1966 Carlos Ortiz (PR)
1971 Ken Buchanan (UK)
1972 Roberto Duran (Pan)
1979 Ernesto Espana (Ven)
1980 Hilmer Kenty (USA)
1981 Sean O'Grady (USA)
1981 Claude Noel (Tri)
1981 Arturo Frias (USA)
1982 Ray Mancini (USA)
1984 Livingstone Bramble (USA)
1986 Edwin Rosario (PR)

JUNIOR LIGHTWEIGHT (130lb)
Undisputed Champions
1921 Johnny Dundee (Ita)
1923 Jack Bernstein (USA)

1923 Johnny Dundee (Ita)
1924 Steve Sullivan (USA)
1925 Mike Balerino (USA)
1925 Tod Morgan (USA)
1929 Benny Bass (USA)
1931 Kid Chocolate (Cub)
1933 Frankie Klick (USA)
1959 Harold Gomes (USA)
1960 Flash Elorde (Phi)
1967 Yoshiaki Numata (Jap)
1967 Hiroshi Kobayashi (Jap)

WBC Super Featherweight Champions
1969 Rene Barrientos (Phi)
1970 Yoshiaki Numata (Jap)
1971 Ricardo Arredondo (Mex)
1974 Kuniaki Shibata (Jap)
1975 Alfredo Escalera (PR)
1978 Alexis Arguello (Nic)
1980 Rafael Limon (Mex)
1981 Cornelius Boza-Edwards (UK)
1981 Rolando Navarette (Phi)
1982 Rafael Limon (Mex)
1982 Bobby Chacon (USA)
1983 Hector Camacho (PR)
1984 Julio Cesar Chavez (Mex)

WBA Champions
1969 Hiroshi Kobayashi (Jap)
1971 Alfredo Marcano (Ven)
1972 Ben Villaflor (Phi)
1973 Kuniaki Shibata (Jap)
1973 Ben Villaflor (Phi)
1976 Sam Serrano (PR)
1980 Yasutsune Uehara (Jap)
1981 Sam Serrano (PR)
1983 Roger Mayweather (USA)
1984 Rocky Lockridge (USA)
1985 Wilfredo Gomez (PR)
1986 Alfredo Layne (Pan)
1986 Brian Mitchell (SAf)

FEATHERWEIGHT (126lb)
Undisputed Champions
1889 Ike Weir (UK)
1890 Billy Murphy (NZ)
1890 Young Griffo (Aus)
1891 George Dixon (Can)
1897 Solly Smith (USA)
1898 Dave Sullivan (Ire)
1898 George Dixon (Can)
1900 Terry McGovern (USA)
1901 Young Corbett II (USA)
1906 Abe Attell (USA)
1912 Johnny Kilbane (USA)
1923 Eugene Criqui (Fra)
1923 Johnny Dundee (Ita)
1925 Louis Kaplan (USA)
1927 Benny Bass (USA)
1928 Tony Canzoneri (USA)
1928 Andre Routis (Fra)
1929 Battling Battalino (USA)
1937 Henry Armstrong (USA)
1939 Joey Archibald (USA)
1946 Willie Pep (USA)

Willie Pep (The Photo Source)

1948 Sandy Saddler (USA)
1949 Willie Pep (USA)
1950 Sandy Saddler (USA)
1957 Hogan Kid Bassey (USA)
1959 Davey Moore (USA)
1963 Sugar Ramos (Cub)
1964 Vicente Saldivar (Mex)

WBC Champions
1968 Howard Winstone (UK)
1968 Jose Legra (Cub)
1969 Johnny Famechon (Fra)
1970 Vicente Saldivar (Mex)
1970 Kuniaki Shibata (Jap)
1972 Clemente Sanchez (Mex)
1972 Jose Legra (Cub)
1973 Eder Jofre (Bra)
1974 Bobby Chacon (USA)
1975 Ruben Olivares (Mex)
1975 David Kotey (Gha)
1976 Danny Lopez (USA)
1980 Salvador Sanchez (Mex)
1982 Juan Laporte (PR)
1984 Wilfredo Gomez (PR)
1984 Azumah Nelson (Gha)

WBA Champions
1968 Raul Rojas (USA)
1968 Shozo Saijyo (Jap)
1971 Antonio Gomez (Ven)
1972 Ernesto Marcel (Pan)
1974 Ruben Olivares (Mex)
1974 Alexis Arguello (Nic)
1977 Rafael Ortega (Pan)
1977 Cecilio Lastra (Spa)
1978 Eusebio Pedroza (Pan)
1985 Barry McGuigan (UK)
1986 Steve Cruz (USA)
1987 Antonio Esparragoza (Ven)

JUNIOR FEATHERWEIGHT (122lb)
WBC Super Bantamweight Champions
1976 Rigoberto Riasco (Pan)
1976 Royal Kobayashi (Jap)
1976 Dong-Kyun Yum (SKo)
1977 Wilfredo Gomez (PR)
1983 Jaime Garza (USA)

1984 Juan Kid Meza (Mex)
1985 Lupe Pintor (Mex)
1986 Samart Payakarum (Tha)
1987 Jeff Fenech (Aus)

WBA Champions
1977 Soo-Hwan Hong (SKo)
1978 Ricardo Cardona (Col)
1980 Leo Randolph (USA)
1980 Sergio Palma (Arg)
1982 Leo Cruz (Dom)
1984 Loris Stecca (Ita)
1984 Victor Callejas (PR)
1987 Louis Espinoza (USA)

BANTAMWEIGHT (118lb)
Undisputed Champions
1891 George Dixon (Can)
1897 Jimmy Barry (USA)
1899 Terry McGovern (USA)
1901 Harry Harris (USA)
1901 Harry Forbes (USA)
1903 Frankie Neil (USA)
1904 Joe Bowker (UK)
1905 Jimmy Walsh (USA)
1911 Johnny Coulon (Can)
1914 Kid Williams (Den)
1917 Pete Herman (USA)
1920 Joe Lynch (USA)
1921 Pete Herman (USA)
1921 Johnny Buff (USA)
1922 Joe Lynch (USA)
1924 Abe Goldstein (USA)
1924 Eddie Martin (USA)
1925 Charlie Rosenberg (USA)
1929 Al Brown (Pan)
1936 Sixto Escobar (PR)
1937 Harry Jeffra (USA)
1938 Sixto Escobar (PR)
1940 Lou Salica (USA)
1942 Manuel Ortiz (USA)
1947 Harold Dade (USA)
1947 Manuel Ortiz (USA)
1950 Vic Toweel (SAf)
1952 Jimmy Carruthers (Aus)
1954 Robert Cohen (Fra)
1957 Alphonse Halimi (Fra)
1959 Joe Becerra (Mex)
1960 Eder Jofre (Bra)
1965 Fighting Harada (Jap)
1968 Lionel Rose (Aus)
1969 Ruben Olivares (Mex)
1970 Jesus Castillo (Mex)
1971 Ruben Olivares (Mex)
1972 Rafael Herrera (Mex)
1972 Enrique Pinder (Pan)

WBC Champions
1973 Rafael Herrera (Mex)
1974 Rodolfo Martinez (Mex)
1976 Carlos Zarate (Mex)
1979 Lupe Pintor (Mex)
1983 Albert Davila (USA)
1985 Daniel Zaragoza (Mex)
1985 Miguel Lora (Col)
1987 Takuya Mugurama (Jap)

1987 Park Chan-Young (SKo)

WBA Champions
1973 Romeo Anaya (Mex)
1973 Arnold Taylor (SAf)
1974 Soo-Hwan Hong (SKo)
1975 Alfonso Zamora (Mex)
1977 Jorge Lujan (Pan)
1980 Julian Solis (PR)
1980 Jeff Chandler (USA)
1984 Richard Sandoval (USA)
1986 Gaby Canizales (USA)
1986 Bernardo Pinango (Ven)

SUPER FLYWEIGHT (115lb)
WBC Champions
1980 Rafael Orono (Ven)
1981 Chul-Ho Kim (SKo)
1982 Rafael Orono (Ven)
1983 Payao Poontarat (Tha)
1984 Jiro Watanabe (Jap)
1986 Gilberto Roman (Mex)
1987 Santos Laciar (Arg)

WBA Junior Bantamweight Champions
1981 Gustavo Ballas (Arg)
1981 Rafael Pedroza (Pan)
1982 Jiro Watanabe (Jap)
1984 Kaosai Galaxy (Tha)

FLYWEIGHT (112lb)
Undisputed Champion
1916 Jimmy Wilde (UK)
1923 Pancho Villa (Phi)
1925 Fidel la Barba (USA)
1928 Frankie Genaro (USA)
1937 Benny Lynch (UK)
1938 Peter Kane (UK)
1943 Jackie Paterson (UK)
1948 Rinty Monaghan (UK)
1950 Terry Allen (UK)
1950 Dado Marino (Haw)
1952 Yoshio Shirai (Jap)
1954 Pascual Perez (Arg)
1960 Pone Kingpetch (Tha)
1962 Fighting Harada (Jap)
1963 Pone Kingpetch (Tha)
1963 Hiroyuki Ebihara (Jap)
1964 Pone Kingpetch (Tha)
1965 Salvatore Burruni (Ita)

WBC Champions
1965 Salvatore Burruni (Ita)
1966 Walter McGowan (UK)
1966 Chartchai Chionoi (Tha)
1969 Efren Torres (Mex)
1970 Chartchai Chionoi (Tha)
1970 Erbito Salavarria (Phi)
1972 Betulio Gonzalez (Ven)
1972 Venice Borkorsor (Tha)
1973 Betulio Gonzalez (Ven)

Left: *Jimmy Wilde* (Syndication International)
Right: *Joe Louis – the "Brown Bomber"* (The Photo Source)

1974 Shoji Oguma (Jap)
1975 Miguel Canto (Mex)
1979 Chan-Hee Park (Sko)
1980 Shoji Oguma (Jap)
1981 Antonio Avelar (Mex)
1982 Prudencio Cardona (Col)
1982 Freddie Castillo (Mex)
1982 Eleoncio Mercedes (Dom)
1983 Charlie Magri (UK)
1983 Frank Cedeno (Phi)
1984 Koji Kobayashi (Jap)
1984 Gabriel Bernal (Mex)
1984 Sot Chitalada (Tha)
1987 Richard Clarke (Jam)

WBA Champions
1966 Horacio Accavallo (Arg)
1969 Hiroyuki Ebihara (Jap)
1969 Bernabe Villacampo (Phi)
1970 Berkrerk Chartvanchai (Tha)
1970 Masao Ohba (Jap)
1973 Chartchai Chionoi (Tha)
1974 Susumu Hanagata (Jap)
1975 Erbito Salavarria (Phi)
1976 Alfonso Lopez (Pan)
1976 Gustavo Espadas (Mex)
1978 Betulio Gonzalez (Ven)
1979 Luis Ibarra (Pan)
1980 Tae-Shik Kim (SKo)
1980 Peter Mathebula (SAf)
1981 Santos Laciar (Arg)

1981 Luis Ibarra (Pan)
1981 Juan Herrera (Mex)
1982 Santos Laciar (Arg)
1985 Hilario Zapata (Pan)
1987 Fidel Bassa (Col)

LIGHT FLYWEIGHT (108LB)
WBC Champions
1975 Franco Udella (Ita)
1975 Luis Estaba (Ven)
1978 Freddie Castillo (Mex)
1978 Sung-Jun Kim (SKo)
1978 Netrnoi Vorasingh (Tha)
1980 Shigeo Nakajima (Jap)
1980 Hilario Zapata (Pan)
1982 Amado Ursua (Mex)
1982 Tadashi Tomori (Jap)
1982 Hilario Zapata (Pan)
1983 Chang Jung-Koo (SKo)

WBA Junior Flyweight Champions
1975 Jaime Rios (Pan)
1976 Juan Jose Guzman (Dom)
1976 Yoko Gushiken (Jap)
1981 Pedro Flores (Mex)
1981 Hwan-Jin Kim (SKo)
1981 Katsuo Takashiki (Jap)
1983 Lupe Madera (Mex)
1984 Francisco Quiroz (Dom)
1985 Joey Olivo (USA)
1985 Yuh Myung-Woo (SKo)

Longest reigning champion: Joe Louis (USA – heavyweight) 11 years 252 days
Most successful defences: 25 Joe Louis (USA – heavyweight) 1937-48
Most titles at one weight: 'Sugar' Ray Robinson (USA) captured the middleweight title five times between 1951-8
World champions at three different weights:
Bob Fitzsimmons (UK) middle, heavy, light-heavy
Tony Canzoneri (USA) feather, light, light-welter

Barney Ross (USA) light, light-welter, welter
Henry Armstrong (USA) feather, welter, light (Armstrong held all three simultaneously)
Wilfred Benitez (USA) light-welter, welter, light-middle
Alexis Arguello (Nic) feather, junior-light, light
Roberto Duran (Pan) light, welter, light-middle
Wilfredo Gomez (PR) super-bantam, feather, junior-light
Sugar Ray Leonard (USA) welter, junior-middle, middle
Thomas Hearns (USA) welter, junior-middle, light-heavy
Oldest world champion: 48 years 59 days Archie Moore (USA) light-heavyweight (Moore may only have been 45 because of a doubt over his date of birth, but he would still have been the oldest world champion)
Youngest world champion: 17 years 176 days Wilfred Benitez (USA) light-welterweight
Heaviest world champion: 270lb (122kg) Primo Carnera (Ita)
Tallest world champion: 6ft 5.4in (196.6cm) Primo Carnera (Ita) (Jess Willard is often quoted as being 6ft 6¼in (199 cm) but he was only 6ft 5in (196cm))

MOST SUCCESSFUL DEFENCES
(In one weight division)
25 Joe Louis (USA) heavyweight 1937-48
20 Larry Holmes (USA) heavyweight 1978-85
19 Henry Armstrong (USA) welterweight 1938-40
19 Manuel Ortiz (USA) bantamweight 1942-6, 1947-9
19 Muhammad Ali (USA) heavyweight 1965-7. 1975-7
19 Eusebio Pedroza (Pan) 1978-85

MOST WORLD TITLE FIGHTS
27 Joe Louis (USA) heavyweight 1937-50
25 Henry Armstrong (USA) middleweight, welterweight, lightweight, flyweight 1937-41
25 Muhammad Ali (USA) heavyweight 1964-80

INTERNATIONAL BOXING FEDERATION (IBF)
The IBF was formed in the United States in 1983 and was initially known as the United States Boxing Association International. It was formed to challenge the status of the two controlling bodies, the WBC and WBA, but has failed to attract the anticipated interest other than in Asia, Australia, and parts of the United States.

Champions as at 1 August 1987
Heavyweight — Mike Tyson (USA)
Cruiserweight — Evander Holyfield (USA)
Light Heavyweight — Bobby Czyz (USA)
Super Middleweight — Chong Pal-Park (SKo)
Middleweight — vacant
Junior Middleweight — Matthew Hilton (Can)
Welterweight — Lloyd Honeyghan (UK)
Junior Welterweight — Terry Marsh (UK)
Lightweight — Vinny Pazienza (USA)
Junior Lightweight — Barry Michael (Aus)
Featherweight — Antonio Rivera (PR)
Light Featherweight — Lee Sung-Hoon (SKo)
Bantamweight — Kelvin Seabrooks (USA)
Junior Bantamweight — Chang Tae-Il (SKo)
Flyweight — Dodie Penalosa (Phi)
Junior Flyweight — Choi Jum-Hwan (SKo)

OLYMPIC GAMES
Boxing was included in the 1904 celebration at St Louis and has been included at every Games since then with the exception of 1912. The weight limits given are those that have been standard since 1952; they were slightly different before then.

SUPER-HEAVYWEIGHT *(Over 91kg)*
1984 Tyrell Biggs (USA)

HEAVYWEIGHT *(91kg; over 81kg prior to 1984)*
1904 Samuel Berger (USA)
1908 Albert Oldham (UK)
1920 Ronald Rawson (UK)
1924 Otto von Porat (Nor)
1928 Arturo Rodriguez Jurado (Arg)
1932 Santiago Lovell (Arg)
1936 Herbert Runge (FRG)
1948 Rafael Iglesias (Arg)
1952 Edward Sanders (USA)
1956 Peter Rademacher (USA)
1960 Francesco De Piccoli (Ita)
1964 Joe Frazier (USA)
1968 George Foreman (USA)
1972 Teofilio Stevenson (Cub)
1976 Teofilio Stevenson (Cub)
1980 Teofilio Stevenson (Cub)
1984 Henry Tillman (USA)

LIGHT-HEAVYWEIGHT *(81kg)*
1920 Edward Eagan (USA)
1924 Harry Mitchell (UK)
1928 Victor Avendano (Arg)
1932 David Carstens (SAf)
1936 Roger Michelot (Fra)
1948 George Hunter (SAf)
1952 Norvel Lee (USA)
1956 James Boyd (USA)
1960 Cassius Clay (USA)
1964 Cosimo Pinto (Ita)
1968 Dan Poznyak (USSR)
1972 Mate Parlov (Yug)
1976 Leon Spinks (USA)
1980 Slobodan Kacar (Yug)
1984 Anton Jospovic (Yug)

MIDDLEWEIGHT *(75kg)*
1904 Charles Mayer (USA)
1908 John Douglas (UK)
1920 Harry Mallin (UK)
1924 Harry Mallin (UK)
1928 Piero Toscani (Ita)
1932 Carmen Barth (USA)
1936 Jean Despeaux (Fra)
1948 Laszlo Papp (Hun)
1952 Floyd Patterson (USA)
1956 Gennadiy Schatkov (USSR)
1960 Edward Crook (USA)
1964 Valeriy Popentschenko (USSR)
1968 Chris Finnegan (UK)
1972 Vyacheslav Lemechev (USSR)
1976 Michael Spinks (USA)
1980 José Gomez (Cub)
1984 Sin-Joon Sup (SKo)

LIGHT-MIDDLEWEIGHT *(71kg)*
1952 Laszlo Papp (Hun)
1956 Laszlo Papp (Hun)
1960 Wilbert McClure (USA)
1964 Boris Lagutin (USSR)
1968 Boris Lagutin (USSR)
1972 Dieter Kottysch (FRG)
1976 Jerzy Rybicki (Pol)
1980 Armando Martinez (Cub)
1984 Frank Tate (USA)

WELTERWEIGHT *(67kg)*
1904 Albert Young (USA)
1920 Albert Schneider (Can)
1924 Jean Delarge (Bel)
1928 Edward Morgan (NZ)
1932 Edward Flynn (USA)
1936 Sten Stuvio (Fin)
1948 Julius Torma (Cs)
1952 Zygmunt Chychla (Pol)
1956 Nicholae Linca (Rom)
1960 Giovanni Benvenuti (Ita)
1964 Marian Kasprzyk (Pol)
1968 Manfred Wolke (GDR)
1972 Emilio Correa (Cub)
1976 Jochen Bachfeld (GDR)
1980 Andres Aldama (Cub)
1984 Mark Breland (USA)

LIGHT-WELTERWEIGHT *(63.5kg)*
1952 Charles Adkins (USA)
1956 Vladimir Yengibaryan (USSR)
1960 Bohumil Numecek (Cs)
1964 Jerzy Kulej (Pol)
1968 Jerzy Kulej (Pol)
1972 Ray Seales (USA)
1976 Ray Leonard (USA)
1980 Patrizio Oliva (Ita)
1984 Jerry Page (USA)

LIGHTWEIGHT *(60kg)*
1904 Harry Spanger (USA)
1908 Frederick Grace (UK)
1920 Samuel Mosberg (USA)
1924 Hans Nielsen (Den)
1928 Carlo Orlandi (Ita)
1932 Lawrence Stevens (SAf)
1936 Imre Harangi (Hun)
1948 Gerald Dreyer (SAf)
1952 Aureliano Bolognesi (Ita)
1956 Dick McTaggart (UK)
1960 Kazimierz Pazdzior (Pol)
1964 Jozef Grudzien (Pol)
1968 Ronnie Harris (USA)
1972 Jan Szczepanski (Pol)
1976 Howard Davis (USA)
1980 Angel Herrera (Cub)
1984 Pernell Whitaker (USA)

FEATHERWEIGHT *(57kg)*
1904 Oliver Kirk (USA)
1908 Richard Gunn (UK)
1920 Paul Fritsch (Fra)
1924 John Fields (USA)
1928 Lambertus van Klaveren (Hol)
1932 Carmelo Robledo (Arg)
1936 Oscar Casanovas (Arg)
1948 Ernesto Formenti (Ita)

1952 Jan Zachara (Cs)
1956 Vladimir Safronov (USSR)
1960 Francesco Musso (Ita)
1964 Stanislav Stepashkin (USSR)
1968 Antonio Roldan (Mex)
1972 Boris Kuznyetsov (USSR)
1976 Angel Herrera (Cub)
1980 Rudi Fink (GDR)
1984 Meldrick Taylor (USA)

BANTAMWEIGHT *(54kg)*
1904 Oliver Kirk (USA)
1908 Henry Thomas (UK)
1920 Clarence Walker (SAf)
1924 William Smith (SAf)
1928 Vittorio Tamagnini (Ita)
1932 Horace Gwynne (Can)
1936 Ulderico Sergo (Ita)
1948 Tibor Csik (Hun)
1952 Pentti Hämäläinen (Fin)
1956 Wolfgang Behrendt (FRG)
1960 Oleg Grigoryev (USSR)
1964 Takao Sakurai (Jap)
1968 Valeriy Sokolov (USSR)
1972 Orlando Martinez (Cub)
1976 Yong-Jo Gu (NKo)
1980 Juan Hernandez (Cub)
1984 Maurizio Stecca (Ita)

FLYWEIGHT *(51kg)*
1904 George Finnegan (USA)
1920 Frank Di Gennara (USA)
1924 Fidel LaBarba (USA)
1928 Antal Kocsis (Hun)
1932 Istvan Enekes (Hun)
1936 Willi Kaiser (FRG)
1948 Pascual Perez (Arg)
1952 Nathan Brooks (USA)
1956 Terry Spinks (UK)
1960 Gyula Török (Hun)
1964 Fernando Atzori (Ita)
1968 Ricardo Delgado (Mex)
1972 Gheorghi Kostadinov (Bul)
1976 Leo Randolph (USA)
1980 Peter Lessov (Bul)
1984 Steve McCrory (USA)

LIGHT-FLYWEIGHT *(48kg)*
1968 Francisco Rodriguez (Ven)
1972 György Gedö (Hun)
1976 Jorge Hernández (Cub)
1980 Shamil Sabirov (USSR)
1984 Paul Gonzales (USA)

Teofilo Stevenson, three Olympic gold medals and three World Amateur titles. (All-Sport)

Leading Medallists	Gold	Silver	Bronze	Total
United States	42	17	26	85
USSR	13	18	15	46
United Kingdom	12	10	19	41
Italy	13	12	13	38
Poland	8	9	21	38
Cuba	12	8	5	25

Most individual gold medals:
3 Laszlo Papp (Hun) middle 1948, lt-middle 1952, 1956
3 Teofilio Stevenson (Cub) heavy 1972, 1976, 1980
Oldest champion: 37 years 254 days Richard Gunn (UK) feather 1908
Youngest champion: 16 years 162 days Jackie Fields (USA) feather 1924

Olympic champions who went on to win professional titles:

	Olympic title	First Professional Title
Fidel LaBarba (USA)	1924 fly	1925 fly
Willie Smith (SAf)	1924 bantam	1927 bantam
(Smith won the British version of the world title)		
Frankie Genaro (USA)	1920 fly	1928 fly
Jackie Fields (USA)	1924 feather	1929 welter
Pascual Perez (Arg)	1948 fly	1954 fly
Floyd Patterson (USA)	1952 middle	1956 heavy
Cassius Clay (USA)	1960 light-heavy	1964 heavy
Giovanni (Nino) Benvenuti (Ita)	1960 welter	1965 light-middle
Joe Frazier (USA)	1964 heavy	1968 heavy
George Foreman (USA)	1968 heavy	1973 heavy
Mate Parlov (Yug)	1972 light-heavy	1978 light-heavy
Leon Spinks (USA)	1976 light-heavy	1978 heavy
'Sugar' Ray Leonard (USA)	1976 light-welter	1979 light-middle
Leo Randolph (USA)	1976 fly	1980 light-fly
Michael Spinks (USA)	1976 middle	1981 light-heavy
Slobodan Kacar (Yug)	1980 light-heavy	1985 middle
Patrizio Oliva (Ita)	1980 light-welter	1986 junior-welter
Mark Breland (USA)	1984 welter	1987 welter

WORLD AMATEUR CHAMPIONSHIPS

First held in Havana in 1974 they are held every four years, in between Olympic Games. Belgrade played host in 1978, Munich in 1982 and Reno in 1986. A challenge series, involving seven of the 1982 champions, was organised in Reno in March 1983, and a second series of challenge bouts for the remaining champions took place in Tokyo two months later.

SUPER-HEAVYWEIGHT *(over 91kg)*
1982 Tyrell Biggs (USA)
1983 Tyrell Biggs (USA)
1986 Teofilio Stevenson (Cub)

HEAVYWEIGHT *(91kg)*
1974 Teofilio Stevenson (Cub)
1978 Teofilio Stevenson (Cub)
1982 Aleksandr Lagubkin (USSR)
1983 Willie DeWitt (Can)
1986 Felix Savon (Cub)

LIGHT-HEAVYWEIGHT *(81kg)*
1974 Mate Parlov (Yug)
1978 Sixto Soria (Cub)
1982 Pablo Romero (Cub)
1983 Pablo Romero (Cub)
1986 Pablo Romero (Cub)

MIDDLEWEIGHT *(75kg)*
1974 Rufat Riskiyev (USSR)
1978 Jose Gomez (Cub)
1982 Bernardo Comas (Cub)
1983 Bernardo Comas (Cub)
1986 Darin Allen (USA)

LIGHT-MIDDLEWEIGHT *(71kg)*
1974 Rolando Garbey (Cub)
1978 Viktor Savchenko (USSR)
1982 Aleksandr Koshkin (USSR)

1983 Shawn O'Sullivan (Can)
1986 Angel Espinosa (Cub)

WELTERWEIGHT *(67kg)*
1974 Emilio Correa (Cub)
1978 Valeriy Rachkov (USSR)
1982 Mark Breland (USA)
1983 Mark Breland (USA)
1986 Kenneth Gould (USA)

LIGHT-WELTERWEIGHT *(63.5kg)*
1974 Ayub Kalule (Uga)
1978 Valeriy Lvov (USSR)
1982 Carlos Garcia (Cub)
1983 Carlos Garcia (Cub)
1986 Vasiliy Shishov (USSR)

LIGHTWEIGHT *(60kg)*
1974 Vasiliy Solomin (USSR)
1978 Andeh Davison (Nig)
1982 Angel Herrera (Cub)
1983 Pernell Whitaker (USA)
1986 Adolfo Horta (Cub)

FEATHERWEIGHT *(57kg)*
1974 Howard Davis (USA)
1978 Angel Herrera (Cub)
1982 Adolfo Horta (Cub)
1983 Adolfo Horta (Cub)
1986 Kelcie Banks (USA)

BANTAMWEIGHT *(54kg)*
1974 Wilfredo Gomez (PR)
1978 Adolfo Horta (Cub)
1982 Floyd Favors (USA)
1983 Floyd Favors (USA)
1986 Moon Sung-Kil (SKo)

FLYWEIGHT *(51kg)*
1974 Douglas Rodriguez (Cub)
1978 Henryk Srednicki (Pol)
1982 Yuriy Aleksandrov (USSR)
1983 Steve McCrory (USA)
1986 Pedro Reyes (Cub)

LIGHT-FLYWEIGHT *(48kg)*
1974 Jorge Hernandez (Cub)
1978 Stephen Muchoki (Ken)
1982 Ismail Mustafov (Bul)
1983 Rafael Saiz (Cub)
1986 Juan Torres (Cub)

WORLDCUP

First held in 1979.
Winners:
1979 USA
1981 USA
1983 North America
1985 Europe

BRIDGE (CONTRACT)

This card game was developed from Whist, with the extra dimension of a competititive auction added. Auction Bridge, in which the highest bidder names trumps was first played in about 1903. It was superseded by Contract, in which no tricks won in the play are counted towards game unless contracted for in the bidding, a principle used earlier in Plafond.

Contract Bridge developed erratically until the present scoring table was devised in 1925 by Harold S.Vanderbilt (USA). Highly publicised matches staged brilliantly by Ely Cuthbertson (USA) against Col.Walter Buller's British team in 1930 and Sydney Lenz's 'official' US team in 1931 attracted worldwide publicity and made Cuthbertson the supreme authority.

The ruling body is the World Bridge Federation.

WORLD TEAM CHAMPIONSHIP

Contested by international teams for the Bermuda Bowl; first held in 1951, at first annually and now biennially.

Wins:

13	Italy	1957-9, 1961-3, 1965-7, 1969, 1973-5
10	USA	1951-4, 1971, 1976-7, 1979, 1981, 1983, 1985
1	Great Britain	1955, France 1956, North America 1970

Women's teams compete for the Venice Trophy, now held concurrently with the Bermuda Bowl.

3	USA	1974, 1976, 1978
2	Great Britain	1981, 1985

WORLD TEAM OLYMPIAD

First held in 1960.

Winners:

Year	Open	Women
1960	France	United Arab Republic
1964	Italy	Great Britain
1968	Italy	Sweden
1972	Italy	Italy
1976	Brazil	USA
1980	France	USA
1984	Poland	USA

WORLD PAIRS OPEN CHAMPIONS

1962 Pierre Jais & Roger Trézel (Fra)
1966 Cornelius Slavenburg & Hans Kreyns (Hol)
1970 Fritz Babsch & Peter Manhardt (Aut)
1974 Robert Hamman & Robert Wolff (USA)
1978 Marcello Branco & Gabino Cintra (Bra)
1982 Chip Martell & Lew Stansby (USA)
1986 Jeff Meckstroth & Eric Rodwell (USA)

Women's champions:
1962 Rixi Markus & Fritzi Gordon (UK)
1966 Joan Durran & Jane Priday (UK)
1970 Mary Jane Farrell & Marilyn Johnson (USA)
1974 Rixi Markus & Fritzi Gordon (UK)
1978 Kathie Wei & Judi Radin (USA)
1982 Carol Sanders & Betty Ann Kennedy (USA)
1986 Jacqui Mitchell & Amalya Kearse (USA)

WORLD KNOCK-OUT TEAMS

Held with the World Pairs.

Winners:
1978 Poland, 1982 France, 1986 USA

The most successful individual at world championship play has been Giorgio Belladonna who played on all 13 Italian Bermuda Bowl winning teams and the 3 Olympiad wins.

EPSON WORLDWIDE BRIDGE CONTEST

Inaugurated in 1986 and based on the use of computer technology. It attracted 66,338 entrants playing exactly the same hands at more than 1000 centres in 76 countries. The 1987 event was contested by 73,256 players at 1537 centres.

Winners: 1986 Fraisnais and Bouteille of Paris.
1987 Peter Thompson and Robin Stretch (UK)

MASTER POINTS

The World Bridge Federation regularly produces a Master Points ranking list. Giorgio Belladonna (Ita) is the top rated male player at 1821¼ points, and the top woman is Jacqui Mitchell (USA) with 347.

Since 1934 the American Contract Bridge League has awarded master points to its players. The first to pass 10,000 points was Oswald Jacoby in 1967. The most points is 35,137.6 by Barry Crane at the time of his murder in 1985. The current leader is Paul Suloway with 27,226 at 1 Apr 1987.

CANOEING

International canoe racing is practised in kayaks or Canadian canoes over flat water or, for canoe slalom, on wild water. Kayak is the Eskimo word for a canoe made of sealskin, originally stretched over a whalebone frame. Kayak canoeists use a paddle with a blade at each end but Canadian canoes are propelled by a paddle with a single blade, from a half-kneeling position. Races are designated with K for kayak and C for Canadian canoes followed by the number of canoeists, e.g. K1, K2, K4, C1, C2.

The most important pioneer of canoeing as a sport was John MacGregor, who founded the Canoe Club in Surrey, England in 1866.

The sport's governing body is the International Canoe Federation, founded in 1924. From then until 1946 its official title was the 'Internationale Representantschaft für Kanusport'. European Championships were first held in 1933, with racing at six categories: K1, C1 and C2 over 1000m; K1, C1 and C2 for folding crafts over 10,000m. Olympic recognition followed in 1936. Wild water and slalom canoeing were introduced in the 1930s.

Speed races on still water are contested at 500m and 1000m in a straight line and 10,000m on a circuit. Slalom competitions are contested over a rapid river course of maximum extent 600m, through a series of 25 gates with scoring both for time and as penalty points for faults in negotiating the course. Wild water competitions are contested on a course of at least 3000m length.

OLYMPIC GAMES
The sport has been held at each Olympic Games from 1936, with slalom events only in 1972.

CANOE RACING WINNERS – MEN

K1 500m
1976 Vasile Diba (Rom) 1:46.41
1980 Vladimir Parfenovich (USSR) 1:43.43
1984 Ian Ferguson (NZ) 1:47.84

K1 1000m
1936 Gregor Hradetzky (Aut) 4:22.9
1948 Gert Fredriksson (Swe) 4:33.2
1952 Gert Fredriksson (Swe) 4:07.9
1956 Gert Fredriksson (Swe) 4:12.8
1960 Erik Hansen (Den) 3:53.00
1964 Rolf Peterson (Swe) 3:57.13
1968 Mihaly Hesz (Hun) 4:02.63
1972 Aleksandr Shaparenko (USSR) 3:48.06
1976 Rüdiger Helm (GDR) 3:48.20
1980 Rüdiger Helm (GDR) 3:48.77
1984 Alan Thompson (NZ) 3:45.73

K1 1000m
1936 Ernst Krebs (Ger) 46:01.6
1948 Gert Fredriksson (Swe) 50:47.7
1952 Thorvald Strömberg (Fin) 47:22.8
1956 Gert Fredriksson (Swe) 47.43.4

K1 4 × 500m relay
1960 Germany 7:39,43

K2 500m
1976 Joachim Mattern & Bernd Olbricht (GDR) 1:35.87
1980 Vladimir Parfenovich & Sergey Chukrai (USSR) 1:32.38
1984 Ian Ferguson & Paul McDonald (NZ) 1:34.21

K2 1000m
1936 Adolf Kainz & Alfons Dorfner (Aut) 4:03.8
1948 Hans Berglund & Lennart Klingström (Swe) 4:07.3
1952 Kurt Wires & Yrjö Hietanen (Fin) 3:51.1
1956 Michel Scheuer & Meinrad Miltenberger (FRG) 3:49.6
1960 Gert Fredriksson & Sven-Olov Sjödelius (Swe) 3:34.7
1964 Sven-Olov Sjödelius & Nils Utterberg (Swe) 3:38.4
1968 Aleksandr Shaparenko & Vladimir Morozov (USSR) 3:37.54
1972 Nikolay Gorbachev & Viktor Kratassyuk (USSR) 3:31.23
1976 Sergey Nagorny & Vladimir Romanovsky (USSR) 3:29.01
1980 Vladimir Parfenovich & Sergey Chukrai (USSR) 3:26.72
1984 Hugh Fisher & Alwyn Morris (Can) 3:24.22

K2 10 000m
1936 Paul Weavers & Ludwig Landen (Ger) 41:45.0
1948 Gunnar Akerlund & Hans Wetterström (Swe) 46:09.4

Aleksandr Shaparenko

1952 Kurt Wires & Yrjö Hietanen (Fin) 44:21.3
1956 Janos Uranyi & Laszlo Fabian (Hun) 43:37.0

K4 1000m
1964 USSR 3:14.67
1968 Norway 3:14.38
1972 USSR 3:14.02
1976 USSR 3:08.69
1980 GDR 3:13.76
1984 New Zealand 3:02.28

C1 500m
1976 Aleksandr Rogov (USSR) 1:59.23
1980 Sergey Postrekhin (USSR) 1:53.37
1984 Larry Cain (Can) 1:57.01

C1 1000m
1936 Francis Amyot (Can) 5:32.1
1948 Josef Holecek (Cs) 5:42.0
1952 Josef Holecek (Cs) 4:56.3
1956 Leon Rotman (Rom) 5:05.3
1960 Janos Parti (Hun) 4:33.93
1964 Jürgen Eschert (GDR) 4:35.14
1968 Tibor Tatai (Hun) 4:36.14
1972 Ivan Patzaichin (Rom) 4:08.94
1976 Matija Ljubek (Yug) 4:09.51
1980 Lubomir Lubenov (Bul) 4:12.38
1984 Ulrich Eicke (FRG) 4:06.32

C1 10 000m
1948 Frantisek Capek (Cs) 62:05.2
1952 Frank Havens (USA) 57:41.1
1956 Leon Rotman (Rom) 56:41.0

C2 500m
1976 Sergey Petrenko & Aleksandr Vinogradov (USSR) 1:45.81
1980 Laszlo Foltan & Istvan Vaskuti (Hun) 1:43.39
1984 Matija Ljubek & Mirko Nisovic (Yug) 1:43.67

C2 1000m
1936 Vladimir Syrovatka & Jan-Felix Brzak (Cs) 4:50.1
1948 Jan-Felix Brzak & Bohumil Kudrna (Cs) 5:07.1

1952 Bent Peder Rasch & Finn Haunstoft (Den) 4:38.3
1956 Alexe Dumitru & Simion Ismailciuc (Rom) 4:47.4
1960 Leonid Geyshtor & Sergey Makarenko (USSR)
      4:17.94
1964 Andrey Khimich & Stepan Oschepkov (USSR)
      4:04.64
1968 Ivan Patzaichin & Serghei Covaliov (Rom) 4:07.18
1972 Vladas Chessyunas & Yuriy Lobanov (USSR)
      3:52.60
1976 Sergey Petrenko & Aleksandr Vinogradov (USSR)
      3:52.76
1980 Ivan Patzaichin & Toma Simionov (Rom) 3:47.65
1984 Ivan Patzaichin & Toma Simionov (Rom) 3:40.60

C2 10000m

1936 Vaclav Mottl & Zdenek Skrdlant (Cs) 50:33.5
1948 Stephen Lysack & Stephen Macknowski (USA)
      55:55.4
1952 Georges Turlier & Jean Laudet (Fra) 54:08.3
1956 Pavel Kharin & Gratsian Botev (USSR) 54:02.4

FOLDING KAYAK 1936

K1: Gregor Hradetzky (Aut) 50:01.2
K2: Sven Johansson & Eric Bladström (Swe) 45:48.9

SLALOM RACING – MEN 1972

K1: Siegbert Horn (GDR) 268.56 pts
C1: Reinhard Eiben (GDR) 315.84
C2: Walter Hofmann & Rolf-Dieter Amend (GDR)
     310.68

Most gold medals: 6 Gert Fredriksson (Swe) 1948-60; 4
Ivan Patzaichin (Rom) 1968-84

Most gold medals at one Games: 3 Vladimir Parfenovich
(USSR) 1980, Ian Ferguson (NZ) 1984.

Most medals: 8 Gert Fredriksson 6 gold as above, silver
K1 10,000m 1952, bronze K1 1000m 1960; 7 Ivan
Patzaichin 4 gold as above, three silver C2 500m
1980-84, C2 1000m 1972.

CANOE RACING WINNERS – WOMEN

K1 500m

1948 Karen Hoff (Den) 2:31.9
1952 Sylvi Saimo (Fin) 2:18.4
1956 Elisaveta Dementyeva (USSR) 2:18.9
1960 Antonina Seredina (USSR) 2:08.08
1964 Lyudmila Khvedosyuk (USSR) 2:12.87
1968 Lyudmila Pinayeva (USSR) 2:11.09
1972 Yulia Ryabchinskaya (USSR) 2:03.17
1976 Carola Zirzow (GDR) 2:01.05
1980 Birgit Fischer (GDR) 1:57.96
1984 Agneta Andersson (Swe) 1:58.72

K2 500m

1960 Maria Zhubina & Antonina Seredina (USSR)
      1:54.76
1964 Anne-Marie Zimmermann & Roswitha Esser (FRG)
      1:56.95
1968 Anne-Marie Zimmermann & Roswitha Esser (FRG)
      1:56.44
1972 Lyudmila Pinayeva & Yekaterina Kuryshko (USSR)
      1:53.50
1976 Nina Gopova & Galina Kreft (USSR) 1:51.15
1980 Carsta Genäuss & Martina Bischof (GDR) 1:43.88
1984 Agneta Andersson & Anna Olsson (Swe) 1:45.25

K4 500m

1984 Romania 1:38.54

Gert Fredriksson – six Olympic gold medals

K1 CANOE SLALOM

1972 Angelika Bahmann (GDR) 364.50 pts

Most gold medals: 3 Lyudmila Pinayeva (née
Khevedosyuk)

Most medals: 4 Lyudmila Pinayeva, 3 gold as above,
bronze K2 500m 1968

CANOE RACING WORLD CHAMPIONSHIPS

First held in 1938, then in 1948, 1950, 1954, 1958,
1963, 1966 and annually from 1970 with the exception
of Olympic years.

*Most individual wins at one event (including Olympic
Games)*

MEN

7 Tamas Wichmann (Hun) C1 10,000m 1970-1, 1974,
  1977, 1979, 1981-2
6 Rüdiger Helm (GDR) K1 1000m 1976, 1978-83
5 Vladimir Parfenovich (USSR) K1 500m 1979-83

WOMEN

5 Lyudmila Pinayeva (USSR) K1 500m 1964, 1966,
  1968, 1970-1
5 Birgit Fischer (GDR) K1 500m 1980-3, 1985

Most gold medals

MEN

13 Gert Fredriksson (Swe) K1 500m 1948, 1954; K1
   1000m 1948, 1950, 1952, 1954, 1956; K1 10000m
   1948, 1956; K1 4×500m relay 1948, 1950, 1954;
   K2 1000m 1960
13 Rüdiger Helm (GDR) K1 1000m 1976, 1978-83; K2
   500m 1978; K4 500m 1983; K4 10,000m 1978-81
13 Ivan Patzaichin (Rom) C1 1000m 1972-3, 1977; C1
   10,000m 1978; C2 500m 1979; C2 1000m 1968,
   1970, 1972, 1980-1, 1983-4; C2 10000m 1982
12 Vladimir Parfenovich (USSR) K1 500m 1979-83; K2
   500m 1979-82; K2 1000m 1980-2

11 Yuriy Lobanov (USSR) C2 500m 1974-5, C2 1000m
1972, 1974, 1977, 1979; C2 10,000m 1973-5,
1977, 1979

WOMEN

17 Birgit Schmidt (née Fischer) (GDR) K1 500m 1980-3,
1985; K2 500m 1977-8, 1981-3, 1985; K4 500m
1978-9, 1981-3, 1985

CANOE SLALOM WORLD CHAMPIONSHIPS

Held biennially since 1949.

Most individual wins:

MEN

3 Manfred Schubert (GDR) C1 1957, 1961, 1963 (also
C1 team 1963, C2 team 1959)

3 Jon Lugbill (USA) C1 1979, 1981, 1983 (also 4 at C1
team 1979-85)

3 Richard Fox (UK) K1 1981, 1983, 1985 (also 3 at K1
team 1981-5)

WILD WATER WORLD CHAMPIONSHIPS

Held biennially since 1959.

Most individual wins:

MEN

4 Jean-Pierre Burny (Bel) K1 1969, 1973, 1975, 1979

3 Gilles Zok (Fra) C1 1981, 1983, 1985 (also 5 at C1
team 1977-85)

WOMEN

3 Gisela Grothaus (FRG) K1 1973, 1975, 1977 (also 4
K1 team 1973-83)

CANOE SAILING WORLD CHAMPIONSHIPS

First held in 1938, and then every 3/4 years from 1961.

Most wins: 3 Alain Emus (UK) 1961, 1965, 1969.

CHESS

A board game played by two players, each with 16 pieces
on a 64-square board. Its origins are uncertain, but it is
thought to have originated in the Punjab, India. The
earliest definite references are to Chaturanga, the Indian
war game imported into Persia. This game evolved into
Shatranj, and thence to the modern game of chess. The
current pieces have been standard for the past 500
years.

The world governing body is the Fédération
Internationale des Echecs (FIDE), formed in 1924.

WORLD CHAMPIONS

The first officially accepted match for the world
championship was in 1888 when Wilhelm Steinitz beat
Johannes Zukertort. However champions had been

Gary Kasparov and Anatoliy Karpov battled long for the World title at chess. (All-Sport)

generally accepted since Adolph Anderssen won the world's first international tournament, held in London. The FIDE took control of the championship in 1948, and there is now a biennial cycle of eliminating contests culminating in a contender to challenge the current champion.

Champions:
1851-8 Adolf Anderssen (Ger)
1858-62 Paul Morphy (USA)
1862-6 Adolf Anderssen (Ger)
1866-94 Wilhelm Steinitz (Aut)
1894-1921 Emanuel Lasker (Ger)
1921-7 José Capablanca (Cub)
1927-35 Alexandre Alekhine (Fra)
1935-7 Max Euwe (Hol)
1937-46 Alexandre Alekhine (Fra)
1948-57 Mikhail Botvinnik (USSR)
1957-8 Vasiliy Smyslov (USSR)
1958-60 Mikhail Botvinnik (USSR)
1960-1 Mikhail Tal (USSR)
1961-3 Mikhail Botvinnik (USSR)
1963-9 Tigran Petrosian (USSR)
1969-72 Boris Spassky (USSR)
1972-5 Robert Fischer (USA)
1975-85 Anatoliy Karpov (USSR)
1985- Gary Kasparov (USSR)

Youngest champion: Gary Kasparov won in 1985 at the age of 22 years 210 days.

Oldest champion: Wilhelm Steinitz was 58 years 10 days when he lost to Lasker in 1894.

WOMEN'S CHAMPIONS
1927-44 Vera Menchik (UK)
1950-3 Lyudmila Rudenko (USSR)
1953-6 Elizaveta Bykova (USSR)
1956-8 Olga Rubtsova (USSR)
1958-62 Elizaveta Bykova (USSR)
1962-78 Nona Gaprindashvili (USSR)
1978- Maya Chiburdanidze (USSR)

Youngest champion: Maya Chiburdanidze was aged 17 when she won the title in 1978.

CHESS OLYMPIADS
The world team championships, which were first held in 1927, and are now held biennially.

Wins:
16	USSR	1952, 1954, 1956, 1958, 1960, 1962, 1964, 1966, 1968, 1970, 1972, 1974, 1980, 1982, 1984, 1986
5	USA	1931, 1933, 1935, 1937, 1976
3	Hungary	1927, 1928, 1978
1	Germany	1939
1	Yugoslavia	1950

Although women may play in the Olympiads, a separate competition for women only was introduced in 1957, and this event has been held concurrently with the men's from 1972.

Wins:
11	USSR	1957, 1963, 1966, 1969, 1972, 1974, 1978, 1980, 1982, 1984, 1986
1	Israel	1976

The USSR have dominated the tournaments. The only time that one of their teams has placed other than first was their second place in 1978. They first competed in 1952 and did not contest in 1976, when the Olympiad was held in Haifa, Israel.

ELO RATINGS
The FIDE issues a list of Elo ratings for the world's leading players twice yearly. The system is named after Professor Elo. Grandmaster level is 2500, a rating currently attained by about 100 players. The highest rating ever achieved is 2785 by Robert Fischer.

COMMONWEALTH GAMES

The Commonwealth Games are multi-sport competitions, held every four years, and contested by representatives of the nations of the British Commonwealth. They were first staged as the British Empire Games at Hamilton, Canada, opening on 16 August 1930. The eleven nations participating were Australia, Bermuda, British Guiana, Canada, England, Ireland, Newfoundland, New Zealand, Scotland, South Africa and Wales. Six sports were included, but there were women's events only in swimming. Women first competed in athletics in 1934.

The idea of staging such an event was first put forward by a Yorkshireman, Rev. J.Astley Cooper in the magazine *Greater Britain* in 1891. The first Inter-Empire Sports meeting was held at Crystal Palace, London in 1911, forming part of the celebrations for the Coronation of King George V. Competitors from Britain, Canada, Australia and New Zealand contested four sports - athletics (five events), heavyweight boxing, swimming (two events) and middleweight wrestling. Canadians won four gold medals, Britain three, and Australia two.

The Games became the British Empire and Commonwealth Games in 1954, and simply the British Commonwealth Games in 1970, in which year the Games went metric for distances and weights.

Ten sports are held at each Games — athletics and swimming are obligatory, and the others are selected from 15 recognised sports, with additionally two demonstration sports. The recognised sports yet to be included officially at any Games are canoeing, judo, table tennis and yachting

VENUES
1930 Hamilton, Canada
1934 London, England
1938 Sydney, Australia
1950 Auckland, New Zealand
1954 Vancouver, Canada
1958 Cardiff, Wales
1962 Perth, Australia
1966 Kingston, Jamaica
1970 Edinburgh, Scotland
1974 Christchurch, New Zealand
1978 Edmonton, Canada
1982 Brisbane, Australia

1986 Edinburgh, Scotland
1990 Auckland, New Zealand

TOP TEN MEDAL WINNING NATIONS

	Nation	Gold	Silver	Bronze	Total
1	England	373	328	326	1027
2	Australia	345	320	266	931
3	Canada	252	260	263	775
4	New Zealand	77	107	134	318
5	Scotland	51	67	99	217
6	South Africa (1930-58)	60	44	47	151
7	Wales	22	36	48	106
8	Kenya	29	16	30	75
9	India	24	28	20	72
10	Northern Ireland #	14	17	29	60

Ireland in 1930

ARCHERY WINNERS

1982 **MEN** Mark Blenkarne (Eng) 2446
      WOMEN Neroli Fairhall (NZ) 2373

ATHLETICS WINNERS

Note that where known fully-automatic times are given as per the current regulations (original official hand times may well have differed).

MEN

100 METRES

Run over 100 yards (91.4m) 1930-66
1930 Percy Williams (Can) 9.9
1934 Arthur Sweeney (Eng) 10.0
1938 Cyril Holmes (Eng) 9.7
1950 John Treloar (Aus) 9.7
1954 Mike Agostini (Tri) 9.6
1958 Keith Gardner (Jam) 9.66
1962 Seraphino Antao (Ken) 9.50
1966 Harry Jerome (Can) 9.41
1970 Don Quarrie (Jam) 10.24w
1974 Don Quarrie (Jam) 10.38
1978 Don Quarrie (Jam) 10.03w
1982 Allan Wells (Sco) 10.05w
1986 Ben Johnson (Can) 10.07

200 METRES

Run over 220 yards (201.17m) 1930-66
1930 Stanley Engelhart (Eng) 21.8
1934 Arthur Sweeney (Eng) 21.9
1938 Cyril Holmes (Eng) 21.2
1950 John Treloar (Aus) 21.5
1954 Donald Jowett (NZ) 21.5
1958 Tom Robinson (Bah) 21.08
1962 Seraphino Antao (Ken) 21.28
1966 Stanley Allotey (Gha) 20.65
1970 Don Quarrie (Jam) 20.56
1974 Don Quarrie (Jam) 20.73
1978 Allan Wells (Sco) 20.12w
1982 Allan Wells (Sco) &
      Mike McFarlane (Eng) 20.43
1986 Atlee Mahorn (Can) 20.31w

400 METRES

Run over 440 yards (402.34m) 1930-66
1930 Alex Wilson (Can) 48.8
1934 Godfrey Rampling (Eng) 48.0
1938 Bill Roberts (Eng) 47.9
1950 Edwin Carr (Aus) 47.9
1954 Kevan Gosper (Aus) 47.2
1958 Milkha Singh (Ind) 46.71
1962 George Kerr (Jam) 46.74
1966 Wendell Mottley (Tri) 45.08
1970 Charles Asati (Ken) 45.01
1974 Charles Asati (Ken) 46.04
1978 Rick Mitchell (Aus) 46.34
1982 Bert Cameron (Jam) 45.89
1986 Roger Black (Eng) 45.57

800 METRES

Run over 880 yards (804.67m) 1930-66
1930 Thomas Hampson (Eng) 1:52.4
1934 Phil Edwards (Guy) 1:54.2
1938 Vernon Boot (NZ) 1:51.2
1950 John Parlett (Eng) 1:53.1
1954 Derek Johnson (Eng) 1:50.7
1958 Herb Elliott (Aus) 1:49.32
1962 Peter Snell (NZ) 1:47.64
1966 Noel Clough (Aus) 1:46.9
1970 Robert Ouko (Ken) 1:46.89
1974 John Kipkurgat (Ken) 1:43.85
1978 Mike Boit (Ken) 1:46.39
1982 Peter Bourke (Aus) 1:45.18
1986 Steve Cram (Eng) 1:43.22

1500 METRES

Run over 1 mile (1609.35m) 1930-66
1930 Reg Thomas (Eng) 4:14.0
1934 Jack Lovelock (NZ) 4:12.8
1938 Jim Alford (Wal) 4:11.6
1950 William Parnell (Can) 4:11.0
1954 Roger Bannister (Eng) 3:58.8
1958 Herb Elliott (Aus) 3:59.03
1962 Peter Snell (NZ) 4:04.58
1966 Kipchoge Keino (Ken) 3:55.34
1970 Kipchoge Keino (Ken) 3:36.6
1974 Filbert Bayi (Tan) 3:32.16
1978 David Moorcroft (Eng) 3:35.48
1982 Steve Cram (Eng) 3:42.37
1986 Steve Cram (Eng) 3:50.87

5000 METRES

Run over 3 miles (4820.04m) 1930-66
1930 Stan Tomlin (Eng) 14:27.4
1934 Walter Beavers (Eng) 14:32.6
1938 Cecil Matthews (NZ) 13:59.6
1950 Len Eyre (Eng) 14:23.6
1954 Chris Chataway (Eng) 13:35.2
1958 Murray Halberg (NZ) 13:14.96
1962 Murray Halberg (NZ) 13:34.15
1966 Kipchoge Keino (Ken) 12:57.4
1970 Ian Stewart (Sco) 13:22.8
1974 Ben Jipcho (Ken) 13:14.4
1978 Henry Rono (Ken) 13:23.04
1982 David Moorcroft (Eng) 13:33.00
1986 Steve Ovett (Eng) 13:24.11

10 000 METRES

Run over 6 miles (9656.07m) 1930-66
1930 John Savidan (NZ) 30:49.6
1934 Arthur Penny (Eng) 31:00.6
1938 Cecil Matthews (NZ) 30:14.5

1950 Harold Nelson (NZ) 30:29.6
1954 Peter Driver (Eng) 29:09.4
1958 David Power (Aus) 28:48.16
1962 Bruce Kidd (Can) 28:26.13
1966 Naftali Temu (Ken) 27:14.21
1970 Lachie Stewart (Sco) 28:11.71
1974 Richard Tayler (NZ) 27:46.4
1978 Brendan Foster (Eng) 28:13.65
1982 Gidamis Shahanga (Tan) 28:10.15
1986 Jonathan Solly (Eng) 27:57.42

MARATHON
(26 miles 385 yards 42.195km)
1930 Duncan McL.Wright (Sco) 2:43:43
1934 Harold Webster (Can) 2:40:36
1938 Johannes Coleman (SAf) 2:30:49.8
1950 Jack Holden (Eng) 2:32:57
1954 Joseph McGhee (Sco) 2:39:36
1958 David Power (Aus) 2:22:45.6
1962 Brian Kilby (Eng) 2:21:17
1966 Jim Alder (Sco) 2:22:07.8
1970 Ron Hill (Eng) 2:09:28
1974 Ian Thompson (Eng) 2:09:12
1978 Gidamis Shahanga (Tan) 2:15:39.8
1982 Rob de Castella (Aus) 2:09:18
1986 Rob de Castella (Aus) 2:10:15

3000 METRES STEEPLECHASE
Held over 8 laps in 1930 and at
2 miles (3218.7m) in 1934
1930 George Bailey (Eng) 9:52.0
1934 Stanley Scarsbrook (Eng) 10:23.4
1962 Trevor Vincent (Aus) 8:43.4
1966 Peter Welsh (NZ) 8:29.44
1970 Tony Manning (Aus) 8:26.2
1974 Ben Jipcho (Ken) 8:20.8
1978 Henry Rono (Ken) 8:26.54
1982 Julius Korir (Ken) 8:23.94
1986 Graeme Fell (Can) 8:24.49

110 METRES HURDLES
Run over 120 yards (109.73m) 1930-66
1930 Lord Burghley (Eng) 14.6
1934 Don Finlay (Eng) 15.2
1938 Tom Lavery (SAf) 14.0w
1950 Peter Gardner (Aus) 14.3
1954 Keith Gardner (Jam) 14.2
1958 Keith Gardner (Jam) 14.20w
1962 Ghulam Raziq (Pak) 14.34
1966 David Hemery (Eng) 14.1
1970 David Hemery (Eng) 13.66w
1974 Fatwel Kimaiyo (Ken) 13.69
1978 Berwyn Price (Wal) 13.70w
1982 Mark McKoy (Can) 13.37
1986 Mark McKoy (Can) 13.31w

400 METRES HURDLES
Run over 440 yards (402.34m) 1930-66
1930 Lord Burghley (Eng) 54.4
1934 Alan Hunter (Sco) 55.2
1938 John Loaring (Can) 52.9
1950 Duncan White (Sri) 52.5
1954 David Lean (Aus) 52.4
1958 Gerhardus Potgieter (SAf) 49.73
1962 Ken Roche (Aus) 51.5
1966 Ken Roche (Aus) 50.95

1970 John Sherwood (Eng) 50.03
1974 Alan Pascoe (Eng) 48.83
1978 Daniel Kimaiyo (Ken) 49.48
1982 Garry Brown (Aus) 49.37
1986 Phil Beattie (NI) 49.60

4 × 100 METRES RELAY
Run over 4 × 110 yards (100.54m) 1930-66
1930 Canada 42.2
1934 England 42.2
1938 Canada 41.6
1950 Australia 42.2
1954 Canada 41.3
1958 England 40.72
1962 England 40.62
1966 Ghana 39.8
1970 Jamaica 39.46
1974 Australia 39.31
1978 Scotland 39.24
1982 Nigeria 39.15
1986 Canada 39.15

4 × 400 METRES RELAY
Run over 4 × 440 yards (402.34m) 1930-66
1930 England 3:19.4
1934 England 3:16.8
1938 Canada 3:16.9
1950 Australia 3:17.8
1954 England 3:11.2
1958 South Africa 3:08.21
1962 Jamaica 3:10.2
1966 Trinidad & Tobago 3:02.8
1970 Kenya 3:03.63
1974 Kenya 3:04.4
1978 Kenya 3:03.54
1982 England 3:05.45
1986 England 3:07.19

HIGH JUMP
1930 Johannes Viljoen (SAf) 1.90
1934 Edwin Thacker (SAf) 1.90
1938 Edwin Thacker (SAf) 1.96
1950 John Winter (Aus) 1.98
1954 Emmanuel Ifeajuna (Nig) 2.03
1958 Ernest Haisley (Jam) 2.06
1962 Percy Hobson (Aus) 2.11
1966 Lawrie Peckham (Aus) 2.08
1970 Lawrie Peckham (Aus) 2.14
1974 Gordon Windeyer (Aus) 2.16
1978 Claude Ferragne (Can) 2.20
1982 Milt Ottey (Can) 2.31
1986 Milt Ottey (Can) 2.30

POLE VAULT
1930 Victor Pickard (Can) 3.73
1934 Sylvanus Apps (Can) 3.81 (3.88 jump-off)
1938 Andries du Plessis (SAf) 4.11
1950 Tim Anderson (Eng) 3.97
1954 Geoff Elliott (Eng) 4.26
1958 Geoff Elliott (Eng) 4.16
1962 Trevor Bickle (Aus) 4.49
1966 Trevor Bickle (Aus) 4.80
1970 Mike Bull (NI) 5.10
1974 Don Baird (Aus) 5.05
1978 Bruce Simpson (Can) 5.10
1982 Ray Boyd (Aus) 5.20

1986 Andrew Ashurst (Eng) 5.20

LONG JUMP
1930 Leonard Hutton (Can) 7.20
1934 Sam Richardson (Can) 7.17
1938 Harold Brown (Can) 7.43
1950 Neville Price (SAf) 7.31
1954 Ken Wilmshurst (Eng) 7.54
1958 Paul Foreman (Jam) 7.47
1962 Michael Ahey (Gha) 8.05w
1966 Lynn Davies (Wal) 7.99
1970 Lynn Davies (Wal) 8.06w
1974 Alan Lerwill (Eng) 7.94
1978 Roy Mitchell (Eng) 8.06
1982 Gary Honey (Aus) 8.13
1986 Gary Honey (Aus) 8.08

TRIPLE JUMP
1930 Gordon Smallacombe (Can) 14.76
1934 Jack Metcalfe (Aus) 15.63
1938 Jack Metcalfe (Aus) 15.49
1950 Brian Oliver (Aus) 15.61
1954 Ken Wilmshurst (Eng) 15.28
1958 Ian Tomlinson (Aus) 15.74
1962 Ian Tomlinson (Aus) 16.20
1966 Samuel Igun (Nig) 16.40
1970 Phil May (Aus) 16.72
1974 Joshua Owusu (Gha) 16.50
1978 Keith Connor (Eng) 17.21
1982 Keith Connor (Eng) 17.81w
1986 John Herbert (Eng) 17.27w

SHOT
1930 Hendrik Hart (SAf) 14.58
1934 Hendrik Hart (SAf) 14.67
1938 Louis Fouche (SAf) 14.48
1950 Maitaika Tuicakau (Fiji) 14.64
1954 John Savidge (Eng) 16.77
1958 Arthur Rowe (Eng) 17.57
1962 Martyn Lucking (Eng) 18.08
1966 David Steen (Can) 18.79
1970 David Steen (Can) 19.21
1974 Geoff Capes (Eng) 20.74
1978 Geoff Capes (Eng) 19.77
1982 Bruno Pauletto (Can) 19.55
1986 Billy Cole (Eng) 18.16

DISCUS
1930 Hendrik Hart (SAf) 41.44
1934 Hendrik Hart (SAf) 41.54
1938 Eric Coy (Can) 44.76
1950 Ian Reed (Aus) 47.72
1954 Stephanus du Plessis (SAf) 51.70
1958 Stephanus du Plessis (SAf) 55.94
1962 Warwick Selvey (Aus) 56.48
1966 Les Mills (NZ) 56.18
1970 George Puce (Can) 59.02
1974 Robin Tait (NZ) 63.08
1978 Borys Chambul (Can) 59.70
1982 Brad Cooper (Bah) 64.04
1986 Raymond Lazdins (Can) 58.86

HAMMER
1930 Malcolm Nokes (Eng) 47.12
1934 Malcolm Nokes (Eng) 48.24
1938 George Sutherland (Can) 48.70
1950 Duncan Clark (Sco) 49.94
1954 Muhammad Iqbal (Pak) 55.38
1958 Mike Ellis (Eng) 62.90
1962 Howard Payne (Eng) 61.64
1966 Howard Payne (Eng) 61.98
1970 Howard Payne (Eng) 67.80
1974 Ian Chipchase (Eng) 69.56
1978 Peter Farmer (Aus) 71.10
1982 Robert Weir (Eng) 75.08
1986 David Smith (Eng) 74.06

JAVELIN
1930 Stanley Lay (NZ) 63.12
1934 Robert Dixon (Can) 60.02
1938 James Courtwright (Can) 62.80
1950 Leo Roininen (Can) 57.10
1954 James Achurch (Aus) 68.52
1958 Colin Smith (Eng) 71.28
1962 Alfred Mitchell (Aus) 78.10
1966 John FitzSimons (Eng) 79.78
1970 David Travis (Eng) 79.50
1974 Charles Clover (Eng) 84.92
1978 Phil Olsen (Can) 84.00
1982 Michael O'Rourke (NZ) 89.48
1986 David Ottley (Eng) 80.62

DECATHLON
All scored on the 1984 Tables
1966 Roy Williams (NZ) 7133
1970 Geoff Smith (Aus) 7420
1974 Mike Bull (NI) 7363
1978 Daley Thompson (Eng) 8470w
1982 Daley Thompson (Eng) 8424
1986 Daley Thompson (Eng) 8663

30 KILOMETRES ROAD WALK
Walked over 20 miles (32.187km) 1966-74
1966 Ron Wallwork (Eng) 2:44:42.8
1970 Noel Freeman (Aus) 2:33:33
1974 John Warhurst (Eng) 2:35:23.0
1978 Ollie Flynn (Eng) 2:22:03.7
1982 Steve Barry (Wal) 2:10:16
1986 Simon Baker (Aus) 2:07:47

WOMEN
100 METRES
Run over 100 yards (91.4m) 1934-66
1934 Eileen Hiscock (Eng) 11.3
1938 Decima Norman (Aus) 11.1
1950 Marjorie Jackson (Aus) 10.8
1954 Marjorie Jackson (Aus) 10.7
1958 Marlene Willard (Aus) 10.70
1962 Dorothy Hyman (Eng) 11.2
1966 Dianne Burge (Aus) 10.6
1970 Raelene Boyle (Aus) 11.26w
1974 Raelene Boyle (Aus) 11.27
1978 Sonia Lannaman (Eng) 11.27w
1982 Angella Taylor (Can) 11.00
1986 Heather Oakes (Eng) 11.20w

200 METRES
Run over 220 yards (201.17m) 1934-66
1934 Eileen Hiscock (Eng) 25.0
1938 Decima Norman (Aus) 24.7
1950 Marjorie Jackson (Aus) 24.3
1954 Marjorie Nelson (née Jackson) (Aus) 24.0

1958 Marlene Willard (Aus) 23.65
1962 Dorothy Hyman (Eng) 24.00
1966 Dianne Burge (Aus) 23.73
1970 Raelene Boyle (Aus) 22.75w
1974 Raelene Boyle (Aus) 22.50
1978 Denise Boyd (Aus) 22.82w
1982 Merlene Ottey (Jam) 22.19w
1986 Angella Issajenko (née Taylor) (Can) 22.91w

400 METRES
Run over 440 yards (402.34m) 1966
1966 Judy Pollock (Aus) 53.0
1970 Marilyn Neufville (Jam) 51.02
1974 Yvonne Saunders (Can) 51.67
1978 Donna Hartley (Eng) 51.69
1982 Raelene Boyle (Aus) 51.26
1986 Debbie Flintoff (Aus) 51.29

800 METRES
Run over 880 yards (804.67m) 1934-66
1934 Gladys Lunn (Eng) 2:19.4
1962 Dixie Willis (Aus) 2:03.85
1966 Abigail Hoffman (Can) 2:04.3
1970 Rosemary Stirling (Sco) 2:06.24
1974 Charlene Rendina (Aus) 2:01.1
1978 Judy Peckham (Aus) 2:02.82
1982 Kirsty McDermott (Wal) 2:01.31
1986 Kirsty Wade (née McDermott) (Wal) 2:00.94

1500 METRES
1970 Rita Ridley (Eng) 4:18.8
1974 Glenda Reiser (Can) 4:07.8
1978 Mary Stewart (Eng) 4:06.34
1982 Christina Boxer (Eng) 4:08.28
1986 Kirsty Wade (Wal) 4:10.91

3000 METRES
1978 Paula Fudge (Eng) 9:12.95
1982 Anne Audain (NZ) 8:45.53
1986 Lynn Williams (Can) 8:54.29

MARATHON
1986 Lisa Martin (Aus) 2:26:07

80 METRES HURDLES
1934 Marjorie Clark (SAf) 11.8
1938 Barbara Burke (SAf) 11.7
1950 Shirley Strickland (Aus) 11.6
1954 Edna Maskell (Zam) 10.9
1958 Norma Thrower (Aus) 10.72w
1962 Pam Kilborn (Aus) 11.07
1966 Pam Kilborn (Aus) 10.9

100 METRES HURDLES
1970 Pam Kilborn (Aus) 13.27
1974 Judy Vernon (Eng) 13.45
1978 Lorna Boothe (Eng) 12.98w
1982 Shirley Strong (Eng) 12.78w
1986 Sally Gunnell (Eng) 13.29

400 METRES HURDLES
1982 Debbie Flintoff (Aus) 55.89
1986 Debbie Flintoff (Aus) 54.94

SPRINT RELAY
2 × 220 yards, 2 × 110 yards
1934 Canada 1:14.4

1938 Australia 1:15.2
1950 Australia 1:13.4

4 × 100 METRES RELAY
Run over 4 × 110 yards 1954-66
1954 Australia 46.8
1958 England 45.37
1962 Australia 46.71
1966 Australia 45.3
1970 Australia 44.14
1974 Australia 43.51
1978 England 43.70
1982 England 43.15
1986 England 43.39

4 × 400 METRES RELAY
1974 England 3:29.2
1978 England 3:27.19
1982 Canada 3:27.70
1986 Canada 3:28.92

HIGH JUMP
1934 Marjorie Clark (SAf) 1.60
1938 Dorothy Odam (Eng) 1.60
1950 Dorothy Tyler (née Odam) (Eng) 1.60
1954 Thelma Hopkins (NI) 1.67
1958 Michele Mason (Aus) 1.70
1962 Robyn Woodhouse (Aus) 1.78
1966 Michele Brown (née Mason) 1.73
1970 Debbie Brill (Can) 1.78
1974 Barbara Lawton (Eng) 1.84
1978 Katrina Gibbs (Aus) 1.93
1982 Debbie Brill (Can) 1.88
1986 Christine Stanton (Aus) 1.92

LONG JUMP
1934 Phyllis Bartholomew (Eng) 5.47
1938 Decima Norman (Aus) 5.80
1950 Yvette Williams (NZ) 5.90
1954 Yvette Williams (NZ) 6.08
1958 Sheila Hoskin (Eng) 6.02
1962 Pam Kilborn (Aus) 6.27
1966 Mary Rand (Eng) 6.36
1970 Sheila Sherwood (Eng) 6.73
1974 Modupe Oshikoya (Nig) 6.46
1978 Sue Reeve (Eng) 6.59
1982 Shonel Ferguson (Bah) 6.91w
1986 Joyce Oladapo (Eng) 6.43

SHOT
1954 Yvette Williams (NZ) 13.96
1958 Valerie Sloper (NZ) 15.54
1962 Valerie Young (née Sloper) (NZ) 15.23
1966 Valerie Young (NZ) 16.50
1970 Mary Peters (NI) 15.93
1974 Jane Haist (Can) 16.12
1978 Gael Mulhall (Aus) 17.31
1982 Judy Oakes (Eng) 17.92
1986 Gael Martin (née Mulhall) (Aus) 19.00

DISCUS
1954 Yvette Williams (NZ) 45.02
1958 Suzanne Allday (Eng) 45.91
1962 Valerie Young (NZ) 50.20
1966 Valerie Young (NZ) 49.78
1970 Rosemary Payne (Sco) 54.46

1974 Jane Haist (Can) 55.52
1978 Carmen Ionescu (Can) 62.16
1982 Margaret Ritchie (Sco) 62.98
1986 Gael Martin (Aus) 56.42

JAVELIN
1934 Gladys Lunn (Eng) 32.18
1938 Robina Higgins (Can) 38.28
1950 Charlotte MacGibbon-Weeks (Aus) 38.84
1954 Magdalena Swanepoel (SAf) 43.82
1958 Anna Pazera (Aus) 57.40
1962 Susan Platt (Eng) 50.24
1966 Margaret Parker (Aus) 51.38
1970 Petra Rivers (Aus) 52.00
1974 Petra Rivers (Aus) 55.48
1978 Tessa Sanderson (Eng) 61.34
1982 Suzanne Howland (Aus) 64.46
1986 Tessa Sanderson (Eng) 69.80

PENTATHLON
Scored on 1971 tables
1970 Mary Peters (NI) 4515 (5148 on tables used)
1974 Mary Peters (NI) 4455
1978 Diane Konihowski (Can) 4768

HEPTATHLON
Scored on 1984 tables
1982 Glynis Nunn (Aus) 6254
1986 Judy Simpson (Eng) 6282w

BADMINTON WINNERS

MEN'S SINGLES
1966 Tan Aik Huang (Mal)
1970 Jamie Paulson (Can)
1974 Punch Gunalan (Mal)
1978 Padukone Prakash (Ind)
1982 Syed Modi (Ind)
1986 Steve Baddeley (Eng)

MEN'S DOUBLES
1966 Tan Aik Huang & Yew Cheng Hoe (Mal)
1970 Ng Boon Bee & Punch Gunalam (Mal)
1974 Derek Talbot & Elliot Stuart (Eng)
1978 Ray Stevens & Michael Tredgett (Eng)
1982 Razif Sidek & Beng Teong Ong (Mal)
1986 Billy Gilliland & Dan Travers (Sco)

WOMEN'S SINGLES
1966 Angela Bairstow (Eng)
1970 Margaret Beck (Eng)
1974 Gillian Gilks (Eng)
1978 Sylvia Ng (Mal)
1982 Helen Troke (Eng)
1986 Helen Troke (Eng)

WOMEN'S DOUBLES
1966 Helen Horton & Ursula Smith (Eng)
1970 Margaret Boxall & Susan Whetnall (Eng)
1974 Margaret Beck & Gillian Gilks (Eng)
1978 Nora Perry & Anne Statt (Eng)
1982 Claire Backhouse & Johanne Falardeau (Can)
1986 Gillian Clark & Gillian Gowers (Eng)

MIXED DOUBLES
1966 Roger Mills & Angela Bairstow (Eng)
1970 Derek Talbot & Margaret Boxall (Eng)

1974 Derek Talbot & Gillian Gilks (Eng)
1978 Michael Tredgett & Nora Perry (Eng)
1982 Martin Dew & Karen Chapman (Eng)
1986 Mike Scandolera & Audrey Tuckey (Aus)

TEAM
1978 England
1982 England
1986 England

BOWLS WINNERS

SINGLES – MEN
1930 Robert Colquhoun (Eng)
1934 Robert Sprot (Sco)
1938 Horace Harvey (SAf)
1950 James Pirret (NZ)
1954 Ralph Hodges (Zim)
1958 Phineas Danilowitz (SAf)
1962 David Bryant (Eng)
1970 David Bryant (Eng)
1974 David Bryant (Eng)
1978 David Bryant (Eng)
1982 William Wood (Sco)
1986 Ian Dickison (NZ)

PAIRS – MEN
1930 Tommy Hills & George Wright (Eng)
1934 Tommy Hills & George Wright (Eng)
1938 Lance Macey & William Denison (NZ)
1950 Robert Henry & Phil Exelby (NZ)
1954 William Rosbotham & Percy Watson (NI)
1958 John Morris & Richard Pilkington (NZ)
1962 Robert McDonald & Hugh Robson (NZ)
1970 Norman King & Peter Line (Eng)
1974 John Christie & Alex McIntosh (Sco)
1978 Eric Liddell & Clementi Delgado (HK)
1982 John Watson & David Gourlay (Sco)
1986 George Adrain & Grant Knox (Sco)

FOURS – MEN
1930 England
1934 England
1938 New Zealand
1950 South Africa
1954 South Africa
1958 England
1962 England
1970 Hong Kong
1974 New Zealand
1978 Hong Kong
1982 Australia
1986 Wales

SINGLES – WOMEN
1986 Wendy Line (Eng)

PAIRS – WOMEN
1986 Freda Elliott & Margaret Johnstone (NI)

TRIPLES – WOMEN
1982 Zimbabwe

FOURS – WOMEN
1986 Wales

BOXING WINNERS

48kg – LIGHT FLYWEIGHT
1970 James Odwori (Uga)
1974 Stephen Muchoki (Ken)
1978 Stephen Muchoki (Ken)
1982 Abraham Wachire (Ken)
1986 Scott Olson (Can)

51kg – FLYWEIGHT
1930 Jacob Smith (SAf)
1934 Patrick Palmer (Eng)
1938 Johannes Joubert (SAf)
1950 Hugh Riley (Sco)
1954 Richard Currie (Sco)
1958 Jackie Brown (Sco)
1962 Robert Mallon (Sco)
1966 Sulley Shittu (Gha)
1970 David Needham (Eng)
1974 David Larmour (NI)
1978 Michael Irungu (Ken)
1982 Michael Mutua (Ken)
1986 John Lyon (Eng)

54kg – BANTAMWEIGHT
1930 Hyman Mizler (Eng)
1934 Freddy Ryan (Eng)
1938 William Butler (Eng)
1950 Johannes van Rensburg (SAf)
1954 John Smillie (Sco)
1958 Howard Winstone (Wal)
1962 Jeffery Dynevor (Aus)
1966 Edward Ndukwu (Nig)
1970 Sulley Shittu (Gha)
1974 Pat Cowdell (Eng)
1978 Barry McGuigan (NI)
1982 Joe Orewa (Nig)
1986 Sean Murphy (Eng)

57kg – FEATHERWEIGHT
1930 F.R.Meachem (Eng)
1934 Charles Catterall (SAf)
1938 Anadale Henricus (Sri)
1950 Henry Gilliland (Sco)
1954 Leonard Leisching (SAf)
1958 Wally Taylor (Aus)
1962 John McDermott (Sco)
1966 Philip Waruinge (Ken)
1970 Philip Waruinge (Ken)
1974 Edward Ndukwa (Nig)
1978 Nelson Azumah (Gha)
1982 Peter Konyegwachie (Nig)
1986 Billy Downey (Can)

60kg – LIGHTWEIGHT
1930 James Rolland (Sco)
1934 Leslie Cook (Aus)
1938 Harry Groves (Eng)
1950 Ronald Latham (Eng)
1954 Piet van Staden (Zim)
1958 Dick McTaggart (Sco)
1962 Eddie Blay (Gha)
1966 Anthony Andeh (Nig)
1970 Abayomi Adeyemi (Nig)
1974 Ayub Kalule (Uga)
1978 Gerard Hamil (NI)

1982 Hussein Khalili (Ken)
1986 Asif Dar (Can)

63.5kg LIGHT WELTERWEIGHT
1954 Mickey Bergin (Can)
1958 Henry Loubscher (SAf)
1962 Clement Quartey (Gha)
1966 James McCourt (NI)
1970 Muhamad Muruli (Uga)
1974 Obisia Nwakpa (Nig)
1978 Winfield Braithwaite (Guy)
1982 Christopher Ossai (Nig)
1986 Howard Grant (Can)

67kg – WELTERWEIGHT
1930 Leonard Hall (SAf)
1934 David McCleave (Eng)
1938 Bill Smith (Aus)
1950 Terence Ratcliffe (Eng)
1954 Nicholas Gargano (Eng)
1958 Joseph Greyling (SAf)
1962 Wallace Coe (NZ)
1966 Eddie Blay (Gha)
1970 Emma Ankudey (Gha)
1974 Muhamad Muruli (Uga)
1978 Michael McCallum (Jam)
1982 Christopher Pyatt (Eng)
1986 Darren Dyer (Eng)

71kg – LIGHT MIDDLEWEIGHT
1954 Wilfred Greaves (Can)
1958 Grant Webster (SAf)
1962 Harold Mann (Can)
1966 Mark Rowe (Eng)
1970 Tom Imrie (Sco)
1974 Lotti Mwale (Zam)
1978 Kelly Perlette (Can)
1982 Shawn O'Sullivan (Can)
1986 Dan Sherry (Can)

75kg – MIDDLEWEIGHT
1930 Frederick Mallin (Eng)
1934 Alf Shawyer (Eng)
1938 Denis Reardon (Wal)
1950 Theunis van Schalkwyk (SAf)
1954 Johannes van der Kolff (SAf)
1958 Terry Milligan (NI)
1962 Cephas Colquhoun (Jam)
1966 Joe Darkey (Gha)
1970 John Conteh (Eng)
1974 Frankie Lucas (SVI)
1978 Philip McElwaine (Aus)
1982 Jimmy Price (Eng)
1986 Rod Douglas (Eng)

81kg – LIGHT HEAVYWEIGHT
1930 Joe Goyder (Eng)
1934 George Brennan (Eng)
1938 Nicholaas Wolmarans (SAf)
1950 Donald Scott (Eng)
1954 Piet Van Vuuren (SAf)
1958 Tony Madigan (Aus)
1962 Tony Madigan (Aus)
1966 Roger Tighe (Eng)
1970 Fatai Ayinla (Nig)
1974 William Knight (Eng)

1978 Roger Fortin (Can)
1982 Fine Sani (Fiji)
1986 James Moran (Eng)

Over 81kg – HEAVYWEIGHT
1930 Victor Stuart (Eng)
1934 Pat Floyd (Eng)
1938 Thomas Osborne (Can)
1950 Frank Creagh (NZ)
1954 Brian Harper (Eng)
1958 Daniel Bekker (SAf)
1962 George Oywello (Uga)
1966 William Kini (NZ)
1970 Benson Masanda (Uga)
1974 Neville Meade (Eng)
1978 Julius Awome (Eng)
1982 Willie DeWit (Can)

91kg – HEAVYWEIGHT
1986 James Peau (NZ)

Over 91kg – SUPER-HEAVYWEIGHT
1986 Lennox Lewis (Can)

CYCLING WINNERS

SPRINT
1934 Ernest Higgins (Eng)
1938 Edgar Gray (Aus)
1950 Russell Mockridge (Aus)
1954 Cyril Peacock (Eng)
1958 Dick Ploog (Aus)
1962 Thomas Harrison (Aus)
1966 Roger Gibbon (Tri)
1970 John Nicholson (Aus)
1974 John Nicholson (Aus)
1978 Kenrick Tucker (Aus)
1982 Kenrick Tucker (Aus)
1986 Gary Neiwand (Aus)

1000 METRES TIME TRIAL
1934 Edgar Gray (Aus) 1:16.4
1938 Robert Porter (Aus) 1:15.2
1950 Russell Mockridge (Aus) 1:13.4
1954 Dick Ploog (Aus) &
     Alfred Swift (SAf) 1:12.5
1958 Neville Tong (Eng) 1:12.1
1962 Peter Bartels (Aus) 1:12.9
1966 Roger Gibbon (Tri) 1:09.6
1970 Harry Kent (NZ) 1:08.69
1974 Dick Paris (Aus) 1:11.85
1978 Jocelyn Lovell (Can) 1:06.00
1982 Craig Adair (NZ) 1:06.954
1986 Martin Vinnicombe (Aus) 1:06.23

4000 METRES INDIVIDUAL PURSUIT
1950 Cyril Cartwright (Eng) 5:16.3
1954 Norman Sheil (Eng) 5:03.5
1958 Norman Sheil (Eng) 5:10.2
1962 Maxwell Langshaw (Aus) 5:08.2
1966 Hugh Porter (Eng) 4:56.6
1970 Ian Hallam (Eng) 5:01.41
1974 Ian Hallam (Eng) 5:05.46
1978 Michael Richards (NZ) 4:49.74
1982 Michael Turtur (Aus) 4:50.990
1986 Dean Woods (Aus) 4:43.92

4000 METRES TEAM PURSUIT
1974 England 4:40.50
1978 Australia 4:29.43
1982 Australia 4:26.090
1986 Australia 4:26.94

100 KILOMETRES ROAD TEAM TIME TRIAL
1982 England 2:09:27
1986 England 2:13:16

TANDEM SPRINT
1970 Gordon Johnson & Ron Jonker (Aus) 11.43
1974 Geoffrey Cooke & Ernest Crutchlow (Eng) 10.74
1978 Jocelyn Lovell & Gordon Singleton (Can) 15.52

10 MILES TRACK
1934 Robert McLeod (Can) 24:26.2
1938 William Maxfield (Eng) 24:44.0
1950 William Heseltine (Aus) 23:23.4
1954 Lindsay Cocks (Aus) 21:59.5
1958 Ian Browne (Aus) 21:40.2
1962 Douglas Adams (Aus) 22:10.8
1966 Ian Alsop (Eng) 21:46.0
1970 Jocelyn Lovell (Can) 20:46.72
1974 Stephen Heffernan (Eng) 20:51.25
1978 Jocelyn Lovell (Can) 20:05.81
1982 Kevin Nichols (Aus) 19:56.559
1986 Wayne McCarney (Aus) 19:40.61

ROAD RACE
Raced over 100km 1938-54, 120 miles (193 km)
1958-66, 164.6 km 1970, 183km 1974, 117 miles (188
km) 1978, 184km 1982, 105 miles (169 km) 1986.
1938 Hendrik Binneman (SAf) 2:53:29.6
1950 Hector Sutherland (Aus) 3:13:06.4
1954 Eric Thompson (Eng) 2:44:08.1
1958 Ray Booty (Eng) 5:16:33.7
1962 Wesley Mason (Eng) 5:20:26.2
1966 Peter Buckley (IOM) 5:07:52.5
1970 Bruce Biddle (NZ) 4:38:05.8
1974 Clyde Sefton (Aus) 5:07:16.87
1978 Philip Anderson (Aus) 4:22:34.41
1982 Malcolm Elliott (Eng) 4:34:40.06
1986 Paul Curran (Eng) 4:08:50

FENCING WINNERS

MEN'S FOIL – INDIVIDUAL
1950 René Paul (Eng)
1954 René Paul (Eng)
1958 Raymond Paul (Eng)
1962 Alexander Leckie (Sco)
1966 Allan Jay (Eng)
1970 Mike Breckin (Eng)

MEN'S FOIL – TEAM
1950 England
1954 England
1958 England
1962 England
1966 England
1970 England

MEN'S EPEE – INDIVIDUAL
1950 Charles-Louis de Beaumont (Eng)
1954 Ivan Lund (Aus)
1958 William Hoskyns (Eng)
1962 Ivan Lund (Aus)
1966 William Hoskyns (Eng)
1970 William Hoskyns (Eng)

MEN'S EPEE – TEAM
1950 Australia
1954 England
1958 England
1962 England
1966 England
1970 England

MEN'S SABRE – INDIVIDUAL
1950 Arthur Pilbrow (Eng)
1954 Michael Amberg (Eng)
1958 William Hoskyns (Eng)
1962 Ralph Cooperman (Eng)
1966 Ralph Cooperman (Eng)
1970 Alexander Leckie (Sco)

MEN'S SABRE – TEAM
1950 England
1954 Canada
1958 England
1962 England
1966 England
1970 England

WOMEN'S FOIL – INDIVIDUAL
1950 Mary Glen-Haig (Eng)
1954 Mary Glen-Haig (Eng)
1958 Gillian Sheen (Eng)
1962 Melody Coleman (NZ)
1966 Janet Wardell-Yerburgh (Eng)
1970 Janet Wardell-Yerburgh (Eng)

WOMEN'S FOIL – TEAM
1966 England
1970 England

GYMNASTICS WINNERS

All 1978:
MEN Philip Delesalle (Can)
MEN'S TEAM Canada
WOMEN Elfi Schlegel (Can)
WOMEN'S TEAM Canada

ROWING WINNERS

SINGLE SCULLS
1930 Bobby Pearce (Aus) 8:03.6
1938 Herbert Turner (Aus) 8:24.0
1950 Mervyn Wood (Aus) 7:46.8
1954 Donald Rowlands (NZ) 8:28.2
1958 Stuart Mackenzie (Aus) 7:20.1
1962 James Hill (NZ) 7:39.7
1986 Steven Redgrave (Eng) 7:28.29

DOUBLE SCULLS
1930 Elswood Bole & Bob Richards (Can) 7:48.0
1938* William Bradley & Cecil Pearce (Aus) 7:29.4
1950 Mervyn Wood & Murray Riley (Aus) 7:22.0
1954 Mervyn Wood & Murray Riley (Aus) 7:54.5
1958 Michael Spracklen & Geoffrey Baker (Eng) 6:54.4
1962 George Justice & Nicholas Birkmyre (Eng) 6:52.4
1986 Pat Walter & Bruce Ford (Can) 6:19.43
* no medals awarded, invitation event

COXLESS PAIRS
1950 Walter Lambert & Jack Webster (Aus) 7:58.0
1954 Robert Parker & Reginald Douglas (NZ) 8:23.9
1958 Robert Parker & Reginald Douglas (NZ) 7:11.1
1962 Stewart Farquharson & James Lee-Nicholson (Eng) 7:03.7
1986 Steven Redgrave & Andrew Holmes (Eng) 6:40.48

COXLESS FOURS
1930 England 7:04.6
1958 England 6:34.4
1962 England 6:31.1
1986 Canada 6:00.56

COXED FOURS
1930 New Zealand 8:02.0
1938 Australia 7:16.8
1950 New Zealand 7:17.2
1954 Australia 7:58.3
1958 England 6:46.5
1962 New Zealand 6:48.2
1986 England 6:08.13

EIGHTS
1930 England 6:37.0
1938 England 6:29.0
1950 Australia 6:27.0
1954 Canada 6:59.0
1958 Canada 5:51.1
1962 Australia 5:53.4
1986 Australia 5:44.42

LIGHTWEIGHT SINGLE SCULLS
1986 Peter Antonie (Aus) 7:16.43

LIGHTWEIGHT COXLESS FOURS
1986 England 6:25.86

WOMEN'S SINGLE SCULLS
1986 Stephanie Foster (NZ) 7:43.22

WOMEN'S DOUBLE SCULLS
1986 Stephanie Foster & Robin Clarke (NZ) 7:21.52

WOMEN'S COXLESS PAIRS
1986 Kathryn Barr & Andrea Schreiner (Can) 7:34.51

WOMEN'S COXED FOURS
1986 Canada 6:50.13

WOMEN'S EIGHTS
1986 Australia 6:43.69

WOMEN'S LIGHTWEIGHT SINGLE SCULLS
1986 Adair Ferguson (Aus) 7:45.49

WOMEN'S LIGHTWEIGHT COXLESS FOURS
1986 England 6:54.70

SHOOTING WINNERS

SMALL BORE RIFLE
(.22 rifle)
1966 Gilmour Boa (Can) 587
1974 Yvonne Gowland (Aus) 594
1978 Alister Allan (Sco) 1194

SMALL BORE RIFLE – PRONE
1982 Alan Smith (Aus) 1184
1986 Alan Smith (Aus) 599

SMALL BORE RIFLE – PRONE – PAIRS
1982 Malcolm Cooper & Mike Sullivan (Eng) 1187
1986 Michael Ashcroft & Gale Stewart (Can) 1175

SMALL BORE RIFLE- THREE POSITIONS
1982 Alister Allan (Sco) 1146
1986 Malcolm Cooper (Eng) 1170

SMALL BORE RIFLE – THREE POSITIONS – PAIRS
1982 Malcolm Cooper & Barry Dagger (Eng) 2301
1986 Malcolm Cooper & Sarah Cooper (Eng) 2278

FULL BORE RIFLE
(.303 rifle 1966, 7.62mm rifle from 1974)
1966 Lord (John) Swansea (Wal) 394
1974 Maurice Gordon (NZ) 387.26
1978 Desmond Vamplew (Can) 391
1982 Arthur Clarke (Sco) 387
1986 Stan Golinski (Aus) 396

FULL BORE RIFLE – PAIRS
1982 Keith Affleck & Geoffrey Ayling (Aus) 572
1986 Alain Marion & William Baldwin (Can) 583

FREE PISTOL
(.22 single shot)
1966 Charles Sexton (Eng) 544
1974 Jules Sobrian (Can) 549
1978 Yvon Trempe (Can) 543
1982 Tom Guinn (Can) 553
1986 Greg Yelavich (NZ) 551

FREE PISTOL – PAIRS
1982 Phillip Adams & John Tremelling (Aus) 1077
1986 Tom Guinn & Claude Beaulieu (Can) 1099

CENTRE FIRE PISTOL
1966 James Lee (Can) 576
1982 John Cooke (Eng) 580
1986 Robert Northover (Eng) 583

CENTRE FIRE PISTOL – PAIRS
1982 Noel Ryan & Alexander Taransky (Aus) 1151
1986 Phillip Adams & Roderick Hack (Aus) 1165

RAPID FIRE PISTOL
(.22 semi automatic)
1966 Anthony Clark (Eng) 585
1974 William Hare (Can) 586
1978 Jules Sobrian (Can) 587
1982 Solomon Lee (HK) 583
1986 Pat Murray (Aus) 591

RAPID FIRE PISTOL – PAIRS
1982 Peter Heuke & Alexander Taransky (Aus) 1160
1986 Brian Girling & Terry Turner (Eng) 1169

OLYMPIC TRAP
(Clay pigeon)
1974 John Primrose (Can) 196
1978 John Primrose (Can) 186
1982 Peter Boden (Eng) 191
1986 Ian Peel (Eng) 195

OLYMPIC TRAP – PAIRS
1982 Jim Ellis & Terry Rumbel (Aus) 190
1986 Ian Peel & Peter Boden (Eng) 185

SKEET
1974 Harry Willsie (Can) 194

1978 John Woolley (NZ) 193
1982 John Woolley (NZ) 197
1986 Nigel Kelly (IOM) 196

SKEET – PAIRS
1982 Brian Gabriel & Fred Altmann (Can) 191
1986 Joe Neville & Kenneth Harman (Eng) 195

AIR PISTOL
1982 George Darling (Eng) 576
1986 Greg Yelavich (NZ) 575

AIR PISTOL – PAIRS
1982 Phillip Adams & Gregory Colbert (Aus) 1128
1986 Paul Leatherdale & Ian Reid (Eng) 1143

AIR RIFLE
1982 Jean-Francois Senecal (Can) 574
1986 Guy Lorion (Can) 588

AIR RIFLE – PAIRS
1982 Alister Allan & Bill McNeil (Sco) 1137
1986 Guy Lorion & Sharon Bowes (Can) 1167

SWIMMING WINNERS

100 METRES FREESTYLE
Swum over 100 yards (91.44m) 1930-4, 110 yards (100.58m) 1938-66
1930 Munroe Bourne (Can) 56.0
1934 George Burleigh (Can) 55.0
1938 Bob Pirie (Can) 59.6
1950 Peter Salmon (Can) 1:00.4
1954 Jon Henricks (Aus) 56.5
1958 John Devitt (Aus) 56.6
1962 Richard Pound (Can) 55.8
1966 Mike Wenden (Aus) 54.0
1970 Mike Wenden (Aus) 53.06
1974 Mike Wenden (Aus) 52.73
1978 Mark Morgan (Aus) 52.70
1982 Neil Brooks (Aus) 51.14
1986 Greg Fasala (Aus) 50.95

200 METRES FREESTYLE
1970 Mike Wenden (Aus) 1:56.69
1974 Stephen Badger (Aus) 1:56.72
1978 Ron McKeon (Aus) 1:52.06
1982 Andrew Astbury (Eng) 1:51.52
1986 Robert Gleria (Aus) 1:50.57

400 METRES FREESTYLE
Swum over 400 yards (365.76m) 1930, 440 yards (402.34m) 1934-66
1930 Noel Ryan (Aus) 4:39.8
1934 Noel Ryan (Aus) 5:03.0
1938 Bob Pirie (Can) 4:54.6
1950 Garrick Agnew (Aus) 4:49.4
1954 Gary Chapman (Aus) 4:39.8
1958 John Konrads (Aus) 4:25.9
1962 Murray Rose (Aus) 4:20.0
1966 Robert Windle (Aus) 4:15.0
1970 Graham White (Aus) 4:08.48
1974 John Kulasalu (Aus) 4:01.44
1978 Ron McKeon (Aus) 3:54.43
1982 Andrew Astbury (Eng) 3:53.29
1986 Duncan Armstrong (Aus) 3:52.25

1500 METRES FREESTYLE
Swum over 1500 yards (1371.6m) 1930-4, 1650 yards (1508.76m) 1938-66
1930 Noel Ryan (Aus) 18:55.4
1934 Noel Ryan (Aus) 18:25.4
1938 Robert Leivers (Eng) 19:46.4
1950 Graham Johnston (SAf) 19:55.7
1954 Graham Johnston (SAf) 19:01.4
1958 John Konrads (Aus) 17:45.4
1962 Murray Rose (Aus) 17:18.1
1966 Ron Jackson (Aus) 17:25.9
1970 Graham Windeatt (Aus) 16:23.82
1974 Steve Holland (Aus) 15:34.73
1978 Max Metzker (Aus) 15:31.92
1982 Max Metzker (Aus) 15:23.94
1986 Jason Plummer (Aus) 15:12.62

4 × 100 METRES FREESTYLE RELAY
Swum over 4 × 110 yards 1962-6
1962 Australia 3:43.9
1966 Australia 3:35.6
1970 Australia 3:36.02
1974 Canada 3:33.79
1978 Canada 3:27.94
1982 Australia 3:24.17
1986 Australia 3:21.58

4 × 200 METRES FREESTYLE RELAY
Swum over 4 × 200 yards 1930-34, 4 x 220 yards 1938-66
1930 Canada 8:42.4
1934 Canada 8:40.6
1938 England 9:19.0
1950 New Zealand 9:27.9
1954 Australia 8:47.6
1958 Australia 8:33.4
1962 Australia 8:13.4
1966 Australia 7:59.5
1970 Australia 7:50.77
1974 Australia 7:50.13
1978 Australia 7:34.83
1982 Australia 7:28.81
1986 Australia 7:23.49

100 METRES BACKSTROKE
Swum over 100 yards (91.44m) 1930-4, 110 yards (100.58m) 1938-66
1930 John Trippett (Eng) 1:05.4
1934 Willie Francis (Sco) 1:05.2
1938 Percy Oliver (Aus) 1:07.9
1950 Jacobus Wiid (SAf) 1:07.7
1954 John Brockway (Wal) 1:06.5
1958 John Monckton (Aus) 1:01.7
1962 Graham Sykes (Eng) 1:04.5
1966 Peter Reynolds (Aus) 1:02.4
1970 Bill Kennedy (Can) 1:01.65
1974 Mark Tonelli (Aus) 59.65
1978 Glenn Patching (Aus) 57.90
1982 Michael West (Can) 57.12
1986 Mark Tewksbury (Can) 56.45

200 METRES BACKSTROKE
Swum over 220 yards (201.17m) 1962-6
1962 Julian Carroll (Aus) 2:20.9
1966 Peter Reynolds (Aus) 2:12.0
1970 Mike Richards (Wal) 2:14.53

1974 Brad Cooper (Aus) 2:06.31
1978 Gary Hurring (NZ) 2:04.37
1982 Cameron Henning (Can) 2:02.88
1986 Sandy Goss (Can) 2:02.55

100 METRES BREASTSTROKE
Swum over 110 yards (100.58m) 1962-6
1962 Ian O'Brien (Aus) 1:11.4
1966 Ian O'Brien (Aus) 1:08.2
1970 Bill Mahony (Can) 1:09.0
1974 David Leigh (Eng) 1:06.52
1978 Graham Smith (Can) 1:03.81
1982 Adrian Moorhouse (Eng) 1:02.93
1986 Victor Davis (Can) 1:03.01

200 METRES BREASTSTROKE
Swum over 200 yards (182.88m) 1930-4, 220 yards (201.17m) 1938-66
1930 Jack Aubin (Can) 2:38.4
1934 Norman Hamilton (Sco) 2:41.4
1938 John Davies (Eng) 2:51.9
1950 David Hawkins (Aus) 2:54.1
1954 John Doms (NZ) 2:52.6
1958 Terry Gathercole (Aus) 2:41.6
1962 Ian O'Brien (Aus) 2:38.2
1966 Ian O'Brien (Aus) 2:29.3
1970 Bill Mahony (Can) 2:30.29
1974 David Wilkie (Sco) 2:24.42
1978 Graham Smith (Can) 2:20.86
1982 Victor Davis (Can) 2:16.25
1986 Adrian Moorhouse (Eng) 2:16.35

100 METRES BUTTERFLY
Swum at 110 yards (100.59m) 1962-6
1962 Kevin Berry (Aus) 59.5
1966 Ron Jacks (Can) 1:00.3
1970 Byron MacDonald (Can) 58.44
1974 Neil Rogers (Aus) 56.58
1978 Dan Thompson (Can) 55.04
1982 Dan Thompson (Can) 54.71
1986 Andrew Jameson (Eng) 54.07

200 METRES BUTTERFLY
Swum over 220 yards (201.17m) 1958-66
1958 Ian Black (Sco) 2:22.6
1962 Kevin Berry (Aus) 2:10.8
1966 David Gerrard (NZ) 2:12.7
1970 Tom Arusoo (Can) 2:08.97
1974 Brian Brinkley (Eng) 2:04.51
1978 George Nagy (Can) 2:01.99
1982 Phil Hubble (Eng) 2:00.98
1986 Anthony Mosse (NZ) 1:57.27

200 METRES INDIVIDUAL MEDLEY
1970 George Smith (Can) 2:13.72
1974 David Wilkie (Sco) 2:10.11
1978 Graham Smith (Can) 2:05.25
1982 Alex Baumann (Can) 2:02.25
1986 Alex Baumann (Can) 2:01.80

400 METRES INDIVIDUAL MEDLEY
Swum over 440 yards (402.34m) 1962-6
1962 Alex Alexander (Aus) 5:15.3
1966 Peter Reynolds (Aus) 4:50.8
1970 George Smith (Can) 4:48.87
1974 Mark Treffers (NZ) 4:35.90
1978 Graham Smith (Can) 4:27.34
1982 Alex Baumann (Can) 4:23.53
1986 Alex Baumann (Can) 4:18.29

4 × 100 METRES MEDLEY RELAY
Swum over 3 × 100 yards 1934, 3 × 110 yards 1938-54, 4 × 110 yards 1958-66. Butterfly leg added from 1958.
1934 Canada 3:11.2
1938 England 3:28.2
1950 England 3:26.6
1954 Australia 3:22.0
1958 Australia 4:14.2
1962 Australia 4:12.4
1966 Canada 4:10.5
1970 Canada 4:01.10
1974 Canada 3:52.93
1978 Canada 3:49.76
1982 Australia 3:47.34
1986 Canada 3:44.00

SPRINGBOARD DIVING
1930 Alfred Phillips (Can)
1934 J.Briscoe Ray (Eng)
1938 Ron Masters (Aus)
1950 George Athans (Can)
1954 Peter Heatly (Sco)
1958 Keith Collin (Eng)
1962 Brian Phelps (Eng)
1966 Brian Phelps (Eng)
1970 Donald Wagstaff (Aus)
1974 Donald Wagstaff (Aus)
1978 Chris Snode (Eng)
1982 Chris Snode (Eng)
1986 Shaun Panayi (Aus)

HIGHBOARD DIVING
1930 Alfred Phillips (Can)
1934 Tommy Mather (Eng)
1938 Doug Tomalin (Eng)
1950 Peter Heatly (Sco)
1954 William Patrick (Can)
1958 Peter Heatly (Sco)
1962 Brian Phelps (Eng)
1966 Brian Phelps (Eng)
1970 Donald Wagstaff (Aus)
1974 Donald Wagstaff (Aus)
1978 Chris Snode (Eng)
1982 Chris Snode (Eng)
1986 Craig Rogerson (Aus)

WATER POLO
1950 Australia

WOMEN
100 METRES FREESTYLE
Swum over 100 yards (91.44m) 1930-4, 110 yards (100.58m) 1938-66
1930 Joyce Cooper (Eng) 1:07.0
1934 Phyllis Dewar (Can) 1:03.0
1938 Evelyn de Lacy (Aus) 1:10.1
1950 Marjorie McQuade (Aus) 1:09.0
1954 Lorraine Crapp (Aus) 1:05.8
1958 Dawn Fraser (Aus) 1:01.4
1962 Dawn Fraser (Aus) 59.5
1966 Marion Lay (Can) 1:02.3
1970 Angela Coughlan (Can) 1:01.22
1974 Sonya Gray (Aus) 59.13

1978 Carol Klimpel (Can) 57.78
1982 June Croft (Eng) 56.97
1986 Jane Kerr (Can) 57.62

200 METRES FREESTYLE
1970 Karen Moras (Aus) 2:09.78
1974 Sonya Gray (Aus) 2:04.27
1978 Rebecca Perrott (NZ) 2:00.63
1982 June Croft (Eng) 1:59.74
1986 Susie Baumer (Aus) 2:00.61

400 METRES FREESTYLE
Swum over 400 yards (365.76m) 1930, 440 yards (402.34m) 1934-66
1930 Joyce Cooper (Eng) 5:25.4
1934 Phyllis Dewar (Can) 5:45.6
1938 Dorothy Green (Aus) 5:39.7
1950 Joan Harrison (SAf) 5:26.4
1954 Lorraine Crapp (Aus) 5:11.4
1958 Ilsa Konrads (Aus) 4:49.4
1962 Dawn Fraser (Aus) 4:51.4
1966 Kathy Wainwright (Aus) 4:38.8
1970 Karen Moras (Aus) 4:27.38
1974 Jenny Turrall (Aus) 4:22.09
1978 Tracey Wickham (Aus) 4:08.45
1982 Tracey Wickham (Aus) 4:08.82
1986 Sarah Hardcastle (Eng) 4:07.68

800 METRES FREESTYLE
1970 Karen Moras (Aus) 9:02.45
1974 Jaynie Parkhouse (NZ) 8:58.49
1978 Tracey Wickham (Aus) 8:24.62
1982 Tracey Wickham (Aus) 8:29.05
1986 Sarah Hardcastle (Eng) 8:24.77

4 × 100 METRES FREESTYLE RELAY
Swum over 4 × 100 yards 1930-34, 4 × 110 yards 1938-66
1930 England 4:32.8
1934 Canada 4:21.8
1938 Canada 4:48.3
1950 Australia 4:44.9
1954 South Africa 4:33.9
1958 Australia 4:17.4
1962 Australia 4:11.0
1966 Canada 4:10.8
1970 Australia 4:06.41
1974 Canada 3:57.14
1978 Canada 3:50.28
1982 England 3:54.23
1986 Canada 3:48.45

4 × 200 METRES FREESTYLE RELAY
1986 Australia 8:12.09

100 METRES BACKSTROKE
Swum over 100 yards (91.44m) 1930-4, 110 yards (100.58m) 1938-66
1930 Joyce Cooper (Eng) 1:15.0
1934 Phyllis Harding (Eng) 1:13.8
1938 Pat Norton (Aus) 1:19.5
1950 Judy-Joy Davies (Aus) 1:18.6
1954 Joan Harrison (SAf) 1:15.2
1958 Judy Grinham (Eng) 1:11.9
1962 Linda Ludgrove (Eng) 1:11.1
1966 Linda Ludgrove (Eng) 1:09.2
1970 Lynne Watson (Aus) 1:07.10

Anita Lonsbrough – Commonwealth, European and Olympic champion. (All-Sport)

1974 Wendy Cook (Can) 1:06.37
1978 Debra Forster (Aus) 1:03.97
1982 Lisa Forrest (Aus) 1:03.48
1986 Sylvia Hume (NZ) 1:04.00

200 METRES BACKSTROKE
Swum over 220 yards (201.17m) 1962-66
1962 Linda Ludgrove (Eng) 2:35.2
1966 Linda Ludgrove (Eng) 2:28.5
1970 Lynne Watson (Aus) 2:22.86
1974 Wendy Cook (Can) 2:20.37
1978 Cheryl Gibson (Can) 2:16.57
1982 Lisa Forrest (Aus) 2:13.36
1986 Georgina Parkes (Aus) 2:14.88

100 METRES BREASTSTROKE
Swum over 110 yards (100.58m) 1962-66
1962 Anita Lonsbrough (Eng) 1:21.3
1966 Diana Harris (Eng) 1:19.7
1970 Beverley Whitfield (Aus) 1:17.40
1974 Catherine Gaskell (Eng) 1:16.42
1978 Robin Corsiglia (Can) 1:13.56
1982 Kathy Bald (Can) 1:11.89
1986 Allison Higson (Can) 1:10.84

200 METRES BREASTSTROKE
Swum over 200 yards (182.88m) 1930-4, 220 yards (201.17m) 1938-66
1930 Celia Wolstenholme (Eng) 2:54.8
1934 Claire Dennis (Aus) 2:50.2
1938 Doris Storey (Eng) 3:06.3
1950 Elenor Gordon (Sco) 3:01.7
1954 Elenor Gordon (Sco) 2:59.2
1958 Anita Lonsbrough (Eng) 2:53.5
1962 Anita Lonsbrough (Eng) 2:51.7
1966 Jill Slattery (Eng) 2:50.3
1970 Beverley Whitfield (Aus) 2:44.12
1974 Pat Beavan (Wal) 2:43.11
1978 Lisa Borsholt (Can) 2:37.70
1982 Anne Ottenbrite (Can) 2:32.07
1986 Allison Higson (Can) 2:31.20

100 METRES BUTTERFLY
Swum at 110 yards (100.59m) 1958-66
1958 Beverley Bainbridge (Aus) 1:13.5
1962 Mary Stewart (Can) 1:10.1

1966 Elaine Tanner (Can) 1:06.8
1970 Diane Lansley (Eng) 1:07.90
1974 Patti Stenhouse (Can) 1:05.38
1978 Wendy Quirk (Can) 1:01.92
1982 Lisa Curry (Aus) 1:01.22
1986 Caroline Cooper (Eng) 1:02.12

200 METRES BUTTERFLY
Swum over 220 yards (201.17m) 1966
1966 Elaine Tanner (Can) 2:29.9
1970 Maree Robinson (Aus) 2:24.67
1974 Sandra Yost (Aus) 2:20.57
1978 Michelle Ford (Aus) 2:11.29
1982 Michelle Ford (Aus) 2:11.89
1986 Donna McGinnis (Can) 2:11.97

200 METRES INDIVIDUAL MEDLEY
1970 Denise Langford (Aus) 2:28.89
1974 Leslie Cliff (Can) 2:24.13
1978 Sharron Davies (Eng) 2:18.37
1982 Lisa Curry (Aus) 2:16.94
1986 Suzanne Landells (Aus) 2:17.02

400 METRES INDIVIDUAL MEDLEY
Swum over 440 yards (402.34m) 1962-66
1962 Anita Lonsbrough (Eng) 5:38.6
1966 Elaine Tanner (Can) 5:26.3
1970 Denise Langford (Aus) 5:10.74
1974 Leslie Cliff (Can) 5:01.35
1978 Sharron Davies (Eng) 4:52.44
1982 Lisa Curry (Aus) 4:51.95
1986 Suzanne Landells (Aus) 4:45.82

4 × 100 METRES MEDLEY RELAY
Swum over 3 × 100 yards 1934, 3 × 110 yards 1938-54, 4 × 110 yards 1958-66. Butterfly leg added from 1958.
1934 Canada 3:42.0
1938 England 3:57.7
1950 Australia 3:53.8
1954 Scotland 3:51.0
1958 England 4:54.0
1962 Australia 4:45.9
1966 England 4:40.6
1970 Australia 4:30.66
1974 Canada 4:24.77
1978 Canada 4:15.26
1982 Canada 4:14.33
1986 England 4:13.48

SPRINGBOARD DIVING
1930 Oonagh Whitsett (SAf)
1934 Judy Moss (Can)
1938 Irene Donnett (Aus)
1950 Edna Child (Eng)
1954 Ann Long (Eng)
1958 Charmian Welsh (Eng)
1962 Susan Knight (Aus)
1966 Kathy Rowlatt (Eng)
1970 Beverley Boys (Can)
1974 Cindy Shatto (Can)
1978 Janet Nutter (Can)
1982 Jenny Donnet (Aus)
1986 Debbie Fuller (Can)

HIGHBOARD DIVING
1930 Pearl Stoneham (Can)
1934 Elizabeth Macready (Eng)
1938 Lurline Hook (Aus)
1950 Edna Child (Eng)
1954 Barbara McAulay (Aus)
1958 Charmian Welsh (Eng)
1962 Susan Knight (Aus)
1966 Joy Newman (Eng)
1970 Beverley Boys (Can)
1974 Beverley Boys (Can)
1978 Linda Cuthbert (Can)
1982 Valerie Beddoe (Aus)
1986 Debbie Fuller (Can)

SYNCHRONISED SWIMMING – SOLO
1986 Sylvie Frechette (Can)

SYNCHRONISED SWIMMING – DUET
1986 Carolyn Waldo & Michelle Cameron (Can)

WEIGHTLIFTING WINNERS

Three lifts 1950-70, two from 1974. All weights in kilograms (originally measured in pounds 1950-66).

FLYWEIGHT – up to 52kg
1970 George Vasiliades (Aus) 290
1974 Precious McKenzie (Eng) 215
1978 Ekambaram Karunakaran (Ind) 205
1982 Nick Voukelatos (Aus) 207.5
1986 Greg Hayman (Aus) 212.5

BANTAMWEIGHT – up to 56kg
1950 Tho Fook Hung (Mal) 297
1954 Maurice Megennis (Eng) 281
1958 Reginald Gaffley (SAf) 299
1962 Chua Phung Kim (Sin) 322
1966 Precious McKenzie (Eng) 319.5
1970 Precious McKenzie (Eng) 335
1974 Michael Adams (Aus) 222.5
1978 Precious McKenzie (NZ) 220
1982 Geoffrey Laws (Eng) 235
1986 Nick Voukelatos (Aus) 245

FEATHERWEIGHT – up to 60kg
1950 Koh Eng Tong (Mal) 310.5
1954 Rodney Wilkes (Tri) 313
1958 Tan Ser Cher (Sin) 310.5
1962 George Newton (Eng) 326.5
1966 Kum Weng Chung (Wal) 337
1970 George Perrin (Eng) 342.5
1974 George Vasiliades (Aus) 237.5
1978 Michel Mercier (Can) 237.5
1982 Dean Willey (Eng) 267.5
1986 Raymond Williams (Wal) 252.5

LIGHTWEIGHT – up to 67.5kg
1950 James Halliday (Eng) 344.5
1954 Verdi Barberis (Aus) 347
1958 Tan Howe Liang (Sin) 358
1962 Carlton Goring (Eng) 351.5
1966 Hugo Gittens (Tri) 367
1970 George Newton (Eng) 372.5
1974 George Newton (Eng) 260
1978 Bill Stellios (Aus) 272.5
1982 David Morgan (Wal) 295
1986 Dean Willey (Eng) 315

MIDDLEWEIGHT – up to 75kg
1950 Gerard Gratton (Can) 360.5

Precious McKenzie, three gold medals for England and one for New Zealand. (All-Sport)

1954 James Halliday (Eng) 362.5
1958 Blair Blenman (Bar) 360.5
1962 Tan Howe Laing (Sin) 390
1966 Pierre St Jean (Can) 404.5
1970 Russell Perry (Aus) 412.5
1974 Tony Ebert (NZ) 275
1978 Sam Castiglione (Aus) 300
1982 Stephen Pinsent (Eng) 312.5
1986 Bill Stellios (Aus) 302.5

**LIGHT-HEAVYWEIGHT –
up to 82.5kg**
1950 James Varaleau (Can) 369.5
1954 Gerry Gratton (Can) 403.5
1958 Phil Caira (Sco) 396.5
1962 Phil Caira (Sco) 408
1966 George Vakakis (Aus) 419.5
1970 Nicolo Ciancio (Aus) 447.5
1974 Tony Ford (Eng) 302.5
1978 Robert Kabbas (Aus) 322.5
1982 Newton Burrowes (Eng) 325
1986 David Morgan (Wal) 350

**MIDDLE HEAVYWEIGHT –
up to 90kg**
1954 Keevil Daly (Can) 399
1958 Manoel Santos (Aus) 403.5
1962 Louis Martin (Eng) 469.5
1966 Louis Martin (Eng) 462
1970 Louis Martin (Eng) 457.5
1974 Nicolo Ciancio (Aus) 330
1978 Gary Langford (Eng) 335
1982 Robert Kabbas (Aus) 337.5
1986 Keith Boxell (Eng) 350

**SUB-HEAVYWEIGHT –
up to 100kg**
1978 John Burns (Wal) 340
1982 Oliver Orok (Nig) 350
1986 Denis Garon (Can) 360

**HEAVYWEIGHT –
up to 110kg**
1950 Harold Cleghorn (NZ) 408
1954 Doug Hepburn (Can) 471.5
1958 Ken McDonald (Eng) 455.5
1962 Arthur Shannos (Aus) 465
1966 Donald Oliver (NZ) 497
1970 Russell Prior (Can) 490
1974 Russell Prior (Can) 352.5
1978 Russell Prior (Can) 347.5
1982 John Burns (Wal) 347.5
1986 Kevin Roy (Can) 375

**SUPER HEAVYWEIGHT –
over 110kg**
1970 Ray Rigby (Aus) 500
1974 Graham May (NZ) 342.5
1978 Jean-Marc Cardinal (Can) 365
1982 Dean Lukin (Aus) 377.5
1986 Dean Lukin (Aus) 392.5

WRESTLING WINNERS

48kg – LIGHT-FLYWEIGHT
1970 Ved Prakash (Ind)

1974 Mitchell Kawasaki (Can)
1978 Ashok Kumar (Ind)
1982 Ram Chander Sarang (Ind)
1986 Ron Moncur (Can)

52kg – FLYWEIGHT
1950 Bert Harris (Aus)
1954 Louis Baise (SAf)
1958 Ian Epton (SAf)
1962 Mohammad Niaz (Pak)
1966 Mohammad Nazir (Pak)
1970 Sudesh Kumar (Ind)
1974 Sudesh Kumar (Ind)
1978 Ray Takahashi (Can)
1982 Mahabir Singh (Ind)
1986 Chris Woodcroft (Can)

57kg – BANTAMWEIGHT
1930 James Trifunov (Can)
1934 Edward Melrose (Sco)
1938 Ted Purcell (Aus)
1950 Douglas Mudgeway (NZ)
1954 Geoffrey Jameson (Aus)
1958 Muhammad Akhtar (Pak)
1962 Siraj-ud-Din (Pak)
1966 Bishambar Singh (Ind)
1970 Sadar Mohd (Pak)
1974 Premnath (Ind)
1978 Satbir Singh (Ind)
1982 Brian Aspen (Eng)
1986 Mitch Ostberg (Can)

62kg – FEATHERWEIGHT
1930 Clifford Chilcott (Can)
1934 Robert McNab (Can)
1938 Roy Purchase (Aus)
1950 John Armitt (NZ)
1954 Abraham Geldenhuys (SAf)
1958 Abraham Geldenhuys (SAf)
1962 Ala-ud-Din (Pak)
1966 Mohammad Akhtar (Pak)
1970 Mohammad Saeed (Pak)
1974 Egon Beiler (Can)
1978 Egon Beiler (Can)
1982 Bob Robinson (Can)
1986 Paul Hughes (Can)

68kg – LIGHTWEIGHT
1930 Howard Thomas (Can)
1934 Richard Garrard (Aus)
1938 Richard Garrard (Aus)
1950 Richard Garrard (Aus)
1954 Godfrey Pienaar (SAf)
1958 Muhammad Ashraf (Pak)
1962 Muhammad Akhtar (Pak)
1966 Mukhtiar Singh (Ind)
1970 Udey Chand (Ind)
1974 Jagrup Singh (Ind)
1978 Zsigmund Kelevitz (Aus)
1982 Jagminder Singh (Ind)
1986 David McKay (Can)

74kg – WELTERWEIGHT
1930 Reg Priestley (Can)
1934 Joseph Schleimer (Can)
1938 Thomas Trevaskis (Aus)

1950 Henry Hudson (Can)
1954 Nicholas Laubscher (SAf)
1958 Muhammad Bashir (Pak)
1962 Muhammad Bashir (Pak)
1966 Muhammad Bashir (Pak)
1970 Mukhtiar Singh (Ind)
1974 Raghunath Pawar (Ind)
1978 Rajinder Singh (Ind)
1982 Rajinder Singh (Ind)
1986 Gary Holmes (Can)

82kg – MIDDLEWEIGHT
1930 Mike Chepwick (Can)
1934 Terry Evans (Can)
1938 Terry Evans (Can)
1950 Maurice Vachon (Can)
1954 Hermanus van Zyl (SAf)
1958 Hermanus van Zyl (SAf)
1962 Muhammad Faiz (Pak)
1966 Muhammad Faiz (Pak)
1970 Harish Rajindra (Ind)
1974 David Aspin (NZ)
1978 Richard Deschatelets (Can)
1982 Chris Rinke (Can)
1986 Chris Rinke (Can)

90kg – LIGHT-HEAVYWEIGHT
1930 Bill McIntyre (Can)
1934 Mick Cubbin (SAf)
1938 Edward Scarf (Aus)
1950 Patrick Morton (SAf)
1954 Jacob Theron (SAf)
1958 Jacob Theron (SAf)
1962 Anthony Buck (Eng)
1966 Robert Chamberot (Can)
1970 Muhammad Faiz (Pak)
1974 Terry Paice (Can)
1978 Stephen Danier (Can)
1982 Clark Davis (Can)
1986 Noel Loban (Eng)

100kg – HEAVYWEIGHT
1930 Earl McCready (Can)
1934 Jack Knight (Aus)
1938 Jack Knight (Aus)
1950 James Armstrong (Aus)
1954 Kenneth Richmond (Eng)
1958 Lila Ram (Ind)
1962 Muhammad Niaz (Pak)
1966 Bhim Singh (Ind)
1970 Edward Millard (Can)
1974 Claude Pilon (Can)
1978 Wyatt Wishart (Can)
1982 Richard Deschatelets (Can)
1986 Clark Davis (Can)

**OVER 100kg –
SUPER-HEAVYWEIGHT**
Limit 130kg from 1986
1970 Ikram Ilahi (Pak)
1974 Bill Benko (Can)
1978 Robert Gibbons (Can)
1982 Wyatt Wishart (Can)
1986 Wayne Brightwell (Can)

CRICKET

Cricket originated in England in the Middle Ages. Its exact origins are obscure, but bat and ball games were played from the 13th century and games similar to the modern one from around 1550. The earliest major match for which the full score survives was that when England played Kent in London in 1744. In that year the first known Laws of the game were issued. The Marylebone Cricket Club (MCC) was founded in 1787, and until the formation of the Cricket Council in 1968 was accepted as the ruling body of the game from its headquarters at Lord's Cricket Ground, London. The MCC remains responsible for the Laws of Cricket. The Imperial (International from 1965) Cricket Conference was formed by representatives of England, Australia and South Africa in 1909. India, New Zealand and West Indies were elected members in 1926, Pakistan in 1953 and Sri Lanka in 1981. South Africa ceased to be a member in 1961. Other, non-Test playing nations have been admitted as associate members.

TEST CRICKET

The first Test match was played at Melbourne on 15-19 Mar 1877 between Australia and England, represented by James Lillywhite's touring side. Neither side was truly representative of their countries and indeed such was the case for many matches, now accepted as Test matches, played over the next fifty years or so. The first match in England was against Australia at The Oval on 6-8 Sep 1880.

W.G. Grace dominated the game of cricket throughout his playing career, 1865 to 1908. (All-Sport)

The first Tests played by each Test-playing nation:

	Against	Date	Venue
Australia (A)	v E	15-19 Mar 1877	Melbourne
England (E)	v A	15-19 Mar 1877	Melbourne
India (I)	v E	25-28 Jun 1932	Lord's
New Zealand (NZ)	v E	10-13 Jan 1930	Christchurch
Pakistan (P)	v I	16-18 Oct 1952	New Delhi
South Africa (SA)	v E	12-13 Mar 1889	Port Elizabeth
Sri Lanka (SL)	v E	17-21 Feb 1982	Colombo
West Indies (WI)	v E	23-26 Jun 1928	Lord's

Summary of Test wins-losses (drawn games omitted) to 1 June 1987

	A	E	I	NZ	P	SA	SL	WI	Wins	Tests
Australia	-	97-88	20-8*	9-5	11-8	29-11	1-0	27-19*	194	472
England	88-97	-	30-11	30-4	13-3	46-18	1-0	21-35	229	633
India	8-20*	11-30	-	10-4	4-7	-	2-1	5-22	40	246
New Zealand	5-9	4-30	4-10	-	3-10	2-9	4-0	4-8	26	183
Pakistan	8-11	3-13	7-4	10-3	-	-	5-1	5-8	38	164
South Africa	11-29	18-46	-	9-2	-	-	-	-	38	172
Sri Lanka	0-1	0-1	1-2	0-4	1-5	-	-	-	2	24
West Indies	19-27*	35-21	22-5	8-4	8-5	-	-	-	92	252

* There have been two tied Tests:
9-14 Dec 1960 at Brisbane Australia v West Indies
18-22 Sep 1986 at Madras Australia v India

TEAM RECORDS

Highest innings totals

903-7 dec	England	v A	The Oval	20-23 Aug 1938
849	England	v WI	Kingston	3-5 Apr 1930
790-3 dec	West Indies	v P	Kingston	27 Feb - 1 Mar 1958

758-8 dec	Australia	v WI	Kingston	13-15 Jun 1955
729-6 dec	Australia	v E	Lord's	28-30 Jun 1930
701	Australia	v E	The Oval	18-20 Aug 1934
695	Australia	v E	The Oval	18-20 Aug 1930
687-8 dec	West Indies	v E	The Oval	12-13 Aug 1976
681-8 dec	West Indies	v E	Port-of-Spain	17-19 Mar 1954
676-7	India	v SL	Kanpur	20-22 Dec 1986

Highest match aggregates
1981 runs South Africa (530 & 481) v England (316 & 654-5) at Durban 3-14 Mar 1939. This was the 'Timeless Test'. The total playing time was 43 hours 16 minutes, over 10 days.
1815 runs West Indies (286 & 408-5) v England (849 & 272-9 dec) at Kingston 3-12 Apr 1930.
1764 runs Australia (533 & 339-9) v West Indies (276 & 616) at Adelaide 24-29 Jan 1969. This is the record for a five day Test.
All the above three Tests were left drawn.

Highest winning margin
Innings and 579 runs England (903-7 dec) beat Australia (201 & 123) at the Oval 20-24 Aug 1938.

Lowest completed innings totals
26	New Zealand	v E	Auckland	28 Mar 1955
30	South Africa	v E	Port Elizabeth	14 Feb 1896
30	South Africa	v E	Birmingham	16 Jun 1924
35	South Africa	v E	Cape Town	4 Apr 1899
36	Australia	v E	Birmingham	30 May 1902
36	South Africa	v A	Melbourne	12 Feb 1932

Lowest declared total
| 32-7 | Australia | v E | Brisbane | 4 Dec 1950 |

Lowest match aggregate
234 runs Australia (153) beat South Africa (36 & 45) 12-15 Feb 1932.

INDIVIDUAL RECORDS – to June 1987
Most Tests
125 Sunil Gavaskar (Ind) 1971-87
114 Colin Cowdrey (Eng) 1954-75
110 Clive Lloyd (WI) 1966-85
108 Geoffrey Boycott (Eng) 1964-82
 96 Rodney Marsh (Aus) 1970-84
 95 Alan Knott (Eng) 1967-81
 95 Dilip Vengsarkar (Ind) 1976-87
 93 Garfield Sobers (WI) 1954-74
 91 David Gower (Eng) 1978-87
 91 Godfrey Evans (Eng) 1946-59
 91 Gundappa Viswanath (Ind) 1969-83
 90 Bob Willis (Eng) 1971-84
 89 Ian Botham (Eng) 1977-87
 89 Allan Border (Aus) 1978-87
 88 Syed Kirmani (Ind) 1976-86
 88 Vivian Richards (WI) 1974-87
 88 Kapil Dev (Ind) 1978-87
 87 Greg Chappell (Aus) 1970-84
 86 Derek Underwood (Eng) 1977-82
 85 Walter Hammond (Eng) 1927-47

Most for other countries
 81 Wasim Bari (Pak) 1967-84
 70 Richard Hadlee (NZ) 1973-87
 50 John Waite (SAf) 1951-65
 23 Sidath Wettimuny (Sri) 1982-7

Youngest player: 15 yr 124 days Mushtaq Mohammed (Pak) v WI Lahore 26 Mar 1959.

Oldest player: 52 yr 165 days Wilfred Rhodes (Eng) v WI Kingston 12 Apr 1930.

Longest Test career: 30 yr 314 days Wilfred Rhodes (Eng) 1 Jun 1899 to 12 Apr 1930.

Most Test appearances as captain
(in brackets no. matches won)
74 (36) Clive Lloyd (WI) 1974-85
48 (21) Greg Chappell (Aus) 1975-83
46 (9) Sunil Gavaskar (Ind) 1976-85
41 (20) Peter May (Eng) 1955-61
40 (9) Nawab of Pataudi Jnr (Ind) 1962-75
39 (12) Bobby Simpson (Aus) 1963-78
39 (9) Garfield Sobers (WI) 1965-72
Other captains to have won 15 or more Tests:
31 (18) Mike Brearley (Eng) 1977-81
30 (15) Ian Chappell (Aus) 1971-5
24 (15) Don Bradman (Aus) 1936-48

Gary Sobers (Patrick Eagar)

BATTING

Highest individual innings scores (over 300)

365*	Garfield Sobers (WI)	v P	Kingston	27 Feb - 1 Mar 1958
364	Leonard Hutton (Eng)	v A	The Oval	20-23 Aug 1938
337	Hanif Mohammad (Pak)	v WI	Bridgetown	20-23 Jan 1958
336*	Walter Hammond (Eng)	v NZ	Auckland	31 Mar - 1 Apr 1933
334	Don Bradman (Aus)	v E	Leeds	11-12 Jul 1930
325	Andrew Sandham (Eng)	v WI	Kingston	3-4 Apr 1930
311	Bobby Simpson (Aus)	v E	Manchester	23-25 Jul 1964
310*	John Edrich (Eng)	v NZ	Leeds	8-9 Jul 1965
307	Bob Cowper (Aus)	v E	Melbourne	12-16 Feb 1966
304	Don Bradman (Aus)	v E	Leeds	21-23 Jul 1934
302	Lawrence Rowe (WI)	v E	Bridgetown	7-10 Mar 1974

Fastest scoring Test Centuries

Mins	Balls				
70	67	Jack Gregory (Aus)	v SA	Johannesburg	12 Nov 1921
75	75	Gilbert Jessop (Eng)	v A	The Oval	13 Aug 1902
78		Richard Benaud (Aus)	v WI	Kingston	15 Jun 1955
80		James Sinclair (SAf)	v A	Cape Town	11 Nov 1902
81	56	Vivian Richards (WI)	v E	St John's	15 Apr 1986

Third fastest century in terms of balls received

116	71	Roy Fredericks (WI)	v A	Perth	13 Dec 1975

Fastest Test double centuries

214	Don Bradman (Aus)	v E	Leeds	11 Jul 1930
223	Stan McCabe (Aus)	v E	Nottingham	11-13 Jun 1938

Fastest 200 in terms of balls received

268	220	Ian Botham (Eng)	v I	The Oval	8-9 Jul 1982

Fastest Test triple century

287	Walter Hammond (Eng) v NZ	Auckland	31 Mar - 1 Apr 1933

During his innings of 336 not out in 318 minutes Hammond hit ten sixes, a record for a Test innings. His third hundred took just 47 minutes, the fastest in Test cricket.

Most Test hundreds (double hundreds in brackets)

34	(4)	Sunil Gavaskar (Ind)	20	(3)	Vivian Richards (WI)
29	(12)	Don Bradman (Aus)	20	(1)	Ken Barrington (Eng)
26	(2)	Garfield Sobers (WI)	20	(-)	Allan Border (Aus)
24	(4)	Greg Chappell (Aus)	19	(4)	Leonard Hutton (Eng)
22	(7)	Walter Hammond (Eng)	19	(1)	Clive Lloyd (WI)
22	(1)	Geoffrey Boycott (Eng)			also scoring 4 double hundreds:
22	(-)	Colin Cowdrey (Eng)	12	(4)	Zaheer Abbas (Pak)
21	(2)	Neil Harvey (Aus)			

Most runs in a Test career

Runs	Name	Average	Tests	Years
10122	Sunil Gavaskar (Ind)	51.12	125	1971-87
8114	Geoffrey Boycott (Eng)	47.72	108	1964-82
8032	Garfield Sobers (WI)	57.78	93	1954-74
7624	Colin Cowdrey (Eng)	44.06	114	1954-75
7515	Clive Lloyd (WI)	46.67	110	1966-85
7249	Walter Hammond (Eng)	58.45	85	1927-47
7110	Greg Chappell (Aus)	53.86	87	1970-84
6996	Don Bradman (Aus)	99.94	52	1928-48
6971	Leonard Hutton (Eng)	56.67	79	1937-55
6917	Allan Border (Aus)	52.80	89	1978-87
6806	Ken Barrington (Eng)	58.67	82	1955-68
6553	David Gower (Eng)	45.50	91	1978-87
6518	Vivian Richards (WI)	52.99	88	1974-87
6227	Rohan Kanhai (WI)	47.53	79	1957-74
6149	Neil Harvey (Aus)	48.41	79	1948-63
6080	Gundappa Viswanath (Ind)	41.93	91	1969-83
5951	Dilip Vengsarkar (Ind)	44.74	95	1976-87

Sunil Gavaskar scored his 10,000th run in Test cricket on 7 Mar 1987. He made a sensational start to his Test career with 774 runs, average 154.80, against the West Indies in 1970-1. Superlatives have flowed ever since. (All-Sport)

5891	Javed Miandad (Pak)	53.55	81	1976-87
5807	Denis Compton (Eng)	50.06	78	1937-57
5509	Gordon Greendige (WI)	48.32	77	1974-87
5410	Jack Hobbs (Eng)	56.94	61	1908-30
5357	Doug Walters (Aus)	48.26	74	1965-81
5345	Ian Chappell (Aus)	42.42	75	1964-80
5234	Bill Lawry (Aus)	47.15	67	1961-71
5138	John Edrich (Eng)	43.54	77	1963-76
5062	Zaheer Abbas (Pak)	44.79	78	1969-85
4882	Tom Graveney (Eng)	44.38	79	1951-69
4869	Bob Simpson (Aus)	46.81	62	1957-78
4825	Ian Botham (Eng)	34.96	89	1977-87
4737	Ian Redpath (Aus)	43.45	66	1964-76
4555	Herbert Sutcliffe (Eng)	60.73	54	1924-35
4537	Peter May (Eng)	46.77	66	1951-61
4502	Edward Dexter (Eng)	47.89	62	1958-68
4455	Everton Weekes (WI)	58.61	48	1948-58
4415	Kim Hughes (Aus)	37.41	70	1977-85
4399	Alvin Kallicharan (WI)	44.43	66	1972-81
4389	Alan Knott (Eng)	32.75	95	1967-81
4334	Roy Fredericks (WI)	42.49	59	1968-77

Don Bradman at 99.94 has the highest average in Test cricket. In addition to those in the table above the following have averages of over 55 for more than 10 Tests:

3798	Clyde Walcott (WI)	56.68	44	1948-60
2256	Graeme Pollock (SAf)	60.97	23	1963-70
2190	George Headley (WI)	60.83	22	1930-54
1540	Edward Paynter (Eng)	59.23	20	1931-39
1072	Sidney Barnes (Aus)	63.05	13	1938-48
995	K.S.Duleepsinhji (Eng)	58.52	12	1929-31
990	Ernest Tyldesley (Eng)	55.00	14	1921-29
947	Dean Jones (Aus)	55.70	10	1984-87
910	Charles Russell (Eng)	56.87	10	1920-23
723	Stewart Dempster (NZ)	65.72	10	1930-33

Fewest innings to reach:
1000 runs: 12 Herbert Sutcliffe (Eng), Everton Weekes (WI)
2000/3000/4000/5000/6000 runs: 22/33/48/56/68 Don Bradman (Aus)
7000 runs: 131 Walter Hammond (Eng)
8000 runs: 157 Garfield Sobers (WI)
9000 runs: 192 Sunil Gavaskar (Ind)
10 000 runs: 212 Sunil Gavaskar (Ind)

Most runs in a Test series

Runs	Tests	Average			
974	5	139.14	Don Bradman (Aus)	v E	1930
905	5	113.12	Walter Hammond (Eng)	v A	1928-9
834	5	92.66	Neil Harvey (Aus)	v SA	1952-3
829	4	118.42	Vivian Richards (WI)	v E	1976
827	5	82.70	Clyde Walcott (WI)	v A	1955
824	5	137.33	Garfield Sobers (WI)	v P	1958
810	5	90.00	Don Bradman (Aus)	v E	1936-7
806	5	201.50	Don Bradman (Aus)	v SA	1931-2

The most runs in a series of three Tests or less:

583	3	194.33	Zaheer Abbas (Pak)	v I	1978
563	2	563.00	Walter Hammond (Eng)	v NZ	1933
558	3	111.60	Seymour Nurse (WI)	v NZ	1969

Most series scoring 500 runs
7 Don Bradman; 6 Sunil Gavaskar, Garfield Sobers

BOWLING

Nine wickets in an innings

10-53	Jim Laker (Eng)	v A	Manchester	30-31 Jul 1956
9-28	George Lohmann (Eng)	v SA	Johannesburg	3 Mar 1896
9-37	Jim Laker (Eng)	v A.	Manchester	27-30 Jul 1956

9-69	Jasubhai Patel (Ind)	v A	Kanpur	20 Dec 1959
9-83	Kapil Dev (Ind)	v WI	Ahmedabad	14-16 Nov 1983
9-86	Sarfraz Nawaz (Pak)	v A	Melbourne	14-15 Mar 1979
9-95	John Noreiga (WI)	v I	Port-of-Spain	7-9 Mar 1971
9-102	Subhash Gupte (Ind)	v WI	Kanpur	12 Dec 1958
9-103	Sydney Barnes (Eng)	v SA	Johannesburg	29-30 Dec 1913
9-113	Hugh Tayfield (SAf)	v E	Johannesburg	19-20 Feb 1957
9-121	Arthur Mailey (Aus)	v E	Melbourne	14-16 Feb 1921

Most wickets in a match

19-90	Jim Laker (Eng)	v A	Manchester	26-31 Jul 1956
17-159	Sydney Barnes (Eng)	v SA	Johannesburg	26-30 Dec 1913
16-137	Bob Massie (Aus)	v E	Lord's	22-26 Jun 1972

Massie's feat (8-84 and 8-53) was on his Test debut.

Five wickets in an innings most times in Tests
(In brackets no. of times ten wickets in match)

28 (7) Richard Hadlee (NZ)	18 (2) Lance Gibbs (WI)
27 (4) Ian Botham (Eng)	17 (6) Derek Underwood (Eng)
24 (7) Sydney Barnes (Eng)	17 (3) Fred Trueman (Eng)
23 (7) Dennis Lillee (Aus)	16 (3) Graham McKenzie (Aus)
21 (7) Clarrie Grimmett (Aus)	16 (2) Bhagwant Chandrasekhar (Ind)
19 (4) Imran Khan (Pak)	16 (1) Richie Benaud (Aus)
19 (2) Kapil Dev (Ind)	16 (–) Bob Willis (Eng)

Most wickets in a Test career

Wkts		Average	Tests	Years
366	Ian Botham (Eng)	27.21	89	1977-87
355	Dennis Lillee (Aus)	23.92	70	1971-84
355	Richard Hadlee (NZ)	22.46	70	1973-87
325	Bob Willis (Eng)	25.20	90	1971-84
311	Kapil Dev (Ind)	29.40	88	1978-87
309	Lance Gibbs (WI)	29.09	79	1958-76
307	Fred Trueman (Eng)	21.57	67	1952-65
297	Derek Underwood (Eng)	25.83	86	1966-82
290	Imran Khan (Pak)	22.23	65	1971-87
266	Bishen Bedi (Ind)	28.71	67	1966-79
259	Joel Garner (WI)	20.97	58	1977-87
252	Brian Statham (Eng)	24.84	70	1951-65
249	Michael Holding (WI)	23.68	60	1975-87
248	Richie Benaud (Aus)	27.03	63	1952-64
246	Graham McKenzie (Aus)	29.78	60	1961-71
242	Bhagwant Chandrasekhar (Ind)	29.74	58	1964-79
240	Malcolm Marshall (WI)	21.64	51	1978-87
236	Alec Bedser (Eng)	24.89	51	1946-55
235	Garfield Sobers (WI)	34.03	93	1954-74
228	Ray Lindwall (Aus)	23.03	61	1946-60
216	Clarrie Grimmett (Aus)	24.21	37	1925-36
202	John Snow (Eng)	26.66	49	1965-76
202	Andy Roberts (WI)	25.61	47	1974-83
200	Jeff Thomson (Aus)	28.00	51	1972-85
193	Jim Laker (Eng)	21.24	46	1948-59
192	Wes Hall (WI)	26.38	48	1958-69
189	Sydney Barnes (Eng)	16.43	27	1901-14
189	Erapalli Prasanna (Ind)	30.38	49	1962-78
186	Alan Davidson (Aus)	20.53	44	1953-63
177	Sarfraz Nawaz (Pak)	32.75	55	1969-84
174	Tony Lock (Eng)	25.58	49	1952-68
170	Keith Miller (Aus)	22.97	55	1946-56
170	Hugh Tayfield (SAf)	25.91	37	1949-60

Fewest Tests to reach:
100 wickets: 16 George Lohmann (Eng)
200 wickets: 35 Clarrie Grimmett (Aus)
300 wickets: 56 Dennis Lillee (Aus)

Jim Laker achieved 19 wickets in the Old Trafford Test against Australia in 1956, even though his Surrey teammate Tony Lock was partnering him. Laker had earlier taken 10-88 in an innings for Surrey against the Australians.
(Sport and General)

In his Test career Lohmann took 112 wickets 1886-96 at 10.75, the lowest average for any bowler taking 25 or more wickets in a Test career. At 34.11 balls per wicket he also has the best striking rate. The next best for both these categories: John Ferris (Eng/Aus) 61 wickets av.12.70, 36.9 balls/wkt; Michael Proctor (SAf) 41 wickets av.15.02, 37.7 balls/wkt.

Most wickets in a Test series

Wkts	Tests	Average			
49	4	10.93	Sydney Barnes (Eng)	v SA	1913-4
46	5	9.60	Jim Laker (Eng)	v A	1956
44	5	14.59	Clarrie Grimmett (Aus)	v SA	1935-6
42	6	21.26	Terry Alderman (Aus)	v E	1981
41	6	12.85	Rodney Hogg (Aus)	v E	1978-9
40	6	13.95	Imran Khan (Pak)	v I	1982-3

The most in a three Test series:

35	3	5.80	George Lohmann (Eng)	v SA	1896
34	3	8.29	Sydney Barnes (Eng)	v SA	1912
33	3	12.15	Richard Hadlee (NZ)	v A	1985

Most series taking 20 wickets

9 Fred Trueman, Dennis Lillee; 7 Lance Gibbs, Malcolm Marshall (in succession); 6 Clarrie Grimmett, Alan Davidson, Jeff Thomson.

WICKET-KEEPING
(ct - caught, st - stumped)

Most dismissals in an innings

7 (all ct) Wasim Bari (Pak) v NZ Auckland 23 Feb 1979
7 (all ct) Bob Taylor (Eng) v I Bombay 15 Feb 1980

Most dismissals in a Test career

Dis		ct	st	Tests	Years
355	Rodney Marsh (Aus)	343	12	96	1970-84
269	Alan Knott (Eng)	250	19	95	1967-81
228	Wasim Bari (Pak)	201	27	81	1967-84
219	Godfrey Evans (Eng)	173	46	91	1946-59
198	Syed Kirmani (Ind)	160	38	88	1976-86
189	Deryck Murray (WI)	181	8	62	1963-80
187	Wally Grout (Aus)	163	24	51	1957-66
174	Bob Taylor (Eng)	167	7	57	1971-84
142	Jeffrey Dujon (WI)	139	3	43	1981-7
141	John Waite (SAf)	124	17	50	1951-65
130	Bert Oldfield (Aus)	78	52	54	1920-37

Most dismissals in a Test series

Dis	ct	st	Tests			
28	28	-	5	Rodney Marsh (Aus)	v E	1982-3
26	23	3	5	John Waite (SAf)	v NZ	1961-2
26	26	-	6	Rodney Marsh (Aus)	v WI	1975-6
24	22	2	5	Deryck Murray (WI)	v E	1963
24	24	-	5	Denis Lindsay (SAf)	v A	1966-7
24	21	3	6	Alan Knott (Eng)	v A	1970-1

The most in a three Test series

22	21	1	3	Amal Silva (Sri)	v I	1985

CATCHES
(By fielders, not wicket-keepers)

Most catches in an innings

5 Victor Richardson (Aus) v SA Durban 3 Mar 1936
5 Yajurvindra Singh (Ind) v E Bangalore 29-30 Jan 1977

Most catches in a Test career

Ct		Tests	Years
122	Greg Chappell (Aus)	87	1970-84

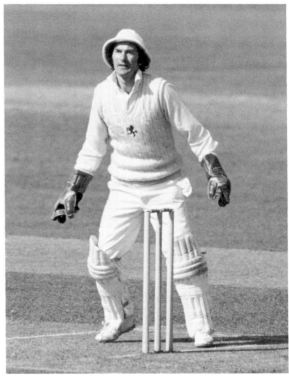

Alan Knott – 4389 runs in his Test career as well as 269 dismissals. (All-Sport)

120	Colin Cowdrey (Eng)	114	1954-75
110	Bob Simpson (Aus)	62	1957-78
110	Walter Hammond (Eng)	85	1927-47
109	Garfield Sobers (WI)	93	1954-74
108	Sunil Gavaskar (Ind)	125	1971-87
106	Ian Botham (Eng)	88	1977-87
105	Ian Chappell (Aus)	75	1964-80
94	Allan Border (Aus)	89	1978-87
90	Clive Lloyd (WI)	110	1966-85
87	Tony Greig (Eng)	58	1972-77
85	Vivian Richards (WI)	88	1974-87
83	Ian Redpath (Aus)	66	1964-76
80	Tom Graveney (Eng)	79	1951-69

Most catches in a Test series

Ct	Tests			
15	5	Jack Gregory (Aus)	v E	1920-1
14	6	Greg Chappell (Aus)	v E	1974-5
13	5	Bob Simpson (Aus)	v SA	1957-8
13	5	Bob Simpson (Aus)	v WI	1960-1

The most in a three Test series

11	3	Tony Greig (Eng)	v P	1974

ALL-ROUNDERS
Best Test career records – over 2000 runs and 150 wickets:
The final column is the ratio of batting average to bowling average, a good test of ability.

	Tests	Runs	Wkts	Catches	Ratio
Ian Botham (Eng)	89	4825	366	106	1.28
Garfield Sobers (WI)	93	8032	235	109	1.70
Richard Hadlee (NZ)	70	2622	355	36	1.23
Kapil Dev (Ind)	88	3668	311	43	1.09

Imran Khan (Pak)	65	2579	290	21	1.45
Richie Benaud (Aus)	63	2201	248	65	0.90
Keith Miller (Aus)	55	2958	170	38	1.61
Vinoo Mankad (Ind)	44	2109	162	33	0.97

Others with ratios of 1.5 or more, and 1000 runs/50 wickets

Walter Hammond (Eng)	85	7249	83	110	1.55
Aubrey Faulkner (SAf)	25	1754	82	20	1.53

Fewest Tests to reach:

1000 runs 100 wickets: 21 Ian Botham, 23 Vinoo Mankad, 25 Kapil Dev

2000 runs 200 wickets: 42 Ian Botham, 50 Kapil Dev, Imran Khan

3000 runs 300 wickets: 71 Ian Botham, 83 Kapil Dev

300 runs and 20 wickets in a Test series

Runs	Wkts	Tests			
475	34	5	George Giffen (Aus)	v E	1894-5
399	34	6	Ian Botham (Eng)	v A	1981
329	30	5	Richie Benaud (Aus)	v SA	1957-8
545	29	5	Aubrey Faulkner (SAf)	v E	1909-10
430	24	5	Tony Greig (Eng)	v WI	1974
442	23	5	Jack Gregory (Aus)	v E	1920-1
424	23	5	Garfield Sobers (WI)	v I	1962
318	22	6	Kapil Dev (Ind)	v E	1981-2
301	21	4	Richard Hadlee (NZ)	v E	1983

Runs	Wkts	Tests			
722	20	5	Garfield Sobers (WI)	v E	1966
439	20	5	Keith Miller (Aus)	v WI	1955
362	20	5	Keith Miller (Aus)	v WI	1951-2
322	20	5	Garfield Sobers (WI)	v E	1963

ONE-DAY INTERNATIONALS

The first ever one-day international match was played at Melbourne on 5 Jan 1971 when Australia beat England by 5 wickets. They have proliferated in recent years, especially in Australia.

WORLD CUP

The first World Cup was held in England in 1975, contested by the six Test playing nations plus Sri Lanka and East Africa at 60-over matches. This tournament was sponsored by the Prudential Assurance Company as were the next World Cup competitions held in England in 1979 and 1983. From 1979 the non-Test playing members of the International Cricket Conference (ICC) have played-off in England for the ICC Trophy and the right to enter the following World Cup tournament. The 1987 World Cup is to be held in India and Pakistan.

World Cup Finals (all held at Lord's)
1975 West Indies (291-8) beat Australia (274) by 17 runs

The prodigious Ian Botham continues to add to his record Test all-round figures.

Gary Sobers — both fast and slow bowler (All-Sport)

1979 West Indies (286-9) beat England (194) by 92 runs
1983 India (183) beat West Indies (140) by 43 runs

World Cup Innings Records
Total: 338-5 Pakistan v Sri Lanka at Swansea 9 Jun 1983
Lowest: 45 Canada v England at Manchester 14 Jun 1979
Individual: 175* Kapil Dev, India v Zimbabwe at Tunbridge Wells 18 Jun 1983
Best bowling: 7-51 Winston Davis, West Indies v Australia at Leeds 11-12 Jun 1983
Dismissals: 5 Syed Kirmani, India v Zimbabwe at Leicester 11 Jun 1983
Economical bowling: 1-6 in 12 overs Bishen Bedi, India v East Africa at Leicester 11 Jun 1975

ICC TROPHY

Winners
1979 Sri Lanka
1982 Zimbabwe
1986 Zimbabwe
Highest innings total: 455-9 off 60 overs Papua New Guinea v Gibraltar at Rugeley 18 Jun 1986.

BENSON & HEDGES WORLD SERIES CUP

Contested each winter since 1979-80 in Australia between the home country and two other teams. At 50 overs per innings.

Year	Winners	2nd	3rd
1980	West Indies	Eng	Aus
1981	Australia	NZ	Ind
1982	West Indies	Aus	Pak
1983	Australia	NZ	Eng
1984	West Indies	Aus	Pak
1985	West Indies	Aus	Sri
1986	Australia	Ind	NZ
1987	England	Aus	WI

Innings Records
Total: 323-2 Australia v Sri Lanka at Adelaide 28 Jan 1985
Lowest: 63 India v Australia at Sydney 3 Jan 1981
Individual: 158 David Gower, England v New Zealand at Brisbane 15 Jan 1983
Best bowling: 5-15 Greg Chappell, Australia v India at Sydney 8 Jan 1981
Dismissals: 4 John Bracewell (all as substitute fielder), New

Zealand v Australia at Adelaide 23 Nov 1980; Rodney Marsh, Australia v India at Sydney 8 Jan 1981; Rodney Marsh, Australia v New Zealand at Perth 6 Feb 1983
Economical bowling: 2-9 in 10 overs Mike Malone, Australia v West Indies at Melbourne 10 Jan 1982

ONE-DAY INTERNATIONAL RECORDS

(Between Test playing nations)

Innings records
Total: 338-5 Pakistan v Sri Lanka at Swansea 9 Jun 1983
Lowest: 63 India v Australia at Sydney 8 Jan 1981
Individual: 189* Vivian Richards, West Indies v England at Manchester 31 May 1984
Best bowling: 7-51 Winston Davis, West Indies v Australia at Leeds 11-12 Jun 1983

Career records

Most runs	Average	100s	Matches
5095 Vivian Richards (WI)	53.07	9	128
4259 Desmond Haynes (WI)	40.95	8	120
3961 Javed Miandad (Pak)	45.52	4	119
3952 Allan Border (Aus)	32.39	3	151
3511 Gordon Greenidge (WI)	46.19	9	84

Most wickets	Average	Matches
146 Joel Garner (WI)	18.84	98
142 Michael Holding (WI)	21.36	102
128 Richard Hadlee (NZ)	21.10	94
122 Kapil Dev (Ind)	26.09	99
116 Ian Botham (Eng)	29.29	95

Most dismissals	Ct	St	Matches
128 Jeffrey Dujon (WI)	118	10	92
123 Rodney Marsh (Aus)	119	4	91

FIRST-CLASS CRICKET

First-class matches are contested over three or more days. Such matches are now specified by the members of the ICC, but prior to 1947 when the term was first defined, there are doubts about the first-class status of many matches. The Association of Cricket Statisticians (ACS) have done much work in studying the problem and deciding about the status of such matches. They have drawn up lists of matches and, as a consequence, consistency can be achieved in statistical compilations. However there is still some disagreement about the status of various matches, and figures compiled as a result are sometimes at variance with traditional figures. We have respected tradition although incorporating corrections agreed by leading statisticians. First-class cricket is taken as having originated in 1815.

TEAM RECORDS
Highest innings totals

1107	Victoria v New South Wales at Melbourne 27-28 Dec 1926
1059	Victoria v Tasmania at Melbourne 2-5 Feb 1923
951-7 dec	Sind v Baluchistan at Karachi 18-20 Feb 1974
918	New South Wales v South Australia at Sydney 5-8 Jan 1901
912-8 dec	Holkar v Mysore at Indore 2-4 Mar 1946
910-6 dec	Railways v Dera Ismail Khan at Lahore 2-4 Dec 1964
903-7 dec	England v Australia at The Oval 20-23 Aug 1938

Highest match aggregate
2376 runs Bombay (651 & 714-8 dec) beat Maharashtra (407 & 604) at Poona over 7 days on 5-11 Mar 1949.

Largest margin of victory
Innings & 851 runs Railways (910-6 dec) beat Dera Ismail Khan (32 & 27) at Lahore on 2-4 Dec 1964.

Lowest completed innings totals
12 Oxford University (batted one short) v MCC and Ground at Oxford 24 May 1877
12 Northamptonshire v Gloucestershire at Gloucester 11 Jun 1907
13 Auckland v Canterbury at Auckland 31 Dec 1877
13 Nottinghamshire v Yorkshire at Nottingham 20-21 Jun 1901

Lowest aggregate in a completed first-class match
105 runs Australians (41 & 12-1) beat MCC (33 & 19) at Lord's 27 May 1878.

INDIVIDUAL RECORDS
BATTING

Highest innings (scores of over 400)

499	Hanif Mohammed	Karachi v Bahawalpur at Karachi 8-11 Jan 1959
452*	Don Bradman	New South Wales v Queensland at Sydney 4-6 Jan 1930
443*	Bhausahib Nimbalkar	Maharashtra v Kathiawar at Poona 16-18 Dec 1948
437	Bill Ponsford	Victoria v Queensland at Melbourne 16-17 Dec 1927
429	Bill Ponsford	Victoria v Tasmania at Melbourne 3-5 Feb 1923
428	Aftab Baloch	Sind v Baluchistan at Karachi 18-20 Feb 1974
424	Archie McLaren	Lancashire v Somerset at Taunton 15-16 Jul 1895

Fastest scoring
either minutes or balls received to reach the following scores:

Score	Mins	Balls	
50	8	13	Clive Inman, Leics v Notts at Nottingham 20 Aug 1965
100	35	40-46	Percy Fender, Surrey v Northants at Northampton 26 Aug 1920
	35	54	Steven O'Shaughnessy, Lancashire v Leics at Manchester 13 Sep 1983
	43	34	David Hookes, South Australia v Victoria at Adelaide 25 Oct 1982
200	113	123	Ravi Shastri, Bombay v Baroda at Bombay 10 Jan 1985
	120	121	Clive Lloyd, West Indians v Glamorgan at Swansea 9 Aug 1976
	120	?	Gilbert Jessop, Gloucestershire v Sussex at Hove 1 Jun 1903

300　181　　　　　Denis Compton, MCC v
North-Eastern Transvaal at Benoni
3-4 Dec 1948

Note that Edwin Alletson scored 189 runs in 90 mins for
Nottinghamshire v Sussex at Hove 20 May 1911, his
final 142 runs being hit off 51 balls in 40 minutes.
Gilbert Jessop scored 191 in 90 minutes (passing 150 in
63 mins) for the Gentlemen of the South v Players at
Hastings 3 Sep 1907.

Six sixes from a six-ball over
Garfield Sobers (Notts) off Malcolm Nash (Glamorgan) at
Swansea 31 Aug 1968
Ravi Shastri (Bombay) off Tilak Raj (Baroda) at Bombay
on 10 Jan 1985

Most sixes in an innings
15 John Reid in an innings of 296 for Wellington v
Northern Districts at Wellington 14-15 Jan 1963.

Sir John Berry 'Jack' Hobbs — "The Master"

Most runs in a first-class career/most 100s, 200s, 300s

All English unless stated. (To start 1987 English season.) The final column shows innings per century.

Runs	Name	Average	Years	100s	200s	300s	Inns/100
61167*	Jack Hobbs	50.67	1905-34	197	16	1	6.7
58959	Frank Woolley	40.77	1906-38	145	9	1	10.6
57611	Patsy Hendren	50.80	1907-38	170	22	1	7.6
55061	Philip Mead	47.67	1905-36	153	13	-	8.8
54896*	W.G.Grace	39.55	1865-1908	126	13	3	11.8
50551	Walter Hammond	56.10	1920-51	167	36	4	6.0
50138*	Herbert Sutcliffe	51.95	1919-45	149	17	1	7.3
48426	Geoffrey Boycott	56.83	1962-86	151	10	1	6.7
47793	Tom Graveney	44.91	1948-72	122	7	-	10.0
43551	Tom Hayward	41.79	1893-1914	104	8	1	10.3
42719	Colin Cowdrey	42.89	1950-76	107	3	2	10.6
42123	Dennis Amiss	43.42	1960-86	100	3	-	10.9
41284	Andrew Sandham	44.82	1911-38	107	11	1	9.3
40140	Len Hutton	55.51	1934-60	129	11	1	6.3
39832	Mike Smith	41.84	1951-75	66	3	-	16.5
39790	John Edrich	45.47	1956-78	103	4	1	9.5
39722*	Wilfred Rhodes	30.79	1896-1930	58	3	-	26.3
39405	Bob Wyatt	40.04	1923-57	85	2	-	13.4
38942	Denis Compton	51.85	1936-64	123	9	1	6.8
38874	Ernest Tyldesley	45.46	1909-36	102	7	-	9.4
37897	Johnny Tyldesley	40.66	1895-1923	86	13	-	11.6
37252	Jack (J.W.) Hearne	40.98	1909-36	96	11	-	10.7
37248	Leslie Ames	43.51	1926-51	102	9	-	9.0
37002	Don Kenyon	33.63	1946-67	74	7	-	15.7
36965	Bill Edrich	42.39	1934-58	86	9	-	11.2
36673	Jim Parks	34.76	1949-76	51	1	-	24.1
36440	David Denton	33.40	1894-1920	69	3	-	16.8
36437	Keith Fletcher	38.19	1962-86	62	2	-	18.0
36272	George Hirst	34.12	1891-1929	60	4	1	20.2
36049	Alan Jones	32.89	1957-83	56	1	-	20.9
36012	Billy Quaife	35.38	1894-1928	72	4	-	16.7
35725	Roy Marshall	35.95	1945-72	68	3	-	15.5
35208	George Gunn	35.96	1902-32	62	1	-	17.1

Others with career averages over 50 and 20000 runs, or 80 100s or 10 200s

Runs	Name	Average	Years	100s	200s	300s	Inns/100
34346	Glenn Turner (NZ)	49.70	1964-83	103	10	1	7.7
34285	Zaheer Abbas (Pak)	52.18	1965-85	107	10	-	7.0

Runs	Name	Average	Years	100s	200s	300s	Inns/100
33659	Maurice Leyland	40.50	1920-48	80	5	-	11.6
31900	Gordon Greenidge (WI)	45.89	1970-87	75	10	-	10.2
31847	Joe Hardstaff Jnr	44.35	1930-55	83	10	-	9.8
31300	Alvin Kallicharan (WI)	45.20	1966-87	84	6	-	9.2
30886	Charles Fry	50.22	1892-1921	94	16	-	7.0
30574	Percy Holmes	42.11	1913-35	67	12	2	12.1
30546	Reg Simpson	38.32	1944-63	64	10	-	13.3
29061	Vivian Richards (WI)	49.67	1971-87	93	9	1	6.7
28774	Rohan Kanhai (WI)	49.01	1955-82	83	7	-	8.1
28358	Barry Richards (SAf)	54.74	1964-83	80	6	1	7.2
28315	Garfield Sobers (WI)	54.87	1953-74	86	6	1	7.1
28067	Don Bradman (Aus)	95.14	1927-49	117	37	6	2.9
27592	Peter May	51.00	1948-63	85	5	-	7.3
26439	Arthur Shrewsbury	36.66	1875-1902	59	10	-	13.7
24749	Sunil Gavaskar (Ind)	51.24	1966-86	78	10	1	6.9
24692	K.S.Ranjitsinhji (Ind)	56.37	1893-1920	72	14	-	6.9
24535	Greg Chappell (Aus)	52.20	1966-84	74	4	-	7.3
23133	Javed Miandad (Pak)	53.30	1973-86	65	8	1	8.0
21699	Neil Harvey (Aus)	50.93	1946-63	67	7	-	6.9
21029	Bobby Simpson (Aus)	56.22	1952-78	60	12	2	7.3
20940	Graeme Pollock (SAf)	54.67	1960-87	62	5	-	6.9

Others with career averages over 55 and 10000 runs, or a century more often than every six innnings

18635	Vijay Hazare (Ind)	57.87	1934-67	60	10	2	6.1
16890	Lindsay Hassett (Aus)	58.24	1932-54	59	8	-	5.5
13819	Bill Ponsford (Aus)	65.18	1920-35	47	13	4	5.0
13392	Bill Woodfull (Aus)	65.00	1921-35	49	7	-	5.0
13248	Vijay Merchant (Ind)	71.22	1929-51	44	11	1	5.2
12762	Alan Kippax (Aus)	57.22	1918-36	43	7	1	6.0
12614	Arthur Morris (Aus)	53.67	1940-64	46	4	-	5.4
12010	Everton Weekes (WI)	55.34	1944-64	36	9	1	6.7
11820	Clyde Walcott (WI)	56.55	1941-64	40	4	1	5.9
9921	George Headley (WI)	69.80	1928-54	33	9	1	5.0

* ACS figures which are at considerable variance: Hobbs 61760 runs (av.50.66), 199 100s; W.G.Grace 54211 runs av. 39.45, 124 centuries (11.9 inns per 100); Sutcliffe 50670 runs (av.52.02), 150 100s; Rhodes 39969 runs (av.30.81).

Least innings to reach 100 centuries:
295 Don Bradman, 552 Denis Compton, 619 Len Hutton, 645 Geoffrey Boycott, 658 Zaheer Abbas, 680 Walter Hammond, 700 Herbert Sutcliffe.

Most times scoring two centuries in a match
8 Zaheer Abbas (including 200 and 100 four times); 7 Walter Hammond; 6 Jack Hobbs, Glenn Turner; 5 Charles Fry.
Uniquely Arthur Fagg scored two double centuries in a match, 244 and 202* Kent v Essex at Colchester 13-15 Jul 1938.

Most centuries in successive innings
6 Charles Fry for Sussex (5) and Rest of England 1901
6 Don Bradman for his XI and for South Australia (5) 1938-9
6 Mike Proctor for Rhodesia 1970-1

Most runs in an English season

Runs		100s	Average	Year
3816	Denis Compton	18	90.85	1947
3539	Bill Edrich	12	80.43	1947
3518	Tom Hayward	13	66.37	1906
3429	Len Hutton	12	68.58	1949
3352	Frank Woolley	12	60.94	1928
3336	Herbert Sutcliffe	14	74.13	1932
3323	Walter Hammond	13	67.81	1933
3311	Patsy Hendren	13	70.44	1928
3309	Bobby Abel	7	55.15	1901

also 14 or more centuries

3024	Jack Hobbs	16	70.32	1925
3011	Walter Hammond	15	75.27	1938

- highest average

2429	Don Bradman	13	115.66	1938
1538	Geoffrey Boycott	6	102.53	1979

Most seasons scoring 3000:
3 Herbert Sutcliffe 1928, 1931, 1932; Patsy Hendren 1923, 1928, 1933; Walter Hammond 1933, 1937, 1938.

Most seasons scoring 2000:
17 Jack Hobbs; 15 Patsy Hendren, Herbert Sutcliffe; 13 Frank Woolley; 12 Walter Hammond; 11 James Langridge, Philip Mead; 10 Tom Hayward; 9 Bill Edrich, Len Hutton, Jack Robertson.

Most seasons (English or overseas) scoring 1000 runs:
28 W.G.Grace, Frank Woolley; 27 Colin Cowdrey, Philip Mead; 26 Geoffrey Boycott, Jack Hobbs; 25 Patsy Hendren; 24 Billy Quaife, Herbert Sutcliffe; 23 Alan Jones.

Most sixes in a season: 80 Ian Botham 1985 (in 1530 runs, av.69.54)

BOWLING

Best bowling

The taking of all ten wickets in an innings by a single bowler has been recorded more than 70 times in first-class cricket. Bowlers to have achieved this feat more than once are:

3 Alfred 'Tich' Freeman, Kent 1929, 1930, 1931
2 Vyell Walker, England 1859 and Middlesex 1865
2 W.G.Grace, MCC 1873, 1886
2 Hedley Verity, Yorkshire 1931, 1932
2 Jim Laker, Surrey and England 1956

The least expensive ten wickets analyses:

10-10 Hedley Verity, Yorkshire v Nottinghamshire at Leeds 12 Jul 1932
10-18 George Geary, Leicestershire v Glamorgan at Pontypridd 15 Aug 1929
10-20 Premansu Chatterjee, Bengal v Assam at Jorhat 28 Jan 1957
10-26 Bert Vogler, Eastern Province v Griqualand West at Johannesburg 28 Dec 1906
10-28 A.E.Moss, Canterbury v Wellington at Christchurch 27-28 Dec 1889 (on his first-class debut)

10-28 William Howell, Australians v Surrey at The Oval 15 May 1899
10-30 Colin Blythe, Kent v Northants at Northampton 1 Jun 1907
10-32 Henry Pickett, Essex v Leicestershire at Leyton 3 Jun 1895

Most wickets in a match: 19 (9-37, 10-53) Jim Laker, England v Australia 26-31 Jul 1956. 17 wickets in a match has been achieved on 18 occasions; the least expensive being for 48 runs by Colin Blythe, 10-30 and 7-18, Kent v Northants 1 Jun 1907.

Most successive wickets

The feat of taking four wickets with consecutive balls has been achieved on 27 occasions. The only man to do this twice has been Bob Crisp for Western Province in Currie Cup matches in 1931-2 and 1934. The most notable spell was by Pat Pocock for Surrey v Sussex at Eastbourne 15 Aug 1972; his records included five wickets in one over, six wickets in nine balls and seven in eleven.

Most hat-tricks (three wickets with consecutive balls):
7 Douglas Wright (Eng) 1937-49; 6 Charlie Parker (Eng) 1922-30, Tom Goddard (Eng) 1924-47.

Most wickets in a first-class career

All English unless stated. The final two columns show the number of occasions on which the bowler has taken 5 wickets in an innings and 10 wickets in a match.

Wkts	Name	Average	Years	5wi	10wm
4187*	Wilfred Rhodes	16.71	1898-1930	287	67
3776	Alfred 'Tich' Freeman	18.42	1914-36	386	140
3278	Charlie Parker	19.46	1903-35	277	91
3061	Jack (J.T.) Hearne	17.75	1888-1923	255	64
2979	Tom Goddard	19.84	1922-52	251	86
2876*	W.G.Grace	17.92	1865-1908	240	64
2874	Alex Kennedy	21.43	1907-36	225	45
2857	Derek Shackleton	18.65	1948-69	194	38
2844	Tony Lock	19.23	1946-71	196	50
2830	Fred Titmus	22.37	1949-82	168	26
2784	Maurice Tate	18.16	1912-37	195	44
2742	George Hirst	18.73	1891-1929	184	40
2503	Colin Blythe	16.81	1899-1914	218	71
2431	Ewart Astill	23.76	1906-39	140	22
2420	Derek Underwood	20.12	1963-86	152	47
2356	Jack White	18.57	1909-37	193	58
2323	Eric Hollies	20.94	1932-57	182	40
2304	Fred Trueman	18.29	1949-69	126	25
2260	Brian Statham	18.36	1950-68	123	11
2233	Reg Perks	24.07	1930-55	143	24
2221	Johnny Briggs	15.93	1879-1900	200	52
2218	Don Shepherd	21.32	1950-72	123	28
2151	George Dennett	19.82	1903-26	211	57
2105	Tom Richardson	18.42	1892-1904	200	72

Others with career average below 15 and 1500 wickets, or more than 50 times taking 10 wickets in a match

2028	Alfred Shaw	12.12	1864-97	177	44
1956	Hedley Verity	14.90	1930-39	164	54
1841	George Lohmann	13.74	1884-98	176	57
1681	James Southerton	14.46	1854-79	192	59
1673	Arthur Mold	15.54	1889-1901	152	56
1571	Tom Emmett	13.56	1866-88	121	29

The best non-English players

1674	Albert Trott (Aus)	21.09	1893-1911	131	41
1571	Intikhab Alam (Pak)	27.67	1957-82	85	13
1560	Bishen Bedi (Ind)	21.69	1961-82	106	20
1424	Clarrie Grimmett (Aus)	22.28	1911-41	127	33

* ACS figures: Rhodes 4204 wickets (av.16.72), W.G.Grace 2808 (av 18.15)

Least matches to reach 1000 wickets:
134 Tom Richardson 1892-6, 147 George Dennett
1903-9, 149 Arthur Mold 1899-1905, 156 Jack (J.T.)
Hearne 1888-96, 159 George Lohmann 1884-8.

Least matches to reach 2000 wickets:
327 Tom Richardson 1892-1903, 347 Jack (J.T.) Hearne
1888-1902, 349 George Dennett 1903-24, 350 Colin
Blythe 1899-1912, 350 'Tich' Freeman 1914-29.

Most wickets in an English season

Wkts		Average	Year
304	Alfred 'Tich' Freeman	18.05	1928
298	Alfred 'Tich' Freeman	15.26	1933
290	Tom Richardson	14.37	1895
283	Charlie Turner	11.68	1888
276	Alfred 'Tich' Freeman	15.60	1931
275	Alfred 'Tich' Freeman	16.84	1930
273	Tom Richardson	14.45	1897

200 wickets in a season most often:
8 'Tich' Freeman; 5 Charlie Parker; 4 Tom Goddard; 3
Jack (J.T.) Hearne, George Lohmann, Wilfred Rhodes,
Tom Richardson, Maurice Tate, Hedley Verity.

100 wickets in a season most often:
23 Wilfred Rhodes; 20 Derek Shackleton; 17 'Tich'
Freeman; 16 Tom Goddard, Charlie Parker, Reg Perks,
Fred Titmus; 15 Jack (J.T.) Hearne, George Hirst, Alex
Kennedy.

*The best average while taking at least 100 wickets in a
season:* 8.54 Alfred Shaw, 186 wkts in 1880.

ALL-ROUNDERS
Best Career Figures
Determined by the best ratios of batting average divided
by bowling average (the figure in the first column), for
those with at least 10000 runs and 1000 wickets:

*Sonny Ramahdin beguiled England when he took 26
Test wickets for West Indies in 1950, having only two
first-class games prior to this tour.* (Sport and General)

	Ratio	Runs	Ave.	Wkts	Ave.	Years
W.G.Grace (Eng)	2.21	54896	39.55	2876	17.92	1865-1908
Frank Tarrant (Aus)	2.06	17857	36.36	1489	17.66	1898-1936
Frank Woolley (Eng)	2.05	58959	40.77	2068	19.85	1906-38
Garfield Sobers (WI)	1.98	28315	54.87	1043	27.74	1953-74
Mike Proctor (SAf)	1.89	21748	36.24	1395	19.19	1960-86
Wilfred Rhodes (Eng)	1.84	39722	30.79	4187	16.71	1895-1930
George Hirst (Eng)	1.82	36272	34.12	2742	18.73	1891-1929
Jack (J.W.) Hearne (Eng)	1.68	37252	40.98	1839	24.43	1909-36
Imran Khan (Pak)	1.66	15807	36.25	1175	21.82	1969-87

Other with 25000 runs and 2000 wickets:

	Ratio	Runs	Ave.	Wkts	Ave.	Years
Trevor Bailey (Eng)	1.44	28642	33.42	2082	23.13	1945-67

Best season's figures in England
2000 runs and 150 wickets in a season

George Hirst	2.78	2385	45.86	208	16.50	1906
Frank Woolley	2.66	2101	42.87	167	16.14	1921
Frank Woolley	2.50	2022	45.95	163	18.37	1922

3000 runs and 100 wickets in a season

James Parks	1.97	3003	50.89	101	25.83	1937

Ratios of over 3.00 for 1000 runs and 100 wickets

W.G.Grace	4.09	1664	52.00	140	12.71	1875
Richard Hadlee (NZ)	3.65	1179	51.26	117	14.05	1981
W.G.Grace	3.30	2622	62.42	130	18.90	1876
Wilfred Rhodes	3.26	1511	39.76	119	12.19	1922
George Hirst	3.16	1844	47.28	128	14.94	1903
W.G.Grace	3.11	1474	39.83	179	12.81	1877
Jack (J.W.) Hearne	3.09	2148	55.07	142	17.83	1920

Best match: George Giffen (Aus) scored 271 and took 9-96 and 7-70, South Australia v Victoria 7-11 Nov 1891.

WICKET-KEEPING DISMISSALS
(ct – caught, st – stumped)

Most dismissals in an innings
8 (all ct) Wally Grout, Queensland v Western Australia at Brisbane 15 Feb 1960
8 (all ct) David East, Essex v Somerset at Taunton 27 Jul 1985

Most stumpings in an innings
6 Hugo Yarnold, Worcestershire v Scotland at Broughty Ferry 2 Jul 1951

Most dismissals in a match
12 (8ct, 4st) Edward Pooley, Surrey v Sussex at The Oval 6-7 Jul 1868
12 (9ct, 3st) Don Tallon, Queensland v New South Wales at Sydney 2-4 Jan 1939
12 (9ct, 3st) Brian Taber, New South Wales v South Australia at Adelaide 13-17 Dec 1968

Most dismissals in a first-class career
All English

Dis	ct	st	Name	Per match	Career
1648	1473	175	Bob Taylor	2.6	1960-86
1527	1270	257	John Murray	2.4	1952-75
1496	1242	254	Herbert Strudwick	2.2	1902-27
1344	1211	133	Alan Knott	2.6	1965-85
1310	933	377	Frederick Huish	2.6	1895-1914
1294	1081	213	Brian Taylor	2.3	1949-73
1265	914	351	David Hunter	2.3	1889-1909
1228	953	275	Harry Butt	2.3	1890-1912
1207	852	355	Jack Board	2.3	1891-1915
1206	904	302	Harry Elliott	2.3	1920-47
1181	1088	93	Jim Parks	1.6	1949-76
1126	949	177	Roy Booth	2.4	1951-70
1121	703	418	Les Ames	1.9	1926-51
1089	754	341	George Duckworth	2.2	1923-47
1082	748	334	Harold Stephenson	2.3	1948-64
1071	895	176	Jimmy Binks	2.1	1955-69
1066	816	250	Godfrey Evans	2.3	1939-69

Best non-English

869	804	65	Rodney Marsh (Aus)	3.4	1968-84
849	741	108	Deryck Murray (WI)	2.3	1961-80
824	703	121	Farokh Engineer (Ind)	2.5	1958-76
812	667	145	Wasim Bari (Pak)	2.9	1964-83

Over 350 dismissals and 3 per match

587	473	114	Wally Grout (Aus)	3.2	1946-66
426	383	43	Ray Jennings (SAf)	3.9	1973-87
395	345	50	Brian Taber (Aus)	3.1	1964-74
385	354	31	John Maclean (Aus)	3.6	1968-79
369	292	77	Gil Langley (Aus)	3.0	1945-57

Most dismissals in an English season

Dis	ct	st	Name	Year
127	79	48	Leslie Ames	1929
121	69	52	Leslie Ames	1928
110	62	48	Hugo Yarnold	1949
107	77	30	George Duckworth	1928
107	96	11	Jimmy Binks	1960
104	82	22	John Murray	1957
102	70	32	Frederick Huish	1913
102	95	7	John Murray	1960

Most catches: 96 Binks 1960
Most stumpings: 64 Ames 1932 (and 36ct)

CATCHES BY FIELDERS
Most catches in an innings
7 Micky Stewart, Surrey v Northants at Northampton 7 Jun 1957
7 Tony Brown, Gloucestershire v Notts at Nottingham 26 Jul 1966

Most catches in a match
10 (4 & 6) Walter Hammond, Gloucestershire v Surrey at Cheltenham 16-17 Aug 1928

Most catches in a first-class career
All English unless stated

Catches	Name	Per match	Career
1018	Frank Woolley	1.04	1906-38
874	W.G.Grace	1.00	1865-1908
831	Tony Lock	1.27	1946-71
819	Walter Hammond	1.29	1920-51
813	Brian Close	1.04	1949-86
786	James Langridge	1.37	1928-55
764	Wilfred Rhodes	0.61	1896-1930
758	Arthur Milton	1.22	1948-74
754	Patsy Hendren	0.91	1907-38
697	Peter Walker	1.49	1956-72
695	John Tunnicliffe	1.40	1891-1907
675	James Seymour	1.22	1900-26
671	Philip Mead	0.82	1905-36
638	Colin Cowdrey	0.92	1950-76
634	Micky Stewart	1.19	1954-72

The highest averages per match of those taking 300 or more:

602	Graham Roope	1.50	1964-86
383	Bobby Simpson (Aus)	1.49	1952-78
328	Hugh Trumble (Aus)	1.54	1887-1904

Most catches in an English season

78	Walter Hammond	1928
77	Micky Stewart	1957
73	Peter Walker	1961
71	Philip Sharpe	1962
70	John Tunnicliffe	1901

COUNTY CHAMPIONSHIP

The first recorded inter-county match was contested in 1709 between Kent and Surrey, and the first county to be acclaimed as champions were Sussex in 1827. Such references became more frequent from 1864, the year in which overarm bowling was legalised, but it was not until the 1890 season that the County Championship was officially recognised and a points system introduced.

From 1827 to 1862 the Southern counties of Kent, Surrey and Sussex generally proved the best, with an occasional challenge from Nottinghamshire. From 1864, when eight counties took part in inter-county matches, to 1889 the following champion counties were proclaimed, principally on the basis of fewest matches lost (* shared):

Surrey	1864, 1887-8, 1889*
Gloucestershire	1873*, 1874, 1876-7
Nottinghamshire	1865, 1868, 1869*, 1871-2, 1873*, 1875, 1879*, 1880, 1882*, 1883-6, 1889*

Middlesex	1866
Yorkshire	1867, 1869*, 1870
Lancashire	1879*, 1881, 1882*, 1889*
Undecided in 1878	

COUNTY CHAMPIONS FROM 1890

The Championship was sponsored by Schweppes in 1977-83 and by Britannic Assurance from 1984.

Wins (including ties for first place)

30 (1T)	Yorkshire	1893, 1896, 1898, 1900-2, 1905, 1908, 1912, 1919, 1922-5, 1931-3, 1935, 1937-9, 1946, 1949*, 1959-60, 1962-3, 1966-8
16 (1T)	Surrey	1890-2, 1894-5, 1899, 1914, 1950*, 1952-8, 1971
10 (2T)	Middlesex	1903, 1920-1, 1947, 1949*, 1976, 1977*, 1980, 1982, 1985
8 (1T)	Lancashire	1897, 1904, 1926-8, 1930, 1934, 1950*
7 (1T)	Kent	1906, 1909-10, 1913, 1970, 1977*, 1978
4	Essex	1979, 1983-4, 1986
3	Nottinghamshire	1907, 1929, 1981
3	Warwickshire	1911, 1951, 1972
3	Worcestershire	1964-5, 1974
2	Glamorgan	1948, 1969
2	Hampshire	1961, 1973
1	Derbyshire	1936
1	Leicestershire	1975

Most appearances: 763 Wilfred Rhodes (Yorkshire) 1898-1930, 707 Frank Woolley (Kent) 1906-38.

GILLETTE CUP / NATWEST BANK TROPHY

Introduced as the Gillette Cup in 1963 as a one-day knock-out event contested by the first-class counties over one innings per side of 65 overs (60 overs from 1964). From 1981 it has been contested for the NatWest Bank Trophy, and Ireland, Scotland, and the leading minor counties also take part.

Winners

1963-4	Sussex	1977	Middlesex
1965	Yorkshire	1978	Sussex
1966	Warwickshire	1979	Somerset
1967	Kent	1980	Middlesex
1968	Warwickshire	1981	Derbyshire
1969	Yorkshire	1982	Surrey
1970-2	Lancashire	1983	Somerset
1973	Gloucestershire	1984	Middlesex
1974	Kent	1985	Essex
1975	Lancashire	1986	Sussex
1976	Northamptonshire		

TEAM RECORDS

(all 60 overs per innings)

Highest innings: 404-3 Worcestershire v Devon at Worcester 24 Jun 1987

Highest in final: 317-4 Yorkshire v Surrey at Lord's 4 Sep 1965

Lowest completed innings: 39 Ireland v Sussex at Hove 3 Jul 1985

Largest runs margin: 299 Worcestershire (404-3) beat Devon (105) at Worcester 24 Jun 1987

INDIVIDUAL INNINGS RECORDS

Highest innings: 206 Alvin Kallicharran, Warwickshire v Oxfordshire at Birmingham 4 Jul 1984

Best bowling: 8-31 Derek Underwood, Kent v Scotland at Edinburgh 24 Jun 1987

Most economical bowling: 1-3 in 12 overs Jack Simmons, Lancashire v Suffolk at Bury St Edmunds 3 Jul 1985

Most dismissals: 6 (5ct 1st) Bob Taylor, Derbyshire v Essex at Derby 19 Aug 1981; 6 (4ct 2st) Terry Davies, Glamorgan v Staffordshire at Stone 25 Jun 1986

INDIVIDUAL CAREER RECORDS 1963-86

Most runs: 1920 Clive Lloyd (Lancs), 1861 Dennis Amiss (Warwicks), 1514 Clive Radley (Middx)

Most wickets: 81 Geoff Arnold (Surrey/Sussex), 78 Peter Lever (Lancs), 71 Jack Simmons (Lancs), 67 Derek Underwood (Kent)

Most dismissals: 66 Bob Taylor (Derby), 65 Alan Knott (Kent), 57 Arnold Long (Surrey/Sussex)

BENSON & HEDGES CUP

A one-day competition played at 55 overs per innings, and contested by 20 teams, the 17 first-class counties and teams representing the Minor Counties, Scotland and the Combined Universities. Played on a zonal basis of four groups of five and then by knock-out.

Winners:

1972	Leicestershire	1980	Northamptonshire
1973	Kent	1981-2	Somerset
1974	Surrey	1983	Middlesex
1975	Leicestershire	1984	Lancashire
1976	Kent	1985	Leicestershire
1977	Gloucestershire	1986	Middlesex
1978	Kent	1987	Yorkshire
1979	Essex		

TEAM RECORDS

Highest innings: 350-3 Essex v Combined Universities at Chelmsford 19 May 1979

Lowest completed innings: 56 Leicestershire v Minor Counties at Wellington 22 May 1982

INDIVIDUAL INNINGS RECORDS

Highest innings: 198* Graham Gooch, Essex v Sussex at Hove 25 May 1982

Best bowling: 7-12 Wayne Daniel, Middlesex v Minor Counties (East) at Ipswich 22 Apr 1978

Most economical bowling: 1-3 in 11 overs Chris Old, Yorkshire v Middlesex at Lord's 6 Jun 1979

Most dismissals: 8 (all ct) Derek Taylor, Somerset v Combined Universities at Taunton 8 May 1982

INDIVIDUAL CAREER RECORDS 1972-86

Most runs: 2938 Graham Gooch (Essex), 2066 Roger Knight (Surrey/Glos/Sussex), 2059 Chris Balderstone (Leics), 2052 Geoff Boycott (Yorks), 2012 Dennis Amiss (Warwicks)

Geoffrey Boycott (Patrick Eagar)

1977	Leicestershire	1982	Sussex
1978	Hampshire	1983	Yorkshire
1979	Somerset	1984-5	Essex
1980	Warwickshire	1986	Hampshire
1981	Essex		

TEAM RECORDS

Highest innings: 310-5 Essex v Glamorgan at Southend 17 Jul 1983

Lowest completed innings: 23 Middlesex v Yorkshire at Leeds 23 Jun 1974

Largest runs margin: 190 runs Kent (257-7) beat Northants (67) at Brackley 22 Jul 1973

INDIVIDUAL INNINGS RECORDS

Highest innings: 176 Graham Gooch, Essex v Glamorgan at Southend 17 Jul 1983

Best bowling: 8-26 Keith Boyce, Essex v Lancashire at Manchester 30 May 1971; 4 wickets in 4 balls Alan Ward, Derbyshire v Sussex, Derby 7 Jun 1970

Most economical bowling: 0-0 in 8 overs Brian Langford, Somerset v Essex at Yeovil 27 Jul 1969

Most dismissals: 7 (6 ct, 1 st) Bob Taylor, Derbyshire v Lancashire at Manchester 4 May 1975

SEASON'S RECORDS

Most runs: 818 (av.58.14) Clive Rice (Notts) 1977

Most wickets: 34 (av.13.17) Bob Clapp (Somerset) 1974

Most dismissals: 28 (22ct 6st) Deryck Murray (Warwicks) 1975

INDIVIDUAL CAREER RECORDS 1969-86

Most runs: 6861 Dennis Amiss (Warwicks), 6536 Clive Radley (Middlesex), 6144 Glenn Turner (Worcs), 6049 Gordon Greenidge (Hants) 5951 Clive Rice (Notts)

Most wickets: 344 John Lever (Essex), 344 Derek Underwood (Kent), 303 Stuart Turner (Essex), 268 Norman Gifford (Worcs/Warwicks), 265 John Shepherd (Kent/Glos)

Most dismissals: 236 Bob Taylor (Derby), 223 Eifion Jones (Glamorgan), 218 Alan Knott (Kent)

Most wickets: 132 John Lever (Essex), 107 Stuart Turner (Essex), 102 John Shepherd (Kent/Glos), 101 Robin Jackman (Surrey), 97 Derek Underwood (Kent)

Most dismissals: 100 David Bairstow (Yorks), 88 Alan Knott (Kent), 77 Bob Taylor (Derby)

JOHN PLAYER LEAGUE / REFUGE ASSURANCE LEAGUE

Introduced in 1969 and played on Sundays by the first-class counties in matches of 40 overs per innings. It became the Refuge Assurance League in 1987.

Winners:

1969-70	Lancashire	1974	Leicestershire
1971	Worcestershire	1975	Hampshire
1972-3	Kent	1976	Kent

FIRST-CLASS COUNTIES

Placings in the first three in the County Championship 1890-1986 and John Player League (JPL) 1969-86, and wins (W), runners-up (RU) or losing semi-finalists (SF) in the Gillette Cup/Nat West Bank Trophy (NW) 1963-86 and Benson & Hedges Cup (B&H) 1972-86. The final column shows the year in which the counties first took part in the Championship or in its preceding inter-county matches from 1864.

County	County Champs			GC/NW			B&H			JPL			First
	1st	2nd	3rd	W	RU	SF	W	RU	SF	1st	2nd	3rd	Year
Derbyshire	1	1	3	1	1	1	-	1	1	-	-	1	1871
Essex	4	1	1	1	-	2	1	3	1	3	4'	2	1895
Glamorgan	2	2	2	-	1	-	-	-	-	-	-	-	1921
Gloucestershire	-	6	7	1	-	2	1	-	1	-	-	-	1870
Hampshire	2	3	4	-	-	5	-	2	3	1	2		1864
Kent	7'	7	9"	2	3	1	3	2	3	3	2	3	1864
Lancashire	8'	12'	10'	4	3	5	1	-	4	2	-	1	1865
Leicestershire	1	1	2'	-	-	1	3	1	1	2	1	2	1895
Middlesex	10"	11	12	3	1	6	2	1	2	-	1	2"	1864
Northamptonshire	-	4	3	1	2	2	1	-	1	-	-	-	1905
Nottinghamshire	3	5	4	-	1	1	-	1	2	-	1	1	1864
Somerset	-	-	5	2	2	4	2	-	2	1	6'	-	1882

County	1st	2nd	3rd	W	RU	SF	W	RU	SF	1st	2nd	3rd	Year
Surrey	16'	7	11	1	2	3	1	2	1	-	-	-	1864
Sussex	-	7	2'	4	3	4	-	-	1	1	1	1	1864
Warwickshire	3	2	1	2	3	4	-	1	4	1	-	1	1895
Worcestershire	3	4'	1	-	2	5	-	2	2	1	1	1	1899
Yorkshire	30'	13"	11'	2	-	2	-	1	2	1	1	-	1864

' Including one tie for place; " including two ties for place
W winner, RU runner-up, SF semi-finalist

CRICKET IN AUSTRALIA

Most Runs in an Australian Season

Runs	Player	Average	Season
1690	Don Bradman (NSW)	93.88	1928-9
1659	Neil Harvey (Vic)	63.80	1952-3
1586	Don Bradman (NSW)	113.28	1929-30
1553	Walter Hammond (Eng)	91.35	1928-9
1552	Don Bradman (SA)	86.22	1936-7

Don Bradman exceeded 1000 runs in a record 12 Australian seasons

Most Wickets in an Australian Season

Wkts	Player	Average	Season
106	Charlie Turner (NSA)	13.59	1887-8
93	George Giffen (SA) *	22.54	1894-5
82	Clarrie Grimmett (SA)	23.69	1929-30
82	Richie Benaud (NSW)	19.25	1958-9
81	Arthur Mailey (NSW)	22.53	1920-1

* George Giffen also scored 902 runs (av.50.11) in 1894-5 for the best ever all-round figures.

Most Dismissals in an Australian Season: 67 (63ct 4 st) Rodney Marsh 1975-6.

SHEFFIELD SHIELD

The annual first-class inter-state competition has been contested for the shield, purchased with money donated by the 3rd Earl of Sheffield, from 1891-2. The original three states were joined by Queensland in 1926-7, Western Australia 1947-8 and Tasmania 1977-8. From 1983 the Shield winner has been determined by a final between the top two teams.

Winners: year shown is that of second half of the season

39	New South Wales	1896-7, 1900, 1902-7, 1909, 1911-2, 1914, 1920-1, 1923, 1926, 1929, 1932-3, 1938, 1940, 1949-50, 1952, 1954-62, 1965-6, 1983, 1985-6
24	Victoria	1893, 1895, 1898-9, 1901, 1908, 1915, 1922, 1924-5, 1928, 1930-1, 1934-5, 1937, 1947, 1951, 1963, 1967, 1970, 1974, 1979-80
12	South Australia	1894, 1910, 1913, 1927, 1936

Dennis Lillee on his way to congratulate wicket-keeper Rod Marsh. They were the most successful combination in Test cricket. (Patrick Eagar)

Don Bradman

		1939, 1953, 1964, 1969, 1971, 1976, 1982
10	Western Australia	1948, 1968, 1972-3, 1975, 1977-8, 1981, 1984, 1987

Most Runs in a Shield Season

Runs	Player	Average	Season	Matches
1217	Bill Ponsford (Vic)	152.12	1927-8	5
1145	Barry Richards (SA)	104.09	1970-1	8
1091	Bill Ponsford (Vic)	136.37	1926-7	5
1062	Don Bradman (SA)	132.75	1939-40	5
1060	David Ogilvie (Qld)	66.25	1977-8	9

Most Runs in a Shield Career

Runs	Player	Average
9685	John Inverarity (WA/SA)	38.58
8926	Don Bradman (NSW/SA)	110.19
8762	Greg Chappell (SA/Qld)	57.26
8647	Sam Trimble (Qld)	39.85
8269	Les Favell (SA)	38.28

Most Wickets in a Shield Season

Wkts	Player	Average	Matches
52	Bill O'Reilly (NSW) (1939-40)	13.80	6
51	Tony Lock (WA) (1966-70)	22.29	8

Most Wickets in a Shield Career

Wkts	Player	Average
513	Clarrie Grimmett (Vic/SA)	25.29
344	Ashley Mallett (SA)	23.75
355	Jeff Thomson (NSW/Qld)	24.48
323	Dennis Lillee (WA)	23.35
302	Tony Lock (WA)	23.89

Limited Overs Competitions

The Australian states currently contest a knock-out competition for the McDonald's Cup at matches of 50 overs per innings. Prior to McDonald's, who took over in 1978-9, sponsors were V&G two years from 1969-70, Coca-Cola two years from 1971-2, and Gillette six years from 1973-4. New Zealand also took part in the first six years.

Winners: year shown is that of second half of the season

6	Western Australia	1971, 1974, 1977-8, 1983, 1986
3	New Zealand	1970, 1973, 1975
3	Queensland	1976, 1981-2
2	Victoria	1972, 1980
2	South Australia	1984, 1987
1	Tasmania	1979
1	New South Wales	1985

INDIA

Most runs in a season: 1604 (av.64.16) Chandu Borde 1964-5. Vijay Hazare scored 1423 runs in 1943-4 at an average of 177.87, the highest ever recorded for 1000 runs in a season.

Most wickets in a season: 88 (av.15.02) Bishen Bedi 1974-5 and 88 (av.19.30) Bishen Bedi 1976-7.

Most dismissals in a season: 43 (32ct 11st) Farokh Engineer 1964-5

In the Indian sub-continent (India, Pakistan, Sri Lanka and Burma):
Most runs in a season: 2121 (av.88.37), including a record 10 centuries, Sunil Gavaskar (Pak) 1978-9
Most wickets in a season: 116 (av.13.78) Maurice Tate (Eng) 1926-7

RANJI TROPHY

The annual Indian first-class inter-state competition was instituted in 1934 in memory of K.S.Ranjitsinhji. It is contested on a zonal basis, culminating in a knock-out competition.

Winners: year given is that of the second half of the season

30	Bombay	1935-6, 1942, 1945, 1949, 1952, 1954, 1956-7, 1959-73, 1975-7, 1981, 1984-5
4	Baroda	1943, 1947, 1950, 1958
4	Holkar	1946, 1948, 1951, 1953
4	Delhi	1979-80, 1982, 1986
3	Karnatka	1974, 1978, 1983
2	Maharashtra	1940-1
2	Hyderabad	1938, 1987
1	Nawanagar 1937, Bengal 1939, Western India 1944, Madras 1955	

NEW ZEALAND

Most runs in season: 1676 (av.93.11) Martin Crowe 1986-7

Most wickets in season: 66 (av.16.48) Stephen Boock 1977-8

Most dismissals in season: 41 (31ct 10st) Ervin McSweeney 1984-5

PLUNKET SHIELD

This first-class competition was run on a challenge basis from 1906 to 1921, and then annually on a league basis from 1921-2 to 1974-5. The Shield was presented by Lord Plunket, Governor-General of New Zealand.

Challenge holders: 1906-7 Canterbury, 1907-11 Auckland, 1911-2 Canterbury, 1912-3 Auckland, 1913-8 Canterbury, 1918-9 Wellington, 1919-20 Canterbury, 1920-1 Auckland, 1921 Wellington.

League wins: year given is the second half of the season

14 Wellington	1924, 1926, 1928, 1930, 1932, 1936, 1950, 1955, 1957, 1961-2, 1966, 1973-4
12 Auckland	1922, 1927, 1929, 1934, 1937-40, 1947, 1959, 1964, 1969
9 Canterbury	1923, 1931, 1935, 1946, 1949, 1952, 1956, 1960, 1965,
9 Otago	1925, 1933, 1948, 1951, 1953, 1958, 1970, 1972, 1975
4 Central Districts	1954, 1967-8, 1971
1 Northern Districts	1963

SHELL SERIES

From 1975-6 the first-class provincial competition has been sponsored by Shell. In the first four years the Shell Cup was awarded to the League winners and the Shell Trophy to winners of a knock-out competition. From 1979-80 the Shell Trophy has been won by the league winners, and the Shell Cup by the winners of the limited-overs competition.

Cup winners 1976-9: 1976 Canterbury, 1977 Northern Districts, 1978 Canterbury, 1979 Otago.

Trophy winners:

3 Otago	1977, 1979, 1986
3 Wellington	1982, 1983, 1985
2 Canterbury	1976, 1984
2 Auckland	1978, 1981
1 Northern Districts 1980, Central Districts 1987	

LIMITED OVERS COMPETITION

Now contested for the Shell Cup, but previously sponsored by the NZ Motor Corporation, 1971-7 and Gillette 1977-9. *Winners:*

6 Auckland	1973, 1979, 1981, 1983-4, 1987
5 Canterbury	1972, 1976-8, 1986
3 Wellington	1974-5, 1982
1 Northern Districts	1980
1 Central Districts	1985

PAKISTAN

Most runs in season: 1649 (av.63.42) Saadat Ali 1983-4

Most wickets in season: 107 (av.16.06) Ijaz Faqih 1985-6

Most dismissals in season: 69 (52ct 17st) Anil Dalpat 1983-4

QUAID-E-AZAM TROPHY

Pakistan's annual national first-class championship is named after Mohammad Ali Jinnah, who was known as Quaid-e-Azam, or 'Great Leader'. From its inception in 1953-4 to 1979-80 it was organised on a zonal basis culminating in a knock-out stage, but it is now run on a league system.

Winners: year given is that of second half of the season

6 Karachi	1955, 1959-60, 1963 (Karachi A), 1968, 1986
4 Karachi Blues	1962, 1964, 1966, 1971
4 National Bank	1976, 1979, 1982, 1984
4 United Bank	1977, 1981, 1983, 1985
2 Bahawalpur	1954, 1958
2 Punjab	1957, 1975 (Punjab A)
2 PIA	1970, 1980
2 Railways	1973-4
1 Lahore 1969, Habib Bank 1978	

SOUTH AFRICA

Most runs in a season: 1915 (av.68.39) John Reid (NZ) 1961-2

Most wickets in a season: 106 (av.19.39) Richie Benaud (Aus) 1957-8

Most dismissals in a season: 65 (57ct 8st) Ray Jennings 1982-3

CURRIE CUP

The annual first-class competition for the South African provinces. The Cup was presented by Sir Donald Currie and first contested in the 1889-90 season. Until 1966 it was not normally contested in the seasons when a touring team visited South Africa.

Winners (shared): year given is second half of season*

27 (4*) Transvaal	1890, 1895, 1903-5, 1907, 1922*, 1924, 1926-7, 1930, 1935, 1938*, 1951, 1959, 1966*, 1969, 1970*, 1971-3, 1979-80, 1983-5, 1987
21 (3*) Natal	1911, 1913, 1922*, 1934, 1937, 1938*, 1947-8, 1952, 1955, 1960-1, 1963-4, 1966*, 1967-8, 1974, 1976-7, 1981
15 (2*) Western Province	1893-4, 1897-8, 1909, 1921, 1922*, 1932, 1953, 1956, 1970*, 1975, 1978, 1982, 1986
1 Kimberley (now Griqualand West) 1891	

NISSAN SHIELD

The South African limited overs competition was contested for the Gillette Cup from 1969-70 to 1976-7, for the Datsun Shield 1977-8 to 1982-3 and for the Nissan Shield from 1983-4.

Winners:

8 Transvaal	1974, 1979-81, 1983-6
4 Western Province	1970-1, 1973, 1982
3 Natal	1975, 1977, 1987
2 Eastern Province	1972, 1976

The Benson & Hedges Trophy limited overs night competition was introduced in 1985-6, when the winners were Western Province, who won again in 1987.

WEST INDIES

Most runs in a season: 1765 (av.135.76) Patsy Hendren (Eng) 1929-30

Most wickets in a season: 80 (av. 12.46) Edward Dowson (Eng) 1901-2

Most dismissals in a season: 33 (31ct 2 st) Jeffrey Dujon 1983

SHELL SHIELD

This annual first-class competition for the West Indian teams has been contested annually from 1966, except in 1968.

Winners (* shared):

12	Barbados	1966-7, 1972, 1974, 1976*, 1977-80, 1982, 1984, 1986
4	Trinidad & Tobago	1970-1, 1976*, 1985
4	Guyana	1973, 1975, 1983, 1987
1	Jamaica	1969
1	Combined Islands	1981

There was a triangular Inter-Colonial tournament first held in 1893, up to 1939, but not resumed after the war. Wins: Trinidad 11, Barbados 10, Demerara/British Guiana 5. Other post-war tournaments prior to the Shell Shield were won by British Guiana in 1957, 1962 and 1964.

WOMEN'S CRICKET

The first women's cricket match recorded was at Gosden Common in Surrey, England in 1745. The first women's club was the White Heather Club, founded at Nun Appleton, Yorkshire in 1887 and the first women's Test match was played between England and Australia at Brisbane on 28-31 December, 1934. The Women's Cricket Association was formed in England in 1926 and the International Women's Cricket Council (IWCC) in 1958.

WORLD CUP

First held in 1973.

Winners:
1973 England, 1978 Australia, 1982 Australia
Highest individual score: 138 not out Jeanette Brittin, England v International XI, Hamilton (NZ) 14 Jan 1982

TEST RECORDS

TEAM

Highest innings: 503-5 dec. England v New Zealand, Christchurch, 16-18 Feb 1935
Lowest innings: 35 England v Australia, St Kilda, Melbourne, 22 Feb 1958

INDIVIDUAL

Highest innings: 190 Sandiya Aggarwal, India v England, Worcester, 14 July 1986 (563 minutes)
189 Betty Snowball, England v New Zealand, Christchurch, 16 Feb 1935 (222 minutes)
Best bowling: 7-6 Mary Duggan, England v Australia, St. Kilda, Melbourne, 22 Feb 1958
7-7 Betty Wilson, Australia v England, St. Kilda, Melbourne, 22 Feb 1958 (including the only test hat-trick)
Best match analyses: 11-16 Betty Wilson, 7-7 and 4-9, as above 22 Feb 1958
11-63 Julia Greenwood, 6-46 and 5-17, England v West Indies, Canterbury 16-18 June 1979
Test career records:
Most Tests: 25 Rachael Heyhoe-Flint, England 1960-79
Most runs: 1814 Rachael Heyhoe-Flint (Eng) in 25 Tests, av 49.02, 1960-79

England's top batswomen, Enid Bakewell and Rachael Heyhoe-Flint, at Hove in 1973. (Women's Cricket Association)

Highest average: 59.88 Enid Bakewell (Eng), 1078 runs in 12 Tests
Most centuries: 4 Enid Bakewell (Eng) and Rachel Heyhoe-Flint
Most wickets: 77 Mary Duggan (Eng) in 17 Tests, av. 13.49, 1949-63

England have played Australia in 29 Tests from 1934 to 1985, England have won 6, Australia 5, and 18 have been drawn.

CROQUET

Croquet is played with ball and mallet, and six hoops with a peg laid out on a grass lawn 35 yd (31.9m) long by 28 yd (25.6m) wide. While its exact origins are obscure, it was probably derived from the French game Jeu de Mail, played from the 12th century. A game resembling croquet, probably of foreign origin, was played in Ireland in the 1830s. Jean Jaques, the sports goods manufacturers, made the first croquet sets in England in the 1850s and published a book on the game in 1857. Ten years later the first championships were held at Evesham, Worcestershire.

The All-England Croquet Club was founded at Wimbledon in 1869 and the current governing body, the Croquet Association, was formed in 1896. The game was played at the 1900 Olympic games, when all the contestants were French.

MACROBERTSON INTERNATIONAL SHIELD

Contested by Australia, Great Britain and New Zealand, first in 1925.

Wins:

7	Great Britain	1925, 1937, 1956, 1963, 1969, 1974, 1982
3	Australia	1928, 1930, 1935
3	New Zealand	1950, 1979, 1986

THE CROQUET CHAMPIONSHIP

The Open Championship was first held in 1867. Women's Championships were first held iin 1869, and separate Men's Championships in 1925. Mixed Doubles were introduced in 1899 and Men's Doubles in 1924. Most wins at each event.

OPEN CHAMPIONSHIP
10 John W.Solomon 1953, 1956, 1959, 1961, 1963-8
 7 Humphrey Hicks 1932, 1939, 1947-50, 1952
 5 Cyril Corbally 1902-3, 1906, 1908, 1913

Most wins by a woman:
 4 Dorothy Steel 1925, 1933, 1935-6

OPEN DOUBLES
10 John W. Solomon & Edmond Cotter 1954-5, 1958-9, 1961-5, 1969

MEN'S CHAMPIONSHIP
10 John W.Solomon 1951, 1953, 1958-60, 1962, 1964-5, 1971-2
 9 Humphrey Hicks 1930, 1932, 1948-50, 1955-6, 1961, 1966

WOMEN'S CHAMPIONSHIP
15 Dorothy Steel 1919, 1921, 1925-7, 1929-30, 1932-9

Most titles at all events:
31 John W. Solomon 10 open, 10 men's, 10 doubles, 1 mixed doubles
31 Dorothy Steel 4 open, 15 women's, 5 doubles, 7 mixed doubles
27 Humphrey Hicks 7 open, 9 men's, 7 doubles, 4 mixed doubles

PRESIDENT'S CUP

An annual invitation event for the best eight players.

Most wins:
11 Nigel Aspinall 1969-70, 1973-6, 1978-80, 1984-5
 9 John W.Solomon 1955, 1957-9, 1962-4, 1968, 1971
 6 Edmond Cotter 1949-50, 1952-3, 1956, 1960
 6 Humphrey Hicks 1947-8, 1951, 1954, 1961, 196?

The lowest ever handicap was minus 5.5 by Humphrey Hicks. The limit is now fixed at minus 5.

CURLING

Curling resembles bowls on ice and is known as the 'roaring game', due to the noise made by the curling stone (which weighs about 40lb/18kg) as it runs over the ice rink. The curlers use brooms to sweep the rink ahead of their stone to remove impediments and smooth the ice. The game became popular in Scotland, but it may have originated in the Netherlands more than 400 years ago. The Grand Caledonian Curling Club was formed in Edinburgh in 1838. Five years later it added Royal to its title and eventually became the international governing body of the sport.

Scots introduced curling to Canada, where the first club was the Royal Montreal Curling Club, founded in 1807. The first club in the USA was the Orchard Lake Club, formed in Michigan in 1832. The first international match was between Canada and the USA in 1884, the start of the Gordon International Medal series, now contested annually by clubs representing the Canadian branch of the Royal Caledonian Curling Club and the Grand National Curling Club of America. The Strathcona Cup series between Canada and Scotland started in 1903. The International Curling Federation was founded in 1966.

WORLD CHAMPIONSHIPS

MEN
Played annually for the Scotch Whisky Cup 1959-67 and for the Air Canada Silver Broom 1968-86.

Winners:

Year	Nation	Skip
1959-60	Canada	Ernie Richardson
1961	Canada	Hec Gervais
1962-3	Canada	Ernie Richardson
1964	Canada	Lyall Dagg
1965	USA	Bud Somerville
1966	Canada	Ron Northcott
1967	Scotland	Chuck Hay
1968-9	Canada	Ron Northcott
1970-1	Canada	Don Duguid
1972	Canada	Orest Meleschuk
1973	Sweden	Kjell Oscarius
1974	USA	Bud Somerville
1975	Switzerland	Otto Danielli
1976	USA	Bruce Roberts
1977	Sweden	Ragnar Kamp
1978	USA	Bob Nichols
1979	Norway	Kristian Sørum

1980	Canada	Rick Falk
1981	Switzerland	Jürg Tanner
1982	Canada	Al Hackner
1983	Canada	Ed Werenich
1984	Norway	Eigel Ramsfjell
1985	Canada	Al Hackner
1986	Canada	Ed Lukovich
1987	Canada	Russ Howard

Most wins: 18 Canada, 4 USA
Most times as winning skip:
4 Ernie Richardson, 3 Ron Northcott

WOMEN
Played annually from 1979.

Winners:

1979	Switzerland	Gaby Casanova
1980	Canada	Mary Mitchell
1981	Sweden	Elisabeth Högström
1982	Denmark	Marianne Jørgensen
1983	Switzerland	Erika Müller
1984	Canada	Connie Laliberte
1985	Canada	Linda Moore
1986	Canada	Marilyn Darte
1987	Canada	Pat Saunders

Most wins: 5 Canada

OLYMPIC GAMES

Curling was included as a demonstration sport at the Games of 1924, 1932 and 1964, and will be again in 1988. A specialised German version of the game was demonstrated in 1936.

CYCLING

The forerunner of the bicycle, the célenifère was demonstrated in the garden of the Palais Royale, Paris in 1791. The first treadle-propelled bicycle was designed by Scottish blacksmith Kirkpatrick Macmillan in 1839. The first cycling club, the Liverpool Velocipede Club, was formed in 1867 and the first race took place the following year. It was over 1200 metres at the Parc St.Cloud, Paris, and won by Englishman James Moore. The first international organisation was the International Cycliste Association (ICA), founded in 1892, which promoted the first world championships the following year. The current governing body, the Union Cycliste International (UCI) was founded in 1900. In 1965 two federations were formed within the UCI – the Fédération de Cyclisme Amateur (FIAC) and the Fédération Internationale de Cyclisme Professional (FICP).

TOUR DE FRANCE

Without doubt, the Tour de France is the greatest cycle race in the world and its popularity attracts the largest audience of any sporting event with more than 10,000,000 watching the annual race. It was first held in 1903 and the successful riders have to cover 4800km/3,000 miles of mixed terrain over a three week period.

1903	Maurice Garin (Fra)
1904	Henri Cornet (Fra)
1905	Louis Trousselier (Fra)
1906	René Pottier (Fra)
1907-8	Lucien Petit-Breton (Fra)
1909	François Faber (Lux)
1910	Octave Lapize (Fra)
1911	Gustave Garrigou (Fra)
1912	Odile Defraye (Bel)
1913-4	Philippe Thys (Bel)
1919	Firmin Lambot (Bel)
1920	Philippe Thys (Bel)
1921	Léon Scieur (Bel)
1922	Firmin Lambot (Bel)
1923	Henri Pélissier (Fra)
1924-5	Ottavio Bottecchia (Ita)
1926	Lucien Buysse (Bel)
1927-8	Nicholas Frantz (Lux)
1929	Maurice De Waele (Bel)
1930	André Leducq (Fra)
1931	Antonin Magne (Fra)
1932	André Leducq (Fra)
1933	Georges Speicher (Fra)
1934	Antonin Magne (Fra)
1935	Romain Maës (Bel)
1936	Sylvere Maës (Bel)
1937	Roger Lapébie (Fra)
1938	Gino Bartali (Ita)
1939	Sylvere Maës (Bel)
1947	Jean Robic (Fra)
1948	Gino Bartali (Ita)
1949	Fausto Coppi (Ita)
1950	Ferdinand Kübler (Swi)
1951	Hugo Koblet (Swi)
1952	Fausto Coppi (Ita)
1953-5	Louison Bobet (Fra)
1956	Roger Walkowiak (Fra)
1957	Jacques Anquetil (Fra)
1958	Charly Gaul (Lux)
1959	Federico Bahamontès (Spa)
1960	Gastone Nencini (Ita)
1961-4	Jacques Anquetil (Fra)
1965	Felice Gimondi (Ita)
1966	Lucien Aimar (Fra)
1967	Roger Pingeon (Fra)
1968	Jan Janssen (Hol)
1969-72	Eddy Merckx (Bel)
1973	Luis Ocana (Spa)
1974	Eddy Merckx (Bel)
1975	Bernard Thevenet (Fra)
1976	Lucien van Impe (Bel)
1977	Bernard Thevenet (Fra)
1978-9	Bernard Hinault (Fra)
1980	Joop Zoetemelk (Hol)
1981-2	Bernard Hinault (Fra)
1983-4	Laurent Fignon (Fra)
1985	Bernard Hinault (Fra)
1986	Greg LeMond (USA)
1987	Stephen Roche (Ire)

Most wins: 5 Jacques Anquetil, Eddy Merckx, Bernard Hinault
Fastest average speed: 37.84 km/h (23.51 mph) Bernard Hinault 1981
Longest race: 5745 km (3569 miles) 1926

TOUR OF ITALY

After the Tour de France, the Tour of Italy (Giro d'Italia) is the second most prestigious of the continental tours. It was first held in 1909 and until 1950 when Switzerland's Hugo Koblet won, all winners had been Italian.

Recent winners:
1977 Michel Pollentier (Bel)
1978 Johan De Muynck (Bel)
1979 Giuseppe Saronni (Ita)
1980 Bernard Hinault (Fra)
1981 Giovani Battaglin (Ita)
1982 Bernard Hinault (Fra)
1983 Giuseppe Saronni (Ita)
1984 Francesco Moser (Ita)
1985 Bernard Hinault (Fra)
1986 Roberto Visentini (Ita)
1987 Stephen Roche (Ire)

Most wins: 5 Alfredo Binda (Ita) 1925, 1927-9, 1933; Fausto Coppi (Ita) 1940, 1947, 1949, 1952-3; Eddy Merckx (Bel) 1968, 1970, 1972-4

TOUR OF SPAIN

The Tour of Spain (Vuelta de España) is the third major tour of the continental season. It was first held in 1935, and annually from 1955.

Recent winners:
1977 Freddie Maertens (Bel)
1978 Bernard Hinault (Fra)
1979 Joop Zoetemelk (Hol)
1980 Faustino Ruperez (Spa)
1981 Giovani Battaglin (Ita)
1982 Marino Lejaretta (Spa)
1983 Bernard Hinault (Fra)
1984 Eric Caritoux (Fra)
1985 Pedro Delgado (Spa)
1986 Alvaro Pino (Spa)
1987 Luis Herrera (Col)

Most wins: 2 Gustave Deloor (Bel) 1935-6; Julio Berrendero (Spa) 1941-2; José Manuel Fuente (Spa) 1972, 1974; Bernard Hinault (Fra) 1978, 1983

THE CLASSICS

The following races make up the major classic races on the continent.

MILAN-SAN REMO (MR)
The first major classic of the season, it is the longest unpaced race of all the classics. First held in 1907 it is known as the *Primavera* in Italy.
Most wins: 7 Eddy Merckx (Bel) 1966-7, 1969, 1971-2, 1975-6; 6 Constante Girardengo (Ita) 1918, 1921, 1923, 1925-6, 1928

TOUR OF FLANDERS (FL)
First held in 1913 the race takes place around Ghent and one of the major features of the race are the steep cobbled climbs, notably the Koppenberg Hill.
Most wins: 3 Achiel Buysse (Bel) 1940-1, 1943; Fiorenzo Magni (Ita) 1949-51; Erik Leman (Bel) 1970, 1972-3

PARIS-ROUBAIX (PR)
Regarded as the toughest one-day race in the world,

Greg LeMond and Bernard Hinault, first and second in the 1986 Tour de France (All-Sport)

hence its nickname, 'The Hell of the North'. The latter stages of the race take place over farm tracks and cobbled roads. It was first held in 1896.
Most wins: 4 Roger de Vlaeminck (Bel) 1972, 1974-5, 1977

FLÈCHE WALLONNE (FW)
There is no fixed course for the Flèche Wallonne but it takes place around the Ardennes district of Belgium and is approximately 250 km (155 miles) in length. It was first held in 1936.
Most wins: 4 Eddy Merckx (Bel) 1967, 1970, 1972, 1975

LIÈGE-BASTOGNE-LIÈGE
First held in 1891 it is the oldest of the Belgian classics. Until 1912 it was for amateurs only. Like the Flèche Wallonne it takes place around the Ardennes district.
Most wins: 5 Eddy Merckx (Bel) 1969, 1971-3, 1975

PARIS-BRUSSELS (PB)
First held in 1893, but not again until 1906 when professionals were allowed to compete. The race was discontinued in 1966 and replaced on the 'Classics' list by the Frankfurt Grand Prix, but it returned in 1973.
Most wins: 3 Octave Lapize (Fra) 1911-3; Felix Sellier (Bel) 1922-4

Eddy Merckx wears the yellow jersey of the Tour de France leader. (All-Sport)

TOUR OF LOMBARDY (TL)

The Tour of Lombardy is one of the Autumn Classics and traditionally marks the end of the road-racing season on the continent. It was first held in 1905 and is often referred to as 'The Race of the Falling Leaves'.
Most wins: 5 Fausto Coppi (Ita) 1946-9, 1954

Other major continental races include:

BORDEAUX-PARIS (BP)

The longest continuous cycle race in the world it is normally around 600 km (375 miles) in length. First held in 1891 it is known as the 'Derby' of road races. The first part of the race, up to Chattellerault, is staged in darkness. Thereafter, the riders are paced by Derny motorcycle riders.
Most wins: 7 (incl.one shared) Herman Van Springel (Bel) 1970, 1974-5, 1977-8, 1980-1

GRAND PRIX DES NATIONS (GN)

The world's premier time trial, it is regarded as the time-trialists 'unofficial' world championship. The venue for the race has varied over the years but has always been held in France. It was first held in 1932.
Most wins: 9 Jacques Anquetil (Fra) 1953-8, 1961, 1965-6; 5 Bernard Hinault (Fra) 1977-9, 1982, 1984

PARIS-NICE (PN)

A gruelling early-season stage race, the riders cover more than 1100km in six days.
Most wins: 6 Sean Kelly (Ire) 1982-7

MOST WINS IN A SEASON

54 Eddy Merckx (Bel) 1971
53 Freddy Maertens (Bel) 1977
52 Freddy Maertens 1976; Eddy Merckx 1970
51 Eddy Merckx 1973
50 Eddy Merckx 1972
42 Rik Van Looy (Bel) 1965

SUPER PRESTIGE PERNOD COMPETITION

During the continental season, various races are designated as counting towards a season-long competition with varying points depending upon status of the race, and the rider's finishing position. The rider with the most points at the end of the season wins the Super Prestige Pernod Trophy. The first award was made in 1959, and won by Henri Anglade (Fra).

Recent winners:
1977 Freddie Maertens (Bel) 326 pts
1978 Francesco Moser (Ita) 323 pts
1979 Bernard Hinault (Fra) 421 pts
1980 Bernard Hinault (Fra) 315 pts
1981 Bernard Hinault (Fra) 325 pts
1982 Bernard Hinault (Fra) 266 pts
1983 Greg LeMond (USA) 245 pts
1984 Sean Kelly (UK) 435 pts
1985 Sean Kelly (UK) 309 pts
1986 Sean Kelly (UK) 910 pts

Most wins: 7 Eddy Merckx (Bel) 1969-75
Most points: 570 Eddy Merckx (Bel) 1971
(Sean Kelly's 910 points under new scoring system in 1986 excluded)

TOUR OF BRITAIN (Milk Race)

Until 1983 the Milk Race was an amateur-only event but it has since gone open. First held in 1951 it was originally sponsored by the *Daily Express* but has been sponsored by the Milk Marketing Board since 1958 when the race resumed after a two year lay-off.

Winners:
1951 Ian Steel (UK)
1952 Ken Russell (UK)
1953 Gordon Thomas (UK)
1954 Eugene Tamburlini (Fra)
1955 Anthony Hewson (UK)
1958 Richard Durlacher (Aut)
1959-60 Bill Bradley (UK)
1961 Billy Holmes (UK)
1962 Eugen Pokorny (Pol)
1963 Peter Chisman (UK)
1964 Arthur Metcalfe (UK)
1965 Les West (UK)
1966 Josef Gawliczek (Pol)
1967 Les West (UK)
1968 Gosta Pettersson (Swe)
1969 Fedor Den Hertog (Hol)
1970 Jiri Mainus (Cs)
1971 Fedor Den Hertog (Hol)
1972 Hennie Kuiper (Hol)
1973 Piet van Katwijk (Hol)
1974 Roy Schuiten (Hol)
1975 Bernt Johansson (Swe)
1976 Bill Nickson (UK)
1977 Said Gusseinov (USSR)
1978 Jan Brzezny (Pol)
1979 Yuriy Kashirin (USSR)
1980 Ivan Mitchtenko (USSR)
1981 Sergey Krivocheyev (USSR)
1982 Yuriy Kashirin (USSR)
1983 Matt Eaton (USA)
1984 Oleg Czougeda (USSR)
1985 Eric van Lancker (Bel)
1986 Joey McLoughlin (UK)
1987 Malcolm Elliott (UK)

Most wins: 2 Bill Bradley, Les West, Fedor Den Hertog, Yuriy Kashirin

OLYMPIC GAMES

Cycling was included in the first Olympics of 1896 and at every Games since except 1904 when there were no official events. Women's races were included in the Games for the first time in 1984.

Winners:

1000 METRES TIME TRIAL

(1896 and 1906 raced over 333.33 metres)
1896 Paul Masson (Fra) 24.0
1906 Francesco Verri (Ita) 22.8
1928 Willy Falck-Hansen (Den) 1:14.4
1932 Edgar Gray (Aus) 1:13.0
1936 Arie van Vliet (Hol) 1:12.0
1948 Jacques Dupont (Fra) 1:13.5
1952 Russell Mockridge (Aus) 1:11.1
1956 Leandro Faggin (Ita) 1:09.8
1960 Sante Gaiardoni (Ita) 1:07.27

1964 Patrick Sercu (Bel) 1:09.59
1968 Pierre Trentin (Fra) 1:03.91
1972 Niels-Christian Fredborg (Den) 1:06.44
1976 Klaus-Jurgen Grunke (GDR) 1:05.93
1980 Lothar Thoms (GDR) 1:02.955
1984 Freddy Schmidtke (FRG) 1:06.10

1000 METRES SPRINT
(1896 and 1900 over 2000 metres. Held over the best of three races with the time over the last 200 metres only being recorded since 1924)
1896 Paul Masson (Fra) 4:56.0
1900 Georges Taillandier (Fra) 2:52.0
1906 Francesco Verri (Ita) 1:42.2
1908 declared void as riders exceeded time limit
1920 Maurice Peeters (Hol) 1:38.3
1924 Lucien Michard (Fra) 12.8
1928 Rene Beaufrand (Fra) 13.2
1932 Jacobus van Egmond (Hol) 12.6
1936 Toni Merkens (Ger) 11.8
1948 Mario Ghella (Ita) 12.0
1952 Enzo Sacchi (Ita) 12.0
1956 Michel Rousseau (Fra) 11.4
1960 Sante Gaiardoni (Ita) 11.1
1964 Giovanni Pettenella (Ita) 13.69
1968 Daniel Morelon (Fra) 10.68
1972 Daniel Morelon (Fra) 11.25
1976 Anton Tkac (Cs) 10.78
1980 Lutz Hesslich (GDR) 11.40
1984 Mark Gorski (USA) 10.49

4000 METRES INDIVIDUAL PURSUIT
1964 Jiri Daler (Cs) 5:04.75
1968 Daniel Rebillard (Fra) 4:41.71
1972 Knut Knudsen (Nor) 4:45.74
1976 Gregor Braun (GDR) 4:47.61
1980 Robert Dill-Bundi (Swi) 4:35.66
1984 Steve Hegg (USA) 4:39.55

4000 METRES TEAM PURSUIT
(1908, held over 1810.5 metres)
1908 Great Britain 2:18.6
1920 Italy 5:20.0
1924 Italy 5:15.0
1928 Italy 5:01.8
1932 Italy 4:53.0
1936 France 4:45.0
1948 France 4:57.8
1952 Italy 4:46.1
1956 Italy 4:37.4
1960 Italy 4:30.90
1964 FR Germany 4:35.67
1968 Denmark 4:22.44
1972 FR Germany 4:22.14
1976 FR Germany 4:21.06
1980 USSR 4:15.70
1984 Australia 4:25.99

TEAM ROAD RACE/TIME-TRIAL
(1912-20 combined times of best four riders in the individual race. 1924-52 combined times of best three. 1956 based on placings. Since 1960 it has been a time-trial.)
1912 Sweden 44h 35:33.6
1920 France 19h 16:43.2
1924 France 19h 13:14.0

1928 Denmark 15h 09:14.0
1932 Italy 7h 27:15.2
1936 France 7h 39:16.2
1948 Belgium 15h 58:17.4
1952 Belgium 15h 20:46.6
1956 France 22 points
1960 Italy 2h 14:33.53
1964 Netherlands 2h 26:31.19
1968 Netherlands 2h 07:49.06
1972 USSR 2h 11:17.8
1976 USSR 2h 08:53.0
1980 USSR 2h 01:21.7
1984 Italy 1h 58:28.0

INDIVIDUAL ROAD RACE

MEN

Year	Winner	Time	Distance (km)
1896	Aristidis Konstantinidis (Gre)	3h 22:31.0	87
1906	Fernand Vast (Fra)	2h 41:28.0	84
1912	Rudolph Lewis (SAf)	10h 42:39.0	320
1920	Harry Stenqvist (Swe)	4h 40:01.8	175
1924	Armand Blanchonnet (Fra)	6h 20:48.0	188
1928	Henry Hansen (Den)	4h 47:18.0	168
1932	Attilio Pavesi (Ita)	2h 28:05.6	100
1936	Robert Charpentier (Fra)	2h 33:05.0	100
1948	José Beyaert (Fra)	5h 18:12.6	194.63
1952	André Noyelle (Bel)	5h 06:03.4	190.4
1956	Ercole Baldini (Ita)	5h 21:17.0	187.73
1960	Viktor Kapitonov (USSR)	4h 20:37.0	175.38
1964	Mario Zanin (Ita)	4h 39:51.63	194.83
1968	Pierfranco Vianelli (Ita)	4h 41:25.24	196.2
1972	Hennie Kuiper (Hol)	4h 14:37.0	182.4
1976	Bernt Johansson (Swe)	4h 46:52.0	175
1980	Sergey Sukhoruchenkov (USSR)	4h 48:28.9	189
1984	Alexi Grewal (USA)	4h 59:57.0	196

WOMEN

Year	Winner	Time	Distance (km)
1984	Connie Carpenter-Phinney (USA)	2h 11:11.0	79.2

POINTS RACE
(Introduced 1984)
1984 Roger Ilegems (Bel)   37 pts

SUPERSEDED TRACK EVENTS
660yd	1908	Victor Johnson (UK)	51.2
5km	1906	Francesco Verri (Ita)	8:35.0
	1908	Benjamin Jones (UK)	8:36.2
10km	1896	Paul Masson (Fra)	17:54.2
20km	1906	William Pett (UK)	29:00.0
	1908	Charles Kingsbury (UK)	34:13.6
50km	1920	Henry George (Bel)	1:16:43.2
	1924	Jacobus Willems (Hol)	1:18:24.0
100km	1896	Léon Flameng (Fra)	3:08:19.2
	1908	Charles Bartlett (UK)	2:41:48.6
12hrs	1896	Adolf Schmal (Aut)	314.997km

2000 METRES TANDEM
From 1924-72 times recorded only over last 200m
1906 John Matthews & Arthur Rushen (UK) 2:57.0
1908 Maurice Schilles & André Auffray (Fra) 3:07.8
1920 Harry Ryan & Thomas Lance (UK) 2:49.4
1924 Lucien Choury & Jean Cugnot (Fra) 12.6
1928 Bernhard Leene & Daan van Dijk (Hol) 11.8
1932 Maurice Perrin & Louis Chaillot (Fra) 12.0
1936 Ernst Ihbe & Carl Lorenz (Ger) 11.8
1948 Renato Perona & Ferdinando Terruzzi (Ita) 11.3
1952 Lionel Cox & Russell Mockridge (Aus) 11.0

1956 Ian Browne & Anthony Marchant (Aus) 10.8
1960 Giuseppe Beghetto & Sergio Bianchetto (Ita) 10.7
1964 Sergio Bianchetto & Angelo Damiano (Ita) 10.75
1968 Daniel Morelon & Pierre Trentin (Fra) 9.83
1972 Vladimir Semenets & Igor Tselovalnikov (USSR) 10.52

ALL EVENTS

Most gold medals: 3 Paul Masson (Fra) 1896, Francisco Verri (Ita) 1906, Robert Charpentier (Fra) 1936, Daniel Morelon (Fra) 1968-72.

Most medals: 5 Morelon, who also won a silver in 1976 and bronze in 1964, both in the sprint.

WORLD CHAMPIONSHIPS

World Championships were first held in 1893 in Chicago, with two events: the sprint and the motor-paced race over 100km. A road race was first held in 1921 and women's events were introduced in 1959. Separate world championships are not contested in Olympic years for events on the Olympic programme (qv).

Events currently contested, with those to have won most often, and winners from 1970 are as follows:

AMATEUR SPRINT
First held 1893
1969-71 Daniel Morelon (Fra)
1973 Daniel Morelon (Fra)
1974 Anton Tkac (Cs)
1975 Daniel Morelon (Fra)
1977 Hans-Jürgen Geschke (GDR)
1978 Anton Tkac (Cs)
1979 Lutz Hesslich (GDR)
1981-2 Sergey Kopylov (USSR)
1983 Lutz Hesslich (GDR)
1985 Lutz Hesslich (GDR)
1986 Michael Hübner (GDR)

Most wins: 7 Daniel Morelon (Fra) 1966-7, 1969-71, 1973, 1975; 4 William Bailey (UK) 1909-11, 1913; 3 Lutz Hesslich as above.

AMATEUR 4KM PURSUIT
First held 1946
1970 Xavier Kurmann (Swi)
1971 Martin-Emilio Rodriguez (Col)
1973 Knut Knudsen (Nor)
1974 Hans Lutz (FRG)
1975 Thomas Huschke (GDR)
1977 Norbert Durpisch (GDR)
1978 Detlef Macha (GDR)
1979 Nikolay Makarov (USSR)
1981-2 Detlef Macha (GDR)
1983 Viktor Kupovets (USSR)
1985-6 Vyacheslav Yekimov (USSR)
Most wins: 3 Tiemen Groen (Hol) 1964-6; Detlef Macha (GDR) as above.

AMATEUR TEAM PURSUIT
First held 1962
Wins:
7 FR Germany 1962, 1964, 1970, 1973-5, 1983
5 USSR 1963, 1965, 1967, 1969, 1982
4 GDR 1977-9, 1981
4 Italy 1966, 1968, 1971, 1985

1 Czechoslovakia 1986

AMATEUR 1KM TIME TRIAL
First held 1966
1970 Niels Fredborg (Den)
1971 Eduard Rapp (USSR)
1973 Janusz Kierzkowski (Pol)
1974 Eduard Rapp (USSR)
1975 Klaus Grünke (GDR)
1977-9 Lothar Thoms (GDR)
1981 Lothar Thoms (GDR)
1982 Fredy Schmidtke (FRG)
1983 Sergey Kopylov (USSR)
1985 Jens Glücklich (GDR)
1986 Maik Malchow (GDR)

Most wins: 4 Lothar Thoms (GDR) as above; 3 Niels Fredborg (Den) 1967-8, 1970.

AMATEUR TEAM TIME TRIAL
First held 1962
Contested at approximately 100km
Wins:
4 USSR 1970, 1977, 1983, 1985
3 Italy 1962, 1964-5
3 Sweden 1967-9, 1974
3 Netherlands 1978, 1982, 1986
2 Poland 1973, 1975
2 GDR 1979, 1981
1 France 1963, Denmark 1966, Belgium 1971

AMATEUR TANDEM SPRINT
First held 1966
1970 Jürgen Barth & Rainer Müller (FRG)
1971 Jürgen Geschke & Werner Otto (GDR)
1973-4 Vladimir Vackar & Miroslav Vymazal (Cs)
1976 Benedykt Kocot & Janusz Kotlinski (Pol)
1977-8 Vladimir Vackar & Miroslav Vymazal (Cs)
1979 Yave Cahard & Frank Depine (Fra)
1980-2 Ivan Kucirek & Pavel Martinek (Cs)
1983 Philippe Vernet & Frank Depine (Fra)
1984 Jürgen Greil & Frank Weber (FRG)
1985-6 Vitezlav Voboril & Roman Rehousek (Cs)

Most wins: 4 Vackar & Vymazal as above

AMATEUR 50KM POINTS RACE
First held 1976
1976 Walter Baumgartner (Swi)
1977 Constant Tourne (Bel)
1978 Noel de Jonckheere (Bel)
1979 Jiri Slama (Cs)
1980 Gary Sutton (Aus)
1981 Lutz Haueisen (GDR)
1982 Hans-Joachim Pohl (GDR)
1983 Michael Marcussen (Den)
1985 Martin Penc (Cs)
1986 Dan Frost (Den)

AMATEUR MOTOR-PACED
Held at 100km 1893-1914, for 1 hour 1958-71, at 50km from 1972
1970 Cees Stam (Hol)
1971-3 Horst Gnas (FRG)
1974 Jean Breuer (FRG)
1975-7 Gaby Minneboo (Hol)
1978 Rainer Podlesch (GDR)
1979 Matthe Pronk (Hol)

1980 Gaby Minneboo (Hol)
1981 Matthe Pronk (Hol)
1982 Gaby Minneboo (Hol)
1983 Rainer Podlesch (GDR)
1984 Jan de Nijs (Hol)
1985 Roberto Dotti (Ita)
1986 Mario Gentilo (Ita)

Most wins: 7 Leon Meredith (UK) 1904-5, 1907-9,
1911, 1913; 5 Gaby Minneboo (Hol) as above; 3 Horst
Gnas (FRG) as above.

AMATEUR ROAD RACE
1970 Joergen Schmidt (Den)
1971 Regis Ovion (Fra)
1973 Ryszard Szurkowski (Pol)
1974 Janusz Kowalski (Pol)
1975 André Gevers (Hol)
1977 Claudio Corti (Ita)
1978 Gilbert Glaus (Swi)
1979 Gianni Giacomini (Ita)
1981 Andrey Vedernikov (USSR)
1982 Bernd Drogan (GDR)
1983 Uwe Raab (GDR)
1985 Lech Piasecki (Pol)
1986 Uwe Ampler (GDR)

Most wins: 2 Giuseppe Martano (Ita) 1930, 1932;
Gustav Adolf Schur (GDR) 1958-9.

PROFESSIONAL SPRINT
1970 Gordon Johnson (Aus)
1971 Leijin Loevesijn (Hol)
1972-3 Robert van Lancker (Bel)
1974 Peder Pedersen (Den)
1975-6 John Nicholson (Aus)
1977-86 Koichi Nakano (Jap)

Most wins: 10 Koichi Nakano (Jap) as above; 7 Jeff
Scherens (Bel) 1932-7, 1947; 7 Antonio Maspes (Ita)
1955-6, 1959-62, 1964; 6 Thorvald Ellegaard (Den)
1901-3, 1906, 1908, 1911; 5 Piet Moeskops (Hol)
1921-4, 1926; 4 Lucien Michard (Fra) 1927-30; 4 Reg
Harris (UK) 1949-51, 1954.

PROFESSIONAL 4KM PURSUIT
First held in 1939, when it was left unfinished, and then
1946.
1970 Hugh Porter (UK)
1971 Dirk Baert (Bel)
1972-3 Hugh Porter (UK)
1974-5 Roy Schuiten (Hol)
1976 Francesco Moser (Ita)
1977-8 Gregor Braun (FRG)
1979 Bert Osterbosch (Hol)
1980 Tony Doyle (UK)
1981-2 Alain Bondue (Fra)
1983 Steele Bishop (Aus)
1984-5 Hans-Henrik Oersted (Den)
1986 Tony Doyle (UK)

Most wins: 4 Hugh Porter (UK) 1968, 1970, 1972-3; 3
Guido Messina (Ita) 1954-6; 3 Roger Rivière 1957-9; 3
Leando Faggin (Ita) 1963, 1965-6.

PROFESSIONAL KEIRIN
First held 1980
1980-1 Danny Clark (Aus)
1982 Gordon Singleton (Can)

Koichi Nakano – a record number of world titles
(All-Sports)

1983 Urs Freuler (Swi)
1984 Robert Dill-Bundi (Swi)
1985 Urs Freuler (Swi)
1986 Michel Vaarten (Bel)

PROFESSIONAL POINTS RACE
First held 1980
1980 Stan Tourne (Bel)
1981-6 Urs Freuler (Swi)

PROFESSIONAL MOTOR-PACED
First held 1895
Held at 100km 1895-1971, over 1 hour from 1972.
1970 Ehrenfried Rudolph (FRG)
1971-2 Theo Verschueren (Bel)
1973-4 Cees Stam (Hol)
1975 Dieter Kemper (FRG)
1976 Wilfried Peffgen (FRG)
1977 Cees Stam (Hol)
1978 Wilfried Peffgen (FRG)
1979 Martin Venix (Hol)
1980 Wilfried Peffgen (FRG)
1981 René Kos (Hol)
1982 Martin Venix (Hol)
1983 Bruno Vicini (Ita)
1984 Horst Schütz (FRG)
1985-6 Bruno Vicini (Ita)

Most wins: 6 Guillermo Timoner (Spa) 1955, 1959-60, 1962, 1964-5; 4 Victor Linart (Bel) 1921, 1924, 1926-7

PROFESSIONAL ROAD-RACE
First held 1927
1970 Jean-Pierre Monseré (Bel)
1971 Eddy Merckx (Bel)
1972 Marino Basso (Ita)
1973 Felice Gimondi (Ita)
1974 Eddy Merckx (Bel)
1975 Hennie Kuiper (Hol)
1976 Freddy Maertens (Bel)
1977 Francesco Moser (Ita)
1978 Gerrie Knetemann (Hol)
1979 Jan Raas (Hol)
1980 Bernard Hinault (Fra)
1981 Freddy Maertens (Bel)
1982 Giuseppe Saronni (Ita)
1983 Greg LeMond (USA)
1984 Claude Criquielion (Bel)
1985 Joop Zoetemelk (Hol)
1986 Moreno Argentin (Ita)

Most wins: 3 Alfredo Binda (Ita) 1927, 1930, 1932; Rik van Steenbergen (Bel) 1949, 1956-7; Eddy Merckx (Bel) 1967, 1971, 1974

WOMEN'S SPRINT
First held 1958
1969-71 Galina Tsareva (USSR)
1972 Galina Yermolayeva (USSR)
1973 Sheila Young (USA)
1974 Tamara Piltsikova (USSR)
1975 Sue Novarra (USA)
1976 Sheila Young (USA)
1977-9 Galina Tsareva (USSR)
1980 Sue Reber (née Novarra) (USA)
1981 Sheila Ochowitz (née Young) (USA)
1982-4 Connie Paraskevin (USA)
1985 Isabelle Nicoloso (Fra)
1986 Christa Rothenburger (GDR)

Most wins: 6 Galina Yermolayeva (USSR) 1958-61, 1963, 1972; 6 Galina Tsareva (USSR) as above.

WOMEN'S 3KM PURSUIT
1970-4 Tamara Garkushina (USSR)
1975-6 Keetie van Oosten-Hage (Hol)
1977 Vera Kuznetsova (USSR)
1978-9 Keetie van Oosten-Hage (Hol)
1980-1 Nadezhda Kibardina (USSR)
1982 Rebecca Twigg (USA)
1983 Connie Carpenter (USA)
1984-5 Rebecca Twigg (USA)
1986 Jeannie Longo (Fra)

Most wins: 6 Tamara Garkushina (USSR) 1967, 1970-4; 5 Beryl Burton (UK) 1959-60, 1962-3, 1966; 4 Keetie van Oosten-Hage (Hol) as above.

WOMEN'S ROAD RACE
First held 1958
1970-1 Anna Konkina (USSR)
1972 Geneviève Gambillon (Fra)
1973 Nicole Vandenbroeck (Bel)
1974 Geneviève Gambillon (Fra)
1975 Trijntje Fopma (Hol)
1976 Keetie van Oosten-Hage (Hol)
1977 Josiane Bost (Fra)
1978 Beate Habetz (FRG)
1979 Petra de Bruin (Hol)
1980 Beth Heiden (USA)
1981 Ute Enzenauer (FRG)
1982 Mandy Jones (UK)
1983 Marianne Berglund (Swe)
1985-6 Jeannie Longo (Fra)

Most wins: 4 Yvonne Reynders (Bel) 1959, 1961, 1963, 1966

A new event, women's 50 km team trial has been added to the championships programme from 1987.

Note that three women's cycling world champions: Beth Heiden, Sheila Young and Christa Rothenburger have also been world champions at speed skating.

THE CLASSIC RIDERS
The riders to have had most wins in the Classic races (MR to BP as shown in text), the Grand Prix des Nations (GN), the World Road Race Championship (WC) and the three prestigious Continental tours: Tour de France (Fr), Tour of Italy (It), Tour of Spain (Sp)

Name	MR	FL	PR	FW	LB	PB	TL	BP	GN	WC	Fr	It	Sp	Total
Eddy Merckx	7	2	3	4	5	1	2	-	1	3	5	5	1	39
Bernard Hinault	-	-	1	2	2	-	2	-	5	1	5	3	2	23
Fausto Coppi	3	-	1	1	-	-	5	-	2	1	2	5	-	20
Jacques Anquetil	-	-	-	-	1	-	-	1	9	-	5	2	1	19
Alfredo Binda	2	-	-	-	-	-	4	-	-	3	-	5	-	14
Roger de Vlaeminck	3	1	4	1	1	1	3	-	-	-	-	-	-	14
Rik van Looy	1	2	3	1	1	2	1	-	-	2	-	-	-	13
Gino Bartali	4	-	-	-	-	-	3	-	-	-	2	3	-	12
Felice Gimondi	1	-	1	-	-	1	2	-	2	1	1	2	1	12
Rik van Steenbergen	1	2	2	2	-	1	-	-	-	3	-	-	-	11
Herman van Springel	-	-	-	-	-	-	1	7	2	-	-	-	-	10
Louison Bobet	1	1	1	-	-	-	1	1	1	1	3	-	-	10

SPEED RECORDS

Records are recognised for both professionals and amateurs on open air and indoor tracks for a variety of distances at unpaced flying and standing starts and for motor-paced. In this selection only the best (amateur or professional) is shown. All marks are outdoors, unless shown as indoors (ind).

MEN

UNPACED STANDING START

Distance	hr:min:sec			
1km	1:02.547	Maic Malchow (GDR)	Mexico City	14 Oct 1980
5km	5:44.700	Gregor Braun (FRG)	La Paz	12 Jan 1986
10km	11:39.720	Francesco Moser (Ita)	Mexico City	19 Jan 1984
20km	23:21.592	Francesco Moser (Ita)	Mexico City	23 Jan 1984
100km	2:11:21.428	Beat Meister (Swi)	Zürich	14 Jul 1986
51.15135km	1 hour	Francesco Moser (Ita)	Mexico City	23 Jan 1984

UNPACED FLYING START

200m	10.123	Nikolay Kovich (USSR)	Moscow (ind)	2 Aug 1987
500m	26.993	Rory O'Reilly (USA)	La Paz	23 Nov 1985
1km	58.269	Dominguez Ruedo Elrain (Col)	La Paz	13 Dec 1986

MOTOR-PACED (Indoors)

50km	32:56.76	Aleksandr Romanov (USSR)	Moscow	21 Feb 1987
100km	1:05:58.03	Aleksandr Romanov (USSR)	Moscow	21 Feb 1987
91.131km	1 hour	Aleksandr Romanov (USSR)	Moscow	21 Feb 1987

WOMEN

UNPACED STANDING START

Distance	hr:min:sec			
1km (ind)	1:13.377	Erika Salumyae (USSR)	Moscow (ind)	21 Sep 1983
5km (ind)	6:22.713	Jeannie Longo (Fra)	Grenoble (ind)	2 Nov 1986
10km (ind)	13:29.395	Jeannie Longo (Fra)	Grenoble (ind)	7 Nov 1986
20km	26:58.152	Jeannie Longo (Fra)	Grenoble (ind)	7 Nov 1986
100km	2:31:30.043	Mieke Havik (Hol)	Rotterdam	19 Sep 1983
44.718km	1 hour	Jeannie Longo (Fra)	Grenoble (ind)	7 Nov 1986

UNPACED FLYING START

200m	11.232	Erika Salumyae (USSR)	Moscow (ind)	2 Aug 1987
500m	29.655	Erika Salumyae (USSR)	Moscow (ind)	6 Aug 1987
1km (ind)	1:05.232	Erika Salumyae (USSR)	Moscow (ind)	30 May 1987

1 HOUR

The classic speed record is that for 1 hour. The current record as in the table above was set at high altitude by Francesco Moser. He also holds the best distance set at sea level: 49.80193 km at Milan on 3 Oct 1986. Similarly Jeannie Longo also holds the women's sea-level best: 43.587 km at Milan on 30 Sep 1986.

The men's 1 hour record at the end of each decade has progressed:

km			
40.781	M.W.Hamilton (USA)	Denver	9 Jul 1898
41.520	Marcel Berthet (Fra)	Paris	20 Jun 1907
44.247	Oscar Egg (Swi)	Paris	18 Jun 1914
45.767	Maurice Archambaud (Fra)	Milan	3 Nov 1937
45.848	Fausto Coppi (Ita)	Milan	7 Nov 1942
47.346	Roger Rivière (Fra)	Milan	23 Nov 1958
48.653	Ole Ritter (Den)	Mexico City	10 Dec 1968
49.431	Eddy Merckx (Bel)	Mexico City	25 Oct 1972

CYCLO-CROSS

The first world cross-country cycling world championships were held in 1950. From 1967 they have been split into amateur and professional categories.

OPEN AND PROFESSIONAL CHAMPIONS

1950 Jean Robic (Fra)
1951-3 Roger Rondeaux (Fra)
1954-8 André Dufraisse (Fra)
1959 Renato Longo (Ita)
1960-1 Rolf Wolfshohl (FRG)
1962 Renato Longo (Ita)
1963 Rolf Wolfshohl (FRG)
1964-5 Renato Longo (Ita)
1966 Eric de Vlaeminck (Bel)
1967 Renato Longo (Ita)
1968-73 Eric de Vlaeminck (Bel)
1974 Albert van Damme (Bel)
1975 Roger de Vlaeminck (Bel)
1976-9 Albert Zweifel (Swi)
1980 Roland Liboton (Bel)
1981 Johannes Stamsnijder (Hol)
1982-4 Roland Liboton (Bel)
1985 Klaus-Peter Thaler (FRG)
1986 Albert Zweifel (Swi)
1987 Klaus-Peter Thaler (FRG)

Most wins: 7 Eric de Vlaeminck; 5 André Dufraisse, Renato Longo

AMATEUR CHAMPIONS

1967 Michel Pelchat (Fra)
1968 Roger de Vlaeminck (Bel)
1969 René Declercq (Bel)
1970-1 Robert Vermeire (Bel)
1972 Norbert De Deckere (Bel)
1973 Klaus-Peter Thaler (FRG)
1974-5 Robert Vermeire (Bel)
1976 Klaus-Peter Thaler (FRG)
1977 Robert Vermeire (Bel)
1978 Roland Liboton (Bel)
1979 Vito di Tano (Ita)
1980 Fritz Saladin (Swi)
1981-2 Milos Fisera (Cs)
1983-4 Radomir Simunek (Cs)
1985 Mike Kluge (FRG)
1986 Vito di Tano (Ita)
1987 Mike Kluge (FRG)

Most wins: 5 Robert Vermeire.

DARTS

Darts, or *Dartes*, were first used as a means of self defence during battles in Ireland in the 16th century. The Pilgrim Fathers played darts aboard the *Mayflower* on their way to discovering the New World in 1620. The modern game, however, dates to 1896 when Brian Gamlin of Bury, Lancashire, devised the present numbering system. The National Darts Association was formed in 1924 and the British Darts Organisation (BDO) was established in 1973. Since then it has developed into a popular television sport, and today more than 6 million people play darts in Britain alone.

WORLD PROFESSIONAL CHAMPIONSHIP

The world professional championship, sponsored by Embassy, is the professional players' leading tournament. It was instituted at the Heart of the Midlands Night Club, Nottingham in 1978. Between 1979 and 1985 all tournaments were held at Jollees Night Club, Stoke-on-Trent. Since 1986 the Lakeside Country Club, Frimley Green, Surrey, has been host to the championship.

Winners	Runners-up	Score
1978 Leighton Rees (Wal)	John Lowe (Eng)	11-7
1979 John Lowe (Eng)	Leighton Rees (Wal)	5-0
1980 Eric Bristow (Eng)	Bobby George (Eng)	5-3
1981 Eric Bristow (Eng)	John Lowe (Eng)	5-3
1982 Jocky Wilson (Sco)	John Lowe (Eng)	5-3
1983 Keith Deller (Eng)	Eric Bristow (Eng)	6-5
1984 Eric Bristow (Eng)	Dave Whitcombe (Eng)	7-1
1985 Eric Bristow (Eng)	John Lowe (Eng)	6-2
1986 Eric Bristow (Eng)	Dave Whitcombe (Eng)	6-0
1987 John Lowe (Eng)	Eric Bristow (Eng)	6-4

(1977 best of 21 legs; 1978-82 best of 9 sets; 1983 best of 11 sets; 1984 best of 13 sets; 1985-7 best of 11 sets)

WORLD MASTERS

The first World Masters took place at the West Centre Hotel, Fulham in 1974.

Winners:
1974 Cliff Inglis (Eng)
1975 Alan Evans (Wal)
1976 John Lowe (Eng)
1977 Eric Bristow (Eng)
1978 Ronnie Davies (Wal)
1979 Eric Bristow (Eng)
1980 John Lowe (Eng)
1981 Eric Bristow (Eng)
1982 Dave Whitcombe (Eng)
1983-4 Eric Bristow (Eng)
1985 Dave Whitcombe (Eng)
1986 Bob Anderson (Eng)

WORLD CUP

A biennial event, the first World Cup was at Wembley in 1977. The winning nation is the team with the most points after a singles, pairs and fours competition. The United States hosted the event in 1979, New Zealand in 1981, Scotland in 1983 and Australia in 1985.

Winners:
1977 Wales
1979 England
1981 England
1983 England
1985 England

Most winning teams: 4 John Lowe, Eric Bristow (both England)

Eric Bristow (Syndication International)

Individual title:
1977 Leighton Rees (Wal)
1979 Nicky Virachkul (USA)
1981 John Lowe (Eng)
1983 Eric Bristow (Eng)
1985 Eric Bristow (Eng)

NATIONS CUP

A tournament for three-man teams, the first Nations Cup was organised in 1977.

Winners:
1977 Scotland
1978 Sweden
1979-80 England
1981 Scotland
1982-4 England
1985 Finland
1986-7 England

Most wins: 7 England
Most winning teams: 7 John Lowe, Eric Bristow (both England)

BRITISH OPEN

Inaugurated 1975.

Winners:
1975 Alan Evans (Wal)
1976 Jack North (Eng)
1977 John Lowe (Eng)
1978 Eric Bristow (Eng)
1979 Tony Brown (Eng)
1980 Cliff Lazarenko (Eng)
1981 Eric Bristow (Eng)
1982 Jocky Wilson (Sco)
1983 Eric Bristow (Eng)
1984 John Cusnett (Eng)
1985-6 Eric Bristow (Eng)
1987 Bob Anderson (Eng)

WORLD PAIRS CHAMPIONSHIP

1986 John Lowe & Bob Anderson (Eng)
1987 Eric Bristow (Eng) & Peter Locke (Wal)

WORLD MATCH-PLAY

Instituted 1984.
1984 John Lowe
1985 Eric Bristow (Eng)
1986 Mike Gregory (Eng)

BRITISH MATCH-PLAY

Instituted 1984.
1984 Mike Gregory (Eng)
1985 John Lowe (Eng)
1986 Eric Bristow (Eng)

BRITISH PROFESSIONAL CHAMPIONSHIP

First contested 1981.
1981 Jocky Wilson (Sco)
1982 Eric Bristow (Eng)
1983 Jocky Wilson (Sco)
1984 Mike Gregory (Eng)
1985 Eric Bristow (Eng)
1986 Jocky Wilson (Sco)

NEWS OF THE WORLD CHAMPIONSHIP

Prior to the World Professional championship the *News of the World* title was the most prestigious in darts. Because of the thousands of entrants from all over the British Isles it remains the most difficult title to win, and is one still sought after by even the best of the the professionals. The first championship was in the London Area only in 1928. Other areas had their own *News of the World* Championships but it was not until 1948 that it became a national event.

Winners (all British unless otherwise stated):
1948 Harry Leadbetter
1949 Jack Boyce
1950 Dixie Newberry
1951 Harry Perryman
1952 Tommy Gibbons
1953 Jimmy Carr
1954 Oliver James
1955 Tom Reddington
1956 Trevor Peachey
1957 Alwyn Mullins
1958 Tommy Gibbons
1959 Albert Welch
1960 Tom Reddington
1961 Alec Adamson
1962 Eddie Brown
1963 Robbie Rumney
1964-5 Tom Barrett
1966 Wilf Ellis
1967 Wally Seaton
1968 Bill Duddy
1969 Barry Twomlow
1970 Henry Barney
1971 Dennis Filkins
1972 Brian Netherton
1973 Ivor Hodgkinson
1974 Peter Chapman
1975 Derek White
1976 Bill Lennard
1977 Mick Norris
1978 Stefan Lord (Swe)
1979 Bobby George
1980 Stefan Lord (Swe)
1981 John Lowe
1982 Roy Morgan
1983-4 Eric Bristow
1985 Dave Lee
1986 Bobby George

Dual winners: Tommy Gibbons, Tom Reddington, Tom Barrett, Stefan Lord, Eric Bristow, Bobby George

THE BRISTOW-LOWE RIVALRY, AND DOMINATION

	World Champs	World Masters	World Cup Team	Ind	Nations Cup	British Open	World Match-Play	British Match-Play	British Pro	News of World
Lowe	2	2	4	1	6	1	1	-	-	1
Bristow	5	5	4	2	6	4	-	1	1	2

WOMEN'S DARTS

WORLD CUP
Instituted in 1983 and played at the same time as the men's competition.

Team:
1983 England
1985 England
Individual:
1983 Sandy Reitan (USA)
1985 Linda Batten (UK)

WORLD MASTERS
1984 Kathy Wones (Eng)
1985 Lilian Barnett (NZ)
1986 Kathy Wones (Eng)

BRITISH OPEN
First held 1979.
1979 Judy Campbell (Sco)
1980 Linda Batten (Eng)
1981 Ann Marie Davies (Wal)
1982 Maureen Flowers (Eng)
1983 Sandy Earnshaw (Eng)
1984 Ann Marie Davies (Wal)
1985 Linda Batten (Eng)
1986 Gwen Sutton (Eng)
1987 Sharon Colclough (Eng)

BRITISH GOLD CUP
Instituted 1984.

Singles:
1984 Linda Batten (Eng)
1985 Barbara Lee (Eng)
1986 Sue Edwards (Eng)

Pairs:
1984 Sandy Earnshaw & Anne Sunderland (Eng)
1985 Linda Smith & Joan Clews (Eng)
1986 Sonya Ralphs & Tammy Montgomery (Eng)

EQUESTRIANISM

The earliest known show jumping competition was at the Agricultural Hall, London in 1869 although some sources say that jumping obstacles on horseback took place at a Paris show three years earlier. The dressage competition derived from the exercises taught at 16th century Italian and French horsemanship academies, while the three-day event developed from cavalry endurance rides. One of the earliest known three-day event competitions was from Vienna to Berlin in 1892. The British Show Jumping Association was formed in 1923 in order to standardise the rules of the sport. It was incorporated under the Companies Act on 31 December 1925. The international governing body, the Fédération Equestre Internationale (FEI), was founded in Brussels in 1921. The current president is HRH Princess Anne, who succeeded her father, HRH Prince Philip in 1986.

SHOW JUMPING

OLYMPIC GAMES

Show Jumping was included in the 1900 Olympic programme, with jumping, high jump and long jump competitions. The sport was not included again until 1912, when the team competition was introduced as well as the individual. The 1956 competition took place in Stockholm, Sweden, because of quarantine restrictions in force in Australia at the time.

INDIVIDUAL

	Horse	Rider
1900	Benton II	Aimé Haegeman (Bel)
1912	Mignon	Jean Cariou (Fra)
1920	Trebecco	Tommaso Lequio (Ita)
1924	Lucette	Alphonse Gemuseus (Swi)
1928	Eliot	Frantisek Ventura (Cs)
1932	Uranus	Takeichi Nishi (Jap)
1936	Tora	Kurt Hasse (Ger)
1948	Arete	Humberto Mariles Cortés (Mex)
1952	Ali Baba	Pierre Jonquères d'Oriola (Fra)
1956	Halla	Hans-Günter Winkler (Ger)
1960	Posillipo	Raimondo d'Inzeo (Ita)
1964	Lutteur B	Pierre Jonquères d'Oriola (Fra)
1968	Snowbound	William Steinkraus (USA)
1972	Ambassador	Graziano Mancinelli (Ita)
1976	Warwick Rex	Alwin Schockemöhle (FRG)
1980	Artemor	Jan Kowalczyk (Pol)
1984	Touch of Class	Joe Fargis (USA)

TEAM
5 FR Germany 1936 (as Germany), 1956, 1960, 1964, 1972
3 Sweden 1912, 1920, 1924
1 Spain 1928, Mexico 1948, Great Britain 1952, Canada 1968, France 1976, USSR 1980, USA 1984
No medals awarded 1932, event not completed as no nation completed the course with three riders.

Most gold medals: 5 Hans-Günter Winkler (FRG) Team 1956, 1960, 1964, 1972; Individual 1956

WORLD CHAMPIONSHIPS

Instituted in 1953, the championships are now held every four years. In 1965, 1970 and 1974, women had a separate competition, but now compete equally with their male counterparts. A team competition was introduced in 1978

Winners:

1953	Quorum	Francisco Goyoago (Spa)
1954	Halla	Hans-Günter Winkler (FRG)
1955	Halla	Hans-Günter Winkler (FRG)
1956	Merano	Raimondo d'Inzeo (Ita)
1960	Gowran Girl	Raimondo d'Inzeo (Ita)
1966	Pomone	Pierre Jonquères d'Oriola (Fra)
1970	Beethoven	David Broome (UK)
1974	Simona	Hartwig Steenken (FRG)
1978	Roman	Gerd Wiltfang (FRG)
1982	Fire II	Norbert Koof (FRG)
1986	Mr.T	Gail Greenhough (Can)

WOMEN

1965	Stroller	Marion Coakes (UK)
1970	Rocket	Janou Lefèbvre (Fra)
1974	Rocket	Janou Tissot (née Lefèbvre)(Fra)

TEAM

Great Britain 1978, France 1982, USA 1986

Most titles: 2 Hans-Günter Winkler, Raimondo d'Inzeo, Janou Tissot (née Lefèbvre)

EUROPEAN CHAMPIONSHIPS

Inaugurated in 1957 men and women had separate competitions until 1975. A biennial event since 1967.

Winners:

MEN

1957	Sonnenglanz	Hans-Günter Winkler (FRG)
1958	Meteor	Fritz Thiedemann (FRG)
1959	Uruguay	Piero d'Inzeo (Ita)
1961	Sunslave	David Broome (UK)
1962	Mister Softee	David Barker (UK)
1963	Rockette	Graziano Mancinelli (Ita)
1965	Dozent	Hermann Schridde (FRG)
1966	Gran Geste	Nelson Pessoa (Bra)
1967	Mister Softee	David Broome (UK)
1969	Mister Softee	David Broome (UK)
1971	Simona	Hartwig Steenken (FRG)
1973	Penwood Forge Mill	Paddy McMahon (UK)
1975	Warwick	Alwin Schockemöhle (FRG)
1977	Seven Valleys	Johan Heins (HOL)
1979	Roman	Gerhard Wiltfang (FRG)
1981	Deister	Paul Schockemöhle (FRG)

David Broome riding Mister Softee in the 1969 European Championships. (E.D.Lacey)

1983 Deister	Paul Schockemöhle (FRG)
1985 Deister	Paul Schockemöhle (FRG)

TEAM
2 Great Britain 1979, 1985; FR Germany 1975, 1981
1 Netherlands 1977, Switzerland 1983

WOMEN

1957 Flanagan	Pat Smythe (UK)
1958 Doly	Giulia Serventi (Ita)
1959 Bandit	Ann Townsend (UK)
1960 Clare Castle	Susan Cohen (UK)
1961 Flanagan	Pat Smythe (UK)
1962 Flanagan	Pat Smythe (UK)
1963 Flanagan	Pat Smythe (UK)
1966 Kenavo	Janou Lefèbvre (Fra)
1967 Untouchable	Kathy Kusner (USA)
1968 Merely-a-Monarch	Anneli Drummond-Hay (UK)
1969 Morning Light	Iris Kellett (Ire)
1971 Psalm	Ann Moore (UK)
1973 Psalm	Ann Moore (UK)

BRITISH SHOW JUMPING DERBY

Held annually at the All-England Jumping Centre
Hickstead in Sussex, the first Derby was in 1961.

1961 Goodbye III	Seamus Hayes (Ire)
1962 Flanagan	Pat Smythe (UK)
1963 Gran Geste	Nelson Pessoa (Bra)
1964 Goodbye III	Seamus Hayes (Ire)
1965 Gran Geste	Nelson Pessoa (Bra)
1966 Mister Softee	David Broome (UK)
1967 Stroller	Marion Coakes (UK)
1968 The Maverick VII	Alison Westwood (UK)
1969 Xanthos	Anneli Drummond-Hay (UK)
1970 Mattie Brown	Harvey Smith (UK)
1971 Mattie Brown	Harvey Smith (UK)
1972 Shirokko	Hendrick Snoek (FRG)
1973 Mr.Banbury	Alison Dawes (née Westwood) (UK)
1974 Salvador	Harvey Smith (UK)
1975 Pele	Paul Darragh (Ire)
1976-9 Boomerang	Eddie Macken (Ire)
1980 Owen Gregory	Michael Whitaker (UK)
1981 Sanyo Video	Harvey Smith (UK)
1982 Deister	Paul Schockemöhle (FRG)
1983 Ryan's Son	John Whitaker (UK)
1984 Gabhram	John Ledingham (Ire)
1985 Lorenzo	Paul Schockemöhle (FRG)
1986 Deister	Paul Schockemöhle (FRG)
1987 Raffles J Nick	Nick Skelton (UK)

Most wins: 4 Eddie Macken, Harvey Smith; 3 Paul Schockemöhle

ROYAL INTERNATIONAL HORSE SHOW

First staged as the International Horse Show at Olympia in 1907. It is now held annually. The two most famous events are the:

KING GEORGE V GOLD CUP

A gold international challenge trophy presented by King George V to be perpetually contested. It was first contested in 1911, and is regarded as the principle show jumping competition for male riders. Any rider winning the event three times keeps the trophy.

Post war winners:

1947 Marquis III	Pierre Jonquères d'Oriola (Fra)
1948 Foxhunter	Harry Llewellyn (UK)
1949 Tankard	Brian Butler (UK)
1950 Foxhunter	Harry Llewellyn (UK)
1951 Ballyneety	Kevin Barry (Ire)
1952 Gracieux	Don Carlos Figueroa (Spa)
1953 Foxhunter	Harry Llewellyn (UK)
1954 Meteor	Fritz Thiedemann (FRG)
1955 Brando	Luigi Cartesegua (Ita)
1956 First Boy	Bill Steinkraus (USA)
1957 Uruguay	Piero d'Inzeo (Ita)
1958 Master William	Hugh Wiley (USA)
1959 Nautical	Hugh Wiley (USA)
1960 Sunsalve	David Broome (UK)
1961-2 The Rock	Piero d'Inzeo (Ita)
1963 Dundrum	Thomas Wade (Ire)
1964 Sinjon	Bill Steinkraus (USA)
1965 Fortun	Hans-Günter Winkler (FRG)
1966 Mister Softee	David Broome (UK)
1967 Firecrest	Peter Robeson (UK)
1968 Enigk	Hans-Günter Winkler (FRG)
1969 Uncle Max	Ted Edgar (UK)
1970 Mattie Brown	Harvey Smith (UK)
1971 Askan	Gerhard Wiltfang (FRG)
1972 Sportsman	David Broome (UK)
1973 Penwood Forge Mill	Paddy McMahon (UK)
1974 Main Spring	Frank Chapot (USA)
1975 Rex the Robber	Alwin Schockemöhle (FRG)
1976 Chain Bridge	Michael Saywell (UK)
1977 Philco	David Broome (UK)
1978 Claret	Jeff McVean (Aus)
1979 Video	Robert Smith (UK)
1980 Scorton	David Bowen (UK)
1981 Mr.Ross	David Broome (UK)
1982 Disney Way	Michael Whitaker (UK)
1983 Deister	Paul Schockemöhle (FRG)
1984 St.James	Nick Skelton (UK)
1985 Towerlands Anglezark	Malcolm Pyrah (UK)
1986 Ryan's Son	John Whitaker (UK)
1987 Towerlands Anglezark	Malcolm Pyrah (UK)

Most wins: 5 David Broome
Outright winners: Talbot Ponsonby 1930, 1932, 1934; Harry Llewellyn (as above), Piero d'Inzeo (as above), David Broome (as above). Only Llewellyn won it three times on the same horse, Foxhunter.

QUEEN ELIZABETH II CUP

The Queen Elizabeth II Cup is the women's equivalent of the King George V Gold Cup. It was inaugurated in 1949.

1949 Rusty	Iris Kellett (Ire)
1950 Silver Cloud	Gill Palethorpe (UK)
1951 Rusty	Iris Kellett (Ire)
1952 Quicksilver III	Gill Rich (UK)
1953 Fanny Rosa	Marie Delfosse (UK)
1954 Charleston	Jose Bonnaud (Fra)
1955 Earlsrath Rambler	Dawn Palethorpe (UK)
1956 Earlsrath Rambler	Dawn Palethorpe (UK)
1957 Sunsalve	Elizabeth Anderson (UK)

1958	Mr.Pollard	Pat Smythe (UK)
1959	Nico	Anna Clement (FRG)
1960	Clare Castle	Susan Cohen (UK)
1961	Oorskiet	Lady Sarah FitzAlan Howard (UK)
1962	Spring Fever	Judy Crago (UK)
1963	Trigger Hill	Julie Nash (UK)
1964	Jubilant	Gillian Makin (UK)
1965	Stroller	Marion Coakes (UK)
1966	Havana Royal	Althea Roger Smith (UK)
1967	Grey Leg	Betty Jennaway (UK)
1968	White Lightning	Mary Chapot (USA)
1969	The Maverick VII	Alison Westwood (UK)
1970	Merely-a-Monarch	Anneli Drummond-Hay (UK)
1971	Stroller	Marion Mould (née Coakes) (UK)
1972	Psalm	Ann Moore (UK)
1973	Psalm	Ann Moore (UK) &
	Mr.Banbury	Alison Dawes (née Westwood) (UK)
1974	All Trumps	Jean Davenport (née Goodwin) (UK)
1975	Hang On	Jean Davenport (née Goodwin) (UK)
1976	Elizabeth Ann	Marion Mould (née Coakes) (UK)
1977	Everest Wallaby	Liz Edgar (UK)
1978	Marius	Caroline Bradley (UK)
1979	Forever	Liz Edgar (UK)
1980	Tigre	Caroline Bradley (UK)
1981-2	Everest Forever	Liz Edgar (UK)
1983	Mandingo	Jean Germany (UK)
1984	Next's Jingo	Veronique Whitaker (UK)
1985	Ned Kelly	Sue Pountain (UK)
1986	Everest Rapier	Liz Edgar (UK)
1987	Monsanta	Gillian Greenwood (UK)

Most wins: 5 Liz Edgar; 3 Marion Mould (née Coakes)
The only horse to win the King George V Gold Cup and Queen Elizabeth II Cup is Sunsalve in 1957 and 1960.

VOLVO WORLD CUP

Instituted in 1979.

1979	Gladstone	Hugo Simon (Aut)
1980	Balbuco	Conrad Homfeld (USA)
1981	Jet Run	Mike Matz (USA)
1982	Calypso	Melanie Smith (USA)
1983	I Love You	Norman Dello Joio (USA)
1984	Aramis	Mario Deslauriers (Can)
1985	Abdullah	Conrad Homfeld (USA)
1986	McLain	Leslie Burr-Lenehan (USA)
1987	On the Natural	Katharine Burdsall (USA)

PRESIDENT'S CUP

The Prix des Nations, inaugurated in 1947, is the official international team jumping competition involving teams of four riders. Selected meetings during the year count towards the Cup, with different countries staging just one Nations Cup meeting, which must be at its official International Horse Show. Since 1965 (the Prince Philip Trophy in 1985) the President's Trophy (now Cup) has been the World Team Championship and is awarded to the country with the best results based on the season's Nations Cup events.

Winners:

12	Great Britain	1965, 1967, 1970, 1972-4, 1977-9, 1983, 1985-6
7	FR Germany	1969, 1971, 1975-6, 1981-2, 1984
2	USA	1966, 1968
1	France	1980

JUMPING RECORDS

The official high jump world record is 8 ft 1¼ in (2.47 m) by Hausó, ridden by Capt. Alberto Larraguibel Morales (Chi) on 5 Feb 1949. The British record is 7 ft 7⁵/₁₆ in (2.32 m) on Everest Lastic, ridden by Nick Skelton on 16 Dec 1978

The world long jump record is 27 ft 6¾ in (8.40 m) by Something, ridden by André Ferreira (SAf) on 26 Apr 1975

THREE-DAY EVENTING

OLYMPIC GAMES

Both individual and team competitions were first held at the 1912 Games.

Winners

INDIVIDUAL

1912	Lady Artist	Axel Nordlander (Swe)
1920	Germania	Helmer Mörner (Swe)
1924	Silver Piece	Adolph van der Voort van Zijp (Hol)
1928	Marcroix	Charles Pahud de Mortanges (Hol)
1932	Marcroix	Charles Pahud de Mortanges (Hol)
1936	Nurmi	Ludwig Stubbendorff (Ger)
1948	Aiglonne	Bernard Chevallier (Fra)
1952	Jubal	Hans von Blixen-Finecke Jr(Swe)
1956	Iluster	Petrus Kastenman (Swe)
1960	Salad Days	Lawrence Morgan (USA)
1964	Surbean	Mauro Checcoli (Ita)
1968	Pitou	Jean-Jacques Guyon (Fra)
1972	Laurieston	Richard Meade (UK) .
1976	Bally-Cor	Edmund Coffin (USA)
1980	Rossinan	Federico Roman (Ita)
1984	Charisma	Mark Todd (NZ)

TEAM

4 USA 1932, 1948, 1976, 1984
3 Sweden 1912, 1920, 1952; Great Britain 1956, 1968, 1972
2 Holland 1924, 1928
1 Germany 1936, Australia 1960, Italy 1964, USSR 1980

Most gold medals: 4 Charles Pahud de Mortanges (Hol) Team 1924, 1928; Individual 1928, 1932 (also won Team silver 1932)

WORLD CHAMPIONSHIP

Instituted in 1966, men and women have competed together at all championships.

INDIVIDUAL

1966	Chalon	Carlos Moratorio (Arg)
1970	Cornishman V	Mary Gordon-Watson (UK)
1974	Irish Cap	Bruce Davidson (USA)
1978	Might Tango	Bruce Davidson (USA)

1982 Regal Realm   Lucinda Green (née Prior-Palmer)
                    (UK)
1986 Priceless   Virginia Leng (née Holgate) (UK)

TEAM

3 Great Britain 1970, 1982, 1986
1 Ireland 1966, USA 1974, Canada 1978

EUROPEAN CHAMPIONSHIP

INDIVIDUAL

1953 Starlight   Lawrence Rook (UK)
1954 Crispin   Albert Hill (UK)
1955 Kilbarry   Frank Weldon (UK)
1957 High and Mighty   Sheila Willcox (UK)
1959 Burn Trout   Hans Schwarzenbach (Swi)
1962 M'Lord Connolly   James Templar (UK)
1965 Volt   Marian Babirecki (Pol)

1967 Durlas Eile   Eddie Boylan (Ire)
1969 Cornishman V   Mary Gordon-Watson (UK)
1971 Doublet   HRH Princess Anne (UK)
1973 Jeger   Aleksandr Yevdokimov (USSR)
1975 Be Fair   Lucinda Prior-Palmer (UK)
1977 George   Lucinda Prior-Palmer (UK)
1979 Monaco   Nils Haagensen (Den)
1981 Oran   Hansueli Schmutz (Swi)
1983 Mystic Minstrel   Rachel Bayliss (UK)
1985 Priceless   Virginia Holgate (IK)

TEAM

10 Great Britain 1953-5, 1957, 1967, 1969, 1971,
     1977, 1981, 1985
3 USSR 1962, 1965, 1975
2 FR Germany 1959, 1973
1 Ireland 1979; Sweden 1983

Lucinda Prior-Palmer (now Mrs Green), six times champion at Badminton. (All-Sport)

BADMINTON

One of the classic Three Day events, the Badminton Horse Trials take place in the grounds of Badminton House in Gloucestershire, home of the Beaufort family. The first event was in 1949.

Winners:

1949	Golden Willow	John Shedden (UK)
1950	Remus	Tony Collings (UK)
1951	Vae Victus	Hans Schwarzenbach (Swi)
1952	Emily Little	Mark Darley (Ire)
1953	Starlight	Lawrence Rook (UK)
1954	Bambi	Margaret Hough (UK)
1955-6	Kilbarry	Frank Weldon (UK) §
1957-8	High and Mighty	Sheila Willcox (UK)
1959	Airs and Graces	Sheila Waddington (née Willcox) (UK)
1960	Our Solo	Bill Roycroft (Aus)
1961	Salad Days	Lawrence Morgan (Aus)
1962	Merely-a-Monarch	Anneli Drummond-Hay (UK)
1963	Gladiator	Susan Fleet (UK) #
1964	M'Lord Connolly	James Templer (UK)
1965	Durlas Eile	Eddie Boylan (Ire)
1966	Not held	
1967	Jonathan	Celia Ross-Taylor (UK)
1968	Our Nobby	Jane Bullen (UK)
1969	Pasha	Richard Walker (UK)
1970	The Poacher	Richard Meade (UK)
1971-2	Great Ovation	Mark Phillips (UK)
1973	Be Fair	Lucinda Prior-Palmer (UK)
1974	Columbus	Mark Phillips (UK)
1975	Cancelled after dressage	
1976	Wideawake	Lucinda Prior-Palmer (UK)
1977	George	Lucinda Prior-Palmer (UK)
1978	Warrior	Jane Holderness-Roddam (née Bullen) (UK)
1979	Killaire	Lucinda Prior-Palmer (UK)
1980	Southern Comfort	Mark Todd (NZ)
1981	Lincoln	Mark Phillips (UK)
1982	Speculator III	Richard Meade (UK)
1983	Regal Realm	Lucinda Green (née Prior-Palmer) (UK)
1984	Beagle Bay	Lucinda Green (UK)
1985	Priceless	Virginia Holgate (UK)
1986	Sir Wattie	Ian Stark (UK)
1987	Not held	

Most wins: 6 Lucinda Green (nee Prior-Palmer); 4 Mark Phillips; 3 Sheila Waddington (née Willcox)
§ Held at Windsor 1955
# reduced to a One Day Event because of the weather

BURGHLEY HORSE TRIALS

Held each September on the estate surrounding Burghley House in Lincolnshire, the Burghley Horse Trials is the major event of the autumn trials season. Burghley House was the home of the former Olympic athlete, David Burghley, the Marquis of Exeter.

Winners:

1961	Merely-a-Monarch	Anneli Drummond-Hay (UK)
1962	European Championship	
1963	St.Finbar	Harry Freeman-Jackson (Ire)
1964	Barberry	Richard Meade (UK)
1965	Victoria Bridge	Jeremy Beale (UK)

1966	World Championship	
1967	Popadom	Lorna Sutherland (UK)
1968	Fair and Square	Sheila Willcox (UK)
1969	Shaitan	Gillian Watson (UK)
1970	Don Camillo	Judy Bradwell (UK)
1971	European Championship	
1972	Larkspur	Janet Hodgson (UK)
1973	Maid Marion	Mark Phillips (UK)
1974	World Championship	
1975	Carawich	Aly Pattinson (UK)
1976	Warrior	Jane Holderness-Roddam (UK)
1977	George	Lucinda Prior-Palmer (UK)
1978	Greco	Lorna Clarke (née Sutherland) (UK)
1979	Davy	Andrew Hoy (Aus)
1980	John of Gaunt	Richard Walker (UK)
1981	Beagle Bay	Lucinda Prior-Palmer (UK)
1982	Ryan's Cross	Richard Walker (UK)
1983	Priceless	Virginia Holgate (UK)
1984	Night Cap	Virginia Holgate (UK)
1985	European Championship	
1986	Murphy Himself	Virginia Leng (née Holgate) (UK)

Most wins: 3 Virginia Leng (née Holgate); 2 Lorna Clarke (née Sutherland), Lucinda Prior-Palmer, Richard Walker

DRESSAGE
OLYMPIC GAMES

The individual competition was included in the 1912 Games, but the team competition was not introduced until 1928.

INDIVIDUAL

1912	Emperor	Carl Bonde (Swe)
1920	Uno	Janne Lundblad (Swe)
1924	Piccolomini	Ernst Linder (Swe)
1928	Draufgänger	Carl von Langen (Ger)
1932	Taine	Xavier Lesage (Fra)
1936	Kronos	Heinz Pollay (Ger)
1948	Hummer	Hans Moser (Swi)
1952	Master Rufus	Henri St.Cyr (Swe)
1956	Juli	Henri St.Cyr (Swe)
1960	Absent	Sergey Filatov (USSR)
1964	Woermann	Henri Chammartin (Swi)
1968	Ichor	Ivan Kizimov (USSR)
1972	Piaff	Liselott Linsenhoff (FRG)
1976	Granat	Christine Stückelberger (Swi)
1980	Mon Cherie	Elisabeth Theurer (Aut)
1984	Ahlerich	Reiner Klimke (FRG)

TEAM
(not held 1960)
6 FR Germany 1928 & 1936 (as Germany), 1964, 1968, 1976, 1984
2 France 1932, 1948; Sweden 1952, 1956; USSR 1972, 1980

Most gold medals: 4 Henri St.Cyr (Swe) Team 1952, 1956; Individual 1952, 1956

WORLD CHAMPIONSHIP

Inaugurated 1966.

INDIVIDUAL

1966	Mariano	Josef Neckermann (FRG)
1970	Pepel	Yelena Petouchkova (USSR)

Christine Stückelberger riding Granat. (Leslie Lane)

1974	Mehmed	Reiner Klimke (FRG)
1978	Granat	Christine Stückelberger (Swi)
1982	Ahlerich	Reiner Klimke (FRG)
1986	Marzog	Anne Grethe Jensen (Den)

TEAM
5 FR Germany 1966, 1974, 1978, 1982, 1986
1 USSR 1970

WORLD CUP

1987 Gauguin de Lully Christine Stückelberger (Swi)

EUROPEAN CHAMPIONSHIP

Inaugurated 1963.

INDIVIDUAL

1963	Wolfdietrich	Henri Chammartin (Swi)
1965	Wolfdietrich	Henri Chammartin (Swi)
1967	Dux	Reiner Klimke (FRG)
1969	Piaff	Liselott Linsenhoff (FRG)
1971	Piaff	Liselott Linsenhoff (FRG)
1973	Mehmed	Reiner Klimke (FRG)
1975	Granat	Christine Stückelberger (Swi)
1977	Granat	Christine Stückelberger (Swi)
1979	Mon Cherie	Elisabeth Theurer (Aut)
1981	Madras	Uwe Schulten-Baumer (FRG)
1983	Marzog	Anne Grethe Jensen (Den)
1985	Ahlerich	Reiner Klimke (FRG)
1987	Corlandus	Margrit Otto-Crepin (Fra)

TEAM
12 FR Germany 1965, 1967, 1969, 1971, 1973, 1975, 1977, 1979, 1981, 1983, 1985, 1987
1 Great Britain 1963

WORLD CARRIAGE DRIVING CHAMPIONSHIPS

Instituted in 1972 and subsequently held every two years.

INDIVIDUAL

1972	August Dubey (Swi)
1974	Sándor Fülöp (Hun)
1976	Imre Abonyi (Hun)
1978	György Bárdos (Hun)
1980	György Bárdos (Hun)
1982	Tjeerd Velstra (Hol)
1984	László Juhász (Hun)
1986	Tjeerd Velstra (Hol)

TEAM
3 Great Britain 1972, 1974, 1980; Hungary 1976, 1978, 1984
2 Netherlands 1982, 1986

WORLD PAIRS CARRIAGE DRIVING
First held (for two horses) at Sandringham in 1985.
Winner: Ekkert Meinecke (FRG). *Team:* Switzerland

FENCING

Fencing, the sport of fighting with a sword, is one of man's oldest pastimes, obviously related to the use of swords in war or single combat. There is evidence of swordsmanship in Egypt as early as 1360 BC. Fencing was widespread in the Middle Ages, and the rapier had been developed as the principal weapon by the end of the 16th century. Modern weapons are the épée, foil and sabre. With the épée (weighing 770 grams) the conditions closely follow those that once appertained to duelling and the whole body is a target area. With the lighter weapons, for the foil (maximum weight 500 grams) the target area is the metallic jacket covering the top half of the body, and for the sabre (500 grams) above the waist, including the head. For the two latter weapons a hit must follow prescribed movements — the "phrase".

The world governing body, the Fédération Internationale d'Escrime (FIE), was founded in Paris in 1913.

OLYMPIC GAMES

Fencing has been included at all Olympic Games, and these tournaments count as world championships in Olympic years. At the early Games between 1896 and 1906, in addition to the competitions, of which the winners are shown below, there were also events for Fencing Masters, at which these professionals competed against the other contestants. Women first competed in 1924 (with the foil); electronic scoring was introduced for the épée in 1936 and for the foil in 1956.

Winners:
MEN

	Foil	Epée	Sabre
1896	Emile Gravelotte (Fra)	Not held	Jean Georgiadis (Gre)
1900	Emile Coste (Fra)	Ramon Fonst (Cub)	Georges de la Falaise (Fra)
1904	Ramon Fonst (Cub)	Ramon Fonst (Cub)	Manuel Diaz (Cub)
1906	Georges Dillon-Kavanagh (Fra)	Georges de la Falaise (Fra)	Jean Georgiadis (Gre)
1908	Not held	Gaston Alibert (Fra)	Jenö Fuchs (Hun)
1912	Nedo Nadi (Ita)	Paul Anspach (Bel)	Jenö Fuchs (Hun)
1920	Nedo Nadi (Ita)	Armand Massard (Fra)	Nedo Nadi (Ita)
1924	Roger Ducret (Fra)	Charles Delporte (Bel)	Sandor Posta (Hun)
1928	Lucien Gaudin (Fra)	Lucien Gaudin (Fra)	Odön Tersztyanszky (Hun)
1932	Gustavo Marzi (Ita)	Giancarlo Cornaggia-Medici (Ita)	György Piller (Hun)
1936	Giulio Gaudini (Ita)	Franco Riccardi (Ita)	Endre Kabos (Hun)
1948	Jean Buhan (Fra)	Luigi Cantone (Ita)	Aladar Gerevich (Hun)
1952	Christian d'Oriola (Fra)	Edoardo Mangiarotti (Ita)	Pal Kovacs (Hun)
1956	Christian d'Oriola (Fra)	Carlo Pavesi (Ita)	Rudolf Karpati (Hun)
1960	Viktor Zhdanovich (USSR)	Giuseppe Delfino (Ita)	Rudolf Karpati (Hun)
1964	Egon Franke (Pol)	Grigoriy Kriss (USSR)	Tibor Pezsa (Hun)
1968	Ion Drimba (Rom)	Gyözö Kulcsar (Hun)	Jerzy Pawlowski (Pol)
1972	Witold Woyda (Pol)	Csaba Fenyvesi (Hun)	Viktor Sidiak (USSR)
1976	Fabio Dal Zotto (Ita)	Alexander Pusch (FRG)	Viktor Krovopuskov (USSR)
1980	Vladimir Smirnov (USSR)	Johan Harmenberg (Swe)	Viktor Krovopuskov (USSR)
1984	Mauro Numa (Ita)	Philippe Boisse (Fra)	Jean-Francois Lamour (Fra)

MEN'S TEAM WINS

Foil

6 France	1924, 1932, 1948, 1952, 1968, 1980
5 Italy	1920, 1928, 1936, 1956, 1984
2 USSR	1960, 1964

1 Cuba, 1904, Poland, 1972, FR Germany, 1976

Epée

6 France	1906, 1908, 1924, 1932, 1948, 1980
6 Italy	1920, 1928, 1936, 1952, 1956, 1960
3 Hungary	1964, 1968, 1972

1 Belgium 1912, Sweden 1976, FR Germany 1984

Sabre

9 Hungary	1908, 1912, 1928, 1932, 1936, 1948, 1952, 1956, 1960
4 Italy	1920, 1924, 1972, 1984
4 USSR	1964, 1968, 1976, 1980
1 Germany	1906

WOMEN'S FOIL

1924	Ellen Osiier (Den)
1928	Helène Mayer (Ger)
1932	Ellen Preis (Aut)
1936	Ilona Elek (Hun)
1948	Ilona Elek (Hun)
1952	Irene Camber (Ita)
1956	Gillian Sheen (UK)
1960	Heidi Schmid (FRG)
1964	Ildiko Ujlaki-Rejtö (Hun)
1968	Yelena Novikova (USSR)
1972	Antonella Ragno-Lonzi (Ita)
1976	Ildiko Schwarczenberger (Hun)
1980	Pascale Trinquet (Fra)
1984	Luan Jujie (Chn)

WOMEN'S FOIL TEAM WINS

4 USSR	1960, 1968, 1972, 1976

1 Hungary 1964, France 1980, FR Germany 1984

MOST MEDALS – individual (*I*) and team (*T*):
Men

Name	Gold		Silver		Bronze		Total	
	I	*T*	*I*	*T*	*I*	*T*		
Edoardo Mangiarotti (Ita)	1	5	1	4	2	-	13	1936-60
Aladar Gerevich (Hun)	1	6	1	-	1	1	10	1932-60
Giulio Gaudini (Ita)	1	2	1	3	2	-	9	1928-36
Roger Ducret (Fra)	1	2	2	2	1	-	8	1920-28
Philippe Cattiau (Fra)	-	3	2	2	-	1	8	1920-36
Pal Kovacs (Hun)	1	5	-	-	1	-	7	1936-60
Others with five or more including four gold medals:								
Christian d'Oriola (Fra)	2	2	1	1	-	-	6	1948-56
Rudolf Karpati (Hun)	2	4	-	-	-	-	6	1948-60
Nedo Nadi (Ita)	3	3	-	-	-	-	6	1912-20
Giuseppe Delfino (Ita)	1	3	1	1	-	-	6	1952-64
Gyözö Kulcsar (Hun)	1	3	-	-	2	-	6	1964-76
Viktor Sidiak (USSR)	1	3	-	1	1	-	6	1968-80
Ramon Fonst (Cub)	3	1	1	-	-	-	5	1900-04
Lucien Gaudin (Fra)	2	2	-	1	-	-	5	1920-28

Nadi won a record five gold medals at one Games in 1920.

Women

Name	Gold		Silver		Bronze		Total	
Ildiko Sagi-Ujlaki-Rejtö (Hun)	1	1	-	3	1	1	7	1960-76
Yelena Byelova (née Novikova) (USSR)	1	3	-	1	1	-	6	1968-80

WORLD CHAMPIONSHIPS

Held annually except in Olympic years (see above). From 1921 to 1935 they were styled as European championships.

Winners:

MEN *Foil*	*Epée*	*Sabre*
1921 -	Lucien Gaudin (Fra)	-
1922 -	R.Herde (Nor)	Adrianus de Jong (Hol)
1923 -	W.Brouwer (Hol)	Adrianus de Jong (Hol)
1925 -	-	Janos Garay (Hun)
1926 Giorgio Chiavacci (Ita)	Georges Tainturier (Fra)	Sandor Gambos (Hun)
1927 Oreste Puliti (Ita)	Georges Buchard (Fra)	Sandor Gambos (Hun)
1929 Oreste Puliti (Ita)	Philippe Cattiau (Fra)	Gyula Glykais (Hun)
1930 Giulio Gaudini (Ita)	Philippe Cattiau (Fra)	György Piller (Hun)
1931 René Lemoine (Fra)	Georges Buchard (Fra)	György Piller (Hun)
1933 Gioacchino Guaragna (Ita)	Georges Buchard (Fra)	Endre Kabos (Hun)
1934 Giulio Gaudini (Ita)	Pal Dunay (Hun)	Endre Kabos (Hun)
1935 shared by four men	Hans Drakenberg (Swe)	Aladar Gerevich (Hun)
1937 Gustavo Marzi (Ita)	Bernard Schmetz (Fra)	Pal Kovacs (Hun)
1938 Gioacchino Guaragna (Ita)	Michel Pécheux (Fra)	Aldo Montano (Ita)
1947 Christian d'Oriola (Fra)	Edouard Artigas (Fra)	Aldo Montano (Ita)
1949 Christian d'Oriola (Fra)	Dario Mangiarotti (Ita)	Gastone Daré (Ita)
1950 Renzo Nostino (Ita)	Mogens Luchow (Den)	Jean Levavasseur (Fra)
1951 Manlio Di Rosa (Ita)	Edoardo Mangiarotti (Ita)	Aladar Gerevich (Hun)
1953 Christian d'Oriola (Fra)	Jozsef Sakovics (Hun)	Pal Kovacs (Hun)
1954 Christian d'Oriola (Fra)	Edoardo Mangiarotti (Ita)	Rudolf Karpati (Hun)
1955 Jozsef Gyuricza (Hun)	Giorgio Anglesio (Ita)	Aladar Gerevich (Hun)
1957 Mihaly Fülöp (Hun)	Armand Mouyal (Fra)	Jerzy Pawlowski (Pol)
1958 Giancarlo Bergamini (Ita)	Bill Hoskyns (UK)	Yakov Rylsky (USSR)
1959 Allan Jay (UK)	Bruno Khabarov (USSR)	Rudolf Karpati (Hun)
1961 Ryszard Parulski (Pol)	Jack Guittet (Fra)	Yakov Rylsky (USSR)
1962 German Sveshnikov (USSR)	Istvan Kausz (Hun)	Zoltan Horvath (Hun)
1963 Jean-Claude Magnan (Fra)	Roland Losert (Aut)	Yakov Rylsky (USSR)
1965 Jean-Claude Magnan (Fra)	Zoltan Nemere (Hun)	Jerzy Pawlowski (Pol)
1966 German Sveshnikov (USSR)	Aleksey Nikanchikov (USSR)	Jerzy Pawlowski (Pol)
1967 Viktor Putyatin (USSR)	Aleksey Nikanchikov (USSR)	Mark Rakita (USSR)
1969 Friedrich Wessel (FRG)	Bogdan Andrzejewski (Pol)	Viktor Sidiak (USSR)
1970 Friedrich Wessel (FRG)	Aleksey Nikanchikov (USSR)	Tibor Pezsa (Hun)

Foil	Epee	Sabre
1971 Vasiliy Stankovich (USSR)	Grigoriy Kriss (USSR)	Michele Maffei (Ita)
1973 Christian Noel (Fra)	Rolf Edling (Swe)	Mario Aldo Monttano (Ita)
1974 Aleksandr Romankov (USSR)	Rolf Edling (Swe)	Mario Aldo Monttano (Ita)
1975 Christian Noel (Fra)	Alexander Pusch (FRG)	Vladimir Nazlimov (USSR)
1977 Aleksandr Romankov (USSR)	Johan Harmenberg (Swe)	Pal Gerevich (Hun)
1978 Didier Flament (Fra)	Alexander Pusch (FRG)	Viktor Krovopuskov (USSR)
1979 Aleksandr Romankov (USSR)	Philippe Riboud (Fra)	Vladimir Nazlimov (USSR)
1981 Vladimir Smirnov (USSR)	Zoltan Szekely (Hun)	Mariusz Wodke (Pol)
1982 Aleksandr Romankov (USSR)	Jenö Pap (Hun)	Viktor Krovopuskov (USSR)
1983 Aleksandr Romankov (USSR)	Ellmar Bormann (FRG)	Vasiliy Etropolski (Bul)
1985 Mauro Numa (Ita)	Philippe Boisse (Fra)	György Nebald (Hun)
1986 Andrea Borella (Ita)	Philippe Ribaud (Fra)	Sergey Mindirgassov (USSR)
1987 Mathias Gey (FRG)	Volker Fischer (FRG)	Jean-Francois Lamour (Fra)

MOST 5 Aleksandr Romankov (USSR)	3 Georges Buchard (Fra)	3 Aladar Gerevich (USSR)
4 Christian d'Oriola (Fra)	3 Aleksey Nikanchikov (USSR)	3 Jerzy Pawlowski (Pol)
		3 Yakov Rylsky (USSR)

Yakov Rylsky congratulates Aladar Gerevich at the 1956 Olympics.

MEN'S TEAM WINS

Foil

14 Italy	1929-31, 1933-5, 1937-8, 1949-50, 1954-5, 1985-6
14 USSR	1959, 1961-3, 1965-6, 1969-70, 1973-4, 1979, 1981-2, 1987
6 France	1947, 1951, 1953, 1958, 1971, 1975
2 FR Germany	1977, 1983
1 Hungary 1957, Romania 1967, Poland 1978	

Epée

10 Italy	1931, 1933, 1937, 1949-50, 1953-5, 1957-8
10 France	1934-5, 1938, 1947, 1951, 1962, 1965-6, 1982-3
5 USSR	1961, 1967, 1969, 1979, 1981
4 Hungary	1959, 1970-1, 1978
4 FR Germany	1973, 1985-7
3 Sweden	1974-5, 1977
1 Belgium 1930, Poland 1963	

Sabre

17 Hungary	1930-1, 1933-5, 1937, 1951, 1953-5, 1957-8, 1966, 1973, 1978, 1981-2
13 USSR	1965, 1967, 1969-71, 1974-5, 1977, 1979, 1983, 1985-7
4 Italy	1938, 1947, 1949-50
4 Poland	1959, 1961-3

WOMEN'S FOIL

1929	Helène Mayer (Ger)
1930	Jenny Addams (Bel)
1931	Helène Mayer (Ger)
1933	Gwen Neligan (UK)
1934-5	Ilona Elek (Hun)
1937	Helène Mayer (Ger)
1938	Marie Sediva (Cs)
1947	Ellen Müller-Preiss (Aut)
1949	Ellen Müller-Preiss (Aut)
1950	Ellen Müller-Preiss (Aut) & Renée Garilhe (Fra)
1951	Ilona Elek (Hun)
1953	Irene Camber (Ita)
1954	Karen Lachman (Den)
1955	Lidia Dömölki (Hun)
1957	Aleksandra Zabelina (USSR)
1958	Valentina Kiselyeva (USSR)
1959	Yelina Yefimova (USSR)
1961	Heidi Schmid (FRG)
1962	Olga Szabo-Orban (Rom)
1963	Ildiko Rejtö (Hun)
1965	Galina Gorokhova (USSR)
1966	Tatyana Samusenko (USSR)
1967	Aleksandra Zabelina (USSR)
1969	Yelena Novikova (USSR)
1970	Galina Gorokhova (USSR)
1971	Marie-Chantal Demaille (Fra)
1973	Valentina Nikonova (USSR)
1974	Ildiko Bobis (Hun)
1975	Ecaterina Stahl (Rom)
1977-8	Valentina Sidorova (USSR)
1979	Cornelia Hanisch (FRG)
1981	Cornelia Hanisch (FRG)
1982	Naila Giliazova (USSR)
1983	Dorina Vaccaroni (Ita)
1985	Cornelia Hanisch (FRG)
1986	Anja Fichtel (FRG)
1987	Elisabeta Tufan (Rom)

Most wins: 3 Helène Mayer, Ilona Elek, Ellen Müller-Preiss, Cornelia Hanisch

WOMEN'S TEAM FOIL

15 USSR	1956, 1958, 1961, 1963, 1965-6, 1970-1, 1974-5, 1977-9, 1981, 1986
13 Hungary	1933-5, 1937, 1952-5, 1959, 1962, 1967, 1973, 1987

3 Denmark   1932, 1947-8
3 Italy   1957, 1982-3
2 France   1950-1
1 Germany 1936, Romania 1969, FR Germany 1985

ETON FIVES

The game of Eton Fives as now known originated at Eton College in 1840, when courts were built which incorporated features of the area where a handball game had been played before (first recorded in 1825). The courts had a distinctive built-in buttress, which had been used by boys playing against the outside of the chapel.

THE AMATEUR CHAMPIONSHIP

Played, as doubles, annually for the Kinnaird Cup. First held in 1928.

Most wins by one pair:
8 Anthony Hughes and Arthur Campbell 1958, 1965-8, 1971, 1973, 1975. Hughes also won in 1963 with D.J.S.Guilford.
6 Brian Matthews & John Reynolds 1981-6
3 A.H.Fabian & J.K.G.Webb 1937, 1939, 1948
3 Peter May & John May 1951-3
3 J.W.Biggs & J.C.Wallis 1961-2, 1964

RUGBY FIVES

This court game was first played around 1850. The court differs from that used for Eton Fives in that there is no buttress.
   The Rugby Fives Association was formed in 1927. It drew up a standard set of rules in 1930 and in the following year established the standard court dimensions, 28ft (8.54m) long and 18ft (5.49m) wide).

AMATEUR SINGLES CHAMPIONSHIP

Contested annually for the Jesters' Club Cup from 1932, except for the war years 1940-7.

Most wins:
13 Wayne Enstone 1973-8, 1980-6
 4 John Pretlove 1953, 1955-6, 1958
 4 Eric Marsh 1960-3
 3 Philip Malt 1933-5
Wayne Enstone has thus dominated in recent years. The winner in 1979 was David Hebden.

AMATEUR DOUBLES CHAMPIONSHIP

Contested annually for the Cyriax Cup, first in 1926, then annually 1930-9 and from 1947.

Most wins:
7 John Pretlove 1952, 1954, 1956-9, 1961 (4 with Dennis Silk 1956-9)
7 David Gardner 1960, 1965-6, 1970-2, 1974
6 Ian Fuller & David Hebden 1980-5
6 Wayne Enstone 1975-9 (with John East), 1986 (with Steve Ashton)
5 John East 1975-9

INVITATION WORLD CHAMPIONSHIPS

First held in 1983, not held in 1986. Winners in all three years 1983-5 at *singles:* Wayne Enstone, at *doubles:* Wayne Enstone & Steve Ashton.

GAELIC FOOTBALL

A 15-a-side game, Gaelic Football has common features with soccer, rugby and Australian Rules football. The first reference of a game resembling Gaelic Football was in 1712 when a match between Meath and Louth took place at Slane. The rules were standardised following the formation of the Gaelic Athletic Association, the governing body in Ireland for Handball, Hurling and Rounders as well as for Gaelic Football, in 1884. Teams played at 21 per side from 1884 to 1913 when they were reduced to 15.

Kerry v Tyrone in the All-Ireland final.

ALL IRELAND CHAMPIONSHIP

The sport's principal championship; the final is played at Dublin's Croke Park on the third Sunday in September each year for the Sam Maguire Trophy. They have been held annually from 1887, except for 1888 when this inter-county event was unfinished.

Most wins:

30 Kerry	1903-4, 1909, 1913-4, 1924, 1926, 1929-32, 1937, 1939-41, 1946, 1953, 1955, 1959, 1962, 1969-70, 1975, 1978-81, 1984-6
21 Dublin	1891-2, 1894, 1897-9, 1901-2, 1906-8, 1921-3, 1942, 1958,1963, 1974, 1976-7, 1983
7 Galway	1925, 1934, 1938, 1956, 1964-6
5 Wexford	1893, 1915-8
5 Cavan	1933, 1935, 1947-8, 1952
4 Tipperary	1889, 1895, 1900, 1920
4 Cork	1890, 1911, 1945, 1973
4 Kildare	1905, 1919, 1927-8
3 Louth	1910, 1912, 1957
3 Mayo	1936, 1950-1
3 Meath	1949, 1954, 1967
3 Down	1960-1, 1968
3 Offaly	1971-2, 1982
2 Limerick	1887, 1896
2 Roscommon	1943-4

Highest score: Dublin 27 Armagh 15, 18 Sep 1977
Highest aggregate: Cork 26 Galway 19, 16 Sep 1973
Most individual appearances: 11, including a record 8 wins by the Kerry players Pat Spillane, Mike Sheehy, Paudie O'Shea, Ger Power, Denis Moran, 1975-86

GLIDING

There is some evidence of the use of gliders in Ancient Egypt about four thousand years ago, and the ability to float in the air like a bird has long been of fascination for man. Gliding (or soaring) as a sport began to gain popular appeal in the 1930s in Europe and the USA.

RECORDS

A wide variety of world records are maintained for single-seater and for multi-seater gliders, for both men and women pilots. There are also records for motor gliders.

SINGLE-SEATERS

(*Category:* Record, Pilot, Glider, Venue, Date)
Straight distance: 1460.8km Hans-Werner Grosse (FRG), ASW-12, Lübeck (FRG) to Biarritz (Fra), 25 Apr 1972
Goal distance: 1254.26km Bruce Drake, David Speight, Dick Georgeson (NZ), all in Nimbus 2s, New Zealand, 14 Jan 1978
Goal and return distance: 1646.68km Tom Knauff (USA), Nimbus 3, Williamsport, Pa. to Knoxville, Tn. USA, 25 Apr 1983
Triangular distance: 1362.68km Tom Knauff USA) Nimbus 3; Lawrence McMaster, J.C.Seymour, Karl-Heinz

Striedick (USA), ASW-20B; Robert Robertson (UK), Ventus A, all on 2 May 1986
Height gain: 12894m Paul Bikle (USA), Schweizer SGS 1-23E, Mojave, Cal., USA, 25 Feb 1961
Absolute altitude: 14938m Robert Harris (USA), Grob G102, California, 17 Feb 1986
Speed over triangular course:

100km	195.30km/h	Ingo Renner (Aus), Nimbus 3, 14 Dec 1982
300km	169.49km/h	Jean-Paul Castel (Fra), Nimbus 3, 15 Nov 1986
500km	164.11km/h	Jean-Paul Castel (Fra), Nimbus 3, 10 Dec 1986
750km	158.40km/h	Hans-Werner Grosse (FRG), ASW-22, 8 Jan 1985
1000km	145.32km/h	Hans-Werner Grosse (FRG), ASW-17, 3 Jan 1979
1250km	133.24km/h	Hans-Werner Grosse (FRG), ASW-17, 9 Dec 1980

WOMEN'S SINGLE-SEATERS

Straight distance: 949.7km Karla Karel (UK), LS-3, Australia, 20 Jan 1980
Goal distance: 748.37km Joann Shaw (USA), Nimbus 2, 17 Aug 1983
Goal and return distance: 1126.68km Doris Grove (USA), Nimbus 2, 28 Sep 1981
Triangular distance: 847.27km Joanne Shaw (USA), Nimbus 2, 5 Aug 1984
Height gain: 9119m Anne Burns (UK), Skylark 3B, South Africa, 13 Jan 1961
Absolute altitude: 12637m Sabrina Jackintell (USA), Astir GS, 14 Feb 1979
Speed over triangular course:

100km	139.45km/h	Susan Martin (Aus), LS-3, 2 Feb 1979
300km	138.71km/h	Inge Müller (FRG), Ventus B, 8 Dec 1984
500km	133.14km/h	Susan Martin (Aus), LS-3, 29 Jan 1979
750km	110.53km/h	Pamela Hawkins (UK), ASW-17, 17 Nov 1984

WORLD CHAMPIONSHIPS

First held in 1937.

Winners:

OPEN CATEGORY

1937	Heini Dittmar (Ger)
1948	Per Persson (Swe)
1950	Billy Nilsson (Swe)
1952	Philip Wills (UK)
1954	Gérard Pierre (Fra)
1956	Paul MacCready (USA)
1958	Ernst Haase (FRG)
1960	Rudolf Hossinger (Arg)
1963	Eduard Makula (Pol)
1965	Jan Wroblewski (Pol)
1968	Harro Wödl (Aut)
1970	George Moffat (USA)
1972	Göran Ax (Swe)
1974	George Moffat (USA)
1976	George Lee (UK)
1978	George Lee (UK)

1981 George Lee (UK)
1983 Ingo Renner (Aus)
1985 Ingo Renner (Aus)
1987 Ingo Renner (Aus)

TWO-SEATER
1952 Luis Juez & J.Ara (Spa)
1954 Z.Rain & P.Komac (Yug)
1956 Nick Goodhart & Frank Foster (UK)

STANDARD CLASS
1958 Adam Witek (Pol)
1960 Heinz Huth (FRG)
1963 Heinz Huth (FRG)
1965 Francois Henry (Fra)
1968 A.J.Smith (USA)
1970 Helmut Reichmann (FRG)
1972 Jan Wroblewski (Pol)
1974 Helmut Reichmann (FRG)
1976 Ingo Renner (Aus)
1978 Baer Selen (Hol)
1981 Marc Schroeder (Fra)
1983 Stig Oye (Den)
1985 Leonardo Brigliadori (Ita)
1987 Markku Kuittinen (Fin)

15 METRES CLASS
1978 Helmut Reichmann (FRG)
1981 Göran Ax (Swe)
1983 Kees Musters (Hol)
1985 Doug Jacobs (USA)
1987 Brian Spreckley (UK)

Most titles: 4 Ingo Renner; 3 Helmut Reichmann,
George Lee

HANG GLIDING

An elementary form of hang glider is reputed to have been used by the monk, Eilmer, to fly from the top of Malmesbury Abbey, Wiltshire. The first modern pioneer of hang gliding was Otto Lilienthal in Germany in the 1890s. Duration and distance records have increased substantially in recent years as pilots have utilised optimum conditions and improved designs.

RECORDS
Records officially recognised by the FAI:
(Category: Record, Pilot, Venue, Date)

MEN
Greatest Distance: (Flexwing) 321.47km Randy Haney (Can), Golden, Canada to Trego, USA, 2 Jun 1986; (Rigid Wing) 161.904km Larry Tudor (USA), Owens Valley, Cal., USA, 12 Jul 1985.
Height gain: (Flexwing) 4343.4m Larry Tudor (USA) at Owens Valley, 4 Aug 1985; (Rigid Wing) 3820m Rainer Scholl (FRG) at Owens Valley, 5 Aug 1985.
Declared goal distance: 272.19km Geoffrey Lyons (UK) at Owens Valley, 11 Jun 1986
Out and return distance: 172.6km Klaus Kohmstedt (FRG), Owens Valley 15 Jul 1985.

Triangular course distance: (Flexwing) 80.83km Denis Cummings (Aus), Parks, NSW, 29 Dec 1985.

WOMEN
Greatest distance: (Flexwing) 233.9km Judy Leden (UK), Owens Valley, 13 Jul1983.
Height gain: (Flexwing) 3291.84km Page Pfieffer (USA), Owens Valley, 12 Jul 1979.
Out and return distance: 118.09km Valerie Wallington (Aus), Australia, 4 Jan 1985.
Declared goal distance: 124.52km Judy Lori (USA), Owens Valley, 15 Jul 1983.

WORLD CHAMPIONSHIPS
An unofficial world championship was held in 1975, won by David Cronk (USA), and the first official championships the following year at Köseen in Austria. They are now held biennially.

Team Champions:
1976 Austria
1979 France
1981 Great Britain
1983 Australia
1985 Great Britain

Individual Champions:
1976 Class I – Standard: Christian Steinbach (Aut)
     Class II – High Aspect Ratio: Terry Dolore (NZ)
     Class III – Open: Ken Battle (Aus)
1979 Class I – Weight Shift: Josef Guggenmos (FRG)
     Class II – Movable Surfaces: Rex Miller (USA)
1981 Class I – Weight Shift: Pepe Lopes (Bra)
Class II – Movable Surfaces: Graeme Bird (NZ)
1983 Steve Moyes (Aus)
1985 John Pendry (UK)

EUROPEAN CHAMPIONSHIPS
Held in 1986, when Great Britain were team champions and Judy Leden (UK) the individual champion.

MICROLIGHTING
The early microlights were foot launched hang gliders with motors attached, the idea being that the motor could be stopped once the desired altitude had been reached. Today's microlights are purpose built aircraft, most commonly of the rogallo (flexwing) type with a trike unit attached, or of the rigid wing type. The pilot's control systems include weight-shift for the rogallo wings and two-axis or three-axis for the rigid wings.

MICROLIGHT RECORDS
Altitude: 7906.5m Richard Rowley (USA), USA, 17 Sep 1983
Distance: 789.5km Alfred Clark (Aus), Phoenix Park, Aus., 2 Aug 1986
Time to climb 6000m: 22 min 36 sec Bob Calvert (UK), Pleasington, 16 Mar 1984
Time to climb 3000m: 8 min 7 sec Bob Calvert (UK), Pleasington, 16 Mar 1984

Speed over 3km straight course at restricted altitude:
126.356km David Green (USA), Camarillo, Cal., 23 Oct
1985

GOLF

The exact roots of golf are uncertain. The Chinese played a
form of golf 1800 years ago, and the French, Dutch and
Belgians played something resembling the sport in the
middle ages. Scotland, must however be regarded as the
home of golf. The game was banned in 1457 but golf was
later played by Scottish royalty such as James IV and Mary.
The world's first golf club, the Honourable Company of
Edinburgh Golfers, was founded in 1744. The ruling body
of the sport, in the eyes of most countries, is the Royal &
Ancient situated at St.Andrews. The Society of St.Andrews
Golfers, the forerunner of the R&A, played its first game of
golf over the famous St.Andrews links on 14 May 1754.

BRITISH OPEN

The Open first took place at Prestwick on 17 October
1860. Eight competitors took part and the lowest score
over three 12-hole rounds was recorded by Willie Park
senior. Prestwick hosted the first 12 Opens and all
subsequent championships have been played over seaside
links. The original prize was a Championship Belt but this
was won outright by Tom Morris junior in 1870 and there
was no event the following year. When it resumed in 1872
the prize was the silver claret jug still awarded to the
champion today. Played over 36 holes 1860-91 and
thereafter at 72 holes

Winners:		Score	Venue
1860	Willie Park, Snr (UK)	174	Prestwick
1861	Tom Morris, Snr (UK)	163	Prestwick
1862	Tom Morris, Snr (UK)	163	Prestwick
1863	Willie Park, Snr (UK)	168	Prestwick
1864	Tom Morris, Snr (UK)	167	Prestwick
1865	Andrew Strath (UK)	162	Prestwick
1866	Willie Park, Snr (UK)	169	Prestwick
1867	Tom Morris, Snr (UK)	170	Prestwick
1868	Tom Morris, Jnr (UK)	157	Prestwick
1869	Tom Morris, Jnr (UK)	154	Prestwick
1870	Tom Morris, Jnr (UK)	149	Prestwick
1872	Tom Morris, Jnr (UK)	166	Prestwick
1873	Tom Kidd (UK)	179	St.Andrews
1874	Mungo Park (UK)	159	Musselburgh
1875	Willie Park, Snr (UK)	166	Prestwick
1876	Bob Martin (UK)	176	St.Andrews
1877	Jamie Anderson (UK)	160	Musselburgh
1878	Jamie Anderson (UK)	157	Prestwick
1879	Jamie Anderson (UK)	169	St.Andrews
1880	Robert Ferguson (UK)	162	Musselburgh
1881	Robert Ferguson (UK)	170	Prestwick
1882	Robert Ferguson (UK)	171	St.Andrews
1883	Willie Fernie (UK)	159*	Musselburgh
1884	Jack Simpson (UK)	160	Prestwick
1885	Bob Martin (UK)	171	St.Andrews
1886	David Brown (UK)	157	Musselburgh

1887	Willie Park, Jnr (UK)	161	Prestwick
1888	Jack Burns (UK)	171	St.Andrews
1889	Willie Park, Jnr (UK)	155*	Musselburgh
1890	John Ball (UK)	164	Prestwick
1891	Hugh Kirkaldy (UK)	166	St.Andrews
1892	Harold H.Hilton (UK)	305	Muirfield
1893	William Auchterlonie (UK)	322	Prestwick
1894	John H.Taylor (UK)	326	Sandwich
1895	John H.Taylor (UK)	322	St.Andrews
1896	Harry Vardon (UK)	316*	Muirfield
1897	Harold H.Hilton (UK)	314	Hoylake
1898	Harry Vardon (UK)	307	Prestwick
1899	Harry Vardon (UK)	310	Sandwich
1900	John H.Taylor (UK)	309	St.Andrews
1901	James Braid (UK)	309	Muirfield
1902	Sandy Herd (UK)	307	Hoylake
1903	Harry Vardon (UK)	300	Prestwick
1904	Jack White (UK)	296	Sandwich
1905	James Braid (UK)	318	St.Andrews
1906	James Braid (UK)	300	Muirfield
1907	Arnaud Massy (Fra)	312	Hoylake
1908	James Braid (UK)	291	Prestwick
1909	John H.Taylor (UK)	295	Deal
1910	James Braid (UK)	299	St.Andrews
1911	Harry Vardon (UK)	303	Sandwich
1912	Edward Ray (UK)	295	Muirfield
1913	John H.Taylor (UK)	304	Hoylake
1914	Harry Vardon (UK)	306	Prestwick
1920	George Duncan (UK)	303	Deal
1921	Jock Hutchison (USA)	296*	St.Andrews
1922	Walter Hagen (USA)	300	Sandwich
1923	Arthur Havers (UK)	295	Troon
1924	Walter Hagen (USA)	301	Hoylake
1925	Jim Barnes (USA)	300	Prestwick
1926	Bobby Jones (USA)	291	Royal Lytham
1927	Bobby Jones (USA)	285	St.Andrews
1928	Walter Hagen (USA)	292	Sandwich
1929	Walter Hagen (USA)	292	Muirfield
1930	Bobby Jones (USA)	291	Hoylake
1931	Tommy Armour (USA)	296	Carnoustie
1932	Gene Sarazen (USA)	283	Prince's
1933	Densmore Shute (USA)	292*	St.Andrews
1934	Henry Cotton (UK)	283	Sandwich
1935	Alfred Perry (UK)	283	Muirfield
1936	Alfred Padgham (UK)	287	Hoylake
1937	Henry Cotton (UK)	290	Carnoustie
1938	Reg Whitcombe (UK)	295	Sandwich
1939	Dick Burton (UK)	290	St.Andrews
1946	Sam Snead (USA)	290	St.Andrews
1947	Fred Daly (UK)	293	Hoylake
1948	Henry Cotton (UK)	284	Muirfield
1949	Bobby Locke (SAf)	283*	Sandwich
1950	Bobby Locke (SAf)	279	Troon
1951	Max Faulkner (UK)	285	Portrush
1952	Bobby Locke (SAf)	287	Royal Lytham
1953	Ben Hogan (USA)	282	Carnoustie
1954	Peter Thomson (Aus)	283	Royal Birkdale
1955	Peter Thomson (Aus)	281	St.Andrews
1956	Peter Thomson (Aus)	286	Hoylake
1957	Bobby Locke (SAf)	279	St.Andrews
1958	Peter Thomson (Aus)	278*	Royal Lytham
1959	Gary Player (SAf)	284	Muirfield
1960	Kel Nagle (Aus)	278	St.Andrews
1961	Arnold Palmer (USA)	284	Royal Birkdale

1962 Arnold Palmer (USA)	276	Troon
1963 Bob Charles (NZ)	277*	Royal Lytham
1964 Tony Lema (USA)	279	St.Andrews
1965 Peter Thomson (Aus)	285	Royal Birkdale
1966 Jack Nicklaus (USA)	282	Muirfield
1967 Roberto de Vicenzo (Arg)	278	Hoylake
1968 Gary Player (SAf)	289	Carnoustie
1969 Tony Jacklin (UK)	280	Royal Lytham
1970 Jack Nicklaus (USA)	283*	St.Andrews
1971 Lee Trevino (USA)	278	Royal Birkdale
1972 Lee Trevino (USA)	278	Muirfield
1973 Tom Weiskopf (USA)	276	Troon
1974 Gary Player (SAf)	282	Royal Lytham
1975 Tom Watson (USA)	279*	Carnoustie
1976 Johnny Miller (USA)	279	Royal Birkdale
1977 Tom Watson (USA)	268	Turnberry
1978 Jack Nicklaus (USA)	281	St.Andrews
1979 Severiano Ballesteros (Spa)	283	Royal Lytham
1980 Tom Watson (USA)	271	Muirfield
1981 Bill Rogers (USA)	276	Sandwich
1982 Tom Watson (USA)	284	Royal Troon
1983 Tom Watson (USA)	275	Royal Birkdale
1984 Severiano Ballesteros (Spa)	276	St.Andrews
1985 Sandy Lyle (UK)	282	Sandwich
1986 Greg Norman (Aus)	280	Turnberry
1987 Nick Faldo (UK)	279	Muirfield

* after play-off

Most wins: 6 Harry Vardon; 5 James Braid, John H.Taylor, Peter Thomson, Tom Watson

UNITED STATES OPEN

First held at Newport, Rhode Island on 4 October 1895. English-born Horace Rawlins was the first winner and he collected a cheque for $150. Played over 72 holes (36 in 1895-7)

Winners (all USA unless otherwise stated)

	Score	Venue
1895 Horace Rawlins	173	Newport
1896 James Foulis	152	Shinnecock Hills
1897 Joe Lloyd	162	Chicago
1898 Fred Herd	328	Myopia Hunt
1899 Willie Smith	315	Baltimore
1900 Harry Vardon (UK)	313	Chicago
1901 Willie Anderson	331*	Myopia Hunt
1902 Laurie Auchterlonie	307	Garden City
1903 Willie Anderson	307*	Baltusrol
1904 Willie Anderson	303	Glen View
1905 Willie Anderson	314	Myopia Hunt
1906 Alex Smith	295	Onwentsia
1907 Alex Ross	302	Philadelphia
1908 Fred McLeod	322*	Myopia Hunt
1909 George Sargent	290	Englewood
1910 Alex Smith	298*	Philadelphia
1911 John McDermott	307*	Chicago
1912 John McDermott	294	Buffalo
1913 Francis Ouimet	304*	Brookline
1914 Walter Hagen	290	Midlothian
1915 Jerome Travers	297	Baltusrol
1916 Charles Evans, Jnr	286	Minikahda
1919 Walter Hagen	301*	Brae Burn
1920 Edward Ray (UK)	295	Inverness

Jack Nicklaus, the only golfer to have won twice each of the four major professional championships and the US Amateur. (All-Sports)

1921	Jim Barnes	289	Columbia
1922	Gene Sarazen	288	Skokie
1923	Bobby Jones	296*	Inwood
1924	Cyril Walker	297	Oakland Hills
1925	Willie Macfarlane	291*	Worcester
1926	Bobby Jones	293	Scioto
1927	Tommy Armour	301*	Oakmont
1928	Johnny Farrell	294*	Olympia Fields
1929	Bobby Jones	294*	Winged Foot
1930	Bobby Jones	287	Interlachen
1931	Billy Burke	292*	Inverness
1932	Gene Sarazen	286	Fresh Meadow
1933	Johnny Goodman	287	North Shore
1934	Olin Dutra	293	Merion
1935	Sam Parks, Jnr	299	Oakmont
1936	Tony Manero	282	Baltusrol
1937	Ralph Guldahl	281	Oakland Hills
1938	Ralph Guldahl	284	Cherry Hills
1939	Byron Nelson	284*	Philadelphia
1940	Lawson Little	287*	Canterbury
1941	Craig Wood	284	Colonial
1946	Lloyd Mangrum	284*	Canterbury
1947	Lew Worsham	282*	St.Louis
1948	Ben Hogan	276	Riviera
1949	Cary Middlecoff	286	Medinah
1950	Ben Hogan	287*	Merion
1951	Ben Hogan	287	Oakland Hills
1952	Julius Boros	281	Northwood
1953	Ben Hogan	283	Oakmont
1954	Ed Furgol	284	Baltusrol
1955	Jack Fleck	287*	Olympic
1956	Cary Middlecoff	281	Oak Hill
1957	Dick Mayer	282*	Inverness
1958	Tommy Bolt	283	Southern Hills
1959	Billy Casper	282	Winged Foot
1960	Arnold Palmer	280	Cherry Hills
1961	Gene Littler	281	Oakland Hills
1962	Jack Nicklaus	283*	Oakmont
1963	Julius Boros	293*	Brookline
1964	Ken Venturi	278	Congressional
1965	Gary Player (SAf)	282*	Bellerive
1966	Billy Casper	278*	Olympic
1967	Jack Nicklaus	275	Baltusrol
1968	Lee Trevino	275	Oak Hill
1969	Orville Moody	281	Champions
1970	Tony Jacklin (UK)	281	Hazeltine
1971	Lee Trevino	280*	Merion
1972	Jack Nicklaus	290	Pebble Beach
1973	Johnny Miller	279	Oakmont
1974	Hale Irwin	287*	Winged Foot
1975	Lou Graham	287	Medinah
1976	Jerry Pate	277	Atlanta
1977	Hubert Green	278	Southern Hills
1978	Andy North	285	Cherry Hills
1979	Hale Irwin	284	Inverness
1980	Jack Nicklaus	272	Baltusrol
1981	David Graham (Aus)	273	Merion
1982	Tom Watson	282	Pebble Beach
1983	Larry Nelson	280	Oakmont
1984	Fuzzy Zoeller	276*	Winged Foot
1985	Andy North	279	Oakland Hills
1986	Ray Floyd	279	Shinnecock Hills
1987	Scott Simpson	277	Olympic

* after play-off

Most wins: 4 Willie Anderson, Bobby Jones, Ben Hogan, Jack Nicklaus

UNITED STATES PGA CHAMPIONSHIP

First held in 1916, the championship was a matchplay event until 1958, when it became a strokeplay competition over four rounds. It is the least publicised of the four majors.

Winners (all USA unless otherwise stated)

		Score	Venue
1916	Jim Barnes	1 up	Siwanoy
1919	Jim Barnes	6 & 5	Engineers
1920	Jock Hutchison	1 up	Flossmoor
1921	Walter Hagen	3 & 2	Inwood
1922	Gene Sarazen	4 & 3	Oakmont
1923	Gene Sarazen	at 38th	Pelham
1924	Walter Hagen	2 up	French Lick
1925	Walter Hagen	6 & 5	Olympia Fields
1926	Walter Hagen	5 & 3	Salisbury
1927	Walter Hagen	1 up	Cedar Crest
1928	Leo Diegel	6 & 5	Five Farms
1929	Leo Diegel	6 & 4	Hill Crest
1930	Tommy Armour	1 up	Fresh Meadow
1931	Tom Creavy	2 & 1	Wannamoisett
1932	Olin Dutra	4 & 3	Keller
1933	Gene Sarazen	5 & 4	Blue Mound
1934	Paul Runyan	at 38th	Park
1935	Johnny Revolta	5 & 4	Twin Hills
1936	Densmore Shute	3 & 2	Pinehurst
1937	Densmore Shute	at 37th	Pittsburgh
1938	Paul Runyan	8 & 7	Shawnee
1939	Henry Picard	at 37th	Pomonok
1940	Byron Nelson	1 up	Hershey
1941	Vic Ghezzi	at 38th	Cherry Hills
1942	Sam Snead	2 & 1	Sea View
1944	Bob Hamilton	1 up	Manito
1945	Byron Nelson	4 & 3	Morraine
1946	Ben Hogan	6 & 4	Portland
1947	Jim Ferrier	2 & 1	Plum Hollow
1948	Ben Hogan	7 & 6	Norwood Hills
1949	Sam Snead	3 & 2	Hermitage
1950	Chandler Harper	4 & 3	Scioto
1951	Sam Snead	7 & 6	Oakmont
1952	Jim Turnesa	1 up	Big Spring
1953	Walter Burkemo	2 & 1	Birmingham
1954	Chick Harbert	4 & 3	Keller
1955	Doug Ford	4 & 3	Meadowbrook
1956	Jack Burke	3 & 2	Blue Hill
1957	Lionel Hebert	2 & 1	Miami Valley
1958	Dow Finsterwald	276	Llanerch
1959	Bob Rosburg	277	Minneapolis
1960	Jay Hebert	281	Firestone
1961	Jerry Barber	277*	Olympia Fields
1962	Gary Player (SAf)	278	Aronomink
1963	Jack Nicklaus	279	Dallas
1964	Bobby Nichols	271	Columbus
1965	Dave Marr	280	Laurel Valley
1966	Al Geiberger	280	Firestone
1967	Don January	281*	Columbine
1968	Julius Boros	281	Pecan Valley
1969	Ray Floyd	276	NCR, Dayton
1970	Dave Stockton	279	Southern Hills

1971	Jack Nicklaus	281	PGA National
1972	Gary Player (SAf)	281	Oakland Hills
1973	Jack Nicklaus	277	Canterbury
1974	Lee Trevino	276	Tanglewood
1975	Jack Nicklaus	276	Firestone
1976	Dave Stockton	281	Congressional
1977	Lanny Wadkins	282*	Pebble Beach
1978	John Mahaffey	276*	Oakmont
1979	David Graham (Aus)	272*	Oakland Hills
1980	Jack Nicklaus	274	Oak Hill
1981	Larry Nelson	273	Atlanta
1982	Ray Floyd	272	Southern Hills
1983	Hal Sutton	274	Riviera
1984	Lee Trevino	273	Shoal Creek
1985	Hubert Green	278	Cherry Hills
1986	Bob Tway	276	Toledo
1987	Larry Nelson	287*	Palm Beach

* after play-off

Most wins: 5 Walter Hagen, Jack Nicklaus; 3 Gene Sarazen, Sam Snead

US MASTERS

Held annually at the Augusta National course in Georgia, the Masters was introduced in 1934. Both the course and the tournament were the idea of the legendary golfer Bobby Jones. Entry to the Masters is by invitation only and the eventual winner is presented with the coveted green jacket. Contested over 72 holes of strokeplay.

Winners (all USA unless otherwise stated)

		Score
1934	Horton Smith	284
1935	Gene Sarazen	282*
1936	Horton Smith	285
1937	Byron Nelson	283
1938	Henry Picard	285
1939	Ralph Guldahl	279
1940	Jimmy Demaret	280
1941	Craig Wood	280
1942	Byron Nelson	280*
1946	Herman Keiser	282
1947	Jimmy Demaret	281
1948	Claude Harmon	279
1949	Sam Snead	282
1950	Jimmy Demaret	283
1951	Ben Hogan	280
1952	Sam Snead	286
1953	Ben Hogan	274
1954	Sam Snead	289*
1955	Cary Middlecoff	279
1956	Jack Burke, Jnr	289
1957	Doug Ford	282
1958	Arnold Palmer	284
1959	Art Wall, Jnr	284
1960	Arnold Palmer	282*
1961	Gary Player (SAf)	280
1962	Arnold Palmer	280*
1963	Jack Nicklaus	286
1964	Arnold Palmer	276
1965	Jack Nicklaus	271
1966	Jack Nicklaus	288*
1967	Gay Brewer	280
1968	Bob Goalby	277
1969	George Archer	281

1970	Billy Casper	279*
1971	Charles Coody	279
1972	Jack Nicklaus	286
1973	Tommy Aaron	283
1974	Gary Player (SAf)	278
1975	Jack Nicklaus	276
1976	Ray Floyd	271
1977	Tom Watson	276
1978	Gary Player (SAf)	277
1979	Fuzzy Zoeller	280*
1980	Severiano Ballesteros (Spa)	275
1981	Tom Watson	280
1982	Craig Stadler	284*
1983	Severiano Ballesteros (Spa)	280
1984	Ben Crenshaw	277
1985	Bernhard Langer (FRG)	282
1986	Jack Nicklaus	279
1987	Larry Mize	285*

* after play-off

Most wins: 6 Jack Nicklaus; 4 Arnold Palmer

Seve Ballesteros (All-Sport)

THE MAJORS

RECORDS

Lowest four round total

BRITISH OPEN	268	Tom Watson, 1977
US OPEN	272	Jack Nicklaus, 1980
US PGA	271	Bobby Nichols, 1964
US MASTERS	271	Jack Nicklaus, 1965
	271	Ray Floyd, 1976

Lowest single round

BRITISH OPEN	63	Mark Hayes (USA),1977
	63	Isao Aoki (Jap), 1980
	63	Greg Norman, 1986
US OPEN	63	Johnny Miller, 1973
	63	Tom Weiskopf (USA), 1980
	63	Jack Nicklaus, 1980
US PGA	63	Bruce Crampton (Aus), 1975
	63	Gary Player, 1984
US MASTERS	63	Nick Price (SAf), 1986

Oldest winners

BRITISH OPEN	46y 99d Tom Morris,Snr., 1867
US OPEN	43y 284d Ray Floyd, 1986
US PGA	48y 140d Julius Boros, 1968
US MASTERS	46y 82d Jack Nicklaus, 1986

Youngest winners

BRITISH OPEN	17y 249d Tom Morris,Jnr., 1868
US OPEN	19y 318d John McDermott, 1911
US PGA	20y 173d Gene Sarazen, 1922
US MASTERS	23y 4d Severiano Ballesteros, 1980

THE CHAMPIONS

		British Open	US Open	US PGA	US Masters
18	Jack Nicklaus	3	4	5	6
11	Walter Hagen	4	2	5	-
9	Ben Hogan	1	4	2	2
9	Gary Player	3	1	2	3
8	Tom Watson	5	1	-	2
7	Harry Vardon	6	1	-	-
7	Bobby Jones	3	4	-	-
7	Gene Sarazen	1	2	3	1
7	Sam Snead	1	-	3	3
7	Arnold Palmer	2	1	-	4

Gene Sarazen was the first man to win all four majors. No man has won all four majors in one year. Ben Hogan won three (British Open, US Open and Masters) in 1953. Greg Norman (1986) led going into the final round of all four championships; he won only one, the British Open.

RYDER CUP

The Ryder Cup started as a result of the efforts of wealthy businessman Samuel Ryder. It was launched in 1927, the year after a successful match between Great Britain and the United States at Wentworth. Held every two years the countries take it in turn to play host. Opposing the USA were Great Britain 1927-71; Great Britain and Ireland 1973-77; Europe from 1979.

Each competition lasts three days with four foursomes and four fourball matches on each of the first two days, and 12 singles on the third and final day.

Year	Venue	Winners	Score
1927	Worcester, Massachusetts	USA	9½-2½
1929	Moortown, Yorkshire	GB	7-5
1931	Scioto, Ohio	USA	9-3
1933	Southport & Ainsdale, Lancs	GB	6½-5½
1935	Ridgewood, New Jersey	USA	9-3
1937	Southport & Ainsdale, Lancs	USA	8-4
1947	Portland, Oregon	USA	11-1
1949	Ganton, Yorkshire	USA	7-5
1951	Pinehurst, North Carolina	USA	9½-2½
1953	Wentworth, Surrey	USA	6½-5½
1955	Thunderbird G&CC, California	USA	8-4
1957	Lindrick, Yorkshire	GB	7½-4½
1959	Eldorado CC, California	USA	8½-3½
1961	Royal Lytham, Lancashire	USA	14½-9½
1963	Atlanta, Georgia	USA	23-9
1965	Royal Birkdale, Lancashire	USA	19½-12½
1967	Houston, Texas	USA	23½-8½
1969	Royal Birkdale, Lancashire	Drawn	16-16
1971	St.Louis, Missouri	USA	18½-13½
1973	Muirfield, Scotland	USA	19-13
1975	Laurel Valley, Pennsylvania	USA	21-11
1977	Royal Lytham, Lancashire	USA	12½-7½
1979	Greenbrier, West Virginia	USA	17-11
1981	Walton Heath, Surrey	USA	18½-9½
1983	PGA National, Florida	USA	14½-13½
1985	The Belfry, Sutton Coldfield	Europe	16½-11½

Most wins: 21 United States
Most selections: 10 Christy O'Connor (Ire), 1955-73
Oldest player: 50y 66d Edward Ray (GB), 1927
Youngest player: 20y 59d Nick Faldo (GB), 1977

WORLD MATCH-PLAY CHAMPIONSHIP

An annual end-of-season knockout competition held at Wentworth, Surrey. The number of entrants was originally eight but has since been increased to 12. Each match consists of two rounds, one in the morning and one in the afternoon. Sponsored by Piccadilly 1964-76, Colgate 1977-8, Suntory from 1979.

Year	Winner	Runner-up	Score
1964	Arnold Palmer (USA)	Neil Coles (UK)	2 & 1
1965	Gary Player (SAf)	Peter Thomson (Aus)	3 & 2
1966	Gary Player (SAf)	Jack Nicklaus (USA)	6 & 4
1967	Arnold Palmer (USA)	Peter Thomson (Aus)	1 up
1968	Gary Player (SAf)	Bob Charles (NZ)	1 up
1969	Bob Charles (NZ)	Gene Littler (USA)	at 37th
1970	Jack Nicklaus (USA)	Lee Trevino (USA)	2 & 1
1971	Gary Player (SAf)	Jack Nicklaus (USA)	5 & 4
1972	Tom Weiskopf (USA)	Lee Trevino (USA)	4 & 3
1973	Gary Player (SAf)	Graham Marsh (Aus)	at 40th
1974	Hale Irwin (USA)	Gary Player (SAf)	3 & 1
1975	Hale Irwin (USA)	Al Geiberger (USA)	4 & 2
1976	David Graham (Aus)	Hale Irwin (USA)	at 38th
1977	Graham Marsh (Aus)	Ray Floyd (USA)	5 & 3
1978	Isao Aoki (Jap)	Simon Owen (NZ)	3 & 2
1979	Bill Rogers (USA)	Isao Aoki (Jap)	1 up
1980	Greg Norman (Aus)	Sandy Lyle (UK)	1 up
1981	Severiano Ballesteros	Ben Crenshaw (USA)	1 up
1982	Severiano Ballesteros	Sandy Lyle (UK)	at 37th
1983	Greg Norman (Aus)	Nick Faldo (UK)	3 & 2
1984	Severiano Ballesteros	Bernhard Langer (FRG)	2 & 1

1985 Severiano Ballesteros Bernhard Langer (FRG) 6 & 5
1986 Greg Norman (Aus)   Sandy Lyle (UK)   2 & 1

Most wins: 5 Gary Player; 4 Severiano Ballesteros (Spa)
Biggest winning margin: 11 & 9 Tom Watson (USA) v Dale Hayes (SAf), 1st round 1979

Greg Norman(All-Sport)

WORLD CUP

The World Cup was the idea of American industrialist Jay Hopkins. He saw the need for an international team competition for male professionals, other than for those of Great Britain and the United States. Contested annually over 72 holes of strokeplay by two-man teams. Interest has fallen in the competition in recent years and the 1986 competition, scheduled for California, was cancelled, but it is to return in Hawaii in November 1987.

Year	Winning Team		Leading Individual	
1953	Argentina (Roberto de Vicenzo & Antonio Cerda)	287*	Antonio Cerda	140*
1954	Australia (Peter Thomson & Kel Nagle)	556	Stan Leonard (Can)	275
1955	United States (Ed Furgol & Chick Harbert)	560	Ed Furgol	279
1956	United States (Ben Hogan & Sam Snead)	567	Ben Hogan	277
1957	Japan (Torakichi Nakamura & Koichi Ono)	557	Torakichi Nakamura	274
1958	Ireland (Harry Bradshaw & Christy O'Connor)	579	Angel Miguel (Spa)	286
1959	Australia (Kel Nagle & Peter Thomson)	563	Stan Leonard (Can)	275
1960	United States (Arnold Palmer & Sam Snead)	565	Flory van Donck (Bel)	279
1961	United States (Jimmy Demaret & Sam Snead)	560	Sam Snead	272
1962	United States (Arnold Palmer & Sam Snead)	557	Roberto de Vicenzo (Arg)	276
1963	United States (Jack Nicklaus & Arnold Palmer)	482*	Jack Nicklaus	237*
1964	United States (Jack Nicklaus & Arnold Palmer)	554	Jack Nicklaus	276
1965	South Africa (Harold Henning & Gary Player)	571	Gary Player	281
1966	United States (Jack Nicklaus & Arnold Palmer)	548	George Knudson (Can)	272
1967	United States (Jack Nicklaus & Arnold Palmer)	557	Arnold Palmer	276
1968	Canada (Al Balding & George Knudson)	569	Al Balding	274
1969	United States (Orville Moody & Lee Trevino)	552	Lee Trevino	275
1970	Australia (Bruce Devlin & David Graham)	544	Roberto de Vicenzo (Arg)	269
1971	United States (Jack Nicklaus & Lee Trevino)	555	Jack Nicklaus	271
1972	Taiwan (Hsieh Min-Nan & Lu Liang-Huan)	438*	Hsieh Min Nan	217*
1973	United States (Johnny Miller & Jack Nicklaus)	558	Johnny Miller	277
1974	South Africa (Bobby Cole & Dale Hayes)	554	Bobby Cole	271
1975	United States (Lou Graham & Johnny Miller)	554	Johnny Miller	275
1976	Spain (Severiano Ballesteros & Manuel Pinero)	574	Ernesto Perez Acosta (Mex)	282
1977	Spain (Severiano Ballesteros & Antonio Garrido)	591	Gary Player (SAf)	289
1978	United States (John Mahaffey & Andy North)	564	John Mahaffey	281
1979	United States (John Mahaffey & Hale Irwin)	575	Hale Irwin	285
1980	Canada (Dan Halldorson & Jim Nelford)	572	Sandy Lyle (Sco)	282
1981	Not held			
1982	Spain (Jose-Maria Canizares & Manuel Pinero)	563	Manuel Pinero	281
1983	United States (Rex Caldwell & John Cook)	565	Dave Barr (Can)	276
1984	Spain (Jose-Maria Canizares & Jose Rivero)	414*	Jose-Maria Canizares	205*
1985	Canada (Dan Halldorson & Dave Barr)	559	Howard Clark (Eng)	272
1986	Not held			

Most wins (Team): 16 United States
(Individual): 6 Jack Nicklaus, Arnold Palmer
(Individual title): 3 Jack Nicklaus
Lowest team score (four rounds): 544 Australia, 1970
Lowest individual score (four rounds): 269 Roberto de Vicenzo, 1970
* at 36 holes in 1953, 63 holes in 1963, 54 holes in 1972 and 1984

LEADING MONEY WINNERS
The following is a list of leading money winners, season-by-season, in Europe and the United States.

EUROPE

		£
1961	Bernard Hunt (UK)	4,492
1962	Peter Thomson (Aus)	5,764
1963	Bernard Hunt (UK)	7,209
1964	Neil Coles (UK)	7,890
1965	Peter Thomson (Aus)	7,011
1966	Bruce Devlin (Aus)	13,205
1967	Gay Brewer (USA)	20,235
1968	Gay Brewer (USA)	23,107
1969	Billy Casper (USA)	23,483
1970	Christy O'Connor (Ire)	31,532
1971	Gary Player (SAf)	11,281
1972	Bob Charles (NZ)	18.538
1973	Tony Jacklin (UK)	24,839
1974	Peter Oosterhuis (UK)	32,127
1975	Dale Hayes (SAf)	20,507
1976	Severiano Ballesteros (Spa)	39,504
1977	Severiano Ballesteros (Spa)	46,436
1978	Severiano Ballesteros (Spa)	54,348
1979	Sandy Lyle (UK)	49,233
1980	Greg Norman (Aus)	74,829
1981	Bernhard Langer (FRG)	95,991
1982	Sandy Lyle (UK)	86,141
1983	Nick Faldo (UK)	140,761
1984	Bernhard Langer (FRG)	160,883
1985	Sandy Lyle (UK)	199,020
1986	Severiano Ballesteros (Spa)	242,208

Most times leading winner: 4 Severiano Ballesteros

UNITED STATES
All winners from United States unless otherwise stated

		$
1934	Paul Runyan	6,767
1935	Johnny Revolta	9,543
1936	Horton Smith	7,682
1937	Harry Cooper	14,138
1938	Sam Snead	19,534
1939	Henry Picard	10,303
1940	Ben Hogan	10,655
1941	Ben Hogan	18,358
1942	Ben Hogan	13,143
1943	Statistics not compiled	
1944	Byron Nelson	37,967*
1945	Byron Nelson	63,335*
1946	Ben Hogan	42,556
1947	Jimmy Demaret	27,936
1948	Ben Hogan	32,112
1949	Sam Snead	31,593
1950	Sam Snead	35,758
1951	Lloyd Mangrum	26,088
1952	Julius Boros	37,032
1953	Lew Worsham	34,002
1954	Bob Toski	65,819
1955	Julius Boros	63,121
1956	Ted Kroll	72,835
1957	Dick Mayer	65,835
1958	Arnold Palmer	42,607
1959	Art Wall, Jnr	53,167
1960	Arnold Palmer	75,262
1961	Gary Player (SAf)	64,450
1962	Arnold Palmer	81,448
1963	Arnold Palmer	128,230
1964	Jack Nicklaus	113,284
1965	Jack Nicklaus	140,752
1966	Billy Casper	121,944
1967	Jack Nicklaus	188,998
1968	Billy Casper	205,168
1969	Frank Beard	164,707
1970	Lee Trevino	157,037
1971	Jack Nicklaus	244,490
1972	Jack Nicklaus	320,542
1973	Jack Nicklaus	308,362
1974	Johnny Miller	353,021
1975	Jack Nicklaus	298,149
1976	Jack Nicklaus	266,438
1977	Tom Watson	310,653
1978	Tom Watson	362,428
1979	Tom Watson	462,636
1980	Tom Watson	530,808
1981	Tom Kite	375,698
1982	Craig Stadler	446,462
1983	Hal Sutton	426,668
1984	Tom Watson	476,260
1985	Curtis Strange	542,321
1986	Greg Norman	653,296

* Nelson received War Bonds
Most times leading winner: 8 Jack Nicklaus

HARRY VARDON TROPHY

Awarded annually in the USA by the USPGA to the tournament player who has the lowest stroke average in PGA events of the year. In Europe a similar trophy is awarded annually to the leading player in the Order of Merit.

Most wins: Europe: 4 Peter Oosterhuis (UK) 1971-4; Severiano Ballesteros (Spa) 1976-8, 1986; 3 Bobby Locke (SAf) 1946, 1950, 1954; Bernard Hunt (UK) 1958, 1960, 1965; Sandy Lyle (UK) 1979-80, 1985
Most wins: USA: 5 Billy Casper 1960, 1963, 1965-6, 1968; Lee Trevino 1970-2, 1974, 1980; 4 Sam Snead 1938, 1949-50, 1955; Arnold Palmer 1961-2, 1964, 1967.

ALL-TIME EARNINGS

EUROPEAN TOUR

Amount		Years	Wins
£989,936	Severiano Ballesteros (Spa)	1974-86	36
£651,272	Bernhard Langer (FRG)	1976-86	15
£640,515	Sandy Lyle (UK)	1977-86	12
£540,396	Sam Torrance (UK)	1971-86	11
£539,634	Nick Faldo (UK)	1976-86	10

UNITED STATES TOUR

Amount		Years	Wins
$4,912,295	Jack Nicklaus (USA)	1962-86	71
$4,085,279	Tom Watson (USA)	1971-86	31
$3,264,291	Lee Trevino (USA)	1966-86	27
$3,249,460	Ray Floyd (USA)	1963-86	21
$2,919,491	Tom Kite (USA)	1972-86	9
$2,811,034	Hale Irwin (USA)	1968-86	17
$2,589,264	Lanny Wadkins (USA)	1971-86	15
$2,484,032	Andy Bean (USA)	1976-86	11

$2,336,891 Ben Crenshaw (USA)   1973-86   12
$2,267,789 Johnny Miller (USA)   1969-86   22

Most wins: 84 Sam Snead; 71 Jack Nicklaus; 62 Ben Hogan; 61 Arnold Palmer; 54 Byron Nelson; 51 Billy Casper; 37 Cary Middlecoff; 34 Lloyd Mangrum; 31 Jimmy Demaret, Tom Watson; 30 Horton Smith

WALKER CUP

Following the success of an international match between amateur teams from the United States and Great Britain (Great Britain and Ireland from 1981) at Hoylake in 1921 the first official series of Walker Cup matches took place the following year. The trophy was donated by George Herbert Walker, a former president of the United States Golf Association. It is a biennial event, alternately in the British Isles and the USA.

Year	Venue	Winners	Score
1922	Long Island, New York	USA	8-4
1923	St.Andrews, Scotland	USA	6½- 5½
1924	Garden City, New York	USA	9-3
1926	St.Andrews, Scotland	USA	6½-5½
1928	Chicago GC, Illinois	USA	11-1
1930	Royal St.George's, Sandwich	USA	10-2
1932	Brookline, Massachusetts	USA	9½-2½
1934	St.Andrews, Scotland	USA	9½-2½
1936	Pine Valley, New Jersey	USA	10½-1½
1938	St.Andrews, Scotland	GB	7½-4½
1947	St.Andrews, Scotland	USA	8-4
1949	Winged Foot, New York	USA	10-2
1951	Royal Birkdale, Southport	USA	7½-4½
1953	Kittansett, Massachusetts	USA	9-3
1955	St.Andrews, Scotland	USA	10-2
1957	Minikhada, Minnesota	USA	8½-3½
1959	Muirfield, Scotland	USA	9-3
1961	Seattle, Washington	USA	11-1
1963	Turnberry, Scotland	USA	14-10
1965	Baltimore, Maryland	Drawn	12-12
1967	Royal St.George's, Sandwich	USA	15-9
1969	Milwaukee, Wisconsin	USA	13-11
1971	St.Andrews, Scotland	GB	13-11
1973	Brookline, Massachusetts	USA	14-10
1975	St.Andrews, Scotland	USA	15½-8½
1977	Shinnecock Hills, New York	USA	16-8
1979	Muirfield, Scotland	USA	15½-8½
1981	Cypress Point, California	USA	15-9
1983	Royal Liverpool, Hoylake	USA	13½-10½
1985	Pine Valley, Philadelphia	USA	13-11
1987	Sunningdale, Berkshire	USA	16½-7½

Most wins: 27 United States
Most appearances: 10 Joe Carr (GB) 1947-67

WORLD AMATEUR TEAM CHAMPIONSHIP

An international team competiition for four-man teams. It has been held biennially from 1958. The winning team receives the Eisenhower Trophy, named after the former United States President Dwight D.Eisenhower. The aggregate of the three lowest scores of each team is taken into consideration when deciding the winners.

Year	Winning Team		Leading Individual	
1958	Australia	918	Bruce Devlin (Aus)	301
			Reid Jack (Sco)	301
			Bill Hyndman (USA)	301
1960	USA	834	Jack Nicklaus (USA)	269
1962	USA	854	Gary Cowan (Can)	280
1964	GB & Ireland	895	Hsieh Min Nan (For)	294
1966	Australia	877	Ronnie Shade (UK)	281
1968	USA	868	Michael Bonallack (UK)	286
			Vinnie Giles (USA)	286
1970	USA	854	Victor Regalado (Mex)	280
1972	USA	865	Tony Gresham (Aus)	285
1974	USA	888	Jerry Pate (USA)	294
			Jaime Gonzalez (Bra)	294
1976	GB & Ireland	892	Ian Hutcheon (UK)	293
			Chen Tze Ming (Tai)	293
1978	USA	873	Bob Clampett (USA)	287
1980	USA	848	Hal Sutton (USA)	276
1982	USA	859	Luis Carbonetti (Arg)	284
1984	Japan	870	Luis Carbonetti (Arg)	286
1986	Canada	838	Eduardo Herrera (Col)	275

Most wins: 9 United States
Lowest score (Team): 834 United States, 1960
Lowest score (Individual): 269 Jack Nicklaus (USA), 1960

US AMATEUR CHAMPIONSHIP

Although unofficial US Amateur championships had been held previously, the first official championship was at Newport, Rhode Island in 1895. They were held during the same week, and at the same venue, as the inaugural US Open. Originally a matchplay competition, it changed to being strokeplay in 1965, but reverted back to matchplay in 1973.

Recent winners (all USA):
1977   John Fought
1978   John Cook
1979   Mark O'Meara
1980   Hal Sutton
1981   Nathaniel Crosby
1982-3   Jay Sigel
1984   Scott Verplank
1985   Sam Randolph
1986   Buddy Alexander
1987

Most wins: 5 Bobby Jones 1924-5, 1927-8, 1930; 4 Jerome Travers 1907-8, 1912-3
Lowest score (stroke-play): 279 Lanny Wadkins , 1970
Biggest winning margin – final (match-play): 12 & 11 Charles Blair Macdonald, 1895

THE AMATEUR CHAMPIONSHIP

In 1885 Thomas Owen Potter of Hoylake organised the first British Amateur Championship at his home course – eight years after the Royal & Ancient showed little interest in running such a competition. Since 1886, however, the championships have been run by the R&A. It has always been a knockout matchplay competition and since 1983 all competitors have to play two medal rounds to reduce the field to 64.

Recent winners:
1977-8   Peter McEvoy (UK)
1979   Jay Sigel (USA)

1980 Duncan Evans (UK)
1981 Phillipe Ploujoux (Fra)
1982 Martin Thompson (UK)
1983 Andrew Parkin (UK)
1984 José-Maria Olazabal (Spa)
1985 Garth McGimpsey (UK)
1986 David Curry (UK)
1987 Paul Mayo (UK)

Most wins: 8 John Ball (UK) 1888, 1890, 1892, 1894, 1899, 1907, 1910, 1912; 5 Michael Bonallack (UK) 1961, 1965, 1968-70; 4 Harold Hilton (UK) 1900-1, 1911, 1913
Biggest winning margin (final): 14 & 13 W.Lawson Little (USA) beat Jack Wallace (UK), 1934

RECORDS

EUROPEAN AND US TOUR RECORDS

	EUROPE	UNITED STATES
Most wins in career:	36 Severiano Ballesteros (Spa) 1976-86	84 Sam Snead (USA) 1937-65
Most wins in a season:	7 Norman Von Nida (Aus) 1947 7 Flory Van Donck (Bel) 1953	18 Byron Nelson (USA) 1945
Most consecutive wins:	4 Alf Padgham (UK) 1935-6 4 Severiano Ballesteros (Spa) 1986	11 Byron Nelson 1945
Lowest score (72 holes):	260 Kel Nagle (Aus) 1961 Irish Hospital's Tournament 260 Mike Clayton (Aus) 1984 Timex Open	257 Mike Souchak (USA) 1955 Texas Open
Lowest score (18 holes):	60 Baldovino Dassu (Ita) 1971 Swiss Open	59 Al Geiberger (USA) 1977 Memphis Classic
Oldest winner:	58y Sandy Herd (UK) 1926 News of the World Matchplay	52y 312d Sam Snead 1965 Greater Greensboro Open
Youngest winner:	19y 121d Severiano Ballesteros (Spa) 1976 Dutch Open	19y 10m John McDermott (USA) 1911 US Open
Most winnings in one season:	£242,208 Severiano Ballesteros (Spa) 1986	$653,296 Greg Norman (Aus) 1986

WOMEN'S GOLF

The Women's Professional Golf Association (WPGA) was formed in the USA in 1944 and reformed in 1948 as the LPGA (Ladies for Women's).

US WOMEN'S OPEN

First held in 1946 at match-play, but at stroke-play annually from 1947.
Winners (all USA, unless stated)

Score

1946	Patty Berg	5 & 4
1947	Betty Jameson	295
1948	Mildred Zaharias	300
1949	Louise Suggs	291
1950	Mildred Zaharias	291
1951	Betsy Rawls	293
1952	Louise Suggs	284
1953	Betsy Rawls	302
1954	Mildred Zaharias	291
1955	Fay Crocker	299
1956	Kathy Cornelius	302
1957	Betsy Rawls	299
1958	Mickey Wright	290
1959	Mickey Wright	287
1960	Betsy Rawls	292
1961	Mickey Wright	293
1962	Murle Lindstrom	301
1963	Mary Mills	289
1964	Mickey Wright	290
1965	Carol Mann	290
1966	Sandra Spuzich	297
1967	Catherine Lacoste (Fra)	294
1968	Susie Berning	289
1969	Donna Caponi	294
1970	Donna Caponi	287
1971	JoAnne Carner	288
1972	Susie Berning	299
1973	Susie Berning	290
1974	Sandra Haynie	295
1975	Sandra Palmer	295
1976	JoAnne Carner	292
1977	Hollis Stacy	292
1978	Hollis Stacy	289
1979	Jerilyn Britz	284
1980	Amy Alcott	280
1981	Pat Bradley	279
1982	Janet Alex	283
1983	Jan Stephenson	290
1984	Hollis Stacy	290
1985	Kathy Baker	280
1986	Jane Geddes	287
1987	Laura Davies (UK)	285

Most wins: 4 Mickey Wright, Betsy Rawls.
Lowest aggregate: 279 Pat Bradley 1981
Biggest margin of victory: 12 strokes Mildred Zaharias 1954
Lowest round: 65 Sally Little 1978, Judy Dickinson 1985

US LPGA CHAMPIONSHIP

First held in 1955. 72 holes except for 1955, when it was match-play.

Winners (all USA)

1955	Beverly Hanson	
1956	Marlene Hagge	291
1957	Louise Suggs	285
1958	Mickey Wright	288
1959	Betsy Rawls	288

1960	Mickey Wright	292
1961	Mickey Wright	287
1962	Judy Kimball	282
1963	Mickey Wright	294
1964	Mary Mills	278
1965	Sandra Haynie	279
1966	Gloria Ehret	282
1967	Kathy Whitworth	284
1968	Sandra Post	294
1969	Betsy Rawls	293
1970	Shirley Englehorn	285
1971	Kathy Whitworth	288
1972	Kathy Ahem	293
1973	Mary Mills	288
1974	Sandra Haynie	288
1975	Kathy Whitworth	288
1976	Betty Burfeindt	287
1977	Chako Higuchi	279
1978	Nancy Lopez	275
1979	Donna Caponi	279
1980	Sally Little	285
1981	Donna Caponi	280
1982	Jan Stephenson	279
1983	Patty Sheehan	279
1984	Patty Sheehan	272
1985	Nancy Lopez	273
1986	Pat Bradley	277

Most wins: 4 Mickey Wright
Lowest aggregate: 272 Patty Sheehan 1984
Biggest margin of victory: 10 strokes Patty Sheehan 1984
Lowest round: 63 Patty Sheehan 1984

BRITISH WOMEN'S OPEN CHAMPIONSHIP

Contested annually at stroke-play from 1976, except for 1983.

Winners (UK unless stated)
1976	Jennifer Lee Smith	299
1977	Vivien Saunders	306
1978	Janet Melville	310
1979	Alison Sheard (SAf)	301
1980	Debbie Massey (USA)	294
1981	Debbie Massey (USA)	295
1982	Marta Figeuras-Dotti (Spa)	296
1984	Ayako Okamoto (Jap)	289
1985	Betsy King (USA)	300
1986	Laura Davies	283
1987	Alison Nicholas	296

LADIES' BRITISH OPEN AMATEUR CHAMPIONSHIP

First held in 1893 and contested annually at match-play.

Recent winners (UK unless stated):
1977 Angela Uzielli
1978 Edwina Kennedy (Aus)
1979 Maureen Madill (Ire)
1980 Ann Sander (USA)
1981 Belle Robertson
1982 Katrina Douglas
1983 Jill Thornhill

1984 Jody Rosenthal (USA)
1985 Lilian Behan (Ire)
1986 Marnie McGuire (NZ)
1987 Janet Collingham

Most wins: 4 Cecil Leitch 1914, 1920-1, 1926; 4 Joyce Wethered 1922, 1924-5, 1929.
Biggest winning margin in final: 9 & 7 Joyce Wethered beat Cecil Leitch 1922
Youngest winner: Marnie McGuire at 17y 112d 1986.

US WOMEN'S AMATEUR CHAMPIONSHIP

Held at stroke-play in 1895, and annually at match-play from 1896.

Most wins: 6 Glenna Vare (née Collett) 1922, 1925, 1928-30, 1935: 5 JoAnne Carner (née Gunderson) 1957, 1960, 1962, 1966, 1968.
Biggest winning margin in final: 14 & 13 Anne Quast beat Phyllis Preuss 1961.

US LPGA TOURNAMENT RECORDS

Lowest score – 72 holes: 268 Nancy Lopez 1985 Henredon Classic, Willow Creek GC, NC.
Lowest score – 18 holes: 62 Mickey Wright 1964 Tall City Open, Hogan Park CC, Texas
Most consecutive wins: 4 Mickey Wright 1962 and in 1963, Kathy Whitworth 1969. Nancy Lopez won five successive tournaments that she contested 1978.
Most wins in a season: 13 Mickey Wright 1963
Oldest winner: 46yr 163d Joanne Carner 1985 Safeco Classic
Youngest winner: 18yr 14d Marlene Hagge 1952 Sarasota Open

ALL-TIME CAREER MONEY LEADERS as at 31.12.86
Money	Wins	
$2,286,218 Pat Bradley	21	1974-86
$2,013,991 JoAnne Carner	42	1970-86
$1,806,648 Amy Alcott	26	1975-86
$1,711,078 Nancy Lopez	34	1977-86
$1,666,762 Kathy Whitworth	88	1959-86
$1,339,444 Donna Caponi	24	1965-86
$1,309,444 Patty Sheehan	17	1980-86
$1,301,110 Beth Daniel	14	1979-86

Others with more than 40 wins: 82 Mickey Wright, 55 Betsy Rawls, 50 Louise Suggs, 42 Sandra Haynie, 41 Patty Berg.

The first to win more than the following amounts in a season:
$20,000: Marlene Hagge $20,235 1956
$50,000: Kathy Whitworth $65,063 1972
$100,000: Judy Rankin $150,734 1976
$200,000: Beth Daniel $231,000 1980
$300,000: Nancy Lopez $416,472 1985
Record: Pat Bradley $492,021 1986.

Most seasons as leading money winner: 8 Kathy Whitworth 1965-8, 1970-3; 4 Mildred 'Babe' Zaharias 1948-51; 4 Mickey Wright 1961-4.

CURTIS CUP

A biennial team competition involving women's teams from the United States and Great Britain and Ireland. It was first held at Wentworth in 1932 and is named after American sisters Margaret and Harriot Curtis.

Year	Venue	Winners	Score
1932	Wentworth, Surrey	USA	5½-3½
1934	Chevy Chase, Maryland	USA	6½-2½
1936	Gleneagles, Scotland	Drawn	4½-4½
1938	Essex, Massachusetts	USA	5½-3½
1948	Royal Birkdale, Southport	USA	6½-2½
1950	Buffalo CC, New York	USA	7½-1½
1952	Muirfield, Scotland	GB&I	5-4
1954	Merion, Pennsylvania	USA	6-3
1956	Prince's, Sandwich	GB&I	5-4
1958	Brae Burn, Massachusetts	Drawn	4½-4½
1960	Lindrick, Sheffield	USA	6½-2½
1962	Broadmoor, Colorado Springs	USA	8-1
1964	Royal Porthcawl, Wales	USA	10½-7½
1966	Hot Springs, Virginia	USA	13-5
1968	Royal County Down, Ireland	USA	10½-7½
1970	Brae Burn, Massachusetts	USA	11½-6½
1972	Western Gailes, Scotland	USA	10-8
1974	San Francisco, California	USA	13-5
1976	Royal Lytham, Lancashire	USA	11½-6½
1978	Apawamis, New York	USA	12-6
1980	St.Pierre, Chepstow	USA	13-5
1982	Denver, Colorado	USA	14½-3½
1984	Muirfield, Scotland	USA	9½-8½
1986	Prairie Dunes, Kansas	GB&I	13-5

Most wins: 19 United States
Most appearances: 8 Mary McKenna (GB&I) 1970-84, 7 Jessie Valentine (née Anderson) (GB&I) 1936-58

WOMEN'S WORLD AMATEUR TEAM CHAMPIONSHIP

Contested biennially from 1964 by teams of three for the Espirito Santo Trophy.

Wins:
9 USA 1966, 1968, 1970, 1972, 1974, 1976, 1980, 1982, 1984
1 France 1964, Australia 1978, Spain 1986.

Lowest aggregate total: 579 USA 1982.
Lowest individual aggregate: 284 Marie-Laurede Lorenzi (Fra) 1986

GREYHOUND RACING

The first greyhound meeting took place at Hendon, North London in September 1876, but the sport became popular following the perfecting of the mechanical hare by Owen Patrick Smith in the USA in 1919. Smith and George Sawyer formed the International Greyhound Racing Association at Tulsa in 1920. The oldest greyhound track in the world, still in operation, is the St Petersburg Kennel Club, at St Petersburg, Florida, opened on 3 Jan 1925. The first meeting with a mechanical hare in Great Britain was at Belle Vue, Manchester, on 24 July 1926, in which year the Greyhound Racing Association was formed.

DERBY

The most prestigious race in British greyhound racing, the Derby was instituted in 1927 and run over 500 yards at the White City. Between 1928-74 it was over 525 yards, and since 1975 over 500 metres. The 1940 race was at Harringay and since 1985, following the closure of the White City, all races have been at Wimbledon.

Winners:

1927	Entry Badge	1960	Duleek Dandy
1928	Boher Ash	1961	Palm's Printer
1929-30	Mick the Miller	1962	The Grand Canal
1931	Seldom Led	1963	Lucky Boy Boy
1932	Wild Woolley	1964	Hack Up Chieftain
1933	Future Cutlet	1965	Chittering Clapton
1934	Davesland	1966	Faithful Hope
1935	Greta Ranee	1967	Tric-Trac
1936	Fine Jubilee	1968	Camera Flash
1937	Wattle Bark	1969	Sand Star
1938	Lone Keel	1970	John Silver
1939	Highland Rum	1971	Dolores Rocket
1940	G.R.Archduke	1972-3	Patricia's Hope
1945	Ballyhennessy Seal	1974	Jimsun
1946	Mondays News	1975	Tartan Khan
1947	Trevs Perfection	1976	Mutts Silver
1948	Priceless Border	1977	Balliniska Band
1949	Narrogar Ann	1978	Lacca Champion
1950	Ballmac Ball	1979	Sarah's Bunny
1951	Ballylanigan Tanist	1980	Indian Joe
1952	Endless Gossip	1981	Parkdown Jet
1953	Daws Dancer	1982	Laurie's Panther
1954	Pauls Fun	1983	I'm Slippy
1955	Rushton Mack	1984	Whisper Wishes
1956	Dunmore King	1985	Pagan Swallow
1957	Ford Spartan	1986	Tico
1958	Pigalle Wonder	1987	Signal Spark
1959	Mile Bush Pride		

Most wins: 2 Mick the Miller, Patricia's Hope

GRAND NATIONAL

The first of the year's classics, for hurdlers, was first run in 1927 at the White City. Since 1985 it has been run at Hall Green, Birmingham. 1927-74 run over 500 yards, since 1975 over 500 metres (five flights).

Winners:

1927	Bonzo	1947	Baytown Pigeon
1928	Cormorant	1948	Joves Reason
1929	Levator	1949-50	Blossom of
1930	Stylish Cutlet		Annagura
1931	Rule the Roost	1951	XPDNC
1932	Long Hop	1952	Whistling Laddie
1933	Scapegoat	1953	Denver Berwick
1934	Lemonition	1954	Prince Lawrence
1935	Quarter Day	1955	Barrowside
1936	Kilganny Bridge	1956	Blue Sand
1937	Flying Wedge	1957	Tanyard Tulip
1938	Juvenile Classic	1958	Fodda Champion
1939	Valiant Bob	1959	Prince Poppit
1940	Juvenile Classic	1960	Bruff Chariot
1946	Barry from Limerick	1961	Ballinatona Special

1962 Corsica Reward	1976 Weston Pete
1963 Indoor Sport	1977 Salerno
1964 Two Aces	1978-9 Top O' The Tide
1965 I'm Crazy	1980 Gilt Edge Flyer
1966 Halfpenny King	1981 Bobcol
1967 The Grange Santa	1982 Face The Mutt
1968 Ballintore Tiger	1983 Sir Winston
1969 Tony's Friend	1984 Kilcoe Foxy
1970-2 Sherry's Prince	1985 Seaman's Star
1973 Killone Flash	1986 Castelyons Cash
1974 Shanney's Darkie	1987 Cavan Town
1975 Pier Hero	

Most wins: 3 Sherry's Pride; 2 Blossom of Annagura, Top O' The Tide

THE LAURELS

An early-season flat race classic it was first held at Wimbledon over 525 yards in 1930. When distances went metric in 1975 it was reduced to 460 metres.

Winners:

1930 Kilbrean Boy	1961 Clonalvy Pride
1931 Future Cutlet	1962 Turturama
1932 Beef Cutlet	1963 Dalcassion Son
1933 Wild Woolley	1964-5 Conna Count
1934 Brilliant Bob	1966 Super Fame
1935 Kitshine	1967 Carry on Oregon
1936 Top O' The Carlow Road	1968 Ambiguous
	1969 Ardine Flame
1937-8 Ballyhennessy Sandhills	1970 Sole Aim
	1971 Black Andrew
1939 Musical Duke	1972 Cricket Bunny
1940 April Burglar	1973 Black Banjo
1945 Burhill Moon	1974 Over Protected
1946 Shannon Shore	1975 Pineapple Grand
1947 Rimmells Black	1976 Xmas Holiday
1948 Good Worker	1977 Greenfield Fox
1949-50 Ballymac Ball	1978 Jet Control
1951 Ballylanigan Tanist	1979 Another Splatter
1952 Endless Gossip	1980 Flying Pursuit
1953 Polonius	1981 Echo Spark
1954 Coolkill Chieftain	1982 Laurie's Panther
1955-6 Duet Leader	1983 Darkie Fli
1957 Ford Spartan	1984 Amenhotet
1958 Granthamian	1985 Ballygroman Jim
1959 Mighty Hassan	1986 Mollifrend Lucky
1960 Dunstown Paddy	

Most wins: 2 Ballyhennessy Sandhills, Ballymac Ball, Duet Leader, Conna Count

SCURRY GOLD CUP

Known as the 'Sprinter's Classic'. It was first run in 1928 and immediately accorded 'Classic' status. Run at Clapton over 400 yards 1928-74, at Slough over 442 metres since 1975.

Winners:

1928 Cruseline Boy	1934 Brilliant Bob
1929 Loose Card	1935 Jack's Joke
1930 Barlock	1936 Mitzvah
1931 Brave Enough	1937 Hexham Bridge
1932 Experts Boast	1938 Orluck's Best
1933 Creamery Boarder	1939 Silver Wire

Ballyregan Bob, 32 successive wins and 16 track records. (All-Sports)

1945 Country Life	1966 Geddy's Blaze
1946 Mischievous Manhattan	1967 Carry On Oregan
1947 Rimmell's Black	1968 Foyle Tonic
1948 Local Interprize	1969 Ace of Trumps
1949 Burndennett Brook	1970-1 Don't Gambol
1950 Gortnagory	1972 Cricket Bunny
1951 Defence Leader	1973 Casa Miel
1952 Monachdy Girlie	1974 Westmead Valley
1953 Rolling Mike	1975 Langnor Lad
1954 Demon King	1976 Xmas Holiday
1955 Chance Me Paddy	1977 Wired to Moon
1956 Belinga's Customer	1978 Greenfield Fox
1957 Lisbrook Chieftain	1979 Northway Point
1958 Beware Champ	1980 Willing Slave
1959-60 Gorey Airways	1981 Smokey
1961 Palm's Printer	1982-4 Yankee Express
1962 Hi Darkie	1985 Daley's Gold
1963 Lucky Joan	1986 Mollifrend Lucky
1964 Salthill Sand	1987 Rapid Mover
1965 After You	

Most wins: 3 Yankee Express; 2 Gorey Airways, Don't Gambol

GREYHOUND RECORDS

Highest speed: 41.72 mph (67.14 km/h) by The Shoe at Richmond, NSW, Australia, 25 Apr 1968
Most career wins: 143 by JR's Ripper (USA) 1982-6
Most consecutive wins: 32 Ballyregan Bob (UK) 1985-6

GYMNASTICS

The ancient Greeks and Romans were exponents of gymnastics and excelled at the Ancient Olympic Games over 2000 years ago. Modern techniques, however, were developed in Germany towards the latter part of the 18th century and the first teacher of modern gymnastics was Johann Friedrich Simon at Basedow's School, Dessau, in 1776. Regarded as the father figure of modern gymnastics was Friedrich Jahn, who founded the Turnverein in Berlin in 1811. In Britain the Amateur Gymnastics Association was formed in 1888. The International Gymnastics Federation was formed in 1891.

APPARATUS

MEN

Parallel bars – two bars of round cross section, 350cm long, set 42cm apart, and supported 160cm above the floor on uprights fixed to a broad stable base.

Horizontal bar – bar 240cm long supported 255cm above the ground by an upright at each end and braced with wires.

Pommel horse – similar to vaulting horse; 110cm high, 163cm long, but with two raised handles at the centre.

Rings – two rigid rings 18cm in diameter suspended 250cm from the floor by two wires 50cm apart attached to a frame, braced with wires, 550 cm high.

Horse vault – Horse is 163cm long, 135cm high. Springboard is 120cm long, placed in line with the long side of the horse.

MEN & WOMEN

Floor exercises – on a 12m square area

WOMEN

Asymmetrical bars – two horizontal bars 350cm long, arranged parallel to one another but at different heights. Lower is 150cm and upper 230cm above the floor. Each is supported by an upright at each end, and these two frames are placed 43cm apart.

Beam – rigid beam of wood 5m long mounted horizontally, 10cm wide at 120cm above the floor.

Horse vault – Horse is 163cm long 120cm high. Springboard as for men's.

MODERN RHYTHMIC GYMNASTICS

Modern Rhythmic Gymnastics world championships were first held in 1963 and was first included in the Olympics in 1984. In this women's sport the disciplines are characterized by the handling of light portable objects, skipping ropes, hoops, clubs, ribbons and balls, to musical accompaniment.

OLYMPIC GAMES

Gymnastics was included in the first Modern Olympics of 1896. A women's competition was first included in 1928.

Winners:

MEN

TEAM

5 Japan 1960, 1964, 1968, 1972, 1976
4 Italy 1912, 1920, 1924, 1932
3 USSR 1952, 1956, 1980
2 USA 1904 (TG Philadelphia), 1984
1 Norway 1906; Sweden 1908; Switzerland 1928; Germany 1936; Finland 1948

INDIVIDUAL COMBINED EXERCISES

1900 Gustave Sandras (Fra)
1904 Julius Lenhart (Aut) §
1906 Pierre Paysse (Fra) *
1906 Pierre Paysse (Fra) *
1908 Alberto Braglia (Ita)
1912 Alberto Braglia (Ita)
1920 Giorgio Zampori (Ita)
1924 Leon Stukelj (Yug)
1928 Georges Miez (Swi)
1932 Romeo Neri (Ita)
1936 Alfred Schwarzmann (Ger)
1948 Veikko Huhtanen (Fin)
1952 Viktor Chukarin (USSR)
1956 Viktor Chukarin (USSR)
1960 Boris Shakhlin (USSR)
1964 Yukio Endo (Jap)
1968 Sawao Kato (Jap)
1972 Sawao Kato (Jap)
1976 Nikolay Andrianov (USSR)
1980 Aleksandr Ditiatin (USSR)
1984 Koji Gushiken (Jap)

* Two competitions in 1906, 5 events and 6 events

§ member of USA Philadelphia Club who won team event

FLOOR EXERCISES

1932 István Pelle (Hun)
1936 Georges Miez (Swi)
1948 Ferenc Pataki (Hun)
1952 William Thoresson (Swe)
1956 Valentin Muratov (USSR)
1960 Nobuyuki Aihara (Jap)
1964 Franco Menichelli (Ita)
1968 Sawao Kato (Jap)
1972 Nikolay Andrianov (USSR)
1976 Nikolay Andrianov (USSR)
1980 Roland Brückner (GDR)
1984 Li Ning (Chn)

PARALLEL BARS

1896 Alfred Flatow (Ger)
1904 George Eyser (USA)
1924 August Güttinger (Swi)
1928 Ladislav Vácha (Cs)
1932 Romeo Neri (Ita)
1936 Konrad Frey (Ger)
1948 Michael Reusch (Swi)
1952 Hans Eugster (Swi)
1956 Viktor Chukarin (USSR)
1960 Boris Shakhlin (USSR)
1964 Yukio Endo (Jap)
1968 Akinori Nakayama (Jap)
1972 Sawao Kato (Jap)
1976 Sawao Kato (Jap)
1980 Aleksandr Tkachev (USSR)
1984 Bart Conner (USA)

POMMEL HORSE

1896 Louis Zutter (Swi)
1904 Anton Heida (USA)
1924 Josef Wilhelm (Swi)
1928 Hermann Hänggi (Swi)
1932 István Pelle (Hun)
1936 Konrad Frey (Ger)

1948 Paavo Aaltonen (Fin), Veikko Huhtanen (Fin) & Heikki Savolainen (Fin)
1952 Viktor Chukarin (USSR)
1956 Boris Shakhlin (USSR)
1960 Eugen Ekman (Fin) & Boris Shakhlin (USSR)
1964 Miroslav Cerar (Yug)
1968 Miroslav Cerar (Yug)
1972 Viktor Klimenko (USSR)
1976 Zoltán Magyar (Hun)
1980 Zoltán Magyar (Hun)
1984 Li Ning (Chn) & Peter Vidmar (USA)

RINGS

1896 Ioannis Mitropoulos (Gre)
1904 Hermann Glass (USA)
1924 Francesco Martino (Ita)
1928 Leon Stukelj (Yug)
1932 George Gulack (USA)
1936 Alois Hudec (Cs)
1948 Karl Frei (Swi)
1952 Grant Shaginyan (USSR)
1956 Albert Azaryan (USSR)
1960 Albert Azaryan (USSR)
1964 Takuji Hayata (Jap)
1968 Akinori Nakayama (Jap)
1972 Akinori Nakayama (Jap)
1976 Nikolay Andrianov (USSR)
1980 Aleksandr Ditiatin (USSR)
1984 Koji Gushiken (Jap) & Li Ning (Chn)

HORIZONTAL BAR

1896 Hermann Weingärtner (Ger)
1904 Anton Heida (USA) & Edward Hennig (USA)
1924 Leon Stukelj (Yug)
1928 Georges Miez (Swi)
1932 Dallas Bixler (USA)
1936 Aleksanteri Saarvala (Fin)
1948 Josef Stadler (Swi)

1952 Jack Günthard (Swi)
1956 Takashi Ono (Jap)
1960 Takashi Ono (Jap)
1964 Boris Shakhlin (USSR)
1968 Mikhail Voronin (USSR) &
Akinori Nakayama (Jap)
1972 Mitsuo Tsukahara (Jap)
1976 Mitsuo Tsukahara (Jap)
1980 Stoyan Deltchev (Bul)
1984 Shinji Morisue (Jap)

HORSE VAULT
1896 Carl Schumann (Ger)
1904 Anton Heida (USA) & George
Eyser (USA)
1924 Frank Kriz (USA)
1928 Eugen Mack (Swi)
1932 Savino Guglielmetti (Ita)
1936 Alfred Schwarzmann (Ger)
1948 Paavo Aaltonen (Fin)
1952 Viktor Chukarin (USSR)
1956 Helmuth Bantz (FRG) &
Valentin Muratov (USSR)
1960 Takashi Ono (Jap) & Boris
Shakhlin (USSR)
1964 Haruhiro Yamashita (Jap)
1968 Mikhail Voronin (USSR)
1972 Klaus Köste (GDR)
1976 Nikolay Andrianov (USSR)
1980 Nikolay Andrianov (USSR)
1984 Lou Yun (Chn)

WOMEN
TEAM
8 USSR 1952, 1956, 1960, 1964,
1968, 1972, 1976, 1980
1 Netherlands 1928; Germany
1936; Czechoslovakia 1948;
Romania 1984

INDIVIDUAL COMBINED
EXERCISES
1952 Maria Gorokhovskaya (USSR)
1956 Larissa Latynina (USSR)
1960 Larissa Latynina (USSR)
1964 Vera Cáslavská (Cs)
1968 Vera Cáslavská (Cs)
1972 Lyudmila Tourischeva (USSR)
1976 Nadia Comaneci (Rom)
1980 Yelena Davydova (USSR)
1984 Mary Lou Retton (USA)

ASYMMETRICAL BARS
1952 Margit Korondi (Hun)
1956 Ágnes Keleti (Hun)
1960 Polina Astakhova (USSR)
1964 Polina Astakhova (USSR)
1968 Vera Cáslavská (Cs)
1972 Karin Janz (GDR)
1976 Nadia Comaneci (Rom)
1980 Maxi Gnauck (GDR)
1984 Ma Yanhong (Chn) & Julianne
McNamara (USA)

BALANCE BEAM
1952 Nina Bocharova (USSR)
1956 Ágnes Keleti (Hun)
1960 Eva Bosakova (Cs)
1964 Vera Cáslavská (Cs)
1968 Natalya Kuchinskaya (USSR)
1972 Olga Korbut (USSR)
1976 Nadia Comaneci (Rom)
1980 Nadia Comaneci (Rom)
1984 Simona Pauca (Rom) &
Ecaterina Szabo (Rom)

FLOOR EXERCISES
1952 Ágnes Keleti (Hun)
1956 Larissa Latynina (USSR) &
Ágnes Keleti (Hun)
1960 Larissa Latynina (USSR)
1964 Larissa Latynina (USSR)
1968 Larissa Petrik (USSR) & Vera
Cáslavská (Cs)
1972 Olga Korbut (USSR)
1976 Nelli Kim (USSR)
1980 Nelli Kim (USSR) & Nadia
Comaneci (Rom)
1984 Ecaterina Szabo (Rom)

HORSE VAULT
1952 Yekaterina Kalinchuk (USSR)
1956 Larissa Latynina (USSR)
1960 Margarita Nikolayeva (USSR)
1964 Vera Cáslavská (Cs)
1968 Vera Cáslavská (Cs)
1972 Karin Janz (GDR)
1976 Nelli Kim (USSR)
1980 Natalya Shaposhnikova (USSR)
1984 Ecaterina Szabo (Rom)

RHYTHMIC GYMNASTICS
1984 Fung Lori (Can)

Olga Korbut (All-Sport)

DISCONTINUED EVENTS
MEN

PARALLEL BARS (Team)
1896 Germany

HORIZONTAl BARS (Team)
1896 Germany

ROPE CLIMBING
1896 Nicolaos Andriakopoulos (Gre)
1904 George Eyser (USA)
1906 Georgios Aliprantis (Gre)
1924 Bedrich Supcik (Cs)
1932 Raymond Bass (USA)

CLUB SWINGING
1904 Edward Hennig (USA)
1932 George Roth (USA)

TUMBLING
1932 Rowland Wolfe (USA)

NINE EVENT COMPETITION
1904 Adolf Spinnler (Swi)

TRIATHLON
(100 yards, long jump, shot)
1904 Max Emmerich (USA)

SEVEN EVENT COMPETITION
1904 Anton Heida (USA)

SIDEHORSE VAULT
1924 Albert Séguin (Fra)

SWEDISH SYSTEM (Team)
1912 Sweden
1920 Sweden

FREE SYSTEM (Team)
1912 Norway
1920 Denmark

WOMEN

PORTABLE APPARATUS (Team)
1952 Sweden
1956 Hungary

MOST MEDALS

MEN

Total	Gymnast	Gold	Silver	Bronze	Years
15	Nikolay Andrianov (USSR)	7	5	3	1972-80
13	Boris Shakhlin (USSR)	7	4	2	1956-64
13	Takashi Ono (Jap)	5	4	4	1956-64
12	Sawao Kato (Jap)	8	3	1	1968-76
11	Viktor Chukarin (USSR)	7	3	1	1952-6
10	Akinori Nakayama (Jap)	6	2	2	1968-72
10	Aleksandr Ditiatin (USSR)	3	6	1	1976-80
9	Mitsuo Tsukahara (Jap)	5	1	3	1968-76
9	Elizo Kenmotsu (Jap)	3	3	3	1968-76
9	Mikhail Voronin (USSR)	2	6	1	1968-72
9	Yuriy Titov (USSR)	1	5	3	1956-64

WOMEN

Total	Gymnast	Gold	Silver	Bronze	Years
18	Larissa Latynina (USSR)	9	5	4	1956-64
11	Vera Cáslavská (Cs)	7	4	0	1964-8
10	Agnes Kaleti (Hun)	5	3	2	1952-6
10	Polina Astakhova (USSR)	5	2	3	1956-64
9	Nadia Comaneci (Rom)	5	3	1	1976-80
9	Lyudmila Tourischeva (USSR)	4	3	2	1968-76

Also 4 gold medals:

MEN Georges Miesz (Swi), Anton Heida (USA), Yukio Endo (Jap), Giorgio Zampori (Ita), Valentin Muratov (USSR)

WOMEN Olga Korbut (USSR), Nellie Kim (USSR)

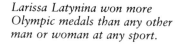

Larissa Latynina won more Olympic medals than any other man or woman at any sport.

WORLD CHAMPIONSHIPS

First held for men at Antwerp in 1903 and every two years until 1913. They were re-introduced in 1922 and held every four years with the Olympic champions also being the world champions. Since 1979 they have reverted to being held biennially. The first women's championships were held in 1934.

Winners

MEN

TEAM

7 Czechoslovakia 1907, 1911, 1913, 1922, 1926, 1930, 1938
5 USSR 1954, 1958, 1979, 1981, 1985; Japan 1962, 1966, 1970, 1974, 1978
3 France 1903, 1905, 1909
1 Switzerland 1950, China 1983
There was no team competition in 1934.

COMBINED EXERCISES

1903 Joseph Martinez (Fra/Alg)
1905 Marcel Lalu (Fra)
1907 Josef Cada (Cs)
1909 Marco Torrès (Fra)
1911 F Steiner (Cs)
1913 Marco Torrès (Fra)
1922 Peter Sumi (Yug) & Frantisek Pechacek (Cs)
1926 Peter Sumi (Yug)
1930 Josip Primozic (Yug)
1934 Eugen Mack (Swi)
1938 Jan Gajdos (Cs)
1950 Walter Lehmann (Swi)
1954 Viktor Chukarin (USSR)
1958 Boris Shakhlin (USSR)
1962 Yuriy Titov (USSR)
1966 Mikhail Voronin (USSR)
1970 Eizo Kenmotsu (Jap)
1974 Shigeru Kasamatsu (Jap)
1978 Nikolay Andrianov (USSR)
1979 Aleksandr Ditiatin (USSR)
1981 Yuriy Korolev (USSR)
1983 Dmitriy Belozerchev (USSR)
1985 Yuriy Korolev (USSR)

FLOOR EXERCISES

1913 Giorgio Zampori (Ita) & V Rabic (Cs)
1930 Josip Primozic (Yug)
1934 Georges Miesz (Swi)
1938 Jan Gajdos (Cs)
1950 Josef Stadler (Swi)
1954 Valentin Muratov (USSR) & Masao Takemoto (Jap)
1958 Masao Takemoto (Jap)
1962 Nobuyuki Aihara (Jap) & Yukio Endo (Jap)
1966 Akinori Nakayama (Jap)
1970 Akinori Nakayama (Jap)
1974 Shigeru Kasamatsu (Jap)
1978 Kurt Thomas (USA)
1979 Kurt Thomas (USA) & Roland Bruckner (GDR)

1981 Yuriy Korolev (USSR) & Li Yuejiu (Chn)
1983 Tong Fei (Chn)
1985 Tong Fei (Chn)

HIGH BAR

1903 Joseph Martinez (Fra/Alg) & N Pissie (Fra)
1905 Marcel Lalu (Fra)
1907 Georges Charmoille (Fra) & Frantisek Erben (Cs)
1909 Joseph Martinez (Fra), Josef Cada & Frantisek Erben (Cs)
1911 Josef Cada (Cs)
1913 Josef Cada (Cs)
1922 Miroslav Klinger (Cs)
1926 Leon Stukelj (Yug)
1930 István Pelle (Hun)
1934 R Winter (Ger)
1950 Paavo Aaltonen (Fin)
1954 Valentin Mouratov (USSR)
1958 Boris Shakhlin (USSR)
1962 Takashi Ono (Jap)
1966 Akinori Nakayama (Jap)
1970 Eizo Kenmotsu (Jap)
1974 Eberhard Gienger (FRG)
1978 Shigeru Kasamatsu (Jap)
1979 Kurt Thomas (USA)
1981 Aleksandr Tkachev (USSR)

1983 Dmitriy Belozerchev (USSR)
1985 Tong Fei (Chn)

PARALLEL BARS

1903 Joseph Martinez (Fra/Alg) &
     Francois Hentges (Lux)
1905 Joseph Martinez (Fra/Alg)
1907 Jos Lux (Fra)
1909 Joseph Martinez (Fra/Alg)
1911 Giorgio Zampori (Ita)
1913 Giorgio Zampori (Ita) & Guido
     Boni (Ita)
1922 Leon Stukelj (Yug), Stane
     Derganc (Yug), N Jindrich (Cs),
     Miroslav Klinger (Cs) & Vlado
     Simoncic (Yug)
1926 Ladislav Vácha (Cs)
1930 Josip Primozic (Yug)
1934 Eugen Mack (Swi)
1938 Michael Reusch (Swi)
1950 Hans Eugster (Swi)
1954 Viktor Chukarin (USSR)
1958 Boris Shakhlin (USSR)
1962 Miroslav Cerar (Yug)
1966 Sergey Diomidov (USSR)
1970 Akinori Nakayama (Jap)
1974 Eizo Kenmotsu (Jap)
1978 Eizo Kenmotsu (Jap)
1979 Bart Conner (USA)
1981 Aleksandr Ditiatin (USSR) &
     Koji Gushiken (Jap)
1983 Vladimir Artemov (USSR) &
     Lou Yun (Chn)
1985 Silvio Kroll (GDR) & Valentin
     Mogilnyi (USSR)

VAULT

1903 N Dejaeghere (Fra), Jos Lux
     (Fra) & N Thysen (Hol)
1905 N Dejaeghere (Fra)
1907 Frantisek Erben (Cs)
1913 Karel Stary (Cs), Ben Sadoun
     (Fra), O Palazzi (Ita) & Stane
     Vidmar (Yug)
1934 Eugen Mack (Swi)
1950 Ernst Gebendinger (Swi)
1954 Leo Sotornik (Cs)
1958 Yuriy Titov (USSR)
1962 Premysel Krbec (Cs)
1966 Haruhiro Matsuda (Jap)
1970 Mitsuo Tsukahara (Jap)
1974 Shigeru Kasamatsu (Jap)
1978 Junichi Shimizu (Jap)
1979 Aleksandr Ditiatin (USSR)
1981 Ralf-Peter Hemmann (GDR)
1983 Artur Akopian (USSR)
1985 Yuriy Korolev (USSR)

RINGS

1903 Joseph Martinez (Fra/Alg) &
     Jos Lux (Lux)
1909 Guido Romano (Ita) & Marco
     Torres (Fra)
1911 F Steiner (Cs), D Follacci (Fra)
     & Pietro Bianchi (Ita)

1913 Laurent Grech (Fra), Marco
     Torres (Fra), Giorgio Zampori
     (Ita) & Guido Boni (Ita)
1922 Laurent Karasek (Cs), N Maly
     (Cs), Leon Stukelj (Yug) &
     Peter Sumi (Yug)
1926 Leon Stukelj (Yug)
1930 Emanuel Löffler (Cs)
1934 Alois Hudec (Cs)
1938 Alois Hudec (Cs)
1950 Walter Lehmann (Swi)
1954 Albert Azarian (USSR)
1958 Albert Azarian (USSR)
1962 Yuriy Titov (USSR)
1966 Mikhail Voronin (USSR)
1970 Akinori Nakayama (Jap)
1974 Nikolay Andrianov (USSR) &
     Dan Grecu (Rom)
1978 Nikolay Andrianov (USSR)
1979 Aleksandr Ditiatin (USSR)
1981 Aleksandr Ditiatin (USSR)
1983 Dmitriy Belozerchev (USSR) &
     Koji Gushiken (Jap)
1985 Li Ning (Chn) & Yuriy Korolev
     (USSR)

POMMEL HORSE

1911 O Palazzi (Ita)
1913 Giorgio Zampori (Ita), N
     Aubrey (Fra) & O Palazzi (Ita)
1922 Miroslav Klinger (Cs), N
     Jindrich (Cs) & Leon Stukelj
     (Yug)
1926 N Karafiat (Cs)
1930 Josip Primozic (Yug)
1934 Eugen Mack (Swi)
1938 Michael Reusch (Swi) &
     Vratislav Petracek (Cs)
1950 Josef Stalder (Swi)
1954 Grant Chaginyan (USSR)
1958 Boris Shakhlin (USSR)
1962 Miroslav Cerar (Yug)
1966 Miroslav Cerar (Yug)
1970 Miroslav Cerar (Yug)
1974 Zoltán Magyar (Hun)
1978 Zoltán Magyar (Hun)
1979 Zoltán Magyar (Hun)
1981 Michael Nikolay (GDR) & Li
     Xiaoping (Chn)
1983 Dmitriy Belozerchev (USSR)
1985 Valentin Mogilnyi (USSR)

WOMEN

TEAM

9 USSR 1954, 1958, 1962, 1970,
  1974, 1978, 1981, 1983, 1985
3 Czechoslovakia 1934, 1938, 1966
1 Sweden 1950; Romania 1979

COMBINED EXERCISES

1934 Vlasta Dekanová (Cs)
1938 Vlasta Dekanová (Cs)
1950 Helena Rakoczy (Pol)

1954 Galina Roudiko (USSR)
1958 Larissa Latynina (USSR)
1962 Larissa Latynina (USSR)
1966 Vera Cáslavská (Cs)
1970 Lyudmila Tourischeva (USSR)
1974 Lyudmila Tourischeva (USSR)
1978 Yelena Mukhina (USSR)
1979 Nelli Kim (USSR)
1981 Olga Bicherova (USSR)
1983 Natalya Yurchenko (USSR)
1985 Oksana Omelianchuk (USSR) &
     Yelena Shushunova (USSR)

PARALLEL BARS

1938 Vlasta Dekanová (Cs)

VAULT

1938 Matylda Pálfyová (Cs) & Marta
     Majowska (Pol)
1950 Helena Rakoczy (Pol)
1954 Tamara Manina (USSR) &
     Anna Petersson (Swe)
1958 Larissa Latynina (USSR)
1962 Vera Cáslavská (Cs)
1966 Vera Cáslabská (Cs)
1970 Erika Zuchold (GDR)
1974 Olga Korbut (USSR)
1978 Nelli Kim (USSR)
1979 Dumitrata Turner (Rom)
1981 Maxi Gnauck (GDR)
1983 Boriana Stoyanova (Bul)
1985 Yelena Shushunova (USSR)

BEAM

1938 Vlasta Dekanová (Cs)
1950 Helena Rakoczy (Pol)
1954 Keiko Tanaka (Jap)
1958 Larissa Latynina (USSR)
1962 Eva Bosakova (Cs)
1966 Natalya Kuchinskaya (USSR)
1970 Erika Zuchold (GDR)
1974 Lyudmila Tourischeva (USSR)
1978 Nadia Comaneci (Rom)
1979 Vera Cerna (Cs)
1981 Maxi Gnauck (GDR)
1983 Olga Mostepanova (USSR)
1985 Daniela Silivas (Rom)

FLOOR EXERCISES

1938 Matylda Pálfyová (Cs)
1950 Helena Rakoczy (Pol)
1954 Tamara Manina (USSR)
1958 Eva Bosakova (Cs)
1962 Larissa Latynina (USSR)
1966 Natalya Kuchinskaya (USSR)
1970 Lyudmila Tourischeva (USSR)
1974 Lyudmila Tourischeva (USSR)
1978 Nelli Kim (USSR) &
     Yelena Mukhina (USSR)
1979 Emilia Eberle (Rom)
1981 Natalya Ilyenko (USSR)
1983 Ecaterina Szabo (Rom)
1985 Oksana Omelianchuk (USSR)

ASYMMETRIC BARS

1950 Helena Rakoczy (Pol)

1954 Ágnes Kaleti (Hun)
1958 Larissa Latynina (USSR)
1962 Irina Pervuschina (USSR)
1966 Natalya Kuchinskaya (USSR)
1970 Karin Janz (GDR)
1974 Annelore Zinke (GDR)
1978 Marcia Frederick (USA)
1979 Ma Yan Hong (Chn) & Maxi
      Gnauck (GDR)
1981 Maxi Gnauck (GDR)
1983 Maxi Gnauck (GDR)
1985 Gabriela Fahnrich (GDR)

MODERN RHYTHMIC GYMNASTICS

Team winners:
5 Bulgaria 1969, 1971, 1981, 1983, 1985
4 USSR 1967, 1973, 1977, 1979
1 Italy 1975

Individual – Overall
1963 Lyudmila Savinkova (USSR)
1965 Hana Micechova (Cs)
1967 Yelena Karpukhina (USSR)
1969 Maria Gigova (Bul)
1971 Maria Gigova (Bul)
1973 Maria Gigova (Bul) & Galina
      Shugarova (USSR)
1975 Carmen Rischer (FRG)
1977 Irina Deryugina (USSR)
1979 Irina Deryugina (USSR)
1981 Anelia Ralenkova (Bul)
1983 Diliana Georgieva (Bul)
1985 Diliana Georgieva (Bul)

MOST INDIVIDUAL GOLD MEDALS, OLYMPICS & WORLD CHAMPIONSHIPS

MEN
10 Boris Shakhlin (USSR) 1956-64
 9 Leon Stukelj (Yug) 1922-8
 9 Akinori Nakayama (Jap) 1966-72
 9 Nikolay Andrianov (USSR)
   1972-80
 7 Joseph Martinez (Fra) 1903-9
 6 Eugen Mack (Swi) 1928-38

WOMEN
12 Larissa Latynina (USSR) 1956-64
10 Vera Caslavska (Cs) 1962-8
 6 Lyudmila Tourischeva (USSR)
   1968-76
 6 Nadia Comaneci (Rom) 1976-80
 6 Nelli Kim (USSR) 1976-80
 6 Maxi Gnauck (GDR) 1979-83

WORLD CHAMPIONSHIPS ONLY
MEN
Most gold medals – individual
5 Eugen Mack, Akinori Nakayama,
  Aleksandr Ditiatin (USSR)

Most medals
12 Eizo Kenmotsu (Jap); 10 Akinori
   Nakayama, Boris Shakhlin,

Nikolay Andrianov

WOMEN
Most gold medals – individual
6 Larissa Latynina, 5 Lyudmila
  Tourischeva

Most medals
9 Larissa Latynina, Lyudmila
  Tourischeva, Eva Bosakova (Cs)

Nadia Comaneci was given seven perfect scores of 10.00, the first ever awarded, at the 1976 Olympic Games.

WORLD CUP

First held 1975

Overall Champions

MEN
1975 Nikolay Andrianov (USSR)
1977 Nikolay Andrianov (USSR) &
      Vladimir Markelov (USSR)
1978 Aleksandr Ditiatin (USSR)
1979 Aleksandr Ditiatin (USSR)
1982 Li Ning (Chn)

1986 Yuriy Korolev (USSR) &
      Li Ning (Chn)

WOMEN
Lyudmila Tourischeva (USSR)
Maria Filatova (USSR

Maria Filatova (USSR)
Stella Zakharova (USSR)
Olga Bicherova (USSR) &
Natalya Yurchenko (USSR)
Yelena Shushunova (USSR)

RHYTHMIC GYMNASTICS WORLD CUP
First held 1983

Overall winners: 1983 Lilia Ignatova (Bul); 1986 Lilia Ignatova (Bul)
Team: 1983 USSR; 1986 Bulgaria

EUROPEAN CHAMPIONSHIPS

First held 1955

Overall Champions

MEN
1955 Boris Shakhlin (USSR)
1957 Joachim Blume (Spa)
1959 Yuriy Titov (USSR)
1961 Miroslav Cerar (Yug)
1963 Miroslav Cerar (Yug)
1965 Franco Menichelli (Ita)
1967 Mikhail Voronin (USSR)
1969 Mikhail Voronin (USSR)
1971 Viktor Klimenko (USSR)

1973 Viktor Klimenko (USSR)
1975 Nikolay Andrianov (USSR)
1977 Vladimir Markelov (USSR)
1979 Stoyan Deltchev (Bul)
1981 Aleksandr Tkachev (USSR)
1983 Dmitriy Belozerchev (USSR)
1985 Dmitriy Belozerchev (USSR)
1987 Valeriy Lyukin (USSR)

WOMEN

Larissa Latynina (USSR)
Natalie Kot (Pol)
Larissa Latynina (USSR)
Mirjana Bilic (Yug)
Vera Caslavska (Cs)
Vera Caslavska (Cs)
Karin Janz (GDR)
Lyudmila Tourischeva (USSR) &
Tamara Lazakovich (USSR)
Lyudmila Tourischeva (USSR)
Nadia Comaneci (Rom)
Nadia Comaneci (Rom)
Nadia Comaneci (Rom)
Maxi Gnauck (GDR)
Olga Bicherova (USSR)
Yelena Shushunova (USSR)
Daniela Silivas (Rom)

HANDBALL

The modern game, similar to association football, with hands substituted for feet, was first played in Germany around 1890. The first international match was played on 3 Sep 1925 when Austria beat Germany 6-3 at Halle/Salle. Germany has long been a stronghold of the game, and it was introduced to the Olympic Games at Berlin in 1936 as an 11-a-side outdoor game. When reintroduced in 1972, again in Germany, at Munich, it was as an indoor 7-a-side game, and this version of the game has been predominant since 1952. The indoor court is 40m long by 20m wide; the goals are 2m high and 3m wide.

Prior to 1928 the International Amateur Athletic Federation looked after the interests of handball, but in that year the International Amateur Handball Federation (FIHA) was founded with Avery Brundage (USA), later the president of the International Olympic Committee, as its first president. The current governing body, the International Handball Federation (IHF), was founded in 1946, replacing the FIHA. The growth of the game is demonstrated by the fact that the IHF comprised 98 member federations by 1987, with further nations applying for membership.

OLYMPIC GAMES

Played outdoors at 11-a-side in 1936, indoors at 7-a-side from 1972 (men) and 1976 (women).

Winners:

MEN	WOMEN
1936 Germany	-
1972 Yugoslavia	-
1976 USSR	USSR
1980 GDR	USSR
1984 Yugoslavia	Yugoslavia

The following USSR players won two gold medals in 1976 and 1980: Larissa Karlova, Zinaida Turchina, Tatyana Kochergina, Lyudmila Poradnik, Aldona Nenenene, Lyubov Odinokova.

WORLD CHAMPIONSHIPS

First held outdoors in 1938 for men and 1949 for women. Men's nations are now divided into three groups A, B and C; and the women into A and B groups.

Winners have been:

MEN OUTDOORS	WOMEN OUTDOORS
1938 Germany	1949 Hungary
1948 Sweden	1956 Romania
1952 FR Germany	1960 Romania
1955 FR Germany	
1959 FR Germany/GDR	**WOMEN INDOORS** (A group)
1963 GDR	1957 Czechoslovakia
1966 FR Germany	1962 Romania
	1965 Hungary
MEN INDOORS (A group)	1971 GDR
1938 Germany	1973 Yugoslavia
1954 Sweden	1975 GDR
1958 Sweden	1979 GDR
1961 Romania	1982 USSR
1964 Romania	1986 USSR

1967 Czechoslovakia
1970 Romania
1974 Romania
1978 FR Germany
1982 USSR
1986 Yugoslavia

EUROPEAN CUP

Contested by national champions. First held in 1957 (men), 1961 (women).

Recent winners:

MEN
1980 TV Grosswallstadt (FRG)
1981 SC Magdeburg (GDR)
1982 Honved SE, Budapest (Hun)
1983 VfL Gummersbach (FRG)
1984 Dukla Praha (Cs)
1985-6 Metaloplastika Sabac (Yug)
1987 SKA Minsk (UUSR)

Most wins: 5 Vfl Gummersbach 1967, 1970-1, 1974, 1983

WOMEN
1980 RK Radnicki Belgrad (Yug)
1981 Spartak Kiev (USSR)
1982 Vasas SC, Budapest (Hun)
1983 Spartak Kiev (USSR)
1984 Radnicki Belgrad (Yug)
1985-7 Spartak Kiev (USSR)

Most wins: 12 Spartak Kiev 1970-3, 1975, 1977, 1979, 1981, 1983, 1985-7

EUROPEAN CUP-WINNERS CUP

First held 1976 (men), 1977 (women).

Winners:

MEN
1976 Balonmano Granollers (Spa)
1977 MAI Moskva (USSR)
1978-9 VfL Gummersbach (FRG)
1980 Calpisa Alicante (Spa)
1981 TuS Nettelstedt (FRG)
1982 SC Empor Rostock (GDR)
1983 SKA Minsk (USSR)
1984-6 FC Barcelona (Spa)
1987 CSKA Moskva (USSR)

Most wins: 3 FC Barcelona

WOMEN
1977 TSC Berlin (GDR)
1978 Ferencvarosi Budapest (Hun)
1979 TSC Berlin (GDR)
1980 Iskra Partizanske (Cs)
1981 Spartacus Budapest (Hun)
1982-3 RK Osiejek (Yug)
1984 Dalma Split (Yug)
1985 Budocnost Titograd (Yug)
1986 Radnicki Belgrad (Yug)
1987 Kubari Krasnodar (USSR)

IHF CUP

First held in the 1982.

Winners:

MEN
1982 Vfl Gummersbach (FRG)
1983 IL Saporozhye (USSR)
1984 TV Grosswallstadt (FRG)
1985 Minaur Baia Mare (Rom)
1986 Raba Vasas Etö Györ (Hun)

WOMEN
1982 IHK Tresnjevka, Zagreb (Yug)
1983 Automobilist Baku (USSR)
1984 Chimistul Vilcea (Rom)
1985 ASK Vorwärts Frankfurt/Oder (GDR)
1986 SC Leipzig (GDR)
1987 Budocnost Titograd (Yug)

A unique achievement in winning all possible competitions in one year was when Vfl Gummersbach (FRG) in 1983 won the FRG national championship and cup, the European Champions Cup and the IHF Super Cup, contested by the winners of the two European Cup competitions.

SCORING RECORDS

Highest score in an international match: USSR beat Afghanistan 86-2 in the 'Friendly Army Tournament' at Miskolc, Hungary, August 1981.

COURT HANDBALL

Handball played against walls or in a court is a game of ancient Celtic origin. The game has been particularly prominent in Ireland and the USA, and the first ever international match was between the champions of these nations in 1887, when Phil Casey (USA) beat Bernard McQuade (Ire). In Ireland and Australia the court is 60 ft (18.3m) long and 30 ft (9.1m) wide, but a smaller court of 40 ft (12m) long and 20ft (6.1m) wide is used in North America.

The first US Championships under the auspices of the AAU were held in 1919 at four-wall singles and doubles. The United States Handball Association (USHA) was founded in 1951.

USHA Professional Championships were first held in 1951.

Most wins:

Singles: 9 Naty Alvarado 1979-80, 1982-7; 6 Jim Jacobs 1955-7, 1960, 1964-5; 6 Fred Lewis 1972, 1974-6, 1978, 1981

Doubles: 8 Marty Decatur 1962-3, 1965, 1967-8, 1975, 1978-9 (the first five with Jim Jacobs); 6 Jim Jacobs 1960, 1962-3, 1965, 1967-8; 5 John Sloan 1957-9, 1961, 1964 1961, 1964

HARNESS RACING

A form of horse racing in which the horses trot or pace while being driven in a light two-wheeled cart, the sulky. Pacers have a lateral gait, as they move their fore and hind legs in unison on one side and then the other; whereas trotters have a diagonal gait, in that their off fore and near hind legs are brought together in unison, followed by their near fore and off hind legs. Standardbred horses (which race up to a certain standard of speed) are raced as opposed to thoroughbreds in horse racing. Race tracks are of dirt surface, oval in shape, of a half a mile to a mile in circumference.

Trotting races were first held in the Netherlands in 1554, and the sulky first appeared in harness racing in 1829. The sport became very popular in the USA in the 19th century, and the National Trotting Association was founded, originally as the National Association for the Promotion of the Interests of the Trotting Turf in 1870. It brought needed controls to a sport that had been threatened by gambling corruption.

1 MILE RECORDS

Trotting race record: 1:53.4 Prakas (driver, Bill O'Donnell) at Du Quoin, Illinois 31 Aug 1985
Pacing record: 1:49.2 Niatross (driver, Clint Galbraith) at Lexington, Kentucky 1 Oct 1980
Pacing race record: 1:49.6 Nihilator (driver, Bill O'Donnell) at East Rutherford, New Jersey 3 Aug 1985.

THE HAMBLETONIAN

The most famous race in North America is the Hambletonian Stakes, run annually for three-year-old trotters. It was first staged at Syracuse, New York in 1926. Previously run at Syracuse, Lexington, and the New York tracks of Yonkers and Goshen, since 1956 it has been run at Du Quoin, Illinois. Hambletonian, born in 1849, although only an ordinary racer, had a most notable influence on the breeding of American trotters.

Winners since 1970:

Year	Horse	Driver
1970	Timothy T	John Simpson Jr.
1971	Speedy Crown	Howard Beissinger
1972	Super Bowl	Stanley Dancer
1973	Flirth	Ralph Baldwin
1974	Christopher T	Bill Haughton
1975	Bonefish	Stanley Dancer
1976	Steve Lobell	Bill Haughton
1977	Green Speed	Bill Haughton
1978	Speedy Somolli	Howard Beissinger
1979	Legend Hanover	George Sholty
1980	Burgomeister	Bill Haughton
1981	Shiaway St.Pat	Ray Remmen
1982	Speed Bowl	Tommy Haughton
1983	Duenna	Stanley Dancer
1984	Historic Freight	Ben Webster
1985	Prakas	Bill O'Donnell
1986	Nuclear Kosmos	Ulf Thoresen

The prize purse first passed $100,000 with $117,118 in

1953, when the winner was Helicopter; $200,000 in 1975 when it was $232,192; $500,000 in 1981 when it was $838,000 and the million dollars in 1983 at $1,080,000.

THE LITTLE BROWN JUG

Pacing's three-year-old classic has been held annually at Delaware, Ohio from 1946. The name honours a great 19th century pacer.

Winners since 1970:

Year	Horse	Driver
1970	Most Happy Fella	Stanley Dancer
1971	Nansemond	Herve Filion
1972	Strike Out	Keith Waples
1973	Melvin's Woe	Joe O'Brien
1974	Ambro Omaha	Bill Haughton
1975	Seatrain	Ben Webster
1976	Keystone Ore	Stanley Dancer
1977	Governor Skipper	John Chapman
1978	Happy Escort	Bill Popfinger
1979	Hot Hitter	Herve Filion
1980	Niatross	Clint Galbraith
1981	Fan Hanover (filly)	Glen Garnsey
1982	Merger	John Campbell
1983	Ralph Hanover	Ron Waples
1984	Colt Forty Six	Chris Boring
1985	Nihilator	Bill O'Donnell
1986	Barbery Spur	Bill O'Donnell

LEADING DRIVERS

The leading money-winning driver of all time is Herve Filion, whose career winnings reached $100 million in May 1987.

The first driver to win $1 million in a year was Stanley Dancer, $1,051,538 in 1964; $2 million was passed by Herve Filion with $2.473,265 in 1972 and the record now is $10,207,372 by Bill O'Donnell in 1985, when he won 419 races. The most wins in a year is 770 by Mike Lauhane in 1986.

Top money winners from 1980:

1980	John Campbell	$3.732,306
1981	Bill O'Donnell	$4,065,608
1982	Bill O'Donnell	$5,755,067
1983	John Campbell	$6,104,082
1984	Bill O'Donnell	$9.059,184
1985	Bill O'Donnell	$10,207,372
1986	John Campbell	$9,515,055

Most years as leading money-winning driver from 1948:
12 Bill Haughton 1952-9, 1963, 1965, 1967-8
 7 Herve Filion 1970-4, 1976-7

TOP MONEY-WINNING HORSES

As at 1 Jan 1987 the leading all-time money winner in North America was Nihilator, with $3,225,653 in 1984-5.

The first to win $1 million in a year:
Pacer: Niatross $1,414,313 in 1980
Trotter: Joie De Vie $1,007,705 in 1983.

The largest ever purse was $2,161,000 for the Woodrow Wilson two-year-old race for pacers at Meadowlands, New Jersey on 16 Aug 1984. The winner, Nihilator, driven by Bill O'Donnell, earned $1,080,500.

Two horses have been three-time winners of the annual Harness Horse of the Year, chosen by the US Trotting Association and the US Harness Writers Association: Bret Hanover 1964-6, Nevele Pride 1967-9

THE INTER-DOMINION CHAMPIONSHIP

The first trotting race in Australia was at Parramatta in 1810. The most important race in the Southern Hemisphere is the Inter-Dominion Championship, first held in 1936. Held annually at various venues in Australia and New Zealand.

Winners from 1970 (shown in brackets is the Australian state or New Zealand ownership)

Year	Horse	Driver
1970	Bold David (Vic)	Alf Simons
1971	Stella Frost (NZ)	Dinny Townley
1972	Welcome Advice (NSW)	Alan Harpley
1973	Hondo Grattan (NSW)	Tony Turnbull
1974	Hondo Grattan (NSW)	Tony Turnbull
1975	Young Quinn (NZ)	John Langdon
1976	Carclew (SA)	Chris Lewis
1977	Stanley Rio (NZ)	John Noble
1978	Markovina (SA)	Bruce Gath
1979	Rondel (NZ)	Peter Wolfenden
1980	Koala King (NSW)	Brian Hancock
1981	San Simeon (WA)	Lyle Austin
1982	Rhett's Law (WA)	Colin Warwick
1983	Gammalite (Vic)	Bill Clarke
1984	Gammalite (Vic)	Bill Clarke
1985	Preux Chevalier (WA)	Barry Perkins
1986	Village Kid (WA)	Chris Lewis
1987	Lightning Blue (Vic)	Jim O'Sullivan

Most wins: 2 Captain Sandy (NZ) 1950, 1953; Hondo Grattan 1973-4; Gammalite 1983-4.

AUSTRALIAN RECORDS

Drivers – most wins in a season: 175 Ted Demmler 1981-2
Top money-winning horse: Gammalite $1,386,480
Highest stakewinner in a season: Village Kid $541,930 1985-6
Most wins in a season: 34 Cane Smoke 1985-6

HOCKEY

Stick and ball games date back some 4000 years, with modern hockey, which is played by teams of 11-a-side, becoming established in the 19th century. The sport's first governing body was an English Hockey Association, formed in London in 1875. The current English men's governing body, the Hockey Association was founded in 1886 and the All-England Women's Hockey Association in 1895, a year after the Irish Ladies' Hockey Union.

The current international governing body, the

Ric Charlesworth, playing for Australia against F.R. Germany. The World Cup Final, when Australia beat England 2-1 in 1986, was Charlesworth's 201st international. (All-Sport)

Fédération Internationale de Hockey (FIH) was formed in 1924. A separate body governed women's hockey until both men's and women's games were united under the auspices of the IHF in 1982.

The sport was long dominated by India and Pakistan, who won every Olympic tournament from 1928 to 1968. From then, however, success has been more widespread, with the amazing result at the 1986 World Cup of India and Pakistan in 11th and 12th places.

OLYMPIC GAMES

Men's winners

England	1908, 1920
India	1928, 1932, 1936, 1948, 1952, 1956, 1964, 1980
Pakistan	1960, 1968, 1984
FR Germany	1972
New Zealand	1976

Highest score: India beat USA 24-1 at Los Angeles 1932
Most gold medals: seven Indian players have won three gold medals: Richard Allen 1928-36, Dhyan Chand 1928-36, Randhir Singh Gentle 1948-56, Leslie Claudius 1948-56, Ranganandan Francis 1948-56, Udham Singh 1952-64. Claudius and Udham Singh also won silver medals in 1960.

Women's winners:
Zimbabwe 1980, Netherlands 1984

IHF WORLD CUP

First contested in 1971.

Winners:

MEN

Pakistan	1971, 1978, 1982
Netherlands	1973
India	1975
Australia	1986

WOMEN

Netherlands	1974, 1978, 1983, 1986
FR Germany	1976, 1981

WOMEN'S WORLD CHAMPIONSHIP

Organised by the International Federation of Women's Hockey Association twice.

Winners: 1975 England, 1979 Netherlands.

CHAMPIONS TROPHY

First held in 1978, the leading six men's teams contest this trophy annually.

Winners:

1978	Pakistan
1980	Pakistan
1981-2	Netherlands
1983-5	Australia
1986-7	FR Germany

The first women's Champions Trophy was held in 1987, when the Netherlands were the winners.

EUROPEAN CUP

Contested by men's national teams at four-yearly intervals from 1970.

Winners:

1970	FR Germany	1978	FR Germany
1974	Spain	1983	Netherlands

The first women's European Cup was contested in 1984, when it was won by the Netherlands.

EUROPEAN CUP FOR CLUB CHAMPIONS

First held unofficially in 1969 and 1970 and officially from 1971.

Winners:

1969-70	Club Egara de Tarrasa (Spa)
1971-5	Frankfurt 1880 (FRG)
1976-8	Southgate (Eng)
1979	Klein Zwitserland (Hol)
1980	Slough (Eng)
1981	Klein Zwitserland (Hol)
1982-3	Dynamo Alma-Ata (USSR)

1984 TG 1846 Frankental (FRG)
1985 Atletico Tarrasa (Spa)
1986 Kampong, Utrecht (Hol)
1987 Bloemendaal (Hol)

WOMEN
1974 Harvetschuder Hamburg (FRG)
1976-82 Amsterdam (Hol)
1983-7 HGC Wassenaar (Hol)

HOCKEY ASSOCIATION CUP

English National Club Champions.
1972-3 Hounslow
1974-5 Southgate
1976 Nottingham
1977 Slough
1978 Guildford
1979-81 Slough
1982 Southgate
1983 Neston
1984 East Grinstead
1985-7 Southgate

ENGLISH NATIONAL INTER-LEAGUE

First held in 1975, and contested by the winners of all the major English leagues.
1975 Bedfordshire Eagles
1976 Slough
1977-8 Southgate
1979 Isca
1980-3 Slough
1984 Neston
1985-6 East Grinstead
1987 Slough

NATIONAL WOMEN'S CLUB CHAMPIONS

1979 Chelmsford
1980 Norton
1981 Sutton Coldfield
1982-3 Slough
1984 Sheffield
1985 Ipswich
1986 Slough
1987 Ealing

COUNTY CHAMPIONSHIP

MEN – first held in 1957/8 season. Moved to December in 1985, so winners in 1985 and 1986 are shown as the following year (i.e. second half of the season).

Wins:
4 Middlesex   1959, 1961, 1977, 1981
4 Kent   1964-5, 1975, 1979
4 Wiltshire   1967-8, 1970, 1972
3 Hertfordshire   1960, 1974, 1976
3 Surrey   1963, 1973, 1986
3 Lancashire   1969, 1978, 1983
2 Worcestershire   1985, 1987

2 Buckinghamshire   1980, 1982
1 Lincolnshire 1958, Durham 1962, Cheshire 1966, Staffordshire 1971, Yorkshire 1984

WOMEN – first held in 1968/9 season (*tied)
9 Lancashire   1969*, 1970, 1971*, 1973-4, 1976-7, 1979, 1985
3 Hertfordshire   1969*, 1971*, 1978
3 Leicestershire   1975*, 1980*, 1983
2 Suffolk   1980*, 1982
2 Staffordshire   1981, 1987
2 Middlesex   1984, 1986
1 Essex 1972, Surrey 1975*

HORSE RACING

The Ancient Egyptians are believed to have participated in horse racing more than 3000 years ago, and the sport certainly formed part of the ancient Olympic Games. Smithfield, in London, staged the first regular race meetings in the 12th century and Britain's oldest race course, at Chester's Roodee, staged its first meeting on 9 February 1540. The Jockey Club was formed around 1750 and in 1752 the earliest recorded steeplechase took place in Co.Cork, Ireland.

THE DERBY

Like all five English classics, the Derby is for three-year-olds, and is open to colts and fillies. The former carry a weight of 9st while fillies carry 8st 9lb. It is raced over 1½ miles at Epsom Downs each June but, between 1915-8 and 1940-5, the race was run at Newmarket.
Since 1984 it has been sponsored by Ever Ready.

Winners:
Year	Winnner	Jockey
1780	Diomed	Sam Arnull
1781	Young Eclipse	Charles Hindley
1782	Assassin	Sam Arnull
1783	Saltram	Charles Hindley
1784	Sergeant	John Arnull
1785	Aimwell	Charles Hindley
1786	Noble	J.White
1787	Sir Peter Teazle	Sam Arnull
1788	Sir Thomas	William South
1789	Skyscraper	Sam Chifney, snr
1790	Rhadamanthus	John Arnull
1791	Eager	Matt Stephenson
1792	John Bull	Frank Buckle
1793	Waxy	Bill Clift
1794	Daedalus	Frank Buckle
1795	Spread Eagle	Anthony Wheatley
1796	Didelot	John Arnull
1797	(unnamed colt)	John Singleton
1798	Sir Harry	Sam Arnull
1799	Archduke	John Arnull
1800	Champion	Bill Clift
1801	Eleanor	John Saunders
1802	Tyrant	Frank Buckle
1803	Ditto	Bill Clift

Year	Horse	Jockey
1804	Hannibal	Bill Arnull
1805	Cardinal Beaufort	Denni Fitzpatrick
1806	Paris	John Shepherd
1807	Election	John Arnull
1808	Pan	Frank Collinson
1809	Pope	Tom Goodison
1810	Whalebone	Bill Clift
1811	Phantom	Frank Buckle
1812	Octavius	Bill Arnull
1813	Smolensko	Tom Goodison
1814	Blucher	Bill Arnull
1815	Whisker	Tom Goodison
1816	Prince Leopold	Will Wheatley
1817	Azor	Jem Robinson
1818	Sam	Sam Chifney, jnr
1819	Tiresias	Bill Clift
1820	Sailor	Sam Chifney, jnr
1821	Gustavus	Sam Day
1822	Moses	Tom Goodison
1823	Emilius	Frank Buckle
1824	Cedric	Jem Robinson
1825	Middleton	Jem Robinson
1826	Lapdog	George Dockeray
1827	Mameluke	Jem Robinson
1828	Cadland	Jem Robinson
1829	Frederick	John Forth
1830	Priam	Sam Day
1831	Spaniel	Will Wheatley
1832	St.Giles	Bill Scott
1833	Dangerous	Jem Chapple
1834	Plenipotentiary	Patrick Conolly
1835	Mundig	Bill Scott
1836	Bay Middleton	Jem Robinson
1837	Phosphorus	George Edwards
1838	Amato	Jim Chapple
1839	Bloomsbury	Sim Templeman
1840	Little Wonder	William MacDonald
1841	Coronation	Patrick Conolly
1842	Attila	Bill Scott
1843	Cotherstone	Bill Scott
1844	Orlando	Nat Flatman
1845	The Merry Monarch	Foster Bell
1846	Pyrrhus the First	Sam Day
1847	Cossack	Sim Templeman
1848	Surplice	Sim Templeman
1849	The Flying Dutchman	Charlie Marlow
1850	Voltigeur	Job Marson
1851	Teddington	Job Marson
1852	Daniel O'Rourke	Frank Butler
1853	West Australian	Frank Butler
1854	Andover	Alfred Day
1855	Wild Dayrell	Robert Sherwood
1856	Ellington	Tom Aldcroft
1857	Blink Bonny	Jack Charlton
1858	Beadsman	John Wells
1859	Musjid	John Wells
1860	Thormanby	Harry Custance
1861	Kettledrum	Ralph Bullock
1862	Caractacus	John Parsons
1863	Macaroni	Tom Challoner
1864	Blair Athol	Jim Snowden
1865	Gladiateur	Harry Grimshaw
1866	Lord Lyon	Harry Custance
1867	Hermit	John Daley
1868	Blue Gown	John Wells
1869	Pretender	John Osborne
1870	Kingcraft	Tom French
1871	Favonius	Tom French
1872	Cremorne	Charlie Maidment
1873	Doncaster	Fred Webb
1874	George Frederick	Harry Custance
1875	Galopin	Jack Morris
1876	Kisber	Charlie Maidment
1877	Silvio	Fred Archer
1878	Sefton	Harry Constable
1879	Sir Bevys	George Fordham
1880	Bend Or	Fred Archer
1881	Iroquois	Fred Archer
1882	Shotover	Tom Cannon
1883	St.Blaise	Charlie Wood
1884	St.Gatien &	Charlie Wood
	Harvester (dead-heated)	Sam Loates
1885	Melton	Fred Archer
1886	Ormonde	Fred Archer
1887	Merry Hampton	Jack Watts
1888	Ayrshire	Fred Barrett
1889	Donovan	Tommy Loates
1890	Sainfoin	Jack Watts
1891	Common	George Barrett
1892	Sir Hugo	Fred Allsopp
1893	Isinglass	Tommy Loates
1894	Ladas	Jack Watts
1895	Sir Visto	Sam Loates
1896	Persimmon	Jack Watts
1897	Galtee More	Charlie Wood
1898	Jeddah	Otto Madden
1899	Flying Fox	Morny Cannon
1900	Diamond Jubilee	Herbert Jones
1901	Volodyovski	Lester Reiff
1902	Ard Patrick	Skeets Martin
1903	Rock Sand	Danny Maher
1904	St.Amant	Kempton Cannon
1905	Cicero	Danny Maher
1906	Spearmint	Danny Maher
1907	Orby	Johnny Reiff
1908	Signorinetta	Billy Bullock
1909	Minoru	Herbert Jones
1910	Lemberg	Bernard Dillon
1911	Sunstar	George Stern
1912	Tagalie	Johnny Reiff
1913	Aboyeur	Edwin Piper
1914	Durbar II	Matt MacGee
1915	Pommern	Steve Donoghue
1916	Fifinella	Joe Childs
1917	Gay Crusader	Steve Donaghue
1918	Gainsborough	Joe Childs
1919	Grand Parade	Fred Templeman
1920	Spion Kop	Frank O'Neill
1921	Humorist	Steve Donoghue
1922	Captain Cuttle	Steve Donoghue
1923	Papyrus	Steve Donoghue
1924	Sansovino	Tommy Weston
1925	Manna	Steve Donoghue
1926	Coronach	Joe Childs
1927	Call Boy	Charlie Elliott
1928	Fellstead	Harry Wragg
1929	Trigo	Joe Marshall
1930	Blenheim	Harry Wragg

Lester Piggott riding The Minstrel, on whom he won his eighth Derby in 1977. (All-Sport)

1931	Cameronian	Freddie Fox	1955	Phil Drake	Freddie Palmer
1932	April the Fifth	Fred Lane	1956	Lavandin	Rae Johnstone
1933	Hyperion	Tommy Weston	1957	Crepello	Lester Piggott
1934	Windsor Lad	Charlie Smirke	1958	Hard Ridden	Charlie Smirke
1935	Bahram	Freddie Fox	1959	Parthia	Harry Carr
1936	Mahmoud	Charlie Smirke	1960	St.Paddy	Lester Piggott
1937	Mid-day Sun	Michael Beary	1961	Psidium	Roger Poincelet
1938	Bois Roussel	Charlie Elliott	1962	Larkspur	Neville Sellwood
1939	Blue Peter	Eph Smith	1963	Relko	Yves Saint-Martin
1940	Pont l'Eveque	Sam Wragg	1964	Santa Claus	Scobie Breasley
1941	Owen Tudor	Billy Nevett	1965	Sea Bird II	Pat Glennon
1942	Watling Street	Harry Wragg	1966	Charlottown	Scobie Breasley
1943	Straight Deal	Tommy Carey	1967	Royal Palace	George Moore
1944	Ocean Swell	Billy Nevett	1968	Sir Ivor	Lester Piggott
1945	Dante	Billy Nevett	1969	Blakeney	Ernie Johnson
1946	Airborne	Tommy Lowrey	1970	Nijinsky	Lester Piggott
1947	Pearl Diver	George Bridgland	1971	Mill Reef	Geoff Lewis
1948	My Love	Rae Johnstone	1972	Roberto	Lester Piggott
1949	Nimbus	Charlie Elliott	1973	Morston	Eddie Hide
1950	Galcador	Rae Johnstone	1974	Snow Knight	Brian Taylor
1951	Arctic Prince	Charlie Spares	1975	Grundy	Pat Eddery
1952	Tulyar	Charlie Smirke	1976	Empery	Lester Piggott
1953	Pinza	Gordon Richards	1977	The Minstrel	Lester Piggott
1954	Never Say Die	Lester Piggott	1978	Shirley Heights	Greville Starkey

1979	Troy	Willie Carson
1980	Henbit	Willie Carson
1981	Shergar	Walter Swinburn
1982	Golden Fleece	Pat Eddery
1983	Teenoso	Lester Piggott
1984	Secreto	Christy Roche
1985	Slip Anchor	Steve Cauthen
1986	Shahrastani	Walter Swinburn
1987	Reference Point	Steve Cauthen

Most wins (Jockey): 9 Lester Piggott; 6 Jem Robinson, Steve Donoghue; 5 John Arnull, Bill Clift, Frank Buckle, Fred Archer; 4 Sam Arnull, Tom Goodison, Bill Scott, Jack Watts, Charlie Smirke

Most wins (Trainer): 7 Robert Robson 1793, 1802, 1809-10, 1815, 1817, 1823; John Porter 1868, 1882-3, 1886, 1890-1, 1899; Fred Darling 1922, 1925-6, 1931, 1938, 1940-1

Most wins (Owner): 5 3rd Earl of Egremont 1782, 1804, 1806-7, 1826; HH Aga Khan III 1930, 1935-6, 1948 (half-share), 1952; 4 John Bowes 1835, 1843, 1852-3; Sir Joseph Hawley 1851, 1858-9, 1868; 1st Duke of Westminster 1880, 1882, 1886, 1899; Sir Victor Sassoon 1953, 1957-8, 1960

Fastest time: 2 min 33.8 sec Mahmoud, 1936. The fastest recorded stalls-started and electrically timed Derby is 2 min 33.90 sec by Reference Point in 1987.

THE OAKS

Raced at Epsom, over 1½ miles, the race is open to fillies only, all of whom carry 9st. It was raced at Newmarket during both World Wars. Since 1984 the race has been sponsored by Gold Seal. Named after the Epsom home of the 12th Earl of Derby, the first race was in 1779.

Post-war winners:

1946	Steady Aim	Harry Wragg
1947	Imprudence	Rae Johnstone
1948	Masaka	Billy Nevett
1949	Musidora	Edgar Britt
1950	Asmena	Rae Johnstone
1951	Neasham Belle	Stan Clayton
1952	Frieze	Edgar Britt
1953	Ambiguity	Joe Mercer
1954	Sun Cap	Rae Johnstone
1955	Meld	Harry Carr
1956	Sicarelle	Freddie Palmer
1957	Carrozza	Lester Piggott
1958	Bella Paola	Max Garcia
1959	Petite Etoile	Lester Piggott
1960	Never Too Late	Roger Poincelet
1961	Sweet Solera	Bill Rickaby
1962	Monade	Yves Saint-Martin
1963	Noblesse	Garnie Bougoure
1964	Homeward Bound	Greville Starkey
1965	Long Look	Jack Purtell
1966	Valoris	Lester Piggott
1967	Pia	Eddie Hide
1968	La Lagune	Gérard Thiboeuf
1969	Sleeping Partner	John Gorton
1970	Lupe	Sandy Barclay
1971	Altesse Royale	Geoff Lewis
1972	Ginevra	Tony Murray
1973	Mysterious	Geoff Lewis

1974	Polygamy	Pat Eddery
1975	Juliette Marny	Lester Piggott
1976	Pawneese	Yves Saint-Martin
1977	Dunfermline	Willie Carson
1978	Fair Salinia	Greville Starkey
1979	Scintillate	Pat Eddery
1980	Bireme	Willie Carson
1981	Blue Wind	Lester Piggott
1982	Time Charter	Billy Newnes
1983	Sun Princess	Willie Carson
1984	Circus Plume	Lester Piggott
1985	Oh So Sharp	Steve Cauthen
1986	Midway Lady	Ray Cochrane
1987	Unite	Walter Swinburn

Most wins (Jockey):
9 Frank Buckle 1797 Niké, 1798 Bellissima, 1799 Bellina, 1802 Scotia, 1803 Theophania, 1805 Meteora, 1817 Neva, 1818 Corinne, 1823 Zinc;
6 Frank Butler 1843 Poison, 1844 The Princess, 1849 Lady Evelyn, 1850 Rhedycina, 1851 Irish, 1852 Songstress;
6 Lester Piggott, as above

Most wins (Trainer):
12 Robert Robson 1802 Scotia, 1804 Pelisse, 1805 Meteora, 1807 Briseïs, 1808 Morel, 1809 Maid of Orleans, 1813 Music, 1815 Minuet, 1818 Corinne, 1822 Pastille, 1823 Zinc, 1825 Wings

Most wins (Owner): 6 4th Duke of Grafton 1813 Music, 1815 Minuet, 1822 Pastille, 1823 Zinc, 1828 Turquoise, 1831 Oxygen

Fastest time: 2 min 34.21 Time Charter, 1982

1000 GUINEAS

The first classic of the English season, the One Thousand Guineas is for fillies only; all carry 9st. It is raced over 1 mile at Newmarket and was first run in 1814. It has been sponsored by General Accident since 1984.

Post-war winners:

Year	Winner	Jockey
1946	Hypericum	Doug Smith
1947	Imprudence	Rae Johnstone
1948	Queenpot	Gordon Richards
1949	Musidora	Edgar Britt
1950	Camaree	Rae Johnstone
1951	Belle of All	Gordon Richards
1952	Zabara	Ken Gethin
1953	Happy Laughter	Manny Mercer
1954	Festoon	Scobie Breasley
1955	Meld	Harry Carr
1956	Honeylight	Edgar Britt
1957	Rose Royal II	Charlie Smirke
1958	Bella Paola	Serge Boullenger
1959	Petite Etoile	Doug Smith
1960	Never Too Late	Roger Poincelet
1961	Sweet Solera	Bill Rickaby
1962	Abermaid	Bill Williamson
1963	Hula Dancer	Roger Poincelet
1964	Pourparler	Garnie Bougoure
1965	Night Off	Bill Williamson
1966	Glad Rags	Paul Cook
1967	Fleet	George Moore
1968	Caergwrle	Sandy Barclay

1969	Full Dress II	Ron Hutchinson
1970	Humble Duty	Lester Piggott
1971	Altesse Royale	Yves Saint-Martin
1972	Waterloo	Eddie Hide
1973	Mysterious	Geoff Lewis
1974	Highclere	Joe Mercer
1975	Nocturnal Spree	Johnny Roe
1976	Flying Water	Yves Saint-Martin
1977	Mrs McArdy	Eddie Hide
1978	Enstone Spark	Ernie Johnson
1979	One in a Million	Joe Mercer
1980	Quick As Lightning	Brian Rouse
1981	Fairy Footsteps	Lester Piggott
1982	On The House	John Reid
1983	Ma Biche	Freddy Head
1984	Pebbles	Philip Robinson
1985	Oh So Sharp	Steve Cauthen
1986	Midway Lady	Ray Cochrane
1987	Miesque	Freddy Head

Most wins (Jockey):
7 George Fordham 1859 Mayonaise, 1861 Nemesis, 1865 Siberia, 1868 Formosa, 1869 Scottish Queen, 1881 Thebais, 1883 Hauteur
6 Frank Buckle 1818 Corinne, 1820 Rowena, 1821 Zeal, 1822 Whizgig, 1823 Zinc, 1827 Arab
5 Jem Robinson 1824 Cobweb, 1828 Zoe, 1830 Charlotte West, 1841 Potentia, 1844 Sorella
5 John Barham Day 1826 Problem, 1834 May-day, 1836 Destiny, 1837 Chapeau d'Espagne, 1840 Crucifix
Most wins (Trainer):
9 Robert Robson 1818 Corinne, 1819 Catgut, 1820 Rowena, 1821 Zeal, 1822 Whizgig, 1823 Zinc, 1825 Tontine, 1826 Problem, 1827 Arab
Most wins (Owner):
8 4th Duke of Grafton 1819 Catgut, 1820 Rowena, 1821 Zeal, 1822 Whizgig, 1823 Zinc, 1825 Tontine, 1826 Problem, 1827 Arab
Fastest time: 1 min 36.85 sec Oh So Sharp 1985

2000 GUINEAS

First run at Newmarket in 1809, it is the other early-season classic. Run over 1 mile it is open to colts, who carry 9st, and fillies, who carry 8st 9lb. Since 1984 sponsored by General Accident.

Post-war winners:

Year	Winnner	Jockey
1946	Happy Knight	Tommy Weston
1947	Tudor Minstrel	Gordon Richards
1948	My Babu	Charlie Smirke
1949	Nimbus	Charlie Elliott
1950	Palestine	Charlie Smirke
1951	Ki Ming	Scobie Breasley
1952	Thunderhead II	Roger Poincelet
1953	Nearula	Edgar Britt
1954	Darius	Manny Mercer
1955	Our Babu	Doug Smith
1956	Gilles de Retz	Frank Barlow
1957	Crepello	Lester Piggott
1958	Pall Mall	Doug Smith
1959	Taboun	George Moore
1960	Martial	Ron Hutchinson
1961	Rockavon	Norman Stirk

1962	Privy Councillor	Bill Rickaby
1963	Only For Life	Jimmy Lindley
1964	Baldric II	Bill Pyers
1965	Niksar	Duncan Keith
1966	Kashmir II	Jimmy Lindley
1967	Royal Palace	George Moore
1968	Sir Ivor	Lester Piggott
1969	Right Tack	Geoff Lewis
1970	Nijinsky	Lester Piggott
1971	Brigadier Gerard	Joe Mercer
1972	High Top	Willie Carson
1973	Mon Fils	Frankie Durr
1974	Nonoalco	Yves Saint-Martin
1975	Bolkonski	Gianfranco Dettori
1976	Wollow	Gianfranco Dettori
1977	Nebbiolo	Gabriel Curran
1978	Roland Gardens	Frankie Durr
1979	Tap On Wood	Steve Cauthen
1980	Known Fact	Willie Carson
1981	To-Agori-Mou	Greville Starkey
1982	Zino	Freddy Head
1983	Lomond	Pat Eddery
1984	El Gran Senor	Pat Eddery
1985	Shadeed	Lester Piggott
1986	Dancing Brave	Greville Starkey
1987	Don't Forget Me	Willie Carson

Most wins (Jockey):
9 Jem Robinson 1825 Enamel, 1828 Cadland, 1831 Riddlesworth, 1833 Clearwell, 1834 Glencoe, 1835 Ibrahim, 1836 Bay Middleton, 1847 Conyngham, 1848 Flatcatcher
6 John Osborne 1857 Vedette, 1869 Pretender, 1871 Bothwell, 1872 Prince Charlie, 1875 Camballo, 1888 Ayrshire
5 Frank Buckle 1810 Hephestion, 1820 Pindarrie, 1821 Reginald, 1822 Pastille, 1827 Turcoman
5 Charlie Elliott 1923 Ellangowan, 1928 Flamingo, 1940 Djebel, 1941 Lambert Simnel, 1949 Nimbus
Most wins (Trainer):
7 John Scott 1842 Meteor, 1843 Cotherstone, 1949 Nunnykirk, 1853 West Australian, 1856 Fazzoletto, 1860 The Wizard, 1862 The Marquis
Most wins (Owner):
5 4th Duke of Grafton 1820 Pindarrie, 1821 Reginald, 1822 Pastille, 1826 Dervise, 1827 Turcoman
5 5th Earl of Jersey 1831 Riddlesworth, 1834 Glencoe, 1835 Ibrahim, 1836 Bay Middleton, 1837 Achmet
Fastest time: 1 min 35.8 sec My Babu 1948

ST.LEGER

The oldest of the five Classics it was first held in 1776. It is run over a distance of 1 mile 6 furlongs 127 yards at Doncaster. Both colts and fillies may enter. Colts carry 9st, filles 8st 11lb. During the First World War the race was held at Newmarket (1915-8) and during the Second World War at Thirsk (1940), Manchester (1941), Newmarket (1942-4), and York (1945). Since 1984 the race has been sponsored by Holsten Pils.

Post-war winners:

Year	Winnner	Jockey
1946	Airborne	Tommy Lowrey
1947	Sayajirao	Edgar Britt

Year	Horse	Jockey
1948	Black Tarquin	Edgar Britt
1949	Ridge Wood	Michael Beary
1950	Scratch II	Rae Johnstone
1951	Talma II	Rae Johnstone
1952	Tulyar	Charlie Smirke
1953	Premonition	Eph Smith
1954	Never Say Die	Charlie Smirke
1955	Meld	Harry Carr
1956	Cambremer	Freddie Palmer
1957	Ballymoss	Tommy Burns
1958	Alcide	Harry Carr
1959	Cantelo	Eddie Hide
1960	St.Paddy	Lester Piggott
1961	Aurelius	Lester Piggott
1962	Hethersett	Harry Carr
1963	Ragusa	Garnie Bougoure
1964	Indiana	Jimmy Lindley
1965	Provoke	Joe Mercer
1966	Sodium	Frankie Durr
1967	Ribocco	Lester Piggott
1968	Ribero	Lester Piggott
1969	Intermezzo	Ron Hutchinson
1970	Nijinsky	Lester Piggott
1971	Athens Wood	Lester Piggott
1972	Boucher	Lester Piggott
1973	Peleid	Frankie Durr
1974	Bustino	Joe Mercer
1975	Bruni	Tony Murray
1976	Crow	Yves Saint-Martin
1977	Dunfermline	Willie Carson
1978	Julio Mariner	Eddie Hide
1979	Son of Love	Alain Lequeux
1980	Light Cavalry	Joe Mercer
1981	Cut Above	Joe Mercer
1982	Touching Wood	Paul Cook
1983	Sun Princess	Willie Carson
1984	Commanche Run	Lester Piggott
1985	Oh So Sharp	Steve Cauthen
1986	Moon Madness	Pat Eddery

Most wins (Jockey):
9 Bill Scott 1821 Memnon, 1828 The Colonel, 1829 Rowton, 1838 Don John, 1839 Charles the Twelfth, 1840 Launcelot, 1841 Satirist, 1846 Sir Tatton Sykes
8 John Jackson 1791 Young Traveller, 1794 Beningbrough, 1796 Ambrosia, 1798 Symmetry, 1805 Staveley, 1813 Altisidora, 1815 Filho da Puta, 1822 Theodore
8 Lester Piggott, as above
Most wins (Trainer):
16 John Scott 1827 Matilda, 1828 The Colonel, 1829 Rowton, 1832 Margrave, 1834 Touchstone, 1838 Don John, 1839 Charles the Twelfth, 1840 Launcelot, 1841 Satirist, 1845 The Baron, 1851 Newminster, 1853 West Australian, 1856 Warlock, 1857 Imperieuse, 1859 Gamester,1862 The Marquis
Most wins (Owner):
7 9th Duke of Hamilton 1786 Paragon, 1787 Spadille, 1788 Young Flora, 1792 Tartar, 1808 Petronius, 1809 Ashton, 1814 William
Fastest time: 3 min 1.6 sec Coronach 1926, Windsor Lad 1934

RECORD WINNING MARGINS

Derby	10 lengths	Shergar (1981)
Oaks	12 lengths	Sun Princess (1983)
1000 Guineas	20 lengths	Mayonaise (1859)
2000 Guineas	8 lengths	Tudor Minstrel (1947)
St.Leger	12 lengths	Never Say Die (1954)

THE LEADING JOCKEYS

	Total	Derby	Oaks	2000	1000	Leger	Years
Lester Piggott	29	9	6	4	2	8	1954-85
Frank Buckle	27	5	9	5	6	2	1792-1827
Jem Robinson	24	6	2	9	5	2	1817-48
Fred Archer	21	5	4	4	2	6	1874-86
Bill Scott	19	4	3	3	-	9	1821-46
Jack Watts	19	4	4	2	4	5	1883-97
John Barham Day	16	-	5	4	5	2	1826-41
George Fordham	16	1	5	3	7	-	1859-83
Joe Childs	15	3	4	2	2	4	1912-33
Frank Butler	14	2	6	2	2	2	1843-53
Steve Donoghue	14	6	2	3	1	2	1915-37
Charlie Elliott	14	3	2	5	4	-	1923-49
Gordon Richards	14	1	2	3	3	5	1930-53

Best record of current jockeys:

	Total	Derby	Oaks	2000	1000	Leger	Years
Willie Carson	10	2	3	3	0	2	1972-87

THE LEADING TRAINERS

	Total	Derby	Oaks	2000	1000	Leger	Years
John Scott	40	5	8	7	4	16	1827-63
Robert Robson	34	7	12	6	9	-	1793-1827
Mat Dawson	28	6	5	5	6	6	1853-95
John Porter	23	7	3	5	2	6	1868-1900
Alec Taylor	21	3	8	4	1	5	1905-27

Best post-war record:

	Total	Derby	Oaks	2000	1000	Leger	Years
Noel Murless	19	3	5	2	6	3	1948-73

THE LEADING OWNERS

	Total	Derby	Oaks	2000	1000	Leger	Years
4th Duke of Grafton	20	1	6	5	8	-	1813-31
17th Earl of Derby	20	3	2	2	7	6	1910-45
HH Aga Khan III	17	5	2	3	1	6	1924-57
6th Viscount Falmouth	16	2	4	3	4	3	1862-83

Note: The 5th Earl of Jersey also had five 2000 Guineas wins and the 3rd Earl of Egremont had a record equalling five Derby successes.

TRIPLE CROWN

The English Triple Crown is the 2000 Guineas, Derby and St.Leger.
The following horses have won all three races:
West Australian (1853), Gladiateur (1865), Lord Lyon (1866), Ormonde (1866), Common (1891), Isinglass (1893), Galtee More (1897), Flying Fox (1899), Diamond Jubilee (1900), Rock Sand (1903), Pommern (1915), Gay Crusader (1917), Gainsborough (1918), Bahram (1935), Nijinsky (1970).
The following horses have won the Fillies Triple Crown - 1000 Guineas, Oaks and St.Leger:
Hannah (1871), Apology (1874), La Flèche (1892), Pretty Polly (1904), Sun Chariot (1942), Meld (1955), Oh So Sharp (1985)
Four classics, all except the Derby, were won by: Formosa (1868) and Sceptre (1902)

GRAND NATIONAL

The most famous steeplechase in the world, it was orginally called the Grand Liverpool Steeplechase and run at a course in Maghull, some four miles from the present site at Aintree, in 1836. The race moved to Aintree in 1839 and it has remained its permanent home with the exception of 1916-8 when it was held at Gatwick. The current course takes in 30 fences over two circuits and is approximately 4 miles long.

Winners: (Amateur riders have their titles, e.g. Mr., Capt.)

Year	Winner	Weight st lb	Jockey
1836	The Duke	-	-
1837	The Duke	12-0	Mr. Potts
1838	Sir William	12-0	Tom Oliver
1839	Lottery	12-0	Jem Mason
1840	Jerry	12-0	Mr. B. Bretherton
1841	Charity	12-0	H. N. Powell
1842	Gay Lad	12-0	Tom Oliver
1843	Vanguard	11-10	Tom Oliver
1844	Discount	10-12	H. Crickmere
1845	Cureall	11-5	Bill Loft
1846	Pioneer	11-12	W. Taylor
1847	Matthew	10-6	Denny Wynne
1848	Chandler	11-12	Capt. Josey Little
1849	Peter Simple	11-0	Tom Cunningham
1850	Abd-el-Kader	9-12	Chris Green
1851	Abd-el-Kader	10-4	T. Abbott
1852	Miss Mowbray	10-4	Mr. Alec Goodman
1853	Peter Simple	10-10	Tom Oliver
1854	Bourton	11-12	J. Tasker
1855	Wanderer	9-8	J. Hanlon
1856	Freetrader	9-6	George Stevens
1857	Emigrant	9-10	Charlie Boyce
1858	Little Charley	10-7	William Archer
1859	Half Caste	9-7	Chris Green
1860	Anatis	9-10	Mr. Tommy Pickernell
1861	Jealousy	9-12	Joe Kendall
1862	Huntsman	11-0	Harry Lamplugh
1863	Emblem	10-10	George Stevens
1864	Emblematic	10-6	George Stevens
1865	Alcibiade	11-4	Capt. Bee Coventry
1866	Salamander	10-7	Mr. Alec Goodman
1867	Cortolvin	11-13	John Page
1868	The Lamb	10-7	Mr. George Ede
1869	The Colonel	10-7	George Stevens
1870	The Colonel	11-12	George Stevens
1871	The Lamb	11-4	Mr. Tommy Pickernell
1872	Casse Tête	10-0	John Page
1873	Disturbance	11-11	Mr. Maunsell Richardson
1874	Reugny	10-12	Mr. Maunsell Richardson
1875	Pathfinder	10-11	Mr. Tommy Pickernell
1876	Regal	11-3	Joe Cannon
1877	Austerlitz	10-8	Mr. Fred Hobson
1878	Shifnal	10-12	Jack Jones
1879	The Liberator	11-4	Mr. Garrett Moore
1880	Empress	10-7	Mr. Tommy Beasley
1881	Woodbrook	11-3	Mr. Tommy Beasley
1882	Seaman	11-6	Lord Manners
1883	Zoëdone	11-0	Count Graf Karl Kinsky
1884	Voluptuary	10-5	Mr. Ted Wilson
1885	Roquefort	11-0	Mr. Ted Wilson
1886	Old Joe	10-9	Tom Skelton
1887	Gamecock	11-0	Bill Daniels
1888	Playfair	10-7	George Mawson
1889	Frigate	11-5	Mr. Tommy Beasley
1890	Ilex	10-5	Arthur Nightingall
1891	Come Away	11-12	Mr. Harry Beasley
1892	Father O'Flynn	10-5	Capt. Roddy Owen
1893	Cloister	12-7	Bill Dollery
1894	Why Not	11-3	Arthur Nightingall
1895	Wild Man from Borneo	10-1	Mr. Joe Widger
1896	The Soarer	9-13	Mr. David Campbell
1897	Manifesto	11-3	Terry Kavanagh
1898	Drogheda	10-12	John Gourley
1899	Manifesto	12-7	George Williamson
1900	Ambush II	11-3	Algy Anthony
1901	Grudon	10-0	Arthur Nightingall
1902	Shannon Lass	10-1	David Read
1903	Drumcree	11-3	Percy Woodland

1904	Moifaa	10-7	Arthur Birch
1905	Kirkland	11-5	Tich Mason
1906	Ascetic's Silver	10-9	Hon. Aubrey Hastings
1907	Eremon	10-1	Alf Newey
1908	Rubio	10-5	Henry Bletsoe
1909	Lutteur III	10-11	George Parfrement
1910	Jenkinstown	10-5	Bob Chadwick
1911	Glenside	10-3	Mr. Jack Anthony
1912	Jerry M	12-7	Ernie Piggott
1913	Covertcoat	11-6	Percy Woodland
1914	Sunloch	9-7	William Smith
1915	Ally Sloper	10-6	Mr. Jack Anthony
1916	Vermouth	11-10	John Reardon
1917	Ballymacad	9-12	Ted Driscoll
1918	Poethlyn	11-6	Ernie Piggott
1919	Poethlyn	12-7	Ernie Piggott
1920	Troytown	11-9	Mr. Jack Anthony
1921	Shaun Spadah	11-7	Dick Rees
1922	Music Hall	11-8	Bilbie Rees
1923	Sergeant Murphy	11-3	Capt.Tuppy Bennett
1924	Master Robert	10-5	Bob Trudgill
1925	Double Chance	10-9	Maj. Jack Wilson
1926	Jack Horner	10-5	Billy Watkinson
1927	Sprig	12-4	Ted Leader
1928	Tipperary Tim	10-0	Mr. Bill Dutton
1929	Gregalach	11-4	Bob Everett
1930	Shaun Goilin	11-0	Tommy Cullinan
1931	Grakle	11-7	Bob Lyall
1932	Forbra	10-7	Jim Hamey
1933	Kellsboro' Jack	11-9	Dudley Williams
1934	Golden Miller	12-2	Gerry Wilson
1935	Reynoldstown	11-4	Mr. Frank Furlong
1936	Reynoldstown	12-2	Mr. Fulke Walwyn
1937	Royal Mail	11-13	Evan Williams
1938	Battleship	11-6	Bruce Hobbs
1939	Workman	10-6	Tim Hyde
1940	Bogskar	10-4	Mervyn Jones
1946	Lovely Cottage	10-8	Capt. Bobby Petre
1947	Caughoo	10-0	Eddie Dempsey
1948	Sheila's Cottage	10-7	Arthur Thompson
1949	Russian Hero	10-8	Leo McMorrow
1950	Freebooter	11-11	Jimmy Power
1951	Nickel Coin	10-1	Johnny Bullock
1952	Teal	10-12	Arthur Thompson
1953	Early Mist	11-2	Bryan Marshall
1954	Royal Tan	11-7	Bryan Marshall
1955	Quare Times	11-0	Pat Taaffe
1956	E. S. B.	11-3	Dave Dick
1957	Sundew	11-7	Fred Winter
1958	Mr. What	10-6	Arthur Freeman
1959	Oxo	10-13	Michael Scudamore
1960	Merryman II	10-12	Gerry Scott
1961	Nicolaus Silver	10-1	Bobby Beasley
1962	Kilmore	10-4	Fred Winter
1963	Ayala	10-0	Pat Buckley
1964	Team Spirit	10-3	Willie Robinson
1965	Jay Trump	11-5	Mr. Tommy Smith
1966	Anglo	10-0	Tim Norman
1967	Foinavon	10-0	John Buckingham
1968	Red Alligator	10-0	Brian Fletcher
1969	Highland Wedding	10-4	Eddie Harty
1970	Gay Trip	11-5	Pat Taaffe
1971	Specify	10-13	John Cook

Red Rum – the only horse to win three Grand Nationals. (All-Sport)

1972	Well To Do	10-1	Graham Thorner
1973	Red Rum	10-5	Brian Fletcher
1974	Red Rum	12-0	Brian Fletcher
1975	L'Escargot	11-3	Tommy Carberry
1976	Rag Trade	10-12	John Burke
1977	Red Rum	11-8	Tommy Stack
1978	Lucius	10-9	Bob Davies
1979	Rubstic	10-0	Maurice Barnes
1980	Ben Nevis	10-12	Mr. Charlie Fenwick
1981	Aldaniti	10-13	Bob Champion
1982	Grittar	11-5	Mr. Dick Saunders
1983	Corbière	11-4	Ben De Haan
1984	Hallo Dandy	10-2	Neale Doughty
1985	Last Suspect	10-5	Hywel Davies
1986	West Tip	10-11	Richard Dunwoody
1987	Maori Venture	10-13	Steve Knight

Most wins (Horse):
3 Red Rum; 2 Abd-el-Kader, Peter Simple, The Colonel, The Lamb, Manifesto, Reynoldstown, Poethlyn
Most wins (Jockey): 5 George Stevens; 3 Tom Oliver, Mr. Tommy Pickernell, Mr. Tommy Beasley, Arthur Nightingall, Ernie Piggott, Mr. Jack Anthony, Brian Fletcher
Most wins (Trainer): 4 Fred Rimell 1956, 1961, 1970, 1976; 4 Aubrey Hastings 1906, 1915, 1917*, 1924; 3 William Holman 1856, 1858, 1860; William Moore 1894, 1896, 1899; Tom Coulthwaite 1907, 1910, 1931; Vincent O'Brien 1953-5; Neville Crump 1948, 1952, 1960; Donald McCain 1973-4, 1977; Tim Forster 1972, 1980, 1985
* Gatwick race
Most wins (Owner): 3 James Machell 1873-4, 1876; Sir Charles Assheton-Smith 1893, 1912-3; Noel Le Mare 1973-4, 1977
Fastest winning time: 9:01. 9 Red Rum (1973)
Record field: 66 in 1929
Richest prize: £64,710 won by Maori Venture in 1987

CHELTENHAM GOLD CUP

The leading race for staying steeplechasers in Great Britain, the Cheltenham Gold Cup is the most prestigious race on the National Hunt calendar. It was first held in 1924; the course has varied over the years but is now over 22 fences and approximately 3 miles in length. Since 1980 the race has been sponsored by the Horserace Totalisator Board. There was no race in 1931, 1937, 1943-4. All horses now carry 12 stone.

Winners:

Year	Winnner	Jockey
1924	Red Splash	Dick Rees
1925	Ballinode	Ted Leader
1926	Koko	Tim Hamey
1927	Thrown In	Mr. Hugh Grosvenor
1928	Patron Saint	Dick Rees
1929	Easter Hero	Dick Rees
1930	Easter Hero	Tommy Cullinan
1932	Golden Miller	Ted Leader
1933	Golden Miller	Billy Stott
1934	Golden Miller	Gerry Wilson
1935	Golden Miller	Gerry Wilson
1936	Golden Miller	Evan Williams
1938	Morse Code	Danny Morgan
1939	Brendan's Cottage	George Owen
1940	Roman Hackle	Evan Williams
1941	Poet Prince	Roger Burford
1942	Médoc II	Frenchie Nicholson
1945	Red Rower	Davy Jones
1946	Prince Regent	Tim Hyde
1947	Fortina	Mr. Dick Black
1948	Cottage Rake	Aubrey Brabazon
1949	Cottage Rake	Aubrey Brabazon
1950	Cottage Rake	Aubrey Brabazon
1951	Silver Fame	Martin Molony
1952	Mont Tremblant	Dave Dick
1953	Knock Hard	Tim Molony
1954	Four Ten	Tommy Cusack
1955	Gay Donald	Tony Grantham
1956	Limber Hill	Jimmy Power
1957	Linwell	Michael Scudamore
1958	Kerstin	Stan Hayhurst
1959	Roddy Owen	Bobby Beasley
1960	Pas Seul	Bill Rees
1961	Saffron Tartan	Fred Winter
1962	Mandarin	Fred Winter
1963	Mill House	Willie Robinson
1964	Arkle	Pat Taaffe
1965	Arkle	Pat Taaffe
1966	Arkle	Pat Taaffe
1967	Woodland Venture	Terry Biddlecombe
1968	Fort Leney	Pat Taaffe
1969	What a Myth	Paul Kelleway
1970	L'Escargot	Tommy Carberry
1971	L'Escargot	Tommy Carberry
1972	Glencaraig Lady	Frank Berry
1973	The Dikler	Ron Barry
1974	Captain Christy	Bobby Beasley
1975	Ten Up	Tommy Carberry
1976	Royal Frolic	John Burke
1977	Davy Lad	Dessie Hughes
1978	Midnight Court	John Francome
1979	Alverton	Jonjo O'Neill
1980	Master Smudge	Richard Hoare
1981	Little Owl	Mr. Jim Wilson
1982	Silver Buck	Robert Earnshaw
1983	Bregawn	Graham Bradley
1984	Burrough Hill Lad	Phil Tuck
1985	Forgive'N'Forget	Mark Dwyer
1986	Dawn Run	Jonjo O'Neill
1987	The Thinker	Ridley Lamb

Most wins (Horse):
5 Golden Miller; 3 Cottage Rake, Arkle; 2 Easter Hero, L'Escargot
Most wins (Jockey):
4 Pat Taaffe; 3 Dick Rees, Aubrey Brabazon, Tommy Carberry
Most wins (Trainer): 5 Tom Dreaper 1946, 1964-6, 1968; 4 Basil Briscoe 1932-5; Vincent O'Brien 1948-50, 1953; Fulke Walwyn 1952, 1962-3, 1973
Most wins (Owner): 7 Miss Dorothy Paget 1932-6, 1940, 1952; 4 Anne, Duchess of Westminster 1964-6, 1975; 3 Frank Vickerman 1948-50
Fastest winning time: 6:23. 4 Silver Fame (1951)

CHAMPION HURDLE

The leading race in England for hurdlers, the Champion Hurdle was inaugurated in 1927. It is raced at Cheltenham during the Spring Festival meeting and is over two miles. Since 1978 it has been sponsored by Waterford Crystal. There was no race in 1931, 1943-4. The current weights are 11st 6lb for 4-year olds, 12st for older horses with a 5lb allowance for mares.

Winners:

Year	Winnner	Jockey
1927	Blaris	George Duller
1928	Brown Jack	Bilbie Rees
1929	Royal Falcon	Dick Rees
1930	Brown Tony	Tommy Cullinan
1932	Insurance	Ted Leader
1933	Insurance	Billy Stott
1934	Chenango	Danny Morgan
1935	Lion Courage	Gerry Wilson
1936	Victor Norman	Frenchie Nicholson
1937	Free Fare	Georges Pellerin
1938	Our Hope	Capt. Perry Harding
1939	African Sister	Keith Piggott
1940	Solford	Sean Magee
1941	Seneca	Ron Smyth
1942	Forestation	Ron Smyth
1945	Brains Trust	Fred Rimell
1946	Distel	Bobby O'Ryan
1947	National Spirit	Danny Morgan
1948	National Spirit	Ron Smyth
1949	Hatton's Grace	Aubrey Brabazon
1950	Hatton's Grace	Aubrey Brabazon
1951	Hatton's Grace	Tim Molony
1952	Sir Ken	Tim Molony
1953	Sir Ken	Tim Molony
1954	Sir Ken	Tim Molony
1955	Clair Soleil	Fred Winter
1956	Doorknocker	Harry Sprague
1957	Merry Deal	Grenville Under-wood
1958	Bandalore	George Slack

1959	Fare Time		Fred Winter
1960	Another Flash		Bobby Beasley
1961	Eborneezer		Fred Winter
1962	Anzio		Willie Robinson
1963	Winning Fair		Mr. Alan Lillingston
1964	Magic Court		Pat McCarron
1965	Kirriemuir		Willie Robinson
1966	Salmon Spray		Johnny Haine
1967	Saucy Kit		Roy Edwards
1968	Persian War		Jimmy Uttley
1969	Persian War		Jimmy Uttley
1970	Persian War		Jimmy Uttley
1971	Bula		Paul Kelleway
1972	Bula		Paul Kelleway
1973	Comedy of Errors		Bill Smith
1974	Lanzarote		Richard Pitman
1975	Comedy of Errors		Ken White
1976	Night Nurse		Paddy Broderick
1977	Night Nurse		Paddy Broderick
1978	Monksfield		Tommy Kinane
1979	Monksfield		Dessie Hughes
1980	Sea Pigeon		Jonjo O'Neill
1981	Sea Pigeon		John Francome
1982	For Auction		Mr. Colin Magnier
1983	Gaye Brief		Richard Linley
1984	Dawn Run		Jonjo O'Neill
1985	See You Then		Steve Smith-Eccles
1986	See You Then		Steve Smith-Eccles
1987	See You Then		Steve Smith-Eccles

Most wins (Horse):
3 Hatton's Grace, Sir Ken, Persian War, See You Then; 2 Insurance, National Spirit, Bula, Comedy of Errors, Night Nurse, Monksfield, Sea Pigeon
Most wins (Jockey): 4 Tim Moloney; 3 Ron Smyth, Fred Winter, Jimmy Uttley, Steve Smith-Eccles
Most wins (Trainer): 5 Peter Easterby 1967, 1976-7, 1980-1; 4 Vic Smyth 1941-2, 1947-8; 3 Vincent O'Brien 1949-51; Willie Stephenson 1952-4; Ryan Price 1955, 1959, 1961; Colin Davies 1968-70; Fred Winter 1971-2, 1974; Nicky Henderson 1985-7
Most wins (Owner): 4 Miss Dorothy Paget 1932-3, 1940, 1946; 3 Mrs. Moya Keogh 1949-51; Maurice Kingsley 1952-4; Henry Alper 1968-70; Stype Wood Stud Ltd. 1985-7
Fastest winning time: 3:51. 7 See You Then (1985)

VINCENT O'BRIEN IRISH GOLD CUP

Ireland's richest steeplechase, first run at Leopardstown in 1987 over 3 miles

1987	Forgive'N'Forget	Mark Dwyer

OTHER PRINCIPAL NATIONAL HUNT RACES

TOTE/SCHWEPPES GOLD TROPHY

A handicap hurdle race, the Schweppes Gold Trophy was first run at Liverpool in 1963 but since 1964 has been run over two miles at Newbury. There was no race in 1969-70, 1974, 1978, 1981, 1983 and 1985-6. The Tote Gold Trophy from 1987.

Winners:

Year	Winner	Weight	Jockey
1963	Rosyth	10-0	Josh Gifford
1964	Rosyth	10-2	Josh Gifford
1965	Elan	10-7	David Nicholson
1966	Le Vermontois	11-3	Josh Gifford
1967	Hill House	10-10	Josh Gifford
1968	Persian War	11-13	Jimmy Uttley
1971	Cala Mesquida	10-9	John Cook
1972	Good Review	10-9	Val O'Brien
1973	Indianapolis	10-6	John King
1975	Tammuz	10-13	Bill Smith
1976	Irish Fashion	10-4	Ron Barry
1977	True Lad	10-4	Tommy Stack
1979	Within the Law	11-4	Alan Brown
1980	Bootlaces	10-9	Paul Leach
1982	Donegal Prince	10-8	John Francome
1984	Ra Nova	10-6	Patrick Farrell
1987	Neblin	10-0	Stan Moore

WHITBREAD GOLD CUP

The Whitbread Gold Cup has a special place in British National Hunt racing. When inaugurated in 1957 it was the first race to attract major commercial sponsorship. Run at Sandown Park over 3 miles 5 furlongs 18 yards. The 1973 race was at Newcastle.

Winners:

Year	Winner	Weight	Jockey
1957	Much Obliged	10-12	Henry East
1958	Taxidermist	10-8	John Lawrence
1959	Done Up	10-13	Harry Sprague
1960	Plummers Plain	10-0	Ron Harrison
1961	Pas Seul	12-0	Dave Dick
1962	Frenchman's Cove	11-3	Stan Mellor
1963	Hoodwinked	10-9	Paddy Buckley
1964	Dormant	9-7	Paddy Buckley
1965	Arkle	12-7	Pat Taaffe
1966	What a Myth	9-8	Paul Kelleway
1967	Mill House	11-11	David Nicholson
1968	Larbawn	10-9	Macer Gifford
1969	Larbawn	11-4	Josh Gifford
1970	Royal Toss	10-0	Richard Pitman
1971	Titus Oates	11-13	Ron Barry
1972	Grey Sombrero	9-10	Willie Shoemark
1973	Charlie Potheen	12-0	Ron Barry
1974	The Dikler	11-13	Ron Barry
1975	April Seventh	9-13	Stephen Knight
1976	Otter Way	10-10	John King
1977	Andy Pandy	10-12	John Burke
1978	Strombolus	10-0	Tommy Stack
1979	Diamond Edge	11-11	Bill Smith
1980	Royal Mail	11-5	Phillip Blacker
1981	Diamond Edge	11-7	Bill Smith
1982	Shady Deal	10-0	Richard Rowe
1983	Drumlargan	10-10	Mr.Frank Codd
1984	Special Cargo	11-2	Kevin Mooney
1985	By The Way	10-0	Robert Earnshaw
1986	Plundering	10-6	Simon Sherwood
1987	Lean Ar Aghaidh	9-10	Guy Landau

MACKESON GOLD CUP

Held annually at Cheltenham since 1960, with the exception of 1976 when it was run at Haydock Park. It is over 2½ miles.

Winners:

Year	Winner	Weight	Jockey
1960	Fortria	12-8	Pat Taaffe
1961	Scottish Memories	10-7	Chris Finnegan
1962	Fortria	12-0	Pat Taaffe
1963	Richard of Bordeaux	10-5	Bobby Beasley
1964	Super Flash	10-5	Stan Mellor
1965	Dunkirk	12-7	Bill Rees
1966	Pawnbroker	11-9	Paddy Broderick
1967	Charlie Worcester	10-11	Josh Gifford
1968	Jupiter Boy	10-3	Eddie Harty
1969	Gay Trip	11-5	Terry Biddlecombe
1970	Chatham	10-3	Ken White
1971	Gay Trip	11-3	Terry Biddlecombe
1972	Red Candle	10-0	Jim Fox
1973	Skymas	10-5	Tommy Murphy
1974	Bruslee	10-7	Andy Turnell
1975	Clear Cut	10-9	Dennis Greaves
1976	Cancello	11-1	Dennis Atkins
1977	Bachelor's Hall	10-6	Martin O'Halloran
1978	Bawnogues	10-7	Craig Smith
1979	Man Alive	10-9	Ron Barry
1980	Bright Highway	11-1	Gerry Newman
1981	Henry Kissinger	10-13	Paul Barton
1982	Fifty Dollars More	11-0	Richard Linley
1983	Pounentes	10-6	Neale Doughty
1984	Half Free	11-10	Richard Linley
1985	Half Free	11-10	Richard Linley
1986	Very Promising	11-13	Richard Dunwoody

HENNESSY COGNAC GOLD CUP

Run at Newbury over 3 miles 2 furlongs 82 yards. Inaugurated in 1957, and run at Cheltenham 1957-9.

Winners:

Year	Winner	Weight	Jockey
1957	Mandarin	11-0	Gerry Madden
1958	Taxidermist	11-1	John Lawrence
1959	Kerstin	11-10	Stan Hayhurst
1960	Knucklecracker	11-1	Derek Ancil
1961	Mandarin	11-5	Willie Robinson
1962	Springbok	10-8	Gerry Scott
1963	Mill House	12-0	Willie Robinson
1964	Arkle	12-7	Pat Taaffe
1965	Arkle	12-7	Pat Taaffe
1966	Stalbridge Colonist	10-2	Stan Mellor
1967	Rondetto	10-1	Jeff King
1968	Man Of The West	10-0	Willie Robinson
1969	Spanish Steps	11-6	John Cooke
1970	Border Mask	11-1	David Mould
1971	Bighorn	10-11	David Cartwright
1972	Charlie Potheen	11-4	Richard Pitman
1973	Red Candle	10-4	Jim Fox
1974	Royal Marshall II	10-0	Graham Thorner
1975	April Seventh	11-2	Andy Turnell
1976	Zeta's Son	10-9	Ian Watkinson
1977	Bachelor's Hall	10-10	Martin O'Halloran
1978	Approaching	10-6	Bob Champion
1979	Fighting Fit	11-7	Richard Linley
1980	Bright Highway	11-6	Gerry Newman
1981	Diamond Edge	11-10	Bill Smith
1982	Bregawn	11-10	Graham Bradley
1983	Brown Chamberlin	11-8	John Francome
1984	Burrough Hill Lad	12-0	John Francome
1985	Galway Blaze	10-0	Mark Dwyer
1986	Broadheath	10-5	Paul Nicholls

KING GEORGE VI CHASE

The traditional Boxing Day fixture at Kempton Park brings together a small, but quality field of steeplechasers. First run in 1947 it is run over three miles. Not held 1961-2, 1967-8, 1970, 1981.

Winners:

Year	Winner	Weight	Jockey
1947	Rowland Roy	11-13	Bryan Marshall
1948	Cottage Rake	12-6	Aubrey Brabazon
1949	Finnure	11-10	Dick Francis
1950	Manicou	11-8	Bryan Marshall
1951	Statecraft	11-11	Anthony Grantham
1952	Halloween	11-13	Fred Winter
1953	Galloway Braes	12-6	Robert Morrow
1954	Halloween	12-10	Fred Winter
1955	Limber Hill	11-13	James Power
1956	Rose Park	11-7	Michael Scudamore
1957	Mandarin	12-0	Gerry Madden
1958	Lochroe	11-7	Arthur Freeman
1959	Mandarin	11-5	Gerry Madden
1960	Saffron Tartan	11-7	Fred Winter
1963	Mill House	12-0	Willie Robinson
1964	Frenchman's Cove	11-7	Stan Mellor
1965	Arkle	12-0	Pat Taaffe
1966	Dormant	11-0	John King
1969	Titus Oates	11-10	Stan Mellor
1971	The Dikler	11-7	Barry Brogan
1972	Pendil	12-0	Richard Pitman
1972	Pendil	12-0	Richard Pitman
1974	Captain Christy	12-0	Bobby Coonan
1975	Captain Christy	12-0	Gerry Newman
1976	Royal Marshall	11-7	Graham Thorner
1977	Bachelor's Hall	11-7	Martin O'Halloran
1978	Gay Spartan	11-10	Tommy Carmody
1979	Silver Buck	11-10	Tommy Carmody
1980	Silver Buck	11-10	Tommy Carmody
1982	Wayward Lad	11-10	John Francome
1983	Wayward Lad	11-10	Robert Earnshaw
1984	Burrough Hill Lad	11-10	John Francome
1985	Wayward Lad	11-10	Graham Bradley
1986	Desert Orchid	11-10	Colin Brown

PRINCIPAL GROUP ONE RACES IN ENGLAND

CORONATION CUP

Raced at Epsom each year, the day after the Derby. It is over 1½ miles. First run 1902. Raced at Newbury 1915-6, Newmarket 1941, 1943-5.

Winners since 1970:

Year	Winner		Jockey
1970	Caliban		Sandy Barclay

Year	Winner	Jockey
1971	Lupe	Geoff Lewis
1972	Mill Reef	Geoff Lewis
1973	Roberto	Lester Piggott
1974	Buoy	Joe Mercer
1975	Bustino	Joe Mercer
1976	Quiet Fling	Lester Piggott
1977	Exceller	Gerard Dubroeucq
1978	Crow	Pat Eddery
1979	Ile de Bourbon	John Reid
1980	Sea Chimes	Lester Piggott
1981	Master Willie	Phillip Waldron
1982	Easter Sun	Bruce Raymond
1983	Be My Native	Lester Piggott
1984	Time Charter	Steve Cauthen
1985	Rainbow Quest	Pat Eddery
1986	Saint Estephe	Pat Eddery
1987	Triptych	Tony Cruz

Most wins: 2 Petty Polly 1905-6, The White Knight 1907-8, Petite Etoile 1960-1

ASCOT GOLD CUP

The highlight of the Royal Ascot meeting, the Gold Cup has been contested since 1807. It is the premier long distance race on the flat, run over 2½ miles. Between 1845-53 it was run as the Emperor's Plate. Held at Newmarket in 1917-8 (as the Newmarket Gold Cup), and in 1941-4.

Winners since 1970:

Year	Winnner	Jockey
1970	Precipice Wood	Jimmy Lindley
1971	Random Shot	Geoff Lewis
1972	Erimo Hawk	Pat Eddery
1973	Lassalle	Jimmy Lindley
1974	Ragstone	Ron Hutchinson
1975	Sagaro	Lester Piggott
1976	Sagaro	Lester Piggott
1977	Sagaro	Lester Piggott
1978	Shangamuzo	Greville Starkey
1979	Le Moss	Lester Piggott
1980	Le Moss	Joe Mercer
1981	Ardross	Lester Piggott
1982	Ardross	Lester Piggott
1983	Little Wolf	Willie Carson
1984	Gildoran	Steve Cauthen
1985	Gildoran	Brent Thomson
1986	Longboat	Willie Carson
1987	Paean	Steve Cauthen

Most wins: 3 Sagaro

KING'S STAND STAKES

The premier sprint race at the Royal Ascot meeting. It is run over 5 furlongs and was first held in 1862.

Winners since 1970:

Year	Winnner	Jockey
1970	Amber Rama	Yves Saint-Martin
1971	Swing Easy	Lester Piggott
1972	Sweet Revenge	Geoff Lewis
1973	Abergwaun	Lester Piggott
1974	Bay Express	Brian Taylor
1975	Flirting Around	Yves Saint-Martin

Year	Winner	Jockey
1976	Lochnager	Eddie Hide
1977	Godswalk	Lester Piggott
1978	Solinus	Lester Piggott
1979	Double Form	John Reid
1980	African Song	Pat Eddery
1981	Marwell	Walter Swinburn
1982	Fearless Lad	Eddie Hide
1983	Sayf El Arab	Taffy Thomas
1984	Habibti	Willie Carson
1985	Never So Bold	Lester Piggott
1986	Last Tycoon	Cash Asmussen
1987	Bluebird	Cash Asmussen

Most wins: 2 Golden Boss 1923-4, Gold Bridge 1933-4

CORAL ECLIPSE STAKES

First run in 1886. Raced over 1¼ miles at Sandown Park each July. Run at Ascot 1946, Kempton Park 1973. Known as the Benson & Hedges Eclipse Stakes 1974-5, Coral since then.

Winners since 1970:

Year	Winnner	Jockey
1970	Connaught	Sandy Barclay
1971	Mill Reef	Geoff Lewis
1972	Brigadier Gerard	Joe Mercer
1973	Scottish Rifle	Ron Hutchinson
1974	Coup de Feu	Pat Eddery
1975	Star Appeal	Greville Starkey
1976	Wollow	Franco Dettori
1977	Artaius	Lester Piggott
1978	Gunner B	Joe Mercer
1979	Dickens Hill	Tony Murray
1980	Ela-Mana-Mou	Willie Carson
1981	Master Willie	Phillip Waldron
1982	Kalaglow	Greville Starkey
1983	Solford	Pat Eddery
1984	Sadlers Wells	Pat Eddery
1985	Pebbles	Steve Cauthen
1986	Dancing Brave	Greville Starkey
1987	Mtoto	Muis Roberts

Most wins: 2 Buchan 1919-20, Polyphontes 1924-5

NORCROS JULY CUP

Run at Newmarket over 6 furlongs. First run 1876. Known as the William Hill July Cup 1978-83.

Winners since 1970:

Year	Winnner	Jockey
1970	Huntercombe	Sandy Barclay
1971	Realm	Brian Taylor
1972	Parsimony	Ron Hutchinson
1973	Thatch	Lester Piggott
1974	Saritamer	Lester Piggott
1975	Lianger	Yves Saint-Martin
1976	Lochnager	Eddie Hide
1977	Gentilhombre	Paul Cook
1978	Solinus	Lester Piggott
1979	Thatching	Lester Piggott
1980	Moorestyle	Lester Piggott
1981	Marwell	Walter Swinburn
1982	Sharpo	Pat Eddery
1983	Habibti	Willie Carson
1984	Chief Singer	Ray Cochrane

1985	Never So Bold	Steve Cauthen
1986	Green Desert	Walter Swinburn
1987	Ajdal	Walter Swinburn

Most wins: 3 Sundridge 1902-4; 2 Spanish Prince 1912-3, Diadem 1919-20, Diomedes 1925-6, Bellacose 1935-6, Abernant 1949-50, Right Boy 1958-9

KING GEORGE VI & QUEEN ELIZABETH II DIAMOND STAKES

First run in 1951 it was originally known as the King George VI & Queen Elizabeth Festival of Britain Stakes. It became the King George VI & Queen Elizabeth Stakes in 1952 and the word 'Diamond' was added in 1975. Raced over 1½ miles at Ascot, it is one of the leading weight-for-age races in Europe.

Winners:

Year	Winnner	Jockey
1951	Supreme Court	Charlie Elliott
1952	Tulyar	Charlie Smirke
1953	Pinza	Gordon Richards
1954	Aureole	Eph Smith
1955	Vimy	Roger Poincelet
1956	Ribot	Enrico Camici
1957	Montaval	Freddie Palmer
1958	Ballymoss	Scobie Breasley
1959	Alcide	Willie Carr
1960	Aggressor	Jimmy Lindley
1961	Right Royal V	Roger Poincelet
1962	Match III	Yves Saint-Martin
1963	Ragusa	Georges Bougoure
1964	Nasram II	Bill Pyers
1965	Meadow Court	Lester Piggott
1966	Aunt Edith	Lester Piggott
1967	Busted	George Moore
1968	Royal Palace	Sandy Barclay
1969	Park Top	Lester Piggott
1970	Nijinsky	Lester Piggott
1971	Mill Reef	Geoff Lewis
1972	Brigadier Gerard	Joe Mercer
1973	Dahlia	Bill Pyers
1974	Dahlia	Lester Piggott
1975	Grundy	Pat Eddery
1976	Pawneese	Yves Saint-Martin
1977	The Minstrel	Lester Piggott
1978	Ile de Bourbon	John Reid
1979	Troy	Willie Carson
1980	Ela-Mana-Mou	Willie Carson
1981	Shergar	Walter Swinburn
1982	Kalaglow	Greville Starkey
1983	Time Charter	Joe Mercer
1984	Teenoso	Lester Piggott
1985	Petoski	Willie Carson
1986	Dancing Brave	Pat Eddery
1987	Reference Point	Steve Cauthen

Most wins: 2 Dahlia

SWETTENHAM STUD SUSSEX STAKES

First run in 1841. Raced over 1 mile at Goodwood. Sponsored from 1985 by the Swettenham Stud (headed by Robert Sangster). For 3-year-olds only 1900-59; 3 & 4-year-olds 1960-74; 3-year-old upwards since 1975.

Winners since 1970:

Year	Winner	Jockey
1970	Humble Duty	Duncan Keith
1971	Brigadier Gerard	Joe Mercer
1972	Sallust	Joe Mercer
1973	Thatch	Lester Piggott
1974	Ace of Aces	Jimmy Lindley
1975	Bolkonski	Franco Dettori
1976	Wollow	Franco Dettori
1977	Artaius	Lester Piggott
1978	Jaazeiro	Lester Piggott
1979	Kris	Joe Mercer
1980	Posse	Pat Eddery
1981	King's Lake	Pat Eddery
1982	On The House	John Reid
1983	Noalcoholic	George Duffield
1984	Chief Singer	Ray Cochrane
1985	Rousillon	Greville Starkey
1986	Sonic Lady	Walter Swinburn
1987	Soviet Star	Greville Starkey

MATCHMAKER INTERNATIONAL

Inaugurated as recently as 1972, it was known as the Benson & Hedges Gold Cup until 1986, when it changed sponsors. The principal race of the three-day August meeting at York; it is run over 1 mile 2 furlongs.

Winners:

Year	Winner	Jockey
1972	Roberto	Braulio Baeza
1973	Moulton	Geoff Lewis
1974	Dahlia	Lester Piggott
1975	Dahlia	Lester Piggott
1976	Wollow	Franco Dettori
1977	Relkino	Willie Carson
1978	Hawaiian Sound	Lester Piggott
1979	Troy	Willie Carson
1980	Master Willie	Phillip Waldron
1981	Beldale Flutter	Pat Eddery
1982	Assert	Pat Eddery
1983	Caerleon	Pat Eddery
1984	Cormorant Wood	Steve Cauthen
1985	Commanche Run	Lester Piggott
1986	Shardari	Walter Swinburn

YORKSHIRE OAKS

For 3-year-old fillies only. Held at York over 1½ miles. First run in 1849.

Winners since 1970:

Year	Winnner	Jockey
1970	Lupe	Sandy Barclay
1971	Fleet Wahine	Geoff Lewis
1972	Attica Meli	Geoff Lewis
1973	Mysterious	Geoff Lewis
1974	Dibidale	Willie Carson
1975	May Hill	Pat Eddery
1976	Sarah Siddons	Christy Roche
1977	Busaca	Pat Eddery
1978	Fair Salinia	Greville Starkey
1979	Connaught Bridge	Joe Mercer
1980	Shoot A Line	Lester Piggott
1981	Condessa	Declan Gillespie

1982 Awaasif	Lester Piggott
1983 Sun Princess	Willie Carson
1984 Circus Plume	Willie Carson
1985 Sally Brown	Walter Swinburn
1986 Untold	Greville Starkey

TATTERSALLS CHEVELEY PARK STAKES

A race for 2-year-old fillies. Run over the last 6 furlongs of the Bunbury Mile at Newmarket. First run in 1870. Tattersalls succeeded William Hill (1973-83) as sponsors in 1985.

Winners since 1970:

Year Winnner	Jockey
1970 Magic Flute	Sandy Barclay
1971 Waterloo	Eddie Hide
1972 Jacinth	John Gorton
1973 Gentle Thoughts	Bill Pyers
1974 Cry Of Truth	John Gorton
1975 Pasty	Pat Eddery
1976 Durtal	Lester Piggott
1977 Sookera	Walter Swinburn
1978 Devon Ditty	Greville Starkey
1979 Mrs. Penny	John Matthias
1980 Marwell	Lester Piggott
1981 Woodstream	Pat Eddery
1982 Ma Biche	Freddy Head
1983 Desirable	Steve Cauthen
1984 Park Appeal	Declan Gillespie
1985 Embla	Angel Cordero
1986 Forest Flower	Tony Ives

TATTERSALLS MIDDLE PARK STAKES

A 6-furlong sprint for 2-year-olds run at Newmarket. First run in 1866 as the Middle Park Plate. Became Middle Park Stakes 1922. 1940 race at Nottingham and run as the New Middle Park Stakes. At one time the race was regarded as the 'Two-Year-Old's Championship', but in recent year's the quality of the fields has declined. Tattersalls became the race's sponsors in 1986.

Winners since 1970:

Year Winnner	Jockey
1970 Brigadier Gerard	Joe Mercer
1971 Sharpen Up	Willie Carson
1972 Tudenham	Jimmy Lindley
1973 Habat	Pat Eddery
1974 Steel Heart	Lester Piggott
1975 Hittite Glory	Frankie Durr
1976 Tachypous	Geoff Lewis
1977 Formidable	Pat Eddery
1978 Junius	Lester Piggott
1979 Known Fact	Willie Carson
1980 Mattaboy	Lester Piggott
1981 Cajun	Lester Piggott
1982 Diesis	Lester Piggott
1983 Creag-An-Sgor	Steve Cauthen
1984 Bassenthwaite	Pat Eddery
1985 Stalker	Joe Mercer
1986 Mister Majestic	Ray Cochrane

DUBAI CHAMPION STAKES

Run at Newmarket over 1¼ miles. First run in 1877. Dubai Champions Stakes from 1982.

Winners since 1970:

Year Winnner	Jockey
1970 Lorenzaccio	Geoff Lewis
1971 Brigadier Gerard	Joe Mercer
1972 Brigadier Gerard	Joe Mercer
1973 Hurry Harriet	Jean Cruguet
1974 Giacometti	Lester Piggott
1975 Rose Bowl	Willie Carson
1976 Vitiges	Pat Eddery
1977 Flying Water	Yves Saint-Martin
1978 Swiss Maid	Greville Starkey
1979 Northern Baby	Philippe Paquet
1980 Cairn Rouge	Tony Murray
1981 Vayrann	Yves Saint-Martin
1982 Time Charter	Billy Newnes
1983 Cormorant Wood	Steve Cauthen
1984 Palace Music	Yves Saint-Martin
1985 Pebbles	Pat Eddery
1986 Triptych	Tony Cruz

Most wins: 2 Lemberg 1910-1, Orpheus 1920-1, Fairway 1928-9, Wychwood Abbot 1935-6, Hippius 1940-1, Dynamite 1951-2, Brigadier Gerard, as above

WILLIAM HILL DEWHURST STAKES

An end-of-season race for 2-year-olds at Newmarket, over 7 furlongs. It was first run in 1875 and has been sponsored by William Hill since 1973.

Winners since 1970:

Year Winnner	Jockey
1970 Mill Reef	Geoff Lewis
1971 Crowned Prince	Lester Piggott
1972 Lunchtime	Pat Eddery
1973 Cellini	Lester Piggott
1974 Grundy	Pat Eddery
1975 Wollow	Franco Dettori
1976 The Minstrel	Lester Piggott
1977 Try My Best	Lester Piggott
1978 Tromos	John Lynch
1979 Monteverdi	Lester Piggott
1980 Storm Bird	Pat Eddery
1981 Wind and Wuthering	Phillip Waldron
1982 Diesis	Lester Piggott
1983 El Gran Senor	Pat Eddery
1984 Kala Dancer	Geoff Baxter
1985 Huntingdale	Michael Hills
1986 Ajdal	Walter Swinburn

MAJOR BRITISH HANDICAPS

WILLIAM HILL LINCOLN HANDICAP

The first big handicap of the season, it is raced over 1 mile at Doncaster in March. Formerly the Lincolnshire Handicap it was raced at Lincoln 1853-1964 except 1916 (Lingfield) and 1952-5 (Pontefract). It became the Lincoln Handicap in 1965 upon moving to its present venue. Irish Sweeps Lincoln Handicap 1969-78, race then sponsored by William Hill.

Recent winners:

Year	Winnner	Jockey
1978	Captain's Wings	Michael Wigham
1979	Fair Season	Greville Starkey
1980	King's Ride	Geoff Baxter
1981	Saher	Ray Cochrane
1982	King's Glory	Bryn Crossley
1983	Mighty Fly	Steve Cauthen
1984	Saving Mercy	Walter Swinburn
1985	Cataldi	Greville Starkey
1986	K-Battery	John Lowe
1987	Star Of A Gunner	John Reid

Most wins: 2 Ob 1906-7, Balmer 1957-8

LADBROKE CHESTER CUP

One of the oldest handicaps still in existence, the Chester Cup dates to 1824. Run over 2 miles 2 furlongs 97 yards. Not held 1983. Sponsored by Ladbroke from 1972.

Recent winners:

Year	Winnner	Jockey
1978	Sea Pigeon	Mark Birch
1979	Charlotte's Choice	Willie Carson
1980	Arapahos	Steve Cauthen
1981	Donegal Prince	Paddy Young
1982	Dawn Johnny	Walter Swinburn
1984	Contester	Geoff Baxter
1985	Morgan's Choice	Willie Carson
1986	Western Dancer	Paul Cook
1987	Just David	Muis Roberts

Most wins: 2 Chivalrous 1922-3, Sea Pigeon 1977-8

ROYAL HUNT CUP

The principal handicap of the Royal Ascot meeting, it was first staged in 1843. Run over 1 mile. The 1941 race was at Newbury.

Recent winners:

Year	Winnner	Jockey
1978	Fear Naught	Michael Wigham
1979	Pipedreamer	Phillip Waldron
1980	Tender Heart	Joe Mercer
1981	Teamwork	Greville Starkey
1982	Buzzard's Bay	Joe Mercer
1983	Mighty Fly	Steve Cauthen
1984	Hawkley	Tyrone Williams
1985	Come On The Blues	Chris Rutter
1986	Patriach	Richard Quinn
1987	Vague Shot	Steve Cauthen

Most wins: 2 Master Vote 1947-8

GOODWOOD CUP

First run 1812. Over 2m 5f at Goodwood.

Recent winners:

Year	Winnner	Jockey
1977	Grey Baron	Geoff Lewis
1978	Tug Of War	Brian Rouse
1979	Le Moss	Joe Mercer
1980	Le Moss	Joe Mercer
1981	Ardross	Lester Piggott

1982	Heighlin	Steve Cauthen
1983	Little Wolf	Willie Carson
1984	Gildoran	Steve Cauthen
1985	Valuable Witness	Pat Eddery
1986	Longboat	Willie Carson
1987	Sergeyevich	Willie Carson

Most wins: 2 Flint Jack 1922-3; Le Moss (as above)

TOTE EBOR HANDICAP

First run 1843. Over 1¾ miles at York. Run at Pontefract over 1½ miles 1943-4. Johnnie Walker Ebor Handicap 1967-73, Terry's All Gold Ebor Handicap 1974-5, Tote from 1976.

Recent winners:

Year	Winnner	Jockey
1977	Move Off	Jimmy Bleasdale
1978	Totowah	Paul Cook
1979	Sea Pigeon	Jonjo O'Neill
1980	Shaftesbury	Greville Starkey
1981	Protection Racket	Mark Birch
1982	Another Sam	Brian Rouse
1983	Jupiter Island	Lester Piggott
1984	Crazy	Walter Swinburn
1985	Western Dancer	Paul Cook
1986	Primary	Greville Starkey

LADBROKES AYR GOLD CUP

Run at Ayr over 6 furlongs. First run 1804. Burmah Castrol Gold Cup 1972-3, Ladbroke from 1974.

Recent winners:

Year	Winnner	Jockey
1977	Jon George	Bruce Raymond
1978	Vaigly Great	Greville Starkey
1979	Primula Boy	Bill Higgins
1980	Sparkling Boy	John Lowe
1981	First Movement	Mick Miller
1982	Famous Star	Paul Eddery
1983	Polly's Brother	Kevin Hodgson
1984	Able Albert	Mark Birch
1985	Camps Heath	Wendyll Woods
1986	Green Ruby	John Williams

WILLIAM HILL CAMBRIDGESHIRE HANDICAP

With the Cesarewitch it completes the Autumn Double. Run over 1 mile 1 furlong, it returned to the Newmarket July course in 1986 after a 45-year spell over the Rowley Mile course. First run 1839, as the Cambridgeshire Stakes until 1970. Run at Nottingham in 1940. Irish Sweeps Cambridgeshire Handicap 1971-7, William Hill since then.

Recent winners:

Year	Winnner	Jockey
1977	Sin Timon	Tony Kimberley
1978	Baronet	Brian Rouse
1979	Smartset	John Reid
1980	Baronet	Brian Rouse
1981	Braughing	Steve Cauthen
1982	Century City	Joe Mercer

1983	Sagamore	Taffy Thomas
1984	Leysh	John Lowe
1985	Tremblant	Pat Eddery
1986	Dallas	Ray Cochrane

Most wins: 2 Hackler's Pride 1903-4, Christmas Daisy 1909-10, Sterope 1948-9, Prince de Galles 1969-70, Baronet (as above)

TOTE CESAREWITCH HANDICAP

The other half of the Autumn Double. Like the Cambridgeshire it was inaugurated in 1839 and is run at Newmarket, but over 2¼ miles.

Recent winners:

Year	Winnner	Jockey
1977	Assured	Philip Waldron
1978	Centurion	John Matthias
1979	Sir Michael	Mark Rimmer
1980	Popsi's Joy	Lester Piggott
1981	Halsbury	Joe Mercer
1982	Mountain Lodge	Willie Carson
1983	Bajan Sunshine	Brian Rouse
1984	Tom Sharp	Steve Dawson
1985	Kayudee	Tony Murray
1986	Orange Hill	Richard Fox

THE IRISH CLASSICS

All Irish Classics are run at the Curragh, situated in County Kildare. The distances of all five races are the same as their English counterparts.

Winners since 1970:

1000 GUINEAS

First run 1922

1970	Black Satin	Ron Hutchinson
1971	Favoletta	Lester Piggott
1972	Pidget	Walter Swinburn, Snr.
1973	Cloonagh	Greville Starkey
1974	Gaily	Ron Hutchinson
1975	Miralla	Ryan Parnell
1976	Sarah Siddons	Christy Roche
1977	Lady Capulet	Tom Murphy
1978	More So	Christy Roche
1979	Godetia	Lester Piggott
1980	Cairn Rouge	Tony Murray
1981	Arctique Royale	Gabriel Curran
1982	Prince's Polly	Walter Swinburn, Jnr.
1983	L'Attrayante	Alain Badel
1984	Katies	Philip Robinson
1985	Al Bahathri	Tony Murray
1986	Sonic Lady	Walter Swinburn, Jnr.
1987	Forest Flower	Tony Ives

2000 GUINEAS

First run 1921

1970	Decies	Lester Piggott
1971	King's Company	Freddy Head
1972	Ballymore	Christy Roche
1973	Sharp Edge	Joe Mercer
1974	Furry Glen	George McGrath
1975	Grundy	Pat Eddery
1976	Northern Treasure	Gabriel Curran

1977	Pampapaul	Franco Dettori
1978	Jaazeiro	Lester Piggott
1979	Dickens Hill	Tony Murray
1980	Nikoli	Christy Roche
1981	King's Lake	Pat Eddery
1982	Dara Monarch	Michael Kinane
1983	Wassl	Tony Murray
1984	Sadlers Wells	George McGrath
1985	Triptych	Christy Roche
1986	Flash of Steel	Michael Kinane
1987	Don't Forget Me	Willie Carson

DERBY

First run 1866

1970	Nijinsky	Liam Ward
1971	Irish Ball	Fredo Gilbert
1972	Steel Pulse	Bill Williamson
1973	Weaver's Hall	George McGrath
1974	English Prince	Yves St.Martin
1975	Grundy	Pat Eddery
1976	Malacate	Philippe Paquet
1977	The Minstrel	Lester Piggott
1978	Shirley Heights	Greville Starkey
1979	Troy	Willie Carson
1980	Tyrnavos	Tony Murray
1981	Shergar	Lester Piggott
1982	Assert	Christy Roche
1983	Shareef Dancer	Walter Swinburn, Jnr.
1984	El Gran Senor	Pat Eddery
1985	Law Society	Pat Eddery
1986	Shahrastani	Walter Swinburn
1987	Sir Harry Lewis	Steve Cauthen

OAKS

First run 1895

1970	Santa Tina	Lester Piggott
1971	Altesse Royale	Geoff Lewis
1972	Regal Exception	Maurice Philipperon
1973	Dahlia	Bill Pyers
1974	Dibidale	Willie Carson
1975	Juliette Marny	Lester Piggott
1976	Lagunette	Philippe Paquet
1977	Olwyn	John Lynch
1978	Fair Salinia	Greville Starkey
1979	Godetia	Lester Piggott
1980	Shoot A Line	Willie Carson
1981	Blue Wind	Walter Swinburn
1982	Swiftfoot	Willie Carson
1983	Give Thanks	Declan Gillespie
1984	Princess Pati	Pat Shanahan
1985	Helen Street	Willie Carson
1986	Colorspin	Pat Eddery
1987	Unite	Walter Swinburn

ST.LEGER

First run 1915

1970	Allangrange	George McGrath
1971	Parnell	A Simpson
1972	Pidget	Thomas Burns
1973	Conor Pass	Peter Jarman
1974	Mistigri	Christy Roche

1975	Caucasus	Lester Piggott
1976	Meneval	Lester Piggott
1977	Transworld	Thomas Murphy
1978	M-Lolshan	Brian Taylor
1979	Niniski	Willie Carson
1980	Gonzales	Raymond Carroll
1981	Protection Racket	Brian Taylor
1982	Touching Wood	Paul Cook
1983	Mountain Lodge	Declan Gillespie
1984	Opale	Darrell McHargue
1985	Leading Counsel	Pat Eddery
1986	Authaal	Christy Roche

THE FRENCH CLASSICS

POULE D'ESSAI DES POULICHES

The equivalent of the 1000 Guineas it is run at Longchamp over 1600 metres (1 mile). First run 1883. Held at Le Tremblay 1943, Maisons-Laffitte 1944-5.

Winners since 1970:

1970	Pampered Miss	Maurice Philipperon
1971	Bold Fascinator	Bill Williamson
1972	Mata Hari	Jean Cruguet
1973	Alles France	Yves Saint-Martin
1974	Dumka	Alain Lequeux
1975	Ivanjica	Freddy Head
1976	Riverqueen	Freddy Head
1977	Madelia	Yves Saint-Martin
1978	Dancing Maid	Freddy Head
1979	Three Troikas	Freddy Head
1980	Aryenne	Maurice Philipperon
1981	Ukraine Girl	Pat Eddery
1982	River Lady	Lester Piggott
1983	L'Attrayante	Alain Badel
1984	Masarika	Yves Saint-Martin
1985	Silvermine	Freddy Head
1986	Baiser Volé	Guy Guignard
1987	Miesque	Freddy Head

POULE D'ESSAI DES POULAINS

Run at Longchamp over 1600 metres, it is the equivalent of the 2000 Guineas. First run 1883. Run at Auteuil 1940, Le Tremblay 1943, Maisons-Laffitte 1944-5.

Winners since 1970:

1970	Caro	Bill Williamson
1971	Zug	Jean-Claude Desaint
1972	Riverman	Jean-Claude Desaint
1973	Kalamoun	Henri Samani
1974	Moulines	Maurice Philipperon
1975	Green Dancer	Freddy Head
1976	Red Lord	Freddy Head
1977	Blushing Groom	Henri Samani
1978	Nishapour	Henri Samani
1979	Irish River	Maurice Philipperon
1980	In Fijar	Georges Doleuze
1981	Recitation	Greville Starkey
1982	Melyno	Yves Saint-Martin
1983	L'Emigrant	Cash Asmussen
1984	Siberian Express	Fredo Gibert
1985	No Pass No Sale	Yves Saint-Martin
1986	Fast Topaze	Cash Asmussen
1987	Soviet Star	Greville Starkey

PRIX DU JOCKEY CLUB

The French Derby, it was first run in 1836. Raced over 2400 metres (1½ miles) at Chantilly. Raced at Longchamp 1919-20, 1941-2, 1945-7, Auteuil 1940, Le Tremblay 1943-4.

Winners since 1970:

1970	Sassafras	Yves Saint-Martin
1971	Rheffic	Bill Pyers
1972	Hard To Beat	Lester Piggott
1973	Roi Lear	Freddy Head
1974	Caracolero	Philippe Paquet
1975	Val de L'Orne	Freddy Head
1976	Youth	Freddy Head
1977	Crystal Palace	Gerard Dubroeucq
1978	Acamas	Yves Saint-Martin
1979	Top Ville	Yves Saint-Martin
1980	Policeman	Willie Carson
1981	Bikala	Serge Gorli
1982	Assert	Christy Roche
1983	Caerleon	Pat Eddery
1984	Darshaan	Yves Saint-Martin
1985	Mouktar	Yves Saint-Martin
1986	Bering	Gary Moore
1987	Natroun	Yves Saint-Martin

PRIX DE DIANE HERMES

The equivalent of the Oaks. It is run over 2100 metres (c.1¼ miles) at Chantilly. First run 1843. Raced at Longchamp 1919-20, 1941-2, 1945-7, Le Tremblay 1943-4.

Winners since 1970:

1970	Sweet Mimosa	Bill Williamson
1971	Pistol Packer	Freddy Head
1972	Rescousse	Yves Saint-Martin
1973	Allez France	Yves Saint-Martin
1974	Highclere	Joe Mercer
1975	No race	
1976	Pawneese	Yves Saint-Martin
1977	Madelia	Yves Saint-Martin
1978	Reine de Saba	Freddy Head
1979	Dunette	Georges Doleuze
1980	Mrs.Penny	Lester Piggott
1981	Madam Gay	Lester Piggott
1982	Harbour	Freddy Head
1983	Escaline	Gary Moore
1984	Northern Trick	Cash Asmussen
1985	Lypharita	Lester Piggott
1986	Lacovia	Freddy Head
1987	Indian Skimmer	Steve Cauthen

PRIX ROYAL OAK

Run over 3100 metres (c. 1 mile 7 furlongs) at Longchamp. The equivalent of the St.Leger it was open only to 3-year-olds until 1978 but since then it has been open to 3-year-olds and upwards. First run 1869. Run at Le Tremblay 1943-4.

Winners since 1970:

1970	Sassafras	Yves Saint-Martin
1971	Bourbon	Freddy Head
1972	Pleben	Marcel Depalmas
1973	Lady Berry	Marcel Depalmas
1974	Busiris	Freddy Head

1975 Henri Le Balafre	Henri Samani
1976 Exceller	Georges Dubroecq
1977 Rex Magan	Philippe Paquet
1978 Brave Johnny	Henri Samani
1979 Niniski	Willie Carson
1980 Gold River	Freddy Head
1981 Ardross	Lester Piggott
1982 Denel	Yves Saint-Martin
1983 Old Country	Pat Eddery
1984 Agent Double	Freddy Head
1985 Mersey	Jean-Luc Kessas
1986 El Cuite	Steve Cauthen

PRIX DE L'ARC DE TRIOMPHE

An end-of-season test for the leading European horses. It is run over 2400 metres (1½ miles) at Longchamp on the first Sunday in October. It was first run in 1920. The 1943-4 races were at Le Tremblay and over 1 miles 3 furlongs.

Winners:

Year	Winner	Jockey
1920	Comrade	Frank Bullock
1921	Ksar	George Stern
1922	Ksar	Frank Bullock
1923	Parth	Frank O'Neill
1924	Massine	Fred Sharpe
1925	Priori	Marcel Allemand
1926	Biribi	Domingo Torterolo
1927	Mon Talisman	Charles Semblat
1928	Kantar	Arthur Esling
1929	Ortello	Paolo Caprioli
1930	Motrico	Marcel Fruhinsholtz
1931	Pearl Cap	Charles Semblat
1932	Motrico	Charles Semblat
1933	Crapom	Paolo Caprioli
1934	Brantôme	Charles Bouillon
1935	Samos	Wally Sibbritt
1936	Corrida	Charlie Elliott
1937	Corrida	Charlie Elliott
1938	Eclair au Chocolat	Charles Bouillon
1941	La Pacha	Paul Francolon
1942	Djebel	Jacko Doyasbère
1943	Verso II	Guy Duforez
1944	Ardan	Jacko Doyasbère
1945	Nikellora	Rae Johnstone
1946	Caracalla	Charlie Elliott
1947	Le Paillon	Fernand Rochetti
1948	Migoli	Charlie Smirke
1949	Coronation	Roger Poincelet
1950	Tantième	Jacko Doyasbère
1951	Tantième	Jacko Doyasbère
1952	Nuccio	Roger Poincelet
1953	La Sorellina	Maurice Larraun
1954	Sica Boy	Rae Johnstone
1955	Ribot	Enrico Camici
1956	Ribot	Enrico Camici
1957	Oroso	Serge Boullenger
1958	Ballymoss	Scobie Breasley
1959	Saint Crespin	George Moore
1960	Puissant Chef	Max Garcia
1961	Molvedo	Enrico Camici
1962	Soltikoff	Marcel Depalmas
1963	Exbury	Jean Deforge

1964	Prince Royal II	Roger Poincelet
1965	Sea Bird II	Pat Glennon
1966	Bon Mot	Freddy Head
1967	Topyo	Bill Pyers
1968	Vaguely Noble	Bill Williamson
1969	Levmoss	Bill Williamson
1970	Sassafras	Yves Saint-Martin
1971	Mill Reef	Geoff Lewis
1972	San San	Freddy Head
1973	Rheingold	Lester Piggott
1974	Allez France	Yves Saint-Martin
1975	Star Appeal	Greville Starkey
1976	Ivanjica	Freddy Head
1977	Alleged	Lester Piggott
1978	Alleged	Lester Piggott
1979	Three Troikas	Freddy Head
1980	Detriot	Pat Eddery
1981	Gold River	Gary Moore
1982	Akiyda	Yves Saint-Martin
1983	All Along	Walter Swinburn
1984	Sagace	Yves Saint-Martin
1985	Rainbow Quest	Pat Eddery
1986	Dancing Brave	Pat Eddery

Most wins (Horse): 2 Ksar, Motrico, Corrida, Tantième, Ribot, Alleged
Most wins (Jockey): 4 Jacko Doyasbère, Freddy Head, Yves Saint-Martin
Most wins (Trainer): 4 Charles Semblat 1942, 1944, 1946, 1949; Alec Head 1952, 1959, 1976, 1981; Francois Mathet 1950-1, 1970, 1982
Most wins (Owner): 6 Marcel Boussac 1936-7, 1942, 1944, 1946, 1949
Fastest winning time: 2:27.7 Dancing Brave (1986)

CHAMPION JOCKEYS (FLAT)

The champion jockeys on the flat in Britain since 1900 have been:

Winners:

Year	Champion	Winners
1900	Lester Reiff	143
1901	Otto Madden	130
1902	Willie Lane	170
1903	Otto Madden	154
1904	Otto Madden	161
1905	Elijah Wheatley	124
1906	Billy Higgs	149
1907	Billy Higgs	146
1908	Danny Maher	139
1909	Frank Wootton	165
1910	Frank Wootton	137
1911	Frank Wootton	187
1912	Frank Wootton	118
1913	Danny Maher	115
1914	Steve Donoghue	129
1915	Steve Donoghue	62
1916	Steve Donoghue	43
1917	Steve Donoghue	42
1918	Steve Donoghue	66
1919	Steve Donoghue	129
1920	Steve Donoghue	143

Year	Jockey	Wins
1921	Steve Donoghue	141
1922	Steve Donoghue	102
1923	Steve Donoghue	89
	Charlie Elliott	89
1924	Charlie Elliott	106
1925	Gordon Richards	118
1926	Tommy Weston	95
1927	Gordon Richards	164
1928	Gordon Richards	148
1929	Gordon Richards	135
1930	Freddy Fox	129
1931	Gordon Richards	145
1932	Gordon Richards	190
1933	Gordon Richards	259
1934	Gordon Richards	212
1935	Gordon Richards	217
1936	Gordon Richards	174
1937	Gordon Richards	216
1938	Gordon Richards	200
1939	Gordon Richards	155
1940	Gordon Richards	68
1941	Harry Wragg	71
1942	Gordon Richards	67
1943	Gordon Richards	65
1944	Gordon Richards	88
1945	Gordon Richards	104
1946	Gordon Richards	212
1947	Gordon Richards	269
1948	Gordon Richards	224
1949	Gordon Richards	261
1950	Gordon Richards	201
1951	Gordon Richards	227
1952	Gordon Richards	231
1953	Gordon Richards	191
1954	Doug Smith	129
1955	Doug Smith	168
1956	Doug Smith	155
1957	Scobie Breasley	173
1958	Doug Smith	165
1959	Doug Smith	157
1960	Lester Piggott	170
1961	Scobie Breasley	171
1962	Scobie Breasley	179
1963	Scobie Breasley	176
1964	Lester Piggott	140
1965	Lester Piggott	166
1966	Lester Piggott	191
1967	Lester Piggott	117
1968	Lester Piggott	139
1969	Lester Piggott	163
1970	Lester Piggott	162
1971	Lester Piggott	162
1972	Willie Carson	132
1973	Willie Carson	163
1974	Pat Eddery	148
1975	Pat Eddery	164
1976	Pat Eddery	162
1977	Pat Eddery	176
1978	Willie Carson	182
1979	Joe Mercer	164
1980	Willie Carson	165
1981	Lester Piggott	179
1982	Lester Piggott	188
1983	Willie Carson	159
1984	Steve Cauthen	130
1985	Steve Cauthen	195
1986	Pat Eddery	177

Most times champion:
26 Gordon Richards, as above
14 George Fordham 1855-63, 1865, 1867-9, 1871*
13 Fred Archer 1874-86; Elnathan Flatman 1840-52
11 Lester Piggott, as above
10 Steve Donoghue, as above
* shared title

Progressive records of most wins in season (since 1840)
 50 Elnathan Flatman (1840)
 68 Elnathan Flatman (1841)
 81 Elnathan Flatman (1845)
 81 Elnathan Flatman (1846)
 89 Elnathan Flatman (1847)
104 Elnathan Flatman (1848)
108 George Fordham (1856)
118 George Fordham (1859)
146 George Fordham (1860)
166 George Fordham (1862)
172 Fred Archer (1875)
207 Fred Archer (1876)
218 Fred Archer (1877)
229 Fred Archer (1878)
232 Fred Archer (1883)
241 Fred Archer (1884)
246 Fred Archer (1885)
259 Gordon Richards (1933)
269 Gordon Richards (1947)

ALL TIME CAREER RECORD OF WINS IN BRITAIN

Wins	Jockey	Years
4870	Gordon Richards	1921-54
4349	Lester Piggott	1948-85
3111	Doug Smith	1931-67
2810	Joe Mercer	1950-85
2748	Fred Archer	1870-86
2600	Willie Carson	1962-86
2591	Eddie Hide	1951-85
2587	George Fordham	1850-84
2313	Eph Smith	1930-65
2161	Scobie Breasley	1950-68
2150	Pat Eddery	1969-86
2067	Bill Nevett	1924-56

LEADING TRAINERS

Since 1945		£
1945	Walter Earl	29,557
1946	Frank Butters	56,140
1947	Fred Darling	65,313
1948	Noel Murless	66,542
1949	Frank Butters	71,721
1950	Charles Semblat (Fra)	57,044
1951	Jack Jarvis	56,397
1952	Marcus Marsh	92,093
1953	Jack Jarvis	71,546
1954	Cecil Boyd-Rochfort	65,326
1955	Cecil Boyd-Rochfort	74,424
1956	Charles Elsey	61,621
1957	Noel Murless	116,898
1958	Cecil Boyd-Rochfort	84,186

1959	Noel Murless	145,727
1960	Noel Murless	118.327
1961	Noel Murless	95,972
1962	Dick Hern	70,206
1963	Paddy Prendergast (Ire)	125,294
1964	Paddy Prendergast (Ire)	128,102
1965	Paddy Prendergast (Ire)	75,323
1966	Vincent O'Brien (Ire)	123,848
1967	Noel Murless	256,899
1968	Noel Murless	141,508
1969	Arthur Budgett	105,349
1970	Noel Murless	199,524
1971	Ian Balding	157,488
1972	Dick Hern	206,767
1973	Noel Murless	132,984
1974	Peter Walwyn	206,445
1975	Peter Walwyn	382,527
1976	Henry Cecil	261,301
1977	Vincent O'Brien (Ire)	439,124
1978	Henry Cecil	382,812
1979	Henry Cecil	683,971
1980	Dick Hern	831,964
1981	Michael Stoute	723,786
1982	Henry Cecil	872,614
1983	Dick Hern	549,598
1984	Henry Cecil	551,939
1985	Henry Cecil	1,148,206
1986	Michael Stoute	1,269,933

Most times leading trainer (since 1896):
12 Alec Taylor 1907, 1909-10, 1914, 1917-23, 1925
 9 Noel Murless, as above
 8 Frank Butters 1927-8, 1932, 1934-5, 1944, 1946, 1949
 6 Fred Darling 1926, 1933, 1940-2, 1947
 6 Henry Cecil, as above

LEADING OWNERS
Since 1945.

		£
1945	17th Earl of Derby	25,067
1946	HH Aga Khan III	24,118
1947	HH Aga Khan III	44,020
1948	HH Aga Khan III	46,393
1949	HH Aga Khan III	68,916
1950	Marcel Boussac	57,044
1951	Marcel Boussac	39,339
1952	HH Aga Khan III	92,518
1953	Sir Victor Sassoon	58,579
1954	HM The Queen	40,993
1955	Lady Zia Wernher	46,345
1956	Major Lionel Holliday	39,327
1957	HM The Queen	62,211
1958	John McShain	63,264
1959	Prince Aly Khan	100,668
1960	Sir Victor Sassoon	90,069
1961	Major Lionel Holliday	39,227
1962	Major Lionel Holliday	70,206
1963	Jim Mullion	68,882
1964	Mrs Howell Jackson	98,270
1965	Jean Ternynck	65,301
1966	Lady Zia Wernher	78,075
1967	Jim Joel	120,925
1968	Raymond Guest	97,075
1969	David Robinson	92,553
1970	Charles Engelhard	182,059

1971	Paul Mellon	138,786
1972	Mrs Jean Hislop	155,190
1973	Nelson Bunker Hunt	124,771
1974	Nelson Bunker Hunt	147,244
1975	Dr Carlo Vittadini	209,492
1976	Daniel Wildenstein	244,500
1977	Robert Sangster	348,023
1978	Robert Sangster	160,405
1979	Sir Michael Sobell	339,751
1980	Simon Weinstock	236,332
1981	HH Aga Khan IV	441,654
1982	Robert Sangster	397,749
1983	Robert Sangster	461,488
1984	Robert Sangster	395,901
1985	Sheikh Mohammed	1,082,502
1986	Sheikh Mohammed	830,121

Most times leading owner (since 1882):
13 HH Aga Khan III 1924, 1929-30, 1932, 1934-5, 1937, 1944, 1946-9, 1952
6 17th Earl of Derby 1923, 1927-8, 1933, 1938, 1945
5 Robert Sangster, as above

LEADING MONEY WINNERS SEASON-BY-SEASON
The leading horses in terms of first prizemoney won each since since 1945 have been:

Year	Horse	£
1945	Sun Stream	13,685
1946	Airborne	20,345
1947	Migoli	17,215
1948	Black Tarquin	21,423
1949	Nimbus	30,236
1950	Palestine	21,583
1951	Supreme Court	36,016
1952	Tulyar	75,173
1953	Pinza	44,101
1954	Never Say Die	30,332
1955	Meld	42,562
1956	Ribot	23,727
1957	Crepello	32,257
1958	Ballymoss	38,686
1959	Petite Etoile	55,487
1960	St.Paddy	71,256
1961	Sweet Solera	36,988
1962	Hethersett	38,497
1963	Ragusa	66,011
1964	Santa Claus	72,067
1965	Sea Bird II	65,301
1966	Charlottown	78,075
1967	Royal Palace	92,998
1968	Sir Ivor	97,075
1969	Blakeney	63,108
1970	Nijinsky	159,681
1971	Mill Reef	121,913
1972	Brigadier Gerard	151,213
1973	Dahlia	79,230
1974	Dahlia	120,771
1975	Grundy	188,375
1976	Wollow	166,389
1977	The Minstrel	201,184
1978	Ile de Bourbon	136,012
1979	Troy	310,359
1980	Ela-Mana-Mou	236,332
1981	Shergar	295,654
1982	Kalaglow	242,304

1983	Sun Princess	221,356
1984	Secreto (USA)	227,680
1985	Oh So Sharp	311,576
1986	Dancing Brave	423,601

All winners 3-year olds except the following: Ribot, Ballymoss, Brigadier Gerard, Dahlia (1974), Kalaglow

CHAMPION JOCKEYS (NATIONAL HUNT)

Prior to the 1925-6 season the championship was decided by winners in a calendar year. Since then it has been taken over the season. Leading jockeys since 1945-6.

Year	Champion	Winners
1944-45	Frenchie Nicholson	15
	Fred Rimell	15
1945-46	Fred Rimell	54
1946-47	Jack Dowdeswell	58
1947-48	Bryan Marshall	66
1948-49	Tim Molony	60
1949-50	Tim Molony	95
1950-51	Tim Molony	83
1951-52	Tim Molony	99
1952-53	Fred Winter	121
1953-54	Dick Francis	76
1954-55	Tim Molony	67
1955-56	Fred Winter	74
1956-57	Fred Winter	80
1957-58	Fred Winter	82
1958-59	Tim Brookshaw	83
1959-60	Stan Mellor	68
1960-61	Stan Mellor	118
1961-62	Stan Mellor	80
1962-63	Josh Gifford	70
1963-64	Josh Gifford	94
1964-65	Terry Biddlecombe	114
1965-66	Terry Biddlecombe	102
1966-67	Josh Gifford	122
1967-68	Josh Gifford	82
1968-69	Bob Davies	77
	Terry Biddlecombe	77
1969-70	Bob Davies	91
1970-71	Graham Thorner	74
1971-72	Bob Davies	89
1972-73	Ron Barry	125
1973-74	Ron Barry	94
1974-75	Tommy Stack	82
1975-76	John Francome	96
1976-77	Tommy Stack	97
1977-78	Jonjo O'Neill	149
1978-79	John Francome	95
1979-80	Jonjo O'Neill	115
1980-81	John Francome	105
1981-82	John Francome	120
	Peter Scudamore	120
1982-83	John Francome	106
1983-84	John Francome	131
1984-85	John Francome	101
1985-86	Peter Scudamore	91
1986-87	Peter Scudamore	123

Most times champion (since 1900):

7 Gerry Wilson 1932/3-1937/8, 1940/1; John Francome, as above

6 Tich Mason 1901-2, 1904-7

5 Bilbie Rees 1920-1, 1924-5, 1926/7; Billy Stott 1927/8-1931/2; Tim Moloney, as above

Progressive record of most wins in a season/year (since 1900):

53	Mr.H.S.Sidney	(1900)
58	Tich Mason	(1901)
67	Tich Mason	(1902)
73	Tich Mason	(1905)
76	W Payne	(1911)
78	I Anthony	(1912)
78	Jack Anthony	(1922)
108	Bilbie Rees	(1924)
121	Fred Winter	(1952/3)
122	Josh Gifford	(1966/7)
125	Ron Barry	(1972/3)
149	Jonjo O'Neill	(1977/8)

LEADING NATIONAL HUNT JOCKEYS

Wins	Jockey	Years
1138	John Francome	1970-85
1035	Stan Mellor	1952-72
923	Fred Winter	1939-64
909	Terry Biddlecombe	1958-74

RACEGOERS CLUB 'RACEHORSE OF THE YEAR' CHAMPIONSHIP

Introduced by the Racecourse Association in 1965 it passed to the Racegoers Club in 1978, whose members take part in a poll each year to decide their 'Horse of the Year'.

Winners:

1965	Sea Bird II
1966	Charlottown
1967	Busted
1968	Sir Ivor
1969	Park Top
1970	Nijinsky
1971	Mill Reef
1972	Brigadier Gerard
1973-4	Dahlia
1975	Grundy
1976	Pawneese
1977	The Minstrel
1978	Shirley Heights
1979	Troy
1980	Moorestyle
1981	Shergar
1982	Ardross
1983	Habibti
1984	Provideo
1985	Pebbles
1986	Dancing Brave

NATIONAL HUNT CHAMPION HORSE OF THE YEAR

Awarded to the champion jumper annually, the voting is along similar lines to that for the flat racehorse of the year.

Winners:

1965/6	Arkle
1966/7	Mill House
1967/8	Persian War
1968/9	Persian War
1969/70	Persian War
1970/1	Bula
1971/2	Bula
1972/3	Pendil

1973/4 Red Rum
1974/5 Comedy of Errors
1975/6 Night Nurse
1976/7 Night Nurse
1977/8 Midnight Court
1978/9 Monksfield
1979/80 Sea Pigeon
1980/1 Sea Pigeon
1981/2 Silver Buck
1982/3 Gaye Brief
1983/4 Dawn Run
1984/5 Forgive'N'Forget
1985/6 Dawn Run
1986/7 Desert Orchid

RACING IN AUSTRALIA

MELBOURNE CUP

The highlight of the racing season in Australia is the Melbourne Cup. Like Royal Ascot it is as much a social occasion as a race-day. Always held on the first Tuesday in November, it was inaugurated in 1861. The race is for 3-year-olds and upwards, and, since 1972 has been over 3200 metres of the Flemington racecourse in Victoria. Prior to then it was over the imperial equivalent of two miles.

Post-war winners:

1945	Rainbird	Billy Cook
1946	Russia	Darby Munro
1947	Hiraji	Jack Purtell
1948	Rimfire	Ray Neville
1949	Foxzami	W Fellows
1950	Comic Court	Pat Glennon
1951	Delta	Neville Sellwood
1952	Dalray	Bill Williamson
1953	Wodalla	Jack Purtell
1954	Rising Fast	Jack Purtell
1955	Toparoa	Neville Sellwood
1956	Evening Peal	G Podmore
1957	Straight Draw	Noel McGrowdie
1958	Baystone	Mel Schumacher
1959	Macdougal	Pat Glennon
1960	Hi Jinx	Bill Smith
1961	Lord Fury	Roy Selkrig
1962	Even Stevens	L Cole
1963	Gatum Gatum	Jim Johnson
1964	Polo Prince	R Taylor
1965	Light Fingers	Roy Higgins
1966	Galilee	Johnny Miller
1967	Red Handed	Roy Higgins
1968	Rain Lover	Jim Johnson
1969	Rain Lover	Jim Johnson
1970	Baghdad Note	E J Didham
1971	Silver Knight	Bruce Marshall
1972	Piping Lane	John Letts
1973	Gala Supreme	Frank Reys
1974	Think Big	Harry White
1975	Think Big	Harry White
1976	Van der Hum	R J Skelton
1977	Gold and Black	John Duggan
1978	Arwon	Harry White
1979	Hyperno	Harry White
1980	Beldale Ball	John Letts

1981	Just a Dash	Peter Cook
1982	Gurner's Lane	Mick Dittman
1983	Kiwi	Jimmy Cassidi
1984	Black Knight	Peter Cook
1985	What A Nuisance	P Hyland
1986	At Talaq	Michael Clarke

Most wins (Jockey): 4 Bobby Lewis (The Victory 1902, Patrobas 1915, Artilleryman 1919, Trivalve 1927); Harry White, as above
Most wins (Trainer): 7 Bart Cummings 1965-7, 1974-5, 1977, 1979
Most wins (Horse): 2 Archer 1861-2, Peter Pan 1932, 1934, Rain Lover 1968-9, Think Big 1974-5
Fastest winning time (2 miles): 3:19.1 Rain Lover (1968) (3200 m): 3:18.4 Gold and Black (1977)

RACING IN THE UNITED STATES

WASHINGTON DC INTERNATIONAL

The Washington International was the idea of John D.Schapiro, the president of Laurel Racecourse in Maryland. The first International was at Laurel Park in October 1952 and was run over 1½ miles. The race showed a steady decline in international status in recent years, and Schapiro sold his interest in the track in 1984.

Winners:

Year	Winnner	Jockey
1952	Wilwyn	Manny Mercer
1953	Worden II	Charlie Smirke
1954	Fisherman	Eddie Arcaro
1955	El Chama	R Bustamante
1956	Master Boing	Guy Chancelier
1957	Mahan	Sam Boulmetis
1958	Sailor's Guide	Howard Grant
1959	Bald Eagle	Manuel Ycaza
1960	Bald Eagle	Manuel Ycaza
1961	T.V.Lark	Johnny Longden
1962	Match III	Yves Saint-Martin
1963	Mongo	Wayne Chambers
1964	Kelso	Ismael Valenzuela
1965	Diatome	Jean Deforge
1966	Behistoun	Jean Deforge
1967	Fort Marcy	Manuel Ycaza
1968	Sir Ivor	Lester Piggott
1969	Karabas	Lester Piggott
1970	Fort Marcy	Jorge Velasquez
1971	Run The Gauntlet	Bobby Woodhouse
1972	Droll Role	Braulio Baeza
1973	Dahlia	Bill Pyers
1974	Admetus	Michael Philipperon
1975	Nobiliary	Sandy Hawley
1976	Youth	Sandy Hawley
1977	Johnny D	Steve Cauthen
1978	Mac Diarmida	Jean Cruguet
1979	Bowl Game	Jorge Velasquez
1980	Argument	Lester Piggott
1981	Providential II	Alain Lequeux
1982	April Run	Cash Asmussen
1983	All Along	Walter Swinburn
1984	Seattle Song	Cash Asmussen

1985 Vanlandingham	Don MacBeth
1986 Lieutenant's Lark	Robbie Davis

Most wins (Horse): 2 Bald Eagle, Fort Marcy,
Most wins (Jockey): 3 Lester Piggott, Manuel Ycaza

THE AMERICAN TRIPLE CROWN

Like the English Classics, the three races that make up the American Triple Crown are for 3-year-olds only.

KENTUCKY DERBY

First run in 1875. Raced at Churchill Downs, Louisville, and over 1¼ miles.

Winners since 1970:

1970 Dust Commander	Mike Manganello
1971 Canonero	Gustavo Avila
1972 Riva Ridge	Ron Turcotte
1973 Secretariat	Ron Turcotte
1974 Cannonade	Angel Cordero, Jnr
1975 Foolish Pleasure	Jacinto Vasquez
1976 Bold Forbes	Angel Cordero, Jnr
1977 Seattle Slew	Jean Cruguet
1978 Affirmed	Steve Cauthen
1979 Spectacular Bid	Ron Franklin
1980 Genuine Risk	Jacinto Vasquez
1981 Pleasant Colony	Jorge Velasquez
1982 Gato Del Sol	Eddie Delahoussaye
1983 Sunny's Halo	Eddie Delahoussaye
1984 Swale	Laffit Pincay, Jnr
1985 Spend A Buck	Angel Cordero
1986 Ferdinand	Willie Shoemaker
1987 Alysheba	Chris McCarron

PREAKNESS STAKES

Raced at Pimlico, Maryland, over 1 mile 1½ furlongs. First run 1873.

Winners since 1970:

1970 Personality	Eddie Belmonte
1971 Canonero	Gustavo Avila
1972 Bee Bee Bee	Eddie Nelson
1973 Secretariat	Ron Turcotte
1974 Little Current	Miguel Rivera
1975 Master Derby	Darrell McHargue
1976 Elocutionist	John Lively
1977 Seattle Slew	Jean Cruguet
1978 Affirmed	Steve Cauthen
1979 Spectacular Bid	Ron Franklin
1980 Codex	Angel Cordero, Jnr
1981 Pleasant Colony	Jorge Velasquez
1982 Aloma's Ruler	Jack Kaenel
1983 Deputed Testamony	Don Miller, Jnr
1984 Gate Dancer	Angel Cordero, Jnr
1985 Tank's Prospect	Pat Day
1986 Snow Chief	Alex Solis
1987 Alysheba	Chris McCarron

BELMONT STAKES

The oldest of the thre Triple Crown races, it was first held in 1867. Run over 1½ miles at Belmont Park, New York.

Winners since 1970:

1970 Echelon	John Rotz
1971 Pass Catcher	Walter Blum
1972 Riva Ridge	Ron Turcotte
1973 Secretariat	Ron Turcotte
1974 Little Current	Miguel Rivera
1975 Avatar	Willie Shoemaker
1976 Bold Forbes	Angel Cordero, Jnr
1977 Seattle Slew	Jean Cruguet
1978 Affirmed	Steve Cauthen
1979 Coastal	Ruben Hernandez
1980 Temperence Hill	Eddie Maple
1981 Summing	George Martens
1982 Conquistador Cielo	Laffit Pincay, Jnr
1983 Caveat	Laffit Pincay, Jnr
1984 Swale	Laffit Pincay, Jnr
1985 Creme Fraiche	Eddie Maple
1986 Danzig Connection	Chris McCarron
1987 Bet Twice	Craig Perret

The following 11 horses have successfully won all legs of the Triple Crown:

1919 Sir Barton
1930 Gallant Fox
1935 Omaha
1937 War Admiral
1941 Whirlaway
1943 Count Fleet
1946 Assault
1948 Citation
1973 Secretariat
1977 Seattle Slew
1978 Affirmed

THE BREEDERS' CUP

An end-of-season gathering at which leading American and European horses compete in seven different races for total prizemoney of $10 million, with the top prize, $3 million, going to the winner of the Breeders' Cup Classic. The winner of the Breeders' Cup Turf receives $2 million, and all other winners each receive $1 million. It was inaugurated in 1984 at Hollywood Park. The meeting was at Aqueduct in 1985 and at Santa Anita in 1986.

Winners:

BREEDERS' CUP SPRINT (6f)

1984 Ellio	Craig Perret
1985 Precisionist	Chris McCarron
1986 Smile	Jacinto Vasquez

BREEDERS' CUP MILE

1984 Royal Heroine	Fernando Toro
1985 Cozzene	Walter Guerra
1986 Last Tycoon	Yves Saint-Martin

BREEDERS' CUP JUVENILE (1m 1f)

1984 Chief's Crown	Don MacBeth
1985 Tasso	Laffit Pincay, Jnr
1986 Capote	Laffit Pincay, Jnr

BREEDERS' CUP JUVENILE FILLIES (1m1f)

1984 Outstandingly	Walter Guerra
1985 Twilight Ridge	Jorge Velasquez
1986 Brave Raj	Pat Valenzuela

BREEDERS' CUP DISTAFF (1¼ m)
1984 Princess Rooney   Eddie Delahoussaye
1985 Life's Magic   Angel Cordero, Jnr
1986 Lady's Secret   Pat Day

BREEDERS' CUP CLASSIC (1¼ m)
1984 Wild Again   Pat Day
1985 Proud Truth   Jorge Velasquez
1986 Skywalker   Laffit Pincay, Jnr

BREEDERS' CUP TURF (1½m)
1984 Lashkari   Yves St.Martin
1985 Pebbles   Pat Eddery
1986 Manila   José Santos

ANNUAL LEADING MONEYWINNING HORSES AND JOCKEYS
from 1946

Year	Leading horse	$	Jockey	
1946	Assault	424,195	Ted Atkinson	1,036,825
1947	Armed	376,325	Doug Dodson	1,429,949
1948	Citation	709,470	Eddie Arcaro	1,686,230
1949	Ponder	321,825	Steve Brooks	1,316,817
1950	Noor	346,940	Eddie Arcaro	1,410,160
1951	Counterpoint	250,525	Willie Shoemaker	1,329,890
1952	Crafty Admiral	277,255	Eddie Arcaro	1,859,591
1953	Native Dancer	513,425	Willie Shoemaker	1,784,187
1954	Determine	328,700	Willie Shoemaker	1,876,760
1955	Nashua	752,550	Eddie Arcaro	1,864,796
1956	Needles	440,850	Bill Hartack	2,343,955
1957	Round Table	600,383	Bill Hartack	3,060,501
1958	Round Table	662,780	Willie Shoemaker	2,961,693
1959	Sword Dancer	537,004	Willie Shoemaker	2,843,133
1960	Bally Ache	455,045	Willie Shoemaker	2,123,961
1961	Carry Back	565,349	Willie Shoemaker	2,690,819
1962	Never Bend	402,969	Willie Shoemaker	2,916,844
1963	Candy Spots	604,481	Willie Shoemaker	2,526,925
1964	Gun Bow	580,100	Willie Shoemaker	2,649,553
1965	Buckpasser	568,096	Braulio Baeza	2,582,702
1966	Buckpasser	669,078	Braulio Baeza	2,951,022
1967	Damascus	817,941	Braulio Baeza	3,088,888
1968	Forward Pass	546,674	Braulio Baeza	2,835,108
1969	Arts and Letters	555,604	Jorge Velasquez	2,542,315
1970	Personality	444,049	Laffit Pincay Jr	2,626,526
1971	Riva Ridge	503,263	Laffit Pincay Jr	3,784,377
1972	Droll Roll	471,633	Laffit Pincay Jr	3,225,827
1973	Secretariat	860,404	Laffit Pincay Jr	4,093,492
1974	Chris Evert	551,063	Laffit Pincay Jr	4,251,060
1975	Foolish Pleasure	716,278	Braulio Baeza	3,695,198
1976	Forego	491,701	Angel Cordero Jr	4,709,500
1977	Seattle Slew	641,370	Steve Cauthen	6,151,750
1978	Affirmed	901,541	Darrel McHargue	6,029,885
1979	Spectacular Bid	1,279,334	Laffit Pincay Jr	8,193,535
1980	Temperance Hill	1,130,452	Chris McCarron	7,663,300
1981	John Henry	1,148,800	Chris McCarron	8,397,604
1982	Perrault	1,197,400	Angel Cordero Jr	9,483,590
1983	All Along	2,138,963	Angel Cordero Jr	10,116,697
1984	Slew O'Gold	2,627,944	Chris McCarron	12,045,813
1985	Spend A Buck	3,552,704	Laffit Pincay	13,415,049
1986	Snow Chief	1,875,200	Jose Santos	11,329,297

TOTAL CAREER EARNINGS (to 1 Jan 1987)

HORSES
	$	
John Henry	6,597,947	1977-84
Spend A Buck	4,220,669	1984-5
Slew O'Gold	3,533,534	1982-4
All Along	3,018,420	1981-4

Willie Shoemaker – still adding to his record number of winning rides. His first race was on 19 Mar 1949 and his first win on 20 Apr 1949. (All-Sport)

JOCKEYS

	$	
Laffit Pincay Jr	116,622,090	1966-86
Willie Shoemaker	110,222,655	1949-86

JOCKEYS

Most wins in a year: 546 Chris McCarron 1974 from 2199 mounts
Most wins in a career: 8514 Willie Shoemaker 1949-86

TRAINERS

Greatest season's earnings: $13,344,595 D.Wayne Lukas in 1986 from 1510 mounts, 259 winners.
Most wins in a year: 496 Jack Van Berg 1976
Most wins in a career: 4800 Jack Van Berg 1957-87

ECLIPSE AWARDS

From 1971 the annual polls conducted by the Thoroughbred Racing Association, the *Daily Racing Form* and the National Turf Writers' Association have been combined to determine the recipients of the Eclipse Award.

Horse of the Year from 1971:

1971 Ack Ack
1972-3 Secretariat
1974-6 Forego
1977 Seattle Slew
1978-9 Affirmed
1980 Spectacular Bid
1981 John Henry
1982 Conquistador Cielo
1983 All Along
1984 John Henry
1985 Spend A Buck
1986 Snow Chief

Most wins in the Thoroughbred Racing Association Poll prior to 1971: 5 Kelso 1960-4

HURLING

A 15-a-side stick and ball game, Hurling is an ancient game dating to around 1800 BC. It was outlawed in Ireland in 1367 by the statute of Kilkenny. The Irish Hurling Union was founded in 1879 and the rules standardized following the formation of the Gaelic Athletic Association in 1884.

ALL-IRELAND CHAMPIONSHIPS

Played on the first Sunday in September each year the All-Ireland Final is the highlight of the Hurling season. The final of this inter-county event takes place at Dublin's Croke Park and the winning team receives the McCarthy Cup. Contested annually from 1887, with the exception of the unfinished championship of 1888.

Cork beat Galway in the 1986 All-Ireland final. (All-Sport)

Wins:

25	Cork	1890, 1892-4, 1902-3, 1919, 1926, 1928-9, 1931,1941-4, 1946, 1952-4, 1970, 1976-8, 1984, 1986
23	Tipperary	1887, 1895-6, 1898-1900, 1906, 1908, 1916, 1925, 1930, 1937, 1945, 1949-51, 1958, 1961-2, 1964-5, 1969, 1971
23	Kilkenny	1904-5, 1907, 1909, 1911-3, 1922, 1932-3, 1935, 1939, 1947, 1957, 1963, 1966-7, 1972, 1974-5, 1979, 1982-3
7	Limerick	1897, 1918, 1921, 1934, 1936, 1940, 1973
6	Dublin	1889, 1917, 1920, 1924, 1927, 1938
5	Wexford	1910, 1955-6, 1960, 1968
2	Galway	1923, 1980
2	Waterford	1948, 1959
2	Offaly	1981, 1985
1	Kerry	1891
1	London Irish	1901
1	Clare	1914
1	Laois	1915

Highest score: Cork 39 Wexford 25
Most individual appearances: 10 Christy Ring (Cork and Munster) and John Doyle (Tipperary)

ICE HOCKEY

Played by teams of 6-a-side with stick and puck. It probably derives from bandy, played on ice-covered pitches, and the 1850s are usually cited for the advent of the puck in Canada, where the game has for long been the major sport. The first rules for Ice Hockey were drawn up by W.F.Robertson and R.F.Smith, students at McGill University, Montreal. The Ontario Hockey Association was formed in 1887.

The sport's governing body is the International Ice Hockey Federation (IIHF), founded in 1908.

OLYMPIC GAMES

An Olympic sport from 1920, it was held at the summer Games of 1920, but thereafter at the Winter Olympics.

Wins:

6	Canada	1920, 1924, 1928, 1932, 1948, 1952
6	USSR	1956, 1964, 1968, 1972, 1976, 1984
2	USA	1960, 1980
1	Great Britain	1936

Most gold medals by an individual: 3 by the USSR players Vitaliy Davidov, Anatoliy Firssov, Viktor Kuzkin and Aleksandr Ragulin 1964-72; Vladislav Tretyak 1972-84.

WORLD CHAMPIONSHIPS

Held annually from 1930, except for the war years and in 1980. In Olympic years up to 1968 those championships were also recognised as the world championships.

Most wins:

20	USSR	1954, 1956, 1963-71, 1973-5, 1978-9, 1981-3, 1986
19	Canada	1920, 1924, 1928, 1930-2, 1934-5, 1937-9, 1948, 1950-2, 1955, 1958-9, 1961
6	Czechoslovakia	1947, 1949, 1972, 1976-7, 1985
4	Sweden	1953, 1957, 1962, 1987
2	USA	1933, 1960
1	Great Britain	1936

Highest score in a world championship match: Australia beat New Zealand 58-0 at Perth, 14 Mar 1987

THE IIHF CANADA CUP

First held in 1979, this tournament is contested by the world's six best teams.

Winners:
1969 Canada, 1981 USSR, 1984 Canada

NATIONAL HOCKEY LEAGUE

Founded in 1917 in Montreal, succeeding the National Hockey Association. It is now contested by 21 teams from Canada and the USA, divided into two divisions within two conferences: Adams and Patrick Divisions in the Wales Conference; Norris and Smythe Divisions in the Campbell Conference. The top teams play-off annually for the Stanley Cup, which was first presented in 1893 by Lord Stanley of Preston, then Governor-General of Canada. From 1894 it was contested by amateur teams for the Canadian Championship. From 1910 it became the award for the winners of the professional league play-offs.

STANLEY CUP

Wins:

23	Montreal Canadiens	1916, 1924, 1930-1, 1944, 1946, 1953, 1956-60, 1965-6, 1968-9, 1971, 1973, 1976-9, 1986
11	Toronto Maple Leafs	1932, 1942, 1945, 1947-9, 1951, 1962-4, 1967
7	Detroit Red Wings	1936-7, 1943, 1950, 1952, 1954-5
6	Ottawa Senators	1909, 1911, 1920-1, 1923, 1927
5	Montreal Victorias	1895-9
5	Boston Bruins	1929, 1939, 1941, 1970, 1972
4	Montreal Wanderers	1906-8, 1910
4	New York Islanders	1980-3
3	Ottawa Silver Seven	1903-5
3	New York Rangers	1928, 1933, 1940
3	Chicago Black Hawks	1934, 1938, 1961
3	Edmonton Oilers	1984-5, 1987
2	Montreal AAA	1894, 1902
2	Quebec Bulldogs	1912-3
2	Montreal Maroons	1926, 1935
2	Philadelphia Flyers	1974-5

1 Montreal Shamrocks 1900, Winnipeg Victorias 1901, Kenora Thistles 1907, Toronto Ontarios 1914, Vancouver Millionaires 1915, Seattle Metropolitans 1917, Toronto Arenas 1918, Toronto St Patricks 1922, Victoria Cougars 1925

Year given is that of second half of season. There were two contests in 1907, and in 1919 the series was unfinished due to an influenza outbreak.

The Conn Smythe Trophy for the most valuable player in the play-offs has been awarded annually from 1965. The only players to win it twice have been: Bobby Orr (Boston) 1970, 1972 and Bernie Parent (Philadelphia) 1974-5.

NATIONAL LEAGUE INDIVIDUAL RECORDS:

CAREER:

Goals	801	Gordie Howe (Detroit Red Wings) 1946-71
Assists:	1049	Gordie Howe (Detroit Red Wings) 1946-71
Points:	1850	Gordie Howe (Detroit Red Wings) 1946-71

SEASON:

Goals:	92	Wayne Gretzky (Edmonton Oilers) 1981-2
Assists:	163	Wayne Gretzky (Edmonton Oilers) 1985-6
Points:	215	Wayne Gretzky (Edmonton Oilers) 1985-6

GAME:

Goals	7	Joe Malone for Quebec Bulldogs v Toronto St Patrick's, 31 Jan 1920
Assists:	7	Billy Taylor for Detroit Red Wings v Chicago Black Hawks, 16 Mar 1947
	7	Wayne Gretzky for Edmonton Oilers v Washington, 15 Feb 1980
Points:	10	Darryl Sittler (6 goals 4 assists) for Toronto Maple Leafs v Boston Bruins, 7 Feb 1976

Wayne Gretzky. (All-Sport)

TEAM GAME:

Goals:	16	Montreal Canadiens beat Quebec Bulldogs 16-3, 3 Mar 1920
Aggregate:	21	Montreal Canadiens beat Toronto St Patrick's 14-7, Montreal, 10 Jan 1930.

HART TROPHY

Awarded annually by the Professional Hockey Writers Association as the Most Valuable Player award of the NHL.

Most wins:
7 Wayne Gretzky (Edmonton Oilers) 1980-6; 5 Gordie Howe (Detroit Red Wings) 1953, 1957-8, 1960, 1963; 3 Eddie Shore (Boston Bruins) 1933, 1936, 1938; 3 Bobby Orr (Boston Bruins) 1970-2; 3 Bobby Clarke (Philadelphia Flyers) 1973, 1975-6.

ROSS TROPHY

Awarded annually from 1947-8 to the NHL season's leading scorer.

Most wins: 6 Gordie Howe (Detroit Red Wings) 1951-4, 1957, 1963; 6 Wayne Gretzky (Edmonton Oilers) 1981-6; 5 Phil Esposito (Boston Bruins) 1969, 1971-4; 4 Stan Mikita (Chicago Black Hawks) 1964-5, 1967-8.

JAMES NORRIS MEMORIAL TROPHY

Awarded annually from the 1953-4 season to the league's leading defenseman.

Most wins: 8 Bobby Orr (Boston Bruins) 1968-75.

WAYNE GRETZKY

To the end of the 1986-7 season, Gretzky's career figures for the Edmonton Oilers are as follows: in 733 NHL games and Stanley Cup play-offs, he has scored 612 goals, with 1117 assists for 1729 points. In his 101 Stanley Cup play-offs he has scored 69 goals, 140 assists for 209 points.

ICE SKATING

Skating in a primitive form is over 2000 years old, but probably first became popular on frozen canals in the Netherlands some 300 years ago. The Dutch were the main exponents of speed skating over the next two hundred years. Figure skating originated in Britain and the first known skating club was the Edinburgh Skating Club, formed c.1742. The first recorded race was in the Fens in 1763 and the earliest artificial rink was opened in Baker Street, London in 1842, although the surface was not of ice. The first artificial ice rink was opened at the Glaciarium, London in 1876, three years before the foundation of the National Skating Association of Great Britain.

Ice skating may be divided into two: figure skating, on rinks of 60m × 30m; and speed skating. The world governing body for both is the International Skating Union (ISU), founded in 1892, and which now has its headquarters in Switzerland.

FIGURE SKATING

Note that in pairs and ice dance competitions the women's name is conventionally listed first.

OLYMPIC GAMES

Winners:

	MEN	**WOMEN**
1908	Ulrich Salchow (Swe) Nikolay Panin (Russia)*	Madge Syers (née Cave) (UK)
1920	Gillis Grafström (Swe)	Magda Julin-Mauroy (Swe)
1924	Gillis Grafström (Swe)	Herma Planck-Szabo (Aut)
1928	Gillis Grafström (Swe)	Sonja Henie (Nor)
1932	Karl Schäfer (Aut)	Sonja Henie (Nor)
1936	Karl Schaäer (Aut)	Sonja Henie (Nor)
1948	Richard Button (USA)	Barbara Ann Scott (Can)

1952 Richard Button (USA)	Jeannette Altwegg (UK)
1956 Hayes Alan Jenkins(USA)	Tenley Albright (USA)
1960 David Jenkins (USA)	Carol Heiss (USA)
1964 Manfred Schnelldorfer (FRG)	Sjoukje Dijkstra (Hol)
1968 Wolfgang Schwarz (Aut)	Peggy Fleming (USA)
1972 Ondrej Nepela (Cs)	Beatrix Schuba (Aut)
1976 John Curry (UK)	Dorothy Hamill (USA)
1980 Robin Cousins (UK)	Anett Pötzsch (GDR)
1984 Scott Hamilton (USA)	Katarina Witt (GDR)

*Special figures competition

PAIRS
1908 Anna Hübler/Heinrich Burger (Ger)
1920 Ludowika Jakobsson/Walter Jakobsson (Fin)
1924 Helene Engelmann/Alfred Berger (Aut)
1928 Andrée Joly/Pierre Brunet (Fra)
1932 Andrée Brunet (née Joly)/Pierre Brunet (Fra)
1936 Maxi Herber/Ernst Baier (Ger)
1948 Micheline Lannoy/Pierre Baugniet (Bel)
1952 Ria Falk/Paul Falk (FRG)
1956 Elisabeth Schwarz/Kurt Oppelt (Aut)
1960 Barbara Wagner/Robert Paul (Can)
1964 Lyudmila Belousova/Oleg Protopopov (USSR)
1968 Lyudmila Belousova/Oleg Protopopov (USSR)
1972 Irina Rodnina/Aleksey Ulanov (USSR)
1976 Irina Rodnina/Aleksandr Zaitsev (USSR)
1980 Irina Rodnina/Aleksandr Zaitsev (USSR)
1984 Yelena Valova/Oleg Vasiliev (USSR)

Most wins: 3 Irina Rodnina

ICE DANCE
1976 Lyudmila Pakhomova/Alexsandr Gorshkov (USSR)
1980 Natalya Linitschuck/Gennadiy Karponosov (USSR)
1984 Jayne Torvill/Christopher Dean (UK)

WORLD CHAMPIONSHIPS
Held annually, first in St,Petersburg (now Leningrad) in 1896. The 1961 championships were cancelled after all the US team were killed in a plane crash.

Winners:

MEN
1896 Gilbert Fuchs (Ger)
1897 Gustav Hügel (Aut)
1898 Henning Grenander (Swe)
1899-1900 Gustav Hügel (Aut)
1901-5 Ulrich Salchow (Swe)
1906 Gilbert Fuchs (Ger)
1907-11 Ulrich Salchow (Swe)
1912-3 Fritz Kachler (Aut)
1914 Gösta Sandahl (Swe)
1922 Gillis Grafström (Swe)
1923 Fritz Kachler (Aut)
1924 Gillis Grafström (Swe)
1925-8 Willy Böckl (Aut)
1929 Gillis Grafström (Swe)
1930-6 Karl Schäfer (Aut)
1937-8 Felix Kaspar (Aut)
1939 Graham Sharp (UK)
1947 Hans Gerschwiler (Swi)
1948-52 Richard Button (USA)
1953-6 Hayes Alan Jenkins (USA)
1957-9 David Jenkins (USA)

1960 Alain Giletti (Fra)
1962 Donald Jackson (Can)
1963 Donald McPherson (Can)
1964 Manfred Schnelldorfer (FRG)
1965 Alain Calmat (Fra)
1966-8 Emmerich Danzer (Aut)
1969-70 Tim Wood (USA)
1971-3 Ondrej Nepela (Cs)
1974 Jan Hoffmann (GDR)
1975 Sergey Volkov (USSR)
1976 John Curry (UK)
1977 Vladimir Kovalyev (USSR)
1978 Charles Tickner (USA)
1979 Vladimir Kovalyev (USSR)
1980 Jan Hoffmann (GDR)
1981-4 Scott Hamilton (USA)
1985 Aleksandr Fadeyev (USSR)
1986 Brian Boitano (USA)
1987 Brian Orser (Can)

Most wins: 10 Ulrich Salchow; 7 Karl Schäfer; 5 Richard Button

WOMEN
1906-7 Madge Syers (née Cave) (UK)
1908-11 Lily Kronberger (Hun)
1912-4 Opika von Méray Horvath (Hun)
1922-4 Herma Szabo (née Planck) (Aut)
1925-6 Herma Jaross (née Planck-Szabo) (Aut)
1927-36 Sonja Henie (Nor)
1937 Cecilia Colledge (UK)
1938-9 Megan Taylor (UK)
1947-8 Barbara Ann Scott (Can)
1949-50 Alena Vrzanova (Cs)
1951 Jeannette Altwegg (UK)
1952 Jacqueline du Bief (Fra)
1953 Tenley Albright (USA)
1954 Gundi Busch (FRG)
1955 Tenley Albright (USA)
1956-60 Carol Heiss (USA)
1962-4 Sjoukje Dijkstra (Hol)
1965 Petra Burka (Can)
1966-8 Peggy Fleming (USA)
1969-70 Gabriele Seyfert (GDR)
1971-2 Beatrix Schuba (Aut)
1973 Karen Magnussen (Can)
1974 Christine Errath (GDR)
1975 Dianne De Leeuw (Hol)
1976 Dorothy Hamill (USA)
1977 Linda Fratianne (USA)
1978 Anett Pötzsch (GDR)
1979 Linda Fratianne (USA)
1980 Anett Pötzsch (GDR)
1981 Denise Biellmann (Swi)
1982 Elaine Zayak (USA)
1983 Rosalynn Sumners (USA)
1984-5 Katarina Witt (GDR)
1986 Debbie Thomas (USA)
1987 Katarina Witt (GDR)

Most wins: 10 Sonja Henie; 6 Carol Heiss

PAIRS
1908 Anna Hübler/Heinrich Burger (Ger)
1909 Phyllis Johnson/James Johnson (UK)
1910 Anna Hübler/Heinrich Burger (Ger)

Jayne Torvill and Christopher Dean. (All-Sport)

1911 Ludowika Eilers/Walter Jakobsson (Fin)
1912 Phyllis Johnson/James Johnson (UK)
1913 Helene Engelmann/Karl Mejstrick (Aut)
1914 Ludowika Eilers/Walter Jakobsson (Fin)
1922 Helene Engelmann/Alfred Berger (Aut)
1923 Ludowika Jakobsson (née Eilers)/Walter Jakobsson (Fin)
1924 Helene Engelmann/Alfred Berger (Aut)
1925 Herma Jaross-Szabo/Ludwig Wrede (Aut)
1926 Andrée Joly/Pierre Brunet (Fra)
1927 Herma Jaross-Szabo/Ludwig Wrede (Aut)
1928 Andrée Joly/Pierre Brunet (Fra)
1929 Lilly Scholz/Otto Kaiser (Aut)
1930 Andrée Brunet (née Joly)/Pierre Brunet (Fra)
1931 Emilie Rotter/Laszlo Szollas (Hun)
1932 Andrée Brunet/Pierre Brunet (Fra)
1933-5 Emilie Rotter/Laszlo Szollas (Hun)
1936-9 Maxi Herber/Ernst Baier (Ger)
1947-8 Micheline Lannoy/Pierre Baugniet (Bel)
1949 Andrea Kékesy/Ede Kiraly (Hun)
1950 Karol Kennedy/Peter Kennedy (USA)
1951-2 Ria Falk (née Baran)/Paul Falk (FRG)
1953 Jennifer Nicks/John Nicks (UK)
1954-5 Frances Dafoe/Norris Bowden (Can)
1956 Elisabeth Schwarz/Kurt Oppelt (Aut)
1957-60 Barbara Wagner/Robert Paul (Can)
1962 Maria Jelinek/Otto Jelinek (Can)
1963-4 Marika Kilius/Hans-Jürgen Bäumler (FRG)

1965-8 Lyudmila Belousova/Oleg Protopopov (USSR)
1969-72 Irina Rodnina/Aleksey Ulanov (USSR)
1973-8 Irina Rodnina/Aleksandr Zaitsev (USSR)
1979 Tai Babilonia/Randy Gardner (USA)
1980 Marina Tcherkassova/Sergey Shakrai (USSR)
1981 Irina Vorobyeva/Igor Lissovsky (USSR)
1982 Sabine Baess/Tassilo Thierbach (GDR)
1983 Yelena Valova/Oleg Vasiliev (USSR)
1984 Barbara Underhill/Paul Martini (Can)
1985 Yelena Valova/Oleg Vasiliev (USSR)
1986-7 Yekaterina Gordeyeva/Sergey Grinkov (USSR)

Most wins: 10 Irina Rodnina; 6 Aleksandr Zaitsev

ICE DANCE
Although the first official world ice dance championships were in 1952, unofficial championships were staged in 1950 and 1951. The winners were: 1950 Lois Waring/Michael McGean (USA); 1951 Jean Westwood/Lawrence Demmy (UK)

Official winners:
1952-5 Jean Westwood/Lawrence Demmy (UK)
1956 Pamela Weight/Paul Thomas (UK)
1957-8 June Markham/Courtney Jones (UK)
1959-60 Doreen Denny/Courtney Jones (UK)
1962-5 Eva Romanova/Pavel Roman (Cs)
1966-9 Diana Towler/Bernard Ford (UK)
1970-4 Lyudmila Pakhomova/Aleksandr Gorshkov (USSR)
1975 Irina Moiseyeva/Andrey Minenkov (USSR)
1976 Lyudmila Pakhomova/Aleksandr Gorshkov (USSR)
1977 Irina Moiseyeva/Andrey Minenkov (USSR)
1978-9 Natalya Linichuk/Gennadiy Karponosov (USSR)
1980 Krisztina Regoczy/András Sallay (Hun)
1981-4 Jayne Torvill/Christopher.Dean (UK)
1985-7 Natalya Bestemianova/Andrey Bukin (USSR)

Most wins: 6 Lyudmila Pakhomova & Aleksandr Gorshkov

SPEED SKATING
A standard outdoor speed skating circuit is 400 metres, with two lanes. The speed skaters race in pairs, the lanes crossing on the straights on either side of the track.
Indoor speed skating is conducted on short tracks, the standard length being 111.12 metres, which can be laid out on a 60m × 30m skating or ice hockey rink.

OLYMPIC GAMES
Held at each Olympic Games from 1924 (for men) and 1960 (for women). Women's races had also been staged as demonstration events in 1932. Winners:

MEN'S 500 METRES
1924 Charles Jewtraw (USA) 44.0
1928 Bernt Eversen (Nor) & Clas Thunberg (Fin) 43.4
1932 John Shea (USA) 43.4
1936 Ivar Ballangrud (Nor) 43.4
1948 Finn Helgesen (Nor) 43.1
1952 Kenneth Henry (USA) 43.2
1956 Yevgeniy Grischin (USSR) 40.2
1960 Yevgeniy Grischin (USSR) 40.2

1964 Terry McDermott (USA) 40.1
1968 Erhard Keller (FRG) 40.3
1972 Erhard Keller (FRG) 39.44
1976 Yevgeniy Kulikov (USSR) 39.17
1980 Eric Heiden (USA) 38.03
1984 Sergey Fokichev (USSR) 38.19

MEN'S 1000 METRES
1976 Peter Mueller (USA) 1:19.32
1980 Eric Heiden (USA) 1:15.18
1984 Gaetan Boucher (Can) 1:15.80

MEN'S 1500 METRES
1924 Clas Thunberg (Fin) 2:20.8
1928 Clas Thunberg (Fin) 2:21.1
1932 John Shea (USA) 2:57.5
1936 Charles Mathiesen (Nor) 2:19.2
1948 Sverre Farstad (Nor) 2:17.6
1952 Hjalmar Andersen (Nor) 2:20.4
1956 Yevgeniy Grischin (USSR) &
      Yuriy Mikhailov (USSR) 2:08.6
1960 Roald Aas (Nor) & Yevgeniy
      Grischin (USSR) 2:10.4
1964 Ants Antson (USSR) 2:10.3
1968 Cornelis Verkerk (Hol) 2:03.4
1972 Ard Schenk (Hol) 2:02.96
1976 Jan Egil Storholt (Nor) 1:59.38
1980 Eric Heiden (USA) 1:55.44
1984 Gaetan Boucher (Can) 1:58.36

MEN'S 5000 METRES
1924 Clas Thunberg (Fin) 8:39.0
1928 Ivar Ballangrud (Nor) 8:50.5
1932 Irving Jaffee (USA) 9:40.8
1936 Ivar Ballangrud (Nor) 8:19.6
1948 Reidar Liaklev (Nor) 8:29.4
1952 Hjalmar Andersen (Nor) 8:10.6
1956 Boris Schilkov (USSR) 7:48.7
1960 Viktor Kositschkin (USSR)
      7:51.3
1964 Knut Johannesen (Nor) 7:38.4
1968 Anton Maier (Nor) 7.22.4
1972 Ard Schenk (Hol) 7:23.61
1976 Sten Stensen (Nor) 7:24.48
1980 Eric Heiden (USA) 7:02.29
1984 Tomas Gustafsson (Swe)
      7:12.28

MEN'S 10000 METRES
1924 Julius Skutnabb (Fin) 18:04.8
1928 event cancelled after five races
1932 Irving Jaffee (USA) 19:13.6
1936 Ivar Ballangrud (Nor) 17:24.3
1948 Äke Seyffarth (Swe) 17:26.3
1952 Hjalmar Andersen (Nor) 16:45.8
1956 Sigvard Ericsson (Swe)16:35.9
1960 Knut Johannesen (Nor) 15:46.6
1964 Jonny Nilsson (Swe) 15:50.1
1968 Johnny Höglin (Swe) 15:23.6
1972 Ard Schenk (Hol) 15:01.35
1976 Piet Kleine (Hol) 14:50.59
1980 Eric Heiden (USA) 14:28.13
1984 Igor Malkov (USSR) 14:39.90

MEN'S ALL-ROUND (aggregate)
1924 Clas Thunberg (Fin)

WOMEN'S 500 METRES
1960 Helga Haase (GDR) 45.9
1964 Lidiya Skoblikova (USSR) 45.0
1968 Lyudmila Titova (USSR) 46.1
1972 Anne Henning (USA) 43.33
1976 Sheila Young (USA) 42.76
1980 Karin Enke (GDR) 41.78

1984 Christa Rothenburger (GDR) 41.02

WOMEN'S 1000 METRES
1960 Klara Guseva (USSR) 1:34.1
1964 Lidiya Skoblikova (USSR) 1:33.2
1968 Carolina Geijssen (Hol) 1:32.6
1972 Monika Pflug (FRG) 1:31.40

Eric Heiden (All-Sport)

1976 Tatyana Averina (USSR) 1:28.43
1980 Natalya Petruseva (USSR) 1:24.10
1984 Karin Enke (GDR) 1:21.61

WOMEN'S 1500 METRES
1960 Lidiya Skoblikova (USSR) 2:25.2
1964 Lidiya Skoblikova (USSR) 2:22.6
1968 Kaija Mustonen (Fin) 2:22.4
1972 Dianne Holum (USA) 2:20.85
1976 Galina Stepanskaya (USSR) 2:16.58
1980 Annie Borckink (Hol) 2:10.95
1984 Karin Enke (GDR) 2:03.42

WOMEN'S 3000 METRES
1960 Lidiya Skoblikova (USSR) 5:14.3
1964 Lidiya Skoblikova (USSR) 5:14.9
1968 Johanna Schut (Hol) 4:56.2
1972 Christina Baas-Kaiser (Hol) 4:52.14
1976 Tatyana Averina (USSR) 4:45.19
1980 Björg Eva Jensen (Nor) 4:32.13
1984 Andrea Schöne (GDR) 4:27.79

MOST OLYMPIC MEDALS

MEN	Gold	Silver	Bronze
7 Clas Thunberg (Nor)	5	1	1
7 Ivar Ballangrud (Nor)	4	2	1
5 Eric Heiden (USA)	5	-	-
5 Yevgeniy Grischin (USSR)	4	1	-
5 Knut Johannesen (Nor)	2	2	1

WOMEN			
6 Lidiya Skoblikova (USSR)	6	-	-
5 Karin Enke (GDR)	3	2	-

Eric Heiden, uniquely, won all five gold medals at one Games (1980).

WORLD CHAMPIONSHIPS

Held annually, first at Amsterdam in 1889. Officially recognized by the ISU from 1893.

Overall champions:

MEN

Contested over four distances: 500m, 1000m, 5000m and 10000m. Titles not awarded 1889-90, 1894, 1902-3, 1906-7.
1891 Joseph Donoghue (USA)
1893 Jaap Eden (Hol)
1895-6 Jaap Eden (Hol)
1897 Jack McCulloch (Can)
1898-9 Peder Oestlund (Nor)
1900 Edvard Engelsaas (Nor)
1901 Franz Frederik Wathen (Fin)
1904 Sigurd Mathisen (Nor)
1905 Coen de Koning (Hol)
1908-9 Oscar Mathisen (Nor)
1910-1 Nikolay Strunnikov (Rus)
1912-4 Oscar Mathisen (Nor)
1922 Harald Ström (Nor)
1923 Clas Thunberg (Fin)
1924 Roald Larsen (Nor)
1925 Clas Thunberg (Fin)
1926 Ivar Ballangrud (Nor)
1927 Bernt Evensen (Nor)
1928-9 Clas Thunberg (Fin)

1930 Michael Staksrud (Nor)
1931 Clas Thunberg (Fin)
1932 Ivar Ballangrud (Nor)
1933 Hans Engnestangen (Nor)
1934 Bernt Evensen (Nor)
1935 Michael Staksrud (Nor)
1936 Ivar Ballangrud (Nor)
1937 Michael Staksrud (Nor)
1938 Ivar Ballangrud (Nor)
1939 Birger Wasenius (Fin)
1947 Lauri Parkkinen (Fin)
1948 Odd Lundberg (Nor)
1949 Kornel Pajor (Hun)
1950-2 Hjalmar Andersen (Nor)
1953 Oleg Goncharenko (USSR)
1954 Boris Schilkov (USSR)
1955 Sigvard Ericsson (Swe)
1956 Oleg Goncharenko (USSR)
1957 Knut Johannesen (Nor)
1958 Oleg Goncharenko (USSR)
1959 Juhani Järvinen (Fin)
1960 Boris Stenin (USSR)
1961 Henk van der Grift (Hol)
1962 Viktor Kosichkin (USSR)
1963 Jonny Nilsson (Swe)
1964 Knut Johannesen (Nor)
1965 Per Ivar Moe (Nor)
1966-7 Cornelis Verkerk (Hol)
1968 Anton Maier (Nor)
1969 Dag Fornaess (Nor)
1970-2 Ard Schenk (Hol)
1973 Göuran Claesen (Swe)
1974 Sten Stensen (Nor)
1975 Harm Kuipers (Hol)
1976 Piet Kleine (Hol)
1977-9 Eric Heiden (USA)
1980 Hilbert van der Duim (Hol)
1981 Amund Sjøbrend (Nor)
1982 Hilbert van der Duim (Hol)
1983 Rolf Falk-Larssen (Nor)
1984 Oleg Bozyiev (USSR)
1985-6 Hein Vergeer (Hol)
1987 Nikolay Gulyayev (USSR)

Most wins: 5 Oscar Mathisen, Clas Thunberg

WOMEN

Contested over four distances: 500m, 1000m, 1500m and 3000m.
1936 Kit Klein (USA)
1937-8 Laila Schou Nilsen (Nor)
1939 Verné Lesche (Fin)
1947 Verné Lesche (Fin)
1948-50 Maria Isakova (USSR)
1951 Eevi Huttunen (Fin)
1952 Lidiya Selikhova (USSR)
1953 Khalida Schegoleyeva (USSR)
1954 Lidiya Selikhova (USSR)
1955 Rimma Zhukova (USSR)
1956 Sofiya Kondakova (USSR)
1957-8 Inga Artamonova (USSR)
1959 Tamara Rylova (USSR)
1960-1 Valentina Stenina (USSR)
1962 Inga Artamonova (USSR)
1963-4 Lidiya Skoblikova (USSR)

1965 Inga Artamonova (USSR)
1966 Valentina Stenina (USSR)
1967-8 Christina Kaiser (Hol)
1969 Lasma Kauniste (USSR)
1970 Atje Keulen-Deelstra (Hol)
1971 Nina Statkevich (USSR)
1972-4 Atje Keulen-Deelstra (Hol)
1975 Karin Kessow (GDR)
1976 Sylvia Burka (Can)
1977 Vera Bryndzey (USSR)
1978 Tatyana Averina (USSR)
1979 Beth Heiden (USA)
1980-1 Natalya Petruseva (USSR)
1982 Karin Enke (then Busch) (GDR)
1983 Andrea Schöne (GDR)
1984 Karin Enke (GDR)
1985 Andrea Schöne (GDR)
1986-7 Karin Kania (née Enke) (GDR)

Most wins: 4 Inga Artamonova, Atje Keulen-Deelstra, Karin Kania

WORLD SPRINT CHAMPIONSHIPS

First held in 1970. Both men's and women's championships are contested over two distances: 500m and 1000m.

Winners

MEN
1970 Valeriy Muratov (USSR)
1971 Erhard Keller (FRG)
1972 Leo Linkovesi (Fin)
1973 Valeriy Muratov (USSR)
1974 Per Bjørang (Nor)
1975 Aleksandr Safranov (USSR)
1976 Johan Granath (Swe)
1977-80 Eric Heiden (USA)
1981 Frode Rømming (Nor)
1982 Sergey Khlebnikov (USSR)
1983 Akira Kuroiwa (Jap)
1984 Gaetan Boucher (Can)
1985-6 Igor Zhelezovskiy (USSR)
1987 Akira Kuroiwa (Jap)

Most wins: 4 Eric Heiden

WOMEN
1970 Lyudmila Titova (USSR)
1971 Ruth Schleiermacher (GDR)
1972 Monika Pflug (FRG)
1973 Sheila Young (USA)
1974 Leah Poulos (USA)
1975-6 Sheila Young (USA)
1977 Sylvia Burka (Can)
1978 Lyubov Sadchikova (USSR)
1979 Leah Muller (née Poulos) (USA)
1980-1 Karin Enke (GDR)
1982 Natalya Petruseva (USSR)
1983-4 Karin Enke (GDR)
1985 Christa Rothenburger (GDR)
1986-7 Karin Kania (née Enke) (GDR)

Most wins: 6 Karin Kania

Karin Enke (All-Sport)

WORLD SHORT TRACK CHAMPIONSHIPS

Held indoors over four distances: 500m, 1000m, 1500m and 3000m. Held unofficially 1978-80 and officially recognized by the ISU from 1981.

Winners:

MEN	**WOMEN**
1978 Jim Lynch (Aus)	Sarah Docter (Can)
1979 Hiroshi Toda (Jap)	Sylvie Daigle (Can)
1980 Gaetan Boucher (Can)	Miyoshi Kato (Jap)
1981 Benoit Baril (Can)	Miyoshi Kato (Jap)
1982 Guy Daigneault (Can)	Maryse Perreault (Can)
1983 Louis Grenier (Can)	Sylvie Daigle (Can)
1984 Guy Daigneault (Can)	Mariko Kinoshita (Jap)
1985 Toshinobu Kawai (Jap)	Eiko Shishii (Jap)
1986 Tatsuyoshi Isihara (Jap)	Bonnie Blair (USA)
1987 Toshinobu Kawai (Jap)	Eiko Shishii (Jap)

SPEED SKATING WORLD RECORDS
MEN

	min:sec	Name	Venue	Date
500m	36.23	Nick Thometz (USA)	Medeo	26 Mar 1987
1000m	1:12.05	Nick Thometz (USA)	Medeo	27 Mar 1987
1500m	1:52.48	Andrey Bobrov (USSR)	Medeo	27 Mar 1987
3000m	3:59.27	Leo Visser (Hol)	Heerenveen	19 Mar 1987
	3:56.65u	Sergey Martyuk (USSR)	Medeo	11 Mar 1977
5000m	6:47.01	Leo Visser (Hol)	Heerenveen	14 Feb 1987
10000m	14:03.92	Geir Karlstad (Nor)	Heerenveen	15 Feb 1987
	13:54.81u	Igor Malkov (USSR)	Medeo	28 Dec 1983

WOMEN

		Name	Venue	Date
500m	39.28	Bonnie Blair (USA)	Medeo	26 Mar 1987
1000m	1:18.84	Karin Kania (née Enke) (GDR)	Karuizawa	23 Feb 1986
1500m	1:59.30	Karin Kania (GDR)	Medeo	22 Mar 1986
3000m	4:16.85	Yvonne van Gennip (Hol)	Heerenveen	19 Mar 1987
5000m	7:20.36	Yvonne van Gennip (Hol)	Heerenveen	20 Mar 1987

u unofficial marks not ratified
Note that marks set at Medeo (USSR) are assisted by high altitude (1691m above sea level)

WORLD SHORT TRACK SPEED SKATING RECORDS
MEN

		Name	Venue	Date
500m	45.08	Louis Grenier (Can)	Amsterdam	16 Mar 1985
1000m	1:34.79	Guy Daignault (Can)	Chamonix	6 Apr 1986
1500m	2:27.27	Tatsuyoshi Ishihara (Jap)	Den Haag	28 Mar 1981
3000m	5:04.24	Tatsuyoshi Ishihara (Jap)	Amsterdam	17 Mar 1985

WOMEN

		Name	Venue	Date
500m	48.12	Bonnie Blair (USA)	Chamonix	5 Apr 1986
1000m	1:41.80	Maryse Perrault (Can)	Chamonix	6 Apr 1986
1500m	2:36.92	Eiko Shishii (Jap)	Montreal	3 Apr 1987
3000m	5:31.65	Nathalie Lambert (Can)	Montreal	5 Apr 1987

JUDO

The combat sport of judo developed from Japanese martial arts, especially from several different schools of ju-jitsu. Dr Jigoro Kano devised the modern sport from these and founded the Kodokan Judo, a training school, in 1882 at Shitaya. Efficiency classes in judo are divided into pupil (kyu) and master (dan) grades. The highest possible grade is 12th dan, awarded only to Jigoro Kano, the only Shihan (or doctor). Apart from him the highest is the red belt awarded for 10th Dan to thirteen men.

The first judo club in Europe was The Budokwai, founded in London in 1918. The first All-Japan Championships were held in 1930. The International Judo Federation was formed in 1951, in which year the first European Championships were held, and world championships were first held in 1956. When the Olympic Games were held in Tokyo in 1964, judo was added to the Olympic programme, initially at three weight categories.

Belt colours for Dan grades:
1st-5th Dan — black
6th-8th Dan — red and white
9th-11th Dan — red
12th Dan — white

OLYMPIC GAMES
Winners:

OPEN
1964 Anton Geesink (Hol)
1972 Willem Ruska (Hol)
1976 Haruki Uemura (Jap)
1980 Dietmar Lorenz (GDR)
1984 Yasuhiro Yamashita (Jap)

OVER 95KG
1980 Angelo Parisi (Fra)
1984 Hitoshi Saito (Jap)

OVER 93KG
1964 Isao Inokuma (Jap)
1972 Willem Ruska (Hol)
1976 Sergey Novikov (USSR)

UNDER 95KG
1980 Robert Van de Walle (Bel)
1984 Hyeung-Zoo Ha (SKo)

UNDER 93KG
1972 Shota Chochoshvili (USSR)
1976 Kazuhiro Ninomiya (Jap)

UNDER 86KG
1980 Jürg Röthlisberger (Swi)
1984 Peter Seisnenbacher (Aut)

UNDER 80KG
1964 Isao Okano (Jap)
1972 Shinobu Sekine (Jap)
1976 Isamu Sonoda (Jap)

UNDER 78KG
1980 Shota Khabareli (USSR)
1984 Frank Weineke (FRG)

UNDER 71KG
1980 Ezio Gamba (Ita)
1984 Byeong-Kuen Ahn (SKo)

UNDER 70KG
1964 Takehide Nakatani (Jap)
1972 Toyokazu Nomura (Jap)
1976 Vladimir Nevzorov (USSR)

UNDER 65KG
1980 Nikolay Solodukhin (USSR)
1984 Yoshiyuki Matsuoka (Jap)

UNDER 63KG
1972 Takao Kawaguchi (Jap)
1976 Hector Rodriguez (Cub)

UNDER 60KG
1980 Thierry Rey (Fra)
1984 Shinji Hosokawa (Jap)

Most titles: 2 Willem Ruska

WORLD CHAMPIONSHIPS

Winners:

OPEN
1956 Shokichi Natsui (Jap)
1958 Koji Sone (Jap)
1961 Anton Geesink (Hol)
1965 Isao Inokuma (Jap)
1967 Matsuo Matsunaga (Jap)
1969 Masatoshi Shinomaki (Jap)
1971 Masatoshi Shinomaki (Jap)
1973 Kazuhiro Ninomiya (Jap)
1975 Haruki Uemura (Jap)
1979 Sumio Endo (Jap)
1981 Yasuhiro Yamashita (Jap)
1983 Hitoshi Saito (Jap)
1985 Yoshimi Masaki (Jap)

OVER 95KG
1979 Yasuhiro Yamashita (Jap)
1981 Yasuhiro Yamashita (Jap)
1983 Yasuhiro Yamashita (Jap)
1985 Yong Chul Cho (SKo)

OVER 93KG
1965 Anton Geesink (Hol)
1967 Willem Ruska (Hol)
1969 Shuji Suma (Jap)
1971 Willem Ruska (Hol)
1973 Chonufuhe Tagaki (Jap)
1975 Sumio Endo (Jap)

UNDER 95KG
1979 Tengiz Khubuluri (USSR)
1981 Tengiz Khubuluri (USSR)
1983 Valeriy Divisenko (USSR)
1985 Hitoshi Sugai (Jap)

UNDER 93KG
1967 Nobuyuki Sato (Jap)
1969 Fumio Sasahara (Jap)
1971 Fumio Sasahara (Jap)
1973 Nobuyuki Sato (Jap)
1975 Jean-Luc Rouge (Fra)

UNDER 86KG
1979 Detlef Ultsch (GDR)
1981 Bernard Tchoullouyan (Fra)
1983 Detlef Ultsch (GDR)
1985 Peter Seisenbacher (Aat)

Yasuhiro Yamashita retired undefeated after 203 successive wins, 1977-85 (All-Sport)

UNDER 80KG
1965 Isao Okano (Jap)
1967 Eiji Maruki (Jap)
1969 Isamu Sonoda (Jap)
1971 Shozo Fujii (Jap)
1973 Shozo Fujii (Jap)
1975 Shozo Fujii (Jap)

UNDER 78KG
1979 Shozo Fujii (Jap)
1981 Neil Adams (UK
1983 Nobutoshi Hikage (Jap)
1985 Nobutoshi Hikage (Jap)

UNDER 71KG
1979 Kyoto Katsuki (Jap)
1981 Chong Hak Park (SKo)
1983 Hidetoshi Nakanishi (Jap)
1985 Byeong-Kuen Ahn (SKo)

UNDER 70KG
1967 Hiroshi Minatoya (Jap)

1969 Hiroshi Minatoya (Jap)
1971 Hizashi Tsuzawa (Jap)
1973 Kazutoyo Nomura (Jap)
1975 Vladimir Nevzorov (USSR)

UNDER 65KG
1979 Nikolai Soludukhin (USSR)
1981 Katsuhiko Kashiwazaki (Jap)
1983 Nikolai Soludukhin (USSR)
1985 Yuriy Sokolov (USSR)

UNDER 63KG
1965 Hiroshi Minatoya (Jap)
1967 Takosumi Shigeoka (Jap)
1969 Yoshio Sonoda (Jap)
1971 Takao Kawaguchi (Jap)
1973 Yoshiharu Minami (Jap)
1975 Yoshiharu Minami (Jap)

UNDER 60KG
1979 Thierry Ray (Fra)
1981 Yasuhiko Moriwaki (Jap)

1983 Khazret Tletseri (USSR)
1985 Shinji Hosokawa (Jap)

Most titles: 4 Yashiro Yamashita, Shozo Fujii

WOMEN'S WORLD CHAMPIONSHIPS

First held in 1980.

Winners:

OPEN
1980 Ingrid Berghmans (Bel)
1982 Ingrid Berghmans (Bel)
1984 Ingrid Berghmans (Bel)
1986 Ingrid Berghmans (Bel)

OVER 72KG
1980 Margarita de Cal (Ita)
1982 Natalina Lupino (Fra)
1984 Maria-Teresa Motta (Ita)
1986 Fenglian Gao (Chn)

UNDER 72KG
1980 Jocelyne Triadou (Fra)
1982 Barbara Classen (FRG)
1984 Ingrid Berghmans (Bel)
1986 Irene de Kok (Hol)

UNDER 66KG
1980 Edith Simon (Aut)
1982 Brigitte Deydier (Fra)
1984 Brigitte Deydier (Fra)
1986 Brigitte Deydier (Fra)

UNDER 61KG
1980 Anita Staps (Hol)
1982 Martine Rothier (Fra)
1984 Natasha Hernandez (Ven)
1986 Diane Bell (UK)

UNDER 56KG
1980 Gerda Winklbauer (Aut)
1982 Béatrice Rodriguez (Fra)
1984 Ann-Maria Burns (USA)
1986 Ann Hughes (UK)

UNDER 52KG
1980 Edith Hrovat (Aut)
1982 Loretta Doyle (UK)
1984 Kaori Yamaguchi (Jap)
1986 Dominique Brun (Fra)

UNDER 48KG
1980 Jane Bridge (UK)
1982 Karen Briggs (UK)
1984 Karen Briggs (UK)
1986 Karen Briggs (UK)

Most titles: 5 Ingrid Berghmans, 3 Brigitte Deydier, Karen Briggs

Ingrid Berghmans (All-Sport)

KARATE

Karate as a martial art was developed in Japan, the name originating as recently as the 1930s. The techniques used, however, were devised from the sixth century Chinese art of Shaolin boxing 'kempo' and its development in Okinawa c.1500 into 'Tang Hand', whereby the island's inhabitants fought bare handed against armed Japanese oppressors.

Tang Hand was introduced to Japan in the 1920s by Funakoshi Gichin, who adopted the word karate, meaning empty hand. The style he practised became known as Shotokan, now one of five major styles in Japan, the others being Wado-ryu, Gojo-ryu, Shito-ryu and Kyokushinkai, each placing different emphasis on technique, speed and power.

Karate spread to the Western world from the 1950s, and the All-Japan Karate-do Organization (FAJKO), founded in 1964, staged the first multi-style world championships in 1970. Following this the World Union of Karate-do Organizations was created.

WORLD CHAMPIONSHIPS

First held in Tokyo in 1970, when there were team and individual championships. Women first competed in 1980. Kumite championships are now staged at different weight categories and there are also Kata (or sequence) events.

Winners:

MEN

TEAM
1970 Japan
1972 France
1975 Great Britain
1977 Netherlands
1980 Spain
1982 Great Britain
1984 Great Britain
1986 Great Britian

INDIVIDUAL
1970 Kouji Wada (Jap)
1972 L.Watanabe-Taske (Bra)
1975 Kazusada Murakami (Jap)
1977 Otti Roethoff (Hol)

INDIVIDUAL KUMITE

Year	Under 60kg	Under 65kg
1980	Ricardo Abad (Spa)	Toshiaki Maeda (Jap)
1982	Jukka-Pekka Väyrinen (Fin)	Yuichi Suzuki (Jap)
1984	Dirk Betzien (FRG)	Ramon Malavé (Swe)
1986	Hideto Nakano (Jap)	Eizou Kondo (Jap)

Year	Under 70kg	Under 75kg
1980	Gonzales (Spa)	Sadao Tajima (Jap)
1982	Seiji Nishimura (Jap)	Javier Gomez (Swi)
1984	Jim Collins (UK)	Toon Stelling (Hol)
1986	Thierry Masci (Fra)	K.Leeuwin (Hol)

Year	Under 80kg	Over 80kg	Open
1980	T.Hill (USA)	J.Montana (Fra)	Ricciardi (Ita)
1982	Pat McKay (UK)	Jeff Thompson (UK)	Hsiao Murase (Jap)

Year	Under 80kg	Over 80kg	Open
1984	Pat McKay (UK)	Jerome Atkinson (UK)	Emmanuel Pinda (Fra)
1986	Jacques Tapol (FRa)	Vic Charles (UK)	Karl Daggfeldt (Swe)

INDIVIDUAL KATA
1977 Keiji Okada (Jap)
1980 Keiji Okada (Jap)
1982 Masashi Koyama (Jap)
1984 Tsuguo Sakumoto (Jap)
1986 Tsuguo Sakumoto (Jap)

WOMEN
INDIVIDUAL KUMITE

Year	Under 53kg	Under 60kg	Over 60kg
1982	Sophie Berger (Fra)	Yukari Yamakawa (Jap)	Guus van Mourik (Hol)
1984	Sophie Berger (Fra)	Tomoko Konishi (Jap)	Guus van Mourik (Hol)
1986	Johanna Kauri (Fin)	Ritva Virelius (Fin)	Guus van Mourik (Hol)

INDIVIDUAL KATA
1980 Suzuko Okamura (Jap)
1982 Mie Nakayama (Jap)
1984 Mie Nakayama (Jap)
1986 Mie Nakayama (Jap)

KENDO

The Japanese martial art of swordsmanship, which was practised by the warrior class, the samurai. The earliest known reference to such arts in Japan was in 789 AD. Kendo is now practised with shiani, or bamboo swords.

WORLD CHAMPIONSHIPS

First held in 1970.

Winners:

Year	Individual	Team
1970	Mitsuru Kobayashi (Jap)	Japan
1973	Tetsushi Sakuragi (Jap)	Japan
1976	Eijo Yoko (Jap)	Japan
1979	Hironori Yamada (Jap)	Japan
1982	Minoru Makita (Jap)	Japan
1985	Kunishide Koda (Jap)	Japan

LACROSSE

The name 'La Crosse', the French word for a crozier or staff, was given by French settlers in North America to the game played by Indians, and known by them as 'baggataway'. The Indians played on a very large pitch, some 500m long, their crosse or racket being a staff curved at one end into a rough circle, into which was fitted a net. The first non-Indian club was the Montreal Lacrosse Club, founded in 1839. The sport was introduced to Britain in 1867 by a party of Caughnawaga Indians.

The first national body was the National Lacrosse Association, formed in Canada in 1867. The International Federation of Amateur Lacrosse (IFAL) was founded in 1928. Women were first reported to have played lacrosse in 1886 and the All-England Women's Lacrosse Association was formed in 1912. The women's game has evolved from the men's game and there are now considerable differences in the rules.

Men's lacrosse is played by teams of 10-a-side and women's principally by 12-a-side, although a major variant is the 6-a-side game.

MEN'S LACROSSE

WORLD CHAMPIONSHIPS

First held in 1967 in Toronto, winners have been:
USA 1967, 1974, 1982, 1986; Canada 1978.

The USA also won the pre-Olympic tournament in 1984. Their only loss at this level was by 16-17 to Canada in the 1978 final, after extra time, the only drawn game at this level.

OLYMPIC GAMES

Lacrosse was played at two Olympics, when the winners were: 1904 Shamrock (Can), 1908 Canada. It was also a demonstration sport in 1928, 1932 and 1948.

ENGLISH CLUB CHAMPIONSHIPS

Contested annually for the Iroquois Cup from 1890.
Most wins:
16 Stockport 1897-1901, 1903, 1905, 1911-3, 1923-4, 1926, 1928, 1934, 1987
11 South Manchester 1890, 1895, 1904, 1906, 1909, 1933, 1966, 1971-3, 1980
10 Old Hulmeians 1907-8, 1910, 1914, 1932, 1949-50, 1962, 1964, 1968
 9 Mellor 1935-7, 1948, 1963, 1965-7, 1969
 7 Old Waconians 1938-9, 1947, 1951-3, 1955
 6 Heaton Mersey 1927, 1954, 1958-60, 1986
 5 Cheadle 1978-9, 1981, 1984-5
 3 Boardman & Eccles 1922, 1929, 1961
 3 Sheffield University 1977, 1982-3

WOMEN'S LACROSSE

WORLD CHAMPIONSHIPS

First held in 1969.
Winners: 1969 GB, 1974 USA, 1978 Canada

WORLD CUP

First held 1982, replacing the World Championships.
Winners: 1982 USA, 1986 Australia.

MODERN PENTATHLON

This is the five sport discipline of cross-country riding, epée fencing, pistol shooting (at 25m), swimming (300m) and cross-country running (4000m). It has been included at every Olympic Games from 1912, and has been known as the military pentathlon. For many years the sport was dominated by members of the armed forces, who have been particularly able to pursue such diverse activities. Military lore explains the origin of the sport: a messenger has to travel across country on horseback, fighting his way through with sword and pistol; he then has to swim across a river, before finishing his journey on foot.

Each event is scored on points, determined either against the other competitors or against scoring tables. Note that the points scores given in the lists of champions are not necessarily comparable. Prior to 1954 the scoring was on the basis of places at each event.

The sport's governing body is L'Union Internationale de Pentathlon Moderne et Biathlon, the UIPMB. It was founded in 1948 as the UIPM, taking on the administration of biathlon (qv) in 1957.

OLYMPIC GAMES

Individual winners:
1912 Gösta Lilliehöök (Swe) 27
1920 Gustaf Dyrssen (Swe) 18
1924 Bo Lindman (Swe) 18
1928 Sven Thofelt (Swe) 47
1932 Johan Oxenstierna (Swe) 32
1936 Gotthardt Handrick (Ger) 31.5
1948 Wille Grut (Swe) 16
1952 Lars Hall (Swe) 32
1956 Lars Hall (Swe) 4843
1960 Ferenc Nemeth (Hun) 5024
1964 Ferenc Torok (Hun) 5116
1968 Björn Ferm (Swe) 4964
1972 Andras Balczo (Hun) 5412
1976 Janusz Pyciak-Peciak (Pol) 5520
1980 Anatoliy Starostin (USSR) 5568
1984 Daniele Masala (Ita) 5469

Team winners (first held 1952):

Hungary	1952, 1960, 1968
USSR	1956, 1964, 1972
Great Britain	1976
Italy	1984

Most gold medals: 3 Andras Balczo (Hun) individual 1972, team 1960 and 1968.
Most medals: 7 Pavel Lednev (USSR): individual 2nd 1976, 3rd 1968, 1972, 1980; team 1st 1972, 1980, 2nd 1968.
Greatest margin of victory: probably by Wille Grut in 1948 as he won three events and was placed fifth and eighth in the other two. On the present scoring system: 77 points Andras Balczo in 1972 over Boris Onischenko (USSR), who four years later was disqualified for using an illegal fencing weapon, which registered hits when no contact had occurred with his opponent.

WORLD CHAMPIONSHIPS

Held annually from 1949 with the exception of Olympic years.

Individual winners:
1949 Tage Bjurefelt (Swe) 19
1950 Lars Hall (Swe) 19
1951 Lars Hall (Swe) 22
1953 Gabor Benedek (Hun) 22
1954 Björn Thofelt (Swe) 4634.5
1955 Konstantin Salnikov (USSR) 4453.5
1957 Igor Novikov (USSR) 4769
1958 Igor Novikov (USSR) 4924
1959 Igor Novikov (USSR) 4847
1961 Igor Novikov (USSR) 5217
1962 Eduards Dobnikov (USSR) 4647
1963 Andras Balczo (Hun) 5267
1965 Andras Balczo (Hun) 5302
1966 Andras Balczo (Hun) 5217
1967 Andras Balczo (Hun) 5056
1969 Andras Balczo (Hun) 5515
1970 Peter Kelemen (Hun) 5220
1971 Boris Onischenko (USSR) 5206
1973 Pavel Lednev (USSR) 5413
1974 Pavel Lednev (USSR) 5302
1975 Pavel Lednev (USSR) 5056
1977 Janusz Pyciak-Peciak (Pol) 5485
1978 Pavel Lednev (USSR) 5498
1979 Robert Nieman (USA) 5483
1981 Janusz Pyciak-Peciak (Pol) 5662
1982 Daniele Masala (Ita) 5680
1983 Anatoliy Starostin (USSR) 5506
1985 Attila Mizser (Hun) 5525
1986 Carlo Massullo (Ita) 5463*

* original winner was Anatoliy Starostin (USSR) 5563, but he and 14 others were subsequently disqualified for illegal drugs use. The USSR also lost their women's team title.

Team wins:

12	USSR	1957-9, 1961-2, 1969, 1971, 1973-4, 1982-3, 1985
8	Hungary	1954-5, 1963, 1965-7, 1970, 1975
4	Sweden	1949-51, 1953
3	Poland	1977-8, 1981
1	USA 1979, Italy 1986	

Most titles: 13 Andras Balczo (Hun) six individual, seven team including Olympics 1960-72.

WOMEN'S WORLD CHAMPIONSHIPS

First held in London in 1981.

Individual winners:
1981 Anne Ahlgren (Swe) 4975
1982 Wendy Norman (UK) 5311
1983 Lynn Chernobrywy (Can) 5328
1984 Svetlana Yakovleva (USSR) 5481
1985 Barbara Kotowska (Pol) 5336
1986 Irina Kiselyeva (USSR) 5323
1987 Irina Kiselyeva (USSR) 5406

Team wins:
3 Great Britain 1981-3
2 USSR 1984, 1987
1 Poland 1985, France 1986

WOMEN'S WORLD CUP

This event which preceded the world championships.

Winners:
1978 Wendy Skipwith (UK)
1979 Kathy Taylor (UK)
1980 Wendy Norman (UK)
Team: Great Britain 1978-80

MOTOR CYCLING

The first known motorcycle race was on 20 September 1896 when eight competitors took part in a race from Paris to Nantes and back. The course covered 152 km (139 miles) and was won by M.Chevalier on a Michelin-Dion tricycle in 4 hr 10 min 37 sec. The first race for two-wheeled motorcycles was held over one mile (1.6 km) of an oval track at Sheen House, Richmond, Surrey on 29 Nov, 1897. The race was won by Charles Jarrott, riding a Fournier, in a time of 2 min 8 sec. The Auto-Cycle Union (ACU) is the governing body of the sport in Britain, and was founded in 1903. The world governing body, the Fédération Internationale Motorcycliste (FIM), was formed in 1904 under the title Fédération Internationale des Clubs Motorcyclistes.

WORLD CHAMPIONSHIPS

World Championships were instituted by the FIM in 1949 for 125, 250, 350 and 500 cc classes, as well as for sidecars. The 50 cc class was introduced in 1962 but this discontinued in 1983 to make way for the larger 80 cc class. In 1977-9 a Formula 750 class was contested. The 350cc class was discontinued at the end of the 1982 season.

50cc
1962 Ernst Degner (FRG) — Suzuki
1963-4 Hugh Anderson (NZ) — Suzuki
1965 Ralph Bryans (Ire) — Honda
1966-8 Hans-Georg Anscheidt (FRG) — Suzuki
1969-70 Angel Nieto (Spa) — Derbi
1971 Jan de Vries (Hol) — Kreidler
1972 Angel Nieto (Spa) — Derbi
1973 Jan de Vries (Hol) — Kreidler
1974 Henk van Kessel (Hol) — Kreidler
1975 Angel Nieto (Spa) — Kreidler
1976-7 Angel Nieto (Spa) — Bultaco
1978 Ricardo Tormo (Spa) — Bultaco
1979-80 Eugenio Lazzarini (Ita) — Kreidler
1981 Ricardo Tormo (Spa) — Bultaco
1982 Stefan Dörflinger (Swi) — MBA
1983 Stefan Dörflinger (Swi) — Krauser Kreidler

80cc
1984 Stefan Dörflinger (Swi) — Zundapp
1985 Stefan Dörflinger (Swi) — Krauser
1986-7 Jorge Martinez (Spa) — Derbi

125cc
1949 Nello Pagani (Ita) — Mondial
1950 Bruno Ruffo (Ita) — Mondial
1951 Carlo Ubbiali (Ita) — Mondial
1952 Cecil Sandford (UK) — MV
1953 Werner Haas (FRG) — NSU
1954 Rupert Hollaus (Aut) — NSU
1955-6 Carlo Ubbiali (Ita) — MV
1957 Tarquinio Provini (Ita) — Mondial
1958-60 Carlo Ubbiali (Ita) — MV
1961 Tom Phillis (Aus) — Honda
1962 Luigi Taveri (Swi) — Honda
1963 Hugh Anderson (NZ) — Suzuki
1964 Luigi Taveri (Swi) — Honda
1965 Hugh Anderson (NZ) — Suzuki
1966 Luigi Taveri (Swi) — Honda
1967 Bill Ivy (UK) — Yamaha
1968 Phil Read (UK) — Yamaha
1969 Dave Simmonds (UK) — Kawasaki
1970 Dieter Braun (FRG) — Suzuki
1971-2 Angel Nieto (Spa) — Derbi
1973-4 Kent Andersson (Swe) — Yamaha
1975 Paolo Pileri (Ita) — Morbidelli
1976-7 Pier-Paolo Bianchi (Ita) — Morbidelli
1978 Eugenio Lazzarini (Ita) — MBA
1979 Angel Nieto (Spa) — Morbidelli
1980 Pier-Paolo Bianchi (Ita) — MBA
1981 Angel Nieto (Spa) — Minarelli
1982-4 Angel Nieto (Spa) — Garelli
1985 Fausto Gresini (Ita) — Garelli
1986 Luca Cadalora (Ita) — Garelli
1987 Fausto Gresini (Ita) — Garelli

250cc
1949 Bruno Ruffo (Ita) — Guzzi
1950 Dario Ambrosini (Ita) — Benelli
1951 Bruno Ruffo (Ita) — Guzzi
1952 Enrico Lorenzetti (Ita) — Guzzi
1953-4 Werner Haas (FRG) — NSU
1955 Herman Müller (FRG) — NSU
1956 Carlo Ubbiali (Ita) — MV
1957 Cecil Sandford (UK) — Mondial
1958 Tarquinio Provini (Ita) — MV
1959-60 Carlo Ubbiali (Ita) — MV
1961 Mike Hailwood (UK) — Honda
1962-3 Jim Redman (Rho) — Honda
1964-5 Phil Read (UK) — Yamaha
1966-7 Mike Hailwood (UK) — Honda
1968 Phil Read (UK) — Yamaha
1969 Kel Carruthers (Aus) — Benelli
1970 Rod Gould (UK) — Yamaha
1971 Phil Read (UK) — Yamaha
1972 Jarno Saarinen (Fin) — Yamaha
1973 Dieter Braun (FRG) — Yamaha

Freddie Spencer, the first man to win 250cc and 500cc world titles in the same year. (All-Sport)

1974-6	Walter Villa (Ita)	Harley-Davidson
1977	Mario Lega (Ita)	Morbidelli
1978-9	Kork Ballington (SAf)	Kawasaki
1980-1	Anton Mang (FRG)	Kawasaki
1982	Jean-Louis Tournadre (Fra)	Yamaha
1983	Carlos Lavado (Ven)	Yamaha
1984	Christian Sarron (Fra)	Yamaha
1985	Freddie Spencer (USA)	Honda
1986	Carlos Lavado (Ven)	Yamaha

350cc

1949	Freddie Frith (UK)	Velocette
1950	Bob Foster (UK)	Velocette
1951-2	Geoff Duke (UK)	Norton
1953-4	Fergus Anderson (UK)	Guzzi
1955-6	Bill Lomas (UK)	Guzzi
1957	Keith Campbell (Aus)	Guzzi
1958-60	John Surtees (UK)	MV
1961	Gary Hocking (Rho)	MV
1962-5	Jim Redman (Rho)	Honda
1966-7	Mike Hailwood (UK)	Honda
1968-73	Giacomo Agostini (Ita)	MV
1974	Giacomo Agostini (Ita)	Yamaha
1975	Johnny Cecotto (Ven)	Yamaha
1976	Walter Villa (Ita)	Harley-Davidson
1977	Takazumi Katayama (Jap)	Yamaha
1978-9	Kork Ballington (SAf)	Kawasaki
1980	Jon Ekerold (SAf)	Yamaha
1981-2	Anton Mang (FRG)	Kawasaki

500cc

1949	Leslie Graham (UK)	AJS
1950	Umberto Masetti (Ita)	Gilera
1951	Geoff Duke (UK)	Norton
1952	Umberto Masetti	Gilera
1953-55	Geoff Duke (UK)	Gilera
1956	John Surtees (UK)	MV
1957	Libero Liberati (Ita)	Gilera
1958-60	John Surtees (UK)	MV
1961	Gary Hocking (Rho)	MV
1962-65	Mike Hailwood (UK)	MV
1966-72	Giacomo Agostini (Ita)	MV
1973-4	Phil Read (UK)	MV
1975	Giacomo Agostini (Ita)	Yamaha

1976-7	Barry Sheene (UK)	Suzuki
1978-80	Kenny Roberts (USA)	Yamaha
1981	Marco Lucchinelli (Ita)	Suzuki
1982	Franco Uncini (Ita)	Suzuki
1983	Freddie Spencer (USA)	Honda
1984	Eddie Lawson (USA)	Yamaha
1985	Freddie Spencer (USA)	Honda
1986	Eddie Lawson (USA)	Yamaha

750cc

1977	Steve Baker (USA)	Yamaha
1978	Johnny Cecotto (Ven)	Yamaha
1979	Patrick Pons (Fra)	Yamaha

SIDECAR

1949-51	Eric Oliver (UK)	Norton
1952	Cyril Smith (UK)	Norton
1953	Eric Oliver (UK)	Norton
1954	Wilhelm Noll (FRG)	BMW
1955	Wilhelm Faust (FRG)	BMW
1956	Wilhelm Noll (FRG)	BMW
1957	Fritz Hillebrand (FRG)	BMW
1958-9	Walter Schneider (FRG)	BMW
1960	Helmut Fath (FRG)	BMW
1961-4	Max Deubel (FRG)	BMW
1965-6	Fritz Scheidegger (Swi)	BMW
1967	Klaus Enders (FRG)	BMW
1968	Helmut Fath (FRG)	URS
1969-70	Klaus Enders (FRG)	BMW
1971	Horst Owesle (FRG)	Munch
1972-3	Klaus Enders (FRG)	BMW
1974	Klaus Enders (FRG)	Busch BMW
1975	Rolf Steinhausen (FRG)	Konig
1976	Rolf Steinhausen (FRG)	Busch Konig
1977	George O'Dell (UK)	Yamaha
1978-9	Rolf Biland (Swi)	Yamaha
1980	Jock Taylor (UK)	Yamaha
1981	Rolf Biland (Swi)	Yamaha
1982	Werner Schwärzel (FRG)	Yamaha
1983	Rolf Biland (Swi)	Yamaha
1984-6	Egbert Streuer (Hol)	Yamaha
1987	Steve Webster (UK)	Yamaha

WORLD ENDURANCE CHAMPIONSHIP

Inaugurated in 1980, it replaced the FIM Coupe d'Endurance.

Winners:

1980	Marc Fontan & Hervé Moineau (Fra)	Honda
1981	Jean Lafond & Raymond Roche (Fra)	Kawasaki
1982	Jean-Claude Chemarin (Fra) & Jacques Cornu (Swi)	Kawasaki
1983	Richard Hubin (Bel) & Hervé Moineau (Fra)	Suzuki
1984-5	Gérard Coudray & Patrick Igoa (Fra)	Honda
1986	Patrick Igoa (Fra)	Honda

TT FORMULA ONE WORLD CHAMPIONSHIP

Formula One, Two and Three World Championships were introduced in 1977. Formula Three discontinued at the end of 1981, and Formula Two in 1986. The Formula One race at the Isle of Man TT forms a round in the championship.

Formula One winners:
1977 Phil Read (UK)   Honda
1978 Mike Hailwood (UK)   Ducati
1979 Ron Haslam (UK)   Honda
1980-1 Graeme Crosby (NZ)   Suzuki
1982-6 Joey Dunlop (Ire)   Honda

WORLD MANUFACTURERS' CHAMPIONSHIP

Most wins:

37 MV Augusta	125cc:	1952-3, 1955-6, 1958-60
	250cc:	1955-6, 1958-60
	350cc:	1958-61, 1968-72,
	500cc:	1956, 1958-65, 1967-73
35 Yamaha/LCR	125cc:	1967-8, 1973-4
Yamaha	250cc:	1964-5, 1968, 1970-4, 1977, 1982-4
	350cc:	1973-7, 1980
	500cc:	1974-5, 1986
	Sidecar:	1977-86
23 Honda	50cc:	1965-6
	125cc:	1961-2, 1964, 1966
	250cc:	1961-3, 1966-7, 1985-6
	350cc:	1962-7
	500cc:	1966, 1983-5
19 BMW	Sidecar:	1955-73
15 Suzuki	50cc:	1962-4, 1967-8
	125cc:	1963, 1965, 1970
	500cc:	1976-82

Giacomo Agostini (All-Sport)

MOST TITLES (Solo)

Total	Rider	50cc	80cc	125cc	250cc	350cc	500cc	750cc	Years
15	Giacomo Agostini (Ita)	-	-	-	-	7	8	-	1966-75
13	Angel Nieto (Spa)	6	-	7	-	-	-	-	1969-84
9	Mike Hailwood (UK)	-	-	-	3	2	4	-	1961-7
9	Carlo Ubbiali (Ita)	-	-	6	3	-	-	-	1951-60
7	Phil Read (UK)	-	-	1	4	-	2	-	1964-74
7	John Surtees (UK)	-	-	-	-	3	4	-	1956-60
6	Geoff Duke (UK)	-	-	-	-	2	4	-	1951-5
6	Jim Redman (Rho)	-	-	-	2	4	-	-	1962-5

Mike Hailwood and Phil Read are the only riders to have won world titles in three classes.

MOST TITLES IN EACH CLASS

  50cc: 6 Angel Nieto; 3 Hans Anscheidt (FRG)
  80cc: 2 Stefan Dörflinger, Jorge Martinez
 125cc: 7 Angel Nieto; 6 Carlo Ubbiali (Ita)
 250cc: 4 Phil Read; 3 Mike Hailwood, Carlo Ubbiali, Walter Villa (Ita)
 350cc: 7 Giacomo Agostini; 4 Jim Redman
 500cc: 8 Giacomo Agostini; 4 Geoff Duke, Mike Hailwood, John Surtees; 3 Kenny Roberts (USA)
 750cc: 1 Steve Baker (USA), Johnny Cecotto (Ven), Patrick Pons (Fra)
Sidecar: 6 Klaus Enders (FRG); 4 Rolf Biland (Swi), Max Deubel (FRG), Eric Oliver (UK); 3 Egbert Streuer (Hol)

MOST GRAND PRIX WINS:

122 Giacomo Agostini (350cc, 54; 500cc, 68)

90 Angel Nieto (50cc, 27; 80cc, 1; 125cc, 62)
76 Mike Hailwood (125cc, 2; 250cc, 21; 350cc, 16; 500cc, 37)
52 Phil Read (125cc, 10; 250cc, 27; 350cc, 4; 500cc, 11)

Hailwood, Read, Jim Redman (Rho) and Charles Mortimer (UK) are the only riders to have won Grands Prix in four different classes.

MOST GRAND PRIX WINS IN EACH CLASS

  50cc: 27 Angel Nieto (Spa)
  80cc: 8 Jorge Martinez (Spa)
 125cc: 62 Angel Nieto (Spa)
 250cc: 27 Phil Read (UK)
 350cc: 54 Giacomo Agostini (Ita)
 500cc: 68 Giacomo Agostini (Ita)
Sidecar: 42 Rolf Biland (Swi)

Fastest race: 1977 Belgian GP at Spa-Francorchamps; won by Barry Sheene (UK) on a 495cc Suzuki at an average speed of 217.37 km/h (135.07 mph)

ISLE OF MAN TT

The most famous of all motor cycle races, the Isle of Man Tourist Trophy races were inaugurated in 1907, two years after motor cycle racing first came to the island. In 1905 the Auto Cycle Club of the RAC held rehersals for the 1906 International Cup Race on the Isle of Man, because road racing on the mainland was banned. It was so popular that it led to the first TT race being staged on 28 May 1907, won by Charlie Collier on a single-cylinder Matchless. The 15.8-mile St.John's course was used until 1911 when the 37½-mile Mountain course was used for the first time. The exact distance of the current Mountain circuit is 37.73 miles (60.72 km). The shorter Clypse course (10.79 miles (17.36 km)) was introduced in 1954 to accommodate the return of sidecar racing, but it was unpopular with riders, and was abandoned at the end of 1959. The most prestigious of all races is the Senior TT.

Winners of the Senior TT have been:
(all UK riders unless otherwise stated)

1911	Oscar Godfrey	Indian
1912	Frank Applebee	Scott
1913	Tim Wood	Scott
1914	Cyril Pullin	Rudge
1920	Tommy de la Hay	Sunbeam
1921	Howard Davies	AJS
1922	Alec Bennett (Ire)	Sunbeam
1923	Tom Sheard	Douglas
1924	Alec Bennett (Ire)	Norton
1925	Howard Davies	HRD
1926	Stanley Woods	Norton
1927	Alec Bennett (Ire)	Norton
1928-9	Charlie Dodson	Sunbeam
1930	Wal Handley	Rudge Whitworth
1931	Tim Hunt	Norton
1932-3	Stanley Woods	Norton
1934	Jimmy Guthrie	Norton
1935	Stanley Woods	Moto Guzzi
1936	Jimmy Guthrie	Norton
1937	Freddie Frith	Norton
1938	Harold Daniell	Norton
1939	Georg Meier (FRG)	BMW
1947	Harold Daniell	Norton
1948	Artie Bell	Norton
1949	Harold Daniell	Norton
1950-1	Geoff Duke	Norton
1952	Reg Armstrong (Ire)	Norton
1953-4	Ray Amm (S Rho)	Norton
1955	Geoff Duke	Gilera
1956	John Surtees	MV
1957	Bob McIntyre	Gilera
1958-60	John Surtees	MV
1961	Mike Hailwood	Norton
1962	Gary Hocking (S Rho)	MV
1963-5	Mike Hailwood	MV
1966-7	Mike Hailwood	Honda
1968-72	Giacomo Agostini (Ita)	MV
1973	Jack Findlay (Aus)	Suzuki
1974	Phil Carpenter	Yamaha
1975	Mick Grant	Kawasaki
1976	Tom Herron (Ire)	Yamaha
1977	Phil Read	Suzuki
1978	Tom Herron (Ire)	Suzuki
1979	Mike Hailwood	Suzuki
1980	Graeme Crosby (NZ)	Suzuki
1981	Mick Grant	Suzuki
1982	Norman Brown	Suzuki
1984	Rob McElnea	Suzuki
1985	Joey Dunlop (Ire)	Honda
1986	Roger Burnett	Honda
1987	Joey Dunlop (Ire)	Honda

Winners of other major classes, since 1977:

JUNIOR 250cc (350cc from 1987)

1977	Charlie Williams	Yamaha
1978	Charles Mortimer	Yamaha
1979-80	Charlie Williams	Yamaha
1981	Steve Tonkin	Armstrong CCM
1982	Con Law	Waddon
1983	Con Law	EMC
1984	Graeme McGregor (Aus)	Yamaha
1985	Joey Dunlop (Ire)	Honda
1986	Steve Cull (Ire)	Honda
1987	Eddie Laycock (Ire)	EMC

FORMULA 1

1977	Phil Read	Honda
1978	Mike Hailwood	Ducati
1979	Alex George	Honda
1980	Mick Grant	Honda
1981	Graeme Crosby (NZ)	Suzuki
1982	Ron Haslam	Honda
1983-7	Joey Dunlop (Ire)	Honda

FORMULA II

1977-9	Alan Jackson	Honda
1980	Charlie Williams	Yamaha
1981-3	Tony Rutter	Ducati
1984	Graeme McGregor (Aus)	Yamaha
1985	Tony Rutter	Ducati
1986	Brian Reid	Yamaha
1987	Steve Hislop	Yamaha

MOST TT WINS:

14 Mike Hailwood 1961-79; 10 Stan Woods 1923-39, Giacomo Agostini (Ita) 1966-75, Joey Dunlop (Ire) 1977-87; 9 Siegfried Schauzu (FRG) 1967-75; 8 Phil Read 1961-77, Charles Mortimer 1970-8, Charlie Williams 1973-80

TT lap record: 190.66 kmh/118.47 mph Joey Dunlop (Honda) 4 June 1984

Three TT wins in one week: Mike Hailwood (1961 Senior, Lightweight 125, Lightweight 250; 1967 Senior, Junior, Lightweight 250); Joey Dunlop (1985 Senior, Junior, Formula One)

Dual Senior/Junior TT winners in one year: Tim Hunt (1931), Stan Woods (1932-3), Jimmy Guthrie (1934), Geoff Duke (1951), Ray Amm (1953), Bob McIntyre (1957), John Surtees (1958-9), Mike Hailwood (1967), Giacomo Agostini (1968-70, 1972), Joey Dunlop (1985)

MOTO-CROSS

Also known as Scrambling, Moto-Cross is a specialised branch of Motor Cycling. The first moto-cross race, over an undulating course, with many climbs, drops, bends, and on a dirt circuit, was at Camberley, Surrey in 1924. It remained primarily a British sport but it became international in 1947 with the introduction of the Moto-Cross des Nations, an international annual team event for 500cc machines. The Trophée des Nations, a team event for 250cc machines, was introduced in 1961. A European Championship for 500cc machines was introduced in 1952 and for 250cc machines in 1957. The 500cc class became the World Championship in 1957 and the 250cc event acquired World Championship status in 1962. A 125cc event was added in 1975, and a sidecar championship in 1980.

WORLD CHAMPIONS

500cc

1957	Bill Nilsson (Swe)	AJS
1958	René Baeten (Bel)	FN
1959	Sten Lundin (Swe)	Monark
1960	Bill Nilsson (Swe)	Husqvarna
1961	Sten Lundin (Swe)	Monark
1962-3	Rolf Tibblin (Swe)	Husqvarna
1964-5	Jeff Smith (UK)	BSA
1966-8	Paul Friedrichs (GDR)	CZ
1969-70	Bengt Aberg (Swe)	Husqvarna
1971-3	Roger de Coster (Bel)	Suzuki
1974	Heikki Mikkola (Fin)	Husqvarna
1975-6	Roger de Coster (Bel)	Suzuki
1977-8	Heikki Mikkola (Fin)	Yamaha
1979	Graham Noyce (UK)	Honda
1980-1	André Malherbe (Bel)	Honda
1982	Brad Lackey (USA)	Suzuki
1983	Håkan Carlqvist (Swe)	Yamaha
1984	André Malherbe (Bel)	Honda
1985-6	Dave Thorpe (UK)	Honda
1987	Georges Jobé (Bel)	Honda

250cc

1962-3	Torsten Hallman (Swe)	Husqvarna
1964	Joël Robert (Bel)	CZ
1965	Viktor Arbekov (USSR)	CZ
1966-7	Torsten Hallman (Swe)	Husqvarna
1968-69	Joël Robert (Bel)	CZ
1970-72	Joël Robert (Bel)	Suzuki
1973	Hakan Andersson (Swe)	Yamaha
1974	Gennadiy Moisseyev (USSR)	KTM
1975	Harry Everts (Bel)	Puch
1976	Heikki Mikkola (Fin)	Husqvarna
1977-8	Gennadiy Moisseyev (USSR)	KTM
1979	Hakan Carlqvist (Swe)	Husqvarna
1980	Georges Jobé (Bel)	Suzuki
1981	Neil Hudson (UK)	Yamaha
1982	Danny la Porte (USA)	Yamaha
1983	Georges Jobé (Bel)	Suzuki
1984-5	Heinz Kinigadner (Aut)	KTM
1986	Jacky Vimond (Fra)	Yamaha

125cc

1975-7	Gaston Rahier (Bel)	Suzuki
1978	Akira Watanabe (Jap)	Suzuki
1979-81	Harry Everts (Bel)	Suzuki
1982-3	Eric Geboers (Bel)	Suzuki
1984	Michèle Rinaldi (Ita)	Suzuki
1985	Pekka Vehkonen (Fin)	Cagira
1986	Dave Strijbos (Hol)	Cagira

SIDECAR

1980	Reinhardt Bohler (FRG)	Yamaha
1981	Tom van Heugten (Hol)	Yamaha Wasp
1982-3	Erik Bollhalder (Swi)	Yamaha
1984-6	Hans Bachtöld (Swi)	EML Jumbo

MOST WORLD TITLES
6 (all 250cc) Joël Robert (Bel) 1964, 1968-72

MOTO-CROSS DES NATIONS

1947-75 for five-man teams (best three to score). From 1976-84 four-man teams, at 500 cc. Since 1985 the Coupe des Nations, Trophée des Nations and Moto-cross des Nations were merged into one three-class (500, 250 and 125cc) competition.

Winners:

15	Great Britain 1947, 1949-50, 1952-4, 1956-7, 1959-60, 1963-7
9	Belgium 1948, 1951, 1969, 1972-3, 1976-7, 1979-80
7	Sweden 1955, 1958, 1961-2, 1970-1, 1974
4	USA 1983-6
2	USSR 1968, 1978; USA 1981-2
1	Czechoslovakia 1975

TROPHÉE DES NATIONS

1961-75 for five-man teams (best three to score). From 1976-84 four-man teams, at 250cc. Merged with the above event in 1985.

Winners:

11	Belgium 1969-78, 1980
5	Sweden 1963-4, 1966-8
4	USA 1981-4
3	Great Britain 1961-2, 1965
1	USSR 1979

1965 – no result, meeting declared null and void.

COUPE DES NATIONS At 125 cc

Winners:
Italy 1982; Belgium 1983; Netherlands 1984

TRIALS

Trials riding, the means of manipulating the cycle around a pre-determined course constituting many obstacles and natural hazards, has existed since the early days of motor cycling. The famous Scottish Six Days Trial, based around Edinburgh, was introduced in 1909, and the first International Six Days Trial took place in 1913. A World Championship was introduced in 1975.

WORLD CHAMPIONS

1975	Martin Lampkin (UK)	Bultaco
1976-8	Yrjö Vesterinen (Fin)	Bultaco
1979	Bernie Schreiber (USA)	Bultaco
1980	Ulf Karlsson (Swe)	Montesa
1981	Gilles Burgat (Fra)	SWM
1982-4	Eddy Lejeune (Bel)	Honda
1985-6	Thierry Michaud (Fra)	Fantic

Most titles: 3 Vesterinen, Lejeune

MOTOR RACING

Following the birth of the motor car in the 19th century, it was inevitable that man would soon start racing. The first race involving motorised vehicles was believed to be the *La*

Alain Prost, driving in the 1986 Australian Grand Prix. (All-Sport)

Velocipede 31km (19.3 miles) race in Paris on 20 April 1887, won by Count Jules Felix Philippe Albert de Dion de Malfiance driving a De Dion steam quadricycle. There is a claim, however, that a race took place in the United States in 1878, and was from Green Bay to Madison, Wisconsin, won by an Oshkosk steamer. The first 'real' motor car race was on 11-14 June 1895, a 1178 km (732 mile) race from Paris to Bordeaux and back. Grand Prix racing started with the 1906 French Grand Prix, and the World Drivers' Championship was instituted in 1950. The sport's international controlling body is the Fédération Internationale de l'Automobile (FIA), whose headquarters are in Paris.

WORLD CHAMPIONSHIP GRANDS PRIX

The FIA took a decision in 1949 to inaugurate a World Championship for Drivers in 1950 and the first World Championship race took place at Silverstone on 13 May 1950 when the Italian Giuseppe Farina won the British Grand Prix. A Constructors' Championship was instituted in 1958. From 1950 to 1960 the Indianapolis 500 formed part of the Championship. The following is a list of winners of all World Championship Grand Prix races.

ARGENTINE GRAND PRIX
At Buenos Aires

1953	Alberto Ascari (Ita)	Ferrari
1954-5	Juan Manuel Fangio (Arg)	Mercedes-Benz
1956	Juan Manuel Fangio (Arg)	Ferrari
1957	Juan Manuel Fangio (Arg)	Maserati
1958	Stirling Moss (UK)	Cooper
1972	Jackie Stewart (UK)	Tyrrell
1973	Emerson Fittipaldi (Bra)	Lotus
1974	Denny Hulme (NZ)	McLaren
1975	Emerson Fittipaldi (Bra)	McLaren
1977	Jody Scheckter (SAf)	Wolf
1978	Mario Andretti (USA)	Lotus
1979	Jacques Laffite (Fra)	Ligier
1980	Alan Jones (Aus)	Williams
1981	Nelson Piquet (Bra)	Brabham

AUSTRALIAN GRAND PRIX
At Adelaide

1985	Keke Rosberg (Fin)	Williams
1986	Alain Prost (Fra)	McLaren

AUSTRIAN GRAND PRIX
At Zeltweg 1964; Österreichring 1970-86

1964	Lorenzo Bandini (Ita)	Ferrari
1970	Jacky Ickx (Bel)	Ferrari
1971	Jo Siffert (Swi)	BRM
1972	Emerson Fittipaldi (Bra)	Lotus
1973	Ronnie Peterson (Swe)	Lotus
1974	Carlos Reutemann (Arg)	Brabham
1975	Vittorio Brambilla (Ita)	March
1976	John Watson (UK)	Penske
1977	Alan Jones (Aus)	Shadow
1978	Ronnie Peterson (Swe)	Lotus
1979	Alan Jones (Aus)	Williams
1980	Jean-Pierre Jabouille (Fra)	Renault
1981	Jacques Laffite (Fra)	Ligier
1982	Elio de Angelis (Ita)	Lotus
1983	Alain Prost (Fra)	Renault
1984	Niki Lauda (Aut)	McLaren
1985-6	Alain Prost (Fra)	McLaren

BELGIAN GRAND PRIX
At Spa-Francorchamps 1950-6, 1958, 1960-8, 1970, 1983, 1985-7; Nivelles 1972, 1974; Zolder 1973, 1975-82, 1984

1950	Juan Manuel Fangio (Arg)	Alfa-Romeo
1951	Giuseppe Farina (Ita)	Alfa-Romeo
1952-3	Alberto Ascari (Ita)	Ferrari
1954	Juan Manuel Fangio (Arg)	Maserati
1955	Juan Manuel Fangio (Arg)	Mercedes-Benz
1956	Peter Collins (UK)	Ferrari
1958	Tony Brooks (UK)	Vanwall
1960	Jack Brabham (Aus)	Cooper
1961	Phil Hill (USA)	Ferrari
1962-5	Jim Clark (UK)	Lotus
1966	John Surtees (UK)	Ferrari
1967	Dan Gurney (USA)	Eagle
1968	Bruce McLaren (NZ)	McLaren

1970	Pedro Rodriguez (Mex)	BRM
1972	Emerson Fittipaldi (Bra)	Lotus
1973	Jackie Stewart (UK)	Tyrrell
1974	Emerson Fittipaldi (Bra)	McLaren
1975-6	Niki Lauda (Aut)	Ferrari
1977	Gunnar Nilsson (Swe)	Lotus
1978	Mario Andretti (USA)	Lotus
1979	Jody Scheckter (SAf)	Ferrari
1980	Didier Pironi (Fra)	Ligier
1981	Carlos Reutemann (Arg)	Williams
1982	John Watson (UK)	McLaren
1983	Alain Prost (Fra)	Renault
1984	Michele Alboreto (Ita)	Ferrari
1985	Ayrton Senna (Bra)	Lotus
1986	Nigel Mansell (UK)	Williams
1987	Alain Prost (Fra)	McLaren

BRAZILIAN GRAND PRIX
At Interlagos 1973-7, 1979-80; Rio de Janeiro 1978, 1981-7

1973	Emerson Fittipaldi (Bra)	Lotus
1974	Emerson Fittipaldi (Bra)	McLaren
1975	Carlos Pace (Bra)	Brabham
1976	Niki Lauda (Aut)	Ferrari
1977-8	Carlos Reutemann (Arg)	Ferrari
1979	Jacques Laffite (Fra)	Ligier
1980	René Arnoux (Fra)	Renault
1981	Carlos Reutemann (Arg)	Williams
1982	Alain Prost (Fra)	Renault
1983	Nelson Piquet (Bra)	Brabham
1984-5	Alain Prost (Fra)	McLaren
1986	Nigel Mansell (UK)	Williams
1987	Alain Prost (Fra)	McLaren

BRITISH GRAND PRIX
At Silverstone 1950-4, 1956, 1958, 1960 and uneven years from 1963; Aintree 1955, 1957, 1959, 1961-2; Brands Hatch, even years from 1964

1950	Giuseppe Farina (Ita)	Alfa-Romeo
1951	José Froilan Gonzalez (Arg)	Ferrari
1952-3	Alberto Ascari (Ita)	Ferrari
1954	José Froilan Gonzalez (Arg)	Ferrari
1955	Stirling Moss (UK)	Mercedes-Benz
1956	Juan Manuel Fangio (Arg)	Ferrari
1957	Stirling Moss (UK) & Tony Brooks (UK)	Vanwall
1958	Peter Collins (UK)	Ferrari
1959-60	Jack Brabham (Aus)	Cooper
1961	Wolfgang von Trips (FRG)	Ferrari
1962-5	Jim Clark (UK)	Lotus
1966	Jack Brabham (Aus)	Brabham
1967	Jim Clark (UK)	Lotus
1968	Jo Siffert (Swi)	Lotus
1969	Jackie Stewart (UK)	Matra
1970	Jochen Rindt (Aut)	Lotus
1971	Jackie Stewart (UK)	Tyrrell
1972	Emerson Fittipaldi (Bra)	Lotus
1973	Peter Revson (USA)	McLaren
1974	Jody Scheckter (SAf)	Tyrrell
1975	Emerson Fittipaldi (Bra)	McLaren
1976	Niki Lauda (Aut)	Ferrari
1977	James Hunt (UK)	McLaren
1978	Carlos Reutemann (Arg)	Ferrari
1979	Clay Regazzoni (Swi)	Williams
1980	Alan Jones (Aus)	Williams

1981	John Watson (UK)	McLaren
1982	Niki Lauda (Aut)	McLaren
1983	Alain Prost (Fra)	Renault
1984	Niki Lauda (Aut)	McLaren
1985	Alain Prost (Fra)	McLaren
1986-7	Nigel Mansell (UK)	Williams

CANADIAN GRAND PRIX
At Mosport 1967, 1969, 1971-7; Mont Tremblant 1968, 1970; Montreal 1978-86

1967	Jack Brabham (Aus)	Brabham
1968	Denny Hulme (NZ)	McLaren
1969	Jacky Ickx (Bel)	Brabham
1970	Jacky Ickx (Bel)	Ferrari
1971-2	Jackie Stewart (UK)	Tyrrell
1973	Peter Revson (USA)	McLaren
1974	Emerson Fittipaldi (Bra)	McLaren
1976	James Hunt (UK)	McLaren
1977	Jody Scheckter (SAf)	Wolf
1978	Gilles Villeneuve (Can)	Ferrari
1979-80	Alan Jones (Aus)	Williams
1981	Jacques Laffite (Fra)	Ligier
1982	Nelson Piquet (Bra)	Brabham
1983	René Arnoux (Fra)	Ferrari
1984	Nelson Piquet (Bra)	Brabham
1985	Michele Alboreto (Ita)	Ferrari
1986	Nigel Mansell (UK)	Williams

DUTCH GRAND PRIX
At Zandvoort

1952-3	Alberto Ascari (Ita)	Ferrari
1955	Juan Manuel Fangio (Arg)	Mercedes-Benz
1958	Stirling Moss (UK)	Vanwall
1959	Jo Bonnier (Swe)	BRM
1960	Jack Brabham (Aus)	Cooper
1961	Wolfgang von Trips (FRG)	Ferrari
1962	Graham Hill (UK)	BRM
1963-5	Jim Clark (UK)	Lotus
1966	Jack Brabham (Aus)	Brabham
1967	Jim Clark (UK)	Lotus
1968-9	Jackie Stewart (UK)	Matra
1970	Jochen Rindt (Aut)	Lotus
1971	Jacky Ickx (Bel)	Ferrari
1973	Jackie Stewart (UK)	Tyrrell
1974	Niki Lauda (Aut)	Ferrari
1975	James Hunt (UK)	Hesketh
1976	James Hunt (UK)	McLaren
1977	Niki Lauda (Aut)	Ferrari
1978	Mario Andretti (USA)	Lotus
1979	Alan Jones (Aus)	Williams
1980	Nelson Piquet (Bra)	Brabham
1981	Alain Prost (Fra)	Renault
1982	Didier Pironi (Fra)	Ferrari
1983	René Arnoux (Fra)	Ferrari
1984	Alain Prost (Fra)	McLaren
1985	Niki Lauda (Aut)	McLaren

EUROPEAN GRAND PRIX
Earlier Grand Prix races were designated 'European Grand Prix' but it was not until 1983 that it became a separate race.
At Brands Hatch 1983, 1985; New Nürburgring 1984

1983	Nelson Piquet (Bra)	Brabham
1984	Alain Prost (Fra)	McLaren
1985	Nigel Mansell (UK)	Williams

FRENCH GRAND PRIX

At Rheims 1950-1, 1953-4, 1956, 1958-61, 1963, 1966; Rouen-les Essarts 1952, 1957, 1962, 1964, 1968; Clermont-Ferrand 1965, 1969-70, 1972; Le Mans 1967; Paul Ricard 1971, 1973, 1975-6, 1978, 1980, 1982-3, 1985-7; Dijon Prenois 1974, 1977, 1979, 1981, 1984

1950	Juan Manuel Fangio (Arg)	Alfa-Romeo
1951	Juan Manuel Fangio (Arg) & Luigi Fagioli (Ita)	Alfa-Romeo
1952	Alberto Ascari (Ita)	Ferrari
1953	Mike Hawthorn (UK)	Ferrari
1954	Juan Manuel Fangio (Arg)	Mercedes-Benz
1956	Peter Collins (UK)	Ferrari
1957	Juan Manuel Fangio (Arg)	Maserati
1958	Mike Hawthorn (UK)	Ferrari
1959	Tony Brooks (UK)	Ferrari
1960	Jack Brabham (Aus)	Cooper
1961	Giancarlo Baghetti (Ita)	Ferrari
1962	Dan Gurney (USA)	Porsche
1963	Jim Clark (UK)	Lotus
1964	Dan Gurney (USA)	Brabham
1965	Jim Clark (UK)	Lotus
1966-7	Jack Brabham (Aus)	Brabham
1968	Jacky Ickx (Bel)	Ferrari
1969	Jackie Stewart (UK)	Matra
1970	Jochen Rindt (Aut)	Lotus
1971-2	Jackie Stewart (UK)	Tyrrell
1973-4	Ronnie Peterson (Swe)	Lotus
1975	Niki Lauda (Aut)	Ferrari
1976	James Hunt (UK)	McLaren
1977-8	Mario Andretti (USA)	Lotus
1979	Jean-Pierre Jabouille (Fra)	Renault
1980	Alan Jones (Aus)	Williams
1981	Alain Prost (Fra)	Renault
1982	René Arnoux (Fra)	Renault
1983	Alain Prost (Fra)	Renault
1984	Niki Lauda (Aut)	McLaren
1985	Nelson Piquet (Bra)	Brabham
1986	Nigel Mansell (UK)	Williams
1987	Nigel Mansell (UK)	Williams

GERMAN GRAND PRIX

At Nürburgring 1951-4, 1956-8, 1961-9, 1971-6; Avus 1959; Hockenheim 1970, 1977-84, 1986-7; New Nürburgring 1985

1951-2	Alberto Ascari (Ita)	Ferrari
1953	Giuseppe Farina (Ita)	Ferrari
1954	Juan Manuel Fangio (Arg)	Mercedes-Benz
1956	Juan Manuel Fangio (Arg)	Ferrari
1957	Juan Manuel Fangio (Arg)	Maserati
1958	Tony Brooks (UK)	Vanwall
1959	Tony Brooks (UK)	Ferrari
1961	Stirling Moss (UK)	Lotus
1962	Graham Hill (UK)	BRM
1963-4	John Surtees (UK)	Ferrari
1965	Jim Clark (UK)	Lotus
1966	Jack Brabham (Aus)	Brabham
1967	Denny Hulme (NZ)	Brabham
1968	Jackie Stewart (UK)	Matra
1969	Jacky Ickx (Bel)	Brabham
1970	Jochen Rindt (Aut)	Lotus
1971	Jackie Stewart (UK)	Tyrrell
1972	Jcky Ickx (Bel)	Ferrari
1973	Jackie Stewart (UK)	Tyrrell

1974	Clay Regazzoni (Swi)	Ferrari
1975	Carlos Reutemann (Arg)	Brabham
1976	James Hunt (UK)	McLaren
1977	Niki Lauda (Aut)	Ferrari
1978	Mario Andretti (USA)	Lotus
1979	Alan Jones (Aus)	Williams
1980	Jacques Laffite (Fra)	Ligier
1981	Nelson Piquet (Bra)	Brabham
1982	Patrick Tambay (Fra)	Ferrari
1983	René Arnoux (Fra)	Ferrari
1984	Alain Prost (Fra)	McLaren
1985	Michele Alboreto (Ita)	Ferrari
1986-7	Nelson Piquet (Bra)	Williams

HUNGARIAN GRAND PRIX

At Budapest

1986-7	Nelson Piquet (Bra)	Williams

ITALIAN GRAND PRIX

At Monza 1950-79, 1981-6; Imola 1980

1950	Giuseppe Farina (Ita)	Alfa-Romeo
1951-2	Alberto Ascari (Ita)	Ferrari
1953	Juan Manuel Fangio (Arg)	Maserati
1954-5	Juan Manuel Fangio (Arg)	Mercedes-Benz
1956	Stirling Moss (UK)	Maserati
1957	Stirling Moss (UK)	Vanwall
1958	Tony Brooks (UK)	Vanwall
1959	Stirling Moss (UK)	Cooper
1960-1	Phil Hill (USA)	Ferrari
1962	Graham Hill (UK)	BRM
1963	Jim Clark (UK)	Lotus
1964	John Surtees (UK)	Ferrari
1965	Jackie Stewart (UK)	BRM
1966	Lodovico Scarfiotti (Ita)	Ferrari
1967	John Surtees (UK)	Honda
1968	Denny Hulme (NZ)	McLaren
1969	Jackie Stewart (UK)	Matra
1970	Clay Regazzoni (Swi)	Ferrari
1971	Peter Gethin (UK)	BRM
1972	Emerson Fittipaldi (Bra)	Lotus
1973-4	Ronnie Peterson (Swe)	Lotus
1975	Clay Regazzoni (Swi)	Ferrari
1976	Ronnie Peterson (Swe)	March
1977	Mario Andretti (USA)	Lotus
1978	Niki Lauda (Aut)	Brabham
1979	Jody Scheckter (SAf)	Ferrari
1980	Nelson Piquet (Bra)	Brabham
1981	Alain Prost (Fra)	Renault
1982	René Arnoux (Fra)	Renault
1983	Nelson Piquet (Bra)	Brabham
1984	Niki Lauda (Aut)	McLaren
1985	Alain Prost (Fra)	McLaren
1986	Nelson Piquet (Bra)	Williams

JAPANESE GRAND PRIX

At Fuji

1976	Mario Andretti (USA)	Lotus
1977	James Hunt (UK)	McLaren

LAS VEGAS GRAND PRIX

At Caeser's Palace

1981	Alan Jones (Aus)	Williams
1982	Michele Alboreto (Ita)	Tyrrell

MEXICAN GRAND PRIX

At Mexico City

1963	Jim Clark (UK)	Lotus

1964 Dan Gurney (USA)	Brabham
1965 Richie Ginther (USA)	Honda
1966 John Surtees (UK)	Cooper
1967 Jim Clark (UK)	Lotus
1968 Graham Hill (UK)	Lotus
1969 Denny Hulme (NZ)	McLaren
1970 Jacky Ickx (Bel)	Ferrari
1986 Gerhard Berger (Aut)	Benetton

MONACO GRAND PRIX
At Monte Carlo

1950 Juan Manuel Fangio (Arg)	Alfa-Romeo
1955 Maurice Trintignant (Fra)	Ferrari
1956 Stirling Moss (UK)	Maserati
1957 Juan Manuel Fangio (Arg)	Maserati
1958 Maurice Trintignant (Fra)	Cooper
1959 Jack Brabham (Aus)	Cooper
1960-1 Stirling Moss (UK)	Lotus
1962 Bruce McLaren (NZ)	Cooper
1963-5 Graham Hill (UK)	BRM
1966 Jackie Stewart (UK)	BRM
1967 Denny Hulme (NZ)	Brabham
1968-9 Graham Hill (UK)	Lotus
1970 Jochen Rindt (Aut)	Lotus
1971 Jackie Stewart (UK)	Tyrrell
1972 Jean-Pierre Beltoise (Fra)	BRM
1973 Jackie Stewart (UK)	Tyrrell
1974 Ronnie Peterson (Swe)	Lotus
1975-6 Niki Lauda (Aut)	Ferrari
1977 Jody Scheckter (SAf)	Wolf
1978 Patrick Depailler (Fra)	Tyrrell
1979 Jody Scheckter (SAf)	Ferrari
1980 Carlos Reutemann (Arg)	Williams
1981 Gilles Villeneuve (Can)	Ferrari
1982 Riccardo Patrese (Ita)	Brabham
1983 Keke Rosberg (Fin)	Williams
1984-5 Alain Prost (Fra)	McLaren
1986 Jacques Laffite (Fra)	Ligier
1987 Ayrton Senna (Bra)	Lotus

MOROCCAN GRAND PRIX
At Ain Diab, Casablanca

1958 Stirling Moss (UK)	Vanwall

PESCARA GRAND PRIX
At Circuit Pescara

1957 Stirling Moss (UK)	Vanwall

PORTUGUESE GRAND PRIX
At Oporto 1958, 1960; Monsanto 1959; Estoril 1984-6

1958 Stirling Moss (UK)	Vanwall
1959 Stirling Moss (UK)	Cooper
1960 Jack Brabham (Aus)	Cooper
1984 Alain Prost (Fra)	McLaren
1985 Ayrton Senna (Bra)	Lotus
1986 Nigel Mansell (UK)	Williams

SAN MARINO GRAND PRIX
At Imola

1981 Nelson Piquet (Bra)	Brabham
1982 Didier Pironi (Fra)	Ferrari
1983 Patrick Tambay (Fra)	Ferrari
1984 Alain Prost (Fra)	McLaren
1985 Elio de Angelis (Ita)	Lotus
1986 Riccardo Patrese (Ita)	Brabham
1987 Nigel Mansell (UK)	Williams

SOUTH AFRICAN GRAND PRIX
At East London 1962-3, 1965; Kyalami 1967-80, 1982-5

1962 Graham Hill (UK)	BRM
1963 Jim Clark (UK)	Lotus
1965 Jim Clark (UK)	Lotus
1967 Pedro Rodriguez (Mex)	Cooper
1968 Jim Clark (UK)	Lotus
1969 Jackie Stewart (UK)	Matra
1970 Jack Brabham (Aus)	Brabham
1971 Mario Andretti (USA)	Ferrari
1972 Denny Hulme (NZ)	McLaren
1973 Jackie Stewart (UK)	Tyrrell
1974 Carlos Reutemann (Arg)	Brabham
1975 Jody Scheckter (SAf)	Tyrrell
1976-7 Niki Lauda (Aut)	Ferrari
1978 Ronnie Peterson (Swe)	Lotus
1979 Gilles Villeneuve (Can)	Ferrari
1980 René Arnoux (Fra)	Renault
1982 Alain Prost (Fra)	Renault
1983 Riccardo Patrese (Ita)	Brabham
1984 Niki Lauda (Aut)	McLaren
1985 Nigel Mansell (UK)	Williams

SPANISH GRAND PRIX
At Pedralbes, Barcelona 1951, 1954; Jarama 1968, 1970, 1972, 1974, 1976-81; Montjuich Park 1969, 1971, 1973, 1975, 1986

1951 Juan Manuel Fangio (Arg)	Alfa-Romeo
1954 Mike Hawthorn (UK)	Ferrari
1968 Graham Hill (UK)	Lotus
1969 Jackie Stewart (UK)	Matra
1970 Jackie Stewart (UK)	March
1971 Jackie Stewart (UK)	Tyrrell
1972-3 Emerson Fittipaldi (Bra)	Lotus
1974 Niki Lauda (Aut)	Ferrari
1975 Jochen Mass (FRG)	McLaren
1976 James Hunt (UK)	McLaren
1977-8 Mario Andretti (USA)	Lotus
1979 Patrick Depailler (Fra)	Ligier
1980 Alan Jones (Aus)	Williams
1981 Gilles Villeneuve (Can)	Ferrari
1986 Ayrton Senna (Bra)	Lotus

SWEDISH GRAND PRIX
At Anderstorp

1973 Denny Hulme (NZ)	McLaren
1974 Jody Scheckter (SAf)	Tyrrell
1975 Niki Lauda (Aut)	Ferrari
1976 Jody Scheckter (SAf)	Tyrrell
1977 Jacques Laffite (Fra)	Ligier
1978 Niki Lauda (Aut)	Brabham

SWISS GRAND PRIX
At Bremgarten, Berne 1950-4; Dijon (France) 1982

1950 Giuseppe Farina (Ita)	Alfa-Romeo
1951 Juan Manuel Fangio (Arg)	Alfa-Romeo
1952 Piero Taruffi (Ita)	Ferrari
1953 Alberto Ascari (Ita)	Ferrari
1954 Juan Manuel Fangio (Arg)	Mercedes-Benz
1982 Keke Rosberg (Fin)	Williams

UNITED STATES GRAND PRIX
At Sebring 1959; Riverside 1960; Watkins Glen 1961-80

1959 Bruce McLaren (NZ)	Cooper
1960 Stirling Moss (UK)	Lotus

1961	Innes Ireland (UK)	Lotus
1962	Jim Clark (UK)	Lotus
1963-5	Graham Hill (UK)	BRM
1966-7	Jim Clark (UK)	Lotus
1968	Jackie Stewart (UK)	Matra
1969	Jochen Rindt (Aut)	Lotus
1970	Emerson Fittipaldi (Bra)	Lotus
1971	Francois Cevert (Fra)	Tyrrell
1972	Jackie Stewart (UK)	Tyrrell
1973	Ronnie Peterson (Swe)	Lotus
1974	Carlos Reutemann (Arg)	Brabham
1975	Niki Lauda (Aut)	Ferrari
1976-7	James Hunt (UK)	McLaren
1978	Carlos Reutemann (Arg)	Ferrari
1979	Gilles Villeneuve (Can)	Ferrari
1980	Alan Jones (Aus)	Williams

Niki Lauda – the most Grand Prix points (All-Sport)

UNITED STATES GRAND PRIX EAST (Detroit GP)
At Detroit

1982	John Watson (UK)	McLaren
1983	Michele Alboreto (Ita)	Tyrrell
1984	Nelson Piquet (Bra)	Brabham
1985	Keke Rosberg (Fin)	Williams
1986	Ayrton Senna (Bra)	Lotus
1987	Ayrton Senna (Bra)	Lotus

UNITED STATES GRAND PRIX WEST (Dallas GP)
At Long Beach 1976-83; Fir Park 1984

1976	Clay Regazzoni (Swi)	Ferrari
1977	Mario Andretti (USA)	Lotus
1978	Carlos Reutemann (Arg)	Ferrari
1979	Gilles Villeneuve (Can)	Ferrari
1980	Nelson Piquet (Fra)	Brabham
1981	Alan Jones (Aus)	Williams
1982	Niki Lauda (Aut)	McLaren
1983	John Watson (UK)	McLaren
1984	Keke Rosberg (Fin)	Williams

WORLD CHAMPIONS & RUNNERS-UP

Year	Winner	Points	Runner-up	Points
1950	Giuseppe Farina (Ita)	30	Juan Manuel Fangio (Arg)	27
1951	Juan Manuel Fangio (Arg)	31	Alberto Ascari (Ita)	25
1952	Alberto Ascari (Ita)	36	Giuseppe Farina (Ita)	24
1953	Alberto Ascari (Ita)	34	Juan Manuel Fangio (Arg)	28
1954	Juan Manuel Fangio (Arg)	42	José Froilán González (Arg)	25½
1955	Juan Manuel Fangio (Arg)	40	Stirling Moss (UK)	23
1956	Juan Manuel Fangio (Arg)	30	Stirling Moss (UK)	27
1957	Juan Manuel Fangio (Arg)	40	Stirling Moss (UK)	25
1958	Mike Hawthorn (UK)	42	Stirling Moss (UK)	41
1959	Jack Brabham (Aus)	31	Tony Brooks (UK)	27
1960	Jack Brabham (Aus)	43	Bruce McLaren (NZ)	34
1961	Phil Hill (USA)	34	Wolfgang von Trips (FRG)	33
1962	Graham Hill (UK)	42	Jim Clark (UK)	30
1963	Jim Clark (UK)	54	Graham Hill (UK) &	29
			Richie Ginther (USA)	29
1964	John Surtees (UK)	40	Graham Hill (UK)	39
1965	Jim Clark (UK)	54	Graham Hill (UK)	40
1966	Jack Brabham (Aus)	42	John Surtees (UK)	28
1967	Denny Hulme (NZ)	51	Jack Brabham (Aus)	46
1968	Graham Hill (UK)	48	Jackie Stewart (UK)	36
1969	Jackie Stewart (UK)	63	Jacky Ickx (Bel)	37
1970	Jochen Rindt (Aut)	45	Jacky Ickx (Bel)	40
1971	Jackie Stewart (UK)	62	Ronnie Peterson (Swe)	33
1972	Emerson Fittipaldi (Bra)	61	Jackie Stewart (UK)	45
1973	Jackie Stewart (UK)	71	Emerson Fittipaldi (Bra)	55
1974	Emerson Fittipaldi (Bra)	55	Clay Regazzoni (Swi)	52
1975	Niki Lauda (Aut)	64	Emerson Fittipaldi (Bra)	45
1976	James Hunt (UK)	69	Niki Lauda (Aut)	68
1977	Niki Lauda (Aut)	72	Jody Scheckter (SAf)	55
1978	Mario Andretti (USA)	64	Ronnie Peterson (Swe)	51
1979	Jody Scheckter (SAf)	51	Gilles Villeneuve (Can)	47
1980	Alan Jones (Aus)	67	Nelson Piquet (Bra)	54
1981	Nelson Piquet (Bra)	50	Carlos Reutemann (Arg)	49
1982	Keke Rosberg (Fin)	44	John Watson (UK) &	39
			Didier Pironi (Fra)	39
1983	Nelson Piquet (Bra)	59	Alain Prost (Fra)	57
1984	Niki Lauda (Aut)	72	Alain Prost (Fra)	71
1985	Alain Prost (Fra)	73	Michele Alboreto (Ita)	53
1986	Alain Prost (Fra)	72	Nigel Mansell (UK)	70

Most wins: 5 Juan Manuel Fangio; 3 Jack Brabham, Jackie Stewart, Niki Lauda; 2 Jim Clark, Alberto Ascari, Graham Hill, Emerson Fittipaldi, Nelson Piquet, Alain Prost.

CONSTRUCTORS' CHAMPIONSHIP

Year	Constructor	Points
1958	Vanwall	48
1959	Cooper-Climax	40
1960	Cooper-Climax	48
1961	Ferrari	45
1962	BRM	42
1963	Lotus-Climax	54
1964	Ferrari	45
1965	Lotus-Climax	54
1966	Brabham-Repco	42
1967	Brabham-Repco	63
1968	Lotus-Ford	62
1969	Matra-Ford	66
1970	Lotus-Ford	59
1971	Tyrrell-Ford	73
1972	Lotus-Ford	61
1973	Lotus-Ford	92
1974	McLaren-Ford	73
1975	Ferrari	72
1976	Ferrari	83
1977	Ferrari	95
1978	Lotus-Ford	86
1979	Ferrari	113
1980	Williams-Ford	120
1981	Williams-Ford	95
1982	Ferrari	74
1983	Ferrari	89
1984	McLaren-Porsche	143½
1985	McLaren-TAG	90
1986	Williams-Honda	141

Most wins: 8 Ferrari; 5 Lotus-Ford; 2 Cooper-Climax, Lotus-Climax, Brabham-Repco, Williams-Ford.

MOST WINS IN A SEASON

7 Jim Clark (UK) 1963, Alain Prost (Fra) 1984; 6 Alberto Ascari (Ita) 1952, Juan Manuel Fangio (Arg) 1954, Jim Clark (UK) 1965, Jackie Stewart (UK) 1969, 1971, James Hunt (UK) 1976, Mario Andretti (USA) 1978

MOST SUCCESSIVE WINS

9 Alberto Ascari (Ita) 1952-3; 5 Jack Brabham (Aus) 1960, Jim Clark (UK) 1965

MOST POLE POSITIONS

33 Jim Clark (UK); 28 Juan Manuel Fangio (Arg); 24 Niki Lauda (Aut); Nelson Piquet (Bra)

Oldest GP driver: 55 yr 292 days Louis Chiron (Mon) 1955 Monaco GP

Youngest GP driver: 19 yr 181 days Mike Thackwell (NZ) 1980 Canadian Grand Prix

Oldest GP winner: 53 yr 22 days Luigi Fagioli (Ita) 1951 French GP

Oldest GP points scorer: 53 yr 248 days Phillipe Etancelin (Fra) 1950 Italian GP (5th)

Youngest GP points scorer: 20 yr 113 days Ricardo Rodriguez (Mex) 1962 Belgian GP (4th)

Oldest world champion: 46 yr 41 days Juan Manuel Fangio (Arg) 1957

Youngest world champion: 25 yr 285 days Emerson Fittipaldi (Bra) 1972

THE MOST SUCCESSFUL CARS

Wins	Constructor	Years
91	Ferrari	1951-85
77	Lotus	1960-86
52	McLaren	1968-86
35	Brabham	1964-85
31	Williams	1979-86
23	Tyrrell	1971-83
17	BRM	1959-72
16	Cooper	1958-67
15	Renault	1979-83
10	Alfa Romeo	1950-1

MOST WINS IN A SEASON

12 McLaren-Porsche 1984; 8 Lotus-Ford 1978; 7 Ferrari 1952-3, Lotus-Climax 1963, Tyrrell-Ford 1971, Lotus-Ford 1973

MOST SUCCESSIVE WINS

14 Ferrari 1952-3; 9 Alfa Romeo 1950-1; 8 McLaren-Porsche 1984-5

LONGEST CIRCUIT

25.57 km/15.89 miles Pescara, Italy (1957 Pecasra GP)

SHORTEST CIRCUIT

3.14 km/1.95 miles Monte Carlo, France (1955-72 Monaco GP)

FASTEST WINNING AVERAGE SPEED

242.62 km/h/150.75 mph 1971 Italian GP at Monza, won by Peter Gethin (UK) in a BRM

SLOWEST WINNING AVERAGE SPEED

98.68 km/h/61.33 mph 1950 Monaco GP, Monte Carlo, won by Juan Manuel Fangio (Arg) in a Alfa Romeo.

FASTEST LAPS

247.02 km/h/153.49 mph Henri Pescarolo (Fra) March-Ford, 1971 Italian GP (Monza)

244.74 km/h/152.08 mph Chris Amon (NZ) March-Ford, 1970 Belgian GP (Spa)

243.07 km/h/151.05 mph Alain Prost (Fra) McLaren-Porsche, 1985 British GP (Silverstone)

LONGEST RACES

805 km/500 miles Indianapolis 500, 1951-60

602 km/374 miles French GP (Rheims), 1951

555 km/345 miles Indianapolis 500, 1950 (shortened race)

508 km/316 miles Belgian GP (Spa) 1951-6

MOST FREQUENTLY USED CIRCUITS (to end 1986)

36 Monza, Italy 1950-86; 33 Monte Carlo, Monaco 1950-86; 22 (Old) Nürburgring, FR Germany 1951-76; 21 Spa, Belgium 1950-86; 20 Silverstone, England 1950-85, Watkins Glen, USA 1961-80

MOST GRAND PRIX WINS IN A CAREER

(to end 1986)

Wins	Driver	Career	Races	Points	Champs.
27	Jackie Stewart (UK)	1965-73	99	360	3
25	Jim Clark (UK)	1960-8	72	274	2
25	Niki Lauda (Aut)	1971-85	171	420	3
25	Alain Prost (Fra)	1980-6	105	355	2
24	Juan Manuel Fangio (Arg)	1950-8	51	277	5
17	Nelson Piquet (Bra)	1978-86	126	305	2
16	Stirling Moss (UK)	1951-61	66	186 9/14	-
14	Graham Hill (UK)	1958-75	176	289	2
14	Jack Brabham (Aus)	1955-70	126	261	3
14	Emerson Fittipaldi (Bra)	1970-80	144	281	2
13	Alberto Ascari (Ita)	1951-5	32	140 1/7	2
12	Mario Andretti (USA)	1968-82	128	183	1
12	Carlos Reutemann (Arg)	1972-82	146	310	-
12	Alan Jones (Aus)	1975-86	116	206	1
10	James Hunt (UK)	1973-9	92	179	1
10	Ronnie Peterson (Swe)	1970-8	123	206	-
10	Jody Scheckter (SAf)	1972-80	112	255	1

INDIANAPOLIS 500

Held at the end of May each year, the Indianapolis 500 forms part of the Memorial Day celebrations. The race is held at the Indianapolis Raceway, Indiana, and covers 200 laps of the 2½-mile oval shaped circuit. The first race was on 30 May 1911 and won by Ray Harroun in a Marmon Wasp.

Between 1950-60 the race formed part of the World Drivers' Championship, but very few European drivers competed in it.

Winners since 1950 (all US unless otherwise stated):

			Av.Speed (mph)
1950	Johnny Parsons	Kurtis Kraft-Offenhauser	124.002
1951	Lee Wallard	Kurtis Kraft-Offenhauser	126.244
1952	Troy Ruttmann	Kuzna-Offenhauser	128.922
1953	Bill Vukovich	Kurtis Kraft 500A-Offenhauser	128.740
1954	Bill Vukovich	Kurtis Kraft 500A-Offenhauser	130.840
1955	Bob Sweikert	Kurtis Kraft 500C-Offenhauser	128.209
1956	Pat Flaherty	Watson-Offenhauser	128.490
1957	Sam Hanks	Epperly-Offenhauser	135.601
1958	Jimmy Bryan	Epperly-Offenhauser	133.791
1959	Rodger Ward	Watson-Offenhauser	135.857
1960	Jim Rathmann	Watson-Offenhauser	138.767
1961	A.J.Foyt,Jr	Watson-Offenhauser	139.130
1962	Rodger Ward	Watson-Offenhauser	140.293
1963	Parnelli Jones	Watson-Offenhauser	143.137
1964	A.J.Foyt,Jr	Watson-Offenhauser	147.350
1965	Jim Clark (UK)	Lotus-Ford	150.686
1966	Graham Hill (UK)	Lola-Ford	144.317
1967	A.J.Foyt,Jr	Coyote-Ford	151.207
1968	Bobby Unser	Eagle-Offenhauser	152.882
1969	Mario Andretti	Hawk-Ford	156.867
1970	Al Unser	P.J.Colt-Ford	155.749
1971	Al Unser	P.J.Colt-Ford	157.735
1972	Mark Donohue	McLaren-Offenhauser	162.962
1973	Gordon Johncock	Eagle-Offenhauser	159.036
1974	Johnny Rutherford	McLaren-Offenhauser	158.589
1975	Bobby Unser	Eagle-Offenhauser	149.213
1976	Johnny Rutherford	McLaren-Offenhauser	148.725
1977	A.J.Foyt,Jr	Coyote-Ford	161.331
1978	Al Unser	Lola-Cosworth	161.363
1979	Rick Mears	Penske-Cosworth	158.899
1980	Johnny Rutherford	Chaparral-Cosworth	142.862
1981	Bobby Unser	Penske-Cosworth	139.085
1982	Gordon Johncock	Wildcat-Cosworth	162.062
1983	Tom Sneva	March-Cosworth	162.117
1984	Rick Mears	March-Cosworth	163.621
1985	Danny Sullivan	March-Cosworth	152.982
1986	Bobby Rahal	March-Cosworth	170.722
1987	Al Unser	March-Cosworth	162.175

Most wins: 4 A.J.Foyt,Jr, and Al Unser, as above; 3 Louis Meyer (1928,1933,1936), Mauri Rose (1941,1947,1948), Bobby Unser, as above, Johnny Rutherford, as above.

Fastest winning speed: 274.692 km/h/170.722 mph Bobby Rahal in a March-Cosworth, 1986

Qualifying record speed for four laps: 348.951 km/h/216.828 mph Rick Mears in a March-Cosworth, 1986

Single lap qualifying record: 351.155 km/h/218.204 mph Mario Andretti, 1987

LE MANS

The most famous of all sports car races, the Le Mans 24 Hour race was inaugurated on 26-27 May 1923, and won by André Lagache and René Leonard in a 3-litre Chenard & Walcker.

The original Le Mans circuit at Sarthe, France, measured 17.26km (10.73 miles) but the present circuit is 13.64km (8.48 miles)

Post-war winners:

		Av.Speed (km/h)
1949 Luigi Chinetti (Ita)/Lord Peter Selsdon (UK)	Ferrari	132.418
1950 Louis Rosier/Jean-Louis Rosier (Fra)	Talbot-Lago	144.379
1951 Peter Walker/Peter Whitehead (UK)	Jaguar	150.466
1952 Hermann Lang/Karl Riess (FRG)	Mercedes-Benz	155.574
1953 Tony Rolt/Duncan Hamilton (UK)	Jaguar	170.335
1954 Froilan Gonzalez (Arg)/ Maurice Trintignant (Fra)	Ferrari	164.386
1955 Mike Hawthorn/Ivor Bueb (UK)	Jaguar	172.308
1956 Ron Flockhart/Ninian Sanderson (UK)	Jaguar	168.120
1957 Ron Flockhart/Ivor Bueb (UK)	Jaguar	183.216
1958 Olivier Gendebien (Bel)/Phil Hill (USA)	Ferrari	170.912
1959 Carroll Shelby/Roy Salvadori (UK)	Aston Martin	181.162
1960 Olivier Gendebien/Paul Frère (Bel)	Ferrari	175.729
1961 Olivier Gendebien (Bel)/Phil Hill (USA)	Ferrari	186.526
1962 Olivier Gendebien (Bel)/Phil Hill (USA)	Ferrari	185.467
1963 Ludovico Scarfiotti/Lorenzo Bandini (Ita)	Ferrari	190.071
1964 Jean Guichet (Fra)/Nino Vaccarella (Ita)	Ferrari	195.638
1965 Jochen Rindt (Aut)/Masten Gregory (USA)	Ferrari	194.879
1966 Chris Amon/Bruce McLaren (NZ)	Ford	201.795
1967 Dan Gurney/A.J.Foyt,Jr (USA)	Ford	218.033
1968 Pedro Rodriguez (Mex)/Lucien Bianchi (Bel)	Ford	185.536
1969 Jacky Ickx (Bel)/Jackie Oliver (UK)	Ford	208.250
1970 Hans Herrmann (FRG)/Richard Attwood (UK)	Porsche	191.992
1971 Helmut Marko (Aut)/Gijs van Lennep (Hol)	Porsche	222.304
1972 Henri Pescarolo (Fra)/Graham Hill (UK)	Matra-Simca	195.472
1973 Henri Pescarolo/Gérard Larrousse (Fra)	Matra-Simca	202.250
1974 Henri Pescarolo/Gérard Larrousse (Fra)	Matra-Simca	191.940
1975 Jacky Ickx (Bel)/Derek Bell (UK)	Mirage-Ford	191.480
1976 Jacky Ickx (Bel)/Gijs van Lennep (Hol)	Porsche	198.750
1977 Jacky Ickx (Bel)/Jürgen Barth (FRG)/ Hurley Haywood (USA)	Porsche	194.802
1978 Jean-Pierre Jaussaud/Didier Pironi (Fra)	Renault Alpine	210.190
1979 Klaus Ludwig (FRG)/Bill Whittington (USA)/ Don Whittington (USA)	Porsche	173.900
1980 Jean-Pierre Jaussaud/Jean Rondeau (Fra)	Rondeau-Ford	192.000
1981 Jacky Ickx (Bel)/Derek Bell (UK)	Porsche	201.060
1982 Jacky Ickx (Bel)/Derek Bell (UK)	Porsche	204.128
1983 Vern Schuppan (Aut)/ Hurley Haywood (USA)/ Al Holbert (USA)	Porsche	210.330
1984 Klaus Ludwig (FRG)/Henri Pescarolo (Fra)	Porsche	204.180
1985 Klaus Ludwig (FRG)/Paulo Barillo (Ita)/ 'John Winter' (FRG)	Porsche	212.021
1986 Hans Stück (FRG)/Derek Bell (UK)/ Al Holbert (USA)	Porsche	203.197
1987 Hans Stück (FRG)/Derek Bell (UK)/ Al Holbert (USA)	Porsche	199.657

Most wins: 6 Jacky Ickx; 5 Derek Bell; 4 Olivier Gendebien, Henri Pescarolo; 3 Woolf Barnato (UK) 1928-30, Luigi Chinetti (Ita/USA) 1932, 1934, 1949, Phil Hill, 1958, 1961-2

Most successful combinations: 3 wins Olivier Gendebien/Phil Hill, and Jacky Ickx/Derek Bell

Fastest winning speed: 222.304 km/h Helmut Marko/Gijs van Lennep, 1971

Greatest distance covered: 5333.72 km/3314.22 miles Helmut Marko/Gijs van Lennep, 1971

Record for current circuit: 5088.507 km/3161.938 miles Klaus Ludwig/Paulo Barillo/'John Winter', 1985

Most successful car: Porsche, with 12 wins between 1970-87 (including seven consecutive 1981-7)

WORLD SPORTS CAR CHAMPIONSHIP

Over the years the format and car specification have changed many times since its introduction in 1953. Between 1953-61 it was known as the Sports Car World Championship, with the title going to the leading manufacturer. The championship ended in 1961 and was revived in 1968 as a championship for competition sports cars and prototypes. With the distinction between competition and prototypes disappearing, a new Championship for Makes was introduced in 1972. In 1981, a championship for drivers was introduced for the first time, and it became known as the World Endurance Championship. This name changed once more in 1986 when it became the Sports-Prototype World Championship, for both cars and drivers. Since 1985 the constructors' championship has been for teams.

Winners – cars:

1953-4 Ferrari	1980 Lancia
1955 Mercedes-Benz	1981-4 Porsche
1956-8 Ferrari	1985 Rothmans-Porsche
1959 Aston Martin	1986 Brun Motorsport
1960-1 Ferrari	*Drivers:*
1968 Ford	1981 Bob Garretson (USA)
1969-71 Porsche	1982-3 Jacky Ickx (Bel)
1972 Ferrari	1984 Stefan Bellof (FRG)
1973-4 Matra-Simca	1985-6 Derek Bell (UK) and
1975 Alfa Romeo	Hans-Joachim Stück (FRG)
1976-9 Porsche	

FORMULA TWO, FORMULA THREE and FORMULA 3000

Formula Two was introduced in 1947 to enable young drivers to gain experience ready for the step up to Formula One. Formula Three was created in the early 1950s for much the same reason. A European Formula Two championship was introduced in 1967 and a Formula Three championship followed in 1975. Both were disontinued in 1984, making way for the new European Formula 3000 Championship. Formula Three remains popular in Britain and championships have existed in various forms since 1966 when Harry Stiller won the Les Leston Championship. It was not until the introduction of the Vandervell British Formula Three Championship in 1979 that the event became unified.

EUROPEAN FORMULA TWO CHAMPIONS

1967 Jacky Ickx (Bel)
1968 Jean-Pierre Beltoise (Fra)
1969 Johnny Servoz-Gavin (Fra)
1970 Clay Regazzoni (Swi)
1971 Ronnie Peterson (Swe)
1972 Mike Hailwood (UK)
1973 Jean-Pierre Jarier (Fra)
1974 Patrick Depailler (Fra)
1975 Jacques Laffite (Fra)
1976 Jean-Pierre Jabouille (Fra)
1977 René Arnoux (Fra)
1978 Bruno Giacomelli (Ita)
1979 Marc Surer (Swi)
1980 Brian Henton (UK)
1981 Geoff Lees (UK)
1982 Corrado Fabi (Ita)

1983 Jonathan Palmer (UK)
1984 Mike Thackwell (NZ)

Most race wins: 11 Jochen Rindt (Aut), Bruno Giacomelli (Ita); 9 Mike Thackwell (NZ); 7 Jean-Pierre Jarier (Fra), Jacques Laffite (Fra)

EUROPEAN FORMULA THREE CHAMPIONS

1975 Larry Perkins (Aus)
1976 Riccardo Patrese (Ita)
1977 Piercarlo Ghinzani (Ita)
1978 Jan Lammers (Hol)
1979 Alain Prost (Fra)
1980 Michele Alboreto (Ita)
1981 Mauro Baldi (Ita)
1982 Oscar Larrauri (Arg)
1983 Pierluigi Martini (Ita)
1984 Ivan Capelli (Ita)

Most race wins: 11 Mauro Baldi (Ita); 8 Oscar Larrauri (Arg), Alain Prost (Fra); 7 Anders Olofsson (Swe); 6 John Nielsen (Den), Emanuele Pirro (Ita)

BRITISH FORMULA THREE CHAMPIONS (Since 1979)

1979 Chico Serra (Bra)
1980 Stefan Johansson (Swe)
1981 Jonathan Palmer (UK)
1982 Tommy Byrne (Ire)
1983 Ayrton Senna (Bra)
1984 Johnny Dumfries (UK)
1985 Mauricio Gugelmin (Bra)
1986 Andy Wallace (UK)

Most race wins: 12 Ayrton Senna (Bra); 11 Andy Wallace (UK); 10 Johnny Dumfries (UK); 8 Jonathan Palmer (UK), Martin Brundle (UK)

EUROPEAN FORMULA 3000 CHAMPIONS

1985 Christian Danner (FRG)
1986 Ivan Capelli (Ita)

Most race wins: 4 Mike Thackwell (NZ), Emanuele Pirro (Ita), Christian Danner (FRG)

RALLYING

The first long-distance rally took place between 10 June-10 August 1907 and was from Peking, China, to Paris. It was won by Prince Scipione Borghese (Ita) driving an Itala. Since then many famous rallies have appeared. The most famous being the Monte Carlo Rally, instituted in 1911 and won by Henri Rougier (Fra) in a Tyrcat-Mery. The RAC International Rally of Great Britain (now known as the Lombard-RAC Rally) was first held in 1927 but it did not gain recognition as an international event by the FIA until 1951.

MONTE CARLO RALLY

Winners

1911	Henri Rougier	Turcat-Mery
1912	J Beutler	Berliet
1924	Jean Ledure	Bignan
1925	Francois Repusseau	Renault 40 CV
1926	Hon.Victor Bruce/	
	W.J.Brunell	AC Bristol
1927	Lefebvre	Amilcar
1928	Jacques Bignan	Fiat

1929	Dr.Sprenger van Eijk	Graham-Paige
1930	Hector Petit	Licorne
1931	Donald Healey	Invicta
1932-3	M Vasselle	Hotchkiss
1934	Gas/Jean Trevoux	Hotchkiss
1935	Christian Lahaye/ R Quatresous	Renault Nervasport
1936	I Zamfirescu/ J Quinlin	Ford
1937	René le Begue/ J Quinlin	Delahaye
1938	G Bakker Schut/ Karel Ton	Ford
1939	Jean Trevoux/M Lesurque Paul Delahaye	Hotchkiss
1949	Jean Trevoux (Fra)/ M Lesurque	Hotchkiss
1950	Marcel Becquart/H Secret	Hotchkiss
1951	Jean Trevoux (Fra)/ R Crovetto	Delahaye
1952	Sidney Allard/ G Warburton	Allard P2
1953	Maurice Gatsonides/ P Worledge	Ford Zephyr
1954	Louis Chiron (Fra)/ C Basadonna	Lancia-Aurelia
1955	Per Malling/ Gunnar Fadum	Sunbeam-Talbot
1956	Ronnie Adams (UK)/ F E A Bigger	Jaguar Mk VII
1957	No race due to Suez crisis	
1958	Guy Monraisse/J Feret	Renault Dauphine
1959	Paul Coltelloni/ P Alexander	Citroen ID19
1960	Walter Schock/R Moll	Mercedes 220SE
1961	Maurice Martin/ R Bateau	Panhard PL17
1962	Erik Carlsson (Swe)/ Gunnar Haggbom	Saab 96
1963	Erik Carlsson (Swe)/ Gunnar Palm	Saab 96
1964	Paddy Hopkirk (Ire)/ Henry Liddon	Mini-Cooper 'S'
1965	Timo Makinen (Fin)/ Paul Easter	Mini-Cooper 'S'
1966	Pauli Toivonen (Fin)/ Ensio Mikander	Citroen DS21
1967	Rauno Aaltonen (Fin)/ Henry Liddon	Mini-Cooper 'S'
1968	Vic Elford (UK)/ David Stone	Porsche 911T
1969-70	Björn Waldegård (Swe)/ Lars Helmer	Porsche 911
1971	Ove Andersson (Swe)/ David Stone	Alpine Renault A110
1972	Sandro Munari (Ita)/ Mario Manucci	Lancia Fulvia
1973	Jean-Claude Andruet (Fra)/ 'Biche' (Michèle Petit)	Alpine Renault A110
1974	No race due to fuel crisis	
1975	Sandro Munari (Ita)/ Mario Manucci	Lancia Stratos
1976	Sandro Munari (Ita)/ Silvio Maiga	Lancia Stratos
1977	Sandro Munari (Ita)/ Mario Manucci	Lancia Stratos
1978	Jean-Pierre Nicolas (Fra)/ Vincent Laverne	Porsche Carrera 911
1979	Bernard Darniche/ Alain Mahe (Fra)	Lancia Stratos
1980	Walter Röhrl/ Christian Geistdörfer (FRG)	Fiat Abarth 131
1981	Jean Ragnotti/ Jean-Marc André (Fra)	Renault 5 Turbo
1982-3	Walter Röhrl/Christian Geistdörfer (FRG)	Opel Ascona
1984	Walter Röhrl/ Christian Geistdörfer (FRG)	Audi Quattro
1985	Ari Vatanen (Fin)/ Terry Harryman (UK)	Peugeot 205 Turbo 16
1986	Henri Toivonen (Fin)/ Sergio Cresto (Ita)	Lancia Delta S4
1987	Mikki Biasion/ Tiziano Siviero (Ita)	Lancia Delta HF4WD

Most wins: 4 Sandro Munari (Ita), Walter Röhrl (FRG); 3 Jean Trevoux (Fra) 1939, 1949, 1951
Most successful co-driver: 4 wins Christian Geistdörfer (FRG) all with Walter Röhrl.

LOMBARD RAC RALLY

Winners since 1951:

1951	Ian Appleyard/ Pat Appleyard(UK)	Jaguar XK120
1952	Godfrey Imhof/ Mrs.B.Fleming(UK)	Allard Cadillac J2
1953	Ian Appleyard/ Pat Appleyard (UK)	Jaguar XK120
1954	Johnny Wallwork/ J.H.Brooks (UK)	Triumph TR2
1955	James Ray/ Brian Horrock (UK)	Standard Ten
1956	Lyndon Sims, R.Jones/ Tony Ambrose (UK)	Aston Martin DB2
1957	Not held due to Suez crisis	
1958	Peter Harper/ Dr.E.W.Deane(UK)	Sunbeam Rapier
1959	Gerald Burgess/ Sam Croft-Pearson(UK)	Ford Zephyr
1960	Erik Carlsson (Swe)/ Stuart Turner (UK)	Saab 96
1961	Erik Carlsson (Swe)/ John Brown (UK)	Saab 96
1962	Erik Carlsson (Swe)/ David Stone (UK)	Saab 96
1963	Tom Trana/ S.Lindstrom (Swe)	Volvo PV544
1964	Tom Trana/ Gunnar Thermanius (Swe)	Volvo 122S
1965	Rauno Aaltonen (Fin)/ Tony Ambrose (UK)	Mini-Cooper 'S'
1966	Bengt Soderström/ Gunnar Palm (Swe)	Ford Cortina Lotus
1967	Not held due to foot and mouth outbreak	
1968	Simo Lampinen (Fin)/ John Davenport (UK)	Saab 96 V4
1969-70	Harry Kallstrom (Fin)/ Gunnar Haggbom (Swe)	Lancia Fulvia

1971 Stig Blomqvist/	
Arne Hertz (Swe)	Saab 96 V4
1972 Roger Clark/	
Tony Mason (UK)	Ford Escort RS
1973-5 Timo Makinen (Fin)/	
Henry Liddon (UK)	Ford Escort RS
1976 Roger Clark/	
Stuart Pegg (UK)	Ford Escort RS
1977 Björn Waldegård (Swe)/	
Hans Thorszelius	Ford Escort RS
1978-9 Hannu Mikkola (Fin)/	
Arne Hertz (Swe)	Ford Escort RS
1980 Henri Toivonen (Fin)/	
Paul White (UK)	Talbot Sunbeam Lotus
1981-2 Hannu Mikkola (Fin)/	
Arne Hertz (Swe)	Audi Quattro A1/A2
1983 Stig Blomqvist/	
Bjorn Cederberg (Swe)	Audi Quattro A2
1984 Ari Vatanen (Fin)/	
Terry Harryman (UK)	Peugeot 205 Turbo 16
1985 Henri Toivonen (Fin)/	
Neil Wilson (UK)	Lancia Delta S4
1986 Timo Salonen (Fin)/	
Seppo Harjanne (Fin)	Peugeot 205 Turbo

Most wins: 4 Hannu Mikola (Fin); 3 Erik Carlsson (Swe), Timo Makinen (Fin)
Most successful co-drivers: 4 wins Arne Hertz (Swe); 3 wins Henry Liddon (UK)

SAFARI RALLY

The longest rally held annually is the Safari Rally, first raced in 1953 as the Coronation Safari in Kenya, Tanzania and Uganda but is now restricted to Kenya. The race has covered up to 6234 km/3874 miles, as it did in 1971. No overall winner was declared in 1953, but the Class A prize went to Alan Dix and Jerry Larsen in their Volkswagen 1200.

Winners:

1954 D Marwaha/	
Vic Preston	Volkswagen 1200
1955 D Marwaha/	
Vic Preston	Ford Zephyr
1956 Eric Cecil/	
Tony Vickers	D.K.W.
1957 Arthur Burton/	
Angus Hofmann	Volkswagen 1200
1958 No outright winner declared	
1959-60 Bill Fritschy/	
Jack Ellis	Mercedes 219
1961 John Manussis/	
Bill Coleridge/David Beckett	Mercedes 220
1962 Tommy Fjastad/	
Bernhard Schneider	Volkswagen 1200
1963 Nick Nowicki/	
Paddy Cliff	Peugeot 404
1964 Peter Hughes/	
Billy Young	Ford Cortina GT
1965 Joginder Singh/	
Jaswant Singh (Ken)	Volvo PV544
1966-7 Bert Shankland/	
Chris Rothwell	Peugeot 404

1968 Nick Nowicki/	
Paddy Cliff	Peugeot 404
1969 Robin Hillyar/	
Jock Aird (UK)	Ford Taunus 20MRS
1970 Edgar Herrmann/	
Hans Schüller (FRG)	Datsun 16000SSS
1971 Edgar Herrmann/	
Hans Schüller (FRG)	Datsun 240Z
1972 Hannu Mikkola (Fin)/	
Gunnar Palm (Swe)	Ford Escort RS1600
1973 Shekhar Mehta/	
Lofty Drews (Ken)	Datsun 250Z
1974 Joginder Singh (Ken)/	
David Doig	Colt Galant 1600
1975 Ove Andersson/	
Arne Hertz (Swe)	Peugeot 504
1976 Joginder Singh (Ken)/	
David Doig	Mitsubishi Colt Lancer
1977 Björn Waldegård (Swe)/	
Hans Thorszelius	Ford Escort RS 1800
1978 Jean-Pierre Nicolas/	
Jean-Claude Lefebvre (Fra)	Peugeot 504 Coupe V6
1979-80 Shekhar Mehta/	
Mike Doughty (Ken)	Datsun 160J
1981-2 Shekhar Mehta/	
Mike Doughty (Ken)	Datsun Violet GT
1983 Ari Vatanen (Fin)/	
Terry Harryman (UK)	Opel Ascona 400
1984 Björn Waldegård (Swe)/	
Hans Thorszelius	Toyota Celica TCT
1985 Juha Kankkunen (Fin)/	
Fred Gallagher (UK)	Toyota Celica TCT
1986 Björn Waldegård (Swe)/	
Fred Gallagher (UK)	Toyota Celica Turbo
1987 Hannu Mikkola (Fin)	
Arne Hertz (Swe)	Audi 200 Quattro

Most wins: 5 Shekhar Mehta; 3 Joginder Singh
Most wins as co-driver: 4 Mike Doughty

WORLD RALLY CHAMPIONSHIPS

A World Championship for makes of car was inaugurated in 1968 and a driver's championship, known as the FIA Cup for Drivers was instituted in 1977; it became the official World Drivers' Championship in 1979. A championship for co-drivers was introduced in 1981.

Winners:
MAKES
1968 Ford (GB)
1969 Ford (Europe)
1970 Porsche
1971 Alpine-Renault
1972 Lancia
1973 Alpine-Renault
1974-6 Lancia
1977-8 Fiat
1979 Ford
1980 Fiat
1981 Talbot
1982 Audi
1983 Lancia
1984 Audi

1985-6 Peugeot
1987 Lancia

DRIVERS
1977 Sandro Munari (Ita)
1978 Markhu Alen (Fin)
1979 Björn Waldegård (Swe)
1980 Walter Röhrl (FRG)
1981 Ari Vatanen (Fin)
1982 Walter Röhrl (FRG)
1983 Hannu Mikkola (Fin)
1984 Stig Blomqvist (Swe)
1985 Timo Salonen (Fin)
1986 Juha Kankkunen (Fin)

CO-DRIVERS
1981 David Richards (UK)
1982 Christian Geistdorfer (FRG)
1983 Arne Hertz (Swe)
1984 Björn Cederberg (Swe)
1985 Seppo Harjanne (Fin)
1987 Juha Piironen (Fin)

DRAG RACING

In this aspect of motor racing two cars (or bikes) race each other over a distance of a quarter of a mile (402.3m). The sport was developed in the 1930s in the USA. The sport's governing body in the USA, the National Hot Rod Association (NHRA) was founded in 1950.

The highest terminal velocity reached at the end of a 440 yards run is 279.24 mph (449.38 km/h) by Joe Amato at Commerce, Georgia on 26 Apr 1987. Darrell Gwynn set the record for the lowest elapsed time of 5.176 seconds at Dallas, Texas on 15 Apr 1987. The official NHRA record is 5.204 by Gwynn at Commerce on 26 Apr 1987.

NETBALL

Invented in the USA in 1891, netball is a women's 7-a-side game, developed from basketball. The first national association was that of New Zealand in 1924, followed by England in 1926. The International Federation of Women's Basketball and Netball Associations (IFWBNA) was formed in 1960.

WORLD CHAMPIONSHIPS

First held in 1963.

Winners:
1963 Australia
1967 New Zealand
1971 Australia
1975 Australia
1979 Australia, New Zealand, Trinidad & Tobago
1983 Australia

OLYMPIC GAMES

The first Olympic Games of the modern era were staged in Athens, Greece from 6 to 15 April 1896. The driving force behind their revival was Pierre de Fredi, Baron de Coubertin, who was born in Paris in 1863. He believed in the Greek athletic ideal of perfection of mind and body, and his energies were devoted to achieving his dream of reintroducing the Olympic Games, which had been staged for more than a thousand years before their prohibition in AD 394.

In 1889 de Coubertin was commissioned by the French government to form a universal sports association and he visited other European nations to gather information. He made public his views on 25 Nov 1892 at the Sorbonne in Paris. These led to the formation of the International Olympic Committee in 1894 and thence to the staging of the Olympic Games, which were opened in Athens on Easter Monday 1896.

VENUES

1896	Athens	1948	London
1900	Paris	1952	Helsinki
1904	St Louis	1956	Melbourne
1906	Athens*	1960	Rome
1908	London	1964	Tokyo
1912	Stockholm	1968	Mexico City
1920	Antwerp	1972	Munich
1924	Paris	1976	Montreal
1928	Amsterdam	1980	Moscow
1932	Los Angeles	1984	Los Angeles
1936	Berlin	1988	Seoul

*Intercalated Games held as the tenth anniversary celebration of the 1896 Games. Results from these 1906 Games have been included in the records in this book.

OLYMPIC CHAMPIONS

See individual sports for winners at all events.

OVERALL OLYMPIC RECORDS

Most medals
18 Larissa Latynina (USSR) Gymnastics
15 Nikolay Andrianov (USSR) Gymnastics
13 Eduardo Mangiorotti (Ita) Fencing
13 Takashi Ono (Jap) Gymnastics
13 Boris Shakhlin (USSR) Gymnastics
12 Sawao Kato (Jap) Gymnastics
12 Paavo Nurmi (Fin) Athletics

Most gold medals
10 Ray Ewry (USA) Athletics
 9 Larissa Latynina (USSR) Gymnastics
 9 Paavo Nurmi (Fin) Athletics
 9 Mark Spitz (USA) Swimming
 8 Sawao Kato (Jap) Gymnastics

Most silver medals
6 Shirley Babashoff (USA) Swimming
6 Aleksandr Ditaitin (USSR) Gymnastics
6 Mikhail Voronin (USSR) Gymnastics

Most bronze medals
6 Heikki Savolainen (Fin) Gymnastics

Most Games winning medals
6 Aladar Gerevich (Hun) Fencing 1932-60

Most Games
8 Raimondo d'Inzeo (Ita) Equestrian 1948-76
7 Ivan Ossier (Den) Fencing 1908-48

7 Durwar Knowles (UK/Bah) Yachting 1948-72
7 Paul Elvstrom (Den) Yachting 1948-84

Longest span of appearances
40 years Ivan Ossier (Den) Fencing 1908-48
40 years Magnus Konow (Nor) Yachting 1908-48

Youngest medallists:
The unknown French boy who coxed the winning Netherlands rowing pair in 1900 was aged 7-10 years.
Next youngest medallists:
10y 215d Dimitrios Loundras (Gre) bronze Gymnastics 1896
12y 34d Inge Sörensen (Den) bronze Swimming 1936
12y 232d Noel Vandernotte (Fra) bronze Rowing 1936
Next youngest gold medallists:
13y 267d Marjorie Gestring (USA) Diving 1936
14y 12d Giorgio Cesana (Ita) Rowing 1936

Oldest medallists:
72y 279d Oscar Swahn (Swe) silver Shooting 1920
68y 194d Samuel Duvall (USA) silver Archery 1904
66y 143d Louis Noverraz (Swi) silver Yachting 1968

Oldest gold medallists:
64y 258d Oscar Swahn (Swe) Shooting 1912
64y 2d Galen Spencer (USA) Archery 1904
63y 244d Robert Williams (USA) Archery 1904

The only man to win gold medals in both Summer and Winter Games in Edward Eagan (USA), Boxing 1920 and Bobsleigh 1932.

ORIENTEERING

Cross-country running with the aid of map and compass, orienteering was invented by Major Ernst Killander in 1918 in Sweden. Their national federation, the Svenska Orienteeringsförbundet, was formed in 1938. The International Orienteering Federation was established in 1961.

WORLD CHAMPIONSHIPS

First held in 1966 and staged biennially.

Winners:

Year	Men's individual	Women's individual
1966	Åge Hadler (Nor)	Ulla Lindqvist (Swe)
1968	Karl Johansson (Swe)	Ulla Lindqvist (Swe)
1970	Stig Berge (Nor)	Ingrid Hadler (Nor)
1972	Åge Hadler (Nor)	Sarolta Monspart (Hun)
1974	Bernt Frilen (Swe)	Mona Norgaard (Den)
1976	Egil Johansen (Nor)	Lia Veijalainen (Fin)
1978	Egil Johansen (Nor)	Anne Berit Eid (Nor)
1979	Öyvin Thon (Nor)	Outi Borgenström (Fin)
1981	Öyvin Thon (Nor)	Annichen Kringstad (Swe)
1983	Morten Berglia (Nor)	Annichen Kringstad (Swe)
1985	Kari Sallinen (Fin)	Annichen Kringstad (Swe)

Men's Relay winners:
Sweden 1966, 1968, 1972, 1974, 1976, 1979
Norway 1970, 1978, 1981, 1983, 1985

Women's Relay winners:
Sweden 1966, 1970, 1974, 1976, 1981, 1983, 1985
Finland 1972, 1978, 1979
Norway 1968

PELOTA

Pelota is the generic name for a number of court games that are played, usually with gloves or baskets, although originally with the hands. *Longue paume* was played in France, having been introduced from Italy in the 13th century, and this developed into Real Tennis (qv), which was for long the French national game. When the game languished in the 17th century, it survived in the Basque country, straddling France and Spain, where the current game of Pelote Basque was developed. The Fédération Francaise de Pelote Basque was formed in 1921 and the Federacion Internacional de Pelota Vasca (FIPV) was founded in 1929 in Spain, where the sport is known as Pelota.

In the Basque country the traditional courts are known as trinquete, while usual in Latin America and Spain are courts of the fronton (enclosed stadium) variety, known in Basque as *jai-alai*, the name of the game in the USA and Latin America.

The chistera, used to propel the ball at great speed, was developed from a wicker fruit basket in the 1860s. Claims for the game to be the fastest of all ball games are reinforced by the highest ball velocity speed measured electronically at 302 km/h by José Ramon Areitio at Newport, Rhode Island in 1979.

WORLD CHAMPIONSHIPS

The FIVP stage world championships every four years, first in 1952 for a variety of events, including long and short court and trinquete court games. The most successful pair have been Roberto Elias and Juan Labat (Arg), who won the Trinquete Share in 1952, 1958, 1962 and 1966. Labat won seven world titles in all.

The most wins in the long court game of Cesta Punta is three by Hamuy (Mex), with different partners, 1958, 1962, 1966.

PÉTANQUE

Also known as 'boules', pétanque is derived from the ancient French game of Jeu Provençal, now differing from that game in that in the latter the bowls are delivered from a short run-up, whereas in pétanque they are delivered from a stationary position.

The steel bowls (or boules) have a diameter of 7–8 cm and weigh 620–800 gm.

The Fédération Francais de Pétanque et Jeu Provençal (FFPJP) was formed in 1945 and subsequently the Fédération Internationale...(FIPJP). The British Petanque Association was founded in 1974.

WORLD CHAMPIONSHIPS

First held in 1959. *Wins:*

8	France	1959, 1961, 1963, 1972, 1974, 1976-7, 1985
4	Switzerland	1965-6, 1973, 1980
3	Italy	1975, 1978-9
2	Tunisia	1986

1 Algeria 1964, Spain 1971, Belgium 1981, Monaco 1982, Morocco 1984

POLO

A four-a-side stick and ball game played on horseback. Polo originated in Central Asia, the earliest date given for such a game being 525 BC in Persia. The name of the game is derived from the Tibetan word 'pulu'. The British learnt of the game in India in the 1850s, and the earliest polo club of the modern era was the Cachar Club, founded in Assam in 1859. The game was first played in England in 1871 and in the USA in 1876.

The game's governing body is the Hurlingham Polo Association. Hurlingham, in London, first staged a match in 1874 and the club committee drew up the first set of English rules a year later.

Polo is played on the largest pitch of any game, with maximum length of 300 yards (274m) and width of 200 yards (182m) without boards, or 160 yards (146m with boards).

WESTCHESTER CUP

The first international match was between Great Britain and the United States at Newport, Rhode Island in 1886 for an international trophy given by the Westchester Club. Last contested in 1939, the winners in this series were:

Great Britain 1886, 1900, 1902, 1914
United States 1909, 1911, 1913, 1921, 1924, 1927, 1930, 1936, 1939.

HIGH GOAL PLAYERS

Polo games are often contested on a handicap basis, each player being awarded a handicap measured in goals up to a maximum of ten, attained by the world's best players. In the history of the game 55 players have been awarded this handicap. A high goal player is one with a handicap of five, so a high goal team rates at 20 or more. The first match between two 40-goal teams, that is all players on the maximum, was played at Palermo, Buenos Aires, Argentina in 1975. The highest handicap ever attained by a woman is five by Claire Tomlinson (UK) in 1986.

CUP OF THE AMERICAS

Contested by Argentina and the USA. The US won the first two matches in 1928 and 1932, and the Argentinians have won all subsequent contests: 1936, 1950, 1966, 1969, 1979, 1980.

OLYMPIC GAMES

Polo has been included at five Olympic Games.

Winners:
1900 Foxhunters (UK/USA)
1908 Roehampton (UK)
1920 Great Britain
1924 Argentina
1936 Argentina

CHAMPION CUP

Britain's premier tournament from its inception in 1876 to 1939, when it was last played at Hurlingham. The teams with most wins were Freebooters 11, and Sussex 10.

COWDRAY PARK GOLD CUP

Played annually at Cowdray Park, Midhurst, Sussex, this competition replaced the Champion Cup. It is the British Open Championship.

Winners:
1956 Los Indios
1957 Windsor Park
1958 Cowdray Park
1959-60 Casarejo
1961-2 Cowdray Park
1963 La Vulci
1964-5 Jersey Lilies
1966 Windsor Park
1967 Woolmer's Park
1968 Pimms
1969 Windsor Park
1970 Boca Raton
1971-2 Pimms
1973-4 Stowell Park
1975 Greenhill Farm
1976 Stowell Park
1977 Foxcote
1978 Stowell Park
1979 Songhai
1980 Stowell Park
1981 Falcons
1982 Southfield
1983 Falcons
1984 Southfield
1985 Maple Leafs
1986 Tramontona

Most wins: 5 Stowell Park

POWERBOATING

Powerboat racing started in about 1900, and there are now a large number of categories of boats that race on either inland waters or offshore. A petrol engine had first been fitted in a boat by Jean Lenoir on the River Seine in 1865.

HARMSWORTH TROPHY

This perpetual trophy was presented by Sir Alfred Harmsworth (later Lord Northcliffe) in 1903. The race for the trophy was for many years the world's most prestigious powerboating event. From 1903 to 1961 it was for circuit races contested by boats of unlimited specification.

Winners:

Year	Boat	Driver	Speed km/h
1903	Napier I (Eng)	Dorothy Levitt	31.43
1904	Trefle-A-Quatre (Fra)	Emile Thubron	42.86
1905	Napier II (Eng)	Lord Montague	41.89
1906	Yarrow-Napier (Eng)	Lionel de Rothschild	24.91
1907	Dixie I (USA)	E.J.Schroeder	51.14
1908	Dixie II (USA)	E.J.Schroeder	50.45
1910	Dixie III (USA)	F.K.Burnham	58.00
1911	Dixie IV (USA)	F.K.Burnham	64.82
1912	Maple Leaf IV (Eng)	Tommy Sopwith	69.49
1913	Maple Leaf IV (Eng)	Tommy Sopwith	92.46
1920	Miss America I (USA)	Garfield Wood	98.99
1921	Miss America II (USA)	Garfield Wood	96.16
1926	Miss America V (USA)	Garfield Wood	98.359
1928	Miss America VII (USA)	Garfield Wood	95.474
1929	Miss America VIII (USA)	Garfield Wood	121.163
1930	Miss America IX (USA)	Garfield Wood	124.294
1932	Miss America X (USA)	Garfield Wood	126.315
1933	Miss America X (USA)	Garfield Wood	139.915
1949	Skip-A-Long (USA)	Stanley Dollar	151.737
1950	Slo-Mo-Shun IV (USA)	Stanley Sayres	162.029
1956	Shanty I (USA)	William Waggoner Jr	144.439
1959	Miss Supertest III (Can)	Bob Hayward	160.595
1960	Miss Supertest III (Can)	Bob Hayward	185.852
1961	Miss Supertest III (Can)	Bob Hayward	158.066

The series then lapsed, but was revised under a new formula in 1977 as the Harmsworth British & Commonwealth Trophy for Motorboats.

Winners:

Year	Boat	Pilot
1977-8	Limit-Up (Eng)	Michael Doxford & Tim Powell
1979	Uno-Mint-Jewellery (Eng)	Derek Pobjoy

From 1980 to 1983 the Harmsworth Trophy was awarded on points gained in a series of offshore races.

Winning drivers:
1980 Bill Elswick and Paul Clauser (USA)
1981 Paul Clauser (USA)
1982 Al Copeland and B Sirois (USA)
1983 George Morales (USA)

The Harmsworth trophy is now contested by two-boat national teams at Formula Two for outboard engines.
1985 (Jan) Jonathan Jones & John Hill (UK)
1985 (Dec) Jonathan Jones & Mark Wilson (UK)

AMERICAN POWER BOAT ASSOCIATION GOLD CUP

The American Power Boat Association was formed in 1903, and held its first Gold Cup race on the Hudson River in 1904, when the winner was Standard, piloted by C.C.Riotto at an average speed of 39 km/h. Now known as the Key West Gold Cup.

Winners from 1970:

Year	Boat	Pilot	Speed km/h
1970	Miss Budweiser	Dean Chenoweth	163.908
1971	Miss Madison	Jim McCormick	163.384
1972	Atlas Van Lines	Bill Muncey	166.643
1973	Miss Budweiser	Dean Chenoweth	167.446
1974	Pay'N Pak	George Henley	180.337

1975 Pay'N Pak	George Henley	182.419
1976 Miss US	Tom d'Eath	173.843
1977 Atlas Van Lines	Bill Muncey	184.832
1978 Atlas Van Lines	Bill Muncey	167.330
1979 Atlas Van Lines	Bill Muncey	173.631
1980 Miss Budweiser	Dean Chenoweth	188.922
1981 Miss Budweiser	Dean Chenoweth	
1982 Atlas Van Lines	Chip Hanauer	193.20
1983 Atlas Van Lines	Chip Hanauer	
1984 Atlas Van Lines	Chip Hanauer	
1985 Miller American	Chip Hanauer	
1986 Miller American	Chip Hanauer	

Most wins: (pilot) 8 Bill Muncey 1956-7, 1961-2, 1972, 1977-9; 5 Garfield Wood 1917-21; (boat) 7 Atlas Van Lines as above.

COWES – TORQUAY OFFSHORE RACE

Instituted in 1961 by Sir Max Aitken of the *Daily Express* at first from Cowes to Torquay, but from 1968 including the return journey, for a distance of 320.4 km.

Winners:

Year	Boat	Pilot	Speed km/h
1961	Thunderbolt	Tommy Sopwith (UK)	40
1962	Tramontana	Jeffrey Quill (UK)	60
1963	A'Speranzella	Renato Levi (Ita)	66
1964	Surfrider	Charles Gardner (UK)	79
1965	Brave Moppie	Dick Bertram (USA)	63
1966	Ghost Rider	Jim Wynne (USA)	66
1967	Surfury	Charles Gardner (UK)	85
1968	Telstar	Tommy Sopwith (UK)	61
1969	The Cigarette	Don Aronow (USA)	107.3
1970	Miss Enfield 2	Tommy Sopwith (UK)	94.1
1971	Lady Nara	Ronny Bonelli (Ita)	63
1972	Aeromarine IX	Carlo Bonomi (Ita)	88
1973	Unowot	Don Shead (UK)	100
1974	Dry Martini	Carlo Bonomi (Ita)	107.7
1975	Uno Embassy	Don Shead (UK)	117.26
1976	I Like It Too	Charles Gill (UK)	112.5
1977	Yellowdrama III	Ken Cassir (UK)	120.91
1978	Kaama	Betty Cook (USA)	124.59
1979	Dry Martini II	Guido Nicolai (Ita)	102.54
1980	Satisfaction	Bill Elswick (USA)	128.16
1981	Rombo	Alberto Smania (Ita)	48.39
1982	Ego Rothman	Renato della Valle (Ita)	65.61
1983	Ego Rothman	Renato della Valle (Ita)	69.72
1984	Ego Rothman	Renato della Valle (Ita)	76.09
1985	Ego Rothman	Renato della Valle (Ita)	63.14
1986	Fresh and Clean	Giovanni Repossi (Ita)	119.5

OLYMPIC GAMES

Motor boating was included in the 1908 Olympic Games.

Winners:

Emile Thubron (Fra) won Class A in *Camille*; Thomas Thornycroft, Bernard Redwood and Captain Field-Richards won Classes B and C in *Gyrinus*.

FORMULA ONE WORLD CHAMPION

1982 Roger Jenkins (UK)
1983-4 Renato Molinari (Ita)
1985 Bob Spalding (UK)
1986 Gene Thibodaux (USA)

FORMULA TWO (FORMULA GRAND PRIX) WORLD CHAMPIONS

1982-3 Michael Werner (FRG)
1984-5 John Hill (UK)
1986 Jonathan Jones (UK) and Buck Thornton (USA)

RACKETBALL

Racquetball (US spelling), using a 40ft by 20ft (12.2m by 6.1m) court, was invented by Joe Sobek at the Greenwich YMCA, Connecticut, USA. He originally named the game Paddle Rackets. The game grew in popular appeal in the 1960s and the International Racquetball Association was founded in 1968 by Bob Kendler (USA). The major event in the USA, the International Racquetball Association Championships was initiated in 1969.

BRITISH CHAMPIONSHIPS

In Britain, racketball is played in squash courts, 32ft by 21ft (9.75 by 6.4m) with a softer ball. The British Racketball Association was formed and staged inaugural British National Championships in 1984.

Winners:

Year	MEN	WOMEN
1984	Denis Secher	Greer Batty
1985	John Hakes	Bett Dryhurst
1986	Murray Scott	Bett Dryhurst

WORLD CHAMPIONSHIPS

Singles winners at the 1986 World Championships sanctioned by the International Amateur Racquetball Association were

Men: Egan Inoue (USA)
Women: Cindy Baxter (USA)

RACKETS

A racket and ball game for two or four players, derived as with other such games from various forms of hand ball games played in the Middle Ages. In England it was often played against walls of buildings, especially those of the Fleet Prison, London in the 18th century. An inmate Robert Mackay claimed the first world title in 1820. The first closed court was the Prince's Club, built at Hans Place, London in 1853. The English governing body, the Tennis and Rackets Association, was formed in 1907.

WORLD CHAMPIONS

Determined on a challenge basis, world champions have been:
1820 Robert Mackay (UK)
1825-34 Thomas Pittman (UK)
1834-8 John Pittman (UK)
1838-40 John Lamb (UK)
1846-60 L.C.Mitchell (UK)
1860 Francis Erwood (UK)
1862-3 Sir William Hart-Dyke (UK)
1863-6 Henry Gray (UK)
1866-75 William Gray (UK)
1876-8 H.B. Fairs (UK)
1878-87 Joseph Gray (UK)
1887-1902 Peter Latham (UK)
1903-11 J.Jamsetji (Ind)
1911-3 Charles Williams (UK)
1913-28 Jock Souter (USA)
1929-35 Charles Williams (UK)
1937-47 David Milford (UK)
1947-54 James Dear (UK)
1954-71 Geoffrey Atkins (UK)
1972-3 William Surtees (USA)
1973-4 Howard Angus (UK)
1975-81 William Surtees (USA)
1981-4 John Prenn (UK)
1984-6 William Boone (UK)
1986- John Prenn (UK)

BRITISH AMATEUR CHAMPIONSHIPS

Held annually, first in 1888 at singles and in 1890 at doubles.

SINGLES

Winners from 1969:
1969 Charles Swallow
1970-1 Martin Smith
1972-5 Howard Angus
1976 William Boone
1977 Charles Hue Williams
1978 William Boone
1979-80 John Prenn
1981 William Boone
1982-3 John Prenn
1984-5 William Boone
1986 James Male (Dec 85)
1987 William Boone

Most wins:
9 Edgar M.Baerlein 1903, 1905, 1908-11, 1920-1, 1923
8 Henry K.Foster 1894-1900, 1904
7 David Milford 1930, 1935-8, 1950-1
6 William Boone 1976, 1978, 1981, 1984-5, 1987
5 John Thompson 1954-5, 1957-9

DOUBLES

Winners from 1969:
1969-71 Richard Gracey & Martin Smith
1972-3 Howard Angus & Charles Hue Williams
1974 Geofrey Atkins & Charles Hue Williams
1975-7 William Boone & Tom Pugh
1978-9 Howard Angus & Andrew Milne
1980-4 William Boone & Randall Crawley (6 wins)
1985 John Prenn & Charles Hue Williams
1986 William Boone & Randall Crawley
1987 James Male & Rupert Owen-Browne

(l-r) William Surtees, Richard Lightfire of the Racquet Club of Chicago, and Howard Angus. (Tennis & Rackets Association)

Most wins by the same pair:
10 David Milford & John Thompson 1948, 1950-2, 1954-9

Most wins by individuals with various partners:
11 David Milford also in 1938
11 John Thompson also in 1966
 9 William Boone 1975-7, 1980-4, 1986
 8 Henry K.Foster 1893-4, 1896-1900, 1903
 8 Lord Aberdare (formerly the Hon.C.N.Bruce) 1921, 1924-8, 1930, 1934

BRITISH OPEN CHAMPIONSHIPS

Held irregularly for the Shepperd Cup 1929-71 on a challenge basis. From 1971 there has been an annual championship, held first as the Louis Roederer Open Invitation Tournament. From 1981 Celestion Loudspeakers have sponsored the sport and the event is now the Celestion Open Championship.

Sheppard Cup champions:
1929-30 Cyril Simpson
1932 Lord Aberdare
1933 Ian Akers-Douglas
1934 Albert Cooper
1936 David Milford

1946 James Dear
1951 James Dear
1954 Geoffrey Atkins
1959 John Thompson
1960 James Dear
1961 Geoffrey Atkins
1964 Geoffrey Atkins
1967 James Leonard
1970 Charles Swallow
1971 Martin Smith
1971 Howard Angus

Open Singles Champions:
1971-3 Howard Angus
1974 William Surtees
1975-6 Howard Angus
1977 John Prenn
1978 Howard Angus
1979 William Boone
1980-3 John Prenn
1984 William Boone
1985 John Prenn
1986 William Boone
1987 James Male

Open Doubles winners (first held 1981):
1981-5 William Boone & Randall Crawley
1986-7 John Prenn & James Male

OLYMPIC GAMES

Rackets was included in the 1908 Olympics, when gold medals were won at singles by Evan Noel (UK) and doubles by Vane Pennel and John Jacob Astor (UK).

REAL TENNIS

An indoor racket and ball game, which was first played as *Jeu de paume* in France in monastery cloisters in the 11th century. From the Middle Ages it was played by royalty, particularly by several Kings of France, where the game was extremely popular around 1600. It spread to other parts of Europe and was played by Henry VII and Henry VIII of England, but declined considerably in popularity in the 17th and 18th centuries.
   The English governing body, the Tennis and Rackets Association was formed in 1907.

WORLD CHAMPIONS

The first recorded world champion is the oldest for any sport, the Frenchman Clergé from 1740.
Determined on a challenge basis, world champions have been:

MEN'S SINGLES
c.1740-50 Clergé (Fra)
1765-85 Raymond Masson (Fra)
1785-1816 Joseph Barcellon (Fra)
1816-9 Marchesio (Ita)
1819-29 Philip Cox (UK)
1829-62 Edmond Barre (Fra)

1862-71 Edmund Tomkins (UK)
1871-85 George Lambert (UK)
1885-90 Tom Pettitt (USA)
1890-95 Charles Saunders (UK)
1895-1905 Peter Latham (UK)
1905-7 Cecil Fairs (UK)
1907-8 Peter Latham (UK)
1908-12 Cecil Fairs (UK)
1912-4 Fred Covey (UK)
1914-6 Jay Gould (USA)
1916-28 Fred Covey (UK)
1928-54 Pierre Etchebaster (Fra)
1955-7 James Dear (UK)
1957-9 Albert Johnson (UK)
1959-69 Northrup Knox (USA)
1969-72 G.H.'Pete' Bostwick (USA)
1972-5 Jimmy Bostwick (USA)
1976-81 Howard Angus (UK)
1981-7 Chris Ronaldson (UK)
1987 Wayne Davies (Aus)

WOMEN'S SINGLES
First played in 1985. *Winners:*
1985 Judy Clarke (Aus)
1987 Judy Clarke (Aus)

WOMEN'S DOUBLES
First played in 1985. *Winners:*
1985 Judy Clarke & Annie Link (Aus)
1987 Lesley Ronaldson & Cathrina Allen (UK)

OLYMPIC GAMES

The sport was once included in the Olympic Games, in 1908, when the title was won by Jay Gould (USA).

BRITISH AMATEUR CHAMPIONSHIPS

Held annually, first in 1888 at singles and in 1920 at doubles.

SINGLES

Winners from 1965:
1965 David Warburg
1966-80 Howard Angus
1981 Alan Lovell
1982 Howard Angus
1983-6 Alan Lovell
1987 Julian Snow

Most wins:
16 Howard Angus 1966-80, 1982
13 Edgar M.Baerlein 1912, 1914, 1919-27, 1929-30
 9 Eustace Miles 1899-1903, 1905-6, 1909-10

DOUBLES

Winners from 1967:
1967-70 Howard Angus & David Warburg
1972-4 Howard Angus & David Warburg
1975 John Clench & Alan Lovell
1976 Howard Angus & David Warburg
1977-9 Alan Lovell & Andrew Windham
1980 Howard Angus & Richard Cooper
1981 Alan Lovell & Michael Dean
1982 Peter Seabrook & John Ward
1983-6 Alan Lovell & Michael Dean
1987 Julian Snow & James Male

Wayne Davies (Tennis & Rackets Association)

Most wins by the same pair:
8 Howard Angus & David Warburg 1967-70, 1972-4, 1976
7 Edgar M.Baerlein & Lowther Lees 1929-31, 1934-7
Most wins by individuals with various partners:
11 Edgar M.Baerlein 1920-2, 1925, 1929-31, 1934-7
10 Lowther Lees 1926, 1928-31, 1934-7, 1946
 9 Alan Lovell 1975, 1977-9, 1981, 1983-6

BRITISH OPEN CHAMPIONSHIPS

The Open championship on a challenge basis for the Prince's Club Shield (to 1976), has been won as follows:
1931 Edgar Baerlein
1931 E.Ratcliffe
1932 W.A.Groom
1934-5 Lowther Lees
1938 James Dear
1950 Ronald Hughes
1951 James Dear
1956 James Dear
1962 Ronald Hughes
1967-8 Frank Willis
1970 Howard Angus
1972 Howard Angus
1975-6 Howard Angus

The Open Invitation tournament was contested annually for the Field Trophy 1965-73; it was sponsored by Cutty Sark 1974-8, then by Unigate, and the sponsors now are George Wimpey.

Singles winners:
1965 Ronald Hughes
1966-7 Frank Willis
1968 Howard Angus
1969 Frank Willis

1970 Howard Angus
1970 (Nov) Frank Willis
1971 Norwood Cripps
1972 Frank Willis
1973 Norwood Cripps
1974 Howard Angus
1975 Chris Ennis
1976-7 Howard Angus
1978 Chris Ronaldson
1979 Howard Angus
1980-5 Chris Ronaldson (two in 1980)
1986-7 Lachlan Deuchar (Aus)

Most wins: 8 Chris Ronaldson, 6 Howard Angus

Open Doubles winners: (first held 1971)
1971 Ronald Hughes & Norwood Cripps
1972 Frank Willis & Chris Ennis
1973-5 Charles Swallow & Norwood Cripps
1976 Frank Willis & David Cull
1977-80 Norwood Cripps & Alan Lovell (5 wins, two in 1977)
1981 Chris Ronaldson & Michael Dean
1982 Norwood Cripps & Alan Lovell
1983 Chris Ronaldson & Michael Dean
1984-7 Wayne Davies & Lachlan Deuchar (Aus)

Women's Open Singles (first held 1978)
1978 Anna Moore (UK)
1979-81 Lesley Ronaldson (UK)
1982 Judy Clarke (Aus)
1983-6 Katrina Allen (UK)
1986 (Nov) Lesley Ronaldson (UK)

RODEO

Rodeo was developed from the 18th century fiestas of the early days of the North American cattle industry. Ranching skills, such as bronc busting, bull riding, steer wrestling and calf roping have become highly competitive activities in the professional rodeos held throughout the USA, in Canada and Mexico. The governing body is the Professional Rodeo Cowboys Association (PRCA), the name taken in 1974 by the Rodeo Cowboys Association, originally formed in 1936, and known as the Cowboys Turtles Association until 1945.

Standard rodeo events are: bareback riding, saddle bronc riding, bull riding, calf roping and steer wrestling with three additional events also often contested: team roping, barrel racing and single-steer roping. In the first three riding events the object is to stay on for a minimum of eight seconds; in the others the object is to complete the task in the minimum time.

NATIONAL FINALS RODEO

Each December the PRCA stage the National Finals Rodeo, which is the culmination of the season's rodeo events. The top 15 money-earning cowboys at each event meet in these grand finals. It was first held in 1959. The venue was Oklahoma for 20 years before the event was moved to Las Vegas in 1985.

Most wins at each event:
Saddle bronc riding: 6 Casey Tibbs 1949, 1951-4, 1959
Bareback bronc riding: 5 Joe Alexander 1971-5
Bull riding: 8 Donnie Gay 1975-81, 1984; 7 Jim Shoulders 1951, 1954-9
Calf roping: 8 Dean Oliver 1955, 1958, 1960-4, 1969; 8 Roy Cooper 1976-8, 1980-4
Steer wrestling: 6 Homer Pettigrew 1940, 1942-5, 1948
Team roping: 4 Jim Rodriguez Jr. 1959-60, 1962, 1965; Leo Camarillo 1972-3, 1975-6
Single steer roping: 6 Everett Shaw 1945-6, 1948, 1951, 1959, 1962
All events: 16 Jim Shoulders 1949-59

ALL-AROUND COWBOY WORLD CHAMPIONS

Won annually by the cowboy who has won the most money in two or more different events.

Winners, with money won:

Year	Winner	Money
1947	Todd Whatley	
1948	Gerald Roberts	21,766
1949	Jim Shoulders	21,496
1950	Bill Linderman	30,715
1951	Casey Tibbs	29,104
1952	Harry Tompkins	30,934
1953	Bill Linderman	33,674
1954	Buck Rutherford	40,404
1955	Casey Tibbs	42,065
1956	Jim Shoulders	43,381
1957	Jim Shoulders	33,299
1958	Jim Shoulders	33,212
1959	Jim Shoulders	32,905
1960	Harry Tompkins	32,522
1961	Benny Reynolds	31,309
1962	Tom Nesmith	32,611
1963	Dean Oliver	31,329
1964	Dean Oliver	31,150
1965	Dean Oliver	33,163
1966	Larry Mahan	40,358
1967	Larry Mahan	51,996
1968	Larry Mahan	49,129
1969	Larry Mahan	57,726
1970	Larry Mahan	41,493
1971	Phil Lyne	49,245
1972	Phil Lyne	60,852
1973	Larry Mahan	64,447
1974	Tom Ferguson	66,929
1975	Leo Camarillo & Tom Ferguson	50,300
1976	Tom Ferguson	87,908
1977	Tom Ferguson	76,730
1978	Tom Ferguson	103,734
1979	Tom Ferguson	96,272
1980	Paul Tierney	105,568
1981	Jimmie Cooper	105,862
1982	Chris Lybbert	123,709
1983	Roy Cooper	153,391
1984	Dee Pickett	122,618
1985	Lewis Feild	130,347
1986	Lewis Feild	166,042

Most wins: 6 Larry Mahan, Tom Ferguson
The leading career earnings winner is Tom Ferguson at $1,049,744 and ten world championships.

ROLLER HOCKEY

An adaptation of hockey and ice hockey, played as a five-a-side game on roller skates. It was first known in Europe as Rink Hockey. The Amateur Rink Hockey Association was formed in Britain c.1898, taking this name in 1908. The NHRA is affiliated to the Fédération Internationale de Roller Skating. The first European Championships were held at Herne Bay, England, in 1926.

WORLD CHAMPIONSHIPS

First held in 1936.

Wins:

12	Portugal	1947-50, 1952, 1956, 1958, 1960, 1962, 1968, 1974, 1982
9	Spain	1951, 1954-5, 1964, 1966, 1970, 1972, 1976, 1980
4	England	1936-9
2	Italy	1953, 1986
2	Argentina	1978, 1984

EUROPEAN CHAMPIONSHIPS

Preceded the world championships, with which it was amalgamated from 1936 to 1957.

Wins:

16	Portugal	1947-50, 1952, 1956, 1959, 1961, 1963, 1965, 1967, 1971, 1973, 1975, 1987
12	England	1926-32, 1934, 1936-9
8	Spain	1951, 1954-5, 1957, 1969, 1979, 1981, 1983
2	Italy	1953, 1985

ROLLER SKATING

The modern four-wheeled roller skate was introduced by James Plympton in the USA in 1863. At first it was used by ice skaters in practice, but soon developed into a sport in its own right. The first roller rink in the USA was opened by Plympton in 1866 at Newport, Rhode Island. The first ever roller skate had been invented by Joseph Merlin of Belgium; when he demonstrated it in 1760, however, it was not a success.

In Britain the National Skating Association assumed control of roller skating in 1893 and staged the first national championships the following year.

The International Roller Skating Federation (Fédération Internationale de Patinage à Roulettes) was founded in 1924; it now has its headquarters in Barcelona. In 1937 the first world championships were held for speed skating (at Monza) and in the same year European championships for figure skating were introduced (at Stuttgart).

WORLD FIGURE SKATING CHAMPIONS

First held in 1947.

Winners:

MEN

1947 Donald Mounce (USA)
1949 Karl Peter (Swi)
1951-2 Freimut Stein (FRG)
1955-6 Franz Ningel (FRG)
1958-9 Karl-Heinz Losch (FRG)
1961-2 Karl-Heinz Losch (FRG)
1965 Hans Dahmen (FRG)
1966 Karl-Heinz Losch (FRG)
1967 Hans Dahmen (FRG)
1968 Jack Courtney (USA)
1970-2 Michael Obrecht (FRG)
1973 Randy Dayney (USA)
1974 Michael Obrecht (FRG)
1975 Leonardo Lienhard (Swi)
1976-8 Thomas Nieder (FRG)
1979-82 Michael Butzke (GDR)
1983 Joachim Helmle (FRG)
1984-5 Michele Biserni (Ita)
1986 Michele Tolomini (Ita)

Most wins: 5 Karl-Heinz Losch

WOMEN

1947 Ursula Wehrli (Swi)
1949 Franca Rio (Ita)
1951 Franca Rio (Ita)
1952 Lotte Cadenbach (FRG)
1955 Helene Kienzle (FRG)
1956 Rita Blumenberg (FRG)
1958 Marika Kilius (FRG)
1959 Ute Kitz (FRG)
1961 Marlies Fahse (FRG)
1962 Fränzi Schmidt (Swi)
1965-8 Astrid Bader (FRG)
1970 Christine Kreutzfeldt (FRG)
1971-2 Petra Häusler (FRG)
1973-5 Sigrid Mullenbach (FRG)
1976-8 Natalie Dunn (USA)
1979-81 Petra Schneider (née Ernert) (FRG)
1982-4 Claudia Bruppacher (FRG)
1985-6 Chiara Sartori (Ita)

Most wins: 4 Astrid Bader

PAIRS

1947 Fernand Leemans & Elvire Collin (Bel)
1949 Ken Byrne & Jean Phethean (UK)
1951 Paul Falk & Ria Baran (FRG)
1952 Günther Koch & Sigrid Knake (FRG)
1955-6 Günther Koch & Sigrid Knake (FRG)
1958 Werner Mensching & Rita Blumenberg (FRG)
1959 Dieter Fingerle & Susu Schneider (FRG)
1961-2 Walther Hoffman & Maria Ludolph (FRG)
1965-7 Dieter Fingerle & Uta Keller (FRG)
1968 Jack Courtney & Sheryl Trueman (USA)
1970-2 Ronald Robovitsky & Gail Robovitsky (USA)
1973 Louis Stovel & Vicki Handyside (USA)
1974 Ron Sabo & Susan McDonald (USA)
1975-6 Ron Sabo & Darlene Waters (USA)
1977 Ray Chapatta & Karen Mejia (USA)
1978 Pat Jones & Rooie Coleman (USA)
1979 Ray Chapatta & Karen Mejia (USA)
1980-2 Paul Price & Tina Kniesley (USA)
1983-6 John Arishita & Tammy Jeru (USA)

Most wins: 4 Dieter Fingerle, John Arishtita & Tammy Jeru

DANCE
1947 Fred Ludwig & Barbara Gallagher (USA)
1949 Ken Byrne & Jean Phethean (UK)
1952 Ted Ellis & Marion Mercer (UK)
1955 Karl-Heinz Beyer & Marga Schäfer (FRG)
1956 Günther Koch & Sigrid Knake (FRG)
1958 Sydney Cooper & Patricia Cooper (UK)
1959 Peter Kwiet & Rita Paucka (FRG)
1961 Peter Kwiet & Rita Kwiet (née Paucka) (FRG)
1962 Brian Colclough & Patricia Colclough (UK)
1965 Brian Colclough & Patricia Colclough (UK)
1966-7 Hans-Jürgen Schamberger & Martha Schamberger (FRG)
1968 Donald Rudalawicz & Rita Smith (USA)
1970-1 Richard Horne & Jane Pankey (USA)
1972 Tom Straker & Bonnie Lambert (USA)
1973 James Stephens & Jane Puracchio (USA)
1974 Udo Donsdorf & Christine Henke (FRG)
1975-6 Kerry Cavazzi & Jane Puracchio (USA)
1977-9 Dan Littel & Florence Arsenault (USA)
1980 Torsten Carels & Gabriele Achenbach (GDR)
1981-2 Mark Howard & Cindy Smith (USA)
1983-4 David Golub & Angela Famiano (USA)
1985 Martin Hauss & Andrea Steudte (FRG)
1986 Scott Myers & Anna Danks (USA)

The following skaters won world titles on both ice and rollers:
Ria and Paul Falk – roller pairs 1951, ice pairs 1951-2
Marika Kilius – roller 1958, ice pairs 1963-4

WORLD SPEED SKATING CHAMPIONS

First contested in 1937 for men and 1953 for women. Held on track or road, men's and women's events at distances from 300m to 10000m.

MOST TITLES WON (TRACK/ROAD)
MEN
15 Giuseppe Cantarella (Ita) 7/8 1964-80
15 Giuseppe Cruciani (Ita) 8/7 1978-83
WOMEN
18 Alberta Vianello (Ita) 8/10 1953-65
18 Annie Lambrechts (Bel) 1/17 1964-81

WORLD RECORDS – TRACK

Distance	MEN min:sec		WOMEN min:sec	
300m	25.947	O. Galliazzo (Ita) 1984	28.145	S. Ghermandi (Ita) 1984
500m	41.233	G. De Persio (Ita) 1980	45.914	C. Stabile (Ita) 1980
1000m	1:25.444	G. De Persio (Ita) 1980	1:32.1	M. Danesi (Ita) 1968
1500m	2:07.770	G. De Persio (Ita) 1980	2:18.3	M. Danesi (Ita) 1968
3000m	4:21.764	G. De Persio (Ita) 1980	4:53.084	A. Lambrechts (Bel) 1985
5000m	7:46.4	V. De Cesaris (Ita) 1969	8:12.978	A. Lambrechts (Bel) 1985
10000m	15:49.7	R. Marotta (Ita) 1968	16:30.484	A. Lambrechts (Bel) 1985
20000m	23:59.6	R. Marotta (Ita) 1968	32:53.970	A. Lambrechts (Bel) 1985
30000m	48:21.4	A. Maestri (Ita) 1968	49:15.906	A. Lambrechts (Bel) 1985
50000m	1:21:25.8	D. Vandeperre (Bel) 1985		

Road world record performance superior to above:

300m	25.088	P.Sarto (Ita) 1984	26.944	S. Ghermandi (Ita) (1984)
5000m	7:44.9	L. Faggioli (Ita) 1957		

ROWING

Rowing dates back to ancient times but the sport in its present form dates to 1715 when Irish comedian Thomas Doggett instituted his famous race for scullers. There were many races at Walton in 1768, but the first known regatta was on the Thames at Ranelagh Gardens, Putney in 1775. The international governing body is the Fédération Internationale des Sociétés d'Aviron (FISA), founded in 1892, two years after the Belgian Federation of Rowing Clubs had staged a 'European Championship', with just one category of boat, the sculling outrigger. The winner over the 2800m course was Edouard Lescrauwaet (Bel). FISA held their first official European Championships in 1893.

OLYMPIC GAMES

The first Olympic rowing competition was on the River Seine over a 1750m course in 1900 but in more recent times rowing courses have been on still waters. The standard length is now 2000m, but the course measured 2 miles (3219m) in 1904, 1½ miles (2414m) in 1908 and 1883m in 1948. Weather and water conditions affect the times recorded.

Winners:
MEN
SINGLE SCULLS
1900 Henri Barrelet (Fra) 7:35.6
1904 Frank Greer (USA) 10:08.5
1906 Gaston Delaplane (Fra) 5:53.4
1908 Harry Blackstaffe (UK) 9:26.0
1912 William Kinnear (UK) 7:47.6
1920 John Kelly Snr (USA) 7:35.0
1924 Jack Beresford Jr (UK) 7:49.2
1928 Henry Pearce (Aus) 7:11.0
1932 Henry Pearce (Aus) 7:44.4
1936 Gustav Schäfer (Ger) 8:21.5
1948 Mervyn Wood (Aus) 7:24.4
1952 Yuriy Tyukalov (USSR) 8:12.8
1956 Vyacheslav Ivanov (USSR) 8:02.5
1960 Vyacheslav Ivanov (USSR) 7:13.96
1964 Vyacheslav Ivanov (USSR) 8:22.51
1968 Henri Jan Wienese (Hol) 7:47.80

1972 Yuriy Malishev (USSR) 7:10.12
1976 Pertti Karppinen (Fin) 7:29.03
1980 Pertti Karppinen (Fin) 7:09.61
1984 Pertti Karppinen (Fin) 7:00.24

DOUBLE SCULLS
1904 John Mulcahy/William Varley (USA) 10:03.2
1920 Paul Costello/John Kelly (USA) 7:09.0
1924 Paul Costello/John Kelly (USA) 7:45.0
1928 Paul Costello/Charles McIlvaine (USA) 6:41.4
1932 William Garrett Gilmore/Kenneth Myers (USA) 7:17.4
1936 Jack Beresford/Leslie Southwood (UK) 7:20.8
1948 Richard Burnell/Herbert Bushnell (UK) 6:51.3
1952 Tranquilo Capozzo/Eduardo Guerrero (Arg) 7:32.2
1956 Aleksandr Berkutov/Yuriy Tyukalov (USSR) 7:24.0
1960 Václav Kozák/Pavel Schmidt (Cs) 6:47.50
1964 Boris Dubrovsky/Oleg Tyurin (USSR) 7:10.66
1968 Anatoliy Sass/Aleksandr Timoshinin (USSR) 6:51.82
1972 Gennadiy Korshikov/Aleksandr Timoshinin (USSR) 7:01.77
1976 Alf Hansen/Frank Hansen (Nor) 7:13.20
1980 Joachim Dreifke/Klaus Kröppelien (GDR) 6:24.33
1984 Bradley Lewis/Paul Enquist (USA) 6:36.87

COXLESS PAIRS
1904 Robert Farnam/Joseph Ryan (USA) 10:57.0
1908 John Fenning/Gordon Thomson (UK) 9:41.0
1924 Antonie Beijnen/Wilhelm Rösingh (Hol) 8:19.4
1928 Kurt Moeschter/Bruno Müller (Ger) 7:06.4
1932 Lewis Clive/Arthur Edwards (UK) 8:00.0
1936 Willie Eichorn/Hugo Strauss (Ger) 8:16.1
1948 George Laurie/John Wilson (UK) 7:21.1
1952 Charles Logg/Thomas Price (USA) 8:20.7
1956 James Fifer/Duvall Hecht (USA) 7:55.4
1960 Valentin Boreyko/Oleg Golovanov (USSR) 7:02.01
1964 George Hungerford/Roger Jackson (Can) 7:32.94
1968 Heinz-Jürgen Bothe/Jörg Lucke (GDR) 7:26.56
1972 Siegfried Brietzke/Wolfgang Mager (GDR) 6:53.16
1976 Bernd Landvoigt/Jörg Landvoigt (GDR) 7:23.31
1980 Bernd Landvoigt/Jörg Landvoigt (GDR) 6:48.01
1984 Petru Iosub/Valer Toma (Rom) 6:45.39

COXED PAIRS
1900 Minerva Amsterdam (Hol) 7:34.2
1906 Bucintoro (Ita) † 4:23.0
1906 Bucintoro (Ita) * 7:32.4
1920 Italy 7:56.0
1924 Switzerland 8:39.0
1928 Switzerland 7:42.6
1932 USA 8:25.8
1936 Germany 8:36.9
1948 Denmark 8:00.5
1952 France 8:28.6
1956 USA 8:26.1
1960 FR Germany 7:29.14
1964 USA 8:21.23
1968 Italy 8:04.81
1972 GDR 7:17.25
1976 GDR 7:58.99
1980 GDR 7:02.54
1984 Italy 7:05.99
† over 1000m * over 1609m

QUADRUPLE SCULLS
1976 GDR 6:18.65

Pertti Karppinen (All-Sport)

1980 GDR 5:49.81
1984 FR Germany 5:57.55

COXLESS FOURS
1904 Century BC, St.Louis (USA) 9:53.8
1908 Magdalen College, Oxford (UK) 8:34.0
1924 Great Britain 7:08.6
1928 Great Britain 6:36.0
1932 Great Britain 6:58.2
1936 Germany 7:01.8
1948 Italy 6:39.0
1952 Yugoslavia 7:16.0
1956 Canada 7:08.8
1960 USA 6:26.26
1964 Denmark 6:59.30
1968 GDR 6:39.18
1972 GDR 6:24.27
1976 GDR 6:37.42
1980 GDR 6:08.17
1984 New Zealand 6:03.48

COXED FOURS
1900 Germania RC, Hamburg (Ger) * 5:59.0
1900 Cercle de l'Aviron (Fra) * 7:11.0
1906 Italy 8:13.0
1912 Germany 6:59.4
1920 Switzerland 6:54.0
1924 Switzerland 7:18.4
1928 Italy 6:47.8
1932 Germany 7:19.0
1936 Germany 7:16.2
1948 USA 6:50.3
1952 Czechoslovakia 7:33.4
1956 Italy 7:19.4
1960 FR Germany 6:39.12
1964 FR Germany 7:00.44
1968 New Zealand 6:45.62
1972 FR Germany 6:31.85
1976 USSR 6:40.22
1980 GDR 6:14.51
1984 Great Britain 6:18.64

* Two finals were held in 1900

EIGHTS
1900 Vesper BC (USA) 6:09.8
1904 Vesper BC (USA) 7:50.0
1908 Leander Club (UK) 7:52.0
1912 Leander Club (UK) 6:15.0
1920 USA 6:02.6
1924 USA 6:33.4
1928 USA 6:03.2
1932 USA 6:37.6
1936 USA 6:25.4
1948 USA 5:56.7
1952 USA 6:25.9
1956 USA 6:35.2
1960 Germany 5:57.18
1964 USA 6:18.23
1968 FR Germany 6:07.00
1972 New Zealand 6:08.94
1976 GDR 5:58.29
1980 GDR 5:49.05
1984 Canada 5:41.32

DISCONTINUED EVENTS

76-Man Naval Rowing Boats (2000m)
1906 Varese (Ita) 10:45.0

17-Man Naval Rowing (3000m)
1906 Poros (Gre) 16:35.0

Coxed Fours Inriggers
1912 Denmark 7:47.0

WOMEN
(all events over 1000m)

SINGLE SCULLS
1976 Christine Scheiblich (GDR) 4:05.56
1980 Sanda Toma (Rom) 3:40.69
1984 Valeria Racila (Rom) 3:40.68

DOUBLE SCULLS
1976 Svetla Otzetova/Zdravka Yordanova (Bul) 3:44.36
1980 Yelena Khlopsteva/Larisa Popova (USSR) 3:16.27
1984 Marioara Popescu/Elisabeta Oleniuc (Rom) 3:26.75

COXLESS PAIRS
1976 Stoyanka Grouitcheva/Siika Kelbetcheva (Bul) 4:01.22
1980 Cornelia Klier/Ute Steindorf (GDR) 3:30.49
1984 Rodica Arba/Elena Horvat (Rom) 3:32.60

QUADRUPLE SCULLS
1976 GDR 3:29.99
1980 GDR 3:15.32
1984 Romania 3:14.11

COXED FOURS
1976 GDR 3:45.08
1980 GDR 3:19.27
1984 Romania 3:19.30

EIGHTS
1976 GDR 3:33.32
1980 GDR 3:03.32
1984 USA 2:59.80

In the summaries that follow, the following abbreviations are used: 1x single sculls, 2x double sculls, 4x quadruple sculls, 4x+ quadruple sculls with coxswain, 2- coxless pairs, 2+ coxed pairs, 4- coxless fours, 4+ coxed fours, 8+ eights.

MOST GOLD MEDALS
3 John B.Kelly (USA) 1x 1920; 2x 1920, 1924
3 Paul Costello (USA) 2x 1920, 1924, 1928
3 Jack Beresford Jr (UK) 1x 1924; 4+ 1932; 2x 1936
3 Vyacheslav Ivanov (USSR) 1x 1956, 1960, 1964
3 Siegfried Brietzke (GDR) 2- 1972; 4- 1976, 1980
3 Pertti Karppinen (Fin) 1x 1976, 1980, 1984

MOST MEDALS (gold/silver/bronze)
5 (3/2/-) Jack Beresford Jr 1920-36 (at five different Games)

The youngest Olympic medallist at any sport is an unknown French boy who coxed the winning Dutch pair in 1900; he was believed to have been between seven and ten years of age.

The oldest Olympic medallist, also a winner, was Robert Zimonyi who coxed the US eights in 1964 at 46 yr 180 days. The oldest oarsman to win a gold medal was Guy Nickalls (UK) at 42 yr 170 days in the eights in 1908.

WORLD CHAMPIONSHIPS

The first World Championships were held at Lucerne in 1962. The first women's championships were in 1974.

Winners

MEN

SINGLE SCULLS
1962 Vyacheslav Ivanov (USSR)
1966 Don Spero (USA)
1970 Alberto Demiddi (Arg)
1974 Wolfgang Hönig (GDR)
1975 Peter-Michael Kolbe (FRG)
1977 Joachim Dreifke (GDR)
1978 Peter-Michael Kolbe (FRG)
1979 Pertti Karppinen (Fin)
1981 Peter-Michael Kolbe (FRG)
1982 Rüdiger Reiche (GDR)
1983 Peter-Michael Kolbe (FRG)
1985 Pertti Karppinen (Fin)
1986 Peter-Michael Kolbe (FRG)

DOUBLE SCULLS
1962 René Duhamel/Bernard Monnereau (Fra)
1966 Melchior Bürgin/Martin Studach (Swi)
1970 Jörgen Engelbrecht/Niels Secher (Den)
1974 Christof Kreuziger/Hans-Ulrich Schmied (GDR)
1975 Alf Hansen/Frank Hansen (Nor)
1977 Chris Baillieu/Michael Hart (UK)
1978-9 Alf Hansen/Frank Hansen (Nor)
1981 Klaus Kröppelien/Joachim Dreifke (GDR)
1982 Alf Hansen/Rolf Thorsen (Nor)
1983 Thomas Lange/Uwe Heppner (GDR)
1985 Thomas Lange/Uwe Heppner (GDR)
1986 Alberto Belgori/Igor Pescialli (Ita)

COXLESS PAIRS
1962 Dieter Bender/Günther Zumkeller (FRG)
1966 Peter Gorny/Werner Klatt (GDR)
1970 Peter Gorny/Werner Klatt (GDR)
1974-5 Bernd Landvoigt/Jörg Landvoigt (GDR)
1977 Vitaliy Yeliseyev/Aleksandr Kulagin (USSR)
1978-9 Bernd Landvoigt/Jörg Landvoigt (GDR)

1981 Yuriy Pimenov/Nikolay Pimenov (USSR)
1982 Magnus Grepperud/Sverre Loken (Nor)
1983 Carl Ertel/Ulf Sauerbrey (GDR)
1985-6 Nikolay Pimenov/Yuriy Pimenov (USSR)

COXED PAIRS
1962 FR Germany
1966 Netherlands
1970 Romania
1974 USSR
1975 GDR
1977 Bulgaria
1978 GDR
1979 GDR
1981 Italy
1982 Italy
1983 GDR
1985 Italy
1986 Great Britain

COXLESS FOURS
1962 FR Germany
1966 GDR
1970 GDR
1974-5 GDR
1977 GDR
1978 USSR
1979 GDR
1981 USSR
1982 Switzerland
1983 FR Germany
1985 FR Germany
1986 USA

COXED FOURS
1962 FR Germany
1966 GDR
1970 FR Germany
1974 GDR
1975 USSR
1977-9 GDR
1981-2 GDR
1983 New Zealand
1985 USSR
1986 GDR

QUADRUPLE SCULLS
1974-5 GDR
1977-9 GDR
1981-2 GDR
1983 FR Germany
1985 Canada
1986 USSR

EIGHTS
1962 FR Germany
1966 FR Germany
1970 GDR
1974 USA
1975 GDR
1977-9 GDR
1981 USSR
1982-3 New Zealand
1985 USSR
1986 Australia

WOMEN

SINGLE SCULLS
1974-5 Christine Scheiblich (GDR)
1977 Christine Scheiblich (GDR)
1978 Christine Hahn (née Scheiblich) (GDR)
1979 Sanda Toma (Rom)
1981 Sanda Toma (Rom)
1982 Irina Fetissova (USSR)
1983 Jutta Hampe (GDR)
1985 Cornelia Linse (GDR)
1986 Jutta Hampe (GDR)

DOUBLE SCULLS
1974-5 Yelena Antonova/Galina Yermoleyeva (USSR)
1977 Anke Borchmann/Roswietha Zobelt (GDR)
1978 Svetla Otzetova/Zdravka Yordanova (Bul)
1979 Cornelia Linse/Heidi Westphal (GDR)
1981 Margarita Kokarevitha/Antonina Makhina (USSR)
1982 Yelena Braticko/Antonina Makhina (USSR)
1983 Jutta Scheck/Martina Schröter (GDR)
1985 Sylvia Schurabe/Martina Schröter (GDR)
1986 Sylvia Schurabe/Beate Schramm (GDR)

COXLESS PAIRS
1974 Marilena Ghita/Cornelia Neascu (Rom)
1975 Sabine Dähne/Angelika Noack (GDR)
1977 Sabine Dähne/Angelika Noack (GDR)
1978-9 Cornelia Bugel/Ute Steindorf (GDR)
1981 Sigrid Anders/Iris Rudolph (GDR)

1982-3 Silvia Fröhlich/Marita Sandig (GDR)
1985 Rodica Arba/Elena Florea (Rom)
1986 Rodica Arba/Olga Homeghi (Rom)

QUADRUPLE SCULLS
1974-5 GDR
1977 GDR
1978 Bulgaria
1979 GDR
1981-2 USSR
1983 USSR
1985-6 GDR

COXED FOURS
1974-5 GDR
1977-8 GDR
1979 USSR
1981-2 USSR
1983 GDR
1985 GDR
1986 Romania

COXLESS FOURS
1986 USA

EIGHTS
1974-5 GDR
1977 GDR
1978-9 USSR
1981-3 USSR
1985-6 USSR

LIGHTWEIGHT SINGLE SCULLS
1974 William Belden (USA)
1975 Reto Wyss (Swi)
1976 Raimund Haberl (Aut)
1977 Reto Wyss (Swi)
1978 José Antonio Montosa (Spa)
1979 William Belden (USA)
1980 Christian Georg Wahrlich (FRG)
1981 Scott Roop (USA)
1982 Raimund Haberl (Aut)
1983-4 Bjarne Eltang (Den)
1985 Ruggero Verroca (Ita)
1986 Peter Antonie (Aus)

LIGHTWEIGHT DOUBLE SCULLS
1978-9 Pal Bornick/Arne Gilje (Nor)
1980-4 Francesco Esposito/Ruggero Verroca (Ita)
1985 Luc Crispon/Thierry Renault (Fra)
1986 Carl Smith/Allan Whitwell (UK)

LIGHTWEIGHT COXLESS FOURS
1974 Australia
1975-7 France
1978 Switzerland
1979 United Kingdom
1980-1 Australia
1982 Italy
1983 Spain
1984 Spain
1985 FR Germany
1986 Italy

LIGHTWEIGHT EIGHTS
1974 USA
1975-6 FR Germany
1977-8 United Kingdom
1979 Spain
1980 United Kingdom
1981 Denmark
1982 Italy
1983 Spain
1984 Denmark
1985-6 Italy

Oxford leads Cambridge in the 1984 Boat Race, when they won for the ninth consecutive year. (All-Sport)

WOMEN'S LIGHTWEIGHT SINGLE SCULLS
1985 Adair Ferguson (Aus)
1986 Maria Sava (Rom)

WOMEN'S LIGHTWEIGHT DOUBLE SCULLS
1985 Lin Clark/Beryl Crockford (UK)
1986 Chris Ernst/C.B.Sands (USA)

WOMEN'S LIGHTWEIGHT COXED FOURS
1985 FR Germany
1986 USA

WORLD CHAMPIONSHIPS AND OLYMPIC GAMES MOST GOLD MEDALS OVERALL

MEN
6 Bernd & Jörg Landvoigt (GDR) 2- 1974-80
6 Joachim Dreifke (GDR) 1x 1977; 2x 1980-1; 4x 1974, 1978-9
6 Karl-Heinz Bussert (GDR) 4x 1976-9, 1981-2
6 Ulrich Diessner (GDR) 4+ 1977-80, 1982; 2+ 1983
6 Siegfried Brietzke & Wolfgang Mager (GDR) 2- 1972; 4- 1974-7, 1979
5 Pertti Karppinen (Fin) 1x 1976, 1979-80, 1984-5
5 Peter-Michael Kolbe (FRG) 1x 1975, 1978, 1981, 1983, 1986
5 Andreas Decker & Stefan Sempler (GDR) 4- 1974-7, 1979
5 Ulrich Karnatz (GDR) 8+ 1975-9

5 Gottfried Döhn (GDR) 4+ 1977-8, 1980; 8+ 1975-6
5 Alf Hansen (Nor) 2x 1975-6, 1978-9, 1982 (first four with his brother Frank)
5 Martin Winter (GDR) 4x 1977-8, 1980-2
5 Uwe Heppner (GDR) 2x 1983, 1985; 4x 1980-2
5 Andreas Gregor (GDR) cox 2+ 1983; 4+ 1977-8, 1980, 1982

LIGHTWEIGHT MEN
6 Ruggero Verroca (Ita) 1x 1985; 2x 1980-4
5 Francesco Esposito (Ita) 2x 1980-4 (all with Verroca)

WOMEN
5 Christine Hahn (née Schieblich) 1x 1974-8
5 Angelika Noack (GDR) 2- 1975, 1977; 4+ 1974, 1978, 1980
5 Yelena Terekhina (USSR) 8+ 1981-3, 1985-6

UNIVERSITY BOAT RACE

The Boat race between the Universities of Oxford and Cambridge is rowed annually on the River Thames from Putney to Mortlake over a distance of 6779km (4 miles 374 yards). It was first contested on 10 June 1829 from Hambledon Lock to Henley Bridge. From 1836 to 1842 it was rowed from Westminster to Putney, and in 1846, 1856 and 1863 from Mortlake to Putney; on all other occasions the present course has been used. Outrigged eights were first used in 1846.

To 1987 Cambridge lead in the series of 133 races with 69 wins to Oxford's 63. There were two races in 1849 and on 24 Mar 1877 there was the only dead-heat in the race's history.

Cambridge wins:	1836, 1839-41, 1845-6, 1849, 1856, 1858, 1860, 1870-4, 1876, 1879, 1884, 1886-9, 1899-1900, 1902-4, 1906-8, 1914, 1920-2, 1924-36, 1939, 1947-51, 1953, 1955-8, 1961-2, 1964, 1968-73, 1975, 1986
Oxford wins:	1829, 1842, 1849, 1852, 1854, 1857, 1859, 1861-9, 1875, 1878, 1880-3, 1885, 1890-8, 1901, 1905, 1909-13, 1923, 1937-8, 1946, 1952, 1954, 1959-60, 1963, 1965-7, 1974, 1976-85, 1987

Race record time: 16 min 45 sec Oxford 18 Mar 1984, an average speed of 24.28 km/h (15.09 mph)
Greatest margin: 20 lengths Cambridge 1900, apart from sinkings
Most successful individual: Boris Rankov (Oxford) rowed in six winning boats 1978-83
Most successful coach: Daniel Topolski of Oxford's ten successive wins 1976-85
Heaviest competitor: Gavin Stewart (Oxford, 1987) 105kg (231lb)
Tallest competitor: Gavin Stewart (Oxford, 1987) 204.5cm (6ft 8½in)
Youngest competitor: Matthew Brittin (Cambridge, 1987) 18yr
Oldest competitor: Donald McDonald (Oxford, 1987) 31yr
The first woman to take part was Susan Brown, who coxed the winning Oxford boats of 1981-2

HENLEY ROYAL REGATTA

Inaugurated in 1839. The course has varied slightly, but has been about 1 mile 550 yards (2112m)

DIAMOND SCULLS

Instituted in 1884, the Diamond Challenge Sculls at Henley is regarded as the Blue Riband of amateur sculling

Winners since 1970:
1970 Jochen Meissner (FRG)
1971 Alberto Demiddi (Arg)
1972 Aleksandr Timoshin (USSR)
1973-5 Sean Drea (Ire)
1976 Edward Hale (Aus)
1977-8 Tim Crooks (UK)
1979 Hugh Matheson (UK)
1980 Riccardo Ibarra (Arg)
1981-2 Chris Baillieu (UK)
1983 Steven Redgrave (UK)
1984 Chris Baillieu (UK)
1985 Steven Redgrave (UK)
1986 Bjarne Eltang (Den)
1987 Peter-Michael Kolbe (FRG)

Most wins: 6 Stuart Mackenzie 1957-62; 5 Guy Nickalls (1888-91, 1893-4), A A Casamajor 1855-8, 1861, J Lowndes 1879-83; 4 Jack Beresford Jr 1920, 1924-6; 3 A C Dicker 1873-5, Frederick Kelly 1902-3, 1905, Sean Drea,

as above, Chris Baillieu, as above
Record time: 7 min 40 sec Sean Drea 5 Jul 1975

GRAND CHALLENGE CUP

The oldest of all the Henley races, it dates to the first Regatta in 1839. It is the world's premier open event for eights.

Winners since 1970:
1970 ASK Rostock (GDR)
1971 Tideway Scullers (UK)
1972 WMF Moscow (USSR)
1973-4 Trud Kolomna (USSR)
1975 Leander/Thames Tradesmen (UK)
1976 Thames Tradesmen (UK)
1977 University of Washington (USA)
1978 Trakia Club (Bul)
1979 Thames Tradesmen (UK)
1980 Charles River RA (USA)
1981 Oxford University/Thames Tradesmen (UK)
1982 Leander/London RC(UK)
1983 London RC/University of London (UK)
1984 Leander/London RC (UK)
1985 Harvard University (USA)
1986 Nautilus (UK)
1987 Soviet Army (USSR)

Most wins: 27 Leander Club 1840, 1875, 1880, 1891-4, 1896, 1898-1901, 1903-5, 1913, 1922, 1924-6, 1929, 1932, 1934, 1946, 1949, 1952-3
Most winning teams: 7 Guy Oliver Nickalls, 1920-2, 1924-6, 1929
Record time: 6 min 13 secs Harvard University (USA) and Leander/Thames Tradesmen, 5 Jul 1975
The Nickalls family, Guy, his brother Vivian, and Guy's son, Guy Oliver, had 43 Henley wins between them.

RUGBY LEAGUE

When the Rugby Union refused permission for players of northern clubs to receive broken-time payments for loss of wages, 22 clubs formed their own breakaway union and, following a meeting at the George Hotel, Huddersfield in 1895, the Northern Union was formed. The number of players per side was reduced from 15 to 13 in 1906 and the union changed its name to the Northern Rugby League in 1922. The word 'Northern' was dropped in 1980.

CHALLENGE CUP

Rugby League's premier knockout tournament; the first final was at Leeds in 1897. The first Wembley final was in 1929 and since 1933 the London stadium has been the final's permanent venue, with the exception of the war years. The Man of the Match winner in the final at Wembley receives the famous Lance Todd Trophy.

Winners:

1897-8	Batley	1903-4	Halifax
1899	Oldham	1905	Warrington
1900	Swinton	1906	Bradford
1901	Batley	1907	Warrington
1902	Broughton Rangers	1908	Hunslet

1909	Wakefield Trinity	1950	Warrington
1910	Leeds	1951	Wigan
1911	Broughton Rangers	1952	Workington Town
1912	Dewsbury	1953	Huddersfield
1913	Huddersfield	1954	Warrington
1914	Hull	1955	Barrow
1915	Huddersfield	1956	St.Helens
1920	Huddersfield	1957	Leeds
1921	Leigh	1958-9	Wigan
1922	Rochdale Hornets	1960	Wakefield Trinity
1923	Leeds	1961	St.Helens
1924	Wigan	1962-3	Wakefield Trinity
1925	Oldham	1964	Widnes
1926	Swinton	1965	Wigan
1927	Oldham	1966	St.Helens
1928	Swinton	1967	Featherstone Rovers
1929	Wigan	1968	Leeds
1930	Widnes	1969-70	Castleford
1931	Halifax	1971	Leigh
1932	Leeds	1972	St.Helens
1933	Huddersfield	1973	Featherstone Rovers
1934	Hunslet	1974	Warrington
1935	Castleford	1975	Widnes
1936	Leeds	1976	St.Helens
1937	Widnes	1977-8	Leeds
1938	Salford	1979	Widnes
1939	Halifax	1980	Hull Kingston Rovers
1941-2	Leeds	1981	Widnes
1943	Dewsbury	1982	Hull
1944	Bradford Northern	1983	Featherstone Rovers
1945	Huddersfield	1984	Widnes
1946	Wakefield Trinity	1985	Wigan
1947	Bradford Northern	1986	Castleford
1948	Wigan	1987	Halifax
1949	Bradford Northern		

Most wins: 10 Leeds; 8 Wigan; 7 Widnes; 6 Huddersfield; 5 Halifax, St.Helens, Wakefield Trinity, Warrington
Highest score (final): Wakefield Trinity 38 Hull 5 (14 May 1960)
Record aggregate (final): 52 pts Wigan 28 Hull 24 (4 May 1985)

LANCE TODD AWARD

The Lance Todd Award goes to the Man-of-the-Match in the Challenge Cup Final at Wembley as decided by a panel of Rugby League writers. The trophy is named after former New Zealand international Lance Todd who played for Wigan and later managed Salford. The first award was made in 1946.

Recent winners:

1976	Geoff Pimblett	St.Helens
1977	Steve Pitchford	Leeds
1978	George Nicholls	St.Helens
1979	Dave Topliss	Wakefield Trinity
1980	Brian Lockwood	Hull Kingston Rovers
1981	Mick Burke	Widnes
1982	Eddie Cunningham	Widnes
1983	David Hobbs	Featherstone Rovers
1984	Joe Lydon	Widnes
1985	Brett Kenny	Wigan
1986	Bob Beardmore	Castleford
1987	Graham Eadie	Halifax

Warrington's Gerry Helme is the only dual winner of the trophy (1950 and 1954).

PREMIERSHIP TROPHY

The Premiership competition replaced the Championship Play-off, and was first contested at the end of the 1974-5 season. It is a knockout competition involving the top eight clubs in the first division with the champions playing the 8th club, 2nd club playing the 7th, and so on. The highest placed club has home advantage, and the final is played at a neutral venue. The Man-of-the-Match in the final receives the coveted Harry Sunderland Trophy.

Winners:
(Figures in brackets indicates final league positions)

1975	Leeds (3)
1976	St.Helens (5)
1977	St.Helens (2)
1978	Bradford Northern (2)
1979	Leeds (4)
1980	Widnes (2)
1981	Hull Kingston Rovers (3)
1982	Widnes (3)
1983	Widnes (5)
1984	Hull Kingston Rovers (1)
1985	St.Helens (2)
1986	Warrington (4)
1987	Wigan (1)

Most wins: 3 St.Helens, Widnes; 2 Hull Kingston Rovers, Leeds
Highest score (final): Warrington 38 Halifax 10 (18 May 1986)
Most appearances (final): 4 Keith Elwell (Widnes) 1978, 1980, 1982-3

SECOND DIVISION PREMIERSHIP

A premiership competition involving the top eight second division sides was inaugurated in 1986-7, when the winners were Swinton.

HARRY SUNDERLAND TROPHY

Named after former Australian team manager, broadcaster and journalist Harry Sunderland, the award is made to the Man-of-the-Match in the Premiership Final (formerly the Championship Play-Off). It was first awarded in 1965.

Recent winners

1976	George Nicholls	St.Helens
1977	Geoff Pimblett	St.Helens
1978	Bob Haigh	Bradford Northern
1979	Kevin Dick	Leeds
1980	Mal Aspey	Widnes
1981	Len Casey	Hull Kingston Rovers
1982	Mick Burke	Widnes
1983	Tony Myler	Widnes
1984	John Dorahy	Hull Kingston Rovers
1985	Harry Pinner	St.Helens
1986	Les Boyd	Warrington
1987	Joe Lydon	Wigan

No player has won the trophy more than once.

The only men to have won the Lance Todd and Harry Sunderland Trophies are:

Geoff Pimblett (St.Helens) 1976 LT 1977 HS
George Nicholls (St.Helens) 1976 HS 1978 LT
Mick Burke (Widnes) 1981 LT 1982 HS
Joe Lydon (Widnes and Wigan) 1984 LT, 1987 HS

LEAGUE CHAMPIONSHIP

Twenty-two clubs formed the original Northern Union in 1895-6, won by Manningham. The 'league' then split into Yorkshire and Lancashire Senior Competitions until 1901-2 when 14 clubs broke away to form the Northern Rugby League. Two divisions were formed the following season. In 1905-6 the two divisions were merged into one and that is how they stayed (excepting the war years) until 1962-3 when two divisions were re-introduced. That lasted just two years, but the present two division system came into being in 1973-4. The title 'Rugby Football League' was adopted in 1922. Because not all clubs played each other twice, or at all in some cases, a Championship Play-off, involving the top four teams, was introduced in 1906-7. This remained unaltered (except during the war years) until 1962 when two divisions were re-introduced. But on the return to just one division in 1964-5 the play-off involved the top 16 teams. It was scrapped altogether at the end of the 1972-3 season.

Championship play-off winners:
9 Wigan 1909, 1922, 1926, 1934, 1946-7, 1950, 1952, 1960
7 Huddersfield 1912-3, 1915, 1929-30, 1949, 1962
6 St.Helens 1932, 1953, 1959, 1966, 1970-1
5 Hull 1920-1, 1936, 1956, 1958
4 Salford 1914, 1933, 1937, 1939; Swinton 1927-8, 1931, 1935
3 Leeds 1961, 1969, 1972; Oldham 1910-1, 1957; Warrington 1948, 1954-5
2 Halifax 1907, 1965; Hull KR 1923, 1925; Hunslet 1908, 1938; Wakefield Trinity 1967-8
1 Batley 1924; Dewsbury 1973; Leigh 1906; Workington Town 1951

Champions since 1973-4

	Division One	Division Two
1973-4	Salford	Bradford Northern
1974-5	St.Helens	Huddersfield
1975-6	Salford	Barrow
1976-7	Featherstone Rovers	Hull
1977-8	Widnes	Leigh
1978-9	Hull Kingston Rovers	Hull
1979-80	Bradford Northern	Featherstone Rovers
1980-1	Bradford Northern	York
1981-2	Leigh	Oldham
1982-3	Hull	Fulham
1983-4	Hull Kingston Rovers	Barrow
1984-5	Hull Kingston Rovers	Swinton
1985-6	Halifax	Leigh
1986-7	Wigan	Hunslet

JOHN PLAYER SPECIAL TROPHY

A knockout competition which was first held in 1971-2. It was originally known as the Player's No.6 Trophy, and then the John Player Trophy until 1983, when it was renamed the John Player Special Trophy.

Winners:
1972 Halifax
1973 Leeds
1974 Warrington
1975 Bradford Northern
1976 Widnes
1977 Castleford
1978 Warrington
1979 Widnes
1980 Bradford Northern
1981 Warrington
1982 Hull
1983 Wigan
1984 Leeds
1985 Hull Kingston Rovers
1986 Wigan
1987 Wigan

Wins: 3 Warrington, Wigan; 2 Bradford Northern, Leeds, Widnes
Highest win (final): Warrington 27 Rochdale Hornets 16 (9 Feb 1974)
Most appearances (final): 6 Mick Adams, Keith Elwell, Eric Hughes (all Widnes) 1975-6, 1978-80, 1984

COUNTY CUPS

Both the Lancashire and Yorkshire County Challenge Cup competitions were first held in the 1905-6 season and are now early-season knock-out competitions.

Most wins:
Lancashire Cup:
Wigan (18) 1906, 1909-10, 1913, 1923, 1929, 1939, 1947-52, 1967, 1972, 1974, 1986-7
Yorkshire Cup:
Leeds (16) 1922, 1929, 1931, 1933, 1935-6, 1938, 1959, 1969, 1971, 1973-4, 1976-7, 1980-1
(Note, years indicate second half of season)

Recent winners:

	Lancashire Cup	Yorkshire Cup
1976-7	Widnes	Leeds
1977-8	Workington	Castleford
1978-9	Widnes	Bradford Northern
1979-80	Widnes	Leeds
1980-1	Warrington	Leeds
1981-2	Leigh	Castleford
1982-3	Warrington	Hull
1983-4	Barrow	Hull
1984-5	St.Helens	Hull
1985-6	Wigan	Hull Kingston Rovers
1986-7	Wigan	Castleford

COUNTY LEAGUES

With the introduction of the two divisions in 1902-3 the Lancashire and Yorkshire Senior competitions were scrapped, but they re-appeared in 1907-8 as the Lancashire and Yorkshire Leagues. Clubs' results in the normal league, against teams from their own county, counted towards the appropriate County League. Both leagues were abandoned in 1970.

Most wins:
Lancashire League: Wigan (18) 1909, 1911-5, 1921, 1923-4, 1926, 1941, 1946-7, 1950, 1952, 1959, 1962, 1970
Yorkshire League: Leeds (15) 1902, 1928, 1931, 1934-5, 1937-8, 1951, 1955, 1957, 1961, 1967-70

CLUB CHAMPIONSHIP (Merit Table)

Following the abolition of the Championship Play-off, a complicated club championship was introduced in 1973-4 and won by Warrington. It was replaced by the Premiership Trophy the following season.

WORLD CUP/INTERNATIONAL CHAMPIONSHIP

Inaugurated in France in 1954, Great Britain, France, New Zealand and Australia played each other on a round-robin basis. In 1975, when the competition was renamed the International Championship, England and Wales replaced Great Britain and the competition was played world wide. The World Cup was discontinued after the 1977 championship but was revived in 1985 when one match from each test series was designated a World Cup game, with the leading two nations due to play off in the final in 1988.

	Winners	Venue
1954	Great Britain	France
1957	Australia	Australia
1960	Great Britain	England
1968	Australia	Australia/New Zealand
1970	Australia	England
1972	Great Britain	France
1975	Australia	World wide
1977	Australia	Australia/New Zealand

Most wins: 5 Australia
Highest score: Great Britain 53 New Zealand 19 at Paris on 4 Nov 1972

EUROPEAN CHAMPIONSHIP

Instituted in 1935 it was a three-cornered tournament involving France, England and Wales. A team representing Other Nationalities competed between 1949-56. It was not held in the following years: 1940-5, 1955, 1957-69, 1971-4, 1976. The competition was discontinued in 1981.

Winners:
England 1935, 1946-8, 1950, 1954, 1970, 1975, 1978-80
France 1939 , 1949, 1951-2, 1977, 1981
Wales 1936-8
Other Nationalities 1953, 1956

SYDNEY PREMIERSHIP

The principal competition in Australia is the Sydney Premiership (sometimes referred to as the New South Wales Premiership), which culminates in the Grand Final each year. The winning team receives the Winfield Cup. The first Grand Final was in 1908.

Most wins:
20 South Sydney   1908-9, 1914, 1918, 1925-9, 1931-2, 1950-1, 1953-5, 1967-8, 1970-1
15 St.George   1941, 1949, 1956-66, 1977, 1979
11 Balmain   1915-7, 1919-20, 1924, 1939, 1944, 1946-7, 1969
11 Eastern Suburbs 1911-3, 1923, 1935-7, 1940, 1945, 1974-5

THE RECORD BREAKERS – RUGBY LEAGUE

ALL MATCHES
Biggest win: 119-2 Huddersfield v Swinton Park Rangers (Challenge Cup) 28 Feb 1914
Most tries in a match: 11 George Henry West (Hull Kingston Rovers) v Brookland Rovers (Challenge Cup) 4 Mar 1905
Most goals in a match: 22 Jim Sullivan (Wigan) v Flimby & Fothergill (Challenge Cup) 14 Feb 1925
Most points in a match: 53 (10 goals, 11 tries) George Henry West (Hull Kingston Rovers) - as above

INTERNATIONALS
Most appearances: 60 Jim Sullivan (Wigan) Wales, GB & Other Nationalities, 1921-39
Most tries: 45 Mick Sullivan (Huddersfield, Wigan, St.Helens, York) GB & England 1954-63
Most goals: 160 Jim Sullivan
Most points: 329 Jim Sullivan
Biggest win: Australia 63 England 13, Paris 31 Dec 1933

SEASON
Most tries: 80 Albert Rosenfeld (Huddersfield) 1913-4
Most goals: 221 David Watkins (Salford) 1972-3
Most points: 496 (194 goals, 36 tries) Lewis Jones (Leeds) 1956-7

CAREER
Most tries: 796 Brian Bevan (Warrington & Blackpool Borough) 1946-64
Most goals: 2,859 Jim Sullivan (Wigan) 1921-46
Most points: 6,220 (2575 goals, 358 tries, 4 drop goals) Neil Fox (Wakefield Trinity, Bradford Northern, Hull Kingston Rovers, York, Bramley, Huddersfield) 1956-60
Most appearances: 921 Jim Sullivan (Wigan) 1921-46
Most consecutive club appearances: 239 Keith Elwell (Widnes) May 1977-Sep 1982
Most consecutive games scoring points: 92 David Watkins (Salford) Aug 1972-Apr 1974

THE TOP TEAMS

Wins by teams in the League in 1986-7.

	Challenge Cup	Championship Play-off	Premiership Trophy	John Player Trophy	Floodlit Final	County Cup	County League	Div 1	Div 2
Barrow	1	-	-	-	-	2	-	-	2
Batley	3	1	-	-	-	1	2	-	-
Blackpool Borough	-	-	-	-	-	-	-	-	-
Bradford Northern	4	-	1	2	-	10	5	3	1
Bramley	-	-	-	-	1	-	-	-	-
Carlisle	-	-	-	-	-	-	-	-	-
Castleford	4	-	-	1	4	3	3	-	-
Dewsbury	2	1	-	-	-	3	1	-	1
Doncaster	-	-	-	-	-	-	-	-	-
Featherstone Rovers	3	-	-	-	-	2	-	1	1
Fulham	-	-	-	-	-	-	-	-	1
Halifax	5	2	-	1	-	5	6	2	-
Huddersfield Barracudas	6	7	-	-	-	12	11	-	2
Hull	2	5	-	1	1	5	4	1	2
Hull Kingston Rovers	1	2	2	1	1	7	2	3	-
Hunslet	2	2	-	-	-	3	3	-	1
Keighley	-	-	-	-	-	-	-	-	-
Leeds	10	3	2	2	1	16	15	-	-
Leigh	2	1	-	-	2	4	-	1	2
Mansfield Marksmen	-	-	-	-	-	-	-	-	-
Oldham	3	3	-	-	-	9	7	1	2
Rochdale Hornets	1	-	-	-	-	3	1	-	-
Runcorn Highfield	-	-	-	-	-	-	1	-	-
(Lancashire League win as Liverpool Stanley)									
St.Helens	5	6	3	-	2	10	8	1	-
Salford	1	4	-	-	1	5	5	2	-
Sheffield Eagles	-	-	-	-	-	-	-	-	-
Swinton	3	4	-	-	-	4	5	2	1
Wakefield Trinity	5	2	-	-	-	9	7	-	1
Warrington	5	3	1	3	-	8	8	-	-
Whitehaven	-	-	-	-	-	-	-	-	-
Widnes	7	-	3	2	1	6	1	1	-
Wigan	8	9	1	3	1	18	18	1	-
Workington Town	1	1	-	-	-	1	-	-	-
York	-	-	-	-	-	3	-	-	1

RUGBY UNION

The game of Rugby Union is traditionally said to have had its beginnings at Rugby School, when William Webb Ellis picked up the ball during a game of football in November 1823, and ran with it. The new 'handling' code of football developed and it was played at Cambridge University in 1839. The first rugby club was formed at Guy's Hospital in 1843 and the Rugby Football Union (RFU) was founded in January 1871.

The International Rugby Football Board (IRFB) was founded in 1886, members are: Australia, England, France, Ireland, New Zealand, Scotland, South Africa and Wales. The Fédération International de Rugby Amateur (FIRA) held its first meeting in 1934. Today there are 16 member nations, all from the continent of Europe.

WORLD CUP

The inaugural World Cup was contested in Australia and New Zealand in 1987 by 16 national teams. The result of the final was New Zealand 29 France 9.

The highest team score was New Zealand's 74-13 victory over Fiji at Christchurch on 27 May 1987. The most points in a match by an individual was 30 by Didier Camberabero (3 tries, 9 conversions) in France's 70-12 win over Zimbabwe at Auckland on 2 June 1987. The highest points scorer in the tournament was the New Zealand goalkicker, Grant Fox with 126 points in 6 games. Craig Green and John Kirwan (NZ) each scored six tries.

INTERNATIONAL CHAMPIONSHIP

First contested by England, Ireland, Scotland and Wales in 1884, France made it a 'Five Nations' tournament when they joined in 1910. Each country plays the other once during each season's championship. The championships of 1885, 1888-9, 1897-8 and 1972 were not completed for various reasons.

Winners:
(outright/shared wins)
21/10 Wales   1893, 1900, 1902, 1905, 1906*, 1908-9, 1911, 1920*, 1922, 1931, 1932*, 1936, 1939*, 1947*, 1950, 1952, 1954*-5*,

18/9 England	1956, 1964*, 1965-6, 1969, 1970*, 1971, 1973*, 1975-6, 1978-9
	1883-4, 1886*, 1890*, 1892, 1910, 1912*, 1913-4, 1921, 1923-4, 1928, 1930, 1932*, 1934, 1937, 1939*, 1947*, 1953, 1954*, 1957-8, 1960*, 1963, 1973*, 1980.
12/8 Scotland	1886*, 1887, 1890*, 1891, 1895, 1901, 1903-4, 1907, 1920*, 1925, 1926*-7*, 1929, 1933, 1938, 1964*, 1973*, 1984, 1986*
10/8 Ireland	1894, 1896, 1899, 1906*, 1912*, 1926*-7*, 1932*, 1935, 1939*, 1948-9, 1951, 1973*, 1974, 1982, 1983*, 1985
8/7 France	1954*, 1955*, 1959, 1960*, 1961-2, 1967-8, 1970*, 1973*, 1977, 1981, 1983*, 1986*, 1987

* denotes shared win (note: there was a quintuple tie in 1973)

GRAND SLAM

The beating of all other four countries during one season's championship has been achieved as follows:

8 Wales 1908-9*, 1911, 1950, 1952, 1971, 1976, 1978
8 England 1913-4, 1921, 1923-4, 1928, 1957, 1980
4 France 1968, 1977, 1981, 1987
2 Scotland 1925, 1984
1 Ireland 1948

* not including France, yet to enter

TRIPLE CROWN

The beating of the other three 'Home Countries' in one season's championship has been achieved as follows:

16 Wales	1893, 1900, 1902, 1905, 1908-9, 1911, 1950, 1952, 1965, 1969, 1971, 1976, 1977-9
15 England	1883-4, 1892, 1913-4, 1921, 1923-4, 1928, 1934, 1937, 1954, 1957, 1960, 1980
9 Scotland	1891, 1895, 1901, 1903, 1907, 1925, 1933, 1938, 1984
6 Ireland	1894, 1899, 1948-9, 1982, 1985

INTERNATIONAL CHAMPIONSHIP RECORDS
TEAM

Highest score: Wales 49 France 14 at Swansea, 1 Jan 1910 (on present day scoring the score would have been 59-16)
Most points in a season: 102 Wales 1975-6
Most tries in a season: 21 Wales 1909-10
Most points in a season: 54 (10 pen, 4 con, 4 dg) Jean-Patrick Lescarboura (Fra), 1984

INDIVIDUAL

Most tries in a season: 8 Cyril Lowe (Eng) 1913-4; Ian Smith (Sco) 1924-5
Most conversions in a season: 11 William Bancroft (Wal) 1908-9
Most penalty goals in a season: 16 Paul Thorburn (Sco) 1985-6
Most points in a match: 19 (8 con, 1 pen) William Bancroft (Wales) v France, 1 Jan 1910 - also a record for most goals in a match
(con – conversion, pen – penalty goal, dg – drop goal)

THE NATIONS' RECORDS AGAINST EACH OTHER

	P	W	D	L
ENGLAND				
v Scotland	103	49	16	38
v Ireland	99	55	8	36
v Wales	92	36	12	44
v France	62	32	7	23
SCOTLAND				
v England	103	38	16	49
v Ireland	97	49	4	44
v Wales	91	38	2	51
v France	57	27	2	28
IRELAND				
v England	99	36	8	55
v Scotland	97	44	4	49
v Wales	89	30	5	54
v France	60	25	5	30
WALES				
v England	92	44	12	36
v Scotland	91	51	2	38
v Ireland	89	54	5	30
v France	60	36	3	21
FRANCE				
v England	62	23	7	32
v Ireland	60	30	5	25
v Wales	60	21	3	36
v Scotland	57	28	2	27

J.P.R.Williams won a record 55 caps for Wales (ASP)

RECENT CHAMPIONSHIP STANDINGS

	1978	1979	1980	1981	1982	1983	1984	1985	1986	1987
England	3	4	1	2=	2=	5	4	3	3=	4=
France	2	2	4=	1	4=	1=	2	2	1=	1
Ireland	4	3	2=	5	1	1=	5	1	5	2=
Scotland	5	5	4=	2=	2=	4	1	5	1=	2=
Wales	1	1	2=	2=	4=	3	3	4	3=	4=

VARSITY MATCH

The first match between the Universities of Oxford and Cambridge took place at The Parks, Oxford on 10 February 1872. It has been contested annually ever since, with the exception of the First World War. During the second war, a special war-time series of matches was played. Cambridge staged the second match in 1873, the Oval 1874-80, Blackheath 1881-7, Queen's Club 1888-1921, and Twickenham thereafter. The years quoted are for the second half of the season, although the match is now played annually in December.

Wins:

47 Cambridge 1873, 1877, 1880, 1886-9, 1892, 1896, 1899-1900, 1905-6, 1913-4, 1920, 1923, 1926-9, 1935, 1937, 1939, 1946, 1948, 1953, 1955, 1957, 1959, 1961-4, 1968-9, 1973-7, 1979, 1981-5

44 Oxford 1872, 1876, 1878, 1882-5, 1890, 1894, 1897-8, 1901-2, 1904, 1907-8, 1910-2, 1921-2, 1924-5, 1930, 1932-4, 1938, 1947, 1949-52, 1956, 1958, 1960, 1965, 1967, 1970-2, 1978, 1980, 1986

13 Drawn 1874-5, 1879, 1881, 1891, 1893, 1895, 1903, 1909, 1931, 1936, 1954, 1966,

War-time series:

Between 1940-45 a total of 12 matches were played and the winners were as follows:

9 Cambridge 1941(2), 1942 (2), 1943 (3), 1944, 1945

2 Oxford 1940, 1944

1 Drawn 1945

COUNTY CHAMPIONSHIP

The English County Championship was introduced in 1889 and Yorkshire were declared the champions by the Rugby Union, after remaining undefeated. The current system, the fifth, divides the counties into Northern, Midland, London and South-Western divisions, with a promotion and relegation system, before the leading four counties play-off in semi-finals to decide which two meet in the final.

Winners:

First system
1889 Yorkshire
1890 Yorkshire

Second system
1891 Lancashire
1892 Yorkshire
1893 Yorkshire
1894 Yorkshire
1895 Yorkshire

Third system

	Winners		Runners-up	
1896	Yorkshire		Surrey	
1897	Kent		Cumberland	
1898	Northumberland		Midlands	
1899	Devon		Northumberland	
1900	Durham		Devon	
1901	Devon		Durham	
1902	Durham		Gloucestershire	
1903	Durham		Kent	
1904	Kent		Durham	
1905	Durham		Middlesex	
1906	Devon		Durham	
1907	Devon & Durham (shared)			
1908	Cornwall		Durham	
1909	Durham		Cornwall	
1910	Gloucestershire		Yorkshire	
1911	Devon		Yorkshire	
1912	Devon		Northumberland	
1913	Gloucestershire		Cumberland	
1914	Midlands		Durham	
1915-19	Not held			
1920	Gloucestershire		Yorkshire	

Fourth System

1921	Gloucestershire	31	Leicestershire	4
1922	Gloucestershire	19	North Midlands	0
1923	Somerset	8	Leicestershire	6
1924	Cumberland	14	Kent	3
1925	Leicestershire	14	Gloucestershire	6
1926	Yorkshire	15	Hampshire	14
1927	Kent	22	Leicestershire	12
1928	Yorkshire	12	Cornwall	8
1929	Middlesex	9	Lancashire	8
			(after 8-8 draw)	
1930	Gloucestershire	13	Lancashire	7
1931	Gloucestershire	10	Warwickshire	9
1932	Gloucestershire	9	Durham	3
1933	Hampshire	18	Lancashire	7
1934	East Midlands	10	Gloucestershire	0
1935	Lancashire	14	Somerset	0
1936	Hampshire	13	Northumberland	6
1937	Gloucestershire	5	East Midlands	0
1938	Lancashire	24	Surrey	12
1939	Warwickshire	8	Somerset	3
1940-46	Not held			
1947	Lancashire	14	Gloucestershire	3
			(after 8-8 draw)	
1948	Lancashire	5	Eastern Counties	0
1949	Lancashire	9	Gloucestershire	3
1950	Cheshire	5	East Midlands	0
1951	East Midlands	10	Middlesex	0
1952	Middlesex	9	Lancashire	6
1953	Yorkshire	11	East Midlands	3
1954	Middlesex	24	Lancashire	6
1955	Lancashire	14	Middlesex	8

1956	Middlesex	13	Devon	9
1957	Devon	12	Yorkshire	3
1958	Warwickshire	16	Cornwall	8
1959	Warwickshire	14	Gloucestershire	9
1960	Warwickshire	9	Surrey	6
1961	Cheshire	5	Devon	3
			(after 0-0 draw)	
1962	Warwickshire	11	Hampshire	6
1963	Warwickshire	13	Yorkshire	10
1964	Warwickshire	8	Lancashire	6
1965	Warwickshire	15	Durham	9
1966	Middlesex	6	Lancashire	0
1967	Surrey & Durham shared after 14-14 & 0-0 draws			
1968	Middlesex	9	Warwickshire	6
1969	Lancashire	11	Cornwall	9
1970	Staffordshire	11	Gloucestershire	9
1971	Surrey	14	Gloucestershire	3
1972	Gloucestershire	11	Warwickshire	6
1973	Lancashire	17	Gloucestershire	12
1974	Gloucestershire	22	Lancashire	12
1975	Gloucestershire	13	Eastern Counties	9
1976	Gloucestershire	24	Middlesex	9
1977	Lancashire	17	Middlesex	6
1978	North Midlands	10	Gloucestershire	7
1979	Middlesex	19	Northumberland	6
1980	Lancashire	21	Gloucestershire	15
1981	Northumberland	15	Gloucestershire	6
1982	Lancashire	7	North Midlands	3
1983	Gloucestershire	19	Yorkshire	7
1984	Gloucestershire	36	Somerset	18
1985	Middlesex	12	Notts, Lincs, Derbys	9
1986	Warwickshire	16	Kent	6
1987	Yorkshire	22	Middlesex	11

Most wins: 15 Gloucestershire; 12 Lancashire; 11 Yorkshire; 9 Warwickshire; 8 Middlesex; 7 Devon (including one shared), Durham (including two shared)
Most individual appearances: 104 Richard Trickey (Lancashire) 1964-78

JOHN PLAYER SPECIAL CUP

The RFU Knockout Competition for English club sides was inaugurated in the 1971-2 season and has been held annually since. The final is at Twickenham.

Finals:

1972	Gloucester	17	Moseley	6
1973	Coventry	27	Bristol	15
1974	Coventry	26	London Scottish	6
1975	Bedford	28	Rosslyn Park	12
1976	Gosforth	23	Rosslyn Park	14
1977	Gosforth	27	Waterloo	11
1978	Gloucester	6	Leicester	3
1979	Leicester	15	Moseley	12
1980	Leicester	21	London Irish	9
1981	Leicester	22	Gosforth	15
1982	Gloucester	12	Moseley	12
			(shared)	
1983	Bristol	28	Leicester	22
1984	Bath	10	Bristol	9
1985	Bath	24	London Welsh	15
1986	Bath	25	Wasps	17
1987	Bath	19	Wasps	12

Most wins: 4 Bath; 3 Leicester, Gloucester (including one shared)

Biggest win: 66-6 Bedford v Bournemouth, 1st round, 2 Nov 1974

SCHWEPPES WELSH CUP

The Welsh Rugby Union Challenge Cup is the Welsh equivalent of the John Player Special Cup. All finals at Cardiff (Arms Park or National Stadium).

Finals:

1972	Neath	15	Llanelli	9
1973	Llanelli	30	Cardiff	7
1974	Llanelli	12	Aberavon	10
1975	Llanelli	15	Aberavon	6
1976	Llanelli	15	Swansea	4
1977	Newport	16	Cardiff	15
1978	Swansea	13	Newport	9
1979	Bridgend	18	Pontypridd	12
1980	Bridgend	15	Swansea	9
1981	Cardiff	14	Bridgend	6
1982	Cardiff *	12	Bridgend	12
1983	Pontypool	18	Swansea	6
1984	Cardiff	24	Neath	19
1985	Llanelli	15	Cardiff	14
1986	Cardiff	28	Newport	21
1987	Cardiff	16	Swansea	15

* Winners on most tries rule

Most wins: 5 Llanelli, Cardiff

SCHWEPPES CLUB CHAMPIONSHIP (SCOTLAND)

The premier club competition in Scotland is the Schweppes Club Championship, instituted 1974. There are currently seven divisions.

Division One winners:
1974-8 Hawick
1979 Heriot's FP
1980 Gala
1982 Hawick
1983 Gala
1984-7 Hawick

Most wins: 10 Hawick

MIDDLESEX SEVENS

The leading Sevens tournament was inaugurated in 1926. The final of the knockout tournament is played at Twickenham and regularly attracts crowds in excess of 50,000. The winners receive the Russell Cargill Trophy.

Winners:

1926	Harlequins	25	St.Mary's Hospital	3
1927	Harlequins	28	Blackheath	6
1928	Harlequins	19	Blackheath	8
1929	Harlequins	16	Rosslyn Park	9
1930	London Welsh	6	Blackheath	0
1931	London Welsh	9	Harlequins	5
1932	Blackheath	18	Harlequins	10
1933	Harlequins	23	Wasps	0
1934	Barbarians	6	Richmond	3*
1935	Harlequins	10	London Welsh	3
1936	Sale	18	Blackheath	6
1937	London Scottish	19	Old Merchant Taylors	3

1938	Metropolitan Police	13	London Scottish	3
1939	Cardiff	11	London Scottish	6
1940	St.Mary's Hospital	14	OCTU Sandhurst	10
1941	Cambridge University	6	Welsh Guards	0
1942	St.Mary's Hospital	8	RAF	6
1943	St.Mary's Hospital	8	Middlesex Hospital	3
1944	St.Mary's Hospital	15	RAF Jurby	5
1945	Nottingham	6	St.Mary's Hospital	3
1946	St.Mary's Hospital	13	Cardiff	3
1947	Rosslyn Park	12	Richmond	6
1948	Wasps	14	Harlequins	5
1949	Heriot's FP	16	London Scottish	6
1950	Rosslyn Park	16	Heriot's FP	0
1951	Richmond II	13	Wasps	10
1952	Wasps	12	St Thomas's Hospital	10
1953	Richmond	10	London Welsh	3
1954	Rosslyn Park	16	London Scottish	0
1955	Richmond	5	St Luke's College	0
1956	London Welsh	24	Emmanuel College Cambridge	10
1957	St.Luke's College	18	London Welsh	5
1958	Blackheath	16	Harlequins	3
1959	Loughborough Colleges	3	London Welsh	0
1960	London Scottish	16	London Welsh	5
1961	London Scottish	20	Stewart's College FP	6
1962	London Scottish	18	Rosslyn Park	6
1963	London Scottish	15	Hawick	11
1964	Loughborough Colleges	18	London Scottish	16
1965	London Scottish	15	Loughborough Colleges	8
1966	Loughborough Colleges	29	Northampton	10
1967	Harlequins	14	Richmond	11
1968	London Welsh	16	Richmond	3
1969	St.Luke's College	21	Edinburgh Wanderers	16
1970	Loughborough Colleges	26	Edinburgh Wanderers	11
1971	London Welsh	18	Harlequins	9
1972	London Welsh	22	Public School Wanderers	18
1973	London Welsh	24	Public School Wanderers	22
1974	Richmond	34	London Welsh	16
1975	Richmond	24	Loughborough Colleges	8
1976	Loughborough Colleges	21	Harlequins	20
1977	Richmond	26	Gosforth	16
1978	Harlequins	40	Rosslyn Park	12
1979	Richmond	24	London Scottish	10
1980	Richmond	34	Rosslyn Park	18
1981	Rosslyn Park	16	London Welsh	14
1982	Stewart's Melville FP	34	Richmond	12
1983	Richmond I	20	London Welsh	13
1984	London Welsh	34	Heriot's FP	18
1985	Wasps	25	Nottingham	6
1986	Harlequins	18	Nottignham	10
1987	Harlequins	22	Rosslyn Park	6

* after extra time

Most wins: 10 Harlequins; 9 Richmond; 8 London Welsh, 6 London Scottish; 5 St.Mary's Hospital, Loughborough Colleges; 4 Rosslyn Park

NATIONAL MERIT TABLES

The RFU approved a plan in 1985 for the leading English clubs to form into two divisions known as Merit Tables 'A' and 'B'. Selected matches throughout the season were designated Merit Table matches, and an end-of-season league table was drawn up. A third Merit Table, C, was added in 1986-7.

Winners:

	Merit Table A	Merit Table B	Merit Table C
1985-6	Gloucester	Orrell	—
1986-7	Bath	Waterloo	Vale of Lune

OLYMPIC GAMES

Rugby has been included in four Olympic celebrations, the first at Paris in 1900. Three teams took part in 1900 and 1924, and played on a round-robin basis, while just two teams entered in 1908 and 1920 with the one match deciding the gold medallists.

	Gold	Silver	Bronze
1900	France	Germany	United Kingdom
1908	Australia	United Kingdom	—
	(Australia won 32-3)		
1920	USA	France	—
	(USA won 8-0)		
1924	USA	France	Romania

INTERNATIONAL RECORDS

The playing records of all major Rugby-playing nations is as follows as at 21 May 1987 (for matches involving the nations in the International Championship see p.265).

ENGLAND	P	W	D	L
v New Zealand	15	3	0	12
v Australia	11	4	0	7
v South Africa	9	2	1	6
SCOTLAND	P	W	D	L
v New Zealand	12	0	2	10
v Australia	10	6	0	4
v South Africa	8	3	0	5
WALES	P	W	D	L
v Australia	11	7	0	4
v New Zealand	11	3	0	8
v South Africa	7	0	1	7
IRELAND	P	W	D	L
v Australia	10	6	0	4
v South Africa	10	1	1	8
v New Zealand	9	0	1	8
FRANCE	P	W	D	L
v New Zealand	20	4	0	16
v South Africa	19	3	4	12
v Australia	15	9	2	9
AUSTRALIA	P	W	D	L
v New Zealand	79	19	4	56
v South Africa	28	7	0	21
v France	15	4	2	9

	P	W	D	L
v England	11	7	0	4
v Wales	11	4	0	7
v Scotland	10	4	0	6
v Ireland	10	4	0	6
NEW ZEALAND	P	W	D	L
v Australia	79	56	4	19
v South Africa	37	15	2	20
v France	20	16	0	4
v England	15	12	0	3
v Scotland	12	10	2	0
v Wales	11	8	0	3
v Ireland	9	8	1	0
SOUTH AFRICA	P	W	D	L
v New Zealand	37	20	2	15
v Australia	28	21	0	7
v France	19	12	4	3
v Ireland	10	8	1	1
v England	9	6	1	2
v Scotland	8	5	0	3
v Wales	7	6	1	0

BLEDISLOE CUP

Contested by New Zealand and Australia, it was instigated in 1931 by Lord Bledisloe, the Governor-General of New Zealand.

Wins:
46 New Zealand; 14 Australia; 3 Drawn

INDIVIDUAL RECORDS

LEADING CAP WINNERS (pre World Cup 1987)
Figures includes caps won for individual countries against other International Board countries and the British Lions, and in other special centenary or celebratory matches. Figures in brackets indicates number of British Lions appearances in addition to those quoted.

69(12) Mike Gibson (Ire) 1964-79
63(17) Willie John McBride (Ire) 1962-75
61(4) Fergus Slattery (Ire) 1970-84
55 Colin Meads (NZ) 1957-71
55(8) J.P.R.Williams (Wal) 1969-81
55(1) Phil Orr (Ire) 1976-87
54(5) Tom Kiernan (Ire) 1960-73
53(10) Gareth Edwards (Wal) 1967-78
52 Roland Bertranne (Fra) 1971-81
51(1) Moss Keane (Ire) 1974-84
51(9) Andy Irvine (Sco) 1972-82
51(1) Jim Renwick (Sco) 1972-84
50 Bernard Dauga (Fra) 1964-72
50 Sandy Carmichael (Sco) 1967-78

Leading cap winners for the other nations:
43(1) Tony Neary (Eng) 1971-80
39 Peter Johnson (Aus) 1959-71 & Greg Davis (Aus) 1963-72
38 Frik Du Preez (SAf) 1960-71 & Jan Ellis (SAf) 1965-76

LEADING POINTS SCORERS
261 Andy Irvine (Sco) 1972-82
225 Dusty Hare (Eng) 1974-84
217 Olly Campbell (Ire) 1976-84

Mike Gibson, of his 69 caps for Ireland 40 were played as centre, 25 as outside-half and four on the wing. (ASP)

207 Don Clarke (NZ) 1956-64
166 Phil Bennett (Wal) 1969-78
162 Paul McLean (Aus) 1974-82
158 Tom Kiernan (Ire) 1960-73
For the other nations, the records are as follows:
France: 139 Jean-Pierre Romeau 1973-77
South Africa: 130 Piet Visagie 1967-71
Most points in a match: 26 Alan Hewson, New Zealand v Australia at Auckland 11 Sept 1982

LEADING TRY SCORERS
24 Ian Smith (Sco) 1924-33
20 Gareth Edwards (Wal) 1967-78
20 Gerald Davies (Wal) 1966-78
19 Stewart Wilson (NZ) 1977-83
18 Cyril Lowe (Eng) 1913-23
16 Ian Kirkpatrick (NZ) 1967-77
For the other nations, the records are as follows:
Ireland: 14 George Stephenson 1920-30
South Africa: 8 John Gainsford 1960-7; Jannie Engelbrecht 1960-9

Most tries in a match: 5 George Lindsay, Scotland v Wales at Raeburn Place, Edinburgh, 26 Feb 1887; Douglas Lambert, England v France at Richmond, 5 Jan 1907

OTHER RECORDS
TEAM:
The highest score in any full international is: 92-0 France v Spain at Oléron, France, 4 Mar 1979
The record score for an International Tour match is: 125-0 New Zealand v Northern New South Wales at Quirindi, Australia, 30 May 1962
The most points scored in a season is: 1607 by Pontypool (Wales) in 1983-4
The most tries in a season is: 269 by Bridgend (Wales) also in 1983-4

INDIVIDUAL
The most points in any international match is: 30 (9 con, 4 pg) Colin Mair (Sco) v Japan at Tokyo, 18 Sep 1977
The most points in an international career (all matches) is: 441 Hugo Porta for Argentina in 46 matches, including 338 in 37 matches v IRB countries
301 Andy Irvine for Scotland (273) and the British Lions (28), 1973-82
The most points scored in a season is: 581 Sam Doble (Moseley) in 52 matches 1971-2
The most points in a career is: 6319 Dusty Hare (Nottingham, Leicester, England, British Lions, and other representative matches) 1971-87

FIRA CHAMPIONSHIP

The first FIRA Championship, for European nations, was held in 1965-6, but they only became officially recognised in 1973-4.
Winners of Group A since 1974:
9 France 1974, 1976, 1978-80, 1982, 1984-6
4 Romania 1975, 1977, 1981, 1983
Earlier winners:
France 1966, 1968, 1970-3
Romania 1969

Jean-Pierre Rives, the inspiration of France. (Colorsport)

CATHAY PACIFIC-HONG KONG BANK SEVENS

The first Hong Kong International sevens was held in 1976, with just 12 teams taking part. Now, it is regarded as the most prestigious international sevens tournament in the world.

Winners:
1976 Cantabrians
1977-8 Fiji
1979 Australia
1980 Fiji
1981 Barbarians
1982-3 Australia
1984 Fiji
1985 Australia
1986-7 New Zealand

BRITISH LIONS

The British Lions went on their first Tour in 1888, when they played a total of 35 matches in Australia and New Zealand. Since then they have been on a further 21 tours. The following is a complete record of all matches on each tour.

Year	Country	P	W	D	L	F	A	Tour captain
1888	Australia	16	14	2	0	210	65	Robert Seddon (Eng)*
	New Zealand	19	13	4	2	82	33	
1891	South Africa	19	19	0	0	224	3	Bill Maclagan (Sco)
1896	South Africa	21	19	1	1	310	45	John Hammond (Eng)#
1899	Australia	21	18	0	3	333	90	Rev.Matthew Mullineaux (Eng)#
1903	South Africa	22	11	3	8	231	138	Mark Morrison (Sco)
1904	Australia	14	14	0	0	265	51	Darky Bedell-Sivright (Sco)
	New Zealand	5	2	1	2	22	33	
1908	Australia	9	7	0	2	139	48	Arthur Harding (Wal)
	New Zealand	17	9	1	7	184	153	
1910	South Africa	24	13	3	8	290	236	Dr.Tom Smyth (Ire)
1924	South Africa	21	9	3	9	175	155	Dr.Ronald Cove-Smith (Eng)
1930	New Zealand	21	15	0	6	420	205	Doug Prentice (Eng)
	Australia	7	5	0	2	204	113	

1938	South Africa	23	17	0	6	407	272	Sam Walker (Ire)
1950	New Zealand	23	17	1	5	420	162	
	Australia	6	5	0	1	150	52	Karl Mullen (Ire)
1955	South Africa	24	18	1	5	418	271	Robin Thompson (Ire)
1959	Australia	6	5	0	1	174	70	Ronnie Dawson (Ire)
	New Zealand	25	20	0	5	582	266	
1962	South Africa	24	15	4	5	351	208	Arthur Smith (Sco)
1966	Australia	8	7	1	0	202	48	Michael Campbell-Lamerton (Sco)
	New Zealand	25	15	2	8	300	281	
1968	South Africa	20	15	1	4	377	181	Tom Kiernan (Ire)
1971	Australia	2	1	0	1	25	27	John Dawes (Wal)
	New Zealand	24	22	1	1	555	204	
1974	South Africa	22	21	1	0	729	207	Willie John McBride (Ire)
1977	New Zealand	25	21	0	4	596	295	Phil Bennett (Wal)
	Fiji	1	0	0	1	21	25	
1980	South Africa	18	15	0	3	401	244	Billy Beaumont (Eng)
1983	New Zealand	18	12	0	6	478	276	Cieran Fitzgerald (Ire)

* Seddon lost his life in a drowning accident while sculling on the Hunter River, NSW, during the tour and was replaced by Arthur Stoddart (Eng)
# Mullineaux and Hammond never played international rugby for one of the home countries

TEST SUMMARIES

BRITISH LIONS	P	W	D	L
v Australia	14	12	0	2
v New Zealand	32	24	3	5
v South Africa	40	14	6	20

BRITISH LIONS RECORDS

Biggest win: 31-0 v Australia at Brisbane, 4 Jun 1966

Biggest defeat: 6-38 by New Zealand at Auckland, 16 Jul 1983

Most caps: 17 Willie John McBride (Ire) 1962-74

Most internationals as captain: 6 Ronnie Dawson (Ire) 1959

Most points in internationals: 44 Phil Bennett (Wal) 1974-77

Most points in one international: 18 Tony Ward (Ire) v South Africa at Cape Town, 31 May, 1980

Most tries in internationals: 6 Tony O'Reilly (Ire) 1955-9

Most tries in one international: 8 players have each scored two tries, the most recent being J.J.Williams (Wal) against South Africa, twice on the 1974 tour.

Most points on a tour: 188 Barry John (Wal) 1971 to Australia and New Zealand

Most tries on a tour: 22 Tony O'Reilly (Ire) 1959 to Australia and New Zealand

Most points in a tour match: 37 Alan Old (Eng) v South Western Districts at Mossel Bay, SAf, 29 May 1974

Most tries in a tour match: 6 David Duckham (Eng) v West Coast-Buller, at Greymouth, NZ, 17 Jun 1971; 6 J.J.Williams (Wal) v South Western Districts at Mossel Bay, SAf, 29 May 1974

AUSTRALIA

Rugby was first played in Australia in 1829 and the first administrative body, the Southern Union, was formed in 1874. It was renamed the NSW Rugby Union in 1892. The first Australian rugby club was that of Sydney University, formed in 1864. New South Wales and Queensland are the predominant states for the game.

SYDNEY PREMIERSHIP

First played in 1900.

Wins:

21 University 1901*, 1904, 1919-20, 1923-4, 1926-8, 1937, 1939, 1945, 1951, 1953-5, 1961-2, 1968, 1970, 1972

18 Randwick 1930, 1934, 1938, 1940, 1948, 1959, 1965-7, 1971, 1973-4, 1978-82, 1984

9 Eastern Suburbs 1903, 1913, 1921, 1931, 1941, 1944, 1946-7, 1969

8 Glebe 1900, 1901*, 1906-7, 1909, 1912, 1914, 1925*,

6 Northern Suburbs 1933, 1935, 1960, 1963-4, 1975

6 Manly 1922, 1932, 1942-3, 1950, 1983

5 Gordon 1949, 1952, 1956, 1958, 1976

3 Newtown 1908, 1910-1,

3 Parramatta 1977, 1985, 1986

2 Western Suburbs 1902, 1929

1 South Sydney 1905

1 Balmain 1925*

1 Drummoyne 1936

1 St.George 1957

* Shared

NEW ZEALAND

Rugby was introduced into New Zealand in 1870. The first New Zealand union was that of Canterbury in 1879, and the New Zealand Rugby Football Union was founded in 1892.

RANFURLY SHIELD

The inter-provincial championship, first held in 1904. It is not a knockout out competition, but one in which the champion state puts its title up for a challenge.

Winners and years when title changed hands:

1904	Wellington	1921	Wellington
1905	Auckland	1922	Hawke's Bay
1913	Taranaki	1927	Wairarapa
1914	Wellington	1927	Manawhenua
1920	Southland	1927	Canterbury

1928 Wairarapa	1959 Auckland
1929 Southland	1960 North Auckland
1930 Wellington	1960 Auckland
1931 Canterbury	1963 Wellington
1934 Hawke's Bay	1963 Taranaki
1934 Auckland	1965 Auckland
1935 Canterbury	1966 Waikato
1935 Otago	1966 Hawke's Bay
1937 Southland	1969 Canterbury
1938 Otago	1971 Auckland
1938 Southland	1971 North Auckland
1947 Otago	1972 Auckland
1950 Canterbury	1972 Canterbury
1950 Wairarapa	1973 Marlborough
1950 South Canterbury	1974 South Canterbury
1950 North Auckland	1974 Wellington
1951 Waikato	1974 Auckland
1952 Auckland	1976 Manawatu
1952 Waikato	1978 North Auckland
1953 Wellington	1979 Auckland
1953 Canterbury	1980 Waikato
1956 Wellington	1981 Wellington
1957 Otago	1982 Canterbury
1957 Taranaki	1985 Auckland
1959 Southland	

Most successive defences: 26 Auckland 1960-3; Canterbury 1982-5
Record attendance: 52,000 Auckland v Canterbury at Lancaster Park 1985

NATIONAL CHAMPIONSHIP

A season-long championship involving 11 states in the first division. Each team plays the other once on a league basis. There are also supplementary divisions enabling promotion to the first division. Inaugurated 1976.

Winners:
1976 Bay of Plenty
1977 Canterbury
1978 Wellington
1979 Counties
1980 Manawatu
1981 Wellington
1982 Auckland
1983 Canterbury
1984-5 Auckland
1986 Wellington

SOUTH AFRICA

Rugby in South Africa, developed from a form of football known as 'Gog's game', was first played in South Africa by a civilian team and a military team at Green Point Common, Cape Town, in 1862. The first union to be formed was Western Province in 1883 and the South African Rugby Board was founded in 1889.

CURRIE CUP

Inter-provincial tournament, first held 1889. Annual from 1968, prior to that it was mostly biennial, avoiding international tours.

Wins:
28 Western Province 1889, 1892, 1894-5, 1897-8, 1904,
1906, 1908, 1914, 1920, 1925, 1927, 1929, 1932*, 1934*, 1936, 1947, 1954, 1959, 1964, 1966, 1979*, 1982-6
14 Northern Transvaal 1946, 1956, 1968-9, 1971*, 1973-8, 1979*, 1980-1
 6 Transvaal 1922, 1939, 1950, 1952, 1971*, 1972
 3 Griqualand West 1899, 1911, 1970
 2 Border 1932*, 1934*
* shared

Highest score: Transvaal beat Far North 99-9 at Ellis Park, Johannesburg, 7 Jul 1973

SHINTY

This 12-a-side curved stick (the caman) and ball game is played almost exclusively in the Scottish Highlands. The pitch is up to 170 yards (155m) long and 80 yards (73m) wide, and the goals 10ft by 12ft (3.0 - 3.65m). The ball is about the size of a tennis ball and has a thick leather covering over a cork and worsted core.

The game's antecedents date back more than 2000 years to the ancient game of *camanachd*, meaning "the sport of the curved stick", and was brought to Scotland from Ireland with the Celtic immigration about 1400 years ago. The sport provided effective battle training, indeed it was probably a crude substitute for battle between clans. The present ruling body, the Camanachd Association, was founded in 1893.

CAMANACHD CUP

The Camanachd Association Challenge Cup, instituted in 1896, is shinty's premier competition.

Most wins:
28 Newtonmore 1907-10, 1929, 1931-2, 1936, 1947-8,
1950-1, 1955, 1957-9, 1967, 1970-2, 1975, 1977-9, 1981-2, 1985-6
19 Kyles Atletic 1904-6, 1920, 1922, 1924, 1927-8,
1935, 1956, 1962, 1965-6, 1968-9, 1974, 1976, 1980, 1983
 9 Kingussie 1896, 1900, 1902-3, 1914, 1921, 1961,
1984, 1987

A record 11 winner's medals have been won by the Newtonmore players Johnnie Campbell, David Ritchie and Hugh Chisholm.

Highest score: 11-3 Newtonmore v. Furnace 1909

SHOOTING

The first shooting club, the Lucerne Shooting Guild (Switzerland), was formed around 1466 and the first recorded shooting match was at Zurich in 1472. The National Rifle Association of Great Britain was formed in 1860 and the Clay Bird Shooting Association was founded in 1903. The American National Rifle Association was formed in 1871. The international governing body, the Union International de Tir (UIT), was formed in Zürich in 1907.

OLYMPIC GAMES

Shooting has been part of the Olympic programme since the first Games in 1896; its inclusion possibly being as a result of the Games' founder, Baron Pierre de Coubertin, being an excellent shot. Separate events for women were first held in 1984 although they had competed alongside their male counterparts since 1968.

Winners:

FREE PISTOL
(60 shots from 50 metres)
1896 Sumner Paine (USA) 442
1900 Conrad Röderer (Swi) 503
1906 Georgios Orphanidis (Gre) 221
1908 Paul van Asbroeck (Bel) 490
1912 Alfred Lane (USA) 499
1920 Karl Frederick (USA) 496
1936 Torsten Ullmann (Swe) 559
1948 Edwin Vazquez Cam (Per) 545
1952 Huelet Benner (USA) 553
1956 Pentti Linnosvuo (Fin) 556
1960 Aleksey Gushchin (USSR) 560
1964 Väinö Markkanen (Fin) 560
1968 Grigory Kossykh (USSR) 562
1972 Ragnar Skanåkar (Swe) 567
1976 Uwe Potteck (GDR) 573
1980 Aleksandr Melentyev (USSR) 581
1984 Xu Haifeng (Chn) 566

SMALL BORE RIFLE (Three Position)
(40 shots each from kneeling, standing and prone positions at a target 50 metres away)
1952 Erling Kongshaug (Nor) 1164
1956 Anatoliy Bogdanov (USSR) 1172
1960 Viktor Shamburkin (USSR) 1149
1964 Lones Wigger (USA) 1164
1968 Bernd Klingner (FRG) 1157
1972 John Writer (USA) 1166
1976 Lanny Bassham (USA) 1162
1980 Viktor Vlasov (USSR) 1173
1984 Malcolm Cooper (UK) 1173

RAPID FIRE PISTOL
(Since 1948; 30 shots at five targets each at 25 metres. The shooter has 8 secs at each target in the first round, then 6 secs and then 4 secs. The set of 15 shots is then repeated)
1896 Jean Phrangoudis (Gre) 344
1900 Maurice Larrouy (Fra) 58
1906 Maurice Lecoq (Fra) 250
1912 Alfred Lane (USA) 287
1920 Guilherme Paraense (Bra) 274
1924 Henry Bailey (USA) 18
1932 Renzo Morigi (Ita) 36
1936 Cornelius van Oyen (Ger) 36
1948 Károly Takács (Hun) 580
1952 Károly Takács (Hun) 579
1956 Stefan Petrescu (Rom) 587
1960 William McMillan (USA) 587
1964 Pentti Linnosvuo (Fin) 592

Malcolm Cooper (All-Sport)

1968 Jozef Zapedzki (Pol) 593
1972 Jozef Zapedzki (Pol) 595
1976 Norbert Klaar (GDR) 597
1980 Corneliu Ion (Rom) 596
1984 Takeo Kamachi (Jap) 595

RUNNING GAME TARGET
(30 shots at a 2in 10-ring target on a simulated boar that does two runs across a 10-metre gap; one at 2½ secs and one at 5 secs)
1900 Louis Debray (Fra) 20
1972 Yakov Zhelezniak (USSR) 569
1976 Aleksandr Gazov (USSR) 579
1980 Igor Sokolov (USSR) 589
1984 Li Yuwei (Chn) 587

TRAP SHOOTING
(200 clay birds are released, one at a time, and at varying angles. The shooter is allowed two shots at each clay)
1900 Roger de Barbarin (Fra) 17
1906 Gerald Merlin (UK)* 24
    Sidney Merlin (UK)** 15
1908 Walter Ewing (Can) 72
1912 James Graham (USA) 96
1920 Mark Arie (USA) 95
1924 Gyula Halasy (Hun) 98

1952 George Généreux (Can) 192
1956 Galliano Rossini (Ita) 195
1960 Ion Dumitrescu (Rom) 192
1964 Ennio Mattarelli (Ita) 198
1968 Bob Braithwaite (UK) 198
1972 Angelo Scalzone (Ita) 199
1976 Don Haldeman (USA) 190
1980 Luciano Giovanetti (Ita) 198
1984 Luciano Giovanetti (Ita) 192
* Single shot ** Double shot

SKEET SHOOTING
(The shooter attempts to hit 200 clay targets which are released either one or two at a time. Unlike trap shooting he or she fires from eight different 'stations' and the birds are released from towers as opposed to ground level)
1968 Yevgeniy Petrov (USSR) 198
1972 Konrad Wirnhier (FRG) 195
1976 Josef Panacek (Cs) 198
1980 Hans Kjeld Rasmussen (Den) 196
1984 Matthew Dryke (USA) 198

SMALL BORE RIFLE (Prone)
(60 shots within two hours at a target with a bullseye diameter of a mere 0.487in, and 50 metres away)
1908 A.A.Carnell (UK) 387
1912 Frederick Hird (USA) 194
1920 Lawrence Nuesslein (USA) 391
1924 Pierre Coquelin de Lisle (Fra) 398
1932 Bertil Rönnmark (Swe) 294
1936 Willy Rögeberg (Nor) 300
1948 Arthur Cook (USA) 599
1952 Iosif Sarbu (Rom) 400
1956 Gerald Ouellette (Can) 600*
1960 Peter Kohnke (FRG) 590
1964 László Hammerl (Hun) 597
1968 Jan Kurka (Cs) 598
1972 Ho-Jun Li (NKo) 599
1976 Karlheinz Smieszek (FRG) 599
1980 Karoly Varga (Hun) 599
1984 Edward Etzel (USA) 599
* Record not allowed, range marginally short.

AIR RIFLE
(60 shots at 10 metres)
1984 Philippe Heberle (Fra) 589

WOMEN:

SPORT PISTOL
(60 shots at 10 metres)
1984 Linda Thom (Can) 585

AIR RIFLE
(40 shots at 10 metres)
1984 Pat Spurgin (USA) 393

SMALL BORE STANDARD RIFLE
(60 shots at 10 metres)
1984 Wu Xiaoxuan (Chn) 581

DISCONTINUED EVENTS

FREE RIFLE (three postions)
(120 shots from 300 metres)
1896 Georgis Orphanidis (Gre)1583
1906 Gudbrand Skattboe (Nor) 973

1908 Albert Helgerud (Nor) 909
1912 Paul Colas (Fra) 987
1920 Morris Fisher (USA) 996
1924 Morris Fisher (USA) 95
1948 Emil Grüning (Swi) 1120
1952 Anatoliy Bogdanov (USSR) 1123
1956 Vasiliy Borissov (USSR) 1138
1960 Hubert Hammerer (Aut) 1129
1964 Gary Anderson (USA) 1153
1968 Gary Anderson (USA) 1157
1972 Lones Wigger (USA) 1155

FREE RIFLE
1896 Pantelis Karasevdas (Gre) 2320: over 200m
1906 Marcel de Stadelhofen (Swi) 243: any position (300m)
1906 Gudbrand Skatteboe (Nor) Prone (300m)
1906 Konrad Stäheli (Swi) Kneeling (300m)
1906 Gudbrand Skatteboe (Nor) Standing (300m)
1908 Jerry Millner (UK) 98: over 1000 yards

FREE RIFLE (TEAM)
1906 Switzerland 4596
1908 Norway 5055
1912 Sweden 5655
1920 USA 4876
1924 USA 676

MILITARY RIFLE
1900 Emil Kellenberger (Swi) 930: Three positions (300m)
1900 Lars Madsen (Den) 305: Standing (300m)
1900 Konrad Stäheli (Swi) 324: Kneeling (300m)
1900 Achille Paroche (Fra) 332: Prone (300m)
1906 Léon Moreaux (Fra) 187: Standing or kneeling (200m)
1906 Louis Richardet (Swi) 238: Standing or kneeling (300m)
1912 Sándor Prokopp (Hun) 97: Three positions (300m)
1912 Paul Colas (Fra) 94: Any position (600m)
1920 Otto Olsen (Nor) 60: Prone (300m)
1920 Carl Osburn (USA) 56: Standing (300m)
1920 Hugo Johansson (Swe) 59: Prone (600m)

MILITARY RIFLE (TEAM)
1900 Switzerland 4399: (300m)
1908 USA 2531: (200, 500, 600, 800, 900, 1000yd)
1912 USA 1687: (200, 400, 500, 600m)
1920 Denmark 266: Standing (300m)
1920 USA 289: Prone (300m)
1920 USA 287: Prone (600m)
1920 USA 573: Prone (300m & 600m)

SMALL BORE RIFLE
1908 J F Fleming (UK) 24: Moving target
1908 William Styles (UK) 45: Disappearing target
1912 Wilhelm Carlberg (Swe) 242: Disappearing target

SMALL BORE RIFLE (TEAM)
1908 United Kingdom 771: (50 & 100yd)
1912 Sweden 925: (25m)
1912 United Kingdom 762: (50m)
1920 USA 1899: (50m)

LIVE PIGEON SHOOTING
1900 Léon de Lunden (Bel) 21

CLAY PIGEONS (TEAM)
1908 United Kingdom 407
1912 USA 532
1920 USA 547
1924 USA 363

RUNNING DEER SHOOTING
1908 Oscar Swahn (Swe) 25 *
1908 Walter Winans (USA) 46 **
1912 Alfred Swahn (Swe) 41 *
1912 Åke Lundeberg (Swe) 79 **
1920 Otto Olsen (Nor) 43 *
1920 Ole Lilloe-Olsen (Nor) 82 **
1924 John Boles (USA) 40 *
1924 Ole Lilloe-Olsen (Nor) 76 **
* Single shot
** Double shot

RUNNING DEER SHOOTING (TEAM)
1908 Sweden 86
1912 Sweden 151
1920 Norway 178 *
1920 Norway 343 **
1924 Norway 160 *
1924 United Kingdom 263 **
* Single shot
** Double shot

RUNNING DEER SHOOTING
(Single and double shot)
1952 John Larsen (Nor) 413
1956 Vitaliy Romanenko (USSR) 441

MILITARY REVOLVER
1896 John Paine (USA) 442: (25m)
1906 Louis Richardet (Swi) 253: (20m)
1906 Jean Fouconnier (Fra) 219 *
* Model 1873

TEAM EVENT
1900 Switzerland 2271
1908 USA 1914
1912 USA 1916 *
1912 Sweden 1145 **
1920 USA 2372 *
1920 USA 1310 **
* Over 50m ** Over 30m

DUELLING PISTOL
1906 Léon Moreaux (Fra) 242: Over 20m
1906 Konstantinos Skarlatos (Gre) 133: Over 25m

MOST OLYMPIC MEDALS
(Min. 4 golds)

Total		Gold	Silver	Bronze	Years
11	Carl Osburn (USA)	5	4	2	1912-24
8	Konrad Stäheli (Swi)	5	2	1	1900
8	Otto Olsen (Nor)	4	3	1	1920-4
7	Gudbrand Skatteboe (Nor)	4	3	-	1906-20
7	Willis Lee (USA)	5	1	1	1920
7	Lloyd Spooner (USA)	4	1	2	1920
7	Einer Liberg (Nor)	4	2	1	1908-24
6	Louis Richardet (Swi)	5	1	-	1900
6	Ole Lilloe-Olsen (Nor)	5	1	-	1920-4
6	Alfred Lane (USA)	5	-	1	1912-20
5	Morris Fisher (USA)	5	-	-	1920-4

Most medals (woman): 2 (1 gold, 1 bronze) Xiaoxuan Wi (Chn), 1984
Most individual gold medals: 3 Gudbrand Skatteboe (Nor) 1906

Oscar Swahn (Swe) was aged 64 years 258 days when he won a gold medal in the team running deer event in 1912 to become the oldest gold medallist in Olympic history. He became the oldest ever Olympic competitor, and indeed medallist, in 1920 when he appeared in Sweden's silver medal winning team, again in the running deer event. He qualified for the 1924 Games, but illness prevented him competing.

WORLD RECORDS
MEN
FREE RIFLE

(Three positions; 3 x 40 shots at 300m)

Score	Maximum		Venue	Date
1166	1200	Malcolm Cooper (UK)	Zürich	7 Jun 1987

(Prone; 60 shots at 300m)

599	600	Malcolm Cooper (UK)	Skouder	28 Aug 1986

STANDARD RIFLE
(Three positions; 3 x 20 shots at 300m)

583	600	Malcolm Cooper (UK)	Zürich	8 Jun 1985

SMALLBORE RIFLE
(Three positions; 3 x 40 shots at 50m)

1175	1200	Kiril Ivanov (USSR)	Osijek	11 Sep 1985

(Prone; 60 shots at 50m)

600	600	Alistair Allan (UK)	Titograd	21 Sep 1981
600	600	Ernest van de Zande (USA)	Rio de Janeiro	10 Nov 1981
600	600	five men	Suhl	10 Sep 1986
600	600	Gale Stewart (Can)	Zürich	5 Jun 1987

FREE PISTOL
(60 shots at 50m)

581	600	Aleksandr Melentev (USSR)	Moscow	20 Jul 1980

RAPID FIRE PISTOL
(60 shots at 25m)

599	600	Igor Puzryev (USSR)	Titograd	21 Sep 1981

CENTRE FIRE PISTOL
(60 shots at 25m)

597	600	Thomas D.Smith (USA)	Sao Paulo	20 Apr 1963

STANDARD PISTOL
(60 shots at 25m)

584	600	Eric Buljong (USA)	Caracas	20 Aug 1983

RUNNING GAME TARGET
(60 shots at 50m with small bore rifle)

595	600	Igor Sokolov (USSR)	Miskulc	9 Aug 1981

OLYMPIC TRAP
(200 birds)

200	200	Danny Carlisle (USA)	Caracas	21 Aug 1983

OLYMPIC SKEET
(200 birds)

200	200	Matthew Dryke (USA)	Sao Paulo	11 Nov 1981
200	200	Jan Hula (Cs)	Zaragossa	16 Jun 1984

AIR RIFLE
(60 shots at 10m)

596	600	Jean-Pierre Amat (Fra)	Zürich	5 Jun 1987

AIR PISTOL
(60 shots at 10m)

591	600	Vladas Tourla (USSR)	Caracas	20 Aug 1983

WOMEN

STANDARD RIFLE
(Three positions; 3 x 20 shots at 50m)

592	600	Marlies Helbig (GDR)	Titograd	17 Sep 1981

(Prone; 60 shots at 50m)

598	600	Eulalia Rolinska (Pol)	Suhl	28 Aug 1971
598	600	Margaret Murdock (USA)	Thun	21 Sep 1974
598	600	Nonka Matova (Bul)	Osijek	8 Sep 1985
598	600	Eva Forian (Hun)	Suhl	9 Sep 1986

SMALLBORE SPORT PISTOL
(60shots at 25m)

594	600	Silvia Kaposztai (Rom)	Osijek	6 Sep 1985

OLYMPIC TRAP
(200 birds)

195	200	Susan Nattrass (Can)	Seoul	4 Oct 1978

OLYMPIC SKEET
(200 birds)

197	200	Svetlana Yakimova (USSR)	Zaragossa	16 Jun 1984

AIR RIFLE
(40 shots at 10m)

395	400	Anna Malekhova (USSR)	The Hague	18 Mar 1982
395	400	Marlies Helbig (GDR)	Innsbruck	22 Sep 1983

AIR PISTOL
(40 shots at 10m)

387	400	Nina Stolyarova (USSR)	Enschede	23 Feb 1974
387	400	Marina Dobrancheva (USSR)	Varna	2 Mar 1985
387	400	Anke Völker (GDR)	Suhl	9 Sep 1986

SKIING

The word *ski* was the Norwegian word for snow-shoe. The earliest ski, recovered from a peat bog in Sweden, has been dated as c.2500 BC. It is 1.1m long and c.20cm wide. Long skis over 2m in length were used in Norway about 4000 years ago, and both long and short skis have been widely used in Scandinavian countries.

In modern times two main categories of skiing have evolved, Nordic, which encompasses cross-country and ski-jumping, and Alpine, which has downhill and slalom events. The first ski races were held in Norway and Australia in the 1850s and 1860s. The first national governing body was that of Norway, formed in 1883, public imagination being caught by the epic Greenland trek using skis of the great Norwegian explorer Fridtjof Nansen in 1888.

Alpine skiing was introduced by British enthusiasts in Switzerland in the 1880s. Sir Henry Lunn pioneered skiing holidays and his son Sir Arnold Lunn introduced the modern slalom event.

The International Ski Federation (FIS) was founded in 1924 to succeed the International Skiing Commission, founded in Oslo in 1910.

See also *Biathlon* for the results of combined skiing and shooting.

ALPINE SKIING

OLYMPIC GAMES

Alpine events were first included at the Olympic Games in 1936.

Winners:

MEN'S ALPINE COMBINATION
downhill and slalom
1936 Franz Pfnür (Ger)
1948 Henri Oreiller (Fra)

MEN'S DOWNHILL
1948 Henri Oreiller (Fra)
1952 Zeno Colo (Ita)
1956 Toni Sailer (Aut)
1960 Jean Vuarnet (Fra)
1964 Egon Zimmermann (Aut)
1968 Jean-Claude Killy (Fra)
1972 Bernhard Russi (Swi)
1976 Franz Klammer (Aut)
1980 Leonhard Stock (Aut)
1984 William Johnson (USA)

MEN'S GIANT SLALOM
1952 Stein Eriksen (Nor)
1956 Toni Sailer (Aut)
1960 Roger Staub (Swi)
1964 Francois Bonlieu (Fra)
1968 Jean-Claude Killy (Fra)
1972 Gustavo Thoeni (Ita)
1976 Heini Hemmi (Swi)

Franz Klammer, the greatest downhill racer (All-Sport)

1980 Ingemar Stenmark (Swe)
1984 Max Julen (Swi)

MEN'S SLALOM
1948 Edy Reinalter (Swi)
1952 Othmar Schneider (Aut)
1956 Toni Sailer (Aut)
1960 Ernst Hinterseer (Aut)
1964 Josef Stiegler (Aut)
1968 Jean-Claude Killy (Fra)
1972 Francisco Fernandez Ochoa (Spa)
1976 Piero Gros (Ita)
1980 Ingemar Stenmark (Swe)
1984 Phil Mahre (USA)

WOMEN'S ALPINE COMBINATION
downhill and slalom
1936 Christel Cranz (Ger)
1948 Trude Beiser (Aut)

WOMEN'S DOWNHILL
1948 Hedy Schlunegger (Swi)
1952 Trude Jochum (née Beiser) (Aut)
1956 Madeleine Berthod (Swi)
1960 Heidi Biebl (FRG)
1964 Christl Haas (Aut)
1968 Olga Pall (Aut)

1972 Marie-Thérèse Nadig (Swi)
1976 Rosi Mittermaier (FRG)
1980 Annemarie Moser-Pröll (Aut)
1984 Michela Figini (Swi)

WOMEN'S GIANT SLALOM
1952 Andrea Mead-Lawrence (USA)
1956 Ossi Reichert (FRG)
1960 Yvonne Rüegg (Swi)
1964 Marielle Goitschel (Fra)
1968 Nancy Greene (Can)
1972 Marie-Thérèse Nadig (Swi)
1976 Kathy Kreiner (Can)
1980 Hanni Wenzel (Lie)
1984 Debbie Armstrong (USA)

WOMEN'S SLALOM
1948 Gretchen Fraser (USA)
1952 Andrea Mead-Lawrence (USA)
1956 Renée Colliard (Swi)
1960 Anne Heggtveit (Can)
1964 Christine Goitschel (Fra)
1968 Marielle Goitschel (Fra)
1972 Barbara Cochran (USA)
1976 Rosi Mittermaier (FRG)
1980 Hanni Wenzel (Lie)
1984 Paoletta Magoni (Ita)

MOST OLYMPIC MEDALS
Four: Hanni Wenzel (Lie) two gold, a silver and a bronze 1976-80.

Three gold medals: Toni Sailer (Aut) 1956, Jean-Claude Killy (Fra) 1968.

WORLD CHAMPIONSHIPS
First held at downhill in 1931 at Mürren. Held annually 1931-9 and bienially post-war. Up to 1980 the Olympic Champions were also world champions, except in 1936 when separate championships were held.

Listed for each event are post-war winners additional to those shown earlier as Olympic Champions and those to have won most titles (including Olympics shown by *):

MEN'S ALPINE COMBINED
1954 Stein Eriksen (Nor)
1956 Toni Sailer (Aut)
1958 Toni Sailer (Aut)
1960 Guy Périllat (Fra)
1962 Karl Schranz (Aut)
1964 Ludwig Leitner (FRG)
1966 Jean-Claude Killy (Fra)
1968 Jean-Claude Killy (Fra)
1970 Bill Kidd (USA)
1972 Gustavo Thoeni (Ita)
1974 Franz Klammer (Aut)
1976 Gustavo Thoeni (Ita)
1978 Andrea Wenzel (Lie)
1980 Phil Mahre (USA)
1982 Michel Vion (Fra)
1985 Pirmin Zurbriggen (Swi)

Ingemar Stenmark, the most successful slalom skier (All-Sport)

1987 Marc Girardelli (Lux)

Most wins: 2 Anton Seelos (Aut) 1933, 1935; Emile Allais (Fra) 1937-8; Sailer, Killy, Thoeni.

MEN'S DOWNHILL
1950 Zeno Colo (Ita)
1954 Christian Pravda (Aut)
1958 Toni Sailer (Aut)
1962 Karl Schranz (Aut)
1966 Jean-Claude Killy (Fra)
1970 Bernhard Russi (Swi)
1974 David Zwilling (Aut)
1978 Josef Walcher (Aut)
1982 Harti Weirather (Aut)
1985 Pirmin Zurbriggen (Swi)
1987 Peter Müller (Swi)

Most wins: 2 Walter Prager (Swi) 1931, 1933; each also one *: Colo, Sailer, Killy, Russi.

MEN'S GIANT SLALOM
1950 Zeno Colo (Ita)
1954 Stein Eriksen (Nor)
1958 Toni Sailer (Aut)
1962 Egon Zimmermann (Aut)
1966 Guy Périllat (Fra)
1970 Karl Schranz (Aut)
1974 Gustavo Thoeni (Ita)
1978 Ingemar Stenmark (Swe)
1982 Steve Mahre (USA)
1985 Markus Wasmaier (FRG)
1987 Pirmin Zurbriggen (Swi)

*Most wins (each also one *):* 2 Eriksen, Sailer, Thoeni, Stenmark

MEN'S SLALOM
1950 Georges Schneider (Swi)
1954 Stein Eriksen (Nor)
1958 Josef Rieder (Aut)
1962 Charles Bozon (Fra)
1966 Carlo Senoner (Ita)
1970 Jean-Noël Augert (Fra)
1974 Gustavo Thoeni (Ita)
1978 Ingemar Stenmark (Swe)
1982 Ingemar Stenmark (Swe)
1985 Jonas Nilsson (Swe)
1987 Frank Wörndl (FRG)

Most wins: 3 Ingemar Stenmark (Swe) also 1980*

MEN'S SUPER-GIANT SLALOM
1987 Pirmin Zurbriggen (Swi)

WOMEN'S ALPINE COMBINATION
1954 Ida Schöpfer (Swi)
1956 Madeleine Berthod (Swi)
1958 Frieda Dänzer (Swi)
1960 Anne Heggtveit (Can)
1962 Marielle Goitschel (Fra)
1964 Marielle Goitschel (Fra)
1966 Marielle Goitschel (Fra)
1968 Nancy Greene (Can)
1970 Michèle Jacot (Fra)
1972 Annemarie Pröll (Aut)
1974 Fabienne Serrat (Fra)
1976 Rosi Mittermaier (FRG)
1978 Annemarie Moser-Pröll (Aut)

1980 Hanni Wenzel (Lie)
1982 Erika Hess (Swi)
1985 Erika Hess (Swi)
1987 Erika Hess (Swi)

Most wins: 5 Christl Cranz (Ger) 1934-5, 1937-9; 3 Marielle Goitschel, Erika Hess.

WOMEN'S DOWNHILL
1950 Trude Beiser-Jochum (Aut)
1954 Ida Schöpfer (Swi)
1958 Lucille Wheeler (Can)
1962 Christl Haas (Aut)
1966 Erika Schinegger (Aut)
1970 Annerösli Zyrd (Swi)
1974 Annemarie Moser-Pröll (Aut)
1978 Annemarie Moser-Pröll (Aut)
1982 Gerry Sorensen (Can)
1985 Michela Figini (Swi)
1987 Maria Walliser (Swi)

Most wins: 3 Christl Cranz (Ger) 1935, 1937, 1939; Moser-Pröll also 1980*

WOMEN'S GIANT SLALOM
1950 Dagmar Rom (Aut)
1954 Lucienne Schmitt (Fra)
1958 Lucille Wheeler (Can)
1962 Marianne Jahn (Aut)
1966 Marielle Goitschel (Fra)
1970 Betsy Clifford (Can)
1974 Fabienne Serrat (Fra)
1978 Maria Epple (FRG)
1982 Erika Hess (Swi)
1985 Diann Roffe (USA)
1987 Vreni Schneider (Swi)

Most wins: 2 Marielle Goitschel also 1964*

WOMEN'S SLALOM
1950 Dagmar Rom (Aut)
1954 Trude Klecker (Aut)
1958 Inger Björnbakken (Nor)
1962 Marianne Jahn (Aut)
1966 Annie Famose (Fra)
1970 Ingrid Lafforgue (Fra)
1974 Hanni Wenzel (Lie)
1978 Lea Sölkner (Aut)
1982 Erika Hess (Swi)
1985 Perrine Pelen (Fra)
1987 Erika Hess (Swi)

Most wins: 4 Christl Cranz (Ger) 1934, 1937-9

WOMEN'S SUPER-GIANT SLALOM
1987 Maria Walliser (FRG)

MOST WINS ALL EVENTS
MEN 7 Toni Sailer (Aut), 6 Jean-Claude Killy (Fra)
WOMEN 12 Christl Cranz (Ger) - and the 1936 Olympic combined; 6 Marielle Goitschel, Erika Hess
All four titles have been won in one year by Sailer 1956 and Killy 1968.

ALPINE SKIING WORLD CUPS

Contested annually from 1967 over a series of events during the winter season. The year given is that of the second half of the season.

Winners:

MEN'S OVERALL
1967-8 Jean-Claude Killy (Fra)
1969-70 Karl Schranz (Aut)
1971-3 Gustavo Thoeni (Ita)
1974 Piero Gros (Ita)
1975 Gustavo Thoeni (Ita)
1976-8 Ingemar Stenmark (Swe)
1979 Peter Lüscher (Swi)
1980 Andreas Wenzel (Lie)
1981-3 Phil Mahre (USA)
1984 Pirmin Zurbriggen (Swi)
1985-6 Marc Girardelli (Lux)
1987 Pirmin Zurbriggen (Swi)

Most: 4 Thoeni; 3 Stenmark, Mahre

MEN'S DOWNHILL
1967 Jean-Claude Killy (Fra)
1968 Gerhard Nenning (Aut)
1969 Karl Schranz (Aut)
1970 Karl Schranz (Aut) & Karl Cordin (Aut)
1971-2 Bernhard Russi (Swi)
1973-4 Roland Collombin (Swi)
1975-8 Franz Klammer (Aut)
1979-80 Peter Müller (Swi)
1981 Harti Weirather (Aut)
1982 Steve Podborski (Can) & Peter Müller (Swi)
1983 Franz Klammer (Aut)
1984 Urs Räber (Swi)
1985 Helmut Höhlehner (Aut)
1986 Peter Wirnsberger (Aut)
1987 Pirmin Zurbriggen (Swi)

Most: 5 Klammer

MEN'S GIANT SLALOM
1967-8 Jean-Claude Killy (Fra)
1969 Karl Schranz (Aut)
1970 Gustavo Thoeni (Ita)
1971 Gustavo Thoeni (Ita) & Patrick Russel (Fra)
1972 Gustavo Thoeni (Ita)
1973 Hans Hinterseer (Aut)
1974 Piero Gros (Aut)
1975-6 Ingemar Stenmark (Swe)
1977 Heini Hemmi (Swi)
1978-81 Ingemar Stenmark (Swe)
1982-3 Phil Mahre (USA)
1984 Ingemar Stenmark (Swe)
1985 Marc Girardelli (Lux)
1986 Joel Gaspoz (Swi)
1987 Pirmin Zurbriggen (Swi)

Most: 7 Stenmark

MEN'S SLALOM
1967 Jean-Claude Killy (Fra)
1968 Dumeng Giovanoli (Swi)
1969 Alfred Matt (Aut), Alain Penz (Fra), Jean-Noël Augert (Fra), Patrick Russel (Fra)
1970 Patrick Russel & Alain Penz (Fra)
1971-2 Jean-Noël Augert (Fra)
1973-4 Gustavo Thoeni (Ita)
1975-81 Ingemar Stenmark (Swe)
1982 Phil Mahre (USA)
1983 Ingemar Stenmark (Swe)
1984-5 Marc Girardelli (Lux)

1986 Rok Petrovic (Yug)
1987 Bojan Krizaj (Yug)

Most: 8 Stenmark

MEN'S SUPER-GIANT SLALOM
1986 Markus Wasmeier (FRG)
1987 Pirmin Zurbriggen (Swi)

WOMEN'S OVERALL
1967-8 Nancy Greene (Can)
1969 Gertrud Gabl (Aut)
1970 Michèle Jacot (Fra)
1971-5 Annemarie Moser-Pröll (Aut)
1976 Rosi Mittermaier (FRG)
1977 Lise-Marie Morerod (Swi)
1978 Hanni Wenzel (Lie)
1979 Annemarie Moser-Pröll (Aut)
1980 Hanni Wenzel (Lie)
1981 Marie-Thérèse Nadig (Swi)
1982 Erika Hess (Swi)
1983 Tamara McKinney (USA)
1984 Erika Hess (Swi)
1985 Michela Figini (Swi)
1986-7 Maria Walliser (Swi)

Most: 6 Moser-Pröll

WOMEN'S DOWNHILL
1967 Marielle Goitschel (Fra)
1968 Isabelle Mir (Fra) & Olga Pall (Aut)
1969 Wiltrud Drexel (Aut)
1970 Isabelle Mir (Fra)
1971-5 Annemarie Moser-Pröll (Aut)
1976-7 Brigitte Habersatter-Totschnig (Aut)
1978-9 Annemarie Moser-Pröll (Aut)
1980-1 Marie-Thérèse Nadig (Swi)
1982 Cécile Gros-Gaudenier (Fra)
1983 Doris De Agostini (Swi)
1984 Maria Walliser (Swi)
1985 Michela Figini (Swi)
1986 Maria Walliser (Swi)
1987 Michela Figini (Swi)

Most: 7 Moser-Pröll

WOMEN'S GIANT SLALOM
1967-8 Nancy Greene (Can)
1969 Marilyn Cochran (USA)
1970 Michèle Jacot & Francoise Macchi (Fra)
1971-2 Annemarie Moser-Pröll (Aut)
1973 Monika Kaserer (Aut)
1974 Hanni Wenzel (Lie)
1975 Annemarie Moser-Pröll (Aut)
1976 Rosi Mittermaier (FRG)
1977-8 Lise-Marie Morerod (Swi)
1979 Christa Kinshoffer (Aut)
1980 Hanni Wenzel (Lie)
1981 Tamara McKinney (USA)
1982 Irene Epple (FRG)
1983 Tamara McKinney (USA)
1984 Erika Hess (Swi)
1985 Michela Figini (Swi) & Marina Kiehl (FRG)
1986 Vreni Schneider (Swi)
1987 Maria Walliser (Swi) & Vreni Schneider (Swi)

Most: 3 Moser-Pröll

WOMEN'S SLALOM

1967 Marielle Goitschel & Annie Famose (Fra)
1968 Annie Famose (Fra)
1969 Gertrud Gabl (Aut)
1970 Ingrid Lafforgue (Fra)
1971 Britt Lafforgue (Fra) & Betsy Clifford (Can)
1972 Britt Lafforgue (Fra)
1973 Patricia Emonet (Fra)
1974 Christa Zechmeister (FRG)
1975-7 Lise-Marie Morerod (Swi)
1978 Hanni Wenzel (Lie)
1979 Regina Sackl (Aut)
1980 Perrine Pelen (Fra)
1981-3 Erika Hess (Swi)
1984 Tamara McKinney (USA)
1985 Erika Hess (Swi)
1986 Roswitha Steiner (Aut)
1987 Corinne Schmidhauser (Swi)

Most: 4 Hess

WOMEN'S SUPER-GIANT SLALOM

1986 Marina Kiehl (FRG)
1987 Maria Walliser (Swi)

MOST WINS

The most wins in World Cup events is 85 by Ingemar Stenmark (Swe) 1974-87. Franz Klammer (Aut) won a record 35 downhill races, 1974-85. Stenmark won a record 13 World Cup races in a season, 1979. The next bests: Jean-Claude Killy (Fra) 12 in 1967, Pirmin Zurbriggen 11 in 1987. The women's career record is 62 by Annemarie Moser (Aut), 1970-9.

NATIONS' CUP

Awarded on the overall results for men and women obtained in the World Cup.

Wins:
11 Austria 1969, 1973-82
 5 France 1967-8, 1970-2
 5 Switzerland 1983-7

HIGHEST SPEED

The highest speed claimed for a skier is 212.514 km/h by Graham Wilkie (UK) on 17 Apr 1987 and the fastest by a woman is 201.005 km/h by Jacqueline Blanc (Fra) on 19 Apr 1987, both at Les Arcs, France.

NORDIC SKIING

OLYMPIC GAMES

The first Winter Olympic Games, held at Chamonix in 1924, included Nordic skiing events, and they have been included on the programme ever since.

Winners:

MEN'S 15 KM CROSS-COUNTRY

Held at 18km 1924, 1936-52, 19.7km 1928, 18.214km 1932
1924 Thorleif Haug (Nor) 1:14:31

Erika Hess (All-Sport)

1928 Johan Grøttumsbraaten (Nor) 1:37:01
1932 Sven Utterström (Swe) 1:23:07
1936 Erik-August Larsson (Swe) 1:14:38
1948 Martin Lundström (Swe) 1:13:50
1952 Hallgeir Brenden (Nor) 1:01:34
1956 Hallgeir Brenden (Nor) 49:39.0
1960 Haakon Brusveen (Nor) 51:55.5
1964 Eero Mäntyranta (Fin) 50:54.1
1968 Harald Grønningen (Nor) 47:54.2
1972 Sven-Åke Lundback (Swe) 45:28.24
1976 Nikolay Bayukov (USSR) 43:58.47
1980 Thomas Wassberg (Swe) 41:57.63
1984 Gunde Svan (Swe) 41:25.6

MEN'S 30 KM CROSS-COUNTRY
1956 Veikko Hakulinen (Fin) 1:44:06.0
1960 Sixten Jernberg (Swe) 1:51:03.9
1964 Eero Mäntyranta (Fin) 1:30:50.7
1968 Franco Nones (Ita) 1:35:39.2
1972 Vyacheslav Vedenin (USSR) 1:36:31.2
1976 Sergey Savelyev (USSR) 1:30:29.38
1980 Nikolay Zimyatov (USSR) 1:27:02.80
1984 Nikolay Zimyatov (USSR) 1:28:56.3

MEN'S 50 KM CROSS-COUNTRY
1924 Thorleif Haug (Nor) 3:44:32
1928 Per-Erik Hedlund (Swe) 4:52:03
1932 Veli Saarinen (Fin) 4:28:00
1936 Elis Wiklund (Swe) 3:30:11
1948 Nils Karlsson (Swe) 3:47:48
1952 Veikko Hakulinen (Fin) 3:33:33
1956 Sixten Jernberg (Swe) 2:50:27
1960 Kalevi Hämäläinen (Fin) 2:59:06.3
1964 Sixten Jernberg (Swe) 2:43:52.6
1968 Ole Ellefsaeter (Nor) 2:28:45.8
1972 Pål Tyldum (Nor) 2:43:14.75
1976 Ivar Formo (Nor) 2:37:30.50
1980 Nikolay Zimyatov (USSR) 2:27:24.60
1984 Thomas Wassberg (Swe) 2:15:55.8

MEN'S 4 × 10 KM CROSS-COUNTRY RELAY
1936 Finland 2:41:33
1948 Sweden 2:32:08
1952 Finland 2:20:16
1956 USSR 2:15:30
1960 Finland 2:18:45.6
1964 Sweden 2:18:34.6
1968 Norway 2:08:33.5
1972 USSR 2:04:47.94
1976 Finland 2:07:59.72
1980 USSR 1:57:03.46
1984 Sweden 1:55:06.30

MEN'S SKI JUMPING – 70 METRE HILL
1924 Jacob Tullin Thams (Nor)
1928 Alf Andersen (Nor)
1932 Birger Ruud (Nor)
1936 Birger Ruud (Nor)
1948 Petter Hugstedt (Nor)
1952 Arnfinn Bergmann (Nor)
1956 Anti Hyvärinen (Fin)
1960 Helmut Recknagel (GDR)
1964 Viekko Kankkonen (Fin)
1968 Jiri Raska (Cs)
1972 Yukio Kasaya (Jap)
1976 Hans-Georg Aschenbach (GDR)

Matti Nykänen (All-Sport)

1980 Toni Innauer (Aut)
1984 Jens Weissflog (GDR)

MEN'S SKI JUMPING – 90 METRE HILL
1964 Toralf Engan (Nor)
1968 Vladimir Byeloussov (USSR)
1972 Wojciech Fortuna (Pol)
1976 Karl Schnabl (Aut)
1980 Jouko Törmänen (Fin)
1984 Matti Nykänen (Fin)

MEN'S NORDIC COMBINED – SKIING AND JUMPING
1924 Thorleif Haug (Nor)
1928 Johan Grøttumsbraaten (Nor)
1932 Johan Grøttumsbraaten (Nor)
1936 Oddbjörn Hagen (Nor)
1948 Heikki Hasu (Fin)
1952 Simon Slåttvik (Nor)
1956 Sverre Stenersen (Nor)

1960 Georg Thoma (FRG)
1964 Tormod Knutsen (Nor)
1968 Franz Keller (FRG)
1972 Ulrich Wehling (GDR)
1976 Ulrich Wehling (GDR)
1980 Ulrich Wehling (GDR)
1984 Tom Sandberg (Nor)

WOMEN'S 5 KM CROSS-COUNTRY
1964 Klaudia Boyarskikh (USSR) 17:50.5
1968 Toini Gustafsson (Swe) 16:45.2
1972 Galina Kulakova (USSR) 17:00.50
1976 Helena Takalo (Fin) 15:48.69
1980 Raisa Smetanina (USSR) 15:06.92
1984 Marja-Liisa Hämäläinen (Fin) 17:04.0

WOMEN'S 10 KM CROSS-COUNTRY
1952 Lydia Wideman (Fin) 41:40.0
1956 Lyubov Kozyryeva (USSR) 38:11.0
1960 Maria Gusakova (USSR) 39:46.6
1964 Klaudia Boyarskikh (USSR) 40:24.3
1968 Toini Gustafsson (Swe) 36:46.5
1972 Galina Kulakova (USSR) 34:17.8
1976 Raisa Smetanina (USSR) 30:13.41
1980 Barbara Petzold (GDR) 30:31.54
1984 Marja-Liisa Hämäläinen (Fin) 31:44.2

WOMEN'S 20 KM CROSS-COUNTRY
1984 Marja-Liisa Hämäläinen (Fin) 1:01:45.0

WOMEN'S 4 × 5 KM CROSS-COUNTRY RELAY
1956 Finland 1:09:01.0
1960 Sweden 1:04:21.4
1964 USSR 59:20.2
1968 Norway 57:30.0
1972 USSR 48:46.15
1976 USSR 1:07:49.75
1980 GDR 1:02:11.10
1984 Norway 1:06:49.70

MOST OLYMPIC MEDALS

	Gold	Silver	Bronze	
9 Sixten Jernberg (Swe)	4	3	2	1956-64
8 Galina Kulakova (USSR)	4	2	2	1968-80
7 Veikko Hakulinen (Fin)	3	3	1	1952-60
7 Eero Mäntyranta (Fin)	3	2	2	1960-8
7 Raisa Smetanina (USSR)	3	4	-	1976-84
6 Johan Grøttumsbraaten (Nor)	3	1	2	1924-32

Also three gold medals: Ulrich Wehling (GDR) 1972-80, Marja-Liisa Hämäläinen (Fin), who also won a bronze at the relay, all in 1984.

WORLD CHAMPIONSHIPS

After Nordic events had been included in the 1924 Olympics, the FIS organised annual competitions until 1937, when for the first time they were given official world championship status. Held annually until 1939, but bienially post-war. Up to 1980 the Olympic Champions were also world champions.

With the advent of new technique, the men's cross-country races are now at 15km and 30km classical, and at 50km freestyle.

Listed for each event are post-war winners additional to those shown earlier as Olympic Champions and those to have won most titles (including Olympics shown by *):

MEN'S 15 KM CROSS-COUNTRY
1950 Karl Erik Äström (Swe)
1954 Veikko Hakulinen (Fin)
1958 Veikko Hakulinen (Fin)
1962 Assar Rönnlund (Swe)
1966 Gjermund Eggen (Nor)
1970 Lars-Göran Åslund (Swe)
1974 Magne Myrmo (Nor)
1978 Josef Luszczek (Pol)
1982 Oddvar Brå (Nor)
1985 Kari Härkönen (Fin)
1987 Marco Albarello (Ita)

Most wins: 2 Johan Gröttumsbraaten (Nor) 1928*, 1931; Hallgeir Brendan 1952*, 1956*; Veikko Hakulinen.

MEN'S 30 KM CROSS-COUNTRY
1954 Vladimir Kusin (USSR)
1958 Kalevi Hämäläinen (Fin)
1962 Eero Mäntyranta (Fin)
1966 Eero Mäntyranta (Fin)
1970 Vyacheslav Vedenin (USSR)
1974 Thomas Magnuson (Swe)
1978 Sergey Savelyev (USSR)
1982 Thomas Eriksson (Swe)
1985 Gunde Svan (Swe)
1987 Thomas Wassberg (Swe)

Most wins: 3 Eero Mäntyranta (Fin) also 1964*

MEN'S 50 KM CROSS-COUNTRY
1950 Gunnar Eriksson (Swe)
1954 Vladimir Kusin (USSR)
1958 Sixten Jernberg (Swe)
1962 Sixten Jernberg (Swe)
1966 Gjermund Eggen (Nor)
1970 Kalevi Oikarainen (Fin)
1974 Gerhard Grimmer (GDR)
1978 Sven-Åke Lundbäck (Swe)
1982 Thomas Wassberg (Swe)
1985 Gunde Svan (Swe)
1987 Maurilio De Zolt (Ita)

Most wins: 4 Sixten Jernberg (Swe) also 1956*, 1964*

MEN'S 4 × 10 KM CROSS-COUNTRY RELAY
Wins including Olympics (*):
9 Finland 1934-5, 1938-9, 1954 and 4*
8 Sweden 1933, 1950, 1958, 1962, 1978, 1987 and 2*
5 Norway 1937, 1966, 1982 tie, 1985 and 1*
5 USSR 1970, 1982 tie and 3*
1 GDR 1974

MEN'S SKI JUMPING – 70 METRES
1950 Hans Bjornstad (Nor)
1954 Matti Pietikäinen (Fin)

1958 Juhanni Kärkinen (Fin)
1962 Toralf Engan (Nor)
1966 Björn Wirkola (Nor)
1970 Gariy Napalkov (USSR)
1974 Hans-Georg Aschenbach (GDR)
1978 Mathias Buse (GDR)
1982 Armin Kogler (Aut)
1985 Jens Weissflog (GDR)
1987 Jiri Parma (Cs)

Most wins: 5 Birger Ruud (Nor) 1931, 1932*, 1935, 1936*, 1937.

MEN'S SKI JUMPING – 90 METRE HILL
1962 Helmut Recknagel (GDR)
1966 Bjöurn Wirkola (Nor)
1970 Gariy Napalkov (USSR)
1974 Hans-Georg Aschenbach (GDR)
1978 Tapio Räisänen (Fin)
1982 Matti Nykänen (Fin)
1985 Per Bergerud (Nor)
1987 Andreas Felder (Aut)
Most wins: 1 each

MEN'S TEAM SKI JUMPING
1982 Norway
1985 Finland
1987 Finland

MEN'S NORDIC COMBINED
1950 Heikki Hasu (Fin)
1954 Sverre Stenersen (Nor)
1958 Paavo Korhonen (Fin)
1962 Arne Larsen (Nor)
1966 Georg Thoma (FRG)
1970 Ladislav Rygel (Cs)
1974 Ulrich Wehling (GDR)
1978 Konrad Winkler (GDR)
1982 Tom Sandberg (Nor)
1985 Hermann Weinbuch (FRG)
1987 Torbjørn Løkken (Nor)

Most wins: 4 Johan Grøttumsbraaten (Nor) 1926, 1928*, 1931, 1932*; 4 Ulrich Wehling with 3*; 3 Oddbjörn Hagen (Nor) 1934-5, 1936*.

MEN'S TEAM NORDIC COMBINED
1982 GDR
1985 FR Germany
1987 FR Germany

WOMEN'S 5 KM CROSS-COUNTRY
1962 Alevtina Koltschina (USSR)
1966 Alevtina Koltschina (USSR)
1970 Galina Kulakova (USSR)
1974 Galina Kulakova (USSR)
1978 Helena Takalo (Fin)
1982 Berit Aunli (Nor)
1985 Anette Böe (Nor)
1987 Marjo Matikainen (Fin)

Most wins: 3 Galina Kulakova also 1972*

WOMEN'S 10 KM CROSS-COUNTRY
1954 Lyubov Kozyryeva (USSR)
1958 Alevtina Koltschina (USSR)
1962 Alevtina Koltschina (USSR)
1966 Klaudia Boyarskikh (USSR)
1970 Alevtina Olyunina (USSR)

1974 Galina Kulakova (USSR)
1978 Zinaida Amosova (USSR)
1982 Berit Aunli (Nor)
1985 Anette Böe (Nor)
1987 Anne Jahren (Nor)

Most wins: 2 Kozyryeva also 1956*, Koltschina, Kulakova also 1972*

WOMEN'S 20 KM CROSS-COUNTRY
1978 Zinaida Amosova (USSR)
1980 Veronika Hesse (GDR)
1982 Raisa Smetanina (USSR)
1985 Grete Nykkelmo (Nor)
1987 Maria-Elena Westin (Swe)

WOMEN'S CROSS-COUNTRY RELAY
3 × 5KM 1954-72, 4 × 5KM from 1974
Wins including Olympics (*):
11 USSR 1954, 1958, 1962, 1966, 1970, 1974, 1985, 1987 and 3*
2 Finland 1978 and 1*
1 Sweden, Norway, GDR all *

MOST WINS – ALL EVENTS (individual/relay)
MEN
8 (5/3) Sixten Jernberg (Swe) 1956-64
6 (6/-) Johan Grøttumsbraaten (Nor) 1926-32
6 (1/5) Klaes Karppinen (Fin) 1934-9
6 (4/2) Thomas Wassberg (Swe) 1980-7

WOMEN
9 (5/4) Galina Kulakova (USSR) 1970-80
8 (4/4) Alevtina Koltschina (USSR) 1958-66
6 (3/3) Raisa Smetanina (USSR) 1974-85

Most medals: 19 Raisa Smetanina, 17 Galina Kulakova

WORLD SKI-FLYING CHAMPIONSHIPS

Held separately from the Nordic World Championships in 1972 and biennially from 1973.

Winners:
1972 Walter Steiner (Swi)
1973 Hans-Georg Aschenbach (GDR)
1975 Karel Kodejska (Cs)
1977 Walter Steiner (Swi)
1979 Armin Kogler (Aut)
1981 Jarri Puikkonen (Fin)
1983 Klaus Ostwald (GDR)
1985 Matti Nykänen (Fin)
1987 Not held

NORDIC SKIING WORLD CUPS

Contested over a series of events during the winter season.

Winners:
CROSS-COUNTRY WORLD CUP

Year	Men	Women
1979	Oddvar Brå (Nor)	Galina Kulakova (USSR)
1980	Juha Mieto (Fin)	Not held
1981	Aleksandr Zavialov (USSR)	Raisa Smetanina (USSR)
1982	Bill Koch (USA)	Berit Aunli (Nor)

1983	Aleksandr Zavialov (USSR)	Marja-Liisa Hämäläinen (Fin)
1984	Gunde Svan (Swe)	Marja-Liisa Hämäläinen (Fin)
1985	Gunde Svan (Swe)	Anette Böe (Nor)
1986	Gunde Svan (Swe)	Marjo Matikainen (Fin)
1987	Torgny Mogren (Swe)	Marjo Matikainen (Fin)

SKI JUMPING WORLD CUP	NORDIC COMBINATION WORLD CUP
1980 Hubert Neupert (Aut)	-
1981 Armin Kogler (Aut)	-
1982 Armin Kogler (Aut)	-
1983 Matti Nykänen (Fin)	Espen Andersen (Nor)
1984 Jens Weissflog (GDR)	Tom Sandberg (Nor)
1985 Matti Nykänen (Fin)	Geir Andersen (Nor)
1986 Matti Nykänen (Fin)	Hermann Weinbuch (FRG)
1987 Vegaard Opaas (Nor)	Torbjørn Løkken (Nor)

SKI JUMPING WORLD RECORDS

MEN
194m Piotr Fijas (Pol) at Planica, Yugoslavia 14 Mar 1987.

WOMEN
110m Tiina Lehtola (Fin) at Ruka, Finland 29 Mar 1981.

WORLD LOPPET
The world's most famous long distance skiing race is the Vasaloppet, contested annually by about 12,000 skiers over a distance of 89km. This race commemorates the flight in 1521 of Gustav Vasa, later King Gustavus Eriksson, from Mora to Sälen in Sweden (85.8km). He was overtaken by speedy, loyal scouts on skis and persuaded to return and lead a rebellion and become king of Sweden. This famous race, for which the fastest recorded time is 3 hr 48 min 55 sec by Bengt Hassis (Swe) in 1986, is one of a series of nine or ten great long distance races staged in various parts of the world which annually form the world loppet.

World loppet champions:
1979-80 Matti Kuosku (Swe)
1981 Sven-Åke Lundbäck (Swe)
1982-3 Lars Frykberg (Swe)
1984 Bengt Hassis (Swe)
1985 Örjan Blomquist (Swe)
1986 Konrad Hallenbarter (Swi)
1987 Örjan Blomquist (Swe)

SNOOKER
Snooker was first played at Jubbulpore, India in 1875 when Neville Chamberlain (not to be confused wth the Prime Minister of the same name) insulted a fellow officer in the Devonshire Regiment by calling him a 'Snooker' after missing an easy shot during a game of Black Pool which they were playing, but with extra coloured balls added. A 'Snooker' was the name given to a new recruit at the Woolwich Military Academy at the time. The name stuck and their new game was called Snooker. The Billiards Association was formed in 1885 and they recognised the sport's first set of rules in 1900.

EMBASSY WORLD PROFESSIONAL CHAMPIONSHIP
The first world professional championship was organised in 1926-7 and was held continuously (except for the war years) until 1952 when the professional players and the governing body, the Billiards Association & Control Club, had a disagreement. A match between Horace Lindrum (Aus) and Clark McConachy (NZ) took place in 1952, and was accorded world championship status. The professional players, however, did not recognise this as the official championship and broke away to organise their own championship, known as the professional match-play championship. This ended in 1957 and it was not until its revival, albeit on a challenge basis, in 1964 that the world championship was held again. It became a knockout event, similar to today's competition, in 1969. Current sponsors Embassy started their association with the

Joe Davis

championship in 1976 and all finals since 1977 have been played at Sheffield's Crucible Theatre.

Winners:
1927-40 Joe Davis (Eng)
1946 Joe Davis (Eng)
1947 Walter Donaldson (Sco)
1948-9 Fred Davis (Eng)
1950 Walter Donaldson (Sco)
1951 Fred Davis (Eng)
1952 Horace Lindrum(Aus)
1952-6(§) Fred Davis (Eng)
1957(§) John Pulman (Eng)
1964-8(*) John Pulman (Eng)
1969 John Spencer (Eng)
1970 Ray Reardon (Wal)
1971 John Spencer (Eng)
1972 Alex Higgins (NI)
1973-6 Ray Reardon (Wal)
1977 John Spencer (Eng)
1978 Ray Reardon (Wal)
1979 Terry Griffiths (Wal)
1980 Cliff Thorburn (Can)
1981 Steve Davis (Eng)
1982 Alex Higgins (NI)
1983-4 Steve Davis (Eng)
1985 Dennis Taylor (NI)
1986 Joe Johnson (Eng)
1987 Steve Davis (Eng)
(§) Professional match-play championship
(*) John Pulman met, and beat, seven challengers between 1964-8

HOW THE WORLD CHAMPIONS HAVE FARED

	Winner	Runner-up	Semi-finalist
Joe Davis	15	-	-
John Pulman	7	1	2
Ray Reardon	6	1	3
Fred Davis	3	6	6
Steve Davis	4	2	-
John Spencer	3	1	2
Walter Donaldson	2	3	2
Alex Higgins	2	2	3
Horace Lindrum	1	3	2
Cliff Thorburn	1	2	2
Dennis Taylor	1	1	3
Terry Griffiths	1	-	-
Joe Johnson	1	1	-

(Professional match-play records excluded)

POT BLACK

BBC Television's *Pot Black* was undoubtedly responsible for the growth of snooker in the 1970s. Although its single-frame format would not be acceptable in today's tournaments, it nevertheless took the sport to millions via the television screen. Sadly the programme was discontinued in 1986.

Winners:
1969 Ray Reardon (Wal)
1970-1 John Spencer (Eng)
1972-3 Eddie Charlton (Aus)
1974-5 Graham Miles (Eng)
1976 John Spencer (Eng)
1977 Perrie Mans (SAf)
1978 Doug Mountjoy (Wal)
1979 Ray Reardon (Wal)
1980 Eddie Charlton (Aus)
1981 Cliff Thorburn (Can)
1982-3 Steve Davis (Eng)
1984 Terry Griffiths (Wal)
1985 Doug Mountjoy (Wal)
1986 Jimmy White (Eng)

Most wins: 3 John Spencer, Eddie Charlton

BENSON & HEDGES MASTERS

One of the most prestigious events after the World Professional Championship, entry to the Benson & Hedges Masters is by invitation only to 16 leading players.

Winners:
1975 John Spencer (Eng)
1976 Ray Reardon (Wal)
1977 Doug Mountjoy (Wal)
1978 Alex Higgins (NI)
1979 Perrie Mans (SAf)
1980 Terry Griffiths (Wal)
1981 Alex Higgins (NI)
1982 Steve Davis (Eng)
1983 Cliff Thorburn (Can)
1984 Jimmy White (Eng)
1985-6 Cliff Thorburn (Can)
1987 Dennis Taylor (NI)

Most wins: 3 Cliff Thorburn

TENNENTS UNITED KINGDOM OPEN

First held at Blackpool in 1977 it was known as the United Kingdom Professional Championship until 1984 when it became open to overseas players. All finals since 1978 have been at the Preston Guildhall. Tennents sponsored the event for the first time in 1986; Super Crystalate were the first sponsors in 1977 and Corals put their name to the championship between 1978-85.

Winners:
1977 Patsy Fagan (Ire)
1978 Doug Mountjoy (Wal)
1979 John Virgo (Eng)
1980-1 Steve Davis (Eng)
1982 Terry Griffiths (Wal)
1983 Alex Higgins (NI)
1984-6 Steve Davis (Eng)
Most wins: 5 Steve Davis

BENSON & HEDGES IRISH MASTERS

The last major championship before the Embassy World Professional Championship, the Benson & Hedges Irish Masters is held at the Goff's Sales Ring in County Kildare.

Winners:
1978 John Spencer (Eng)
1979 Doug Mountjoy (Wal)
1980-2 Terry Griffiths (Wal)
1983-4 Steve Davis (Eng)

1985-6 Jimmy White (Eng)
1987 Steve Davis (Eng)

WORLD TEAM CHAMPIONSHIP

Despite a checkered history the world team championship is still going after seven years. State Express sponsored the event from 1979-83. Guinness then had one year, when the event was moved to the second half of the season, before handing over to Car Care Plan in 1986. The format changed yet again in 1987 when Tuborg took over the sponsorship.

Winners:
1979 Wales
1980 Wales
1981 England
1982 Canada
1983 England
1985 All-Ireland
1986-7 All-Ireland 'A'

DULUX BRITISH OPEN

The British Open started life as the British Gold Cup in 1980. Between 1981-4 it was known as the Yamaha International, and in 1985 it acquired the sponsorship of ICI Paints, who used their Dulux brand name.

Winners:
1980 Alex Higgins (NI)
1981-2 Steve Davis (Eng)
1983 Ray Reardon (Wal)
1984 Steve Davis (Eng)
1985 Silvino Francisco (SAf)
1986 Steve Davis (Eng)
1987 Jimmy White (Eng)

MERCANTILE CREDIT CLASSIC

Mercantile succeeded Lada as sponsors of the Classic in 1984. Lada had, in turn, succeeded the event's first sponsors, Wilsons Brewery, in 1981.

Winners:
1980 (Jan) John Spencer (Eng)
1980 (Dec) Steve Davis (Eng)
1982 Terry Griffiths (Wal)
1983-4 Steve Davis (Eng)
1985 Willie Thorne (Eng)
1986 Jimmy White (Eng)
1987 Steve Davis (Eng)

BCE INTERNATIONAL

Like the BCE International, its forerunner, the Jameson International was also an early-season event and carried world ranking points. The Jameson was the first tournament after the world championship to be accorded ranking status. It was replaced by the Goya Matchroom Trophy in 1985, and in 1986 BCE became the new sponsors.

Winners:
1981 Steve Davis (Eng)
1982 Tony Knowles (Eng)
1983-4 Steve Davis (Eng)

1985 Cliff Thorburn (Can)
1986 Neal Foulds (Eng)

LANGS SCOTTISH MASTERS

Sponsored by Lang's since 1981, this early-season competition carries no ranking points as the field is limited to eight invited professionals.

Winners:
1981 Jimmy White (Eng)
1982-4 Steve Davis (Eng)
1985-6 Cliff Thorburn (Can)

ROTHMANS GRAND PRIX

Previous known as the Professional Players Tournament, it became the Rothmans Grand Prix in 1984.

Winners:
1982 Ray Reardon (Wal)
1983 Tony Knowles (Eng)
1984 Dennis Taylor (NI)
1985 Steve Davis (Eng)
1986 Jimmy White (Eng)

HOFMEISTER WORLD DOUBLES

The idea of a doubles championship was conceived in 1982 and its format has proved popular with players and spectators.

Winners:
1982-3 Steve Davis & Tony Meo (Eng)
1984 Alex Higgins (NI) & Jimmy White (Eng)
1985-6 Steve Davis & Tony Meo (Eng)

BREAKS

While the maximum break of 147 has been achieved many times, only the following have done so under official conditions:

Joe Davis (Eng) London, 1955
Rex Williams (Eng) South Africa, 1965
Steve Davis (Eng) Oldham, 1982
Cliff Thorburn (Can) Sheffield, 1983
Kirk Stevens (Can) London, 1984

BREAK RECORDS

The following is a list of the break records in all the current major professional tournaments, or their predecessors.

Scottish Masters:
142 Cliff Thorburn (1985)
BCE International:
140 Neal Foulds (1984)
Rothmans Grand Prix:
138 Jimmy White (1986)
Tennents United Kingdom Open:
144 Jimmy White (1986)
Hofmeister World Doubles:
217(*) Steve Davis/Tony Meo (1986)
Mercantile Credit Classic:
147 Steve Davis (1982)
Benson & Hedges Masters:
147 Kirk Stevens (1984)

Dulux British Open:
145 Dave Martin (1986)
World Team Championship:
127 Terry Griffiths (1981)
Benson & Hedges Irish Masters:
133 Steve Davis (1983)
Embassy World Professional Championship:
147 Cliff Thorburn (1983)

(*) Combined total of best breaks of both players in any one match
(As at the end of the 1986-7 season)

WORLD RANKINGS

The World Professional Billiards & Snooker Association (1987 membership, 128 players) published its first set of world rankings in 1976. The following is a list of top ranked players. A revised list is produced after the World Championship each year.
1976-80 Ray Reardon (Wal)
1981 Cliff Thorburn (Can)
1982 Ray Reardon (Wal)
1983-7 Steve Davis (Eng)

WORLD AMATEUR CHAMPIONSHIP

First held in Calcutta, India in 1963, it was a biennial event until 1984 when it became an annual competition. The championships are run by the International Billiards & Snooker Federation (1987 membership, 29 nations) which became the non-professional game's governing body in 1985.

Winners:
1963 Gary Owen (Eng)
1966 Gary Owen (Eng)
1968 David Taylor (Eng)
1970 Jonathan Barron (Eng)
1972 Ray Edmonds (Eng)
1974 Ray Edmonds (Eng)
1976 Doug Mountjoy (Wal)
1978 Cliff Wilson (Wal)
1980 Jimmy White (Eng)
1982 Terry Parsons (Wal)
1984 O.B.Agrawal (Ind)
1985-6 Paul Mifsud (Malta)

Most wins: 2 Gary Owen, Ray Edmonds, Paul Mifsud
Highest break: 132 Tony Drago (Malta) 1984
The highest officially recognised break by an amateur is 141 by Martin Clark (Eng) in the 1986 Home International Championship at Heysham, near Morecambe.

Steve Davis – the player of the 1980s. (All-Sport)

STEVE DAVIS'S DOMINATION

Since winning his first major professional title, the 1980 Coral United Kingdom Championship at Preston, Steve Davis has won 33 of the 78 major championships in Britain up to May 1987. His domination is clearly seen by the following chart.

	Steve DAVIS	Cliff THORBURN	Jimmy WHITE	Alex HIGGINS	Tony MEO	Terry GRIFFITHS	Dennis TAYLOR	Tony KNOWLES
World Champs.	4	-	-	1	-	-	1	-
B&H Masters	1	3	1	1	-	-	1	-
UK Open	5	-	-	1	-	1	-	-
B&H Irish Masters	3	-	2	-	-	2	-	-
World Team Cup	1	1	-	3	1	-	3	1
British Open	4	-	1	-	-	-	-	-
Mercantile	4	-	1	-	-	1	-	-
BCE International	3	1	-	-	-	-	-	1
Scottish Masters	3	2	1	-	-	-	-	1
Rothmans GP	1	-	1	-	-	-	1	1
World Doubles	4	-	1	1	4	-	-	-
TOTAL WINS	33	7	8	7	5	4	6	3

(Note: wins in competitions that were forerunners of the above are included)

SOFTBALL

Softball, invented by George Hancock of the Farragut Boat Club, Chicago in 1887, began as an indoor version of baseball. The game was originally known as 'kitten-ball' or 'mush-ball', the name softball being introduced by Walter Hakanson in 1926. The Amateur Softball Association of America was formed in 1933 and introduced US Championships for both men's and women's teams that year.

Played by nine-a-side teams, the game developed internationally following the formation in 1950 of the International Softball Federation. There are slow pitch and fast pitch varieties.

WORLD CHAMPIONSHIPS

World championships for women were introduced in 1965 and for men a year later.

Winners: (men's title shared in 1976)

MEN
USA 1966, 1968, 1976 (=), 1980
Canada 1972, 1976 (=)
New Zealand 1976 (=), 1984

WOMEN
Australia 1965
Japan 1970
USA 1974, 1978, 1986
New Zealand 1982

World Championship tournament records:

	MEN
Most runs:	14 Takayuki Ietke (Japan) 1984
Best average:	.583 Takayuki Ietke (Japan) 1984
Most strikeouts:	98 Ty Stofflet (USA) 1976
	WOMEN
Most runs:	13 Kathy Elliott (USA) 1974
Best average:	.550 Tamara Bryce (Pan) 1978
Most strikeouts:	76 Joan Joyce (USA) 1974

US NATIONAL FAST PITCH CHAMPIONS

Most annual Championships won:

MEN
10 Clearwater (Florida) Bombers 1950, 1954, 1956-7, 1960, 1962-3, 1966, 1968, 1973
 7 Raybestos (Franklin) Cardinals, Stratford, Ct. 1955, 1958, 1969-70, 1972, 1976, 1983

WOMEN
19 Raybestos (Hi Ho) Brakettes, Stratford, Ct. 1958-60, 1963, 1966-8, 1971-8, 1980, 1982-3, 1985
 9 Orange (Cal.) Lionettes 1950-2, 1955-6, 1962, 1965, 1969-70

US NATIONAL SLOW PITCH CHAMPIONS

Slow pitch championships were first held in 1953 for men and 1962 for women.

Most championships won:

MEN
3 Skip Hogan A.C., Pittsburgh 1962, 1964-5; Joe Gatliff Auto Sales, Newport, Ky. 1956-7, 1963

WOMEN
5 Dots, Miami, Fla as Converse Dots 1969, Marks Brothers, N.Miami Dots 1974-5, Bob Hoffman Dots 1978-9
4 Dana Gardens, Cincinnati 1962-4, 1966

SPEEDWAY

Although dirt track racing on motorcycles in the United States dates to 1902, the first Speedway meeting, as the sport is known today, was not until 1923, when a meeting took place at the West Maitland Agricultural Show, New South Wales. The first meeting in Britain was at Droylesden, Greater Manchester in 1927. The first meeting on a cinder track took place at High Beech, Essex the following year.

WORLD CHAMPIONSHIPS

The first World Championships, for individual riders, was held at Wembley in 1936. The team competition was introduced in 1960, and the Pairs in 1970. Two Pairs championships, in 1968 and 1969, had claimed the status of 'World' championship, but the governing body does not recognise these two events for record purposes. The Long Track championship was inaugurated in 1971. Ice Speedway world championships were instituted in 1966 with an individual competition; a team competition was added in 1979.

Winners:

INDIVIDUAL
1936 Lionel Van Praag (Aus)
1937 Jack Milne (USA
1938 Bluey Wilkinson (Aus)
1949 Tommy Price (Eng)
1950 Freddie Williams (Wal)
1951-2 Jack Young (Aus)
1953 Freddie Williams (Wal)
1954 Ronnie Moore (NZ)
1955 Peter Craven (Eng)
1956 Ove Fundin (Swe)
1957-8 Barry Briggs (NZ)
1959 Ronnie Moore (NZ)
1960-1 Ove Fundin (Swe)
1962 Peter Craven (Eng)
1963 Ove Fundin (Swe)
1964 Barry Briggs (NZ)
1965 Björn Knutsson (Swe)
1966 Barry Briggs (NZ)
1967 Ove Fundin (Swe)
1968-70 Ivan Mauger (NZ)
1971 Ole Olsen (Den)
1972 Ivan Mauger (NZ)
1973 Jerzy Szczakiel (Pol)
1974 Anders Michanek (Swe)

1975 Ole Olsen (Den)
1976 Peter Collins (Eng)
1977 Ivan Mauger (NZ)
1978 Ole Olsen (Den)
1979 Ivan Mauger (NZ)
1980 Michael Lee (Eng)
1981-2 Bruce Penhall (USA)
1983 Egon Müller (FRG)
1984-5 Erik Gundersen (Den)
1986 Hans Nielsen (Den)

Most wins: 6 Ivan Mauger; 5 Ove Fundin; 4 Barry Briggs; 3 Ole Olsen
Most appearances: 17 (all consecutive) Barry Briggs, 1957-70

PAIRS
Winners (unofficial 1968-9)
1968 Sweden (Ove Fundin/Torbjörn Harryson)
1969 New Zealand (Ivan Mauger/Bob Andrews)
1970 New Zealand (Ronnie Moore/Ivan Mauger)
1971 Poland (Jerzy Szczakiel/Andrzej Wyglenda)
1972 England (Ray Wilson/Terry Betts)
1973 Sweden (Anders Michanek/Tommy Jansson)
1974 Sweden (Anders Michanek/Soren Sjösten)
1975 Sweden (Anders Michanek/Tommy Jansson)
1976 England (John Louis/Malcolm Simmons)
1977 England (Peter Collins/Malcolm Simmons)
1978 England (Malcolm Simmons/Gordon Kennett)
1979 Denmark (Ole Olsen/Hans Nielsen)
1980 England (David Jessup/Peter Collins)
1981 USA (Bruce Penhall/Bobby Schwartz)
1982 USA (Dennis Sigalos/Bobby Schwartz)
1983 England (Kenny Carter/Peter Collins)
1984 England (Peter Collins/Chris Morton)
1985 Denmark (Erik Gundersen/Tommy Knudsen)
1986-7 Denmark (Hans Nielsen/Erik Gundersen)

Most wins (Team): 7 England; 3 Sweden, Denmark; 2 United States
Most wins (Individual): 4 Peter Collins (Eng); 3 Anders Michanek (Swe), Malcolm Simmons (Eng), Erik Gundersen (Den)

TEAM
Winners:
8 Great Britain 1968, 1971-3/England 1974-5, 1977, 1980
6 Sweden 1960, 1962-4, 1967, 1970
6 Denmark 1978, 1981, 1983-6
4 Poland 1961, 1965-6, 1969
1 Australia 1976, New Zealand 1979, USA 1982

Most wins (Individual):
6 Ove Fundin (Swe) 1960, 1962-4, 1967, 1970
6 Hans Nielsen (Den) 1978, 1981, 1983-6
5 Peter Collins (GB/Eng) 1973-5, 1977, 1980
5 Erik Gundersen (Den) 1981, 1983-6
4 Malcolm Simmons (GB/Eng) 1973-5, 1977
4 Ivan Mauger (GB/NZ) 1968, 1971-2, 1979
4 Rune Sormander (Swe) 1960, 1962-4
4 Björn Knutsson (Swe) 1960, 1962-4
4 Gote Nordin (Swe) 1962-4, 1967

LONG TRACK
Winners:
1971-2 Ivan Mauger (NZ)

Erik Gundersen, the first man to hold world titles simultaneously at individual, pairs, team and long track (All-Sport)

1973 Ole Olsen (Den)
1974-6 Egon Müller (FRG)
1977 Anders Michanek (Swe)
1978 Egon Müller (FRG)
1979 Alois Weisbock (FRG)
1980 Karl Maier (FRG)
1981 Michael Lee (Eng)
1982 Karl Maier (FRG)
1983 Shawn Moran (USA)
1984 Erik Gundersen (Den)
1985 Simon Wigg (Eng)
1986 Erik Gundersen (Den)

Most wins: 4 Egon Müller

MOST WORLD TITLES

	Total	Ind	Pairs	Team	L.Track
Ivan Mauger (NZ)	14	6	2*	4	2
Erik Gundersen (Den)	12	2	3	5	2
Peter Collins (Eng)	10	1	4	5	-
Hans Nielsen (Den)	10	1	3	6	-
Ole Olsen (Den)	8	3	1	3	1
Malcolm Simmons (Eng)	7	-	3	4	-
Barry Briggs (NZ)	6	4	-	2	-
Ove Fundin (Swe)	12	5	1*	6	-
Björn Knutsson (Swe)	5	1	-	4	-

* including one unofficial Pairs win

WORLD ICE SPEEDWAY CHAMPIONSHIP
INDIVIDUAL
Winners:
1966 Gabdrahman Kadirov (USSR)
1967 Boris Samorodov (USSR)
1968-9 Gabdrahman Kadirov (USSR)
1970 Antonin Svaab (Cs)
1971-3 Gabdrahman Kadirov (USSR)
1974 Milan Spinka (Cs)
1975-8 Sergey Tarabanko (USSR)

1979-80 Anatoliy Bondarenko (USSR)
1981 Vladimir Lyubich (USSR)
1982-3 Sergey Kosakov (USSR)
1984 Erik Stenlund (Swe)
1985 Vladimir Suchov (USSR)
1986 Juriy Ivanov (USSR)

TEAM
7 USSR 1979-84, 1986
1 Sweden 1985

BRITISH SPEEDWAY LEAGUE

The British League was founded in 1932 as the National League. A second division was added in 1936 and a third division existed 1947-51. From 1957 there was only one division again. A rival league, the Provincial League came into being in 1960 and the two leagues merged in 1965. A second division was created in 1968. The new division was renamed the New National League in 1975, and since 1976 it has been known as the National League.

National League
1932 Wembley
1933 Belle Vue
1934 Belle Vue
1935 Belle Vue

	Division 1	Division 2
1936	Belle Vue	Southampton
1937	West Ham	Bristol
1938	New Cross	Hackney Wick
1939	Belle Vue	Newcastle
1946	Wembley	-

	Division 1	Division 2	Division 3
1947	Wembley	Middlesbrough	Eastbourne
1948	New Cross	Bristol	Exeter
1949	Wembley	Bristol	Stoke
1950	Wembley	Norwich	Oxford
1951	Wembley	Norwich	Poole
1952	Wembley	Poole	-
1953	Wembley	Coventry	-
1954	Wimbledon	Bristol	-
1955	Southampton	Poole	-
1956	Wimbledon	Swindon	-
1957	Swindon	-	-
1958	Wimbledon	-	-
1959	Wimbledon	-	-
1959	Wimbledon	-	-

	National League	Provincial League
1960	Wimbledon	Rayleigh
1961	Wimbledon	Poole
1962	Southampton	Poole
1963	Belle Vue	Wolverhampton
1964	Oxford	Newcastle

British League

1965	West Ham	-
1966	Halifax	-
1967	Swindon	-

	Division 1	Division 2
1968	Coventry	Belle Vue Colts
1969	Poole	Belle Vue Colts
1970	Belle Vue	Canterbury
1971	Belle Vue	Eastbourne
1972	Belle Vue	Crewe
1973	Reading	Boston
1974	Exeter	Birmingham

	British League	New National League
1975	Ipswich	Birmingham

	British League	National League
1976	Ipswich	Newcastle
1977	White City	Eastbourne
1978	Coventry	Canterbury
1979	Coventry	Mildenhall
1980	Reading	Rye House
1981	Cradley Heath	Middlesbrough
1982	Belle Vue	Newcastle
1983	Cradley Heath	Newcastle
1984	Ipswich	Long Eaton
1985	Oxford	Ellesmere Port
1986	Oxford	Eastbourne

Most wins (Div.1): 10 Belle Vue; 8 Wembley; 7 Wimbledon; 3 Coventry

BRITISH LEAGUE RIDERS' CHAMPIONSHIP
1965-70 Barry Briggs (Swindon)
1971 Ivan Mauger (Belle Vue)
1972 Ole Olsen (Wolverhampton)
1973 Ivan Mauger (Exeter)
1974-5 Peter Collins (Belle Vue)
1976-8 Ole Olsen (Coventry)
1979 John Louis (Ipswich)
1980 Les Collins (Leicester)
1981-2 Kenny Carter (Halifax)
1983 Erik Gundersen (Cradley Heath)
1984 Chris Morton (Belle Vue)
1985 Erik Gundersen (Cradley Heath)
1986 Hans Nielsen (Oxford)

SQUASH

Squash rackets developed from rackets, being played with a softer ball, first at Harrow School in 1817 but it was not until the formation of the Squash Rackets Association in 1928 that the game grew in popularity world-wide. The first recognised champion was John Miskey, who won the US Amateur Championship in 1907, the year of formation of the United States Squash Racquets Association. The Women's Squash Rackets Association was founded in 1934, and the International Squash Rackets Federation (ISRF) was founded in 1967. The Women's International Squash Rackets Federation was formed in 1976.

WORLD OPEN CHAMPIONSHIP

The first World Open Championships were held in 1976. There were no championships in 1978 but since 1979 it has been an annual event for men, and a biennial event for women.

MEN
1976-7 Geoff Hunt (Aus)
1979-80 Geoff Hunt (Aus)
1981-5 Jahangir Khan (Pak)
1986 Ross Norman (NZ)

Most wins: 5 Jahangir Khan; 4 Geoff Hunt

Jahangir Khan (All-Sport)

WOMEN

	Individual	Team
1976	Heather McKay (Aus)	-
1979	Heather McKay (Aus)	Great Britain
1981	Rhonda Thorne(Aus)	Australia
1983	Vicki Cardwell (Aus)	Australia
1985	Susan Devoy (NZ)	England

Most wins: 2 Heather McKay

WORLD AMATEUR/ISRF CHAMPIONSHIPS

First held in 1967 the championship became known as the I.S.R.F. World Championship in 1979 after the sport went Open. There is an individual and team competition.

Winners:

	Individual	Team
1967	Geoff Hunt (Aus)	Australia
1969	Geoff Hunt (Aus)	Australia
1971	Geoff Hunt (Aus)	Australia
1973	Cam Nancarrow (Aus)	Australia
1975	Kevin Shawcross (Aus)	Great Britain
1977	Maqsood Ahmed (Pak)	Pakistan
1979	Jahangir Khan (Pak)	Great Britain
1981	Steve Bowditch (Aus)	Pakistan
1983	Jahangir Khan (Pak)	Pakistan
1985	Jahangir Khan (Pak)	Pakistan

Most wins (Ind): 3 Geoff Hunt, Jahangir Khan
(Team): 4 Australia, Pakistan

WORLD MASTERS

First held in 1979, it has not been held since 1984.

MEN

1979 Qamar Zaman (Pak)
1980 Mohibullah Khan (Pak)
1981-4 Jahangir Khan (Pak)

WOMEN

1984 Lucy Soutter (UK)

WORLD CUP

First held 1984

	Singles	Pairs
1984	Jahangir Khan (Pak)	Ross Thorne & Dean Williams (Aus)

BRITISH OPEN CHAMPIONSHIPS

First held in 1922 for women, and in 1930 for men, the British Open was regarded as the unofficial World Championship until the creation of the World Amateur Championship in 1967.

MEN

1930-1 Don Butcher (UK)
1932-7 Abdul Fattah Amr Bey (Egy)
1938 James Dear (UK)
1946-9 Mahmoud Karim (Egy)
1950-5 Hashim Khan (Pak)
1956 Roshan Khan (Pak)
1957 Hashim Khan (Pak)
1958-61 Azam Khan (Pak)
1962 Mohibullah Khan (Pak)
1963-6 Abdel Abou Taleb (Egy)
1967-8 Jonah Barrington (UK)
1969 Geoff Hunt (Aus)
1970-3 Jonah Barrington (UK)
1974 Geoff Hunt (Aus)
1975 Qamar Zaman (Pak)
1976-81 Geoff Hunt (Aus)
1982-7 Jahangir Khan (Pak)

Most wins: 8 Geoff Hunt; 7 Hashim Khan; 6 Abdel Fattah Amr Bey, Jonah Barrington, Jahangir Khan

WOMEN

1922 Joyce Cave (UK)
1922 Sylvia Huntsman(UK)
1923 Nancy Cave (UK)
1924 Joyce Cave (UK)
1925-6 Cecily Fenwick (UK)
1928 Joyce Cave (UK)
1929-30 Nancy Cave (UK)
1931 Cecily Fenwick (UK)
1932-4 Susan Noel (UK)
1934-9 Margot Lumb (UK)
1947-9 Joan Curry (UK)
1950-8 Janet Morgan (UK)
1960 Sheila Macintosh (UK)

1961 Fran Marshall (UK)
1962-5 Heather Blundell (Aus)
1966-77 Heather McKay (née Blundell)
1978 Susan Newman (Aus)
1979 Barbara Wall (Aus)
1980-1 Vicki Hoffman (Aus)
1982-3 Vicki Cardwell (née Hoffman)(Aus)
1984-7 Susan Devoy (NZ)

Most wins: 16 Heather McKay; 9 Janet Morgan; 6 Margot Lumb; 4 Vicki Cardwell (née Hoffman), Susan Devoy

BRITISH AMATEUR CHAMPIONSHIP

Instituted in 1922. With the distinction between amateurs and professionals disappearing in 1979, the tournament came to an end.

Winners, all UK unless otherwise stated.
1922-3 Tommy Jameson
1924 Dugald Macpherson
1925 Victor Cazalet
1926 Jimmy Tomkinson
1927 Victor Cazalet
1928 Dugald McPherson
1929-30 Victor Cazalet
1931-3 Abdul Fattah Amr Bey (Egy)
1934 Cyril Hamilton
1935-7 Abdul Fattah Amr Bey (Egy)
1938 Kenneth Gandar Dower
1946-50 Norman Borrett
1951 Gavin Hildick-Smith
1952-3 Alan Fairbairn
1954 Roy Wilson
1955 Ibrahim Amin (Egy)
1956 Roy Wilson
1957-8 Nigel Broomfield
1959 Ibrahim Amin (Egy)
1960-1 Michael Oddy
1962 Ken Hiscoe (Aus)
1963-5 Aftab Jawaid (Pak)
1966-8 Jonah Barrington
1969 Geoff Hunt (Aus)
1970-1 Gogi Alauddin (Pak)
1972 Cam Nancarrow (Aus)
1973-4 Mohibullah Khan (Pak)
1975 Kevin Shawcross (Aus)
1976 Bruce Brownlee (NZ)
1977-8 Gamal Awad (Egy)
1979 Jonathan Leslie

Most wins: 6 Abdul Fattah Amr Bey; 5 Norman Borrett; 4 Victor Cazalet; 3 Aftab Jawaid

US PROFESSIONAL (SOFTBALL) SQUASH CHAMPIONSHIP

Held for the first time in 1986, when the winners were: **MEN** Jahangir Khan (Pak), **WOMEN** Lisa Opie (UK)

NORTH AMERICAN OPEN

Played with a harder ball, standard in North America where the courts are also narrower and longer. First held 1953 after the amalgamation of the US and Canadian Open championships.

Winners:
1953 Henri Salaun (USA)
1954 Diehl Mateer Jr (USA)
1955-6 Hashim Khan (Pak)
1957 Roshan Khan (Pak)
1958 Diehl Mateer Jr (USA)
1959-60 Roshan Khan (Pak)
1961 Azam Khan (Pak)
1962 Hashim Khan (Pak)
1963-5 Mohibullah Khan (Pak)
1966 Ralph Howe (USA)
1967 Mohibullah Khan (Pak)
1968-73 Sharif Khan (Pak)
1974 Victor Niederhoffer (USA)
1975-81 Sharif Khan (Pak) (6 wins)
1982 Mike Desaulniers (Can)
1983 Mark Talbot (USA)
1984-5 Jahangir Khan (Pak)
1986 Mark Talbott (USA)
1987 Ned Edwards (USA)

Heather McKay (née Blundell) was unbeaten in women's squash from 1962 to 1980. She won 16 British Open titles and 14 consecutive Australian amateur titles 1960-73 before turning professional. After winning her second world title in 1979 she concentrated on a new sport - racquetball, and became the best player in Canada (to where she had moved in 1975) within a year.

When Jahangir Khan lost to Ross Norman in the World Championship final at Toulouse, France, in November 1986, it was his first defeat since April 1981 when Geoff Hunt beat him in the final of the British Open.

SURFING

Surfing was a traditional Polynesian activity, which has long been popular on suitable coast lines, such as off California, Hawaii or Australia. It was developed as a sporting activity in the 1950s and 1960s.

WORLD AMATEUR CHAMPIONSHIPS

First held in 1964. The only triple winner is Michael Novakov (Aus), who won all three men's Kneeboard titles in 1982, 1984, and 1986.

Open winners:

Year	Men's Open	Women's Open
1964	Bernard Farrelly (Aus)	Phyllis O'Donnell (Aus)
1965	Felipe Pomar (Per)	Joyce Hoffmann (USA)
1966	Robert 'Nat' Young (USA)	Joyce Hoffmann (USA)
1968	Fred Hemmings (Haw)	Margo Godfrey (USA)
1970	Ralph Arness (USA)	Sharon Webber (Haw)
1972	Jimmy Blears (Haw)	Sharon Webber (Haw)
1980	Mark Scott (Aus)	Alisa Schwarzstein (USA)
1982	Tommy Curren (USA)	Jenny Gill (Aus)
1984	Scott Farnsworth (USA)	Janice Aragon (USA)
1986	Mark Sainsbury (Aus)	Connie Nixon (Aus)

WORLD PROFESSIONAL CHAMPIONSHIPS

First held in 1970. The Grand Prix circuit is held throughout the year in Japan, USA, South Africa, France, Great Britain and Australia. Winners (year given from 1983 is the second half of each May–April season):

MEN
1970 Robert Young (Aus)
1971 Paul Neilsen (Aus)
1972 Jonathan Paarman (SAf)
1973 Ian Cairns (Aus)
1974 Reno Abellira (Haw)
1975 Mark Richards (Aus)
1976 Peter Townend (Aus)
1977 Shaun Tomson (SAf)
1978 Wayne Bartholomew (Aus)
1979 Mark Richards (Aus)
1980 Mark Richards (Aus)
1981 Mark Richards (Aus)
1983 Mark Richards (Aus)
1984 Tom Carroll (Aus)
1985 Tom Carroll (Aus)
1986 Tommy Curren (USA)

WOMEN
1979 Margo Oberg (Haw)
1980 Lyne Boyer (Haw)
1981 Margo Oberg (Haw)
1983 Margo Oberg (Haw)
1984 Kim Mearig (USA)
1985 Frieda Zamba (USA)
1986 Frieda Zamba (USA)

SWIMMING & DIVING

Although swimming may have been popular in ancient times, it was not included in the Greek Olympic Games. The earliest references to swimming races were in Japan in 36 BC. In modern times competitive swimming was popularised in Britian from at least 1791. The first national swimming association was the Metropolitan Swimming Clubs Association, later to become the Amateur Swimming Association (ASA), founded in London in 1869. The first national champion was Tom Morris, who won a mile race in the Thames that year. Swimming has been held at every Olympic Games from the first in 1896.

The international governing body for swimming, diving and water polo, the Fédération International de Natation Amateur (FINA) was founded in 1908.

OLYMPIC GAMES

Winners of all events on the current programme. Olympic records are indicated by OR, or as listed at the end of each event if not set in a final.

MEN

100 METRES FREESTYLE
1896 Alfred Hajos (Hun) 1:22.2
1904 Zoltan von Halmay (Hun) 1:02.08 (100y)
1906 Charles Daniels (USA) 1:13.4
1908 Charles Daniels (USA) 1:05.6
1912 Duke Kahanamoku (USA) 1:03.4
1920 Duke Kahanamoku (USA) 1:01.4
1924 Johnny Weissmuller (USA) 59.0
1928 Johnny Weissmuller (USA) 58.6
1932 Yasuji Miyazaki (Jap) 58.2
1936 Ferenc Csik (Hun) 57.6
1948 Walter Ris (USA) 57.3
1952 Clarke Scholes (USA) 57.4
1956 Jon Henricks (Aus) 55.4
1960 John Devitt (Aus) 55.2
1964 Don Schollander (USA) 53.4
1968 Mike Wenden (Aus) 52.2
1972 Mark Spitz (USA) 51.22
1976 Jim Montgomery (USA) 49.99
1980 Jörg Woithe (GDR) 50.40
1984 Rowdy Gaines (USA) 49.80 OR

200 METRES FREESTYLE
1900 Frederick Lane (Aus) 2:25.2
1904 Charles Daniels (USA) 2:44.2 (220y)
1968 Mike Wenden (Aus) 1:55.2
1972 Mark Spitz (USA) 1:52.78
1976 Bruce Furniss (USA) 1:50.29
1980 Sergey Koplyakov (USSR) 1:49.81
1984 Michael Gross (FRG) 1:47.44 OR

400 METRES FREESTYLE
1896 Paul Neumann (Aut) 8:12.6 (500m)
1904 Charles Daniels (USA) 6:16.2 (440y)
1906 Otto Scheff (Aut) 6:23.8
1908 Henry Taylor (UK) 5:36.8
1912 George Hodgson (Can) 5:24.4
1920 Norman Ross (USA) 5:26.8
1924 Johnny Weissmuller (USA) 5:04.2
1928 Albeto Zorilla (Arg) 5:01.6
1932 Buster Crabbe (USA) 4:48.4
1936 Jack Medica (USA) 4:44.5
1948 William Smith (USA) 4:41.0
1952 Jean Boiteux (Fra) 4:30.7
1956 Murray Rose (Aus) 4:27.3
1960 Murray Rose (Aus) 4:18.3
1964 Don Schollander (USA) 4:12.2
1968 Mike Burton (USA) 4:09.0
1972 Brad Cooper (Aus) 4:00.27
1976 Brian Goodell (USA) 3:51.93
1980 Vladimir Salnikov (USSR) 3:51.31
1984 George Dicarlo (USA) 3:51.23
OR Thomas Fahrner (FRG) 3:50.91 (1984)

1500 METRES FREESTYLE
1896 Alfred Hajos (Hun) 18:22.2 (1200m)
1900 John Jarvis (UK) 13:40.2 (1000m)
1904 Emil Rausch (Ger) 27:18.2 (1 Mile)
1906 Henry Taylor (UK) 28:28.0
1908 Henry Taylor (UK) 22:48.4
1912 George Hodgson (Can) 22:00.0
1920 Norman Ross (USA) 22:23.2
1924 Andrew Charlton (Aus) 20:06.6
1928 Arne Borg (Swe) 19:51.8
1932 Kusuo Kitamura (Jap) 19:12.4
1936 Noboru Terada (Jap) 19:13.7
1948 James McLane (USA) 19:18.5

Michael Gross, known as "The Albatross", due to his exceptional arm span. (All-Sport)

1952 Ford Konno (USA) 18:30.0
1956 Murray Rose (Aus) 17:58.9
1960 John Konrads (Aus) 17:19.6
1964 Bob Windle (Aus) 17:01.7
1968 Mike Burton (USA) 16:38.9
1972 Mike Burton (USA) 15:52.58
1976 Brian Goodell (USA) 15:02.40
1980 Vladimir Salnikov (USSR) 14:58.27 OR
1984 Michael O'Brien (USA) 15:05.20

4×100 METRES FREESTYLE RELAY
1964 USA 3:33.2
1968 USA 3:31.7
1972 USA 3:26.42
1984 USA 3:19.03 OR

4×200 METRES FREESTYLE RELAY
1906 Hungary 16:52.4
1908 United Kingdom 10:55.6
1912 Australasia 10:11.6
1920 USA 10:04.4
1924 USA 9:53.4
1928 USA 9:36.2
1932 Japan 8:58.4
1936 Japan 8:51.5
1948 USA 8:46.0
1952 USA 8:31.1
1956 Australia 8:23.6
1960 USA 8:10.2
1964 USA 7:52.1
1968 USA 7:52.3
1972 USA 7:35.78
1976 USA 7:23.22
1980 USSR 7:23.50
1984 USA 7:15.69 OR

100 METRES BACKSTROKE
1904 Walter Brack (Ger) 1:16.8 (100y)
1908 Arno Bieberstein (Ger) 1:24.6
1912 Harry Hebner (USA) 1:21.2
1920 Warren Kealoha (USA) 1:15.2
1924 Warren Kealoha (USA) 1:13.2
1928 George Kojac (USA) 1:08.2
1932 Masaji Kiyokawa (Jap) 1:08.6
1936 Adolf Kiefer (USA) 1:05.9
1948 Allen Stack (USA) 1:06.4
1952 Yoshinobu Oyakawa (USA) 1:05.4
1956 David Thiele (Aus) 1:02.2
1960 David Thiele (Aus) 1:01.9
1968 Roland Matthes (GDR) 58.7
1972 Roland Matthes (GDR) 56.58
1976 John Naber (USA) 55.49 OR
1980 Bengt Baron (Swe) 56.53
1984 Rick Carey (USA) 55.79

200 METRES BACKSTROKE
1900 Ernst Hoppenberg (Ger) 2:47.0
1964 Jed Graef (USA) 2:10.3
1968 Roland Matthes (GDR) 2:09.6
1972 Roland Matthes (GDR) 2:02.82
1976 John Naber (USA) 1:59.19
1980 Sandor Wladar (Hun) 2:01.93
1984 Rick Carey (USA) 2:00.23
OR Rick Carey (USA) 1:58.99 (1984)

100 METRES BREASTSTROKE
1968 Don McKenzie (USA) 1:07.7
1972 Nobutaka Taguchi (Jap) 1:04.94
1976 John Hencken (USA) 1:03.11
1980 Duncan Goodhew (UK) 1:03.34
1984 Steve Lundquist (USA) 1:01.65 OR

200 METRES BREASTSTROKE
1908 Frederick Holman (UK) 3:09.2
1912 Walter Bathe (Ger) 3:01.8
1920 Häken Malmroth (Swe) 3:04.4
1924 Robert Skelton (USA) 2:56.5
1928 Yoshiyuki Tsuruta (Jap) 2:48.8
1932 Yoshiyuki Tsuruta (Jap) 2:45.4
1936 Tetsuo Hamuro (Jap) 2:41.5
1948 Joseph Verdeur (USA) 2:39.3
1952 John Davies (Aus) 2:34.4

1956 Masaru Furukawa (Jap) 2:34.7
1960 William Mulliken (USA) 2:37.4
1964 Ian O'Brien (Aus) 2:27.8
1968 Felipe Munoz (Mex) 2:28.7
1972 John Hencken (USA) 2:21.55
1976 David Wilkie (UK) 2:15.11
1980 Robertas Zhulpa (USSR) 2:15.85
1984 Victor Davis (Can) 2:13.34 OR

100 METRES BUTTERFLY
1968 Doug Russell (USA) 55.9
1972 Mark Spitz (USA) 54.27
1976 Matt Vogel (USA) 54.35
1980 Pär Arvidsson (Swe) 54.92
1984 Michael Gross (FRG) 53.08 OR

200 METRES BUTTERFLY
1956 William Yorzyk (USA) 2:19.3
1960 Mike Troy (USA) 2:12.8
1964 Kevin Berry (Aus) 2:06.6
1968 Carl Robie (USA) 2:08.7
1972 Mark Spitz (USA) 2:00.70
1976 Mike Bruner (USA) 1:59.23
1980 Sergey Fesenko (USSR) 1:59.76
1984 Jon Sieben (Aus) 1:57.04 OR

200 METRES INDIVIDUAL MEDLEY
1968 Charles Hickcox (USA) 2:12.0
1972 Gunnar Larsson (Swe) 2:07.17
1984 Alex Baumann (Can) 2:01.42 OR

400 METRES INDIVIDUAL MEDLEY
1964 Richard Roth (USA) 4:45.4
1968 Charles Hickcox (USA) 4:48.4
1972 Gunnar Larsson (Swe) 4:31.98
1976 Rod Strachan (USA) 4:23.68
1980 Aleksandr Sidorenko (USSR) 4:22.89
1984 Alex Baumann (Can) 4:17.41 OR

4×100 METRES MEDLEY RELAY
1960 USA 4:05.4
1964 USA 3:58.4
1968 USA 3:54.9
1972 USA 3:48.16
1976 USA 3:42.22
1980 Australia 3:45.70
1984 USA 3:39.30 OR

SPRINGBOARD DIVING
1908 Albert Zürner (Ger)
1912 Paul Günther (Ger)
1920 Louis Kuehn (USA)
1924 Albert White (USA)
1928 Peter Desjardins (USA)
1932 Michael Galitzen (USA)
1936 Richard Degener (USA)
1948 Bruce Harlan (USA)
1952 David Browning (USA)
1956 Robert Clotworthy (USA)
1960 Gary Tobian (USA)
1964 Kenneth Sitzberger (USA)
1968 Bernard Wrightson (USA)
1972 Vladimir Vasin (USSR)
1976 Philip Boggs (USA)
1980 Aleksandr Portnov (USSR)
1984 Greg Louganis (USA)

HIGHBOARD PLATFORM DIVING
1904 George Sheldon (USA)
1906 Gottlob Walz (Ger)
1908 Hjalmar Johansson (Swe)
1912 Erik Adlerz (Swe)
1920 Clarence Pinkston (USA)
1924 Albert White (USA)
1928 Peter Desjardins (USA)
1932 Harold Smith (USA)
1936 Marshall Wayne (USA)
1948 Samuel Lee (USA
1952 Samuel Lee (USA)
1956 Joaquin Capilla Perez (Mex)
1960 Robert Webster (USA)
1964 Robert Webster (USA)
1968 Klaus Dibiasi (Ita)
1972 Klaus Dibiasi (Ita)
1976 Klaus Dibiasi (Ita)
1980 Falk Hoffmann (GDR)
1984 Greg Louganis (USA)

WOMEN

100 METRES FREESTYLE
1912 Fanny Durack (Aus) 1:22.2
1920 Etheleda Bleibtrey (USA) 1:13.6
1924 Ethel Lackie (USA) 1:12.4
1928 Albina Osipowich (USA) 1:11.0
1932 Helene Madison (USA) 1:06.8
1936 Hendrika Mastenbroek (Hol) 1:05.9
1948 Greta Andersen (Den) 1:06.3
1952 Katalin Szöke (Hun) 1:06.8
1956 Dawn Fraser (Aus) 1:02.0
1960 Dawn Fraser (Aus) 1:01.2
1964 Dawn Fraser (Aus) 59.5
1968 Jan Henne (USA) 1:00.0
1972 Sandra Neilson (USA) 58.59
1976 Kornelia Ender (GDR) 55.65
1980 Barbara Krause (GDR) 54.79 OR
1984 Nancy Hogshead (USA) &
     Carrie Steinseifer (USA) 55.92

200 METRES FREESTYLE
1968 Debbie Meyer (USA) 2:10.5
1972 Shane Gould (Aus) 2:03.56
1976 Kornelia Ender (GDR) 1:59.26
1980 Barbara Krause (GDR) 1:58.33 OR
1984 Mary Wayte (USA) 1:59.23

400 METRES FREESTYLE
1920 Ethelda Bleibtrey (USA) 4:34.0 (300m)
1924 Martha Norelius (USA) 6:02.2
1928 Martha Norelius (USA) 5:42.8
1932 Helene Madison (USA) 5:28.5
1936 Hendrika Mastenbroek (Hol) 5:26.4
1948 Ann Curtis (USA) 5:17.8
1952 Valeria Gyenge (Hun) 5:12.1
1956 Lorraine Crapp (Aus) 4:54.6
1960 Chris von Saltza (USA) 4:50.6
1964 Virginia Duenkel (USA) 4:43.3
1968 Debbie Meyer (USA) 4:31.8
1972 Shane Gould (Aus) 4:19.04
1976 Petra Thümer (GDR) 4:09.89
1980 Ines Diers (GDR) 4:08.76
1984 Tiffany Cohen (USA) 4:07.10 OR

Dawn Fraser (All-Sport)

800 METRES FREESTYLE
1968 Debbie Meyer (USA) 9:24.0
1972 Keena Rothhammer (USA) 8:53.68
1976 Petra Thümer (GDR) 8:37.14
1980 Michelle Ford (Aus) 8:28.90
1984 Tiffany Cohen (USA) 8:24.95 OR

4×100 METRES FREESTYLE RELAY
1912 United Kingdom 5:52.8
1920 USA 5:11.6
1924 USA 4:58.8
1928 USA 4:47.6
1932 USA 4:38.0
1936 Netherlands 4:36.0
1948 USA 4:29.2
1952 Hungary 4:24.4
1956 Australia 4:17.1
1960 USA 4:08.9
1964 USA 4:03.8
1968 USA 4:02.5
1972 USA 3:55.19
1976 USA 3:44.82
1980 GDR 3:42.71 OR
1984 USA 3:43.43

100 METRES BACKSTROKE
1924 Sybil Bauer (USA) 1:23.2
1928 Maria Braun (Hol) 1:22.0
1932 Eleanor Holm (USA) 1:19.4
1936 Nida Senff (Hol) 1:18.9
1948 Karen Harup (Den) 1:14.4
1952 Joan Harrison (SAf) 1:14.3
1956 Judy Grinham (UK) 1:12.9
1960 Lynn Burke (USA) 1:09.3
1964 Cathy Ferguson (USA) 1:07.7
1968 Kaye Hall (USA) 1:06.2
1972 Melissa Belote (USA) 1:05.78
1976 Ulrike Richter (GDR) 1:01.83
1980 Rica Reinisch (GDR) 1:00.86 OR
1984 Theresa Andrews (USA) 1:02.55

200 METRES BACKSTROKE
1968 Pokey Watson (USA) 2:24.8
1972 Melissa Belote (USA) 2:19.19

1976 Ulrike Richter (GDR) 2:13.43
1980 Rica Reinisch (GDR) 2:11.77 OR
1984 Jolanda de Rover (Hol) 2:12.38

100 METRES BREASTSTROKE
1968 Djurdjica Bjedov (Yug) 1:15.8
1972 Catherine Carr (USA) 1:13.58
1976 Hannelore Anke (GDR) 1:11.16
1980 Ute Geweniger (GDR) 1:10.22
1984 Petra Van Staveren (Hol) 1:09.88 OR

200 METRES BREASTSTROKE
1924 Lucy Morton (UK) 3:33.2
1928 Hilde Schrader (Ger) 3:12.6
1932 Claire Dennis (Aus) 3:06.3
1936 Hideko Maehata (Jap) 3:03.6
1948 Petronella van Vliet (Hol) 2:57.2
1952 Eva Szekely (Hun) 2:51.7
1956 Ursula Happe (FRG) 2:53.1
1960 Anita Lonsbrough (UK) 2:49.5
1964 Galina Prozumenshchikova (USSR) 2:46.4
1968 Sharon Wichman (USA) 2:44.4
1972 Beverley Whitfield (Aus) 2:41.71
1976 Marina Koshevaya (USSR) 2:33.35
1980 Lina Kachushite (USSR) 2:29.54 OR
1984 Anne Ottenbrite (Can) 2:30.38

100 METRES BUTTERFLY
1956 Shelley Mann (USA) 1:11.0
1960 Carolyn Schuler (USA) 1:09.5
1964 Sharon Stouder (USA) 1:04.7
1968 Lynette McClements (Aus) 1:05.0
1972 Mayumi Aoki (Jap) 1:03.34
1976 Kornelia Ender (GDR) 1:00.13
1980 Caren Metschuck (GDR) 1:00.42
1984 Mary T. Meagher (USA) 59.26
OR Mary T.Meagher (USA) 59.05 (1984)

200 METRES BUTTERFLY
1968 Ada Kok (Hol) 2:24.7
1972 Karen Moe (USA) 2:15.57
1976 Andrea Pollack (GDR) 2:11.41
1980 Ines Geissler (GDR) 2:10.44
1984 Mary T.Meagher (USA) 2:06.90 OR

200 METRES INDIVIDUAL MEDLEY
1968 Claudia Kolb (USA) 2:24.7
1972 Sharon Gould (Aus) 2:23.07
1984 Tracy Caulkins (USA) 2:12.64 OR

400 METRES INDIVIDUAL MEDLEY
1964 Donna De Varona (USA) 5:18.7
1968 Claudia Kolb (USA) 5:08.5
1972 Gail Neall (Aus) 5:02.97
1976 Ulrike Tauber (GDR) 4:42.77
1980 Petra Schneider (GDR) 4:36.29 OR
1984 Tracy Caulkins (USA) 4:39.24

4×100 METRES MEDLEY RELAY
1960 USA 4:41.1
1964 USA 4:33.9
1968 USA 4:28.3
1972 USA 4:20.75
1976 GDR 4:07.95
1980 GDR 4:06.67 OR
1984 USA 4:08.34

SPRINGBOARD DIVING
1920 Aileen Riggin (USA)
1924 Elizabeth Becker (USA)
1928 Helen Meany (USA)
1932 Georgia Coleman (USA)
1936 Marjorie Gestring (USA)
1948 Victoria Draves (USA)
1952 Pat McCormick (USA)
1956 Pat McCormick (USA)
1960 Ingrid Krämer (GDR)
1964 Ingrid Engel (née Krämer)(GDR)
1968 Sue Gossick (USA)
1972 Micki King (USA)
1976 Jennifer Chandler (USA)
1980 Irina Kalinina (USSR)
1984 Sylvie Bernier (Can)

HIGHBOARD PLATFORM DIVING
1912 Greta Johansson (Swe)
1920 Stefani Fryland-Clausen (Den)
1924 Caroline Smith (USA)
1928 Elizabeth Pinkston (USA)
1932 Dorothy Poynton (USA)
1936 Dorothy Hill (née Poynton) (USA)
1948 Victoria Draves (USA)
1952 Pat McCormick (USA)
1956 Pat McCormick (USA)
1960 Ingrid Krämer (GDR)
1964 Lesley Bush (USA)
1968 Milena Duchkova (Cs)
1972 Ulrika Knape (Swe)
1976 Yelena Vaytsekhovskaya (USSR)
1980 Martina Jäschke (GDR)
1984 Zhou Jihong (Chn)

SYNCHRONISED SWIMMING

SOLO
1984 Tracie Ruiz (USA)

DUET
1984 Candy Costie & Tracie Ruiz (USA)

MOST OLYMPIC GOLD MEDALS: (INDIVIDUAL/RELAY)
MEN
9 (4/5) Mark Spitz (USA) 1968-72
5 (4/1) Charles Daniels (USA) 1904-8
5 (3/2) Johnny Weissmuller (USA) 1924-8
5 (2/3) Don Schollander (USA) 1964-8
4 (4/-) Roland Matthes (GDR) 1968-72
4 (3/1) Henry Taylor (UK) 1906-8
4 (3/1) Murray Rose (Aus) 1956-60
4 (2/2) John Naber (USA) 1976
WOMEN
4 (4/-) Pat McCormick (USA) 1952-6
4 (3/1) Dawn Fraser (Aus) 1956-64
4 (3/1) Kornelia Ender (GDR) 1976

Spitz won a record seven gold medals at one games, in 1972.

Most Olympic medals: (gold/silver/bronze)

MEN
11 (9/1/1) Mark Spitz (USA) 1968-72
 8 (5/1/2) Charles Daniels (USA) 1904-8
 8 (4/2/2) Roland Matthes (GDR) 1968-72
 8 (4/1/3) Henry Taylor (UK) 1906-20

WOMEN
8 (4/4/-) Dawn Fraser (Aus) 1956-64
8 (4/4/-) Kornelia Ender (GDR) 1972-6
8 (2/6/-) Shirley Babashoff (USA) 1972-6

Youngest gold medallist:
MEN 14yr 309d Kusuo Kitamura (Jap) 1500 freestyle 1932
WOMEN 13yr 268d Marjorie Gestring (USA) springboard diving 1936

Oldest gold medallist:
MEN 34yr 186d Hjalmar Johansson (Swe) highboard diving 1908
WOMEN 30yr 41d Ursula Happe (FRG) 200m breaststroke 1956

Youngest medallist:
MEN 14yr 10d Nils Skoglund (Swe) silver highboard diving 1928
WOMEN 12yr 24d Inge Sörensen (Den) bronze 200m breaststroke 1936

WORLD CHAMPIONSHIPS
World Championships separate from the Olympic Games were first held in 1973, and are now staged every four years. Venues have been: 1973 Belgrade; 1975 Cali, Colombia; 1978 West Berlin; 1982 Guayaquil, Ecuador; 1986 Madrid.

Champions have been:

MEN
50 METRES FREESTYLE
1986 Tom Jager (USA) 22.49

100 METRES FREESTYLE
1973 Jim Montgomery (USA) 51.70
1975 Andrew Coan (USA) 51.25
1978 David McCagg (USA) 50.24
1982 Jörg Woithe (GDR) 50.18
1986 Matt Biondi (USA) 48.94

200 METRES FREESTYLE
1973 Jim Montgomery (USA) 1:53.02
1975 Tim Shaw (USA) 1:51.04
1978 William Forrester (USA) 1:51.02
1982 Michael Gross (FRG) 1:49.84
1986 Michael Gross (FRG) 1:47.92

400 METRES FREESTYLE
1973 Rick DeMont (USA) 3:58.18
1975 Tim Shaw (USA) 3:54.88
1978 Vladimir Salnikov (USSR) 3:51.94
1982 Vladimir Salnikov (USSR) 3:51.30
1986 Rainer Henkel (FRG) 3:50.05

1500 METRES FREESTYLE
1973 Steve Holland (Aus) 15:31.85
1975 Tim Shaw (USA) 15:28.92
1978 Vladimir Salnikov (USSR) 15:03.99
1982 Vladimir Salnikov (USSR) 15:01.77
1986 Rainer Henkel (FRG) 15:05.31

4 × 100 METRES FREESTYLE RELAY
1973 USA 3:27.18
1975 USA 3:24.85
1978 USA 3:19.74
1982 USA 3:19.26

1986 USA 3:19.89

4 × 200 METRES FREESTYLE RELAY
1973 USA 7:33.22
1975 FRG 7:39.44
1978 USA 7:20.82
1982 USA 7:21.09
1986 GDR 7:15.91

100 METRES BACKSTROKE
1973 Roland Matthes (GDR) 57.47
1975 Roland Matthes (GDR) 58.15
1978 Robert Jackson (USA) 56.36
1982 Dirk Richter (GDR) 55.95
1986 Igor Polyanski (USSR) 55.58

200 METRES BACKSTROKE
1973 Roland Matthes (GDR) 2:01.87
1975 Zoltan Verraszto (Hun) 2:05.05
1978 Jesse Vassallo (USA) 2:02.16
1982 Rick Carey (USA) 2:00.82
1986 Igor Polyanski (USSR) 1:58.78

100 METRES BREASTSTROKE
1973 John Hencken (USA) 1:04.02
1975 David Wilkie (UK) 1:04.26
1978 Walter Kusch (GDR) 1:03.56
1982 Steve Lundquist (USA) 1:02.75
1986 Victor Davis (Can) 1:02.71

200 METRES BREASTSTROKE
1973 David Wilkie (UK) 2:19.28
1975 David Wilkie (UK) 2:18.23
1978 Nick Nevid (USA) 2:18.37
1982 Victor Davis (Can) 2:14.77
1986 Jozsef Szabo (Hun) 2:14.27

100 METRES BUTTERFLY
1973 Bruce Robertson (Can) 55.69
1975 Greg Jagenburg (USA) 55.63
1978 Joe Bottom (USA) 54.30
1982 Matt Gribble (USA) 53.88
1986 Pablo Morales (USA) 53.54

200 METRES BUTTERFLY
1973 Robin Backhaus (USA) 2:03.32
1975 William Forrester (USA) 2:01.95
1978 Michael Bruner (USA) 1:59.38
1982 Michael Gross (FRG) 1:58.85
1986 Michael Gross (FRG) 1:56.53

Mark Spitz, winner of nine Olympic gold medals (All-Sport)

200 METRES INDIVIDUAL MEDLEY
1973 Gunnar Larsson (Swe) 2:08.36
1975 Andras Hargitay (Hun) 2:07.72
1978 Graham Smith (Can) 2:03.65
1982 Aleksey Sidorenko (USSR) 2:03.30
1986 Tamas Darnyi (Hun) 2:01.57

400 METRES INDIVIDUAL MEDLEY
1973 Andras Hargitay (Hun) 4:31.11
1975 Andras Hargitay (Hun) 4:32.57
1978 Jesse Vassallo (USA) 4:20.05
1982 Ricardo Prado (Bra) 4:19.78
1986 Tamas Darnyi (Hun) 4:18.98

4 × 100 METRES MEDLEY RELAY
1973 USA 3:49.49
1975 USA 3:49.00
1978 USA 3:44.63
1982 USA 3:40.84
1986 USA 3:41.25

SPRINGBOARD DIVING
1973 Phil Boggs (USA)
1975 Phil Boggs (USA)
1978 Phil Boggs (USA)
1982 Greg Louganis (USA)
1986 Greg Louganis (USA)

HIGHBOARD DIVING
1973 Klaus Dibiasi (Ita)
1975 Klaus Dibiasi (Ita)
1978 Greg Louganis (USA)
1982 Greg Louganis (USA)
1986 Greg Louganis (USA)

WOMEN

50 METRES FREESTYLE
1986 Tamara Costache (Rom) 25.28

100 METRES FREESTYLE
1973 Kornelia Ender (GDR) 57.54
1975 Kornelia Ender (GDR) 56.50
1978 Barbara Krause (GDR) 55.68
1982 Birgit Meineke (GDR) 55.79
1986 Kristin Otto (GDR) 55.05

200 METRES FREESTYLE
1973 Keena Rothhammer (USA) 2:04.99
1975 Shirley Babashoff (USA) 2:02.50
1978 Cynthia Woodhead (USA) 1:58.53
1982 Annemarie Verstappen (Hol) 1:59.53
1986 Heike Friedrich (GDR) 1:58.26

400 METRES FREESTYLE
1973 Heather Greenwood (USA) 4:20.28
1975 Shirley Babashoff (USA) 4:16.87
1978 Tracey Wickham (Aus) 4:06.28
1982 Carmela Schmidt (GDR) 4:08.98
1986 Heike Friedrich (GDR) 4:07.45

800 METRES FREESTYLE
1973 Novella Calligaris (Ita) 8:52.97
1975 Jenny Turrall (Aus) 8:44.75
1978 Tracey Wickham (Aus) 8:24.94
1982 Kim Lineham (USA) 8:27.48
1986 Astrid Strauss (GDR) 8:28.24

4 × 100 METRES FREESTYLE RELAY
1973 GDR 3:52.45
1975 GDR 3:49.37
1978 USA 3:43.43
1982 GDR 3:43.97
1986 GDR 3:40.57

4 × 200 METRES FREESTYLE RELAY
1986 GDR 7:59.33

100 METRES BACKSTROKE
1973 Ulrike Richter (GDR) 1:05.42
1975 Ulrike Richter (GDR) 1:03.30
1978 Linda Jezek (USA) 1:02.55
1982 Kristin Otto (GDR) 1:01.30
1986 Betsy Mitchell (USA) 1:01.74

200 METRES BACKSTROKE
1973 Melissa Belote (USA) 2:20.52
1975 Birgit Treiber (GDR) 2:15.46
1978 Linda Jezek (USA) 2:11.93
1982 Cornelia Sirch (GDR) 2:09.91
1986 Cornelia Sirch (GDR) 2:11.37

100 METRES BREASTSTROKE
1973 Renate Vogel (GDR) 1:13.74
1975 Hannelore Anke (GDR) 1:12.72
1978 Yulia Bogdanova (USSR) 1:10.31
1982 Ute Geweniger (GDR) 1:09.14
1986 Sylvia Gerasch (GDR) 1:08.11

200 METRES BREASTSTROKE
1973 Renate Vogel (GDR) 2:40.01
1975 Hannelore Anke (GDR) 2:37.25
1978 Lina Kachushite (USSR) 2:31.42
1982 Svetlana Varganova (USSR) 2:28.82
1986 Silke Hörner (GDR) 2:27.40

100 METRES BUTTERFLY
1973 Kornelia Ender (GDR) 1:02.53
1975 Kornelia Ender (GDR) 1:01.24
1978 Mary-Joan Pennington (USA) 1:00.20
1982 Mary T.Meagher (USA) 59.41
1986 Kornelia Gressler (GDR) 59.51

200 METRES BUTTERFLY
1973 Rosemarie Kother (GDR) 2:13.76
1975 Rosemarie Kother (GDR) 2:13.82
1978 Tracy Caulkins (USA) 2:09.87
1982 Ines Geissler (GDR) 2:08.66
1986 Mary T.Meagher (USA) 2:08.41

200 METRES INDIVIDUAL MEDLEY
1973 Angela Hübner (GDR) 2:20.51
1975 Kathy Heddy (USA) 2:19.80
1978 Tracy Caulkins (USA) 2:14.07
1982 Petra Schneider (GDR) 2:11.79
1986 Kristin Otto (GDR) 2:15.56

400 METRES INDIVIDUAL MEDLEY
1973 Gudrun Wegner (GDR) 4:57.31
1975 Ulrike Tauber (GDR) 4:52.76
1978 Tracy Caulkins (USA) 4:40.83
1982 Petra Schneider (GDR) 4:36.10
1986 Kathleen Nord (GDR) 4:43.75

4 × 100 METRES MEDLEY RELAY
1973 GDR 4:16.84
1975 GDR 4:14.74

Mary T. Meagher (All-Sports)

1978 USA 4:08.21
1982 GDR 4:05.88
1986 GDR 4:04.82

SPRINGBOARD DIVING
1973 Christine Kohler (GDR)
1975 Irina Kalinina (USSR)
1978 Irina Kalinina (USSR)
1982 Megan Neyer (USA)
1986 Min Gao (Chn)

HIGHBOARD DIVING
1973 Ulrike Knape (Swe)
1975 Janet Ely (USA)
1978 Irina Kalinina (USSR)
1982 Wendy Wyland (USA)
1986 Lin Chen (Chn)

SYNCHRONISED SWIMMING SOLO
1973 Teresa Andersen (USA)
1975 Gail Buzonas (USA)
1978 Helen Vanderburg (Can)
1982 Tracie Ruiz (USA)
1986 Carolyn Waldo (Can)

SYNCHRONISED SWIMMING DUET
1973 Teresa Andersen & Gail Johnson (USA)
1975 Robin Curren & Amanda Norrish (USA)
1978 Michele Calkins & Helen Vanderburg (Can)
1982 Kelly Kryczka & Sharon Hambrook (Can)
1986 Carolyn Waldo & Michelle Cameron (Can)

SYNCHRONISED SWIMMING TEAM
1973 USA
1975 USA
1978 USA
1982 Canada
1986 Canada

MOST GOLD MEDALS (individual/relay)
MEN
6 (2/4) Jim Montgomery (USA) 1973-5
5 (5/0) Greg Louganis (USA) 1978-86
5 (0/5) Rowdy Gaines (USA) 1978-82
WOMEN
8 (4/4) Kornelia Ender (GDR) 1973-5
7 (3/4) Kristin Otto (GDR) 1982-6

MOST MEDALS (gold/silver/bronze)
MEN
8 (5/3/0) Rowdy Gaines (USA) 1978-82
WOMEN
10 (8/2/0) Kornelia Ender (GDR) 1973-5
9 (7/2/0) Kristin Otto (GDR) 1982-6
9 (2/5/2) Mary T.Meagher (USA) 1978-82
MOST MEDALS AT ONE CHAMPIONSHIPS
(gold/silver/bronze)
MEN
7 (3/1/3) Matt Biondi (USA) 1986
WOMEN
6 (5/1/0) Tracy Caulkins (USA) 1978
6 (4/2/0) Kristin Otto (GDR) 1986
6 (1/3/2) Mary T.Meagher (USA) 1986

WORLD CUP
Held in 1979 when both men's and women's competitions were won-by the USA.

WORLD CUP – DIVING
First held in 1979, it is now a team competition held biennially.
Team winners:
1981 China 1983 China 1985 China

EUROPEAN CUP
The European inter-nation competitions for men and women were first held in 1969. Staged biennially at first, they are now held annually in the winter in a 25m pool.
Winners:
MEN 8 USSR 1971, 1975-6, 1979-83; 3 GDR 1969, 1973, 1984; 2 FRG 1985-6.
WOMEN 12 GDR 1969, 1971, 1973, 1975, 1979-86; 1 USSR 1976.

EUROPEAN CHAMPIONSHIPS
First held in Budapest in 1926, and subsequently in 1927, 1931, 1934, 1938, 1947, at four-yearly intervals 1950-74, in 1977 and biennially from 1981.

Winners in 1983 and 1985, championship records if set before 1983, and swimmers to have won a particular event twice:
MEN

100 METRES FREESTYLE
1983 Per Johansson (Swe) 50.20
1985 Stéphane Caron (Fra) 50.20

Most: 2 Istvan Barany (Hun) 1926, 1931; Alex Jany (Fra) 1947, 1950; Peter Nocke (FRG) 1974, 1977; Per Johansson (Swe) 1981, 1983

200 METRES FREESTYLE
1983 Michael Gross (FRG) 1:47.87
1985 Michael Gross (FRG) 1:47.95

Most: 2 Peter Nocke (FRG) 1974, 1977; Gross

400 METRES FREESTYLE
1983 Vladimir Salnikov (USSR) 3:49.80
1985 Uwe Dassler (GDR) 3:51.52

Most: 2 Arne Borg (Swe) 1926-7; Alex Jany (Fra) 1947, 1950

1500 METRES FREESTYLE
1983 Vladimir Salnikov (USSR) 15:08.84
1985 Uwe Dassler (GDR) 15:08.56

Most: 3 Vladimir Salnikov (USSR) 1977, 1981, 1983; 2 Arne Borg (Swe) 1926-7

4 × 100 METRES FREESTYLE RELAY
1983 USSR 3:20.88
1985 FRG 3:22.18

4 × 200 METRES FREESTYLE RELAY
1983 FRG 7:20.40
1985 FRG 7:19.23

100 METRES BACKSTROKE
1983 Dirk Richter (GDR) 56.10
1985 Igor Polyanski (USSR) 55.24

Most: 2 Roland Matthes (GDR) 1970, 1974

200 METRES BACKSTROKE
1983 Sergey Zabolotnov (USSR) 2:01.00
1985 Igor Polyanski (USSR) 1:58.50

Most: 2 Roland Matthes (GDR) 1970, 1974

100 METRES BREASTSTROKE
1983 Robertas Zhulpa (USSR) 1:03.32
1985 Adrian Moorhouse (UK) 1:02.99

Most: 2 Nikolay Pankin (USSR) 1970, 1974

200 METRES BREASTSTROKE
1983 Adrian Moorhouse (UK) 2:17.49
1985 Dmitriy Volkov (USSR) 2:19.53

Most: 2 Erich Rademacher (Ger) 1926-7; Georgy Prokopenko (USSR) 1962, 1966

100 METRES BUTTERFLY
1983 Michael Gross (FRG) 54.00
1985 Michael Gross (FRG) 54.02

Most: 2 Roger Pyttel (GDR) 1974, 1977; Gross

200 METRES BUTTERFLY
1983 Michael Gross (FRG) 1:57.05
1985 Michael Gross (FRG) 1:56.65

Most: 3 Gross 1981, 1983, 1985; 2 Valentin Kuzmin (USSR) 1962, 1966

200 METRES INDIVIDUAL MEDLEY
1983 Giovanni Franceshi (Ita) 2:02.48
1985 Tamas Darnyi (Hun) 2:03.23

400 METRES INDIVIDUAL MEDLEY
1983 Giovanni Franceshi (Ita) 4:20.41
1985 Tamas Darnyi (Hun) 4:20.70

Most: 2 Sergey Fesenko (USSR) 1977, 1981

4 × 100 METRES MEDLEY RELAY
1983 USSR 3:43.99
1985 FRG 3:43.59

SPRINGBOARD DIVING
1983 Petar Georgiev (Bul)
1985 Nikolay Droschin (USSR)

Most: 2 Ewald Riebschlager (Ger) 1927, 1932

HIGHBOARD DIVING
1983 David Ambarzumyan (USSR)
1985 Thomas Knuths (GDR)

Most: 2 Hans Luber (Ger) 1926-7; Brian Phelps (UK) 1958, 1962; Klaus Dibiasi (Ita) 1966, 1974

WOMEN
100 METRES FREESTYLE
1983 Birgit Meineke (GDR) 55.18
1986 Heike Friedrich (GDR) 55.71

200 METRES FREESTYLE
1983 Birgit Meineke (GDR) 1:59.45
1985 Heike Friedrich (GDR) 1:59.55

400 METRES FREESTYLE
1983 Astrid Strauss (GDR) 4:08.07
1985 Astrid Strauss (GDR) 4:09.22

Most: 2 Marie Bruan (Hol) 1927, 1931; Strauss

800 METRES FREESTYLE
1983 Astrid Strauss (GDR) 8:32.12
1985 Astrid Strauss (GDR) 8:32.45

Most: 2 Strauss

4 × 100 METRES FREESTYLE RELAY
1983 GDR 3:44.72
1985 GDR 3:44.48

4 × 200 METRES FREESTYLE RELAY
1983 GDR 8:02.27
1985 GDR 8:03.82

100 METRES BACKSTROKE
1983 Ina Kleber (GDR) 1:01.79
1985 Birte Weigang (GDR) 1:02.16

Most: 2 Kleber 1981, 1983

200 METRES BACKSTROKE
1983 Cornelia Sirch (GDR) 2:12.05
1985 Cornelia Sirch (GDR) 2:10.89

Most: 2 Sirch

100 METRES BREASTSTROKE
1983 Ute Geweniger (GDR) 1:08.51
1985 Sylvia Gerasch (GDR) 1:08.62

Most: 2 Geweniger 1981, 1983

200 METRES BREASTSTROKE
1983 Ute Geweniger (GDR) 2:30.64
1985 Tamara Bogomilova (Bul) 2:28.57

Most: 2 Galina Prozumeshikova/Stepanova (USSR) 1966, 1970; Geweniger 1981, 1983

100 METRES BUTTERFLY
1983 Ines Geissler (GDR) 1:00.31
1985 Kornelia Gressler (GDR) 59.46

Most: 2 Ada Kok (Hol) 1962, 1966

200 METRES BUTTERFLY
1983 Cornelia Polit (GDR) 2:07.82
1985 Jacqueline Alex (GDR) 2:11.78

200 METRES INDIVIDUAL MEDLEY
1983 Ute Geweniger (GDR) 2:13.07
1986 Kathleen Nord (GDR) 2:16.07

Most: 2 Ulrike Tauber (GDR) 1974, 1977; Geweniger 1981 (2:12.64 rec), 1983

400 METRES INDIVIDUAL MEDLEY
1983 Kathleen Nord (GDR) 4:39.95
1985 Kathleen Nord (GDR) 4:47.08

Rec: 1981 Petra Schneider (GDR) 4:39.30
Most: 2 Ulrike Tauber (GDR) 1974, 1977; Nord

4 × 100 METRES MEDLEY RELAY
1983 GDR 4:05.79
1985 GDR 4:06.93

SPRINGBOARD DIVING
1983 Brita Baldus (GDR)
1985 Zhanna Tsirulnikova (USSR)

Most: 2 Olga Jensch (née Jordan) (Ger) 1931, 1934; Mady Moreau (Fra) 1947, 1950

HIGHBOARD DIVING
1983 Alla Lobankina (USSR)
1985 Anzyela Stasyulevich (USSR)

Most: 2 Nicole Pelissard (Fra) 1947, 1950

SYNCHRONISED SWIMMING SOLO
1983 Carolyn Wilson (UK)
1985 Carolyn Wilson (UK)

Most: 2 Wilson

SYNCHRONISED SWIMMING DUET
1983 Carolyn Wilson & Amanda Dodd (UK)
1985 Eva-Maria Edinger & Alexandra Worisch (Aut)

SYNCHRONISED SWIMMING TEAM
1983 UK
1985 France

MOST GOLD MEDALS (individual/relay)

MEN 11(7/4) Michael Gross (FRG) 1981-5
WOMEN 8(7/1) Ute Geweniger (GDR) 1981-3

Michael Gross won three individual events in both 1983 and 1985; in the latter he also swam on three winning FRG relay teams, for a record six golds at one Championships. He also won two silvers and a bronze, for a record 14 medals in the three Championships 1981-5. Birgit Meineke won a women's record five gold medals in 1983, two individual and three relay for the GDR.

Others to have won three individual events at one Championships: Arne Borg (Swe) 1927, Ian Black (UK) 1958, Gunnar Larsson (Swe) 1970, Ute Geweniger (GDR) 1981.

(For *Commonwealth Games* swimming, see separate section)

WORLD RECORDS

World records for swimming were first recognised by FINA in 1908. At that time records for distances under 800m could be set in pools of any length over 25 yards, and it was possible for times to be taken in mid-course, and not just at the end of the pool. The range of distances proliferated, but was cut back in 1948 and in 1952, when, also, records for the breast-stroke and butterfly were separated. In 1957 FINA decreed that henceforth only times set in 50m or 55y pools would be accepted and no mid-pool times would be recognised. As short-course times are quicker (by c.0.7 sec. per turn), due to more turns, at some events it took a few years before the old records were surpassed. In 1968 Imperial distances were cut from the lists.

Records are shown for each of the currently recognised events, with the records at 15-year intervals:

\# records set in short-course pools (up to 1957)
y mark made at the longer equivalent Imperial distance.
Also listed are those swimmers to have set most records at each distance.

MEN *min:sec*   *Name*   *Date*

50 METRES FREESTYLE
1987   22.33   Matt Biondi (USA)   26 Jun 1986 & 31 Jul 1987

100 METRES FREESTYLE
1912	1:01.6	Duke Kahanamoku (USA)	20 Jul 1912
1927	57.4 #	Johnny Weissmuller (USA)	17 Feb 1924
1942	56.4 #	Peter Fick (USA)	11 Feb 1936
1957	54.6	John Devitt (Aus)	28 Jan 1957
1972	51.22	Mark Spitz (USA)	3 Sep 1972
1987	48.74	Matt Biondi (USA)	24 Jun 1986

Most: 4 Jim Montgomery (USA) 51.12 - 49.99 1975-6
        3 Duke Kahanamoku (USA) 61.6 - 60.4 1912-20
        3 Peter Fick (USA) 56.8# - 56.4# 1934-6
        3 Mark Spitz (USA) 51.9 - 51.22 1970-2
        3 Matt Biondi (USA) 49.24 - 48.74 1985-6

200 METRES FREESTYLE (y- 220 yards)
1912	2:25.4y #	Charles Daniels (USA)	26 Mar 1909
1927	2:08.0 #	Johnny Weissmuller (USA)	5 Apr 1927
1942	2:07.2 #	Jack Medica (USA)	12 Apr 1935
1957	2:01.5 #	Dick Hanley (USA)	8 Mar 1957
1972	1:52.78	Mark Spitz (USA)	29 Aug 1972
1987	1:47.44	Michael Gross (FRG)	29 Jul 1984

Most: 9 Don Schollander (USA) 1:58.8 - 1:54.3 1963-8
5 Tsuyoshi Yamanaka (Jap) 2:03.0 - 2:00.4 1958-61
4 Mark Spitz (USA) 1:54.3 - 1:52.78 1969-72
4 Bruce Furniss (USA) 1:51.41 - 1:50.29 1975-6
4 Michael Gross (FRG) 1:48.28 - 1:47.44 1983-4

400 METRES FREESTYLE (y- 440 yards)

1912	5:21.6 #	Jack Hatfield (UK)	26 Sep 1912
1927	4:50.3 #	Arne Borg (Swe)	11 Sep 1925
1942	4:38.5 #	Bill Smith (USA)	13 May 1941
1957	4:25.9	Murray Rose (Aus)	12 Jan 1957
1972	4:00.11	Kurt Krumpholtz (USA)	4 Aug 1972
1987	3:47.80	Michael Gross (FRG)	27 Jun 1985

Most: 6 Vladimir Salnikov (USSR) 3:51.41 - 3:48.32 1979-83
4 John Konrads (Aus) 4:25.9y - 4:15.9y 1958-60
4 Tim Shaw (USA) 3:56.96 - 3:53.31 1974-5

800 METRES FREESTYLE (y- 880 yards)

1912	11:25.4y	Henry Taylor (UK)	21 Jul 1906
1927	10:22.2y	Johnny Weissmuller (USA)	27 Jul 1927
1942	9:50.9	Bill Smith (USA)	24 Jul 1941
1957	9:19.2y	George Breen (USA)	27 Oct 1956
1972	8:23.8	Brad Cooper (Aus)	12 Jan 1972
1987	7:50.64	Vladimir Salnikov (USSR)	4 Jul 1986

Most: 6 Steve Holland (Aus) 8:17.6 - 8:02.91 1973-6
4 Shozo Makino (Jap) 10:16.6 - 9:55.8 1931-5
4 Vladimir Salnikov (USSR) 7:56.43 - 7:50.64 1979-86

1500 METRES FREESTYLE

1912	22:00.0	George Hodgson (Can)	10 Jul 1912
1927	19:07.2	Arne Borg (Swe)	2 Sep 1927
1942	18:58.8	Tomikatsu Amano (Jap)	10 Aug 1938
1957	17:52.9	George Breen (USA)	5 Dec 1956
1972	15:52.58	Mike Burton (USA)	4 Sep 1972
1987	14:54.76	Vladimir Salnikov (USSR)	22 Feb 1983

Most: 5 Arne Borg (Swe) 21:35.3 - 19:07.2 1923-7
5 Mike Burton (USA) 16:41.6 - 15:52.58 1966-72
4 Steve Holland (Aus) 15:37.8 - 15:10.59 1973-6

4 × 100 METRES FREESTYLE RELAY

1942	3:50.8 #	Yale University (USA)	18 Mar 1942
1957	3:46.8	Japan	6 Aug 1955
1972	3:26.42	USA	28 Aug 1972
1987	3:17.08	USA	17 Aug 1985

(Scott McAdam, Mike Heath, Paul Wallace, Matt Biondi)

4 × 200 METRES FREESTYLE RELAY

1942	8:51.5	Japan	11 Aug 1936
1957	8:23.6	Australia	3 Dec 1956
1972	7:35.78	USA	31 Aug 1972
1987	7:15.69	USA	30 Jul 1984

(Mike Heath, David Larson, Jeffrey Float, Bruce Hayes)

100 METRES BACKSTROKE

1912	1:15.6 #	Otto Fahr (Ger)	29 May 1912
1927	1:10.2 #	P.A.House (USA)	22 Mar 1927
1942	1:04.8 #	Adolph Kiefer (USA)	18 Jan 1936
1957	1:02.2	David Theile (Aus)	6 Dec 1956
1972	56.30	Roland Matthes (GDR)	4 Sep 1972
1987	55.19	Rick Carey (USA)	21 Aug 1983

Most: 8 Roland Matthes (GDR) 58.4 - 56.30 1967-72
4 Warren Kealoha (USA) 1:14.8 - 1:11.4 # 1920-6
4 Adolph Kiefer (USA) 1:07.0 #- 1:04.8 # 1935-6

200 METRES BACKSTROKE

| 1912 | 2:48.4 # | Otto Fahr (Ger) | 3 Apr 1912 |

Johnny Weissmuller won five Olympic gold medals. He was the first man to swim 100 metres in less than a minute and the first to swim 440 yds in under five minutes. He was undefeated from 1921 to his retirement in 1928, after which he became famous as Tarzan in many films.

1927	2:38.8 #	Walter Laufer (USA)	13 Jul 1926
1942	2:23.0 #	Adolph Kiefer (USA)	23 May 1941
1957	2:18.3 #	Gilbert Bozon (Fra)	26 Jun 1953
1972	2:02.82	Roland Matthes (GDR)	10 Jul 1972
1987	1:58.14	Igor Polyanskiy (USSR)	3 Mar 1985

Most: 9 Roland Matthes (GDR) 2:07.9 - 2:01.87 1967-73
4 Tom Stock (USA) 2:16.0 - 2:10.9 1960-2

100 METRES BREASTSTROKE (* with butterfly stroke)

1912	1:17.8	Walther Bathe (Ger)	18 Dec 1910
1927	1:14.0 #	Walter Spence (USA)	28 Oct 1927
1942	1:07.3*#	Dick Hough (USA)	15 Apr 1939
1957	1:11.5	Vladimir Minashkin (USSR)	15 Sep 1957
1972	1:04.94	Nobutaka Taguchi (Jap)	30 Aug 1972
1987	1:01.65	Steven Lundquist (USA)	29 Jul 1984

Most: 7 John Hencken (USA) 1:05.68 - 1:03.11 1972-6
6 Chet Jastremski (USA) 1:11.1 - 1:07.5 1961
5 Leonid Meshkov (USSR) 1:07.2*#- 1:06.5*# 1949-51
5 Steven Lundquist (USA) 1:02.62 - 1:01.65 1982-4

200 METRES BREASTSTROKE (* with butterfly stroke)
(u under-water swimming, permitted at breaststroke until 1957)

1912	3:00.8 #	Felicien Coubert (Bel)	2 Oct 1910
1927	2:48.0 #	Erich Rademacher (Ger)	11 Mar 1927
1942	2:36.8*#	Alfred Nakache (Fra)	6 Jul 1941
1957	2:31.0u#	Masaru Furukawa (Jap)	1 Oct 1955
1972	2:21.55	John Hencken (USA)	2 Sep 1972
1987	2:13.34	Victor Davis (Can)	2 Aug 1984

Most: 6 Joe Verdeur (USA) 2:35.6*#- 2:28.3*# 1946-50
5 John Hencken (USA) 2:22.79 - 2:18.21 1972-4
4 Masaru Furukawa (Jap) 2:36.6u#- 2:31.0u# 1954-5

100 METRES BUTTERFLY

1957	1:01.0	Takashi Ishimoto (Jap)	14 Sep 1957
1972	54.27	Mark Spitz (USA)	31 Aug 1972
1987	52.84	Pablo Morales (USA)	23 Jun 1986

Most: 7 Mark Spitz (USA) 56.3 - 54.27 1967-72
6 György Tumpek (Hun) 1:04.3# - 1:03.4 1953-7
5 Takashi Ishimoto (Jap) 1:01.5 - 1:00.1 1957-8

200 METRES BUTTERFLY (y- 220 yards)

1957	2:16.7 #	Bill Yorzyk (USA)	14 Apr 1956
1972	2:00.70	Mark Spitz (USA)	28 Aug 1972
1987	1:56.24	Michael Gross (FRG)	28 Jun 1986

Most: 9 Mark Spitz (USA) 2:06.4 - 2:00.70 1967-72
6 Mike Troy (USA) 2:19.0 - 2:12.8 1959-60
5 Kevin Berry (Aus) 2:12.5y - 2:06.6 1962-4

200 METRES INDIVIDUAL MEDLEY

| 1972 | 2:07.17 | Gunnar Larsson (Swe) | 3 Sep 1972 |
| 1987 | 2:01.42 | Alex Baumann (Can) | 4 Aug 1984 & 4 Mar 1986 |

Most: 4 Alex Baumann (Can) 2:02.78 - 2:01.42 1981-6

400 METRES INDIVIDUAL MEDLEY (y- 440 yards)

1957	5:08.3 #	Vladimir Strouyanov (USSR)	17 Mar 1957
1972	4:30.81	Gary Hall (USA)	3 Aug 1972
1987	4:17.41	Alex Baumann (Can)	30 Jul 1984

Most: 5 Gary Hall (USA) 4:43.3 - 4:30.81 1968-72
4 Ted Stickles (USA) 5:04.3 - 4:51.0y 1961-2

4 × 100 METRES MEDLEY RELAY

1957	4:14.8 #	USSR	14 Aug 1956
1972	3:48.16	USA	4 Sep 1972
1987	3:38.28	USA	18 Aug 1985

(Rick Carey, John Moffett, Pablo Morales, Matt Biondi)

WOMEN

50 METRES FREESTYLE

1987	25.28	Tamara Costache (Rom)	23 Aug 1986

Most: 4 Tamara Costache (Rom) 25.50 - 25.28 1986

100 METRES FREESTYLE

1912	1:18.8	Fanny Durack (Aus)	21 Jul 1912
1927	1:10.0 #	Ethel Lackie (USA)	28 Jan 1926
1942	1:04.6 #	Willy den Ouden (Hol)	27 Feb 1936
1957	1:02.0	Dawn Fraser (Aus)	1 Dec 1956
1972	58.5	Shane Gould (Aus)	8 Jan 1972
1987	54.73	Kristin Otto (GDR) (relay leg)	19 Aug 1986

Most: 11 Dawn Fraser (Aus) 1:04.5 - 58.9 1956-64
       10 Kornelia Ender (GDR) 58.25 - 55.65 1973-6

200 METRES FREESTYLE (y- 220 yards)

1927	2:40.6y#	Martha Norelius (USA)	28 Feb 1926
1942	2:21.7 #	Ragnhild Hveger (Den)	11 Sep 1938
1957	2:18.5	Lorraine Crapp (Aus)	20 Oct 1956
1972	2:03.56	Shane Gould (Aus)	1 Sep 1972
1987	1:57.55	Heike Friedrich (GDR)	18 Jun 1986

Most: 4 Dawn Fraser (Aus) 2:20.7 - 2:11.6y 1956-60
       4 Kornelia Ender (GDR) 2:03.22 - 1:59.26 1974-6

400 METRES FREESTYLE (y- 440 yards)

1927	5:51.4y	Martha Norelius (USA)	23 Jan 1927
1942	5:00.1 #	Ragnhild Hveger (Den)	15 Sep 1940
1957	4:47.2	Lorraine Crapp (Aus)	20 Oct 1956
1972	4:19.04	Shane Gould (Aus)	30 Aug 1972
1987	4:06.28	Tracey Wickham (Aus)	24 Aug 1978

Most: 8 Ragnhild Hveger (Den) 5:14.2# - 5:00.1# 1937-40
       5 Debbie Meyer (USA) 4:32.6 - 4:24.3 1967-70
       4 Martha Norelius (USA) 5:51.4y - 5:39.2# 1927-8

800 METRES FREESTYLE (y- 880 yards)

1927	12:17.8y#	Martha Norelius (USA)	31 Jul 1927
1942	10:52.5	Ragnhild Hveger (Den)	13 Aug 1941
1957	10:27.3	Mary Kok (Hol)	16 Feb 1957
1972	8:53.68	Keena Rothhammer (USA)	3 Sep 1972
1987	8:22.44	Janet Evans (USA)	28 Jul 1987

Most: 5 Debbie Meyer (USA) 9:35.8 - 9:10.4 1967-8
       4 Ilsa Konrads (Aus) 10:17.7y - 10:11.4y 1958-9
       4 Petra Thümer (GDR) 8:40.68 - 8:35.04 1976-7

1500 METRES FREESTYLE

1927	23:44.6	Martha Norelius (USA)	28 Jul 1927
1942	20:57.0	Ragnhild Hveger (Den)	20 Aug 1941
1957	20:03.1	Jans Koster (Hol)	27 Jul 1957
1972	17:00.6	Shane Gould (Aus)	12 Dec 1971
1987	16:00.73	Janet Evans (USA)	1 Aug 1987

Most: 5 Jenny Turrall (Aus) 16:49.9 - 16:33.94 1973-4
       4 Debbie Meyer (USA) 18:11.1 - 17:19.9 1967-9

4 × 100 METRES FREESTYLE RELAY

1942	4:27.6	Denmark	7 Aug 1938
1957	4:17.1	Australia	6 Dec 1956
1972	3:55.19	USA	30 Aug 1972
1987	3:40.57	GDR	19 Aug 1986

(Kristin Otto, Manuela Stellmach, Sabine Schulze, Heike Friedrich)

4 × 200 METRES FREESTYLE RELAY

1987	7:59.33	GDR	17 Aug 1986

(Manuela Stellmach, Astrid Strauss, Nadja Bergknecht, Heike Friedrich)

100 METRES BACKSTROKE

1927	1:22.0 #	Willy van den Turk (Hol)	10 Jul 1927
1942	1:10.9 #	Cor Kint (Hol)	22 Sep 1939
1957	1:12.9	Judy Grinham (UK)	5 Dec 1956
1972	1:05.6	Karen Muir (SAf)	6 Jul 1969
1987	1:00.59	Ines Kleber (GDR)	24 Aug 1984

Most: 9 Ulrike Richter (GDR) 1:05.39 - 1:01.51 1973-6
4 Ria van Velsen (Hol) 1:12.3 - 1:10.9 1958-60
4 Lynn Burke (USA) 1:10.1 - 1:09.0 1960

200 METRES BACKSTROKE (y- 220 yards)

1927	3:03.8 #	Sybil Bauer (USA)	9 Feb 1924
1942	2:38.8 #	Cor Kint (Hol)	29 Nov 1939
1957	2:38.5y	Lenie de Nijs (Hol)	17 May 1957
1972	2:19.19	Melissa Belote (USA)	4 Sep 1972
1987	2:08.60	Betsy Mitchell (USA)	27 Jun 1986

Most: 10 Satoko Tanaka (Jap) 2:37.1 - 2:28.2 1959-63
4 Karen Muir (SAf) 2:27.1 - 2:23.8 1966-8

100 METRES BREASTSTROKE (* with butterfly stroke)

1927	1:28.8 #	Agnes Geraghty (USA)	13 Feb 1926
1942	1:20.2 #	Johanna Holzner (Ger)	13 Mar 1936
1957	1:16.9*#	Eva Szekely (Hun)	9 May 1951
1972	1:13.58	Cathy Carr (USA)	2 Sep 1972
1987	1:08.11	Sylvia Gerasch (GDR)	21 Aug 1986

Most: 6 Ute Geweniger (GDR) 1:10.20 - 1:08.51 1980-3
5 Catie Ball (USA) 1:15.6 - 1:14.2 1966-8
3 Nel van Vliet (Hol) 1:19.4# - 1:18.2# 1946-7

200 METRES BREASTSTROKE (y- 220 yards)

1927	3:16.6	Else Jacobsen (Den)	20 Aug 1927
1942	2:56.0 #	Maria Lenk (Bra)	8 Nov 1939
1957	2:46.4 #	Ada den Haan (Hol)	13 Nov 1956
1972	2:38.5	Catie Ball (USA)	26 Aug 1968
1987	2:27.40	Silke Hörner (GDR)	18 Aug 1986

Most: 4 Ada den Haan (Hol) 2:46.4# - 2:51.3 1956-7
4 Galina Prozumenshikova (USSR) 2:47.7y - 2:40.8 1964-6

100 METRES BUTTERFLY

1957	1:10.5	Atie Voorbij (Hol)	4 Aug 1957
1972	1:03.34	Mayumi Aoki (Jap)	1 Sep 1972
1987	57.93	Mary T.Meagher (USA)	16 Aug 1981

Most: 6 Atie Voorbij (Hol) 1:13.7# - 1:10.5 1955-7
6 Kornelia Ender (GDR) 1:03.05 - 1:00.13 1973-6

200 METRES BUTTERFLY (y- 220 yards)

1957	2:38.1 #	Tineke Lagerberg (Hol)	19 Mar 1957
1972	2:15.57	Karen Moe (USA)	4 Sep 1972
1987	2:05.96	Mary T.Meagher (USA)	13 Aug 1981

Most: 5 Rosemarie Kother (GDR) 2:15.45 - 2:11.22 1973-6
5 Mary T.Meagher (USA) 2:09.77 - 2:05.96 1979-81
4 Ada Kok (Hol) 2:25.8 - 2:21.0y 1965-7
4 Karen Moe (USA) 2:20.7 - 2:15.27 1970-2

200 METRES INDIVIDUAL MEDLEY

| 1972 | 2:23.07 | Shane Gould (Aus) | 28 Aug 1972 |
| 1987 | 2:11.73 | Ute Geweniger (GDR) | 4 Jul 1981 |

Most: 6 Ulrike Tauber (GDR) 2:18.97 - 2:15.85 1974-7
5 Claudia Kolb (USA) 2:27.8 - 2:23.5 1966-8

400 METRES INDIVIDUAL MEDLEY

1957	5:38.9 #	Mary Kok (Hol)	2 Dec 1956
1972	5:02.97	Gail Neall (USA)	31 Aug 1972
1987	4:36.10	Petra Schneider (GDR)	1 Aug 1982

Most: 6 Donna de Varona (USA) 5:36.5 - 5:14.9 1960-4
  5 Claudia Kolb (USA) 5:11.7 - 5:04.7 1967-8
  4 Sylvia Ruuska (USSR) 5:46.6 - 5:40.2y 1958-9
  4 Petra Schneider (GDR) 4:39.96 - 4:36.10
    1980-2

4 × 100 METRES MEDLEY RELAY

1957	4:53.1 #	Netherlands	8 Dec 1956
1972	4:20.75	USA	3 Sep 1972
1987	4:03.69	GDR	24 Aug 1984

(Ina Kleber, Sylvia Gerasch, Ines Geissler, Birgit Meineke)

MOST WORLD RECORDS AT INDIVIDUAL EVENTS
Including now obsolete distances the most world records set is:

MEN
32 Arne Borg (Swe) 1921-9

WOMEN
42 Ragnhild Hveger (Den) 1936-42.

The most for the currently recognised events:

MEN
26 Mark Spitz (USA) 3 100fr, 4 200fr, 3 400fr,
  7 100bu, 9 200bu 1967-72
17 Roland Matthes (GDR) 8 100ba, 9 200ba 1967-73
13 Vladimir Salnikov (USSR) 6 400fr, 4 800fr, 3 1500fr,
  1979-86
12 John Konrads (Aus) 3 200fr, 4 400fr, 3 800fr,
  2 1500fr, 1958-60
12 Don Schollander (USA) 9 200fr, 3 400fr 1963-8
12 John Hencken (USA) 7 100br, 5 200br 1972-6
10 Arne Borg (Swe) 3 400fr, 2 800fr, 5 1500fr 1922-7
10 Gary Hall (USA) 1 200ba, 1 200bu, 3 200im,
  5 400im 1968-72
10 Steve Holland (Aus) 6 800fr, 4 1500fr 1973-6
10 Michael Gross (FRG) 4 200fr, 1 400fr, 1 100bu,
  4 200bu 1983-6

WOMEN
23 Kornelia Ender (GDR) 10 100fr, 4 200fr, 1 100ba,
  6 100bu, 2 200im 1973-6
15 Ragnhild Hveger (Den) 1 200fr, 8 400fr, 2 800fr,
  3 1500fr, 1 200ba 1937-41
15 Dawn Fraser (Aus) 11 100fr, 4 200fr 1956-64
15 Debbie Meyer (USA) 1 200fr, 5 400fr, 5 800fr,
  4 1500fr 1967-70
11 Claudia Kolb (USA) 5 200im, 5 400im, 1 100br
  1964-8
11 Shane Gould (Aus) 2 100fr, 3 200fr, 2 400fr,
  1 800fr, 2 1500fr, 1 200im 1971-2
11 Ulrike Richter (GDR) 9 100ba, 2 200ba 1973-6

Helene Madison (USA) 1930-2 and Shane Gould (Aus)
1971-2 set records at each freestyle distance: 100m,
200m, 400m, 800m and 1500m.

*Kornelia Ender won four gold and four silver medals
at the Olympic Games, and set 23 world records
(All-Sport)*

WORLD SHORT-COURSE BESTS – IN 25M POOLS

Event	min:sec	Name	Date
MEN			
50m freestyle	21.84	Matt Biondi (USA)	26 Apr 1987
100m freestyle	48.52	David McCagg (USA)	2 Jan 1978
200m freestyle	1:44.5	Michael Gross (FRG)	30 Nov 1982
400m freestyle	3:42.4	Michael Gross (FRG)	2 Feb 1985
800m freestyle	7:38.75	Michael Gross (FRG)	8 Feb 1985

Vladimir Salnikov, the greatest ever freestyle swimmer at the longer distances (All-Sport)

1500m freestyle	14:37.60	Vladimir Salnikov (USSR)	19 Dec 1982
100m backstroke	54.20	Dirk Richter (GDR)	15 Dec 1985
200m backstroke	1:56.60	Tamas Darnyi (Hun)	8 Feb 1987
100m breaststroke	59.75	Adrian Moorhouse (UK)	8 Feb 1987
200m breaststroke	2:08.82	Victor Davis (Can)	7 Feb 1987
100m butterfly	52.9 *	Michael Gross (FRG)	24 Nov 1984
200m butterfly	1:54.78	Michael Gross (FRG)	9 Feb 1985
200m individual medley	1:58.18	Pablo Morales (USA)	26 Apr 1987
400m individual medley	4:10.67	Alex Baumann (Can)	26 Jan 1984

WOMEN

50m freestyle	24.94	Tamara Costache (Rom)	8 Feb 1987
100m freestyle	53.99	Birgit Meineke (GDR)	9 Jan 1983
200m freestyle	1:56.35	Birgit Meineke (GDR)	7 Jan 1983
400m freestyle	4:02.05	Astrid Strauss (GDR)	8 Feb 1987
800m freestyle	8:15.34	Astrid Strauss (GDR)	6 Feb 1987
1500m freestyle	15:43.31	Petra Schneider (GDR)	11 Jan 1982
100m backstroke	59.89	Betsy Mitchell (USA)	26 Apr 1987
200m backstroke	2:07.74	Cornelia Sirch (GDR)	9 Jan 1983
100m breaststroke	1:07.05	Silke Hörner (GDR)	8 Feb 1986
200m breaststroke	2:25.71	Silke Hörner (GDR)	9 Feb 1987
100m butterfly	58.91*	Mary T.Meagher (USA)	3 Jan 1981
200m butterfly	2:05.65	Mary T.Meagher (USA)	2 Jan 1981
200m individual medley	2:10.60	Petra Schneider (GDR)	8 Jan 1982
400m individual medley	4:31.36	Noemi Lung (Rom)	31 Jan 1987

* slower than the world long-course records (qv)

TABLE TENNIS

The origins of table tennis are uncertain, but sports goods manufacturers were selling equipment for the game in England in the 1880s. The use of a celluloid table tennis ball was pioneered by James Gibb. This ball, called 'Gossima', was manufactured by J.Jacques & Son, and it was probably Jacques who conceived the onomatopoeic name 'Ping Pong', by which the game was popularly known in the early part of this century. The use of pimpled rubber stuck on to a wooden bat was introduced around this time. A Ping Pong Association was formed in 1902, when the craze for the game was at a peak. This organisation was renamed the Table Tennis Association, but became defunct, before being reconstituted as the English Table Tennis Association in 1927.

The world governing body is the International Table Tennis Federation (ITTF), which was founded in 1926.

WORLD CHAMPIONSHIPS

European Championships were contested in December 1926, when the ITTF was formed, and the event was retrospectively designated as the World Championships. Subsequent championships were contested annually until 1957, except for the war years, and biennially from 1959.

Note that two events are shown for 1933, and none for 1934, as the 1933-4 tournament was held in December 1933.

SWAYTHLING CUP

The trophy for the men's team championship was given in 1926 by Lady Swaythling, mother of the Hon. Ivor Montagu, the first President of the ITTF. Matches are played over the best of nine singles, by teams of three.

Wins:

12	Hungary	1926, 1928-31, 1933 (2), 1935, 1938, 1949, 1952, 1979
10	China	1961, 1963, 1965, 1971, 1975, 1977, 1981, 1983, 1985, 1987
7	Japan	1954-7, 1959, 1967, 1969
6	Czechoslovakia	1932, 1939, 1947-8, 1950-1
1	Austria 1936, USA 1937, England 1953, Sweden 1973	

CORBILLON CUP

The Marcel Corbillon Cup was presented in 1934 by M.Corbillon, President of the French Table Tennis Association, for the winners of the women's team event. Matches are contested as the best of four singles and a doubles.

Wins:

8	Japan	1952, 1954, 1957, 1959, 1961, 1963, 1967, 1971
8	China	1965, 1975, 1977, 1979, 1981, 1983, 1985, 1987
5	Romania	1950-1, 1953, 1955-6
3	Czechoslovakia	1935-6, 1938
2	Germany	1933, 1939
2	USA	1937, 1949
2	England	1947-8
1	USSR 1969, South Korea 1973	

MEN'S SINGLES

Contested for the St. Bride Vase, presented in 1929 by the St. Bride Institute Table Tennis Club, London in recognition of the title won in 1929 by Fred Perry, later triple Wimbledon champion at lawn tennis.

Winners:

1926 Roland Jacobi (Hun)
1928 Zoltan Mechlovits (Hun)
1929 Fred Perry (Eng)
1930 Viktor Barna (Hun)
1931 Miklos Szabados (Hun)
1932-5 Viktor Barna (Hun)
1936 Standa Kolar (Cs)
1937 Richard Bergmann (Aut)
1938 Bohumil Vana (Cs)
1939 Richard Bergmann (Aut)
1947 Bohumil Vana (Cs)
1948 Richard Bergmann (Eng)
1949 Johnny Leach (Eng)
1950 Richard Bergmann (Eng)

Jiang Jialiang (All-Sport)

1951 Johnny Leach (Eng)
1952 Hiroji Satoh (Jap)
1953 Ferenc Sido (Hun)
1954 Ichiro Ogimura (Jap)
1955 Toshiaki Tanaka (Jap)
1956 Ichiro Ogimura (Jap)
1957 Toshiaki Tanaka (Jap)
1959 Jung Kuo-tuan (Chn)
1961 Chuang Tse-tung (Chn)
1963 Chuang Tse-tung (Chn)
1965 Chuang Tse-tung (Chn)
1967 Nobuhiko Hasegawa (Jap)
1969 Shigeo Ito (Jap)
1971 Stellan Bengtsson (Swe)
1973 Hsi En-ting (Chn)
1975 Istvan Jonyer (Hun)
1977 Mitsuru Kohno (Jap)
1979 Seiji Ono (Jap)
1981 Guo Yuehua (Chn)
1983 Guo Yuehua (Chn)
1985 Jiang Jialiang (Chn)
1987 Jiang Jialiang (Chn)

Most wins: 5 Viktor Barna, 4 Richard Bergmann

WOMEN'S SINGLES

Contested for the G.Geist Prize, donated in 1931 by Dr.Gaspar Geist, President of the Hungarian Association.

Winners:

1926 Maria Mednyanszky (Hun)

1928-31 Maria Mednyanszky (Hun)
1932-3 Anna Sipos (Hun)
1933 Marie Kettnerova (Cs)
1935 Marie Kettnerova (Cs)
1936 Ruth Aarons (USA)
1937 Vacant; finalists: Ruth Aarons (USA) and Trudi Pritzi (Aut)
1938 Trudi Pritzi (Aut)
1939 Vlasha Depetrisova (Cs)
1947-9 Gizi Farkas (Hun)
1950-5 Angelica Rozeanu (Rom)
1956 Timo Okawa (Jap)
1957 Fujie Eguchi (Jap)
1959 Kimiyo Matsuzaki (Jap)
1961 Chiu Chung-hui (Chn)
1963 Kimiyo Matsuzaki (Jap)
1965 Naoko Fukazu (Jap)
1967 Sachiko Morisawa (Jap)
1969 Toshiko Kowada (Jap)
1971 Lin Hui-ching (Chn)
1973 Hu Yu-lan (Chn)
1975 Pak Yung-Sun (NKo)
1977 Pak Yung-Sun (NKo)
1979 Ge Xinai (Chn)
1981 Tong Ling (Chn)
1983 Cao Yanhua (Chn)
1985 Cao Yanhua (Chn)
1987 He Zhili (Chn)

Most wins: 6 Angelica Rozeanu, 5 Maria Mednyanszky

MEN'S DOUBLES

Contested for the Iran Cup, presented by the Shah of Iran in Paris in 1947.

Winners:
1926 Roland Jacobi & Dani Pecsi (Hun)
1928 Alfred Liebster & Robert Thum (Aut)
1929-32 Viktor Barna & Miklos Szabados (Hun)
1933 Viktor Barna & Sandor Glancz (Hun)
1933 Viktor Barna & Miklos Szabados (Hun)
1935 Viktor Barna & Miklos Szabados (Hun)
1936-7 Robert Blattner & James McClure (USA)
1938 James McClure & Sol Schiff (USA)
1939 Viktor Barna & Richard Bergmann (Eng)
1947 Adolf Slar & Bohumil Vana (Cs)
1948 Ladislav Stipek & Bohumil Vana (Cs)
1949 Ivan Andreadis & Ferko Tokar (Cs)
1950 Ferenc Sido & Ferenc Soos (Hun)
1951 Ivan Andreadis & Bohumil Vana (Cs)
1952 Norikazu Fujii & Tadaski Hayashi (Jap)
1953 Josef Koczian & Ferenc Sido (Hun)
1954 Zarko Dolinar & Vilim Harangozo (Yug)
1955 Ivan Andreadis & Ladislav Stipek (Cs)
1956 Ichiro Ogimura & Yoshio Tomita (Jap)
1957 Ivan Andreadis & Ladislav Stipek (Cs)
1959 Teruo Murakami & Ichiro Ogimura (Jap)
1961 Nobuyo Hoshino & Koji Kimura (Jap)
1963 Chang Shih-lin & Wang Chih-liang (Chn)
1965 Chuang Tse-tung & Hsu Yin-sheng (Chn)
1967 Hans Alser & Kjell Johansson (Swe)
1969 Hans Alser & Kjell Johansson (Swe)
1971 Istvan Jonyer & Tibor Klampar (Hun)
1973 Stellan Bengtsson & Kjell Johansson (Swe)
1975 Gabor Gergely & Istvan Jonyer (Hun)

1977 Li Zhenshi & Liang Geliang (Chn)
1979 Dragutin Surbek & Anton Stipancic (Yug)
1981 Cai Zhenhua & Li Zhenshi (Chn)
1983 Dragutin Surbek & Zoran Kalinic (Yug)
1985 Mikael Applegren & Ulf Carlsson (Swe)
1987 Chen Longcan & Wei Qinguang (Chn)

Most wins: 8 Viktor Barna, 6 Miklos Szabados

WOMEN'S DOUBLES

Contested for the W.J.Pope Trophy. Mr Pope, Honorary Secretary of the ITTF 1947-50, presented the trophy in 1948.

Winners:
1928 Erika Flamm (Aut) & Maria Mednyanszky (Hun)
1929 Erika Metzger & Erika Rüster (Ger)
1930-5 Maria Mednyanszky & Anna Sipos (Hun)
1936 Marie Kettnerova & Maria Smidova (Cs)
1937-8 Vlasha Depetrisova & Vera Votrubcova (Cs)
1939 Hilde Bussmann & Trudi Pritzi (Ger)
1947 Gizi Farkas (Hun) & Trudi Pritzi (Aut)
1948 Margaret Franks & Vera Thomas (Eng)
1949 Helen Elliot (Sco) & Gizi Farkas (Hun)
1950 Dora Beregi (Eng) & Helen Elliot (Sco)
1951 Diane Rowe & Rosalind Rowe (Eng)
1952 Shizuka Narahara & Tomi Nishimura (Jap)
1953 Gizi Farkas (Hun) & Angelica Rozeanu (Rom)
1954 Diane Rowe & Rosalind Rowe (Eng)
1955-6 Angelica Rozeanu & Ella Zeller (Rom)
1957 Livia Mosoczy & Agnes Simon (Hun)
1959 Taeko Namba & Kazuko Yamaizumi (Jap)
1961 Maria Alexandru & Geta Pitica (Rom)
1963 Kimiyo Matsuzaki & Masako Seki (Jap)
1965 Cheng Min-chih & Lin Hui-ching (Chn)
1967 Saeko Hirota & Sachiko Morisawa (Jap)
1969 Svetlana Grinberg & Zoya Rudnova (USSR)
1971 Cheng Min-chih & Lin Hui-ching (Chn)
1973 Maria Alexandru (Rom) & Miho Hamada (Jap)
1975 Maria Alexandru (Rom) & Shoko Takashima (Jap)
1977 Pak Yong Ok (NKo) & Yang Yin (Chn)
1979 Zhang Li & Zhang Deying (Chn)
1981 Zhang Deying & Cao Yanhua (Chn)
1983 Shen Jianping & Dai Lili (Chn)
1985 Dai Lili & Geng Lijuan (Chn)
1987 Yang Young-Ja & Hyun Jung-Hwa (SKo)

Most wins: 7 Maria Mednyanszky, 6 Anna Sipos

MIXED DOUBLES

Contested for the Heydusek Prize, presented in 1948 by Zdenek Heydusek, Secretary of the Czechoslovak Association.

Winners:
1927-8 Zoltan Mechlovits & Maria Mednyanszky (Hun)
1929 Istvan Kelen & Anna Sipos (Hun)
1930-1 Miklos Szabados & Maria Mednyanszky (Hun)
1932 Viktor Barna & Anna Sipos (Hun)
1933 Istvan Kelen & Maria Mednyanszky (Hun)
1933 Miklos Szabados & Maria Mednyanszky (Hun)
1935 Viktor Barna & Anna Sipos (Hun)
1936 Mila Hamr & Traute Kleinova (Cs)
1937 Bohumil Vana & Vera Votrubcova (Cs)
1938 Laszlo Bellak (Hun) & Wendy Woodhead (Eng)
1939 Bohumil Vana & Vera Votrubcova (Cs)
1947 Ferenc Soos & Gizi Farkas (Hun)
1948 Richard Miles & Thelma Thall (USA)

1949-50 Ferenc Sido & Gizi Farkas (Hun)
1951 Bohumil Vana (Cs) & Angelica Rozeanu (Rom)
1952-3 Ferenc Sido (Hun) & Angelica Rozeanu (Rom)
1954 Ivan Andreadis (Cs) & Gizi Farkas (Hun)
1955 Kalman Szepesi & Eva Koczian (Hun)
1956 Erwin Klein & Leah Neuberger (USA)
1957 Ichiro Ogimura & Fujie Eguchi (Jap)
1959 Ichiro Ogimura & Fujie Eguchi (Jap)
1961 Ichiro Ogimura & Kimiyo Matsuzaki (Jap)
1963 Koji Kimura & Kazuko Ito (Jap)
1965 Koji Kimurra & Masako Seki (Jap)
1967 Nobuhiko Hasegawa & Noriko Yamanaka (Jap)
1969 Nobuhiko Hasegawa & Yasuka Konno (Jap)
1971 Chang Shih-ling & Lin Hui-ching (Chn)
1973 Liang Geliang & Li Li (Chn)
1975 Stanislav Gomozkov & Anna Ferdman (USSR)
1977 Jacques Secretin & Claude Bergeret (FRa)
1979 Liang Geliang & Ge Xinai (Chn)
1981 Xie Saike & Huang Junqun (Chn)
1983 Guo Yuehua & Ni Xialian (Chn)
1985 Cai Zhenhua & Cao Yanhua (Chn)
1987 Hui Jun & Geng Lijuan (Chn)

Most wins: 6 Maria Mednyanszky

Most individual world titles overall:
MEN: 15 Viktor Barna (Hun/Eng), 10 Miklos Szabados (Hun)
WOMEN: 18 Maria Mednyanszky (Hun), 12 Angelica Rozeanu (Rom)
11 Anna Sipos (Hun), 10 Gizi Farkas (Hun)

WORLD CUP

Held annually from 1980.

Men's winners:
1980 Guo Yuehua (Chn)
1981 Tibor Klampar (Hun)
1982 Guo Yuehua (Chn)
1983 Mikael Appelgren (Swe)
1984 Jiang Jialiang (Chn)
1985 Chen Xinhua (Chn)
1986 Chen Longcan (Chn)
1987 Teng Yi (Chn)

EUROPEAN CHAMPIONSHIPS

Held biennially from 1958.

Most singles championships:
MEN 2 Zoltan Berczik 1958, 1960; Kjell Johansson (Swe) 1964, 1966; Hans Alser (Swe) 1962, 1970.
WOMEN 3 Eva Földi (née Koczian) 1958, 1960, 1964; 2 Zoya Rudnova (USSR) 1970, 1972; Judit Magos (Hun) 1974, 1978; Valentina Popova (USSR) 1980, 1984.

ENGLISH OPEN CHAMPIONSHIPS

Instituted in 1921, this is the longest established national championship and has attracted many of the world's best players. Held annually to 1980. but biennially since then.

Most titles:
Men's singles: 6 Richard Bergmann (Aut/Eng) 1939-40, 1948, 1950, 1952, 1954; 5 Viktor Barna (Hun) 1933-5, 1937-8

Women's singles: 6 Maria Alexandru (Rom) 1963-4, 1970-2, 1974
Men's doubles: 7 Viktor Barna (Hun/Eng) 1931, 1933-5, 1938-9, 1949
Women's doubles: 12 Diane Rowe (Eng) 1950-6, 1960, 1962-5 (first 6 with her twin Rosalind)
Mixed doubles: 8 Viktor Barna (Hun/Eng) 1933-6, 1938, 1940, 1951, 1953
All events:
MEN 20 Viktor Barna (as above)
WOMEN 17 Diane Rowe (singles 1962, doubles as above, mixed 1952, 1954, 1956, 1960)

TAEKWON-DO

Taekwon-Do is a martial art, developed in Korea by General Choi Hong Hi, 9th Dan, the highest Dan awarded in the sport. It was officially recognised as part of Korean tradition and culture in 1955. Thereafter the sport spread internationally.

The International Taekwon-Do Federation was formed in 1966. World Championships are held at pattern, sparring (different weight categories) and power test. They were first held in 1974.
Overall team winners were not awarded in 1974 and 1978, but since then have been:
1981 Great Britain
1984 Canada
1987 North Korea

TENNIS (LAWN)

Lawn Tennis evolved from Real Tennis and while accounts of various forms of 'Field Tennis' were recorded in the 18th century, the real 'father' of Lawn Tennis is regarded as Major Wingfield who showed off his new game, which he called Sphairistike, at a Christmas Party at a country house at Nantclwyd, Wales, in 1873. The Marylebone Cricket Club were responsible for revising Wingfield's initial rules and in 1877 the All England Croquet Club added the name Lawn Tennis to their title.

WIMBLEDON CHAMPIONSHIPS

The All-England Championships at Wimbledon are regarded as the most prestigious championships in the world. They were first held in 1877 and, until 1922, were organised on a challenge round basis.

Winners:
MEN'S SINGLES
1877 Spencer Gore (UK)
1878 Frank Hadow (UK)
1879-80 Rev.John Hartley (UK)
1881-6 William Renshaw (UK)
1887 Herbert Lawford (UK)
1888 Ernest Renshaw (UK)
1889 William Renshaw (UK)
1890 Willoughby Hamilton (UK)
1891-2 Wilfred Baddeley (UK)

1893-4 Joshua Pim (UK)
1895 Wilfred Baddeley (UK)
1896 Harold Mahoney (UK)
1897-1900 Reginald Doherty (UK)
1901 Arthur Gore (UK)
1902-5 Lawrence Doherty (UK)
1907 Norman Brookes (Aus)
1908-9 Arthur Gore (UK)
1910-3 Tony Wilding (NZ)
1914 Norman Brookes (Aus)
1919 Gerald Patterson (Aus)
1920-1 Bill Tilden (USA)
1922 Gerald Patterson (Aus)
1923 William Johnston (USA)
1924 Jean Borotra (Fra)
1925 René Lacoste (Fra)
1926 Jean Borotra (Fra)
1927 Henri Cochet (Fra)
1928 René Lacoste (Fra)
1929 Henri Cochet (Fra)
1930 Bill Tilden (USA)
1931 Sidney Wood (USA)
1932 Ellsworth Vines (USA)
1933 Jack Crawford (Aus)
1934-6 Fred Perry (UK)
1937-8 Donald Budge (USA)
1939 Bobby Riggs (USA)
1946 Yvon Petra (Fra)
1947 Jack Kramer (USA)

1948 Bob Falkenburg (USA)
1949 Ted Schroeder (USA)
1950 Budge Patty (USA)
1951 Dick Savitt (USA)
1952 Frank Sedgman (Aus)
1953 Vic Seixas (USA)
1954 Jaroslav Drobny (Egy)
1955 Tony Trabert (USA)
1956-7 Lew Hoad (Aus)
1958 Ashley Cooper (Aus)
1959 Alex Olmedo (USA)
1960 Neale Fraser (Aus)
1961-2 Rod Laver (Aus)
1963 Chuck McKinley (USA)
1964-5 Roy Emerson (Aus)
1966 Manuel Santana (Spa)
1967 John Newcombe (Aus)
1968-9 Rod Laver (Aus)
1970-1 John Newcombe (Aus)
1972 Stan Smith (USA)
1973 Jan Kodes (Cs)
1974 Jimmy Connors (USA)
1975 Arthur Ashe (USA)
1976-80 Bjorn Borg (Swe)
1981 John McEnroe (USA)
1982 Jimmy Connors (USA)
1983-4 John McEnroe (USA)
1985-6 Boris Becker (FRG)
1987 Pat Cash (Aus)

Most wins (pre-1922):
7 William Renshaw 1881-6, 1889
(post-1922): 5 Bjorn Borg 1976-80
WOMEN'S SINGLES
1884-5 Maud Watson (UK)
1886 Blanche Bingley (UK)
1887-8 Lottie Dod (UK)
1889 Blanche Hillyard (UK)
1890 Helene Rice (UK)
1891-3 Lottie Dod (UK)
1894 Blanche Hillyard (UK)
1895-6 Charlotte Cooper (UK)
1897 Blanche Hillyard (UK)
1898 Charlotte Cooper (UK)
1899-1900 Blanche Hillyard (UK)
1901 Charlotte Sterry (née Cooper) (UK)
1902 Muriel Robb (UK)
1903-4 Dorothea Douglass (UK)
1905 May Sutton (USA)
1906 Dorothea Douglass (UK)
1907 May Sutton (USA)
1908 Charlotte Sterry (UK)
1909 Dora Boothby (UK)
1910-1 Dorothea Lambert Chambers (UK)
1912 Ethel Larcombe (UK)
1913-4 Dorothea Lambert Chambers (UK)

Fred Perry and Pat Hughes won Wimbledon titles at men's singles and doubles respectively in 1936, since when there have been no British winners at these events. (Popperfoto)

1919-23 Suzanne Lenglen (Fra)
1924 Kathleen McKane (née Godfree) (UK)
1925 Suzanne Lenglen (Fra)
1926 Kathleen Godfree (UK)
1927-9 Helen Wills (USA)
1930 Helen Moody (née Wills) (USA)
1931 Cilly Aussem (Ger)
1932-3 Helen Moody (USA)
1934 Dorothy Round (UK)
1935 Helen Moody (USA)
1936 Helen Jacobs (USA)
1937 Dorothy Round (UK)
1938 Helen Moody (USA)
1939 Alice Marble (USA)
1946 Pauline Betz (USA)
1947 Margaret Osborne (USA)
1948-50 Louise Brough (USA)
1951 Doris Hart (USA)
1952-4 Maureen Connolly (USA)
1955 Louise Brough (USA)
1956 Shirley Fry (USA)
1957-8 Althea Gibson (USA)
1959-60 Maria Bueno (Bra)
1961 Angela Mortimer (UK)
1962 Karen Susman (USA)
1963 Margaret Smith (Aus)
1964 Maria Bueno (Bra)
1965 Margaret Smith (Aus)
1966-8 Billie Jean King (USA)
1969 Ann Jones (UK)
1970 Margaret Court (Aus)
1971 Evonne Goolagong (Aus)
1972-3 Billie Jean King (USA)
1974 Chris Evert (USA)
1975 Billy Jean King (USA)
1976 Chris Evert (USA)
1977 Virginia Wade (UK)
1978-9 Martina Navratilova (Cs)
1980 Evonne Cawley (Aus)
1981 Chris Evert-Lloyd (USA)
1982-7 Martina Navratilova (USA)

Most wins (pre-1922):
7 Dorothea Lambert Chambers (née Douglass) 1903-4, 1906, 1910-1, 1913-4
(post-1922): 8 Helen Moody (née Wills) 1927-30, 1932-3, 1935, 1938; Martina Navratilova 1978-9, 1982-7

MEN'S DOUBLES
1879 L.R.Erskine & Herbert Lawford (UK)
1880-1 Ernest Renshaw & William Renshaw (UK)
1882 Rev.John Hartley & R.T.Richardson (UK)
1883 C.W.Grinstead & C.E.Welldon (UK)
1884-6 Ernest Renshaw & William Renshaw (UK)
1887 Patrick Bowes-Lyon & Herbert Wilberforce (UK)
1888-9 Ernest Renshaw & William Renshaw (UK)
1890 Joshua Pim & Frank Stoker (UK)
1891 Herbert Baddeley & Wilfred Baddeley (UK)
1892 Harry Barlow & Ernest Lewis (UK)
1893 Joshua Pim & Frank Stoker (UK)
1894-6 Herbert Baddeley & Wilfred Baddeley (UK)
1897-1901 Lawrence Doherty & Reginald Doherty (UK)
1902 Frank Riseley & Sidney Smith (UK)
1903-5 Lawrence Doherty & Reginald Doherty (UK)
1906 Frank Riseley & Sidney Smith (UK)

Helen Wills-Moody did not lose a set at Wimbledon from 1927 to 1933. (Popperfoto)

1907 Norman Brookes (Aus) & Anthony Wilding (NZ)
1908 Josiah Ritchie (UK) & Anthony Wilding (NZ)
1909 Arthur Gore & Roper Barrett (UK)
1910 Josiah Ritchie (UK) & Anthony Wilding (NZ)
1911 Max Decugis & André Gobert (Fra)
1912-3 Charles Dixon & Roper Barrett (UK)
1914 Norman Brookes (Aus) & Anthony Wilding (NZ)
1919 Pat O'Hara Wood & Ronald Thomas (Aus)
1920 Charles Garland & Richard Williams (USA)
1921 Randolph Lycett & Max Woosnam (UK)
1922 James Anderson (Aus) & Randolph Lycett (UK)
1923 Leslie Godfree & Randolph Lycett (UK)
1924 Frank Hunter & Vincent Richards (USA)
1925 Jean Borotra & René Lacoste (Fra)
1926 Jacques Brugnon & Henri Cochet (Fra)
1927 Frank Hunter & William Tilden (USA)
1928 Jacques Brugnon & Henri Cochet (Fra)
1929-30 William Allison & John Van Ryn (USA)
1931 George Lott & John Van Ryn (USA)
1932-3 Jean Borotra & Jacques Brugnon (Fra)
1934 George Lott & Lester Stoefen (USA)
1935 Jack Crawford & Adrian Quist (Aus)
1936 Pat Hughes & Raymond Tuckey (UK)
1937-8 Don Budge & Gene Mako (USA)

1939 Ellwood Cooke & Bobby Riggs (USA)
1946 Tom Brown & Jack Kramer (USA)
1947 Bob Falkenburg & Jack Kramer (USA)
1948 John Bromwich & Frank Sedgman (Aus)
1949 Ricardo Gonzales & Frank Parker (USA)
1950 John Bromwich & Adrian Quist (Aus)
1951-2 Ken McGregor & Frank Sedgman (Aus)
1953 Lew Hoad & Ken Rosewall (Aus)
1954 Rex Hartwig & Mervyn Rose (Aus))
1955 Rex Hartwig & Lew Hoad (Aus)
1956 Lew Hoad & Ken Rosewall (Aus)
1957 Gardnar Mulloy & Budge Patty (USA)
1958 Sven Davidson & Ulf Schmidt (Swe)
1959 Roy Emerson & Neale Fraser (Aus)
1960 Rafael Osuna (Mex) & Dennis Ralston (USA)
1961 Roy Emerson & Neale Fraser (Aus)
1962 Bob Hewitt & Fred Stolle (Aus)
1963 Rafael Osuna & Antonio Palafox (Mex)
1964 Bob Hewitt & Fred Stolle (Aus)
1965 John Newcombe & Tony Roche (Aus)
1966 Ken Fletcher & John Newcombe (Aus)
1967 Bob Hewitt & Frew McMillan (SAf)
1968-70 John Newcombe & Tony Roche (Aus)
1971 Roy Emerson & Rod Laver (Aus)
1972 Bob Hewitt & Frew McMillan (SAf)
1973 Jimmy Connors (USA) & Ilie Nastase (Rom)
1974 John Newcombe & Tony Roche (Aus)
1975 Vitas Gerulaitis & Sandy Mayer (USA)
1976 Brian Gottfried (USA) & Raul Ramirez (Mex)
1977 Ross Case & Geoff Masters (Aus)
1978 Bob Hewitt & Frew McMillan (SAf)
1979 Peter Fleming & John McEnroe (USA)
1980 Pete McNamara & Paul McNamee (Aus)
1981 Peter Fleming & John McEnroe (USA)
1982 Peter McNamara & Paul McNamee (Aus)
1983-4 Peter Fleming & John McEnroe (USA)
1985 Heinz Gunthardt (Swi) & Balazs Taroczy (Hun)
1986 Joakim Nystrom & Mats Wilander (Swe)
1987 Ken Flack & Robert Seguso (USA)

Most wins: 8 Lawrence Doherty and Reginald Doherty 1897-1901, 1903-5

WOMEN'S DOUBLES
1913 Winifred McNair & Dora Boothby (UK)
1914 Agnes Morton (UK) & Elizabeth Ryan (USA)
1919-23 Suzanne Lenglen (Fra) & Elizabeth Ryan (USA)
1924 Hazel Wightman & Helen Wills (USA)
1925 Suzanne Lenglen (Fra) & Elizabeth Ryan (USA)
1926 Mary Browne & Elizabeth Ryan (USA)
1927 Helen Wills & Elizabeth Ryan (USA)
1928 Peggy Saunders & Phyllis Watson (UK)
1929 Peggy Michell & Phyllis Watson (UK)
1930 Helen Moody (née Wills) & Elizabeth Ryan (USA)
1931 Dorothy Barron & Phyllis Mudford (UK)
1932 Doris Metaxa (Fra) & Josane Sigart (Bel)
1933-4 Simone Mathieu (Fra) & Elizabeth Ryan (USA)
1935-6 Freda James & Kay Stammers (UK)
1937 Simone Mathieu (Fra) & Billie Yorke (UK)
1938-9 Sarah Fabyan & Alice Marble (USA)
1946 Louise Brough & Margaret Osborne (USA)
1947 Doris Hart & Pat Todd (USA)
1948-50 Louise Brough & Margaret Du Pont (USA)
1951-3 Shirley Fry & Doris Hart (USA)
1954 Louise Brough & Margaret Du Pont (USA)

1955 Angela Mortimer & Anne Shilcock (UK)
1956 Angela Buxton (UK) & Althea Gibson (USA)
1957 Althea Gibson & Darlene Hard (USA)
1958 Maria Bueno (Bra) & Althea Gibson (USA)
1959 Jean Arth & Darlene Hard (USA)
1960 Maria Bueno (Bra) & Darlene Hard (USA)
1961 Karen Hantze & Billie Jean Moffitt (USA)
1962 Billie Jean Moffitt & Karen Susman (USA)
1963 Maria Bueno (Bra) & Darlene Hard (USA)
1964 Margaret Smith & Lesley Turner (Aus)
1965 Maria Bueno (Bra) & Billie Jean Moffitt (USA)
1966 Maria Bueno (Bra) & Nancy Richey (USA)
1967-8 Rosemary Casals & Billie Jean King (USA)
1969 Margaret Court & Judy Tegart (Aus)
1970-1 Rosemary Casals & Billie Jean King (USA)
1972 Billie Jean King (USA) & Betty Stove (Hol)
1973 Rosemary Casals & Billie Jean King (USA)
1974 Evonne Goolagong (Aus) & Peggy Michel (USA)
1975 Ann Kiyomura (USA) & Kazuko Sawamatsu (Jap)
1976 Chris Evert (USA) & Martina Navratilova (Cs)
1977 Helen Cawley (Aus) & Joanne Russell (USA)
1978 Kerry Reid & Wendy Turnbull (Aus)
1979 Billie Jean King (USA) & Martina Navratilova (Cs)
1980 Kathy Jordan & Anne Smith (USA)
1981-4 Martina Navratilova & Pam Shriver (USA)
1985 Kathy Jordan (USA) & Elizabeth Smylie (Aus)
1986 Martina Navratilova & Pam Shriver (USA)
1987 Claudia Kohde-Kilsch (FRG) & Helena Sukova (Cs)

Most wins: 12 Elizabeth Ryan 1914, 1919-23, 1925-7, 1930, 1933-4

MIXED DOUBLES
1913 Hope Crisp & Agnes Tuckey (UK)
1914 James Parke & Ethel Larcombe (UK)
1919 Randolph Lycett (UK) & Elizabeth Ryan (USA)
1920 Gerald Patterson (Aus) & Suzanne Lenglen (Fra)
1921 Randolph Lycett (UK) & Elizabeth Ryan (USA)
1922 Pat O'Hara Wood (USA) & Suzanne Lenglen (Fra)
1923 Randolph Lycett (UK) & Elizabeth Ryan (USA)
1924 Brian Gilbert & Kitty McKane (UK)
1925 Jean Borotra & Suzanne Lenglen (Fra)
1926 Leslie Godfree & Kitty Godfree (UK)
1927 Frank Hunter & Elizabeth Ryan (USA)
1928 Pat Spence (SAf) & Elizabeth Ryan (USA)
1929 Frank Hunter & Helen Wills (USA)
1930 Jack Crawford (Aus) & Elizabeth Ryan (USA)
1931 George Lott & Anna Harper (USA)
1932 Enrique Maier (Spa) & Elizabeth Ryan (USA)
1933 Gottfried von Cramm & Hilda Krahwinkel (Ger)
1934 Ryuki Miki (Jap) & Dorothy Round (UK)
1935-6 Fred Perry & Dorothy Round (UK)
1937-8 Don Budge & Alice Marble (USA)
1939 Bobby Riggs & Alice Marble (USA)
1946 Tom Brown & Louise Brough (USA)
1947-8 John Bromwich (Aus) & Louise Brough (USA)
1949 Eric Sturgess & Sheila Summers (SAf)
1950 Eric Sturgess (SAf) & Louise Brough (USA)
1951-2 Frank Sedgman (Aus) & Doris Hart (USA)
1953-5 Vic Seixas & Doris Hart (USA)
1956 Vic Seixas & Shirley Fry (USA)
1957 Mervyn Rose (Aus) & Darlene Hard (USA)
1958 Bob Howe & Lorraine Coghlan (Aus)
1959-60 Rod Laver (Aus) & Darlene Hard (USA)
1961 Fred Stolle & Lesley Turner (Aus)

1962 Neale Fraser (Aus) & Margaret Du Pont (USA)
1963 Ken Fletcher & Margaret Smith (Aus)
1964 Fred Stolle & Lesley Turner (Aus)
1965-6 Ken Fletcher & Margaret Smith (Aus)
1967 Owen Davidson (Aus) & Billie Jean King (USA)
1968 Ken Fletcher & Margaret Court (Aus)
1969 Fred Stolle (Aus) & Ann Jones (UK)
1970 Ilie Nastase (Rom) & Rosemary Casals (USA)
1971 Owen Davidson (Aus) & Billie Jean King (USA)
1972 Ilie Nastase (Rom) & Rosemary Casals (USA)
1973-4 Owen Davidson (Aus) & Billie Jean King (USA)
1975 Marty Riessen (USA) & Margaret Court (Aus)
1976 Tony Roche (Aus) & Francoise Durr (Fra)
1977 Bob Hewitt & Greer Stevens (SAf)
1978 Frew McMillan (SAf) & Betty Stove (Hol)
1979 Bob Hewitt & Greer Stevens (SAf)
1980 John Austin & Tracy Austin (USA)
1981 Frew McMillan (SAf) & Betty Stove (Hol)
1982 Kevin Curren (SAf) & Anne Smith (USA)
1983-4 John Lloyd (UK) & Wendy Turnbull (Aus)
1985 Paul McNamee (Aus) & Martina Navratilova (USA)
1986 Ken Flach & Kathy Jordan (USA)
1987 Jeremy Bates & Jo Durie (UK)

Most wins (Men): 4 Vic Seixas 1953-6, Owen Davidson 1967, 1971, 1973-4; Ken Fletcher 1963, 1965-6, 1968 *(Women):* 7 Elizabeth Ryan 1919, 1921, 1923, 1927-8, 1930, 1932

MOST WIMBLEDON TITLES

	Tot	*Sngles*	*Dbls*	*Mixed*	*Years*
Billie Jean King (USA)	20	6	10	4	1961-79
Elizabeth Ryan (USA)	19	-	12	7	1914-34
Martina Navratilova (Cs/USA)	16	8	7	1	1976-87
Suzanne Lenglen (Fra)	15	6	6	3	1919-25
Lawrence Doherty (UK)	13	5	8	-	1897-1905
Louise Brough (USA)	13	4	5	4	1946-55

UNITED STATES CHAMPIONSHIPS

The first official US Championships were in 1891 and remained in existence until 1969, the year after the sport went open. In 1968 and 1969, however, there were two Championships, the Amateur and Open events. Since 1970 there has only been an Open competition.

Post-war winners
MEN'S SINGLES
1946-7 Jack Kramer (USA)
1948-9 Ricardo Gonzales (USA)
1950 Arthur Larsen (USA)
1951-2 Frank Sedgman (USA)
1953 Tony Trabert (USA)
1954 Vic Seixas (USA)
1955 Tony Trabert (USA)
1956 Ken Rosewall (Aus)
1957 Malcolm Anderson (Aus)
1958 Ashley Cooper (Aus)
1959-60 Neale Fraser (Aus)
1961 Roy Emerson (Aus)
1962 Rod Laver (Aus)
1963 Raphael Osuna (Mex)
1964 Roy Emerson (Aus)
1965 Manuel Santana (Spa)
1966 Fred Stolle (Aus)
1967 John Newcombe (Aus)

1968 Arthur Ashe (USA)
Open Arthur Ashe (USA)
1969 Stan Smith (USA)
Open Rod Laver (Aus)
1970 Ken Rosewall (Aus)
1971 Stan Smith (USA)
1972 Ilie Nastase (Rom)
1973 John Newcombe (Aus)
1974 Jimmy Connors (USA)
1975 Manuel Orantes (Spa)
1976 Jimmy Connors (USA)
1977 Guillermo Vilas (Arg)
1978 Jimmy Connors (USA)
1979-81 John McEnroe (USA)
1982-3 Jimmy Connors (USA)
1985-6 Ivan Lendl (Cs)

Most wins: 7 Bill Tilden 1920-5, 1929; Richard Sears 1881-7; Bill Larned 1901-2, 1907-11

WOMEN'S SINGLES
1946 Pauline Betz (USA)
1947 Louise Brough (USA)
1948-50 Margaret Du Pont (USA)
1951-3 Maureen Connolly (USA)
1954-5 Doris Hart (USA)
1956 Shirley Fry (USA)
1957-8 Althea Gibson (USA)
1959 Maria Bueno (Bra)
1960-1 Darlene Hard (USA)
1962 Margaret Smith (Aus)
1963-4 Maria Bueno (Bra)
1965 Margaret Smith (Aus)
1966 Maria Bueno (Bra)
1967 Billie Jean King (USA)
1968 Margaret Court (Aus)
Open Virginia Wade (UK)
1969 Margaret Court (Aus)
Open Margaret Court (Aus)
1970 Margaret Court (Aus)
1971-2 Billie Jean King (USA)
1973 Margaret Court (Aus)
1974 Billie Jean King (USA)
1975-8 Chris Evert (USA)
1979 Tracy Austin (USA)
1980 Chris Evert-Lloyd (USA)
1981 Tracy Austin (USA)
1982 Chris Evert-Lloyd (USA)
1983-4 Martina Navratilova (USA)
1985 Hana Mandlikova (Cs)
1986 Martina Navratilova (USA)

Most wins: 7 Molla Mallory (née Bjurstedt) 1915-6, 1918 1920-2, 1926; Helen Moody (née Wills) 1923-5, 1927-9, 1931

MEN'S DOUBLES
1946 Gardnar Mulloy & William Talbert (USA)
1947 Jack Kramer & Ted Schroeder (USA)
1948 Gardnar Mulloy & William Talbert (USA)
1949 John Bromwich & William Sidwell (Aus)
1950 John Bromwich & Frank Sedgman (Aus)
1951 Ken McGregor & Frank Sedgman (Aus)
1952 Mervin Rose (Aus) & Vic Siexas (USA)
1953 Rex Hartwig & Mervyn Rose (Aus)
1954 Vic Seixas & Tony Trabert (USA)
1955 Kosei Kano & Atushi Miyagi (Jap)

Billie-Jean King (All-Sport)

1956 Lew Hoad & Ken Rosewall (Aus)
1957 Ashley Cooper & Neale Fraser (Aus)
1958 Alex Olmedo & Ham Richardson (USA)
1959-60 Roy Emerson & Neale Fraser (Aus)
1961 Charles McKinley & Dennis Ralston (USA)
1962 Antonio Palafox & Rafael Osuna (Mex)
1963-4 Charles McKinley & Dennis Ralston (USA)
1965-6 Roy Emerson & Fred Stolle (Aus)
1967 John Newcombe & Tony Roche (Aus)
1968 Bob Lutz & Stan Smith (USA)
Open Bob Lutz & Stan Smith (USA)
1969 Dick Crealy & Allan Stone (Aus)
Open Ken Rosewall & Fred Stolle (Aus)
1970 Pierre Barthes (Fra) & Nikki Pilic (Yug)
1971 John Newcombe (Aus) & Roger Taylor (UK)
1972 Cliff Drysdale (SAf) & Roger Taylor (UK)
1973 Owen Davidson & John Newcombe (Aus)
1974 Bob Lutz & Stan Smith (USA)
1975 Jimmy Connors (USA) & Ilie Nastase (Rom)
1976 Tom Okker (Hol) & Marty Riessen (USA)
1977 Bob Hewitt & Frew McMillan (SAf)
1978 Bob Lutz & Stan Smith (USA)
1979 Peter Fleming & John McEnroe (USA)
1980 Bob Lutz & Stan Smith (USA)
1981 Peter Fleming & John McEnroe (USA)

1982 Kevin Curren (SAf) & Steve Denton (USA)
1983 Peter Fleming & John McEnroe (USA)
1984 John Fitzgerald (Aus) & Tomas Smid (Cs)
1985 Ken Flach & Robert Seguso (USA)
1986 Andres Gomez (Ecu) & Slobodan Zivojinovic (Yug)

Most wins: 6 Richard Sears 1882-7; Holcombe Ward 1899-1901, 1904-6

WOMEN'S DOUBLES
1946-50 Louise Brough & Margaret Osborne (USA)
1951-4 Shirley Fry & Doris Hart (USA)
1955-7 Louise Brough & Margaret Du Pont (USA)
1958-9 Jean Arth & Darlene Hard (USA)
1960 Maria Bueno (Bra) & Darlene Hard (USA)
1961 Darlene Hard (USA) & Lesley Turner (Aus)
1962 Maria Bueno (Bra) & Darlene Hard (USA)
1963 Robyn Ebbern & Margaret Smith (Aus)
1964 Karen Susman & Billie Jean Moffitt (USA)
1965 Nancy Richey & Carole Graebner (USA)
1966 Maria Bueno (Bra) & Nancy Richey (USA)
1967 Rosemary Casals & Billie Jean King (USA)
1968 Maria Bueno (Bra) & Margaret Court (Aus)
Open Maria Bueno (Bra) & Margaret Court (Aus)
1969 Margaret Court (Aus) & Virginia Wade (UK)
Open Francoise Durr (Fra) & Darlene Hard (USA)
1970 Margaret Court & Judy Dalton (Aus)
1971 Rosemary Casals (USA) & Judy Dalton (Aus)
1972 Francoise Durr (Fra) & Betty Stove (Hol)
1973 Margaret Court (Aus) & Virginia Wade (UK)
1974 Rosemary Casals & Billie Jean King (USA)
1975 Margaret Court (Aus) & Virginia Wade (UK)
1976 Linda Boshoff & Ilana Kloss (SAf)
1977 Martina Navratilova (Cs) & Betty Stove (Hol)
1978 Billie Jean King (USA) & Martina Navratilova (Cs)
1979 Betty Stove (Hol) & Wendy Turnbull (Aus)
1980 Billie Jean King (USA) & Martina Navratilova (Cs)
1981 Kathy Jordan & Anne Smith (USA)
1982 Rosemary Casals (USA) & Wendy Turnbull (Aus)
1983-4 Martina Navratilova & Pam Shriver (USA)
1985 Claudia Kohde-Kilsch (FRG) & Helena Sukova (Cs)
1986 Martina Navratilova & Pam Shriver (USA)

Most wins: 13 Margaret Du Pont (née Osborne) 1941-50, 1955-7

MIXED DOUBLES
1946 William Talbert & Margaret Osborne (USA)
1947 John Bromwich (Aus) & Louise Brough (USA)
1948 Tom Brown & Louise Brough (USA)
1949 Eric Sturgess (SAf) & Louise Brough (USA)
1950 Ken McGregor (Aus) & Margaret Du Pont (USA)
1951-2 Frank Sedgman (Aus) & Doris Hart (USA)
1953-5 Vic Seixas & Doris Hart (USA)
1956 Ken Rosewall (Aus) & Margaret Du Pont (USA)
1957 Kurt Nielsen (Den) & Althea Gibson (USA)
1958-60 Neale Fraser (Aus) & Margaret Du Pont (USA)
1961 Robert Mark & Margaret Smith (Aus)
1962 Fred Stolle & Margaret Smith (Aus)
1963 Ken Fletcher & Margaret Smith (Aus)
1964 John Newcombe & Margaret Smith (Aus)
1965 Fred Stolle & Margaret Smith (Aus)
1966 Owen Davidson (Aus) & Donna Fales (USA)
1967 Owen Davidson (Aus) & Billie Jean King (USA)
1968 Peter Curtis (UK) & Mary-Ann Eisel (USA)
1969 Paul Sullivan & Patty Hogan (USA)

Open Marty Riessen (USA) & Margaret Court (née Smith) (Aus)
1970 Marty Riessen (USA) & Margaret Court (Aus)
1971 Owen Davidson (Aus) & Billie Jean King (USA)
1972 Marty Riessen (USA) & Margaret Court (Aus)
1973 Owen Davidson (Aus) & Billie Jean King (USA)
1974 Geoff Masters (Aus) & Pam Teeguarden (USA)
1975 Dick Stockton & Rosemary Casals (USA)
1976 Phil Dent (Aus) & Billie Jean King (USA)
1977-8 Frew McMillan (SAf) & Betty Stove (Hol)
1979 Bob Hewitt & Greer Stevens (SAf)
1980 Marty Riessen & Wendy Turnbull (USA)
1981-2 Kevin Curren (SAf) & Anne Smith (USA)
1983 John Fitzgerald & Elizabeth Sayers (Aus)
1984 Tom Gullikson (USA) & Manuela Maleeva (Bul)
1985 Heinz Gunthardt (Swi) & Martina Navratilova (USA)
1986 Sergio Casal (Spa) & Raffaella Reggi (Ita)

Most wins (Men): 4 Edwin Fischer 1894-6, 1898; Wallace Johnson 1907, 1909, 1911, 1920; Bill Tilden 1913-4, 1922-3; William Talbert 1943-6; Owen Davidson 1966-7, 1971, 1973; Marty Riessen 1969-70, 1972, 1980
(Women): 9 Margaret Du Pont (née Osborne) 1943-6, 1950, 1956, 1958-60; 8 Margaret Court (née Smith) as above

MOST UNITED STATES TITLES

	Tot	Sngls	Dbls	Mixed	Years
Margaret Du Pont (USA)	25	3	13	9	1941-60
Margaret Court (Aus)	22	7	7	8	1961-75
Louise Brough (USA)	17	1	12	4	1942-57
Bill Tilden (Aus)	16	7	5	4	1913-29
Hazel Wightman (USA)	16	4	6	6	1909-28
Sarah Fabyan (USA)	15	2	9	4	1930-45

FRENCH CHAMPIONSHIPS

The French Championships were first held in 1891 but they remained 'closed', open only to members of French clubs, until 1925 when they became a fully international event. They have always been held on hard courts.

Post-war winners

MEN'S SINGLES

1946 Marcel Bernard (Fra)
1947 Jozsef Asboth (Hun)
1948-9 Frank Parker (USA)
1950 Budge Patty (USA)
1951-2 Jaroslav Drobny (Egy)
1953 Ken Rosewall (Aus)
1954-5 Tony Trabert (USA)
1956 Lew Hoad (Aus)
1957 Sven Davidson (Swe)
1958 Mervyn Rose (Aus)
1959-60 Nicola Pietrangeli (Ita)
1961 Manuel Santana (Spa)
1962 Rod Laver (Aus)
1963 Roy Emerson (Aus)
1964 Manuel Santana (Spa)
1965 Fred Stolle (Aus)
1966 Tony Roche (Aus)
1967 Roy Emerson (Aus)
1968 Ken Rosewall (Aus)
1969 Rod Laver (Aus)
1970-1 Jan Kodes (Cs)

1972 Andres Gimeno (Spa)
1973 Ilie Nastase (Rom)
1974-5 Bjorn Borg (Swe)
1976 Adriano Panatta (Ita)
1977 Guillermo Vilas (Arg)
1978-81 Bjorn Borg (Swe)
1982 Mats Wilander (Swe)
1983 Yannick Noah (Fra)
1984 Ivan Lendl (Cs)
1985 Mats Wilander (Swe)
1986-7 Ivan Lendl (Cs)

Most wins (since 1925): 6 Bjorn Borg

WOMEN'S SINGLES

1946 Margaret Osborne (USA)
1947 Pat Todd (USA)
1948 Nelly Landry (Fra)
1949 Margaret Du Pont (née Osborne) (USA)
1950 Doris Hart (USA)
1951 Shirley Fry (USA)
1952 Doris Hart (USA)
1953-4 Maureen Connolly (USA)
1955 Angela Mortimer (UK)
1956 Althea Gibson (USA)
1957 Shirley Bloomer (UK)
1958 Zsuzsi Kormoczy (Hun)
1959 Christine Truman (UK)
1960 Darlene Hard (USA)
1961 Ann Haydon (UK)
1962 Margaret Smith (Aus)
1963 Lesley Turner (Aus)
1964 Margaret Smith (Aus)
1965 Lesley Turner (Aus)
1966 Ann Jones (UK)
1967 Francoise Durr (Fra)
1968 Nancy Richey (USA)
1969 Margaret Court (née Smith) (Aus)
1970 Margaret Court (Aus)
1971 Evonne Goolagong (Aus)
1972 Billie Jean King (USA)
1973 Margaret Court (Aus)
1974-5 Chris Evert (USA)
1976 Sue Barker (UK)
1977 Mimi Jausovec (Yug)
1978 Virginia Ruzici (Rom)
1979-80 Chris Evert-Lloyd (USA)
1981 Hana Mandlikova (Cs)
1982 Martina Navratilova (USA)
1983 Chris Evert-Lloyd (USA)
1984 Martina Navratilova (USA)
1985-6 Chris Evert-Lloyd (USA)
1987 Steffi Graf (FRG)

Most wins (since 1925): 7 Chris Evert-Lloyd

MEN'S DOUBLES

1946 Marcel Bernard & Yvon Petra (Fra)
1947 Eustace Fannin & Eric Sturgess (SAf)
1948 Lennart Bergelin (Swe) & Jaroslav Drobny (Cs)
1949 Richard Gonzales & Frank Parker (USA)
1950 William Talbert & Tony Trabert (USA)
1951-2 Ken McGregor & Frank Sedgman (Aus)
1953 Lew Hoad & Ken Rosewall (Aus)
1954-5 Vic Seixas & Tony Trabert (USA)
1956 Don Candy (Aus) & Robert Perry (USA)

1984 Henri Leconte & Yannick Noah (Fra)
1985 Mark Edmondson & Kim Warwick (Aus)
1986 John Fitzgerald (Aus) & Tomas Smid (Cs)
1987 Anders Jarryd (Swe) & Robert Seguso (USA)

Most wins (since 1925): 6 Roy Emerson (Aus)

WOMEN'S DOUBLES
1946-7 Louise Brough & Margaret Osborne (USA)
1948 Doris Hart & Pat Todd (USA)
1949 Louise Brough & Margaret Du Pont (née Osborne) (USA)
1950-3 Shirley Fry & Doris Hart (USA)
1954 Maureen Connolly (USA) & Nell Hopman (Aus)
1955 Beverley Fleitz & Darlene Hard (USA)
1956 Angela Buxton (UK) & Althea Gibson (USA)
1957 Shirley Bloomer (UK) & Darlene Hard (USA)
1958 Yola Ramirez & Rosa Reyes (Mex)
1959 Sandra Reynolds & Renee Schuurman (SAf)
1960 Maria Bueno (Bra) & Darlene Hard (USA)
1961 Sandra Reynolds & Renee Schuurman (SAf)
1962 Sandra Price (née Reynolds) & Renee Schuurman (SAf)
1963 Ann Jones (UK) & Renee Schuurman (SAf)
1964-5 Margaret Smith & Lesley Turner (Aus)
1966 Margaret Smith & Judy Tegart (Aus)
1967 Francoise Durr (Fra) & Gail Sheriff (Aus)
1968-9 Francoise Durr (Fra) & Ann Jones (UK)
1970 Francoise Durr & Gail Chanfreau (Fra)
1971 Francoise Durr & Gail Chanfreau (Fra)
1972 Billie Jean King (USA) & Betty Stove (Hol)
1973 Margaret Court (Aus) & Virginia Wade (UK)
1974 Chris Evert (USA) & Olga Morozova (USSR)
1975 Chris Evert (USA) & Martina Navratilova (Cs)
1976 Fiorella Bonicelli (Uru) & Gail Lovera (Fra)
1977 Regina Marsikova (Cs) & Pam Teeguarden (USA)
1978 Mimi Jausovec (Yug) & Virginia Ruzici (Rom)
1979 Betty Stove (Hol) & Wendy Turnbull (Aus)
1980 Kathy Jordan & Anne Smith (USA)
1981 Ros Fairbank & Tanya Harford (SAf)
1982 Martina Navratilova & Anne Smith (USA)
1983 Ros Fairbank (SAf) & Candy Reynolds (USA)
1984-5 Martina Navratilova & Pam Shriver (USA)
1986 Martina Navratilova (USA) & Andrea Temesvari (Hun)
1987 Martina Navratilova & Pam Shriver (USA)

Most wins (since 1925): 6 Simone Mathieu (Fra) 1933-4, 1936-9, Martina Navratilova

MIXED DOUBLES
1946 Budge Patty & Pauline Betz (USA)
1947 Eric Sturgess & Sheila Summers (SAf)
1948 Jaroslav Drobny (Cs) & Pat Todd (USA)
1949 Eric Sturgess & Sheila Summers (SAf)
1950 Enrique Morea (Arg) & Barbara Scofield (USA)
1951-2 Frank Sedgman (Aus) & Doris Hart (USA)
1953 Vic Seixas & Doris Hart (USA)
1954 Lew Hoad (Aus) & Maureen Connolly (USA)
1955 Gordon Forbes (SAf) & Darlene Hard (USA)
1956 Luis Ayala (Chl) & Thelma Long (Aus)
1957 Jan Javorsky & Vera Puzejova (Cs)
1958 Nicola Pietrangeli (Ita) & Shirley Bloomer (UK)
1959 Billy Knight (UK) & Yola Ramirez (Mex)
1960 Bob Howe (Aus) & Maria Bueno (Bra)
1961 Rod Laver (Aus) & Darlene Hard (USA)

Martina Navratilova (All-Sport)

1957 Mal Anderson & Ashley Cooper (Aus)
1958 Ashley Cooper & Neale Fraser (Aus)
1959 Nicola Pietrangeli & Orlando Sirola (Ita)
1960 Roy Emerson & Neale Fraser (Aus)
1961 Roy Emerson & Rod Laver (Aus)
1962 Roy Emerson & Neale Fraser (Aus)
1963 Roy Emerson (Aus) & Manuel Santana (Spa)
1964 Roy Emerson & Ken Fletcher (Aus)
1965 Roy Emerson & Fred Stolle (Aus)
1966 Clark Graebner & Dennis Ralston (USA)
1967 John Newcombe & Tony Roche (Aus)
1968 Ken Rosewall & Fred Stolle (Aus)
1969 John Newcombe & Tony Roche (Aus)
1970 Ilie Nastase & Ion Tiriac (Rom)
1971 Arthur Ashe & Marty Riessen (USA)
1972 Bob Hewitt & Frew McMillan (SAf)
1973 John Newcombe (Aus) & Tom Okker (Hol)
1974 Dick Crealy (Aus) & Onny Parun (NZ)
1975 Brian Gottfried (USA) & Raul Ramirez (Mex)
1976 Fred McNair & Sherwood Stewart (USA)
1977 Brian Gottfried (USA) & Raul Ramirez (Mex)
1978 Gene Mayer & Hank Pfister (USA)
1979 Sandy Mayer & Gene Mayer (USA)
1980 Victor Amaya & Hank Pfister (USA)
1981 Heinz Gunthardt (Swi) & Balazs Taroczy (Hun)
1982 Sherwood Stewart & Ferdi Taygan (USA)
1983 Anders Jarryd & Hans Simonsson (Swe)

1962 Bob Howe (Aus) & Renee Schuurman (SAf)
1963-5 Ken Fletcher & Margaret Smith (Aus)
1966 Frew McMillan & Annette Van Zyl (SAf)
1967 Owen Davidson (Aus) & Billie Jean King (USA)
1968 Jean-Claude Barclay & Francoise Durr (Fra)
1969 Marty Riessen (USA) & Margaret Court (née Smith) (Aus)
1970 Bob Hewitt (SAf) & Billie Jean King (USA)
1971 Jean-Claude Barclay & Francoise Durr (Fra)
1972 Kim Warwick & Evonne Goolagong (Aus)
1973 Jean-Claude Barclay & Francoise Durr (Fra)
1974 Ivan Molina (Col) & Martina Navratilova (Cs)
1975 Thomaz Koch (Bra) & Fiorella Bonicelli (Uru)
1976 Kim Warwick (Aus) & Ilana Kloss (SAf)
1977 John McEnroe & Mary Carillo (USA)
1978 Pavel Slozil & Renata Tomanova (Cs)
1979 Bob Hewitt (SAf) & Wendy Turnbull (Aus)
1980 Bill Martin & Anne Smith (USA)
1981 Jimmy Arias & Andrea Jaeger (USA)
1982 John Lloyd (UK) & Wendy Turnbull (Aus)
1983 Eliot Teltscher & Barbara Jordan (USA)
1984 Dick Stockton & Anne Smith (USA)
1985 Heinz Gunthardt (Swi) & Martina Navratilova (USA)
1986 Ken Flach & Kathy Jordan (USA)
1987 Emilio Sanchez (Spa) & Pam Shriver (USA)

Most wins (Men): 3 Ken Fletcher, Jean-Claude Barclay
(Women): 4 Margaret Court (née Smith)

MOST FRENCH TITLES

	Tot	Sngls	Dbls	Mixed	Years
Margaret Court (Aus)	13	5	4	4	1962-73
Simone Mathieu (Fra)	10	2	6	2	1933-9
Doris Hart (USA)	10	2	5	3	1948-53
Martina Navratilova (Cs/USA)	10	2	6	2	1974-87
Henri Cochet (Fra)	9	4	3	2	1926-30
Francoise Durr (Fra)	9	1	5	3	1967-73
Chris Evert-Lloyd (USA)	9	7	2	-	1974-86

AUSTRALIAN CHAMPIONSHIPS

The first championships were held in 1905 and were known as the Australasian Championships; it was not until 1925 that the title changed to its present style. New Zealand twice hosted the championship, in 1906 and 1912. There were two championships in 1977 because the event was moved from early-season (January) to December. It reverted to a January date in 1987, which meant there was no championship in 1986.

Post-war winners:

MEN'S SINGLES
1946 John Bromwich (Aus)
1947 Dinny Pails (Aus)
1948 Adrian Quist (Aus)
1949-50 Frank Sedgman (Aus)
1951 Dick Savitt (USA)
1952 Ken McGregor (Aus)
1953 Ken Rosewall (Aus)
1954 Mervyn Rose (Aus)
1955 Ken Rosewall (Aus)
1956 Lew Hoad (Aus)
1957-8 Ashley Cooper (Aus)
1959 Alex Olmedo (USA)
1960 Rod Laver (Aus)

1961 Roy Emerson (Aus)
1962 Rod Laver (Aus)
1963-7 Roy Emerson (Aus)
1968 Bill Bowrey (Aus)
1969 Rod Laver (Aus)
1970 Arthur Ashe (USA)
1971-2 Ken Rosewall (Aus)
1973 John Newcombe (Aus)
1974 Jimmy Connors (USA)
1975 John Newcombe (Aus)
1976 Mark Edmondson (Aus)
1977 Roscoe Tanner (USA)
     Vitas Gerulaitis (USA)
1978-9 Guillermo Vilas (Arg)
1980 Brian Teacher (USA)
1981-2 Johan Kriek (SAf)
1983-4 Mats Wilander (Swe)
1985 Stefan Edberg (Swe)
1987 Stefan Edberg (Swe)

Most wins: 6 Roy Emerson

WOMEN'S SINGLES
1946-8 Nancye Bolton (Aus)
1949 Doris Hart (USA)
1950 Louise Brough (USA)
1951 Nancye Bolton (Aus)
1952 Thelma Long (Aus)
1953 Maureen Connolly (USA)
1954 Thelma Long (Aus)
1955 Beryl Penrose (Aus)
1956 Mary Carter (Aus)
1957 Shirley Fry (USA)
1958 Angela Mortimer (UK)
1959 Mary Reitano (Aus)
1960-6 Margaret Smith (Aus)
1967 Nancy Richey (USA)
1968 Billie Jean King (USA)
1969 Margaret Court (née Smith) (Aus)
1970-1 Margaret Court (Aus)
1972 Virginia Wade (UK)
1973 Margaret Court (Aus)
1974-5 Evonne Goolagong (Aus)
1976 Evonne Cawley (née Goolagong) (Aus)
1977 Kerry Reid (Aus)
     Evonne Cawley (Aus)
1978 Christine O'Neill (Aus)
1979 Barbara Jordan (USA)
1980 Hana Mandlikova (Cs)
1981 Martina Navratilova (USA)
1982 Chris Evert-Lloyd (USA)
1983 Martina Navratilova (USA)
1984 Chris Evert-Lloyd (USA)
1985 Martina Navratilova (USA)
1987 Hana Mandlikova (Cs)

Most wins: 11 Margaret Court (née Smith); 6 Nancye Bolton (née Wynne) 1937, 1940, 1946-8, 1951

MEN'S DOUBLES
1946-50 John Bromwich & Adrian Quist (Aus)
1951-2 Ken McGregor & Frank Sedgman (Aus)
1953 Lew Hoad & Ken Rosewall (Aus)
1954 Rex Hartwig & Mervyn Rose (Aus)
1955 Vic Seixas & Tony Trabert (USA)
1956 Lew Hoad & Ken Rosewall (Aus)
1957 Neale Fraser & Lew Hoad (Aus)

1958 Ashley Cooper & Neale Fraser (Aus)
1959-61 Rod Laver & Robert Mark (Aus)
1962 Roy Emerson & Neale Fraser (Aus)
1963-4 Bob Hewitt & Fred Stolle (Aus)
1965 John Newcombe & Tony Roche (Aus)
1966 Roy Emerson & Fred Stolle (Aus)
1967 John Newcombe & Tony Roche (Aus)
1968 Dick Crealy & Allan Stone (Aus)
1969 Roy Emerson & Rod Laver (Aus)
1970 Bob Lutz & Stan Smith (USA)
1971 John Newcombe & Tony Roche (Aus)
1972 Owen Davidson & Ken Rosewall (Aus)
1973 Mal Anderson & John Newcombe (Aus)
1974 Ross Case & Geoff Masters (Aus)
1975 John Alexander & Phil Dent (Aus)
1976 John Newcombe & Tony Roche (Aus)
1977 Arthur Ashe (USA) & Tony Roche (Aus)
       Ray Ruffels & Allan Stone (Aus)
1978 Wojtek Fibak (Pol) & Kim Warwick (Aus)
1979 Peter McNamara & Paul McNamee (Aus)
1980-1 Mark Edmondson & Kim Warwick (Aus)
1982 John Alexander & John Fitzgerald (Aus)
1983 Mark Edmonson & Paul McNamee (Aus)
1984 Mark Edmondson (Aus) & Sherwood Stewart (USA)
1985 Paul Annacone (USA) & Christo Van Rensburg (SAf)
1987 Stefan Edberg & Anders Jarryd (Swe)

Most wins: 10 Adrian Quist 1936-40, 1946-50; 8 John Bromwich 1938-40, 1946-50

WOMEN'S DOUBLES
1946 Mary Bevis & Joyce Fitch (Aus)
1947-9 Nancye Bolton & Thelma Long (Aus)
1950 Louise Brough & Doris Hart (USA)
1951-2 Nancye Bolton & Thelma Long (Aus)
1953 Maureen Connolly & Julie Sampson (USA)
1954 Mary Hawton (née Bevis) & Beryl Penrose (Aus)
1955 Mary Hawton & Beryl Penrose (Aus)
1956 Mary Hawton & Thelma Long (Aus)
1957 Shirley Fry & Althea Gibson (USA)
1958 Mary Hawton & Thelma Long (Aus)
1959 Sandra Reynolds & Renee Schuurman (SAf)
1960 Maria Bueno (Bra) & Christine Truman (UK)
1961 Mary Reitano & Margaret Smith (Aus)
1962-3 Robyn Ebbern & Margaret Smith (Aus)
1964 Judy Tegart & Lesley Turner (Aus)
1965 Margaret Smith & Lesley Turner (Aus)
1966 Carole Graebner & Nancy Richey (USA)
1967 Judy Tegart & Lesley Turner (Aus)
1968 Karen Krantzcke & Kerry Melville (Aus)
1969 Margaret Court (née Smith) & Judy Tegart (Aus)
1970 Margaret Court & Judy Dalton (née Tegart) (Aus)
1971 Margaret Court & Evonne Goolagong (Aus)
1972 Helen Gourlay & Kerry Harris (Aus)
1973 Margaret Court (Aus) & Virginia Wade (UK)
1974-5 Evonne Goolagong (Aus) & Peggy Michel (USA)
1976 Evonne Cawley (née Goolagong) & Helen Gourlay (Aus)
1977 Diane Fromholtz & Helen Gourlay (Aus)
Evonne Cawley & Helen Cawley (Aus) shared the December title with Ramona Guerrant (USA) & Kerry Reid (née Melville) (Aus). Final not played.
1978 Betsy Nagelsen (USA) & Renata Tomanova (Cs)

Margaret Court

1979 Judith Chaloner (NZ) & Dianne Evers (Aus)
1980 Betsy Nagelsen (USA) & Martina Navratilova (Cs)
1981 Kathy Jordan & Anne Smith (USA)
1982-5 Martina Navratilova & Pam Shriver (USA)
1987 Martina Navratilova & Pam Shriver (USA)

Most wins: 12 Thelma Long (née Coyne) 1936-40, 1947-9, 1951-2, 1956, 1958; 10 Nancye Bolton (née Wynne) 1936-40, 1947-9,1951-2; 8 Margaret Court (née Smith)

MIXED DOUBLES
1946-8 Colin Long & Nancye Bolton (Aus)
1949-50 Frank Sedgman (Aus) & Doris Hart (USA)
1951-2 George Worthington & Thelma Long (Aus)
1953 Rex Hartwig (Aus) & Julie Sampson (USA)
1954 Rex Hartwig & Thelma Long (Aus)
1955 George Worthington & Thelma Long (Aus)
1956 Neale Fraser & Beryl Penrose (Aus)
1957 Mal Anderson & Fay Muller (Aus)
1958 Bob Howe & Mary Hawton (Aus)
1959 Robert Mark (Aus) & Sandra Reynolds (SAf)
1960 Trevor Fancutt (SAf) & Jan Lehane (Aus)
1961 Bob Hewitt & Jan Lehane (Aus)
1962 Fred Stolle & Lesley Turner (Aus)
1963-4 Ken Fletcher & Margaret Smith (Aus)
1965 John Newcombe & Margaret Smith (Aus) shared title with Owen Davidson & Robyn Ebbern (Aus). Final not played.
1966 Tony Roche & Judy Tegart (Aus)
1967 Owen Davidson & Lesley Turner (Aus)
1968 Dick Crealy (Aus) & Billie Jean King (USA)
1969 Marty Riessen (USA) & Margaret Court (née Smith) (Aus) shared title with Fred Stolle (Aus) & Ann Jones (UK). Final not played.
1970-85 not held
1987 Sherwood Stewart & Zina Garrison (USA)

Most wins (Men): 4 Harry Hopman 1930, 1936-7, 1939, Colin Long 1940, 1946-8
(Women): 4 Nell Hopman (née Hall) 1930, 1936-7, 1939, Nancye Bolton (née Wynne) 1940, 1946-8, Thelma Long (née Coyne) 1951-2, 1954-5, Margaret Court (née Smith) 1963-5, 1969

MOST AUSTRALIAN TITLES

	Tot	Singles	Dbls	Mixed	Years
Margaret Court (Aus)	21	11	8	2	1960-73
Nancye Bolton (Aus)	20	6	10	4	1936-51
Thelma Long (Aus)	18	2	12	4	1936-58
Daphne Akhurst (Aus)	13	5	4	4	1924-30
Adrian Quist (Aus)	13	3	10	-	1936-50
Best record by a non-Australian:					
Martina Navratilova (Cs/USA)	9	3	6	-	1980-87

THE ALL TIME GREATS

A summary of the all-time greats' performances (singles and doubles) in the four Grand Slam events – Wimbledon, US Open, French Championship, and Australian Championship.

	Tot	Wimb	US	Fr	Aus	Singles Wins
Margaret Court (Aus)	66	10	22	13	21	24
Martina Navratilova (Cs/USA)	46	16	11	10	9	16
Billie Jean King (USA)	39	20	13	4	2	12
Margaret Du Pont (USA)	37	7	25	5	-	6
Louise Brough (USA)	35	13	17	3	2	6
Doris Hart (USA)	35	10	11	10	4	6
Helen Wills-Moody (USA)	31	12	13	6	-	19
Roy Emerson (Aus)	28	5	6	8	9	12
Elizabeth Ryan (USA)	26	19	3	4	-	0
John Newcombe (Aus)	25	9	6	3	7	7

GRAND SLAM

To achieve the Grand Slam is to hold simultaneously the titles of the four major tournaments as above. Originally one had to win all four in the same year to claim the Grand Slam.

The following players have achieved the Grand Slam: (Single years indicates all four titles won in one year)

MEN'S SINGLES
Donald Budge (USA) 1937/8, 1938
Rod Laver (Aus) 1962
Rod Laver (Aus) 1969

WOMEN'S SINGLES
Maureen Connolly (USA) 1952/3, 1953
Margaret Court (Aus) 1969/70, 1970, 1970/1
Martina Navratilova (USA) 1983/4

MEN'S DOUBLES
Frank Sedgman (Aus) 1950/1, 1951, 1951/2
Ken McGregor (Aus) 1951, 1951/2

WOMEN' DOUBLES
Louise Brough (USA) 1949/50
Maria Bueno (Bra) 1960
Martina Navratilova (USA) 1983/4, 1984, 1984/5, 1985/6
Pam Shriver (USA) 1983/4, 1984, 1984/5

MIXED DOUBLES
Margaret Smith (Aus) 1962/3, 1963, 1963/4
Ken Fletcher (Aus) 1963, 1963/4
Owen Davidson (Aus) 1966/7, 1967
Billie Jean King (USA) 1967/8

DAVIS CUP

The American player Dwight F. Davis donated a cup in 1900 to be contested by national teams. Up to 1971 the winning nation accepted a challenge from the country winning a knockout competition. But since 1972 the entire competition has been on a knockout basis with countries divided into zonal groups with a promotion and relegation system into the World Group of 16 nations who play-off for the Cup. There was no competition in 1901 and 1910, or during the war years. Each match is contested over two pairs of singles and a doubles.

Finals:

	Winners	Runners-Up	
1900	United States	British Isles	3-0
1902	United States	British Isles	3-2
1903	British Isles	United States	4-1
1904	British Isles	Belgium	5-0
1905	British Isles	United States	5-0
1906	British Isles	United States	5-0
1907	Australasia	British Isles	3-2
1908	Australasia	United States	3-2
1909	Australasia	United States	5-0
1911	Australasia	United States	5-0
1912	British Isles	Australasia	3-2
1913	United States	British Isles	3-2
1914	Australasia	United States	3-2
1919	Australasia	British Isles	4-1
1920	United States	Australasia	5-0
1921	United States	Japan	5-0
1922	United States	Australasia	4-1
1923	United States	Australia	4-1
1924	United States	Australia	5-0
1925	United States	France	5-0
1926	United States	France	4-1
1927	France	United States	3-2
1928	France	United States	4-1
1929	France	United States	3-2
1930	France	United States	4-1
1931	France	Great Britain	3-2
1932	France	United States	3-2
1933	Great Britain	France	3-2
1934	Great Britain	United States	4-1
1935	Great Britain	United States	5-0
1936	Great Britain	Australia	3-2
1937	United States	Great Britain	4-1
1938	United States	Australia	3-2
1939	Australia	United States	3-2
1946	United States	Australia	5-0
1947	United States	Australia	4-1
1948	United States	Australia	5-0
1949	United States	Australia	4-1
1950	Australia	United States	4-1
1951	Australia	United States	3-2
1952	Australia	United States	4-1
1953	Australia	United States	3-2
1954	United States	Australia	3-2
1955	Australia	United States	5-0
1956	Australia	United States	5-0
1957	Australia	United States	3-2
1958	United States	Australia	3-2
1959	Australia	United States	3-2
1960	Australia	Italy	4-1
1961	Australia	Italy	5-0

1962	Australia	Mexico	5-0
1963	United States	Australia	3-2
1964	Australia	United States	3-2
1965	Australia	Spain	4-1
1966	Australia	India	4-1
1967	Australia	Spain	4-1
1968	United States	Australia	4-1
1969	United States	Romania	5-0
1970	United States	West Germany	5-0
1971	United States	Romania	3-2
1972	United States	Romania	3-2
1973	Australia	United States	5-0
1974	South Africa	India	walkover
1975	Sweden	Czechoslovakia	3-2
1976	Italy	Chile	4-1
1977	Australia	Italy	3-1
1978	United States	Great Britain	4-1
1979	United States	Italy	5-0
1980	Czechoslovakia	Italy	4-1
1981	United States	Argentina	3-1
1982	United States	France	4-1
1983	Australia	Sweden	3-2
1984	Sweden	United States	4-1
1985	Sweden	West Germany	3-2
1986	Australia	Sweden	3-2

Wins: 28 United States; 26 Australia/Australasia; 9 British Isles/Great Britain; 6 France; 3 Sweden; 1 Czechoslovakia, Italy, South Africa

Most Davis Cup Appearances

	Total Rubbers	Years	Wins
Nicola Pietrangeli (Ita)	163	1954-72	120
Ilie Nastase (Rom)	146	1966-85	110
Jacques Brichant (Bel)	120	1949-65	71
Manuel Santana (Spa)	119	1958-73	91
Thomaz Koch (Bra)	118	1962-81	75

Most appearances for Great Britain:

Mike Sangster	65	1960-8	43

Most wins for Great Britain:

Fred Perry	52	1931-6	45

Most appearances in a Cup-winning team:
8 Roy Emerson (Aus) 1959-62, 1964-7

WIGHTMAN CUP

The former American player Hazel Wightman (née Hotchkiss) donated the trophy in 1920 to be contested by national female teams. However, none showed any interest until 1923 when the United States and Great Britain played for the trophy. Since then all Wightman Cup matches have been between the two nations. The format is five singles and two doubles.

Wins:
48 United States 1923, 1926-7, 1929, 1931-9, 1946-57, 1959, 1961-7, 1969-73, 1976-7, 1979-86
10 Great Britain 1924-5, 1928, 1930, 1958, 1960, 1968, 1974-5, 1978
The United States have 'whitewashed' Great Britain 12 times by inflicting a 7-0 defeat upon them. The years in which they performed the feat were: 1923, 1946-7, 1949-50, 1952-4*, 1977, 1979, 1981, 1985-6
* In 1954 only six matches were played, the USA won 6-0. Great Britain has not inflicted such a defeat on the American team.

Most Wightman Cup Appearances

	Total Rubbers	Years	Wins
Virginia Wade (UK)	56	1965-85	19
Chris Evert-Lloyd (USA)	38	1971-85	34*
Ann Jones (UK)	32	1957-75	16
Helen Moody (USA)	30	1923-38	21
Helen Jacobs (USA)	30	1927-39	19

* won all her 26 singles

Others with 20 or more wins:

Billie Jean King (USA)	26	1961-78	21
Doris Hart (USA)	24	1946-55	22
Louise Brough (USA)	22	1946-57	22

FEDERATION CUP

An international women's team competition played on a knockout basis at one venue each year. It was first held in 1963.

Winners:
1963 United States
1964-5 Australia
1966-7 United States
1968 Australia
1969 United States
1970-1 Australia
1972 South Africa
1973-4 Australia
1975 Czechoslovakia
1976-82 United States
1983-5 Czechoslovakia
1986 United States
1987 F.R. Germany

Wins: 12 United States; 7 Australia; 4 Czechoslovakia; 1 South Africa, F.R. Germany
Most appearances: Virginia Wade (UK) played in a record 100 rubbers (56 singles, 44 doubles) 1967-83, winning 66 (36 singles, 30 doubles).
Chris Evert-Lloyd won her first 29 singles in the competition 1977-86. In all she won 35/37 singles, 17/19 doubles 1977-87. Margaret Court won all her 20 singles matches for Australia 1963-71.

WORLD TEAM CUP

Formerly known as the Nations Cup, it is an eight-nation men's team event. First held in Kingston, Jamaica, in 1975, it was not held the next two years but was revived in 1977.

Winners:
1975 United States
1978 Spain
1979 Australia
1980 Argentina
1981 Czechoslovakia
1982 United States
1983 Spain
1984-5 United States
1986 France
1987 Czechoslovakia

Most wins: 4 United States

MEN'S GRAND PRIX MASTERS

Throughout the season various tournaments count towards the Masters and points are gained according to performances. The value of points available per tournament is geared to the stature of the tournament. At the end of the season the leading 16 players play-off for the Masters singles title, and eight pairs play-off for the doubles title. There was no event in 1977 because the date of the final was switched from December to the following January. There were two tournaments in 1986 because it reverted back to a December final.

Winners:

SINGLES
1970 Stan Smith (USA)
1971-3 Ilie Nastase (Rom)
1974 Guillermo Vilas (Arg)
1975 Ilie Nastase (Rom)
1976 Manuel Orantes (Spa)
1978 Jimmy Connors (USA)
1979 John McEnroe (USA)
1980-1 Bjorn Borg (Swe)
1982-3 Ivan Lendl (Cs)
1984-5 John McEnroe (USA)
1986 Ivan Lendl (Cs)
1986 Ivan Lendl (Cs)

Most wins: 4 Ilie Nastase, Ivan Lendl
Jimmy Connors qualified for the play-offs for a record 14 years 1972-85

DOUBLES
1970 Arthur Ashe & Stan Smith (USA)
1971-4 Not held
1975 Juan Gisbert & Manuel Orantes (Spa)
1976 Fred McNair & Sherwood Stewart (USA)
1978 Bob Hewitt & Frew McMillan (SAf)
1979-85 Peter Fleming & John McEnroe (USA)
1986 Stefan Edberg & Anders Jarryd (Swe)
1986 Stefan Edberg & Anders Jarryd (Swe)

Most wins: 7 John McEnroe & Peter Fleming

WOMEN'S INTERNATIONAL SERIES

As with the men, so women have had an international championship played after a season-long series of tournaments.

Winners: (see also Virginia Slims/Avon Series below)
SINGLES
1977-8 Chris Evert (USA)
1979* Martina Navratilova (Cs)
1980* Tracy Austin (USA)
1981 Tracy Austin (USA)
1982 Martina Navratilova (USA)
1983* Martina Navratilova (USA)
1984* Martina Navratilova (USA)

DOUBLES
1977 Francoise Durr (Fra) & Virginia Wade (UK)
1978 Billie Jean King (USA) & Martina Navratilova (Cs)
1979* Billie Jean King (USA) & Martina Navratilova (Cs)
1980* Rosemary Casals (USA) & Wendy Turnbull (Aus)
1981 Martina Navratilova (Cs) & Pam Shriver (USA)
1982 Martina Navratilova & Pam Shriver (USA)
1983* Martina Navratilova & Pam Shriver (USA)

John McEnroe (All-Sport)

1984* Martina Navratilova & Pam Shriver (USA)
* played the following year

VIRGINIA SLIMS/AVON SERIES
From 1971 there was an annual series of Virginia Slims tournaments, with the Championships as the climax. Avon Products took over the sponsorship 1979-82, with Virginia Slims back again in 1983 when their initial series ran for 15 months to March 1984.

Championship winners (the Doubles event has not been staged each year):

SINGLES
1971 Billie Jean King (USA)
1972-3 Chris Evert (USA)
1974 Evonne Goolagong (Aus)
1975 Chris Evert (USA)
1976 Evonne Cawley (née Goolagong) (Aus)
1977 Chris Evert (USA)
1978-9 Martina Navratilova (Cs)
1980 Tracy Austin (USA)
1981 Martina Navratilova (Cs)
1982 Sylvia Hanika (FRG)
1983* Martina Navratilova (USA)
1984* Martina Navratilova (USA)
1985* Martina Navratilova (USA)
1986 Martina Navratilova (USA)

DOUBLES
1971 Rosemary Casals & Billie Jean King (USA)
1973 Rosemary Casals (USA) & Margaret Court (Aus)
1974 Rosemary Casals & Billlie Jean King (USA)
1979 Francoise Durr (Fra) & Betty Stove (Hol)
1980 Billie Jean King (USA) & Martina Navratilova (Cs)
1981 Martina Navratilova (Cs) & Pam Shriver (USA)
1982 Martina Navratilova & Pam Shriver (USA)
1984* Martina Navratilova & Pam Shriver (USA)
1985* Hana Mandlikova (Cs) & Wendy Turnbull (Aus)
1986 Martina Navratilova & Pam Shriver (USA)
* played the following year

WORLD CHAMPIONSHIP TENNIS

World Championship Tennis Incorporated (WCT) was founded in 1967 to promote professional tennis. Following a series of qualifying tournaments, a finals tournament was held annually for men from 1971.

Winners:
1971-2 Ken Rosewall (Aus)
1973 Stan Smith (USA)
1974 John Newcombe (Aus)
1975 Arthur Ashe (USA)
1976 Bjorn Borg (Swe)
1977 Jimmy Connors (USA)
1978 Vitas Gerulaitas (USA)
1979 John McEnroe (USA)
1980 Jimmy Connors (USA)
1981 John McEnroe (USA)
1982 Ivan Lendl (Cs)
1983-4 John McEnroe (USA)
1985 Ivan Lendl (Cs)
1986 Anders Jarryd (Swe)
1987 Miloslav Mecir (Cs)

WCT DOUBLES
Introduced in 1973

Winners:
1973 Bob Lutz & Stan Smith (USA)
1974 Bob Hewitt & Frew McMillan (SAf)
1975 Brian Gottfried (USA) & Raul Ramirez (Mex)
1976 Wojtek Fibak (Pol) & Tom Okker (Hol)
1977 Vijay Amritraj (Ind) & Dick Stockton (USA)
1978 Wojtek Fibak (Pol) & Tom Okker (Hol)
1979 Peter Fleming & John McEnroe (USA)
1980 Brian Gottfried (USA) & Raul Ramirez (Mex)
1981 Peter McNamara & Paul McNamee (Aus)
1982-3 Heinz Gunthardt (Swi) & Balazs Taroczy (Hun)
1984 Pavel Slozil & Tomas Smid (Cs)
1985 Ken Flach & Robert Seguso (USA)
1986 Heinz Gunthardt (Swi) & Balazs Taroczy (Hun)
1986§ Stefan Edberg & Anders Jarryd (Swe)
§ brought forward from January to December

ITF WORLD CHAMPIONS

A panel of former champions decide annually who are the International Tennis Federation's World Champions.

Winners since the inauguration of the award in 1978 have been:

MEN	**WOMEN**
1978 Bjorn Borg (Swe)	Chris Evert (USA)
1979 Bjorn Borg (Swe)	Martina Navratilova (Cs)
1980 Bjorn Borg (Swe)	Chris Evert-Lloyd (USA)

Bjorn Borg (All-Sport)

1981	John McEnroe (USA)	Chris Evert-Lloyd (USA)
1982	Jimmy Connors (USA)	Martina Navratilova (USA)
1983	John McEnroe (USA)	Martina Navratilova (USA)
1984	John McEnroe (USA)	Martina Navratilova (USA)
1985	Ivan Lendl (Cs)	Martina Navratilova (USA)§
1986	Ivan Lendl (Cs)	Martina Navratilova (USA)

§ Points from the Virginia Slims series decided the Ladies world champion

THE MONEY WINNERS

All time money list (as at the end of 1986):

	MEN	**$**
1	Ivan Lendl (Cs)	10,294,375
2	John McEnroe (USA)	9,194,859
3	Jimmy Connors (USA)	7,067,951
4	Guillermo Vilas (Arg)	4,746,486
5	Mats Wilander (Swe)	3,940,658
6	Bjorn Borg (Swe)	3,607,206
7	Tomas Smid (Cs)	2,908,222
8	Brian Gottfried (USA)	2,781,614
9	Vitas Gerulaitis (USA)	2,777,614
10	Wojtek Fibak (Pol)	2,683,619

WOMEN	$
1 Martina Navratilova (USA)	11,792,315
2 Chris Evert-Lloyd (USA)	7,195,918
3 Pam Shriver (USA)	2,672,747
4 Hana Mandlikova (Cs)	2,664,681
5 Wendy Turnbull (Aus)	2,407,237
6 Billie Jean King (USA)	1,965,412
7 Tracy Austin (USA)	1,908,715
8 Helena Sukova (Cs)	1,579,693
9 Virginia Wade (UK)	1,542,014
10 Evonne Cawley (née Goolagong) (Aus)	1,399,434

WORLD YOUNG MASTERS

The inaugural World Young Masters for players under the age of 21 was held in 1985 and won by Boris Becker (FRG), who retained the title in his home country the following year.

OLYMPIC GAMES

Lawn Tennis was included in the Olympic Games from 1896 to 1924 and as a demonstration sport in 1968. Following the staging of an international tournament at the 1984 Games, at which the singles winners were Stefan Edberg (Swe) and Steffi Graf (FRG), Tennis is due to be re-introduced to the Olympics in 1988.

Most medals: 6 Max Decugis (Fra) a record 4 gold 1920-4, 1 silver and 1 bronze; 5 Kathleen McKane (UK) 1 gold, 2 silver, 2 bronze, 1920-4

MAIDEN NAMES/MARRIED NAMES

Married Name	Maiden Name
Nancye BOLTON	WYNNE
Evonne CAWLEY	GOOLAGONG
Helen CAWLEY	GOURLAY
Gail CHANFREAU (see also LOVERA)	SHERRIFF
Margaret COURT	SMITH
Judy DALTON	TEGART
Margaret DU PONT	OSBORNE
Chris EVERT-LLOYD	EVERT
Sarah FABYAN	PALFREY
Kathleen GODFREE	McKANE
Mary HAWTON	BEVIS
Blanche HILLYARD	BINGLEY
Ann JONES	HAYDON
Billie Jean KING	MOFFITT
Dorothea LAMBERT CHAMBERS	DOUGLASS
Thelma LONG	COYNE
Gail LOVERA (see also CHANFREAU)	SHERRIFF
Peggy MICHEL	SAUNDERS
Helen MOODY	WILLS
Kerry REID	MELVILLE
Mary REITANO	CARTER
Elizabeth SMYLIE	SAYERS
Charlotte STERRY	COOPER
Vera SUKOVA	PUZEJOVA
Karen SUSMAN	HANTZE

TRAMPOLINING

Trampolining has formed part of circus acts for many years but it only started to attract interest as a sport after the design of trampolines similar to modern day ones, by George Nissen in the United States in 1936. The first official Trampolining tournament took place in the United States in 1947.

WORLD CHAMPIONSHIPS

Instituted in 1964, they have been held biennially since 1968.

Winners:

MEN

INDIVIDUAL
1964 Danny Millman (USA)
1965 George Irwin (USA)
1966 Wayne Miller (USA)
1967-8 David Jacobs (USA)
1970 Wayne Miller (USA)
1972 Paul Luxon (UK)
1974 Richard Tison (FRA)
1976 Richard Tison (FRA) & Yevgeniy Yanes (USSR)
1978 Yevgeniy Yanes (USSR)
1980 Stewart Matthews (UK)
1982 Carl Furrer (UK)
1984 Lionel Pioline (FRA)
1986 Lionel Pioline (FRA)

SYNCHRONISED PAIRS
1965 Gary Irwin & Frank Smith (USA)
1966 Wayne Miller & David Jacobs (USA)
1967 Hartmut Riehler & Kurt Treiter (FRG)
1968 Klaus Forster & Michael Budenberg (FRG)
1970 Don Waters & Gary Smith (USA)
1972 Paul Luxon & Robert Hughes (UK)
1974 Robet Nealy & Jim Cartledge (USA)
1976 Yevgeniy Yakovenko & Yevgeniy Yanes (USSR)
1978 Yevgeniy Yanes & Vladimir Zhadoyev (USSR)
1980 Stewart Matthews & Carl Furrer (UK)
1982 Stuart Ransom & Mark Calderon (USA)
1984 Igor Bogachev & Vadim Krasnochapka (USSR)
1986 Igor Bogachev & Vadim Krasnochapka (USSR)

TUMBLING
1965 Frank Schmitz (USA)
1966 Frank Fortier (USA)
1976 Jim Bertz (USA)
1978 JIm Bertz (USA)
1980 Kevin Eckberg (USA)
1982 Steve Elliott (USA)
1984 Steve Elliott (USA)
1986 Jerry Hardy (USA)

DOUBLE MINI TRAMPOLINE
1976 Ron Merriott (USA)
1978 Stuart Ransom (USA)
1980 Derrick Lotz (SAf)
1982 Brett Austine (Aus)
1984 Brett Austine (Aus)
1986 Brett Austine (Aus)

WOMEN
INDIVIDUAL
1964-8 Judy Wills (USA)
1970 Renee Ransom (USA)
1972 Alexandra Nicholson (USA)
1974 Alexandra Nicholson (USA)
1976 Svetlana Levina (USSR)
1978 Tatyana Anisimova (USSR)
1980 Ruth Keller (Swi)
1982 Ruth Keller (Swi)
1984 Sue Shotton (UK)
1986 Tatyana Lushina (USSR)

Most wins: 5 Judy Wills

SYNCHRONISED PAIRS
1966-7 Judy Wills & Nancy Smith (USA)
1968 Ute Czech & Agathe Jarosch (FRG)
1970 Jennifer Liebenberg & Lucia Odendaal (SAf)
1972 Marilyn Stieg & Bobby Grant (USA)
1974 Ute Scheile & Petra Wenzel (FRG)
1976 Svetlana Levina & Olga Starikova (USSR)
1978 Ute Luxon & Ute Scheile (FRG)
1980 Gabriele Bahr & Beate Kruswicki (FRG)
1982 Jacqueline de Ruiter & Marjo van Diermen (Hol)
1984 Kirsty McDonald & Sue Shotton (UK)
1986 Tatyana Lushina & Yelena Merkulova (USSR)

TUMBLING
1965-6 Judy Wills (USA)
1976 Tracey Long (USA)
1978 Nancy Quattrochi (USA)
1980 Tracy Contour (USA)
1982 Jill Hollembeak (USA)
1984 Jill Hollembeak (USA)
1986 Jill Hollembeak (USA)

DOUBLE MINI TRAMPOLINE
1976 Leigh Hennessy (USA)
1978 Leigh Hennessy (USA)
1980 Beth Fairchild (USA)
1982 Christine Tough (Can)
1984 Gabi Dreier (FRG)
1986 Bettina Lehmann (FRG)

WORLD CUP

Held annually from 1980.

Most titles at each discipline:

Men's individual:	3 Carl Furrer (UK) 1980-1, 1983
Women's individual:	3 Sue Shotton (UK) 1981, 1983, 1986
Men's synchro:	2 John Hansen & Anders Christiansen (Den) 1982, 1985
	2 Lionel Pioline & Daniel Pean (Fra) 1983-4
Women's synchro:	3 Gabriel Bahr & Beate Kruswicki (FRG) 1983-5

TRIATHLON

The triathlon combines long distance swimming, cycling and running. A group of Americans first established the sport in 1974. Their efforts led to the first Hawaii 'Ironman', which was contested by 15 intrepid sportsmen, of whom 12 finished, on 18 Feb 1978. The growth in popularity of the event can be seen from the numbers of contestants in the 'Ironman', from 15 in its first two years to 108 in 1980, 326 in 1981, 580 and 850 in the two held in 1982, to reach 1000 in 1984.

The Federation International Triathlon (FIT), the world governing body, was founded in 1984.

HAWAII IRONMAN

Contestants first swim 2.4 miles (3.8km), then cycle 112 miles (180km) and finally run a full marathon of 26 miles 385 yards (42.195km). The 1978-80 course was in Oahu, from 1981 it has been in Kona, Hawaii.

Winners:

MEN
1978 Gordon Haller (USA) 11:46:58
1979 Tom Warren (USA) 11:15:56
1980 Dave Scott (USA) 9:24:33
1981 John Howard (USA) 9:38:29
1982 (Feb) Scott Tinley (USA) 9:19:41
1982 (Oct) Dave Scott (USA) 9:08:23
1983 Dave Scott (USA) 9:05:57
1984 Dave Scott (USA) 8:54:30
1985 Scott Tinley (USA) 8:50:54
1986 Dave Scott (USA) 8:28:37

WOMEN
1979 Lyn Lemaire (USA) 12:55:38
1980 Robin Beck (USA) 11:21:24
1981 Linda Sweeney (USA) 12:00:32
1982 (Feb) Kathleen McCartney (USA) 11:09:40
1982 (Oct) Julie Leach (USA) 10:54:08
1983 Sylviane Puntous (Can) 10:43:36
1984 Sylviane Puntous (Can) 10:25:13
1985 Joanne Ernst (USA) 10:25:22
1986 Paula Newby-Fraser (USA) 9:49:14*

* Sylviane Puntous was disqualified after finishing in 9:47:49.

EUROPEAN IRONMAN

Contested over the same distances as in Hawaii, world best times were set in 1986, when the event was staged in Sofia: *men:* 8:27:46 Scott Tinley (USA), *women:* Erin Baker (NZ) 9:27:36.

WORLD CHAMPIONSHIP TRIATHLON AT NICE

Contested annually from 1982 over shorter distances than the 'Ironman': 3.2km swim, 120km cycle, 32km run.

Winners:

MEN
1982 Mark Allen (USA) 6:33:52
1983 Mark Allen (USA) 6:04:51
1984 Mark Allen (USA) 6:05:23
1985 Mark Allen (USA) 5:53:13
1986 Mark Allen (USA) 5:46:10

WOMEN
1982 Lyn Brooks (USA) 7:40:44
1983 Linda Buchanan (USA) 7:06:03
1984 Colleen Cannon (USA) 7:05:15
1985 Erin Baker (NZ) 6:37:21

The Swedish team, which won the inaugural world women's tug-of-war title at 580kg in 1986 (Ake Owetz)

1986 Linda Buchanan (USA) 6:50:56*

* Erin Baker was disqualified after finishing in 6:40:26

BUD LIGHT US TRIATHLON SERIES CHAMPIONSHIPS

The championship race is the culmination of 12 races held throughout the USA each year since 1982. These races are contested over yet shorter distances: 1.5km swim, 40km cycle, 10km run (2km/40km/15km in 1982-3). There were a record 2383 contestants in the race at Chicago in 1986. Winners of the Championship race held at Bass Lake, California in 1983-4, Hilton Head Island, South Carolina 1985-6:

MEN
1983 Scott Molina (USA) 2:29:58
1984 Scott Molina (USA) 1:59:04
1985 Scott Molina (USA) 1:57:16
1986 Scott Molina (USA) 1:49:23

WOMEN
1983 Sylviane & Patricia Puntous (Can) 2:48:18
1984 Beth Mitchell (USA) 2:15:45
1985 Linda Buchanan (USA) 2:07:42
1986 Kirsten Hanssen (USA) 2:02:27

TUG-OF-WAR

The term 'Tug-of-War' is thought to have originated in Suffolk, England in the 19th century. Such a trial of strength and skill, involving two teams of eight pulling against each other on opposite ends of a long, thick rope, is believed to be of great antiquity. The standard rope now used is 35 metres long and 10.5 cm in circumference.

The first rules were framed by the New York AC in 1879 and the sport was included in the Olympic Games from 1900 until 1920. In Britain tug-of-war was administered by the Amateur Athletic Association until 1958 when the Tug-of-War Association was formed. National Championships are held annually. The world governing body is the International Tug-of-War Federation.

OLYMPIC GAMES

Winners:
1900 Sweden/Denmark
1904 Milwaukee AC (USA)
1906 Germany
1908 City Police (UK)
1912 Sweden
1920 Great Britain

WORLD CHAMPIONSHIPS

European Championships for men were first held in 1965, and these were followed by World Championships for men in 1975 and for women in 1986. There are categories depending on the total weight of the team, and catch-weight competitions in which there are no weight limits.

World champions:

720KG
England 1975-8, 1980, 1982
Ireland 1984, 1986
Switzerland 1985

640KG
England 1975-6, 1978, 1980
Ireland 1982, 1984, 1986
Wales 1977
Switzerland 1985

560KG
Switzerland 1982, 1985
England 1984, 1986

CATCHWEIGHT
England 1984

The most successful team has been the Sheen Farmers, who competed for England, winning at 640kg in 1975-6 and at 720kg 1977-8 and 1980.

In England the Wood Treatment team (formerly the Bosley Farmers) from Cheshire won 20 consecutive catchweight titles 1959-78, as well as two world (1975-6) and ten European titles (1964-81) at 720kg.

VOLLEYBALL

The game was invented, originally as "Mintonette", in 1895 by William G.Morgan, director of physical training at the YMCA, Holyoke, Massachusetts, USA. His aim was to provide a more recreational, non-contact game than basketball, which had been invented just four years earlier by James Naismith, whom Morgan had met while a student at Springfield YMCA. The number of players per side was fixed at six in 1918.

Volleyball was first played at an international games, at the 1913 Far Eastern Games in Manila, Philippines. The International Volleyball Federation (FIVB) was formed in 1947 and world championships first held in 1949, with the game introduced to the Olympics in 1964. It is now one of the most widely practised games in the world, with 163 members of the FIVB.

OLYMPIC GAMES

Held for men and women at all Olympics from 1964.

Winners:

MEN		WOMEN
1964	USSR	Japan
1968	USSR	USSR
1972	Japan	USSR
1976	Poland	Japan
1980	USSR	USSR
1984	USA	China

Most medals:
MEN 2 gold, 1 bronze Yuriy Poyarkov (USSR) 1964-72; 1 gold, 1 silver, 1 bronze Katsutoshi Nekoda (Jap) 1964-72.
WOMEN 2 gold, 2 silver Inna Ryskal (USSR) 1964-76.

WORLD CHAMPIONSHIPS

Now held every four years.

Wins:

MEN

6	USSR	1949, 1952, 1960, 1962, 1978, 1982
2	Czechoslovakia	1956, 1966
1	GDR 1970, Poland 1974, USA 1986	

WOMEN

4	USSR	1952, 1956, 1960, 1970
3	Japan	1962, 1967, 1974
2	China	1982, 1986
1	Cuba	1978

WORLD CUP

Held every four years from 1965 (men) and 1973 (women).

Wins:

MEN
3 USSR 1965, 1977, 1981
1 GDR 1969, USA 1985

WOMEN
2 China 1981, 1985
1 USSR 1973, Japan 1977

EUROPEAN CHAMPIONSHIPS

First held in 1948 for men and 1949 for women. Now held biennially.

Wins:

MEN

10	USSR	1950-1, 1967, 1971, 1975, 1977, 1979, 1981, 1983, 1985
3	Czechoslovakia	1948, 1955, 1958
1	Romania	1963

WOMEN

12	USSR	1949-51, 1958, 1963, 1967, 1971, 1975, 1977, 1979, 1983, 1985
1	Czechoslovakia 1955, Bulgaria 1981	

BEACH VOLLEYBALL

World Championships were first held at Ipanema Beach, Rio de Janeiro, Brazil in February 1987. Winners of the doubles event were Smith and Stoklos (USA).

WATER POLO

Played by teams of 7-a-side (from squads of 11). Originally known as 'football in the water', it was developed in Britain from 1869 and was first given official recognition by the Swimming Association of Great Britain in 1885. It has been an Olympic event since 1900. The first women's International competition was in 1978. Governed by FINA (see Swimming).

OLYMPIC GAMES

The first two winning teams were club sides: Osborne Swimming Club, Manchester, representing Great Britain in 1900, and New York AC in 1904.

Wins:

6	Hungary	1932, 1936, 1952, 1956, 1964, 1976
4	Great Britain	1900, 1908, 1912, 1920
2	Italy	1948, 1960
2	USSR	1972, 1980
2	Yugoslavia	1968, 1984

1 USA (New York AC) 1904, France 1924, Germany 1928.

Individuals to have won three gold medals:
George Wilkinson (UK) 1900-12, Paul Radmilovic & Charles Smith (UK) 1908-20, Dezsö Gyarmati & György Karpati (Hun) 1952-64. Gyarmati won most medals, adding silver in 1948 and bronze in 1960.

WORLD CHAMPIONSHIPS

First held at the world swimming championships in 1973.

Winners:

MEN
1973 Hungary
1975 USSR
1978 Italy
1982 USSR
1986 Yugoslavia

WOMEN
1986 Australia

FINA WORLD CUP

First held in 1979.

Winners:

MEN
1979 Hungary
1981 USSR
1983 USSR
1985 FR Germany
1987 Yugoslavia

WOMEN – winners of unofficial championships:
1979 USA, 1981 Canada.

EUROPEAN CHAMPIONSHIPS

MEN

10	Hungary	1926-7, 1931, 1934, 1938, 1954, 1958, 1962, 1974, 1977
4	USSR	1966, 1970, 1983, 1985
1	Italy 1947, Netherlands 1950, FR Germany 1981

WOMEN
Netherlands 1985

WATER SKIING

Water-skiing, as practised today, was pioneered in the 1920s, particularly by Ralph Samuelson on Lake Pepin, Minnesota, USA. The sport's origins, however, can be traced back hundreds of years through people walking on planks and aquaplaning. The development of the motor boat to tow skiers was clearly the key factor in the sport's growth.

The world governing body is the World Water Ski Union (WWSU), first formed as the Union Internationale de Ski Nautique in Geneva in 1946. World championships were instituted in 1949.

WORLD CHAMPIONSHIPS

First held at Juan Les Pins, France in 1949 and now staged biennially.

Winners:

MEN

Year	Overall	Slalom
1949	Christian Jourdan (Fra) & Guy de Clercq (Bel)	Christian Jourdan (Fra)
1950	Dick Pope Jr (USA)	Dick Pope Jr (USA)
1953	Alfredo Mendoza (USA)	Charles Blackwell (Can)
1955	Alfredo Mendoza (USA)	Alfredo Mendoza (USA)
1957	Joe Cash (USA)	Joe Cash (USA)
1959	Chuck Stearns (USA)	Chuck Stearns (USA)
1961	Bruno Zaccardi (Ita)	Jimmy Jackson (USA)
1963	Billy Spencer (USA)	Billy Spencer (USA)
1965	Roland Hillier (USA)	Roland Hillier (USA)
1967	Mike Suyderhoud (USA)	Tito Antunano (Mex)
1969	Mike Suyderhoud (USA)	Victor Palomo (Spa)
1971	George Athans (Can)	Mike Suyderhoud (USA)
1973	George Athans (Can)	George Athans (Can)
1975	Carlos Suarez (Ven)	Roby Zucchi (Ita)
1977	Mike Hazelwood (UK)	Bob LaPoint (USA)
1979	Joel McClintock (Can)	Bob LaPoint (USA)
1981	Sammy Duvall (USA)	Andy Mapple (UK)
1983	Sammy Duvall (USA)	Bob LaPoint (USA)
1985	Sammy Duvall (USA)	Patrice Martin (Fra)

Year	Tricks	Jumping
1949	Pierre Gouin (Fra)	Guy de Clercq (Bel)
1950	Jack Andresen (USA)	Guy de Clercq (Bel)
1953	Warren Witherall (USA)	Alfredo Mendoza (USA)
1955	Scotty Scott (USA)	Alfredo Mendoza (USA)
1957	Mike Amsbury (USA)	Joe Mueller (USA)
1959	Philippe Logut (Fra)	Buster McCalla (USA)
1961	Jean Marie Muller (Fra)	Larry Penacho (USA)
1963	Billy Spencer (USA)	Jimmy Jackson (USA)
1965	Ken White (USA)	Larry Penacho (USA)
1967	Alan Kempton (USA)	Alan Kempton (USA)
1969	Bruce Cockburn (Aus)	Wayne Grimditch (USA)
1971	Ricky McCormick (USA)	Mike Suyderhoud (USA)
1973	Wayne Grimditch (USA)	Ricky McCormick (USA)
1975	Wayne Grimditch (USA)	Ricky McCormick (USA)
1977	Carlos Suarez (Ven)	Mike Suyderhoud (USA)
1979	Patrice Martin (Fra)	Mike Hazelwood (UK)
1981	Cory Pickos (USA)	Mike Hazelwood (UK)
1983	Cory Pickos (USA)	Sammy Duvall (USA)
1985	Bob LaPoint (USA)	Geoff Carrington (Aus)

WOMEN

Year	Overall	Slalom
1949	Willa Worthington (USA)	Willa Worthington (USA)
1950	Willa McGuire* (USA)	Evie Wolford (USA)
1953	Leah Marie Rawls (USA)	Evie Wolford (USA)
1955	Willa McGuire (USA)	Willa McGuire (USA)
1957	Marina Doria (Swi)	Marina Doria (Swi)
1959	Vickie Van Hook (USA)	Vickie Van Hook (USA)
1961	Sylvie Hulsemann (Lux)	Janelle Kirkley (USA)
1963	Jeanette Brown (USA)	Jeanette Brown (USA)
1965	Liz Allan (USA)	Barbara Cooper-Clack (USA)
1967	Jeanette Stewart-Wood (UK)	Liz Allan (USA)
1969	Liz Allan (USA)	Liz Allan (USA)
1971	Christy Weir (USA)	Christy Freeman (USA)
1973	Lisa St John (USA)	Sylvie Maurial (Fra)

Mike Hazelwood (All-Sport)

1975	Liz Shetter* (USA)	Liz Shetter (USA)
1977	Cindy Todd (USA)	Cindy Todd (USA)
1979	Cindy Todd (USA)	Pattsie Messner (USA)
1981	Karin Roberge (USA)	Cindy Todd (USA)
1983	Ana Maria Carrasco (Ven)	Cindy Todd (USA)
1985	Karen Neville (Aus)	Camille Duvall (USA)

Year	Tricks	Jumping
1949	Madeleine Boutellier (Fra)	
1950	Willa McGuire* (USA)	Willa Worthington (USA)
		Johnette Kirkpatrick (USA)
1953	Leah Marie Rawls (USA)	Sandra Swaney (USA)
1955	Marina Doria (Swi)	Willa McGuire (USA)
1957	Marina Doria (Swi)	Nancie Rideout (USA)
1959	Piera Castelvetri (Ita)	Nancie Rideout (USA)
1961	Sylvie Hulsemann (Lux)	Renate Hansluvka (Aut)
1963	Guyonne Dalle (Fra)	Renate Hansluvka (Aut)
1965	Dany Duflot (Fra)	Liz Allan (USA)
1967	Dany Duflot (Fra)	Jeanette Stewart-Wood (UK)
1969	Liz Allan (USA)	Liz Allan (USA)
1971	Willi Stahle (Hol)	Christy Weir (USA)
1973	Maria Victoria Carrasco (Ven)	
1975	M.V. Carrasco (Ven)	Liz Shetter* (USA)
1977	M.V. Carrasco (Ven)	Liz Shetter* (USA)
		Linda Giddens (USA)
1979	Natalya Rumyantseva (USSR)	Cindy Todd (USA)

1981	Ana Maria Carrasco (Ven)	Deena Brush (USA)
1983	Natalya Ponomaryeva (USSR)	Cindy Todd (USA)
1985	Judy McClintock (Can)	Deena Brush (USA)

* Shetter née Allan, McGuire née Worthington, Ponomaryeva née Rumyantseva

MOST WINS

Overall **MEN** 3 Sammy Duvall
      WOMEN 3 Willa McGuire (née Worthington), Liz Shetter (née Allan).
Individual: **MEN** 5 Bob LaPoint
      WOMEN 8 Liz Shetter (née Allan)
Liz Allan is the only water skier to win all four titles in one year, 1969.
Team: Title won by the USA at all 15 championships 1957-85.

EUROPEAN CHAMPIONSHIPS

Held annually since 1947.

Recent overall champions and those with most wins:

Year	MEN	WOMEN
1980	Mike Hazelwood (UK)	Marlon van Dijk (Hol)
1981	Mike Hazelwood (UK)	Anita Carlmann (Swe)
1982	Mike Hazelwood (UK)	Natalya Rumyantseva (USSR)
1983	Mike Hazelwood (UK)	Anita Carlmann (Swe)

1984 Patrice Martin (Fra)   Natalya Ponomaryeva
(née Rumyantseva) (USSR)
1985 Patrice Martin (Fra)   Helena Kjellander (Swe)
1986 Mike Hazelwood (UK) Philippa Roberts (UK)
1987 Andre Alessi (Ita)   Natalya Rumyantseva
(USSR)

Most wins:
MEN Mike Hazelwood (UK) 1976-83, 1986; 4 Claude
de Clercq (Bel) 1947, 1950-2; 4 Bruno Zaccardi (Ita)
1959-61, 1966.
WOMEN: 4 Marina Doria (Swi) 1953-6

WORLD CUP

First held 1970, current
format adopted 1980.
Wins:
Great Britain 1980, 1984
USA 1982, 1986

EUROPEAN CUP

First held 1980.
Wins:
Italy 1980
France 1982
Great Britain 1983
Sweden 1984, 1985

WORLD RECORDS

MEN
Slalom 5 buoys on a 10.75m line: Bob LaPoint (USA)
1984, Andy Mapple (UK) 1985
Tricks 10550 points Patrice Martin (France) 1986
Jump 61.9m Mike Hazelwood (UK) 1986

WOMEN
Slalom 4 buoys on a 11.25m line: Deena Brush (USA)
1983, Jennifer Leachman (USA) 1985
Tricks 8350 points Ana Maria Carrasco (Ven) 1984
Jump 46.0m Deena Brush (USA) 1987

WORLD BAREFOOT WATER SKIING CHAMPIONSHIPS

The first person reported to water ski barefoot was Dick
Pope Jr in Florida in 1947. World barefoot championships,
which have been dominated by Australians, were first held
in 1978; events include wake slalom, tricks, start methods
and jump events.

Overall winners:

Year	MEN	WOMEN
1978	Brett Wing (Aus)	Colleen Wilkinson (Aus)
1980	Brett Wing (Aus)	Kim Lampard (Aus)
1982	Brett Wing (Aus)	Kim Lampard (Aus)
1985	Mike Seipel (USA)	Kim Lampard (Aus)
1986	Mike Seipel (USA)	Kim Lampard (Aus)

Brett Wing won all five titles in 1980.
Team: Championship won by Australia on all five
occasions 1978-86.
Barefoot world jump record: 20.1m Mike Seipel (USA)
1984

WORLD SKI RACING CHAMPIONSHIPS

First held in 1979. *Winners:*

Year	MEN	WOMEN
1979	Wayne Ritchie (Aus)	Bronwyn Wright (Aus)
1981	Danny Bertels (Bel)	Liz Hobbs (UK)
1983	Danny Bertels (Bel)	Liz Hobbs (UK)
1985	Mark Pickering (Aus)	Debbie Nordblad (USA)

In 1986 Stephen Moore (UK) won the inaugural ski racing
World Cup, winning all three races. The World Cup and
the World Championships now take place in alternate
years.

The fastest speed recorded on water skis is 230.26 km/h
by Christoper Massey (Aus) on the Hawkesbury River, New
South Wales, Australia in 1983.

The official barefoot speed record for two runs is 177.06
km/h by Lee Kirk (USA) on Firebird Lake, Phoenix, Arizona,
USA in 1977. The fastest by a woman is 118.56 km/h by
Karen Toms (Aus) on the Hawkesbury River in 1984.

WEIGHTLIFTING

Strength testing by lifting heavy weights is an ancient
sport and competitions for lifting weights of stone were
included in the ancient Olympic Games. Just five years
after a world championship competition was held in 1891,
weightlifting was included in the first of the modern
Olympic Games. The events were for one-arm and
two-arm lifts. During the couple of centuries preceding
that, professional strongmen had demonstrated awesome
feats of strength, but some of the advertised weights may
be doubted.

Modern weightlifting, as included on the Olympic
programme, is a combination of strength and skill. There
are two standard lifts: the snatch, which is a one-
movement lift from the floor to an extended arm position
above the head; and the jerk, which is a two movement
lift, the clean from floor to shoulders, and then the jerk
itself from the shoulders to a fully extended arm position
above the head. Competitors have up to three attempts at
each weight, and three referees determine whether lifts
are correct. Until 1972 the press was also included as a
standard lift, but it was then dropped due to the
difficulties involved in judging it. There are ten bodyweight
categories for lifters.

The world governing body, the Interntional Weightlifting Federation (IWF), was formed in 1920 as the
Fédération Haltérophile Internationale.

WORLD AND OLYMPIC CHAMPIONS

Although the IWF first ran world championships at Tallinn,
Estonia in 1922, they have subsequently recognised 18
championships held from those in Vienna, Austria in 1898
to 1920. Championships were held again in 1923, but not
again until 1937 and 1938. They have been held annually
from 1946 (except for 1967), with the Olympic Games
recognised as the official championships during those
years.

Olympic Games weightlifting was contested at one-
hand jerk and two-hand jerk with no weight categories in
1896, 1904 and 1906. Weight categories were introduced
at the 1920 Olympic Games and have expanded over the
years. From 1920 to 1946 there were five: 60kg, 67.5kg,
75kg, 82.5kg, over 82.5kg. Further additions have been:
56kg 1947, 90kg 1951, 52kg and 110kg 1969, 100kg
1977, with the super-heavyweights now over 110kg.
Somewhat confusingly, the heavyweight class was thus

over 82.5kg until 1950, over 90kg until 1968, and at the 110kg limit when the super-heavyweight class was introduced in 1969.

At the 1920 Olympics three lifts were totalled, with one-hand snatch added to the one- and two-handed jerk. In 1924 two additional lifts were added, two-hands press and snatch. From 1928 to 1972 the results were decided on the aggregate of press, snatch and jerk, and from 1973 on snatch and jerk.

a Most World and Olympic (*) titles 1896-1924

6 Josef Grafl (Aut) 67.5+kg 1910; 80+kg 1908-11, 1913

4 Josef Steinbach (Aut) overall 1904, 1905, 80+kg 1905; one-hand jerk 1906*

4 Leopold Hennermüller (Aut) 67.5kg 1910, 80kg 1911 (twice), 1913

4 Emil Kliment (Aut) 60kg 1910, 1911 (twice), 1913

b World and Olympic Champions (*) from 1928

Totals are shown in kilograms; 1928-72 three lifts, since 1973 two lifts.

52KG

Formerly Flyweight

1969 Vladimir Krishchisin (USSR) 337.5
1970 Sandor Holczreiter (Hun) 342.5
1971 Zygmunt Smalcerz (Pol) 340
1972* Zygmunt Smalcerz (Pol) 337.5
1973 Mohammed Nassiri (Irn) 240
1974 Mohammed Nassiri (Irn) 232.5
1975 Zygmunt Smalcerz (Pol) 237.5
1976* Aleksandr Voronin (USSR) 242.5
1977 Aleksandr Voronin (USSR) 247.5
1978 Kanybek Osmonalyev (USSR) 240
1979 Kanybek Osmonalyev (USSR) 242.5
1980* Kanybek Osmonalyev (USSR) 245
1981 Kanybek Osmonalyev (USSR) 247.5
1982 Stefan Leletko (Pol) 250
1983 Neno Terziyski (Bul) 260
1984* Zeng Guoqiang (Chn) 235
1985 Sevdalim Marinov (Bul) 252.5
1986 Sevdalim Marinov (Bul) 257.5

56KG

Formerly Bantamweight

1947 Joseph de Pietro (USA) 300
1948* Joseph de Pietro (USA) 307.5
1949 Mahmoud Namdjou (Irn) 315
1950 Mahmoud Namdjou (Irn) 310
1951 Mahmoud Namdjou (Irn) 317.5
1952* Ivan Udodov (USSR) 315
1953 Ivan Udodov (USSR) 315
1954 Bakir Farhutdinov (USSR) 315
1955 Vladimir Stogov (USSR) 335
1956* Charles Vinci (USA) 342.5
1957 Vladimir Stogov (USSR) 345
1958 Vladimir Stogov (USSR) 342.5
1959 Vladimir Stogov (USSR) 332.5
1960* Charles Vinci (USA) 345
1961 Vladimir Stogov (USSR) 345
1962 Yoshinobu Miyake (Jap) 352.5
1963 Aleksey Vakhonin (USSR) 345
1964* Aleksey Vakhonin (USSR) 357.5
1965 Imre Földi (Hun) 360
1966 Aleksey Vakhonin (USSR) 362.5

1968* Mohammad Nassiri (Irn) 367.5
1969 Mohammed Nassiri (Irn) 360
1970 Mohammed Nassiri (Irn) 362.5
1971 Gennadiy Chetin (USSR) 370
1972* Imre Földi (Hun) 377.5
1973 Atanas Kirov (USSR) 257.5
1974 Atanas Kirov (USSR) 255
1975 Atanas Kirov (USSR) 255
1976* Norair Nurikyan (Bul) 262.5
1977 Jiro Hosotani (Jap) 252.5
1978 Daniel Nunez (Cub) 260
1979 Anton Kodiabashev (Bul) 267.5
1980* Daniel Nunez (Cub) 275
1981 Anton Kodiabashev (Bul) 272.5
1982 Anton Kodiabashev (Bul) 280
1983 Oksen Mirzoyan (USSR) 292.5
1984* Wu Shude (Chn) 267.5
1985 Neno Terziyski (Bul) 280
1986 Mitko Grablev (Bul) 290

60KG

Formerly Featherweight

1928* Franz Andrysek (Aut) 287.5
1932* Raymond Suvigny (Fra) 287.5
1936* Anthony Terlazzo (USA) 312.5
1937 Georg Liebsch (Ger) 297.5
1938 Georg Liebsch (Ger) 305
1946 Arvid Andersson (Swe) 320
1947 Robert Higgins (USA) 310
1948* Mahmoud Fayad (Egy) 332.5
1949 Mahmoud Fayad (Egy) 332.5
1950 Mahmoud Fayad (Egy) 327.5
1951 Sayed Gouda (Egy) 310
1952* Rafael Chimiskyan (USSR) 337.5
1953 Nikolay Saksonov (USSR) 337.5
1954 Rafael Chimiskyan (USSR) 350
1955 Rafael Chimiskyan (USSR) 350
1956* Isaac Berger (USA) 352.5
1957 Yevgeniy Minayev (USSR) 362.5
1958 Isaac Berger (USA) 372.5
1959 Marian Zielinski (Pol) 365
1960* Yevgeniy Minayev (USSR) 372.5
1961 Isaac Berger (USA) 367.5
1962 Yevgeniy Minayev (USSR) 362.5
1963 Yoshinobu Miyake (Jap) 375
1964* Yoshinobu Miyake (Jap) 397.5
1965 Yoshinobu Miyake (Jap) 385
1966 Yoshinobu Miyake (Jap) 387.5
1968* Yoshinobu Miyake (Jap) 392.5
1969 Yoshiyuki Miyake (Jap) 385
1970 Mieczyslaw Nowak (Pol) 392.5
1971 Yoshiyuki Miyake (Jap) 387.5
1972* Norair Nurikyan (Bul) 402.5
1973 Dito Shanidze (USSR) 272.5
1974 Georgi Todorov (Bul) 280
1975 Georgi Todorov (Bul) 285
1976* Nikolay Kolesnikov (USSR) 285
1977 Nikolay Kolesnikov (USSR) 280
1978 Nikolay Kolesnikov (USSR) 270
1979 Marek Severyn (USSR) 290
1980* Viktor Mazin (USSR) 290
1981 Beloslav Manolov (Bul) 302.5
1982 Yurik Sarkisyan (USSR) 302.5
1983 Yurik Sarkisyan (USSR) 312.5

Naim Suleimanov (now Neum Shalamanov) set his first world record, at 56kg in 1983, at the age of 15yrs 123 days. (All-Sport)

1984* Chen Weiqiang (Chn) 282.5
1985 Neum Shalamanov (Bul) 322.5
1986 Neum Shalamanov (Bul) 335

67.5KG
Formerly Lightweight
1928* Kurt Helbig (Ger) 322.5
    & Hans Haas (Aut) 322.5
1932* René Duverger (Fra) 325
1936* Anwar Mohammed Mesbah (Egy) 342.5
    & Robert Fein (Aut) 342.5
1937 Anthony Terlazzo (USA) 357.5
1938 Anthony Terlazzo (USA) 350
1946 Stanley Stanczyk (USA) 367.5
1947 Peter George (USA) 352.5
1948* Ibrahim Shams (Egy) 360
1949 Ibrahim Shams (Egy) 352.5
1950 Joseph Pitman (USA) 352.5
1951 Ibrahim Shams (Egy) 342.5
1952* Tommy Kono (USA) 362.5
1953 Peter George (USA) 370
1954 Dmitriy Ivanov (USSR) 367.5
1955 Nikolay Kostilyev (USSR) 382.5
1956* Igor Rybak (USSR) 380
1957 Viktor Bushuyev (USSR) 380
1958 Viktor Bushuyev (USSR) 390
1959 Viktor Bushuyev (USSR) 385
1960* Viktor Bushuyev (USSR) 397.5
1961 Waldemar Baszanowski (Pol) 402.5
1962 Vladimir Kaplunov (USSR) 415
1963 Marian Zielinski (Pol) 417.5
1964* Waldemar Baszanowski (Pol) 432.5
1965 Waldemar Baszanowski (Pol) 427.5
1966 Yevgeniy Katsura (USSR) 437.5
1968* Waldemar Baszanowski (Pol) 437.5
1969 Waldemar Baszanowski (Pol) 445
1970 Zbigniew Kaczmarek (Pol) 440
1971 Zbigniew Kaczmarek (Pol) 440
1972* Mukharbi Kirzhinov (USSR) 460

1973 Mukharbi Kirzhinov (USSR) 305
1974 Pyotr Korol (USSR) 305
1975 Pyotr Korol (USSR) 312.5
1976* Pyotr Korol (USSR) 305
1977 Roberto Urrutia (Cub) 315
1978 Yanko Rusev (Bul) 310
1979 Yanko Rusev (Bul) 332.5
1980* Yanko Rusev (Bul) 342.5
1981 Joachim Kunz (GDR) 340
1982 Piotr Mandra (Pol) 325
1983 Joachim Kunz (GDR) 340
1984* Yao Jingyuan (Chn) 320
1985 Mikhail Petrov (Bul) 335
1986 Mikhail Petrov (Bul) 342.5

75KG
Formerly Middleweight
1928* Roger Francois (Fra) 335
1932* Rudolf Ismayr (Ger) 345
1936* Khadr El Touni (Egy) 387.5
1937 John Terpak (USA) 352.5
1938 Adolf Wagner (Ger) 367.5
1946 Khadr El Touni (Egy) 377.5
1947 Stanley Stanczyk (USA) 405
1948* Frank Spellman (USA) 390
1949 Khadr El Touni (Egy) 397.5
1950 Khadr El Touni (Egy) 400
1951 Peter George (USA) 395
1952* Peter George (USA) 400
1953 Tommy Kono (USA) 407.5
1954 Peter George (USA) 405
1955 Peter George (USA) 405
1956* Fyodor Bogdanovskiy (USSR) 420
1957 Tommy Kono (USA) 420
1958 Tommy Kono (USA) 430
1959 Tommy Kono (USA) 425
1960* Aleksandr Kurinov (USSR) 437.5
1961 Aleksandr Kurinov (USSR) 435
1962 Aleksandr Kurinov (USSR) 422.5

1963 Aleksandr Kurinov (USSR) 437.5
1964* Hans Zdrazila (Cs) 445
1965 Viktor Kurentsov (USSR) 437.5
1966 Viktor Kurentsov (USSR) 450
1968* Viktor Kurentsov (USSR) 475
1969 Viktor Kurentsov (USSR) 467.5
1970 Viktor Kurentsov (USSR) 462.5
1971 Vladimir Kanygin (USSR) 477.5
1972* Yordan Bikov (Bul) 485
1973 Nedelcho Kolev (Bul) 337.5
1974 Nedelcho Kolev (Bul) 335
1975 Peter Wenzel (GDR) 335
1976* Yordan Mitkov (Bul) 335
1977 Yurik Vardanyan (USSR) 345
1978 Roberto Urrutia (Cub) 347.5
1979 Roberto Urrutia (Cub) 345
1980* Asen Zlatev (Bul) 360
1981 Yanko Rusev (Bul) 360
1982 Yanko Rusev (Bul) 365
1983 Alexander Varbanov (Bul) 370
1984* Karl-Heinz Radschinsky (FRG) 340
1985 Alexander Varbanov (Bul) 370
1986 Alexander Varbanov (Bul) 377.5

82.5KG
Formerly Light-heavyweight
1928* Said Nosseir (Egy) 355
1932* Louis Hostin (Fra) 372.5
1936* Louis Hostin (Fra) 372.5
1937 Fritz Haller (Aut) 375
1938 John Davis (USA) 387.5
1946 Grigoriy Novak (USSR) 425
1947 John Terpak (USA) 387.5
1948* Stanley Stanczyk (USA) 417.5
1949 Stanley Stanczyk (USA) 412.5
1950 Stanley Stanczyk (USA) 420
1951 Stanley Stanczyk (USA) 402.5
1952* Trofim Lomakin (USSR) 417.5
1953 Arkadiy Vorobyev (USSR) 430
1954 Tommy Kono (USA) 435
1955 Tommy Kono (USA) 435
1956* Tommy Kono (USA) 447.5
1957 Trofim Lomakin (USSR) 450
1958 Trofim Lomakin (USSR) 440
1959 Rudolf Plyukfelder (USSR) 457.5
1960* Ireneusz Palinski (Pol) 442.5
1961 Rudolf Plyukfelder (USSR) 450
1962 Gyözö Veres (Hun) 460
1963 Gyözö Veres (Hun) 477.5
1964* Rudolf Plyukfelder (USSR) 475
1965 Norbert Osimek (Pol) 472.5
1966 Vladimir Belyayev (USSR) 485
1968* Boris Syelitskiy (USSR) 485
1969 Masashi Ohuchi (Jap) 487.5
1970 Gennadiy Ivanchenko (USSR) 505
1971 Boris Pavlov (USSR) 495
1972* Leif Jensen (Nor) 507.5
1973 Vladimir Rizhenkov (USSR) 350
1974 Trendafil Stoychev (Bul) 350
1975 Valeriy Shariy (USSR) 357.5
1976* Valeriy Shariy (USSR) 365
1977 Gennadiy Bessonov (USSR) 352.5
1978 Yurik Vardanyan (USSR) 377.5
1979 Yurik Vardanyan (USSR) 370

1980* Yurik Vardanyan (USSR) 400
1981 Yurik Vardanyan (USSR) 392.5
1982 Asen Zlatev (Bul) 400
1983 Yurik Vardanyan (USSR) 392.5
1984* Petre Becheru (Rom) 355
1985 Yurik Vardanyan (USSR) 397.5
1986 Asen Zlatev (Bul) 405

82.5+KG
Heavyweight
1928* Josef Strassberger (Ger) 372.5
1932* Jaroslav Skobla (Cs) 380
1936* Josef Manger (Aut) 410
1937 Josef Manger (Ger) 420
1938 Josef Manger (Ger) 410
1946 John Davis (USA) 435
1947 John Davis (USA) 455
1948* John Davis (USA) 452.5
1949 John Davis (USA) 442.5
1950 John Davis (USA) 462.5

90KG
Formerly Middle-heavyweight
1951 Norbert Schemansky (USA) 427.5
1952* Norbert Schemansky (USA) 445
1953 Norbert Schemansky (USA) 442.5
1954 Arkadiy Vorobyev (USSR) 460
1955 Arkadiy Vorobyev (USSR) 455
1956* Arkadiy Vorobyev (USSR) 462.5
1957 Arkadiy Vorobyev (USSR) 470
1958 Arkadiy Vorobyev (USSR) 465
1959 Louis Martin (UK) 445
1960* Arkadiy Vorobyev (USSR) 472.5
1961 Ireneusz Palinski (Pol) 475
1962 Louis Martin (UK) 480
1963 Louis Martin (UK) 480
1964* Vladimir Golovanov (USSR) 487.5
1965 Louis Martin (UK) 487.5
1966 Geza Toth (Hun) 487.5
1968* Kaarlo Kangasniemi (Fin) 517.5
1969 Kaarlo Kangasniemi (Fin) 515
1970 Vasiliy Kolotov (USSR) 537.5
1971 David Rigert (USSR) 542.5
1972* Andon Nikolov (Bul) 525
1973 David Rigert (USSR) 365
1974 David Rigert (USSR) 387.5
1975 David Rigert (USSR) 377.5
1976* David Rigert (USSR) 382.5
1977 Sergey Poltoratskiy (USSR) 375
1978 Rolf Milser (FRG) 377.5
1979 Gennadiy Bessonov (USSR) 380
1980* Peter Baczako (Hun) 377.5
1981 Blagoi Blagoyev (Bul) 405
1982 Blagoi Blagoyev (Bul) 415
1983 Blagoi Blagoyev (Bul) 417.5
1984* Nicu Vlad (Rom) 392.5
1985 Anatoliy Khrapatiy (USSR) 395
    & Viktor Solodov (USSR) 395
1986 Anatoliy Khrapatiy (USSR) 412.5

90KG+
Heavyweight
1951 John Davis (USA) 432.5
1952* John Davis (USA) 460
1953 Douglas Hepburn (Can) 467.5

Vasiliy Alekseyev, the most prolific world record setter (80 between 1970 and 1977) at any sport.

1954 Norbert Schemansky (USA) 487.5
1955 Paul Anderson (USA) 512.5
1956* Paul Anderson (USA) 500
1957 Aleksey Medvedev (USSR) 500
1958 Aleksey Medvedev (USSR) 485
1959 Yuriy Vlasov (USSR) 500
1960* Yuriy Vlasov (USSR) 537.5
1961 Yuriy Vlasov (USSR) 525
1962 Yuriy Vlasov (USSR) 540
1963 Yuriy Vlasov (USSR) 557.5
1964* Leonid Zhabotinskiy (USSR) 572.5
1965 Leonid Zhabotinskiy (USSR) 552.5
1966 Leonid Zhabotinskiy (USSR) 567.5
1968* Leonid Zhabotinskiy (USSR) 572.5

100KG
1977 Anatoliy Kozlov (USSR) 367.5
1978 David Rigert (USSR) 390
1979 Pavel Sirchin (USSR) 385
1980* Otto Zaremba (Cs) 395
1981 Viktor Sots (USSR) 407.5
1982 Viktor Sots (USSR) 422.5
1983 Pavel Kuznyetsov (USSR) 422.5
1984* Rolf Milser (FRG) 385
1985 Sandor Szanyi (Hun) 415
1986 Nicu Vlad (Rom) 437.5

110KG
Formerly Heavyweight
1969 Robert Bednarski (USA) 555
1970 Jan Talts (USSR) 565
1971 Yuriy Kozin (USSR) 552.5
1972* Jan Talts (USSR) 580
1973 Pavel Pervushin (USSR) 385
1974 Valeriy Ustyuzhin (USSR) 380
1975 Valentin Khristov (Bul) 417.5
1976* Yuriy Zaitsev (USSR) 385
1977 Valentin Khristov (Bul) 405
1978 Yuriy Zaitsev (USSR) 402.5
1979 Sergey Arakelov (USSR) 410
1980* Leonid Taranenko (USSR) 422.5
1981 Valeriy Kravchuk (USSR) 415
1982 Sergey Arakelov (USSR) 427.5
1983 Vyacheslav Klokov (USSR) 440
1984* Norberto Oberburger (Ita) 390
1985 Yuriy Zakharevich (USSR) 422.5
1986 Yuriy Zakharevich (USSR) 447.5

110KG+
Formerly Super-heavyweight
1969 Joseph Dube (USA) 577.5
1970 Vasiliy Alekseyev (USSR) 612.5
1971 Vasiliy Alekseyev (USSR) 635

1972* Vasiliy Alekseyev (USSR) 640
1973 Vasiliy Alekseyev (USSR) 402.5
1974 Vasiliy Alekseyev (USSR) 425
1975 Vasiliy Alekseyev (USSR) 427.5
1976* Vasiliy Alekseyev (USSR) 440
1977 Vasiliy Alekseyev (USSR) 430
1978 Jürgen Heuser (GDR) 417.5
1979 Sultan Rakhmanov (USSR) 430
1980* Sultan Rakhmanov (USSR) 440
1981 Anatoliy Pisarenko (USSR) 425
1982 Anatoliy Pisarenko (USSR) 445
1983 Anatoliy Pisarenko (USSR) 450
1984* Dean Lukin (Aus) 412.5
1985 Antonio Krastev (Bul) 437.5
1986 Antonio Krastev (Bul) 460

Most titles:

OLYMPIC GAMES: ten men have won two gold medals. The most medals is four by Norbert Schemansky (USA) gold 90kg 1952; silver 82+kg 1948; bronze 90+kg 1960, 1964.

WORLD AND OLYMPIC:
8 John Davis (USA) 1938-52
8 Tommy Kono (USA) 1952-9

8 Vasiliy Alekseyev (USSR) 1970-7
7 Arkadiy Vorobyev (USSR) 1953-60
7 Yurik Vardanyan (USSR) 1977-85
6 Stanley Stanczyk (Pol) 1946-51
6 Peter George (USA) 1947-55
6 Yoshinobu Miyake (Jap) 1962-8
6 David Rigert (USSR) 1971-8

WORLD CUP

Awarded on a points basis to the best lifter at an annual gala, attended by the world's best, who qualify from a worldwide series of events.

World Cup winners:	*Gala winners:*
1980 György Szalai (Hun)	Janos Solyomvari (Hun)
1981 Yanko Rusev (Bul)	Blagoi Blagoyev (Bul)
1982 Blagoi Blagoyev (Bul)	Blagoi Blagoyev (Bul)
1983 Blagoi Blagoyev (Bul)	Oksen Mirzoyan (USSR)
1984 Naim Suleimanov (Bul)	Naim Suleimanov (Bul)
1985 Neum Shalamanov* (Bul)	Neum Shalamanov* (Bul)
1986 Neum Shalamanov (Bul)	Asen Zlatev (Bul)

* Change of name from Naim Suleimanov

WORLD WEIGHTLIFTING RECORDS

Bodyweight Class	Lift	kg	Name and country	Venue	Date
52kg	Snatch	116.5	He Zhuqqiang (Chn)	Ageo, Japan	17 Apr 1987
	Jerk	152.5	Neno Terziyski (Bul)	Vitoria, Spain	27 Apr 1984
	Total	262.5	Neno Terziyski (Bul)	Vitoria, Spain	27 Apr 1984
56kg	Snatch	133	Oksen Mirzoyan (USSR)	Varna	12 Sep 1984
	Jerk	170.5	Neum Shalamanov (Bul)	Varna	12 Sep 1984
		173	Neum Shalamanov (Bul)	Belgrade	20 Oct 1984 u
	Total	300	Neum Shalamanov (Bul)	Varna	11 May 1984
		305	Neum Shalamanov (Bul)	Belgrade	20 Oct 1984 u
60kg	Snatch	148	Neum Shalamanov (Bul)	Melbourne	7 Dec 1986
	Jerk	188	Neum Shalamanov (Bul)	Sofia	9 Nov 1986
	Total	335	Neum Shalamanov (Bul)	Sofia	9 Nov 1986
67.5kg	Snatch	157.5	Mikhail Petrov (Bul)	Reims	4 May 1987
	Jerk	200	Alexander Varbanov (Bul)	Varna	13 Sep 1984
	Total	352.5	Andreas Behm (GDR)	Schwedt, GDR	20 Jul 1984
75kg	Snatch	168.5	Borislav Gydikov (Bul)	Sofia	11 Nov 1986
	Jerk	215	Alexander Varbanov (Bul)	Sofia	11 Nov 1986
	Total	377.5	Zdravko Stoichkov (Bul)	Varna	14 Sep 1984
82.5kg	Snatch	183	Asen Zlatev (Bul)	Melbourne	7 Dec 1986
	Jerk	225	Asen Zlatev (Bul)	Sofia	12 Nov 1986
	Total	405	Yurik Vardanyan (USSR)	Varna	14 Sep 1984
90kg	Snatch	195.5	Blagoi Blagoyev (Bul)	Varna	1 May 1983
	Jerk	233.5	Anatoliy Khrapatiy (USSR)	Lvov	5 Mar 1987
	Total	422.5	Viktor Solodov (USSR)	Varna	15 Sep 1984
		422.5	Anatoliy Khrapatiy (USSR)	Lvov	5 Mar 1987
100kg	Snatch	200.5	Nicu Vlad (Rom)	Sofia	14 Nov 1986
	Jerk	242.5	Pavel Kuznyetsov (USSR)	Arkhangelsk	4 Jul 1987
	Total	440	Yuriy Zakharevich (USSR)	Odessa	4 Mar 1983
110kg	Snatch	202.5	Yuriy Zakharevich (USSR)	Reims	9 May 1987
	Jerk	248	Yuriy Zakharevich (USSR)	Sofia	15 Nov 1986
	Total	447.5	Yuriy Zakharevich (USSR)	Sofia	15 Nov 1986
110kg+	Snatch	215.5	Antonio Krastev (Bul)	Reims	10 May 1987
	Jerk	265.5	Leonid Taranenko (USSR)	Arkhangelsk	4 Jul 1984
	Total	472.5	Leonid Taranenko (USSR)	Arkhangelsk	4 Jul 1987

u unofficial

PROGRESSION OF WORLD RECORD FOR THE SUPER-HEAVYWEIGHT JERK

An idea of the tremendous progress that has been made in weightlifting is shown by charting the record for the jerk by the heaviest men at approximately five-yearly intervals, including the final records made by the leading names:

kg
161.5 Charles Rigoulot (Fra) 1925
167   Said Nossier (Egy) 1931
167.5 Arnold Luhäär (Est) 1937
174   Yakov Kuchenko (USSR) 1947
182   John Davis (USA) 1951
192.5 Norbert Schemansky (USA) 1954
197   Paul Anderson (USA) 1955
215.5 Yuriy Vlasov (USSR) 1964
220   Leonid Zhabotinskiy (USSR) 1968
256   Vasiliy Alekseyev (USSR) 1977
265   Anatoliy Pisarenko (USSR) 1984

Most improvements:
31	Vasiliy Alekseyev (USSR)	221.5 - 256 kg	1970-7
9	Yuriy Vlasov (USSR)	197.5 - 215.5 kg	1959-64
6	Norbert Schemansky (USA)	185 - 192.5 kg	1952-4
6	Leonid Zhabotinskiy (USSR)	213 - 220 kg	1964-8

Alekseyev's 31 improvements is by far the most by any lifter at any category at any event.

The youngest world record holder: Naim Suleimanov (Bul), who has changed his name to Neum Shalamanov, set his first world records, jerk 160kg and total 285kg at 56kg, when aged 15 years 123 days on 26 Mar 1983.

The first man to clean and jerk three times his own bodyweight: Stefan Topurov (Bul) 180kg in the 60kg class on 24 Oct 1983.

WOMEN'S WORLD CHAMPIONSHIPS

The first World Championships for women is to be held in October 1987 in Miami.

POWERLIFTING

From the many different lifts that have been practised by weightlifters and incorporated in tests of strength, powerlifting now recognises the squat, bench press and dead lift, all performed two-handed. The competitor is allowed three attempts at each lift and the best successful attempt on each lift is totalled. There are eleven weight categories for men and ten for women.

The sport of powerlifting was first contested at national level in Great Britain in 1958. The first US Championships were held in 1964. The International Powerlifting Federation was founded in 1972.

WORLD CHAMPIONSHIP

First held for men as unofficial championships in 1971 and officially in 1973, and for women in 1980.
Recent champions: (totals given are the total of the three lifts in kilograms)

MEN

52KG
1981 Hideaki Inaba (Jap) 560
1982 Hideaki Inaba (Jap) 552.5
1983 Hideaki Inaba (Jap) 565
1984 Chuck Dunbar (USA) 532.5
1985 Hideaki Inaba (Jap) 562.5
1986 Hideaki Inaba (Jap) 577.5

56KG
1981 Hiroyuki Isagawa (Jap) 577.5
1982 Lamar Gant (USA) 590
1983 Lamar Gant (USA) 575
1984 Lamar Gant (USA) 580
1985 Hiroyuki Isagawa (Jap) 562.5
1986 Hiroyuki Isagawa (Jap) 572.5

60KG
1981 Lamar Gant (USA) 625
1982 Kullervo Lampela (Fin) 582.5
1983 Göran Henrysson (Swe) 605
1984 Göran Henrysson (Swe) 600
1985 Göran Henrysson (Swe) 605
1986 Lamar Gant (USA) 647.5

67.5KG
1981 Joe Bradley (USA) 732.5
1982 Stefan Nentis (Swe) 697.5
1983 Bob Wahl (USA) 705
1984 Dan Austin (USA) 722.5
1985 Eddie Pengelly (UK) 667.5
1986 Dan Austin (USA) 712.5

75KG
1981 Steve Alexander (USA) 752.5
1982 Rickey Crain (USA) 772.5
1983 Rickey Crain (USA) 762.5
1984 Gene Bell (USA) 762.5
1985 Eric Coppin (Bel) 765
1986 Rick Crilly (Can) 732.5

82.5KG
1981 Mike Bridges (USA) 945
1982 Mike Bridges (USA) 845
1983 Mike Bridges (USA) 807.5
1984 Ed Coan (USA) 875
1985 Jarmo Virtanen (Fin) 842.5
1986 Jarmo Virtanen (Fin) 850

90KG
1981 Walter Thomas (USA) 930
1982 Walter Thomas (USA) 857.5
1983 Kenneth Mattsson (Swe) 872.5
1984 Dennis Wright (USA) 840
1985 David Caldwell (UK) 832.5
1986 Jari Tahtinen (Fin) 822.5

100KG
1981 Jim Cash (USA) 922.5
1982 Kenneth Mattsson (Swe) 880
1983 Fred Hatfield (USA) 920
1984 Tony Stevens (UK) 915
1985 Tony Stevens (UK) 907.5
1986 Tony Stevens (UK) 882.5

110KG
1981 Reijo Kiviranta (Fin) 920
1982 Hannu Saarelainen (Fin) 887.5

1983 Steve Wilson (USA) 910
1984 Dave Jacoby (USA) 935
1985 Dave Jacoby (USA) 907.5
1986 Fred Hatfield (USA) 902.5

125KG
1981 Ernie Hackett (USA) 962.5
1982 John Gamble (USA) 907.5
1983 Lars Noren (Swe) 890
1984 Ab Wolders (Hol) 945
1985 Tom Henderson (USA) 935
1986 Lars Noren (Swe) 942.5

Over 125KG
1981 Paul Wrenn (USA) 1027.5
1982 Tom Maggee (Can) 942.5
1983 Bill Kazmaier (USA) 975
1984 Lee Moran (USA) 977.5
1985 George Hechter (USA) 947.5
1986 Mike Hall (USA) 980

Most world titles:
12 Hideaki Inaba (Jap) 52kg 1974-83, 1985-6
11 Lamar Gant (USA) 56kg 1975-7, 1979, 1982-4; 60kg
   1978, 1980-1, 1986
 8 Larry Pacifico (USA) 90kg 1976; 100kg 1974-5,
   1977-9; 110kg 1972-3

WOMEN
44KG
1981 D.Wicker (USA) 287.5
1982 Ginger Lord (USA) 300
1983 Cheryl Jones (USA) 317.5
1984 Cheryl Jones (USA) 347.5
1985 Cheryl Jones (USA) 350
1986 Judy Gedney (USA) 322.5

48KG
1981 Terry Dillard (USA) 340
1982 Terry Dillard (USA) 347.5
1983 Diana Rowell (USA) 355
1984 Majik Jones (USA) 390
1985 Bernadette Plouviez (Bel) 345
1986 Marie Vassart (Bel) 350

52KG
1981 Sue Roberts (Aus) 370
1982 Sue Jordan (Aus) 365
1983 Kali Bogias (Can) 390
1984 Kali Bogias (Can) 392.5
1985 Sisi Dolman (Hol) 400
1986 Sisi Dolman (Hol) 400

56KG
1981 Gayla Crain (USA) 395
1982 Julie Thomas (USA) 365
1983 Julie Thomas (USA) 440
1984 Vicky Steenrod (USA) 475
1985 Tina van Duyn-Woodley (Hol) 415
1986 Felecia Johnson (USA) 407.5

60KG
1981 T.Todaro (USA) 387.5
1982 Ruth Shafer (USA) 450
1983 Ruth Shafer (USA) 500
1984 Diane Frantz (USA) 435
1985 Vicky Steenrod (USA) 502.5
1986 Rita Bass (UK) 420

67.5KG
1981 Jennifer Weyland (USA) 467.5
1982 Angie Ross (USA) 435
1983 Linda Miller (Aus) 435
1984 Ruth Shafer (USA) 552.5
1985 Ruth Shafer (USA) 427.5
1986 Heidi Wittesch (Aut) 470

75KG
1981 Judith Oakes (UK) 462.5
1982 Beverley Francis (Aus) 497.5
1983 Pamela Matthews (Aus) 487.5
1984 Deborah McElroy-Patton (USA) 475
1985 Heidi Wittesch (Aut) 470
1986 Deborah Patton (USA) 462.5

82.5KG
1981 Beverley Francis (Aus) 575
1982 Judith Oakes (UK) 502.5
1983 Beverley Francis (Aus) 577.5
1984 Beverley Francis (Aus) 557.5
1985 Beverley Francis (Aus) 565
1986 Juanita Trujillo (USA) 537.5

OVER 82.5KG
1981 Wanda Sander (USA) 550

90KG
1982 Rebecca Waibler (FRG) 475
1983 Gael Mulhall (Aus) 525
1984 Annette Bohach (USA) 500
1985 Tore Eriksen (Nor) 465
1986 Lorraine Costango (USA) 550

OVER 90KG
1982 Annie McElroy (USA) 502.5
1983 Wanda Sander (USA) 522.5
1984 Annie McElroy (USA) 485
1985 Annie McElroy (USA) 527.5
1986 Annie McElroy (USA) 527.5

Most women's world titles: 6 Beverley Francis (Aus) 75kg
1980, 1982; 82.5kg 1981, 1983-5

WORLD RECORDS all weights in kilograms
MEN

Class	SQUAT	
52 kg	243	Hideaki Inaba (Jap) 1986
56 kg	237.5	Hideaki Inaba (Jap) 1982
60 kg	295	Joe Bradley (USA) 1980
67.5 kg	297	Robert Wahl (USA) 1982
75 kg	327.5	Mike Bridges (USA) 1980
82.5 kg	379.5	Mike Bridges (USA) 1982
90 kg	375	Fred Hatfield (USA) 1980
100 kg	400	Fred Hatfield (USA) 1982
110 kg	393.5	Dan Wohleber (USA) 1981
125 kg	412.5	David Waddington (USA) 1982
125+ kg	445	Dwayne Fely (USA) 1982

Class	BENCH PRESS	
52 kg	146.5	Joe Cunha (Jap) 1982
56 kg	155	Hiroyaki Isagawa (Jap) 1986
60 kg	180	Joe Bradley (USA) 1980
67.5 kg	200	Kristoffer Hulecki (Swi) 1985
75 kg	217.5	James Rouse (USA) 1980
82.5 kg	240	Mike Bridges (USA) 1981
90 kg	255	Mike McDonald (USA) 1980

100 kg	261.5	Mike McDonald (USA) 1977
110 kg	270	Jeffrey Magruder (USA) 1982
125 kg	278.5	Tom Hardman (USA) 1982
125+ kg	300	Bill Kazmeier (USA) 1981

Class	DEAD LIFT	
52 kg	235	Hideaki Inaba (Jap) 1986
56 kg	289.5	Lamar Gant (USA) 1982
60 kg	300.5	Lamar Gant (USA) 1986
67.5 kg	312.5	Raimo Valineva (Fin) 1981
75 kg	325.5	Eric Coppin (Bel) 1985
82.5 kg	357.5	Veli Kumpuniemi (Fin) 1980
90 kg	372.5	Walter Thomas (USA) 1982
100 kg	377.5	James Cash (USA) 1982
110 kg	395	John Kuc (USA) 1980
125 kg	385	Terry McCormick (USA) 1982
125+ kg	403.5	Lars Noren (Swe) 1987

Class	TOTAL	
52 kg	577.5	Hideaki Inaba (Jap) 1986
56 kg	625	Lamar Gant (USA) 1982
60 kg	707.5	Joe Bradley (USA) 1982
67.5 kg	732.5	Joe Bradley (USA) 1981
75 kg	850	Rick Gaugler (USA) 1982
82.5 kg	952.5	Mike Bridges (USA) 1982
90 kg	937.5	Mike Bridges (USA) 1980
100 kg	952.5	James Cash (USA) 1982
110 kg	1000	John Kuc (USA) 1980
125 kg	1005	Ernie Hackett (USA) 1980
125+ kg	1100	Bill Kazmaier (USA) 1981

WOMEN

Class	SQUAT	
44 kg	140	Anna-Liisa Prinkkala (Fin) 1984
48 kg	147	Majik Jones (USA) 1984
52 kg	173	Sisi Dolman (Hol) 1986
56 kg	190	Vicky Steenrod (USA) 1984
60 kg	200.5	Ruth Shafer (USA) 1983
67.5 kg	230	Ruth Shafer (USA) 1984
75 kg	214.5	Terry Byland (USA) 1987
82.5 kg	230	Juanita Trujillo (USA) 1986
90 kg	237.5	Lorraine Constanzo (USA) 1986
90+ kg	247.5	Jan Todd (USA) 1983

Class	BENCH PRESS	
44 kg	75	Teri Hoyt (USA) 1982
48 kg	82.5	Michelle Evris (USA) 1981
52 kg	95	Mary Ryan (USA) 1984
56 kg	112	Vicky Steenrod (USA) 1984
60 kg	105	Vicky Steenrod (USA) 1985
67.5 kg	107.5	Heidi Wittsech (Aus) 1986
75 kg	140	Beverley Francis (Aus) 1981
82.5 kg	150	Beverley Francis (Aus) 1981
90 kg	120.5	Gael Martin (Aus) 1983
90+ kg	130	Gael Martin (Aus) 1982

Class	DEAD LIFT	
44 kg	165	Nancy Belliveau (Can) 1985
48 kg	182.5	Majik Jones (USA) 1984
52 kg	197	Diana Rowell (USA) 1984
56 kg	200	Diana Rowell (USA) 1984
60 kg	213	Ruth Shafer (USA) 1983
67.5 kg	244	Ruth Shafer (USA) 1984
75 kg	210	Pamela Matthews (Aus) 1982
82.5 kg	227.5	Vicky Gagne (USA) 1981
90 kg	212	Lorraine Constanzo (USA) 1987
90+ kg	230	Wanda Sander (USA) 1983

Class	TOTAL	
44 kg	352.5	Marie Vassart (Bel) 1985
48 kg	390	Majik Jones (USA) 1984
52 kg	427.5	Diana Rowell (USA) 1984
56 kg	482.5	Vicky Steenrod (USA) 1984
60 kg	502.5	Vicky Steenrod (USA) 1985
67.5 kg	565	Ruth Shafer (USA) 1984
75 kg	550	Beverley Francis (Aus) 1981
82.5 kg	577.5	Beverley Francis (Aus) 1983
90 kg	560	Lorraine Constanzo (USA) 1987
90+ kg	567.5	Gael Martin (Aus) 1982

WRESTLING

Wrestling was part of the Ancient Olympics, and wall drawings from nearly 6000 years ago depict it as taking place long before then. Wrestling was included in the first Modern Olympics in 1896, sixteen years before the formation of the International Amateur Wrestling Association. The two forms of wrestling at international level are Freestyle and Greco-Roman. The principle difference between the two is that use of the legs is completely prohibited in the Greco-Roman style. Holds below the waist are also prohibited in this style of wrestling.

OLYMPIC GAMES

A heavyweight division of Greco-Roman wrestling was included in the first Modern Olympics. The freestyle event did not make its debut until 1904.

Winners
FREESTYLE

UP TO 48KG
1904 Robert Curry (USA)
1972 Roman Dmitriyev (USSR)
1976 Hassan Issaev (Bul)
1980 Claudio Pollio (Ita)
1984 Robert Weaver (USA)

UP TO 52KG
(1904 weight up to 115lb/52.16kg)
1904 George Mehnert (USA
1948 Lennart Viitala (Fin)
1952 Hasan Gemici (Tur)
1956 Mirian Tsalkalamanidze (USSR)
1960 Ahmet Bilek (Tur)
1964 Yoshikatsu Yoshida (Jap)
1968 Shigeo Nakata (Jap)
1972 Kiyomi Kato (Jap)
1976 Yuji Takada (Jap)
1980 Anatoliy Beloglazov (USSR)
1984 Saban Trstena (Yug)

UP TO 57KG
(1904 up to 125lb/56.70kg; 1908 up to 119lb/54kg; 1924-36 up to 56kg)
1904 Isidor Niflot (USA)
1908 George Mehnert (USA)
1924 Kustaa Pihlajamäki (Fin)

1928 Kaarlo Mäkinen (Fin)
1932 Robert Pearce (USA)
1936 Odön Zombori (Hun)
1948 Nasuh Akar (Tur)
1952 Shohachi Ishii (Jap)
1956 Mustafa Dagistanli (Tur)
1960 Terrence McCann (USA)
1964 Yojiro Uetake (Jap)
1968 Yojiro Uetake (Jap)
1972 Hideaki Yanagida (Jap)
1976 Vladimir Yumin (USSR)
1980 Sergey Beloglazov (USSR)
1984 Hideaki Tomiyama (Jap)

UP TO 62KG
(1904 up to 135lb/61.24kg; 1908 up to 133lb/60.30 kg; 1920 up to 60kg; 1924-36 up to 61kg; 1948-60, since 1972 up to 62 kg; 1964-8 up to 63 kg)
1904 Benjamin Bradshaw (USA)
1908 George Dole (USA)
1920 Charles Ackerly (USA)
1924 Robin Reed (USA)
1928 Allie Morrison (USA)
1932 Hermanni Pihlajamaki (Fin)
1936 Kustaa Pihlajamaki (Fin)
1948 Gazanfer Bilge (Tur)
1952 Bayram Sit (Tur)
1956 Shozo Sasahara (Jap)
1960 Mustafa Dagistanli (Tur)
1964 Osamu Watanabe (Jap)
1968 Masaaki Kaneko (Jap)
1972 Zagalav Abdulbekov (USSR)
1976 Jung-Mo Yang (SKo)
1980 Magomedgasan Abushev (USSR)
1984 Randy Lewis (USA)

UP TO 68KG
(1904 up to 145lb/65.77kg; 1908 up to 146¾lb/66.60kg; 1920 up to 67.5kg; 1924-36 up to 66kg; 1948-60 up tp 67kg; 1964-8 up to 70kg)
1904 Otto Roehm (USA)
1908 George de Relwyskow (UK)
1920 Kalle Anttila (Fin)
1924 Russell Vis (USA)
1928 Osväld Käpp (Est)
1932 Charles Pacôme (Fra)
1936 Károly Kárpáti (Hun)
1948 Celál Atik (Tur)
1952 Olle Anderberg (Swe)
1956 Emamali Habibi (Iran))
1960 Shelby Wilson (USA)
1964 Enyu Valchev (Bul) *
1968 Abdollah Movahed Ardabili (Iran)
1972 Dan Gable (USA)
1976 Pavel Pinigin (USSR)
1980 Saipulla Absaidov (USSR)
1984 In-Tak You (SKo)
* competed as Dimov in 1960

UP TO 74KG
(1904 up to 158lb/71.67kg; 1924-36 up to 72kg; 1948-60 up to 73kg)
1904 Charles Erickson (USA)
1924 Hermann Gehri (Swi)
1928 Arvo Haavisto (Fin)

1932 Jack Van Bebber (USA)
1936 Frank Lewis (USA)
1948 Yasar Dogu (Tur)
1952 William Smith (USA)
1956 Mitsuo Ikeda (Jap)
1960 Douglas Blubaugh (USA)
1964 Ismail Ogan (Tur)
1968 Mahmut Atalay (Tur)
1972 Wayne Wells (USA)
1976 Jiichiro Date (Jap)
1980 Valentin Raitchev (Bul)
1984 David Schultz (USA)

UP TO 82KG
(1908 up to 161lb/73kg; 1920 up to 165¼lb/75kg; 1924-60 up to 79kg; 1964-8 up to 87kg)
1908 Stanley Bacon (UK)
1920 Eino Leino (Fin)
1924 Fritz Hagmann (Swi)
1928 Ernst Kyburz (Swi)
1932 Ivar Johansson (Swe)
1936 Emile Poilvé (Fra)
1948 Glen Brand (USA)
1952 David Tsimakuridze (USSR)
1956 Nikola Stanchev (Bul)
1960 Hasan Güngör (Tur)
1964 Prodan Gardschev (Bul)
1968 Boris Gurevich (USSR)
1972 Levan Tediashvili (USSR)
1976 John Peterson (USA)
1980 Ismail Abilov (Bul)
1984 Mark Schultz (USA)

UP TO 90KG
(1920 up to 82.5kg; 1924-60 up to 87kg; 1964-8 up to 97kg)
1920 Anders Larsson (Swe)
1924 John Spellman (USA)
1928 Thure Sjöstedt (Swe)
1932 Peter Mehringer (USA)
1936 Knut Fridell (Swe)
1948 Henry Wittenberg (USA)
1952 Wiking Palm (Swe)
1956 Gholam Takhti Reza (Iran)
1960 Ismet Atli (Tur)
1964 Aleksandr Medved (USSR)
1968 Ahmet Ayik (Tur)
1972 Ben Peterson (USA)
1976 Levan Tediashvili (USSR)
1980 Sanasar Oganesyan (USSR)
1984 Ed Banach (USA)

UP TO 100KG
(1904 over 158lb/71.60kg; 1908 over 73kg; 1920 over 82.5kg; 1924-60 over 87kg; 1964-8 over 97kg)
1904 Bernhuff Hansen (USA)
1908 George O'Kelly (UK)
1920 Robert Roth (Swi)
1924 Harry Steel (USA)
1928 Johan Richthoff (Swe)
1932 Johan Richthoff (Swe)
1936 Kristjan Palusalu (Est)
1948 Gyula Bóbis (Hun)
1952 Arsen Mekokishvili (USSR)
1956 Hamit Kaplan (Tur)

1960 Wilfried Dietrich (FRG)
1964 Aleksandr Ivanitskiy (USSR)
1968 Aleksandr Medved (USSR)
1972 Ivan Yarygin (USSR)
1976 Ivan Yarygin (USSR)
1980 Ilya Mate (USSR)
1984 Lou Banach (USA)

OVER 100KG
1972 Aleksandr Medved (USSR
1976 Soslan Andiyev (USSR)
1980 Soslan Andiyev (USSR)
1984 Bruce Baumgartner (USA)

GRECO-ROMAN
UP TO 48KG
1972 Gheorghe Berceanu (Rom)
1976 Aleksey Schumakov (USSR)
1980 Zaksylik Ushkempirov (USSR)
1984 Vincenzo Maenza (Ita)

UP TO 52KG
1948 Pietro Lombardi (Ita)
1952 Boris Gurevich (USSR)
1956 Nikolay Solovyov (USSR)
1960 Dumitru Pirvulescu (Rom)
1964 Tsutomu Hanahara (Jap)
1968 Petar Kirov (Bul)
1972 Petar Kirov (Bul)
1976 Vitaliy Konstantinov (USSR)
1980 Vakhtang Blagidze (USSR)
1984 Atsuji Miyahara (Jap)

UP TO 57KG
(1924-8 up to 58kg; 1932-6 up to 56kg)
1924 Eduard Pütsep (Est)
1928 Kurt Leucht (Ger)
1932 Jakob Brendel (Ger)
1936 Márton Lörincz (Hun)
1948 Kurt Pettersén (Swe)
1952 Imre Hódos (Hun)
1956 Konstantin Vyrupayev (USSR)
1960 Oleg Karavayev (USSR)
1964 Masamitsu Ichiguchi (Jap)
1968 János Varga (Hun)
1972 Rustem Kazakov (USSR)
1976 Pertti Ukkola (Fin)
1980 Shamil Serikov (USSR)
1984 Pasquale Passarelli (FRG)

UP TO 62KG
(1912-20 up to 60kg; 1924-8, 1948-60, since 1972 up to 62kg; 1932-6 up to 61kg; 1964-8 up to 63kg)
1912 Kaarlo Koskelo (Fin)
1920 Oskari Friman (Fin)
1924 Kalle Antila (Fin)
1928 Voldemar Väli (Est)
1932 Giovanni Gozzi (Ita)
1936 Yasar Erkan (Tur)
1948 Mehmet Oktav (Tur)
1952 Yakov Punkin (USSR)
1956 Rauno Mäkinen (Fin)
1960 Müzahir Sille (Tur)
1964 Imre Polyák (Hun)

1968 Roman Rurua (USSR)
1972 Gheorghi Markov (Bul)
1976 Kazimierz Lipién (Pol)
1980 Stylianos Migiakis (Gre)
1984 Weon-Kee Kim (SKo)

UP TO 68KG
(1906 up to 75kg; 1908 up to 66.60 kg; 1912-28 up to 67.5kg; 1932-6 up to 66kg; 1948-60 up to 67kg; 1964-8 up to 70kg)
1906 Rudolf Watzl (Aut)
1908 Enrico Porro (Ita)
1912 Eemil Väre (Fin)
1920 Eemil Väre (Fin)
1924 Oskari Friman (Fin)
1928 Lajos Keresztes (Hun)
1932 Erik Malmberg (Swe)
1936 Lauri Koskela (Fin)
1948 Gustaf Freij (Swe)
1952 Schazam Safin (USSR)
1956 Kyösti Lehtonen (Fin)
1960 Avtandil Koridze (USSR)
1964 Kazim Ayvaz (Tur)
1968 Munji Mumemura (Jap)
1972 Shamil Khisamutdinov (USSR)
1976 Suren Nalbandyan (USSR)
1980 Stefan Rusu (Rom)
1984 Vlado Lisjak (Yug)

UP TO 74KG
(1932-6 up to 72kg; 1948-60 up to 73kg; 1964-8 up to 78kg)
1932 Ivar Johansson (Swe)
1936 Rudolf Svedberg (Swe)
1948 Gösta Andersson (Swe)
1952 Miklós Szilvási (Hun)
1956 Mithat Bayrak (Tur)
1960 Mithat Bayrak (Tur)
1964 Anatoliy Kolesov (USSR)
1968 Rudolf Vesper (GDR)
1970 Vitezslav Mácha (Cs)
1976 Anatoliy Bykov (USSR)
1980 Ferenc Kocsis (Hun)
1984 Jouko Salomaki (Fin)

UP TO 82KG
(1906 up to 85kg; 1908 up to 73kg; 1912-28 up to 75kg; 1932-60 up to 79kg; 1964-8 up to 87kg)
1906 Verner Weckman (Fin)
1908 Frithiof Mårtensson (Fin)
1912 Claes Johansson (Swe)
1920 Carl Westergren (Swe)
1924 Edvard Westerlund (Fin)
1928 Väinö Kokkinen (Fin)
1932 Väinö Kokkinen (Fin)
1936 Ivar Johansson (Swe)
1948 Axel Grönberg (Swe)
1952 Axel Grönberg (Swe)
1956 Givy Kartoziya (USSR)
1960 Dimiter Dobrev (Bul)
1964 Branislav Simic (Yug)
1968 Lothar Metz (GDR)
1972 Csaba Hegedüs (Hun)
1976 Momir Petkovic (Yug)
1980 Gennadiy Korban (USSR)
1984 Ion Draica (Rom)

UP TO 90KG

(1908 up to 93kg; 1912-28 up to 82.5kg; 1932-60 up to 87kg; 1964-8 up to 97kg)

1908 Verner Weckman (Fin)
1912 No winner declared after Anders Ahlgren (Swe) and Ivan Böhling (Fin) fought out a draw after nine hours
1920 Claes Johansson (Swe)
1924 Carl Westergren (Swe)
1928 Ibrahim Moustafa (Egy)
1932 Rudolf Svensson (Swe)
1936 Axel Cadier (Swe)
1948 Karl-Eric Nilsson (Swe)
1952 Koelpo Gröndahl (Fin)
1956 Valentin Nikolayev (USSR)
1960 Tevfik Kis (Tur)
1964 Boyan Radev (Bul)
1968 Boyan Radev (Bul)
1972 Valeriy Rezantsev (USSR)
1976 Valeriy Rezantsev (USSR)
1980 Norbert Növényi (Hun)
1984 Steven Fraser (USA)

UP TO 100KG

(1896, Open; 1906 over 85kg; 1908 over 93kg; 1912-28 over 82.5kg; 1932-60 over 81kg; 1964-8 over 91kg)

1896 Carl Schuhmann (Ger)
1906 Sören Jensen (Den)
1908 Richárd Weisz (Hun)
1912 Yrjö Saarela (Fin)
1920 Adolf Lindfors (Fin)
1924 Henri Deglane (Fra)
1928 Rudolf Svensson (Swe)
1932 Carl Westergren (Swe)
1936 Kristjan Palusalu (Eat)
1948 Ahmet Kirecci (Tur)
1952 Johannes Kotkas (USSR)
1956 Anatoliy Parfenov (USSR)
1960 Ivan Bogdan (USSR)
1964 István Kozma (Hun)
1968 István Kozma (Hun)
1972 Nicolae Martinescu (Rom)
1976 Nikolay Balboshin (USSR)
1980 Gheorghi Raikov (Bul)
1984 Vasile Andrei (Rom)

OVER 100 KG

1972 Anatoliy Roschin (USSR)
1976 Aleksandr Kolchinsky (USSR)
1980 Aleksandr Kolchinsky (USSR)
1984 Jeffrey Blatnick (USA)

WORLD CHAMPIONSHIPS

The first Greco-Roman world championships were held in Scandinavia in 1921 and the first Freestyle championships at Helsinki in 1951. Olympic champions are automatically world champions in Olympic years.

Winners:

FREESTYLE

UP TO 48KG

1969-71 Ebrahim Javadpour (Iran)
1973 Roman Dmitriyev (USSR)
1974 H Murselov (Bul)
1975 Hasan Issaev (Bul)
1977 Anatoliy Beloglazov (USSR)
1978-9 Sergey Kornilayev (USSR)
1981-2 Sergey Kornilayev (USSR)
1983 Kim-Chol Hwan (SKo)
1985 Kim-Chol Hwan (SKo)
1986 Yae-Sik Li (NKo)

UP TO 52KG

1951 Yucel (Tur)
1953 Georgiy Saydov (USSR)
1954 Hüseyin Akbas (Tur)
1957 M Kartel (Tur)
1959 Ali Aliyev (USSR)
1961-2 Ali Aliyev (USSR)
1963 Y Cemal (Tur)
1965 Yoshikatsu Yoshida (Jap)
1966 Chang-Sun Chang (SKo)
1967 Shigeo Nakata (Jap)
1969 Richard Sanders (USA)
1970 Riza Ali (Tur)
1971 Mohamad Ghorbani (Iran)
1973 Ebrahim Javadpour (Iran)
1974-5 Yuji Takada (Jap)
1977 Yuji Takada (Jap)
1978 Anatoliy Beloglazov (USSR)
1979 Juyi Takada (Jap)
1981 Toshio Asakura (Jap)
1982 Hartmut Reich (GDR)
1983 Valentin Jordanov (Bul)
1985 Valentin Jordanov (Bul)
1986 Kim-Yong Sik (NKo)

UP TO 57KG

1951 Nasuk Akar (Tur)
1953 Hüseyin Akbas (Tur)
1954 Mustafa Dagistanli (Tur)
1957 Hüseyin Akbas (Tur)
1959 Hüseyin Akbas (Tur)
1961 Mohamad Saifpour Saidabadi (Iran)
1962 Hüseyin Akbas (Tur)
1963 Aidyn Ibragimov (USSR)
1965 Tomiaki Fukada (Jap)
1966-7 Ali Aliyev (USSR)
1969 Tadamichi Tanaki (Jap)
1970-1 Hideaki Yanagida (Jap)
1973 Mohamad Farahvashi-Fashandi (Iran)
1974 Vladimir Yumin (USSR)
1975 Masao Arai (Jap)
1977 Tadashi Sasaki (Jap)
1978-9 Hideaki Tomiyama (Jap)
1981 Sergey Beloglazov (USSR)
1982 Anatoliy Beloglazov (USSR)
1983 Sergey Beloglazov (USSR)
1985-6 Sergey Beloglazov (USSR)

UP TO 62KG

1951 Haydar Zafer (Tur)
1953 N Moucheguian (USSR)
1954 Shozo Sasahara (Jap)
1957 Mustafa Dagistanli (Tur)
1959 Mustafa Dagistanli (Tur)
1961 Vladimir Rubashvili (USSR)
1962-3 Osamu Watanabe (Jap)
1965 Mohamad Saifpour Saidabadi (Iran)

1966-7 Masaki Kaneko (Jap)
1969 Takeo Morita (Jap)
1970 Shamseddin Seyed-Abbassi (Iran)
1971 Zagalav Abdulbekov (USSR)
1973 Zagalav Abdulbekov (USSR)
1974 I Zeveg (Mgl)
1975 Zevgi Oydov (Mgl)
1977-9 Vladimir Yumin (USSR)
1981 Simeon Sterev (Bul)
1982 Sergeiy Beloglazov (USSR)
1983 Viktor Alekseyev (USSR)
1985 Viktor Alekseyev (USSR)
1986 Hetar Isayev (USSR)

UP TO 68KG
1951 Olle Anderberg (Swe)
1953 Viktor Sinyavskiy (USSR)
1954 Djahanbakte Tovfighe (Iran)
1957 Alimberg Bestayev (USSR)
1959 Viktor Sinyavskiy (USSR)
1961 Mohamad-Ali Sanatkaram (Iran)
1962 Enyu Valtchev (Bul)
1963 Iwao Horiuchi (Jap)
1965-7 Abdollah Movahed (Iran)
1969-70 Abdollah Movahed (Iran)
1971 Dan Gable (USA)
1973 Lloyd Keaser (USA)
1974 N Nasrullayev (USSR)
1975 Pavel Pinigin (USSR)
1977-8 Pavel Pinigin (USSR)
1979 Mikhail Kharachura (USSR)
1981 Saipulla Absaidov (USSR)
1982 Mikhail Kharachura (USSR)
1983 Arsen Fadzeyev (USSR)
1985-6 Arsen Fadzeyev (USSR)

UP TO 74KG
1951 Celál Atik (Tur)
1953 Ismail Ogan (Tur)
1954 Vakhtang Balavadze (USSR)
1957 Vakhtang Balavadze (USSR)
1959 Emamali Habibi (Iran)
1961-2 Emamali Habibi (Iran)
1963 Guliko Sagaradze (USSR)
1965 Guliko Sagaradze (USSR)
1966 Mahmut Atalay (Tur)
1967 Daniel Robin (Fra)
1969 Zarbeg Beriashvili (USSR)
1970 Wayne Wells (USA)
1971 Yuri Gusov (USSR)
1973 Mansour Barzegar (Iran)
1974-5 Ruslan Ashuraliyev (USSR)
1977 Stan Dziedzic (USA)
1978-9 Leroy Kemp (USA)
1981 Martin Knosp (FRG)
1982 Leroy Kemp (USA)
1983 Dave Schultz (USA)
1985-6 Raul Cascaret (Cub)

UP TO 82KG
1951 Haydar Zafer (Tur)
1953 Hasan Güngör (Tur)
1954 Abbas Zandi (Iran)
1957 Nabi Sorouri (Iran)
1959 Georgiy Shkirtladze (USSR)
1961-2 Mansour Mehdizadeh (Iran)

1963 Prodan Gardschev (Bul)
1965 Menisade (Iran)
1966 Prodan Gardschev (Bul)
1967 Boris Gurevich (USSR)
1969 Fred Fozzard (USA)
1970 Yuriy Shakhmuradov (USSR)
1971 Levan Tediashvili (USSR)
1973 V Syulzhin (USSR)
1974 Viktor Novozhilov (USSR)
1975 Adolf Seger (FRG)
1977 Adolf Seger (FRG)
1978 Magomed Aratsilov (USSR)
1979 István Kovacs (Hun)
1981 Chris Campbell (USA)
1982-3 Tejmuraj Dzgoev (USSR)
1985 Mark Schultz (USA)
1986 Vladimir Modosyan (USSR)

UP TO 90KG
1951 Yasar Dogu (Tur)
1953 Anatoliy Albul (USSR)
1954 Avgus Englas (USSR)
1957 Mitious Petkov (Bul)
1959 Golam Reza Takhti (Iran)
1961 Golam Reza Takhti (Iran)
1962-3 Aleksandr Medved (USSR)
1965 Ahmet Ayik (Tur)
1966 Aleksandr Medved (USSR)
1967 Ahmet Ayik (Tur)
1969 Boris Gurevich (USSR)
1970 Gennadiy Strakhov (USSR)
1971 Rusi Petrov (Bul)
1973-5 Levan Tediashvili (USSR)
1977 Anatoliy Prokopchuk (USSR)
1978 Uwe Neupert (GDR)
1979 Khasan Ortzuyev (USSR)
1981 Sanasar Oganesyan (USSR)
1982 Uwe Neupert (GDR)
1983 Piotr Naneyev (USSR)
1985 Bill Sherr (USA)
1986 Macharbek Khadartsev (USSR)

UP TO 100KG
1951 Bertil Antonsson (Swe)
1953 Lyutvi Akhmedov (Bul)
1954 Arsen Mekokishvili (USSR)
1957 Hamit Kaplan (Tur)
1959 Lyutvi Ahmedov (Bul)
1961 Wilfried Dietrich (FRG)
1962-3 Aleksandr Ivanitskiy (USSR)
1965-6 Aleksandr Ivanitskiy (USSR)
1967 Aleksandr Medved (USSR)
1969 Shota Lomidze (USSR)
1970 V Gulyutkin (USSR)
1971 Shota Lomidze (USSR)
1973 Ivan Yarygin (USSR)
1974 V Gulyutkin (USSR)
1975 Khorloo Bayanminkh (Mgl)
1977 Aslanbek Bisultanov (USSR)
1978 Harald Buttner (GDR)
1979 Ilya Mate (USSR)
1981 Roland Gehrke (GDR)
1982 Ilya Mate (USSR)
1983 Aslan Khadartsev (USSR)
1985 Levy Khabelov (USSR)

1986 Aslan Khadartsev (USSR)

OVER 100KG (now 130KG)
1969-71 Aleksandr Medved (USSR)
1973 Soslan Andiyev (USSR)
1974 S Ladislav (Rom)
1975 Soslan Andiyev (USSR)
1977 Soslan Andiyev (USSR)
1979 Salman Khasimikov (USSR)
1981-3 Salman Khasimikov (USSR)
1985 David Gobedichviliy (USSR)
1986 Bruce Baumgartner (USA)

GRECO-ROMAN

(Post-war winners)

UP TO 48KG
1969-70 Gheorghe Berceanu (Rom)
1971 Vladimir Zubkov (USSR)
1973-5 Vlademir Zubkov (USSR)
1977 Aleksey Shumakov (USSR)
1978 Constantin Alexandru (Rom)
1981 Zaksylik Ushkempirov (USSR)
1982 Temur Karashvili (USSR)
1983 Bratan Tsenov (Bul)
1985-6 Magyatdin Allakhverdyev (USSR)

UP TO 52KG
1950 Bengt Johansson (Swe)
1953 Boris Gurevitch (USSR)
1955 Ignazio Fabra (Ita)
1958 Boris Gurevitch (USSR)
1961 A Saydov (USSR)
1962 S Rybalko (USSR)
1963 Borivoje Vukov (Yug)
1965 Rybalko (USSR)
1966 Angel Kerezov (Bul)
1967 Vladimir Bakulin (USSR)
1969 Ferodz Aluzadeh (Iran)
1970-1 Petar Kirov (Bul)
1973 Gheorge Guergue (Rom)
1974 Peter Kirov (USSR)
1975 Vitaliy Konstantinov (USSR)
1977 Nicu Ginga (Rom)
1978 Vakhtang Blagidze (USSR)
1979 Lajos Racz (Hun)
1981 Vakhtang Blagidze (USSR)
1982-3 Benyur Pashayan (USSR)
1985 Jan Rønningen (Nor)
1986 Sergey Dyudyayev (USSR)

UP TO 57KG
1950 Ali Mahmoud Hassan (Egy)
1953 Artem Teryan (USSR)
1955 V Stashevich (USSR)
1958 Oleg Karavayev (USSR)
1961 Oleg Karavayev (USSR)
1962 Masamitsu Ichiguchi (Jap)
1963 János Varga (Hun)
1965 I Chernya (USSR)
1966 Fritz Strange (FRG)
1967 Ion Baciu (Rom)
1969 Rustem Kazakov (USSR)
1970 János Varga (Hun)
1971 Rustem Kazakov (USSR)
1973 Jozef Lipien (Pol)

1974-5 Farhat Mustafin (USSR)
1977 Pertti Ukkola (Fin)
1978-9 Shamil Serikov (USSR)
1981 Pasquale Passarelli (FRG)
1982 Piotr Mikhalik (Pol)
1983 Eto Masaki (Jap)
1985 Stojan Balov (Bul)
1986 Emil Ivanov (Bul)

UP TO 62KG
1950 Olle Anderberg (Swe)
1953 Olle Anderberg (Swe)
1955 Imre Polyák (Hun)
1958 Imre Polyák (Hun)
1961 Mostafa Mansour (Egy)
1962 Imre Polyák (Hun)
1963 Gennadiy Sapunov (USSR)
1965 Y Grigoryev (USSR)
1966-7 Roman Rurua (USSR)
1969 Roman Rurua (USSR)
1970 Hideo Fujimoto (Jap)
1971 Gheorgi Markov (Bul)
1973-4 Kazimierz Lipien (Pol)
1975 Nelson Davidyan (USSR)
1977 Laszlo Reczi (Hun)
1978 Boris Kramarenko (USSR)
1979 Istvan Toth (Hun)
1981 Istvan Toth (Hun)
1982 Ryszard Swierad (Pol)
1983 Hnanu Lahtinen (Fin)
1985 Zhivko Vangelov (Bul)
1986 Kamandar Madzidov (USSR)

UP TO 68KG
1950 J Gal (Hun)
1953 Gustav Freij (Swe)
1955 Grigoriy Gamarnik (USSR)
1958 Riza Dogan (Tur)
1961 Avtandil Koridze (USSR)
1962 Kazim Ayvaz (Tur)
1963 Stevan Horvat (Yug)
1965 Gennadiy Supanov (USSR)
1966 Stevan Horvat (Yug)
1967 Eero Tapio (Fin)
1969 Simon Popescu (Rom)
1970 Roman Rurua (USSR)
1971 Srejan Damyanovic (Yug)
1973 Shamil Khisamutdinov (USSR)
1974 Nelson Davidyan (USSR)
1975 Shamil Khisamutdinov (USSR)
1977 Heinz-Helmut Wehling (GDR)
1978 Stefan Rusu (Rom)
1979 Andrzej Supron (Pol)
1981-2 Gennadiy Yermilov (USSR)
1983 Tapio Sipilä (Fin)
1985 Stefan Negrisan (Rom)
1986 Levon Dzyolfalakyan (USSR)

UP TO 74KG
1950 M Simanainen (Fin)
1953 G Chatvorjan (USSR)
1955 Vladimir Maneyev (USSR)
1958 Kazim Ayvaz (Tur)
1961 Valeriu Bularca (Rom)
1962-3 Anatoliy Kolesov (USSR)

1965 Anatoliy Kolesov (USSR)
1966-7 Viktor Igumenov (USSR)
1969-71 Viktor Igumenov (USSR)
1973 Ivan Kolev (Bul)
1974 Viteslav Mácha (Cs)
1975 Anatoliy Bykov (USSR)
1977 Viteslav Mácha (Cs)
1978 Arif Niftulayev (USSR)
1979 Ferenc Kocsis (Hun) & Ianko Chopov (Bul)
1981 A Kudryavtsev (USSR)
1982 Stefan Rusu (Rom)
1983 Mikhail Mamiashvili (USSR)
1985-6 Mikhail Mamiashvili (USSR)

UP TO 82KG
1950 Axel Grönberg (Swe)
1953 Givy Kartozlya (USSR)
1955 Givy Kartozlya (USSR)
1958 Givy Kartozlya (USSR)
1961 V Zenin (USSR)
1962-3 Tevfik Kis (Tur)
1965 R Bogdanas (USSR)
1966 Valentin Olenik (USSR)
1967 Laszlo Sillai (Hun)
1969 Petar Petrov Kroumov (Bul)
1970 Anatoliy Nazarenko (USSR)
1971 Csada Hegedus (Hun)
1973 L Liberman (USSR)
1974-5 Anatoliy Nazarenko (USSR)
1977 Vladimir Cheboskarov (USSR)
1978 Ion Draica (Rom)
1979 Gennadiy Korban (USSR)
1981 Gennadiy Korban (USSR)
1982-3 Temur Abkhasava (USSR)
1985 Bogdan Daras (Pol)
1986 Bogdan Daras (Pol) & Tibor Komaroni (Hun)

UP TO 90KG
1950 M Candas (Tur)
1953 A Englas (USSR)
1955 Valentin Nikolayev (USSR)
1958 Rostom Abashidze (USSR)
1961 György Gurics (Hun)
1962-3 Rostom Abashidze (USSR)
1965 J Anisimov (USSR)
1966 Boyan Radev (Bul)
1967 Nikolay Yakovenko (USSR)
1969 A Yurkevich (USSR)
1970-1 Valeriy Rezantsev (USSR)
1973-5 Valeriy Rezantsev (USSR)
1977 Frank Andersson (Swe)
1978 Stojan Nikolov (Bul)
1979 Frank Andersson (Swe)
1981 Igor Kanygin (USSR)
1982 Frank Andersson (Swe)
1983 Igor Kanygin (USSR)
1985 Michael Houk (USA)
1986 Andrjez Malina (Pol)

UP TO 100KG
1950 Bertil Antonsson (Swe)
1953 Bertil Antonsson (Swe)
1955 A Mazur (USSR)
1958 Ivan Bogdan (USSR)
1961 Ivan Bogdan (USSR)

1962 István Kozma (Hun)
1963 Anatoliy Rochin (USSR)
1965 N Shmakov (USSR)
1966-7 István Kozma (Hun)
1969 Nikolay Yakovenko (USSR)
1970 Per Svensson (Swe)
1971 Nicolae Martinescu (Rom)
1973-4 Nikolay Balboshin (USSR)
1975 K Losano (Bul)
1977-9 Nikolay Balboshin (USSR)
1981 Mikhail Saladze (USSR)
1982 Roman Wroclawski (Pol)
1983 Andrej Dmitrov (Bul)
1985 Andrej Dmitrov (Bul)
1986 Támas Gáspár (Hun)

OVER 100KG (now 130KG)
1969-70 Anatoliy Roshin (USSR)
1971 Per Svensson (Swe)
1973-5 Anatoliy Tomov (Bul)
1977 Nikolai Dinev (Bul)
1978 Aleksandr Kolinchskiy (USSR)
1979 Aleksandr Tomov (USSR)
1981 Refik Memisevic (Yug)
1982 Nikolai Denev (Bul)
1983 Jevgeniy Artiochin (USSR)
1985 Igor Rostozotskiy (USSR)
1986 Thomas Johansson (Swe)

MOST WORLD & OLYMPIC TITLES
10 Aleksandr Medved (USSR) Freestyle: 90kg 1962-4, 1966; 100kg 1967-8; Over 100kg 1969-72
7 Nikolay Balboshin (USSR) Greco Roman: 100kg 1973-4, 1976, 1978-9; Over 100kg 1971, 1977
7 Valeriy Rezantsev (USSR) Greco-Roman: 90kg 1970-6
6 Ali Aliev (USSR) Freestyle: 52kg 1959, 1961-2; 57kg 1966-8
6 Abdollah Movahed (Iran) Freestyle: 68kg 1965-70
6 Levan Tediashvili (USSR) Freestyle: 82kg 1971-2; 90kg 1973-5, 1976
6 Soslan Andiev (USSR) Freestyle: Over 100kg 1973, 1975-8, 1980
6 Sergey Beloglazov (USSR) Freestyle: 57kg 1980-1, 1983, 1985-6; 62kg 1982
5 Viktor Igumenov (USSR) Greco Roman: 74kg 1966-7, 1969-71
5 Roman Rurua (USSR) Greco Roman: 62kg 1966-70
5 Yuji Takada (Jap) Freestyle: 52kg 1964-7, 1979

YACHTING

The first known yacht race was in September 1661 when Charles II challenged the Duke of York to a race over a 23-mile stretch of the River Thames from Greenwich to Gravesend. The sport became popular towards the end of the 19th century, nearly 150 years after the formation of the world's first yacht club, at Cork, Ireland in 1720.

AMERICA'S CUP

One of the most famous of all sporting trophies, the Cup was donated by the Royal Yacht Squadron for a race around the Isle of Wight in 1851. The American schooner *America* won the race and took the trophy to the United States. The New York Yacht club then offered it as a challenge trophy but, despite many challenges over the years, the cup stayed in American hands until 1983 when it temporarily became Australian property.

	Winner	Winning skipper	Score	Challenger
1870	Magic	Andrew Comstock	-	Cambria (Eng)
1871	Columbia & Sappho	Nelson Comstock Sam Greenwood	4-1	Livonia (Eng)
1876	Madeleine	Josephus Williams	2-0	Countess of Dufferin (Can)
1881	Mischief	Nathaniel Clock	2-0	Atalanta (Can)
1885	Puritan	Aubrey Crocker	2-0	Genesta (Eng)
1886	Mayflower	Martin Stone	2-0	Galatea (Eng)
1887	Volunteer	Henry Haff	2-0	Thistle (Sco)
1893	Vigilant	William Hansen	3-0	Valkyrie II (Eng)
1895	Defender	Henry Haff	3-0	Valkyrie III (Eng)
1899	Columbia	Charlie Barr	3-0	Shamrock (Eng)
1901	Columbia	Charlie Barr	3-0	Shamrock II (Eng)
1903	Reliance	Charlie Barr	3-0	Shamrock III (Eng)
1920	Resolute	Charles Adams	3-2	Shamrock IV (Eng)
1930	Enterprise	Harold Vanderbilt	4-0	Shamrock V (Eng)
1934	Rainbow	Harold Vanderbilt	4-2	Endeavour (Eng)
1937	Ranger	Harold Vanderbilt	4-0	Endeavour II (Eng)
1958	Columbia	Briggs Cunningham	4-0	Sceptre (Eng)
1962	Weatherly	Emil Mosbacher Jr	4-1	Gretel (Aus)
1964	Constellation	Bob Bavier Jr	4-0	Sovereign (Eng)
1967	Intrepid	Emil Mosbacher Jr	4-0	Dame Pattie (Aus)
1970	Intrepid	Bill Ficker	4-1	Gretel II (Aus)
1974	Courageous	Ted Hood	4-0	Southern Cross (Aus)
1977	Courageous	Ted Turner	4-0	Australia (Aus)
1980	Freedom	Dennis Conner	4-1	Australia (Aus)
1983	Australia II	John Bertrand	4-3	Liberty (USA)
1987	Stars & Stripes	Dennis Conner	4-0	Kookaburra III (Aus)

Most times winning skipper: 3 Charlie Barr, Harold Vanderbilt; 2 Henry Haff, Emil Mosbacher Jr, Dennis Conner
Most times skippered challenger: 3 Jim Hardy 1970, 1974, 1980

ADMIRAL'S CUP

The Royal Ocean Racing Club donated the trophy in 1957 to encourage yachtsmen from abroad to race in English waters. Up to three boats per nation are allowed to enter and in 1975, 1977 and 1979, a record 19 nations competed. The biennial series of races take place in the English Channel, at Cowes, and around the Fastnet rock.

Winners:
8 Great Britain 1957, 1959, 1963, 1965, 1971, 1975, 1977, 1981
3 FR Germany 1973, 1983, 1985
2 USA 1961, 1969; Australia 1967, 1979

OLYMPIC GAMES

Yachting did not make its Olympic debut until 1900; it should have been included in the first Modern Olympics programme four years earlier, but bad weather prevented any competition. The classes of competition have varied over the years, but all Olympic champions are listed below.

SOLING
1972 USA (Harry Melges, William Bentsen, William Allen)
1976 Denmark (Poul Jensen, Valdemar Bandolowski, Erik Hermann Hansen)
1980 Denmark (Poul Jensen, Valdemar Bandolowski, Erik Hermann Hansen)
1984 USA (Robert Haines Jr, Edward Trevelyan, Roderick Davis)

FLYING DUTCHMAN
(1956 Sharpie class)
1956 Peter Mander/John Cropp (NZ)
1960 Peder Lunde Jr/Björn Bergvall (Nor)
1964 Helmer Pedersen/Earle Wells (NZ)
1968 Rodney Pattisson/Iain Macdonald-Smith (UK)
1972 Rodney Pattisson/Christopher Davies (UK)
1976 Jörg Diesch/Eckert Diesch (FRG)
1980 Alejandro Abascal/Miguel Noguer (Spa)
1984 Jonathan McKee/William Carl Buchan (USA)

STAR
1932 Gilbert Gray/Andrew Libano Jr(USA)
1936 Peter Bischoff/Hans-Joachim Weise (Ger)
1948 Hilary Smart/Paul Smart (USA)
1952 Agostino Straulino/Nicolo Rode (Ita)
1956 Herbert Williams/Lawrence Low (USA)
1960 Timir Pinegin/Fyodor Shutkov (USSR)
1964 Durward Knowles/Cecil Cooke (Bah)
1968 Lowell North/Peter Barrett (USA)

1972 David Forbes/John Anderson (Aus)
1980 Valentin Mankin/Aleksandr Muzychenko (USSR)
1984 Bill Buchan/Stephen Erickson (USA)

FINN

(12-foot and 18-foot (2-handed) dinghy classes. 1920, Meulan class 1924, International 12-foot class 1928, Snowbird class 1932, International Olympia class 1936, Firefly class 1948)

1920 Franciscus Hin/Johannes Hin(Hol) 12-foot dinghy
1920 Francis Richards/T.Hedburg(UK) 18-foot dinghy
1924 Léon Huybrechts (Bel)
1928 Sven Thorell (Swe)
1932 Jacques Lebrun(Fra)
1936 Daniel Kagchelland (Hol)
1948 Paul Elvström (Den)
1952 Paul Elvström (Den)
1956 Paul Elvström (Den)
1960 Paul Elvström (Den)
1964 Willi Kuhweide (FRG)
1968 Valentin Mankin (USSR)
1972 Serge Maury (Fra)
1976 Jochen Schümann (GDR)
1980 Esko Rechardt (Fin)
1984 Russell Coutts (NZ)

470

1976 Frank Hübner/Harro Bode (FRG)
1980 Marcos Soares/Eduardo Penido (Bra)
1984 Luis Doreste/Roberto Molina (Spa)

TORNADO

1976 Reg White/John Osborn (UK)
1980 Alexandre Welter/Lars Björkström (Bra)
1984 Rex Sellers/Christopher Timms (NZ)

BOARDSAILING (Windglider)

1984 Stephan van den Berg (Hol)

Most Individual Gold medals: 4 Paul Elvström

DISCONTINUED EVENTS

SWALLOW

1948 Stewart Morris/David Bond (UK)

TEMPEST

1972 Valentin Mankin/Vitaliy Dyrdyra (USSR)
1976 John Albrechtson/Ingvar Hansson (Swe)

DRAGON

1948 Norway
1952 Norway
1956 Sweden

Rodney Pattisson, twice Olympic champion at the Flying Dutchman class. (All-Sport)

1960 Greece
1964 Denmark
1968 USA
1972 Australia

30 SQUARE METRES
1920 Sweden

40 SQUARE METRES
1920 Sweden

5.5 METRES
1952 USA
1956 Sweden
1960 USA
1964 Australia
1968 Sweden

6 METRES
1908 Great Britain
1912 France
1920 Norway
1924 Norway
1928 Norway
1932 Sweden
1936 Great Britain
1948 USA
1952 USA

6 METRES (1907 rating)
1920 Belgium

6.5 METRES
1920 Netherlands

7 METRES
1908 Great Britain
1920 Great Britain

8 METRES
1908 Great Britain
1912 Norway
1920 Norway
1924 Norway
1928 France
1932 USA
1936 Italy

8 METRES (1907 rating)
1920 Norway

10 METRES
1912 Sweden
1920 Norway (1907 rating)
1920 Norway (1919 rating)

12 METRES
1908 Great Britain
1912 Norway
1920 Norway (1907 rating)
1920 Norway (1919 rating)

TONNAGE CATEGORIES IN 1900
½ Ton: France
½-1 Ton: France
1-2 Ton: Switzerland
2-3 Ton: Great Britain
3-10 Ton: France
10-20 Ton: France
Open: Great Britain

THE WHITBREAD ROUND THE WORLD RACE

The longest race in the world, it was inaugurated in August 1973, and is organised by the Royal Naval Sailing Association. Held quadrennially, the distance is 26,180 nautical miles and starts and finishes at Portsmouth.

Year	Winning Skipper	Yacht	Time
1974	Ramon Carlin (Mex)	Sayula II	152d 9hr
1978	Cornelius van Rietschoten (Hol)	Flyer	
1982	Cornelius van Rietschoten (Hol)	Flyer	120d 6hr 35min
1986	Pierre Fehlmann (Swi)	UBS Switzerland	117d 14hr 31min

Fastest winning time: 117 days 14 hr 31 min Pierre Fehlmann, 1986

SINGLE HANDED TRANSATLANTIC RACE

Sponsored by the *Observer* newspaper, the race is now held every four years. It was the idea of Colonel 'Blondie' Hasler. The race is from Plymouth to Newport, Rhode Island, and is approximately 3000 miles.

Year	Winner	Yacht	Time
1960	Francis Chichester (UK)	Gypsy Moth III	40d 12hr 30min
1962	Francis Chichester (UK)	Gypsy Moth III	33d 15hr 7min
1964	Eric Tabarly (Fra)	Pen Duick II	27d 3hr 56min
1968	Geoffrey Williams (UK)	Sir Thomas Lipton	25d 20hr 33min
1972	Alain Colas (Fra)	Pen Duick IV	20d 13hr 15min
1976	Eric Tabarly (Fra)	Pen Duick VI	23d 20hr 12min
1980	Phil Weld (USA)	Moxie	17d 23hr 12min
1984	Yvon Fauconnier (Fra)	Umupro Jardin V	16d 6hr 25min

BOARDSAILING

Boardsailing (often called Windsurfing, which is a trade name) was pioneered as a sport by Henry Hoyle Schweitzer and Jim Drake in California, USA, in 1968, but the origin of boardsailing dates back to 1958 when 12-year-old Peter Chilvers of England devised the first prototype sailboard. The sport became popular in the 1970s and a world championship was instituted in 1973. Boardsailing was included in the Olympic Games for the first time in 1984.

SPEED RECORDS

The highest speed reached under sail on water by any craft over a 500m timed run is by the boardsailer Pascal Maka (Fra) at 38.86 knots (71.96 km/h) in a 50 knot wind at Fuerteventura, Canary Island on a Gaastra 4 sq.m. Limited Edition Speed Trial Sailboard on 21 Jul 1986. The women's record was set at the same venue by Britt Dunkerbeke at 33.77 knots (62.58 km/h).

The previous speed sailing record had been 36.04 knots (66.78 km/h) by the 22.4m proa Crossbow II in Portland Harbour, UK on 17 Nov 1980. Crossbow II is thought to have reached a top burst of speed of 45 knots.

ASIAN GAMES

The first Asian Games were held at New Delhi, India on 8-11 Mar 1951, when ten nations took part. These multi-sport Games have since 1954 been held at four-yearly intervals.

A predecessor of the Asian Games were the Far Eastern Games, first held in 1913 in Manila, with China, the Philippines and two Japanese athletes taking part. These Games were held every two years to 1927 and then in 1930 and 1934.

VENUES

1951 New Delhi, 1954 Manila, 1958 Tokyo, 1962 Djakarta, 1966 Bangkok, 1970 Bangkok, 1974 Teheran, 1978 Bangkok, 1982 New Delhi, 1986 Seoul.

Shigenobu Murofushi (Jap) has the unique feat of winning his event, the hammer, at five Games, 1970-74-78-82-86

MEDAL TABLE – ALL SPORTS AT THE 1986 GAMES

	G	S	B	Total
China	94	82	46	222
S.Korea	93	55	76	224
Japan	58	76	77	211
Iran	6	6	10	22
India	5	9	23	37
Phillipines	4	5	9	18
Thailand	3	10	13	26
Pakistan	2	3	4	9
Indonesia	1	5	14	20

22 nations won medals.

CENTRAL AMERICAN AND CARIBBEAN GAMES

First held in 1926 in Mexico City, and at four-yearly intervals ever since except for 1942. The 15th Games were staged in Santiago, Dominican Republic in 1986.

PAN-ARAB GAMES

These Games were instituted by decree of the Arab League in 1951, and first held in 1953. Thereafter they were staged every four years until 1965, but then a gap until 1985 (at 18 sports). The next Games will be at Baghdad in 1989.

PAN-AMERICAN GAMES

The Pan-American Games are multi-sport competitions open to athletes from North, Central and South American nations. They have been held every four years from 1951, when the Games were opened at Buenos Aires by the Argentinian President, Juan Peron, in front of a 100,000 crowd. They were originally planned for 1942, but delayed due to the outbreak of war.

VENUES

1951 Buenos Aires, Arg.	1971 Cali, Colombia
1955 Mexico City, Mexico	1975 Mexico City, Mexico
1959 Chicago, USA	1979 San Juan, Puerto Rico
1963 Sao Paulo, Brazil	1983 Caracas, Venezuela
1967 Winnipeg, Canada	1987 Indianapolis, USA

In Indianapolis 27 sports were scheduled to be contested, all 23 Olympic summer sports with the addition of Baseball, Roller Skating, Softball and Taekwon-Do. 34 nations are affiliated to the controlling body, the Pan-American Sports Organization.

WORLD STUDENT GAMES

The 'Universiade' or World Student Games, organised by the Fédération Internationale du Sport Universitaire (FISU), is well established as one of the world's most important sports meetings, although it has been somewhat under-regarded in the UK and perhaps in the USA. The first 'International Universities' Games was held in Warsaw, organised by the Confederation Internationale des Etudiants (CIE). From 1951-1962 rival Games were staged by FISU and the UIE. The latter, Communist inspired, were known as the World Youth Games from 1954 and these had the higher standards. From 1963, however, the Games merged and are now held biennially.

VENUES

(from 1951-62: U - UIE, F - FISU)
1924 Warsaw, 1927 Rome, 1928 Paris, 1930 Darmstadt, 1933 Turin, 1935 Budapest, 1937 Paris, 1939 Monaco, 1947 Paris, 1949 Budapest, 1951 Berlin (U) & Luxembourg (F), 1953 Bucharest (U) & Dortmund (F), 1954 Budapest (U), 1955 Warsaw (U) & San Sebastian (F), 1957 Moscow (U) & Paris (F), 1959 Vienna (U) and Turin (F), 1961 Sofia (F), 1962 Helsinki (U), 1963 Porto Alegre, 1965 Budapest, 1967 Tokyo, 1970 Turin, 1973 Moscow, 1975 Rome (unofficial), 1977 Sofia, 1979 Mexico City, 1981 Bucharest, 1983 Edmonton, 1985 Kobe, 1987 Zagreb

Ten sports are included at the Games: Association Football, Athletics, Basketball, Fencing, Gymnastics, Judo, Swimming, Tennis, Volleyball and Water Polo.

INDEX OF SPORTS AND MAJOR EVENTS

The index contains all the sports included in this book, with cross-references to alternative names. It also includes various competitions, but excludes most of those that are, by their name, obviously included in their respective sports.

ACKNOWLEDGEMENTS

The authors wish to acknowledge with grateful thanks the assistance of the following experts and officials of governing bodies:
All England Women's Lacrosse Association
American Amateur Racquetball Federation
Maria Elena Assenza, Fédération Internationale de Tir à l'Arc
Jörg Bahrke, International Handball Federation
Max Bangerter, International Gymnastics Federation
Howard Bass, winter sports
Gisele Bertrand, International Motorcycling Federation
Pat Besford, swimming
Dennis Bird, ice and roller skating
Arnold Böstrom, International Powerlifting Federation
Glenna Brouse, The Thoroughbred Record, USA
M. Collin, Women's Cricket Association
Peter Craft, The Tug-of-War Association
Mike Cunningham, British Surfing Association
Pat Davis, Badminton
Domenico Di Gianfrancesco, Federazione Italiana Hockey e Pattinaggio
Albert Dormer, World Bridge Federation

A. Duttmann, Deutscher Rollsport-Bund
Ron Ferguson, Australian Water Ski Association
Mike Getty, British Darts Organisation
Maurice Glazer, British Tenpin Bowling Association
Peter Grekulovic, Yugoslav Gymnastics Federation
Col. Harper, the Hurlingham Polo Association
Kris Murphy Henion, Professional Rodeo Cowboys Association
Gillian Hill, British Water Ski Federation
International Softball Association
Naoshi Ito, Japan
M. Jekiel, Union Cycliste Internationale
Ove Karlsson, Idrottsböken
Darren P. Kingsley, US Squash Racquets Association
Rodney Knight, Eton Fives Association
Roger Koo, Taekwon-Do
Graham Lester, Lacrosse
Paula McMartin, Women's International Bowling Congress
Andy Milroy, ultra-distance running
John Moody, British Amateur Weight Lifters' Association
Anthony Needell, powerboating
Joseph and Pauline New, National Skating Association of Great Britain
Keith Osmin, Autosport

Tony Pawson, fly fishing
David Pickup, trampolining
Cathy Plant, CAT Sports Inc., triathlon
Bruce Pluckhahn, National Bowling Hall of Fame and Museum
Mike Price, cycling
John Randall, horse racing
P. J. Reeder, Rugby Fives Association
Jack Richmond, The Camanachd Association
Barry Rolfe, British Gliding Association
Jack Rollin, soccer
George Sarahete, International Federation of Tenpin Bowling
Len Smith, Australian harness racing
William Stephens, Racquets Association
Roy Stobbs and Bernard Franks, Billiards & Snooker Control Council
Lance Tingay, lawn tennis
E. Tummers, International Hockey Federation
Mel Welch, English Basket Ball Association
Dr. R. Wheatley, National Roller Hockey Association of Great Britain
Rick Wilson, British Hang Gliding Association
Anne Woodley, Powerboat Secretary, Royal Yachting Association
Hugh Wrampling, pétanque
Ian Wright, racquetball and squash